THE LAST VALLEY

THE LAST VALLEY

Dien Bien Phu and the French Defeat in Vietnam

Martin Windrow

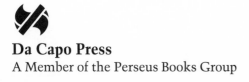

Da Capo Press
A Member of the Perseus Books Group

For Dick, best of brothers,

who started the whole thing.

Cataloging-in-Publication data for this book is available from the Library of Congress.

First Da Capo Press edition 2004
Originally published in Great Britain in 2004 by Weidenfeld & Nicolson; reprinted by arrangement
ISBN 0-306-81386-6

Published by Da Capo Press
A Member of the Perseus Books Group
www.dacapopress.com

Da Capo Press books are available at special discounts for bulk purchases in the U.S. by corporations, institutions, and other organizations. For more information, please contact the Special Markets Department at the Perseus Books Group, 11 Cambridge Center, Cambridge, MA 02142, or call (800) 255-1514 or (617) 252-5298, or e-mail special.markets@perseusbooks.com.

1 2 3 4 5 6 7 8 9—08 07 06 05 04

Contents

The Maps

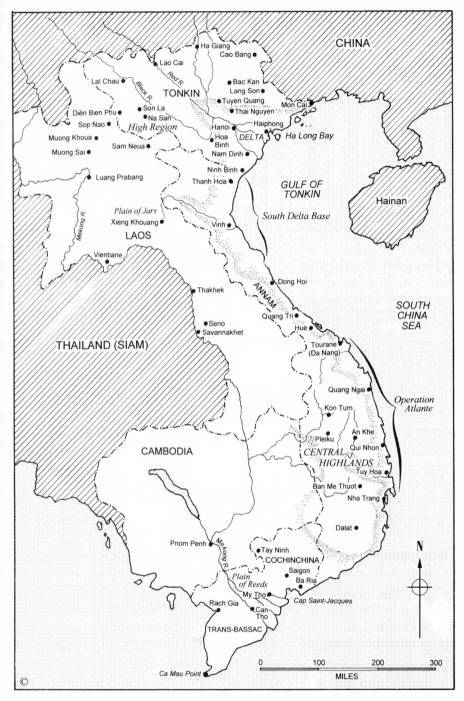

MAP 1 The Indochinese peninsula, *c.* 1953.

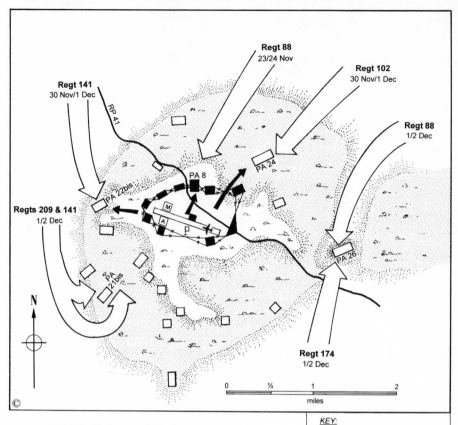

MAP 2 Defence of Na San perimeter,
23 November – 2 December 1952.

KEY:

= Hills with scrub & tree cover

= Inner strongpoints

M = Mortar company

A = Artillery

P = Col Gilles command post

= Paratroop counter-attacks

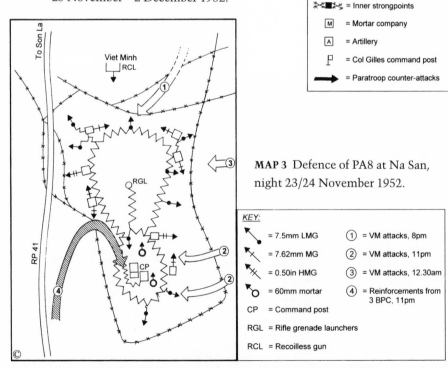

MAP 3 Defence of PA8 at Na San,
night 23/24 November 1952.

KEY:

= 7.5mm LMG

= 7.62mm MG

= 0.50in HMG

= 60mm mortar

CP = Command post

RGL = Rifle grenade launchers

RCL = Recoilless gun

① = VM attacks, 8pm

② = VM attacks, 11pm

③ = VM attacks, 12.30am

④ = Reinforcements from 3 BPC, 11pm

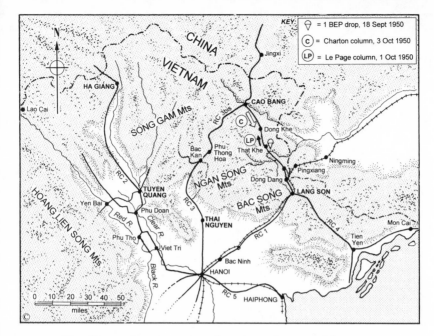

MAP 4 The Chinese frontier region of Tonkin. The area of the *Viet Bac* was approximately that enclosed by the place names in bold type: clockwise from top left, Ha Giang, Cao Bang, Lang Son, Thai Nguyen, and Tuyen Quang.

MAP 5 The Red River delta.

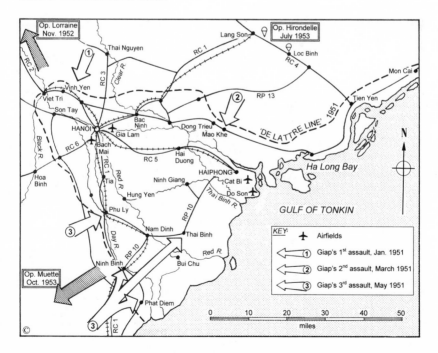

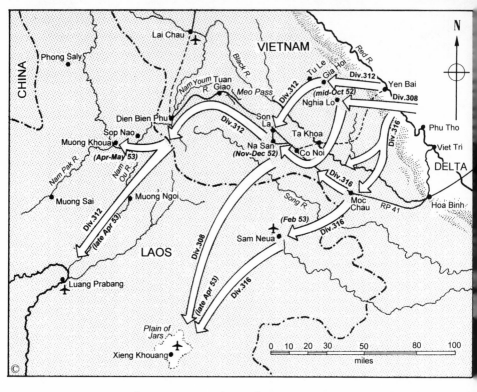

MAP 6 Viet Minh operations in the High Region, winter 1952 and spring 1953.

MAP 7 Main Viet Minh supply routes, winter 1953 and spring 1954.

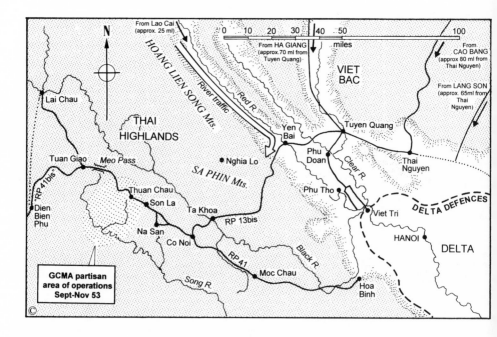

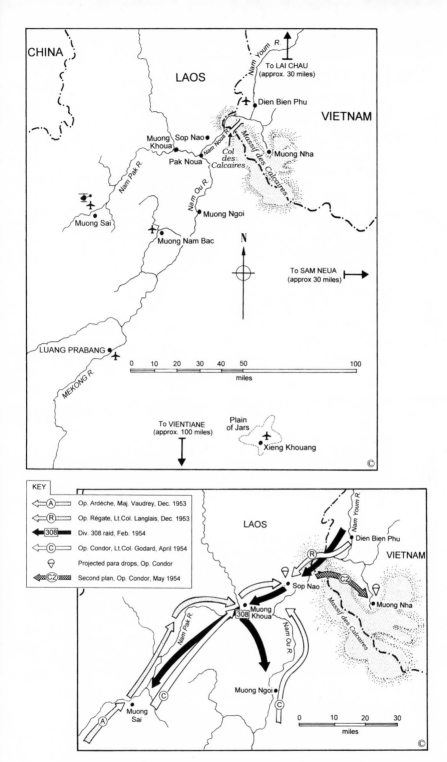

MAP 8 Northern Laos, 1953–4.

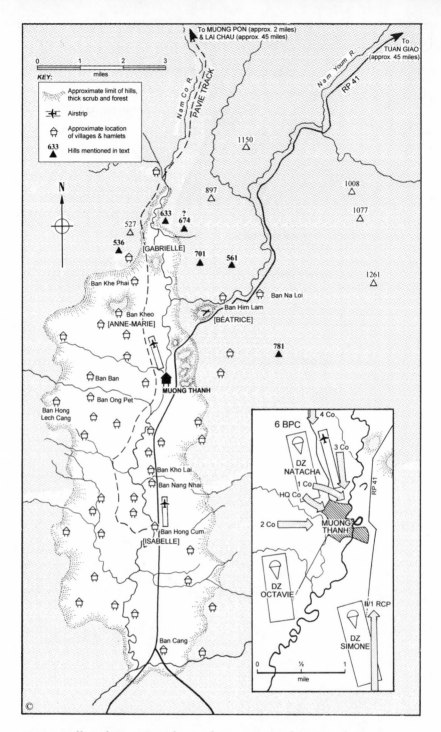

MAP 9 Valley of Dien Bien Phu, with approximate location of some surrounding hills. (Spot heights are in metres above sea level.) *(Inset)* Sketch map of Operation 'Castor', 20 November 1953.

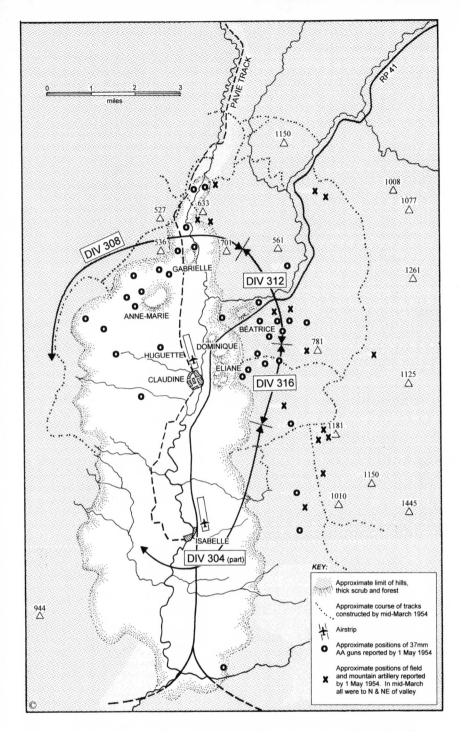

MAP 10 Approximate deployment of Viet Minh siege army at Dien Bien Phu.

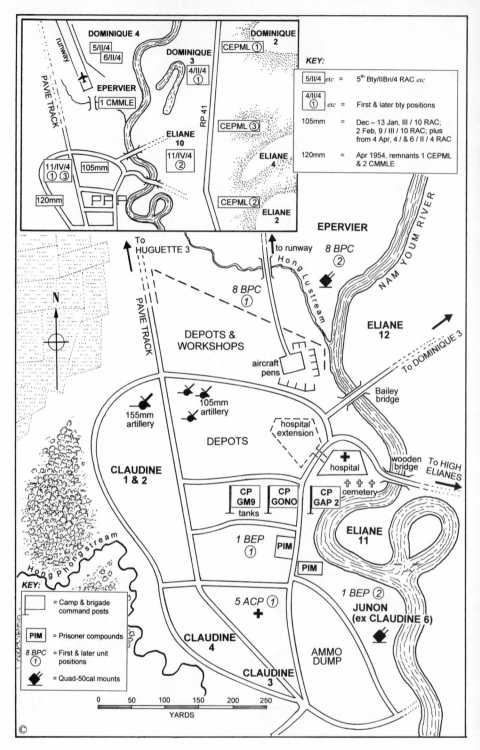

MAP 11 Dien Bien Phu central camp. *(Inset)* Artillery battery and mortar company deployments.

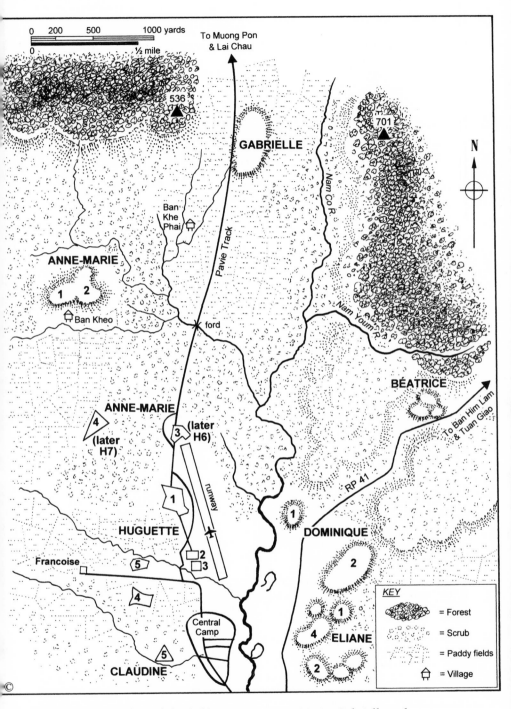

MAP 12 The northern defended locations – Anne-Marie, Gabrielle and Béatrice, as in mid March 1954.

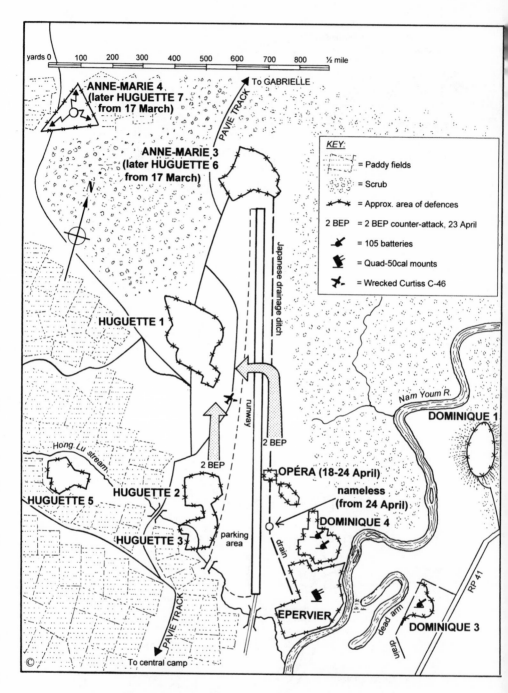

MAP 13 The airfield and the northern Huguettes and Dominiques as in late March, with additional positions mid to late April.

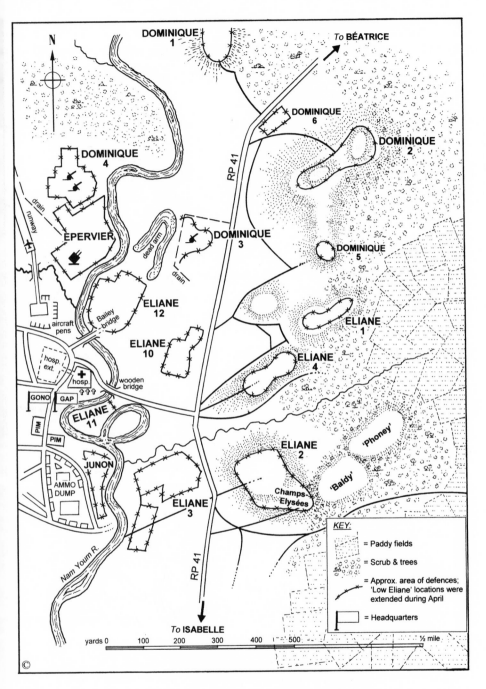

MAP 14 The east bank and the 'Five Hills' of Dominique and Eliane.

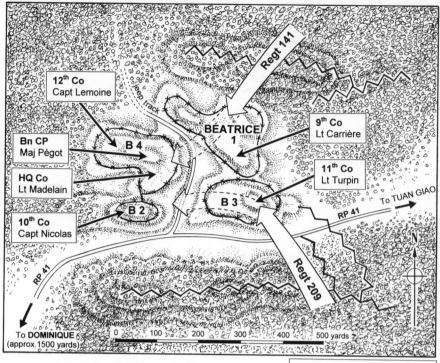

12th Co Capt Lemoine

jeep track

Regt 141

BÉATRICE 1

9th Co Lt Carrière

Bn CP Maj Pégot

B 4

HQ Co Lt Madelain

11th Co Lt Turpin

10th Co Capt Nicolas

B 2

B 3

To TUAN GIAO

RP 41

N

Regt 209

RP 41

To **DOMINIQUE** (approx.1500 yards)

0   100   200   300   400   500 yards

MAP 15 Defence of Béatrice, night 13/14 March 1954.

KEY:

= Forest

= Approx. positions VM approach trenches

= Approx. defended areas

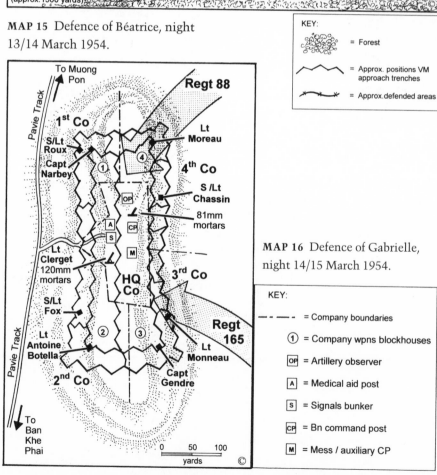

To Muong Pon

Pavie Track

Regt 88

1st Co

S/Lt Roux

Capt Narbey

① ④

Lt Moreau

4th Co

S/Lt Chassin

OP

= 81mm mortars

A

CP

S

M

Lt Clerget 120mm mortars

HQ Co

3rd Co

S/Lt Fox

Pavie Track

Lt Antoine

② ③

Botella

2nd Co

Capt Gendre

Regt 165

Lt Monneau

To Ban Khe Phai

0   50   100
yards

MAP 16 Defence of Gabrielle, night 14/15 March 1954.

KEY:

- - - - = Company boundaries

① = Company wpns blockhouses

OP = Artillery observer

A = Medical aid post

S = Signals bunker

CP = Bn command post

M = Mess / auxiliary CP

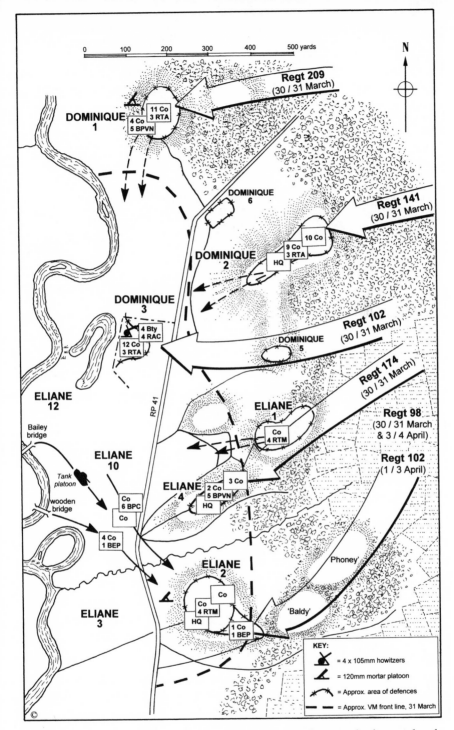

MAP 17 Engagements on the east bank on 30/31 March 1954, the first night of the 'Battle of the Five Hills'.

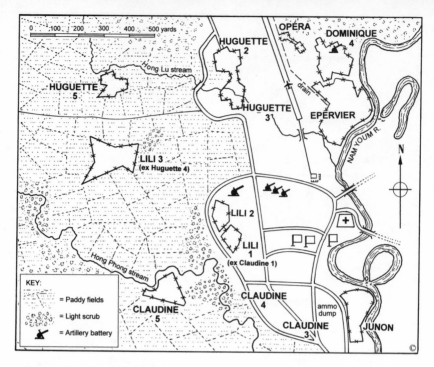

MAP 18 West bank defences, including southern Huguettes and Lilianes, from mid April 1954.

MAP 19 Defences of Isabelle.

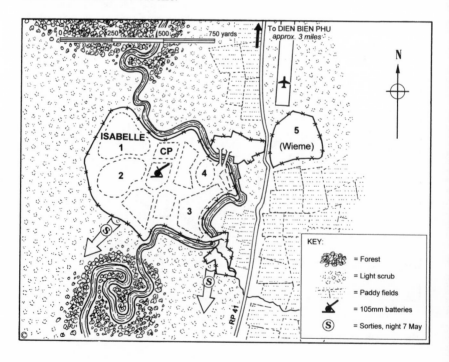

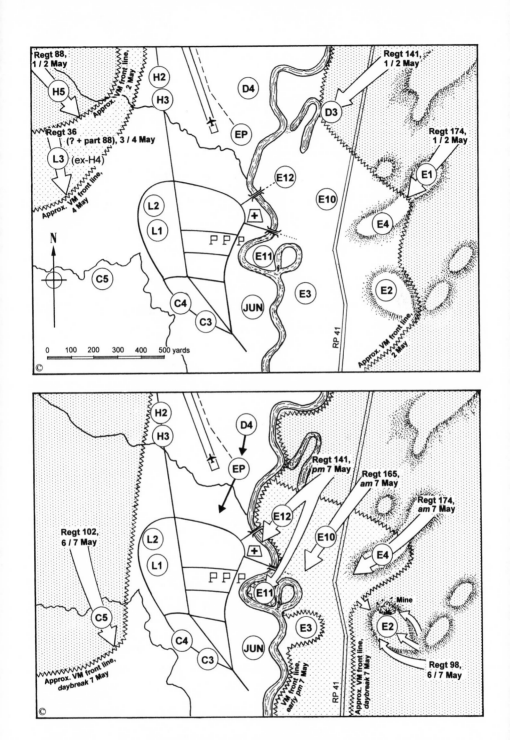

MAPS 20 & 21 The fall of Dien Bien Phu, 2–7 May 1954.

Glossary

Services, commands, etc.

ANV	Vietnamese National Army (French-led)
CEF	French Expeditionary Corps (Italy, WWII)
CEFEO	French Far East Expeditionary Corps
FAEO	French Far East Air Forces
FFI	French Interior Forces (WWII)
FMEO	French Far East Naval Forces
FTL	Land Forces Laos
FTNV	Land Forces North Vietnam
GATAC/Nord	Tactical Air Group North
GCMA	Composite Airborne Commando Group (French-led partisans)
GMI	Composite Intervention Group (formerly, GCMA)
GOMRN	Operational Group Middle Black River (Na San garrison)
GONO	Operational Group North-West (Dien Bien Phu garrison)
NATO	North Atlantic Treaty Organization
SAS	Special Air Service (British, WWII)
SDECE	French foreign intelligence service
S/GMMTA	French Air Force transport command in Indochina
TAPI	Airborne Troops Indochina

Types of unit, and *other military terms*

AA	*anti-aircraft*
ACM	Mobile Surgical Team
ACP	Parachute Surgical Team
BCCP	Colonial Commando Parachute Battalion

BCL	Laotian Light Infantry Battalion
BEP	Foreign Legion Parachute Battalion
BG	Engineer Battalion
BGP	Parachute Engineer Battalion
BM	Marching Battalion (for short-term deployment); or, Montagnard Battalion
BMEP	Foreign Legion Parachute Marching Battalion
BMTS	Marching Battalion, Senegalese Rifles
BPC	Colonial (also Shock) Parachute Battalion; formerly, BCCP
BPL	Laotian Parachute Battalion
BPVN	Vietnamese Parachute Battalion
BT	Thai Battalion
C-in-C	*commander in chief*
CCF	*Fire Control Co-ordination committee*
CEPML	Foreign Legion Parachute Heavy Mortar Company
CM	Marching Company
CMLE	Foreign Legion Composite Mortar Company
CMMLE	Foreign Legion Composite Heavy Mortar Company
CO	*commanding officer*
CP	*command post*
CR	*defended battalion location*
CRA	Air Resupply Company
CRALE	Foreign Legion Auto Repair Company
CSLT	Thai Light Auxiliary Company
CSM	Military Auxiliary Company
DB	Armoured Division
DBLE	Foreign Legion Half-Brigade (regiment)
Dinassaut	Naval riverine assault unit
DZ	*drop zone*
ELA	Air Liaison Flight
EROM	Overseas Reconnaissance Flight
FOO	*forward observation officer (artillery)*
GAOA	Artillery Air Observation Squadron
GAP	Airborne Brigade
GAVN	Vietnamese Artillery Battalion

GB	Bomber Squadron
GC	Fighter Squadron
GFHAT	Combined Army Helicopter Unit
GM	Motorized Brigade; or, Marching Group
GT	Transport Squadron
HQ	*headquarters*
LMG	*light machine gun, automatic rifle*
LZ	*landing zone*
MG	*machine gun*
MO	*medical officer*
NCO	*non-commissioned officer – the non-officer leadership ranks, from sergeant upwards*
PA	*strongpoint*
PC Feux	*artillery fire control post*
PCIA	*air traffic control post*
PIM	*military internee (prisoner labour)*
PSP	*pierced steel plates (prefabricated runway surface)*
RAC	Colonial Artillery Regiment
RALP	Parachute Light Artillery Regiment
RC	Cuirassier Regiment (light tanks)
RC	*Colonial Highway (major road)*
RCC	Light Horse Regiment (light tanks)
RCL	*recoilless gun*
RCP	Parachute Light Infantry Regiment
REI	Foreign Legion Infantry Regiment
REP	Foreign Legion Parachute Regiment
RHQ	*regimental headquarters*
RIC	Colonial Infantry Regiment
RICM	Moroccan Colonial Infantry Regiment (armoured)
RP	*Provincial Highway (minor road)*
RTA	Algerian Rifle Regiment
RTM	Moroccan Rifle Regiment
SMG	*sub-machine gun*
TM	Moroccan Irregular Battalion (Tabor Marocain)

Vietnamese terms

Bo Dai Dia Phuong	Viet Minh regional troops
Bo Doi	Viet Minh regular soldier; also, general term for any military unit
Can Bo	political officers, commissars
Chi Doi	regiment
Chu Luc	Viet Minh regular forces
Cong An	Viet Minh security service
Dai Doi	company
Dan Quan	popular revolutionary organization (DQ)
Dan Quan Du Kich	guerrilla arm of Dan Quan (DQDK)
Dong Minh Hoi	provisional government
Du Kich Tap Trung	concentration of popular guerrilla units
Lien Khu	Viet Minh integrated politico-military zone
Quan Doi Nhan Dan	People's Army
Su Doan	division
Sung Khong Ziat	recoilless gun (SKZ)
Tam Tam Che	system of three-man teams
Tieu Doan	battalion (TD)
Tieu Doan Kinh Quan	light battalion (TDKQ)
Tieu Doan Luu Dong	mobile battalion
Tinh Doi Bo	Viet Minh provincial command
Trinh Sat	reconnaissance unit
Trung Doan	regiment
Trung Doan Doc Lap	independent regiment
Tu Ve	popular forces (DQ and DQDK)
Viet Bac	Viet Minh heartland provinces, NE Tonkin
Viet Minh	national independence front

Note: Viet Minh terms for military units were used loosely, the same word often being applied to units of very different size.

Ranks

Most French service ranks used in this text are straightforward translations into English language equivalents, but these do not always exist; note in particular:

Corporal Chief	*Caporal chef, brigadier chef*
Sergeant	*Sergent, maréchal des logis*
Sergeant Chief	*Sergent chef, maréchal des logis chef*
Warrant Officer	*Adjudant, adjudant-chef* (French Army);
	officier d'équipage de la flotte (French Navy)
Sub-lieutenant (second lieutenant)	*Sous-lieutenant* (French Army)
Lieutenant Commander	*Lieutenant de vaisseau* (French Navy)
Major	*Commandant, chef de bataillon, chef d'escadrons*

Specific French *general officer* ranks are translated as Brigadier General (two star), Major General (three star), Lieutenant General (four star), and General (five star). There is no one-star rank. Most references in the text use the generic 'General Cogny', etc., for all grades.

The author has attempted to refer to individuals by the ranks they held at the date of the particular reference – e.g. Lieutenant Colonel Langlais pre-16 April 1954, Colonel Langlais thereafter – but is conscious that these are not invariably correct.

Picture captions

Picture section between pages 352 and 353

1 During a visit to Dien Bien Phu in December 1953, the C-in-C Lieutenant General Henri Navarre (left) photographed with the commander of Airborne Troops Indochina, Brigadier General Jean Gilles. In US camouflage uniform behind Navarre is the commander of 1st Airborne Brigade, Lieutenant Colonel Alain Fourcade. Behind Gilles, wearing a képi, is Navarre's chief-of-staff Brigadier General Fernand Gambiez, whose son would be killed at Dien Bien Phu on 23 March. *(ECPA)*

2 General Vo Nguyen Giap, then Defence Minister and Deputy Prime Minister of the Democratic Republic, photographed on Dominique 2 in May 1984 during ceremonies to mark the 30th anniversary of his victory. He was then aged 74. *(Courtesy TRH Pictures)*

3 Colonel Christian de Castries, commanding officer of Operational Group North-West, posed for this famous photograph in his command post at Claudine before the outbreak of the battle. He wears his trademark scarlet Spahi sidecap and matching silk scarf. *(ECPA)*

4 Operation 'Castor', 20 November 1953: while others still fall on drop zone Natacha, a paratrooper from GAP 1, armed with a folding-butt CR39 rifle, organizes his kit bag and pack after freeing himself from his harness. His unit has been variously identified, but from the relaxed attitude of the background man this photo was probably taken during the second lift in the afternoon, which dropped Major Souquet's 1 BPC. The viewpoint is west to east; the darkly wooded hill just left of the background man seems to be the future Dominique 2, which would fall to the People's Army on 30/31 March 1954. It is easy to appreciate how dangerously its mortars, RCLs and artillery observers dominated the Huguette positions that would be installed in the foreground area. *(ECPA)*

5 Operation 'Castor', 20 November: Vietnamese paratroopers and French NCOs of Major Bréchignac's II/1 RCP slog up to the village of Muong Thanh from DZ Simone. Indochinese soldiers made up half of this nominally Metropolitan French battalion. These men carry French MAT49 sub-machine guns, issued on a generous scale to paratroopers. *(ECPA)*

6 24 November: the first lucky column of Thai auxiliaries from the Lai Chau garrison, led by Captain Bordier, arrive at Dien Bien Phu. *(ECPA)*

7 Late afternoon, 20 November: two paratroopers from 6th Colonial carry in one of the battalion's ten dead from DZ Natacha for burial. *(ECPA)*

8 Early evening, 20 November: paras of 6 BPC load their wounded on to one of the two Sikorsky S-55 helicopters from Muong Sai that flew in the radios for the Air Force ground control team. The helicopters' range limited them to running a shuttle service for casualties to Muong Sai, where they were triaged; serious cases were then flown out by Dakota to Hanoi. *(ECPA)*

9 Eight 120mm mortars of the Legion's 1 CEPML were dropped at Dien Bien Phu on 21 November. This photo taken near the village houses of Muong Thanh before the mortars were dug in shows a ranging or 'bedding-in' shot being fired; in the background men work peacefully, and there is very little ammunition stacked by the weapon. One of the most important memoirists of the battle, Lieutenant Erwan Bergot, initially commanded one of 1 CEPML's two platoons, and subsequently the combined remnants of the whole unit and a Legion infantry mortar company. The 120mm, of which the People's Army also had large numbers at Dien Bien Phu, would play a central part in the battle; it did at least as much damage to the French artillery as General Giap's 105mm howitzers. *(ECPA)*

10 Photographed during midnight mass on 24 December 1953 (left to right): Lieutenant Colonel Jules Gaucher of the Foreign Legion, CO of 13 DBLE and GM 9; Colonel de Castries, and Lieutenant General Navarre. The C-in-C made a quick inspection of Dien Bien Phu but, typically, was unable to concentrate on this one problem for more than a few hours; on 26 December a message would call him away to deal with the crisis in central Laos. Basing himself at Seno, Navarre quickly stabilized the situation by calling in General Gilles' paratroopers from the strategic reserve – the same units which had captured Dien Bien Phu the month before, and which would soon be returning there. *(ECPA)*

11 In his command post in the main HQ bunker, the one-armed artillery commander Colonel Charles Piroth. His staff and units were inadequately equipped for counter-battery work in wooded hill country – not so much in firepower, as in maps and the means for target location. *(ECPA)*

12 A famous group photo of five of the most prominent paratroop officers of the garrison, taken during a conference in Lieutenant Colonel Langlais' headquarters bunker. (*Left to right*) Captain André Botella of 5 BPVN, Major Marcel Bigeard of 6 BPC, Captain Pierre Tourret of 8 BPC, Langlais, and Major Hubert de Seguin-Pazzis, who took command of GAP 2 when Langlais became chief of operations for the whole garrison. Note on the table a stereoscopic viewer for aerial photos, on which the GONO staff had to rely in the absence of adequate maps. *(ECPA)*

13 Lieutenant Colonel Pierre Langlais, commanding officer of 2nd Airborne Brigade (GAP 2) for Operation 'Castor', but effectively Colonel de Castries' chief of operations from the night of 13 March onwards; seen here wearing his red paratrooper's beret, which he burned at the fall of the camp rather than let it be taken as a souvenir by the enemy. *(ECPA)*

14 Major Marcel Bigeard, commanding officer of 6 BPC for Operation
'Castor', who led it back to Dien Bien Phu – after operations in Laos –
on 16 March. Soon afterwards Langlais co-opted Bigeard to his staff as
officer responsible for planning counter-attacks, and Major Thomas
took over command of 6th Colonial for the rest of the battle. Bigeard
copied his unit's jaunty camouflaged field cap from the wartime
Japanese model; it would become standard issue for French paras in the
Algerian War, universally known as the *'casquette Bigeard'*. *(ECPA)*

15 Major Jean Bréchignac of II/1 RCP. Like Bigeard's 6 BPC, his unit
took part in the capture of Dien Bien Phu in November 1953 and in
early sorties into the hills. They were then flown out and returned to
the strategic reserve in the second week of December, being airlifted to
Seno in central Laos late that month for operations against Division
325, before being dropped back into Dien Bien Phu at the beginning of
April 1954. Here 'Brèche' wears the popular 'sausageskin' camouflage
uniform – the lightweight British wartime windproofs. Bréchignac was
one of the many distinguished combat officers whose careers would be
brought to a premature end by the events in Algeria in April 1961. *(ECPA)*

16 Captain Yves Hervouët of 1 RCC, who commanded the 'bisons' of
the composite tank squadron throughout the battle despite having both
arms in plaster casts from 1 April onwards. Captured on 7 May, he was
one of those who died on the march before even reaching the prison
camps. *(ECPA)*

17 The central valley, photographed at the turn of November/ December
1953 from perhaps 1,500 feet above the southern end of the runway,
looking roughly from north-west to south-east – the viewpoint of a
paratrooper of one of the first sticks of 6 BPC on 20 November. See Map
14 for orientation. Below (A) are Baldy and Phoney, much the same
height as (B), the terraced hill which became Eliane 2, on which the
'governor's house' and other brick buildings show as faint light patches
in front of the trees. Later their rubble would provide the dug-outs on
this hill with the unique advantage of a proper 'bursting layer' in their
overhead cover, which had a significant effect during the fighting on the

night of 30/31 March 1954. Note the paddy-fields east and south of these features; highway RP41 shows only as a faint trace right of Eliane 2. Much foreshortened, (C) is the 'horseshoe' of the Nam Youm; around (D), the houses of Muong Thanh village are almost completely hidden by trees. The airfield is open, dating the photo after 25 November, as three Dakotas are parked in the central foreground. Note at (E) the dogleg of the old Japanese drainage ditch, the dark shadow showing its depth – in April 1954 it was the only safe route north up the airfield. The area immediately left of it, where lines of bivouac tents can be seen, became Dominique 4; brush fires are burning on the future Epervier. (F) is the Pavie Track, which became the main north–south road in the central camp – see Map 11. *(ECPA)*

18 Paratroopers unload the rear body of a Dodge 4 × 4 'weapons carrier' truck from the clamshell doors of one of the Bristol 170 transports requisitioned from the civilian airline SIRA. Dien Bien Phu relied upon these for all heavy equipment that could not be parachuted; although their six-ton capacity was similar to that of the Bristol, fully loaded Fairchild C-119 Packets needed a longer runway than the 1,260 yards at 'Torri Rouge'. The most impressive loads flown in by the Bristols were the complete hulls of the ten M24 Chaffee tanks. Many of these paras have turned their red berets inside out, showing a pale-looking lining tailored in old US camouflage cloth. *(ECPA)*

19 The central camp in early March, from much the same angle as the photo opposite but slightly further south; see Map 11 – the Bailey bridge is just off the left-hand edge of the picture. The width of the foreground is about 350 yards from the river in the east to the bottom right hand edge in the west; the depth from the crossroads at bottom centre to the track junction at top right is about 500 yards. The village and trees have completely disappeared, and the whole west bank is crammed with diggings. (A) is the western base of Eliane 2; its vital position only some 500 yards from the heart of Dien Bien Phu is obvious. (B) is the wooden bridge; immediately below it is the underground hospital. (C) is Eliane 11, on the promontory west of the 'horseshoe'. Aircraft dispersal pens can be seen above (D). The gunpits for 105mm artillery (E) and the 155mm battery (F) flank the Pavie Track, slanting away down the spine of the camp. (G) is the headquarters area, with the command posts for GONO, GM 9 and GAP 2. (H) is the ammunition dump; left of it, strongpoint Junon would be planted on the river-bank. *(ECPA)*

20 19 February 1954: Colonel de Castries personally drives visiting Defence Minister René Pleven and FTNV commander Major General René Cogny on a tour of the camp; his jeep has a pennant staff topped with the star-and-crescent insignia of Castries' old regiment, the Spahis. Cogny holds a heavy walking stick, and Castries has stowed his beside his seat; both officers suffered from the permanent effects of earlier leg wounds and, in Cogny's case, nearly two years in a Gestapo prison and the concentration camps. *(ECPA)*

21 One of the hilltop strongpoints – unidentified, it could be on Béatrice or one of the 'Five Hills'. The scrub has been cleared from most of the summit. Above the sandbag 'blockhouse' at bottom right, two dark figures on the crest give an idea of scale. A flagged aerial at top left indicates a command post; under magnification the dark silhouette to the right of it is revealed as a raised blockhouse surrounded by zig-zagging trenches. The barbed wire of the internal barricades is very sparse. *(ECPA)*

22 One of the 105mm howitzers of 5th or 6th Battery, II/4 RAC in its large open gunpit on Dominique 4. Note the Bailey bridge silhouetted on the skyline top right, its position signposted by a surviving tree; the photographer was looking roughly from north to south-east (*see Map 11*). Ready use ammunition is piled at the right; at left a communication trench leads to a dug-out roofed with logs and sandbags. Cave-like shelters are dug into the walls of the gunpit and trench, but the complete vulnerability of the crew to enemy fire while serving the gun is strikingly obvious. *(ECPA)*

23 Before 14 March GONO's local air support was provided by Bearcat F8F-1 fighter-bombers of squadron GC 1/22 'Saintonge', detached from Hanoi–Bach Mai to 'Torri Rouge' – the airfield at Dien Bien Phu. Here armourers load a 500lb bomb to one of the wing shackles; above this are the ports for the two 0.50in wing guns, and outboard of it are two mounting points for 5in unguided rockets. Beneath the fighter's individual call-sign 'S' the cowling is emblazoned with the badge of GC 1/22. French Bearcats in Indochina retained the dark blue US Navy colourscheme of their original owners. *(ECPA)*

24 December 1953: specialists from 2nd Platoon, 5th Foreign Legion Medium Repair Company work beside the Dien Bien Phu airstrip to reassemble the flown-in M24 Chaffee tanks of 3rd Squadron, 1st Light Horse Regiment (1RCC). Lieutenant Bugeat's 25 fitters and mechanics of 2/5 CMRLE completed all ten tanks between 18 December and 15 January 1954. Note the pierced steel plates providing a hard surface, as also used on the runway. *(ECPA)*

25 Lieutenant Henri Préaud's M24 tank 'Auerstaedt' photographed at Isabelle. The Chaffees arrived painted plain olive drab, and were then individually camouflaged by their crews with streaks of pale dried mud. *(Photo Henri Préaud, courtesy Simon Dunstan)*

26 Warrant Officer Carette's tank 'Bazeilles', abandoned on the summit of Eliane 2 in the early hours of 1 April 1954 after a serious engine fire caused by several bazooka or RCL hits. It has been claimed that the hulk's machine gun, manned by two NCOs of 1 BPC, was the last French gun firing on Eliane 2 when the strongpoint finally fell on the night of 6/7 May 1954. *(Photo Kieran Lynch, 1996)*

27 14 December 1953: Vietnamese paratroopers photographed by Jean Péraud in action in thick cover during GAP 2's return from the failed sortie to Muong Pon. The smoke in the background is from a napalm strike by B-26s called in to help the brigade break free from their attackers; it also killed several paras of 5 BPVN. *(ECPA)*

28 Legion paratroopers of 1 BEP take what cover they can find in the fallow paddy-fields during one of the road-opening missions southward to Isabelle in late March. Note the heavy cover afforded to enemy blocking forces by the tree lines around the deserted village; this photo may have been taken near the often contested creek crossing at Ban Kho Lai/Ban Nang Nhai. The foreground para is a rifle-grenadier armed with a semi-automatic MAS49 rifle. *(ECPA)*

29 Photographed during one of 1 BEP's sorties into the hills north of Dien Bien Phu during December 1953, Captain Cabiro, 4th Company commander, provides a classic image of a French paratroop officer. The US steel helmet (fitted locally with extra paratroop chin strapping) was standard issue, although many Legion and North African infantry received the French M1951 equivalent; the slang for a helmet was a 'locomotive-skin hat'. The holstered P08 Luger pistol is a souvenir of World War II; and note the US SCR536 'handie-talkie' radio – the generous scale of issue in para battalions put radios in every platoon and allowed superior command and control. 'Cab' was badly wounded in both legs in an encounter battle north-west of Hill 781 during the second week of February, and was flown out of the valley. As second-in-command of 2 REP, Major Cabiro would lead them in their last major action of the Algerian War, at Chélia in the Aurès Mountains on 2 December 1960. *(ECPA)*

30 Typical terrain of the High Region, over which both the assembling Viet Minh siege army and the garrison's sortie columns had to operate. Here, photographed from a narrow track clinging to the left-hand slope, a river cuts through the hills between Lai Chau and Tuan Giao. The valley bottom is thickly wooded, and on the steep slopes rough grass alternates with almost impenetrable scrub. *(Photo Kieran Lynch)*

31 Paratroop medics treating shellfire or mortar casualties on one of the eastern hilltops; the doctor crouching at left is tentatively identified as Lieutenant Patrice de Carfort of 8 BPC. The configuration of the background suggests that this may have been taken on Dominique 2. This is supported by the presence of 120mm mortar bomb packing tubes *(far right)*; a platoon of 1 CEPML equipped with these weapons was deployed on that hill in March. *(ECPA)*

32 A fuel dump hit by shellfire blazes in the background; in the foreground are the arched iron roofs of the main headquarters bunkers. Note the many radio aerials on the right; and under magnification the turrets of two of the Chaffee tanks can be made out at centre and left. This photo, like so many others flown out of Dien Bien Phu before the 'air bridge' was cut on 28 March, has been variously dated. It has been suggested that it was taken on 14 March, but under magnification it shows no evidence of the heavy shelling which fell around the command posts on 13/14 March, and it probably records a fire started by the intermittent shelling of the previous weeks. *(ECPA)*

33 A youthful Viet Minh prisoner is marched into the camp after an engagement on the eastern hills; by the end of the battle the ranks of the People's Army were filled with barely trained teenagers. His clothing is typically topped off with a quilted jerkin. Behind him is one of the internal barbed wire fences which hampered movement around the camp after dark. *(ECPA)*

34 Paratroopers trying to improve their trenches in one of the locations east of the airstrip; note the sacks made of rattan – *cai phen* – which did not pack as well as classic hessian sandbags, particularly when wet. Judging from the pickets beyond, the barbed wire defences are unimpressive. In the far background are wrecked aircraft along the parking strip west of the runway; the light-coloured tailplane at extreme top right is that of the Curtiss C-46 Commando south of Huguette 1 which became a landmark during the battle. This seems to place these trenches in Dominique 4 or Epervier; Opéra was not constructed until mid April. After the airfield was closed on 28 March the French photographic record of the battle ceases apart from aerial reconnaissance images. *(ECPA)*

35 Marked prominently but vainly with the Geneva cross, a C-47 Dakota of GT 2/62 'Franche-Comté' comes under shellfire while attempting a daylight casualty evacuation flight during the third week of March. From the position of the tail wheel it has just turned 180°, so is at the north end of the runway facing south, and has not yet picked up a load of wounded. The photo appears to be looking west from the drainage ditch that ran down the east side of the airstrip, where the wounded waited their chance to board. *(ECPA)*

36 On 18 March the photographer Jean Péraud slipped a film and some notes on to an ambulance aircraft for delivery to a colleague in Hanoi, but the notes were seized by the French censor. They read, in part: 'Counting on your discretion – film shows medical evacuation of 17th – catastrophic under VM fire – attempt fruitless. Tried again twice on 18th, but still under VM fire, though Red Cross apparent – atmosphere of anxiety, terror even – screams, crying – rush of the wounded for the door – haven't seen anything like it since the concentration camp... Morale is still very high, even under VM fire... '. Dakota '77011' was probably that flown by Lieutenant Ruffray and Captain Cornu. *(ECPA)*

37 Daniel Camus' well-known photograph taken in the underground hospital shows Dr Paul Grauwin *(left)* examining a casualty whose foot has been partially blown off. Grauwin, the commander of Mobile Surgical Team 29, was not a regular officer, although he had long experience in Indochina (where he would return following the ceasefire). At centre, in the helmet, is Signaller Julot Vandamme; at right, Theatre Aide Bacus of Dr Gindrey's team. *(ECPA)*

38 Operation 'Condor', second half of April 1954: légionnaires of II/2 REI and Laotian troops make a halt in the jungle of the Nam Ou river valley of northern Laos during the northwards march of Lieutenant Colonel Yves Godard's column in a vain attempt to link up with the Dien Bien Phu garrison. Their dress and equipment is also typical of the légionnaires in GONO; and note *(right)* an 81mm mortar base-plate slung on the pony's pack saddle. This battalion was the only European unit in Colonel de Crèvecoeur's small force in upper Laos, and 'Condor' was their third operation in the border country since December 1953. In that month's Operation 'Ardèche' they had made an exhausting march to the rendezvous at Sop Nao with Langlais' paratroopers coming down from Dien Bien Phu; and in early February they had suffered heavy casualties at Muong Khoua while trying to block Division 308's 'raid' towards Luang Prabang. *(ECPA)*

39 High-altitude aerial photo of Isabelle shortly before the end of the battle; see Map 19. At upper right the broad, straight line of the secondary airstrip crosses the edge of the picture, with the narrow stripe of RP41 just left of it. The darkest patches at upper centre are thick woodland along the banks of the Nam Youm; the web of pale lines showing against the paddy-fields and dark scrub are the Viet Minh approach trenches dug by Regiment 57. (We have not attempted to show these on the various sketch maps, since the dating of photos to show their daily development is very uncertain.) The hundreds of tiny white dots on the dark terrain surrounding the strongpoint are discarded parachutes. During April most of the tens of thousands of canopies were not bundled up but left where they lay; from the air the whole camp looked as if it was scattered with confetti. *(ECPA, courtesy Simon Dunstan)*

40 The victors: watched by a member of the International Control Commission, a propaganda section of People's Army Division 308 clap and sing on the streets of Hanoi as they march in to take possession of the northern capital on 14 October 1954. *(USIA, courtesy Howard R. Simpson)*

Preface

IN THE TEN YEARS FOLLOWING World War II, three major conflicts were fought in the former colonial territories of mainland East Asia between Western armies and local forces supported to varying degrees by Communist China.

The largely Chinese guerrilla rising against the British in Malaya from June 1948 was handicapped by its geographical remoteness from China; by the ethnic divisions of the population; and by British willingness to negotiate Malaya's independence. Only a tiny proportion of the Malay majority were ever involved, and although the so-called Malayan Emergency continued officially until July 1960, British and local forces had confined the remnants of the Malayan Races Liberation Army to remote jungle refuges by mid 1955.

In the former Japanese colony of South Korea the Communist challenge took the form of outright invasion by the conventional army of the Democratic Republic (North Korea) in June 1950, openly supported by Chinese forces from that November. This aggression was met and defeated by the conventional forces of the United Nations (predominantly, the United States), resulting in stalemate from mid 1952 and a negotiated ceasefire in July 1953.

Against the background of these simultaneous conflicts, the rising of the Communist Viet Minh movement against the post-war restoration of French colonial government in Indochina (predominantly, Vietnam) in 1946–54 came to have a special significance. Benefiting from particularly favourable circumstances, and especially from a common border with China, the Viet Minh succeeded in a unique achievement: the wartime transformation of a clandestine guerrilla movement into a powerful conventional army. The final vindication of that army was the destruction at Dien Bien Phu in spring 1954 of a US-equipped French force eventually 15,000 strong, including artillery, tanks, two crack parachute brigades and Foreign Legion infantry, with tactical air support.

This was the first time that a non-European colonial independence movement had evolved through all the stages from guerrilla bands to a conventionally organized and equipped army able to defeat a modern Western occupier in pitched battle. Following this defeat, which shocked the Western world and gave huge encouragement to nascent independence movements elsewhere, the collapse of French confidence led within a few months to French withdrawal and a negotiated (though ostensibly temporary) partition of Vietnam at the 17th parallel, between the Democratic People's Republic in the north and the new American-supported Republic of Vietnam in the south. American agencies were active in the affairs of this state from its birth, and the USA would become ever more involved in its troubles over the next decade, culminating in the landing of major US ground forces in 1965. These direct consequences of Dien Bien Phu were the first steps down a road that only ended with the departure of the last helicopters from the roof of the US Embassy in Saigon in April 1975.

DIEN BIEN PHU IS ONE OF those battles which has been so loaded down with historical significance that the actual events are trapped behind an unusually thick distorting lens of hindsight. This has tended to limit the questions we ask about it, and to suggest simplistic answers: crudely, 'How could the French Army have got itself into such an obvious trap?' We know how the story ended, and what is known cannot be un-known, whatever a judge's instructions to the jury; but it is important to hold in mind that on a battlefield nothing is inevitable. The defenders of Dien Bien Phu were not foredoomed, but were caught up in the interplay of particular events and circumstances. If we are to understand what happened on the ground we should study the experience of the men in the trenches and the physical facts which governed that experience; and we should also pull back far enough to catch at least a glimpse of the broader choices which their commanders had to make.

There is another distortion that we should try to dispel, in simple justice to those whose lives or happiness ended in the valley of the Nam Youm river 50 years ago. Throughout history, the ancient customs of war have held that a fortress garrison which chooses to resist to the end, forcing the attackers to pay the bloody price of storming the walls, forfeits all claim on the victors' mercy. But it is not only on the physical plane that the winner takes all: the spectacle of the fall of a great fortress has such impact that the victors may also take the entire psychological reward. Mesmerized by the ruin of what once seemed so strong, we tend to forget what the purpose of the fortress was in the first place, and what resistance could ever realistically have been expected of its defenders. Dien Bien Phu was a shocking defeat; but it was also one of the 20th century's great epics of military endurance.

If France herself had not been overwhelmed by a sense of hopeless catastrophe, Dien Bien Phu could easily have proved a Pyrrhic victory for General Vo Nguyen Giap, the Viet Minh's military commander-in-chief, who lost something between a third and a half of his infantry on its ghastly slopes. That she was so overwhelmed, and that it did not so prove, was due to the context created by the events of the previous seven years; and since some of these were central to the decisions taken by the commanders on both sides, it seems doubly important to summarize them in these pages. If not literally, then Dien Bien Phu was at least psychologically the last act in a connected process.

MY INTEREST IN DIEN BIEN PHU was sparked more than 30 years ago when I was enthralled by Bernard Fall's classic *Hell in a Very Small Place*. As an exciting account of battle drawing upon the testimony of survivors it could hardly be bettered; but even while I devoured it I was aware that my ignorance of the context was denying me many of the rewards of the story. What paths had led these exotically named regiments to this particular valley in an Asian wilderness? Why were there so many Vietnamese faces in photographs of the élite French parachute battalions? If we close an eye to the easy perspective of hindsight, can we understand why the French commanders were initially so confident, and General Giap so hesitant? Why did the defeat of 15,000 men lead so immediately to the collapse of an army with a theoretical strength more than twenty times as great? Unevenly, I began to find out; and each step in my education pointed me further back, towards a line of other questions receding across the years.

My occasional hobby became more absorbing and my curiosity more wide-ranging with the gradual publication of authoritative French material not available to the earliest historians of the battle, and perhaps under-valued by some subsequent writers. The terms in which some of these analytical papers were written, even thirty years after the event, were sur-prisingly intense. It had always been clear how much Dien Bien Phu had mattered in 1954; it was instructive to discover how much it still mattered. The tragic climax to the Algerian War in 1961–2 had alerted even the most casual British observer to the wholly foreign relationship between gov-ernment, citizens and army which then existed among our fellow Europeans just 20 miles across the Channel, and Dien Bien Phu seemed to be embedded like a tumour at the heart of that relationship.

It is perhaps Britain's greatest historical blessing that since 1689 the continuity of our institutions has saved the British Army from making political choices. By contrast, France's 200 troubled years as a serial republic, interspersed with brief periods of less than constitutional monarchy and of foreign occupation, have confronted her army on at least six occasions with disputed claims to the legitimate leadership of the state. Like a human personality, a country's and an army's sense of itself at any particular moment is the product of its memories of the past, and the choices it makes in moments of crisis will be dictated to a great extent by its particular tribal myths. Every generation in France's military history between at least 1870 and 1962 was connected, by chains which have been held up to the light for English readers by Alistair Horne in his several fascinating books. Dien Bien Phu was an important link in one of those chains.

Anyone who approaches the events of the French Indochina War of 1946–54 at even a superficial level soon becomes aware not only of their legacy in Algeria in 1954–62, but also of their origins in France between 1940 and 1944 – in defeat, occupation, liberation and their long aftermath. During the 1960s one of the more empty-headed slogans parroted by fash-ionably Leftist adolescents of all ages was 'better Red than dead'. Political France in the 1930s may not inspire much admiration; but the wrenching distortions inflicted on French society and its army in the aftermath of June 1940 are surely sufficient arguments for national self-defence at any cost. The wounds of military occupation by a foreign power are deep, disgusting and take generations to heal. (The same consideration applies, of course, to Vietnam, whose occupation lasted a great deal longer and whose divisions were even more brutal.)

France's defeat and subjection to four years of ruin and humiliation not only shaped her post-war response to the challenge of the Vietnamese independence movement; it also determined the timing of that challenge in the first place. The unsustainable contradictions of France's occupation of Indochina made an eventual native independence movement inevitable. But it was the French defeat in 1940 that allowed Japan to impose her garrisons on French Indochina, shaming the colonial rulers in the eyes of Japan's fellow Asians. It was the vacuum left by Japan's destruction of the residual French administration in March 1945, followed by her own abrupt surrender six months later, that gave Ho Chi Minh his priceless opportunity to build a truly nationwide political organization, and Vo Nguyen Giap the freedom and the weapons to expand a negligible guerrilla force into the beginnings of an army. And it was liberated France's burning need to reassert her power and dignity through her imperial role that ensured a fairly primitive military response to this challenge.

How differently would the history of Indochina – and of America – have unfolded if the French had not been defeated at Dien Bien Phu, and if the war had dragged on in parallel with the peace negotiations at Geneva? The almost contemporary example of the Pan Mun Jon talks in Korea suggests one model; but while the exploration of historical 'what ifs' is intriguing, it is usually pointless. The game only works if one accepts a narrowly determinist view of history – history with very few 'moving parts', any one of which can supposedly be removed with only limited and predictable consequences. In the real world the alternative possibilities branch out at an exponential rate. Everything is connected, and the specifics of geography, date, national moods, armies and personalities (together with blind chance) determine most of history's outcomes.

These particularities seem to emerge clearly from even brief examinations of the French Expeditionary Corps and the Viet Minh. The more we read about the French Indochina War, the more struck we must be by the perfect combination of factors which coincided to give Giap his eventual victory. This was hailed as an elegant laboratory demonstration of the Maoist equation for revolutionary warfare, and many argued that Mao's manuals provided an invincible formula whose results could be duplicated in any colonial situation. In fact, the exact pattern of advantages which Giap enjoyed in 1950–54 was absent from most other colonial wars – and, most immediately, from the Algerian struggle that began just months after Dien Bien Phu and which enmeshed some of the same French officers. Obviously, the tactical similarities between Giap's wars against the French and the American expeditionary armies are also seductive; but attempts to draw parallels of worldwide application should surely be viewed with caution. People and nations are what they are, and events happen when they happen.

I AM NOT AN ACADEMICALLY trained historian, and this book does not for a moment pretend to be a work of primary research; it is a synthesis of secondary sources, the most important of them in French and therefore perhaps unfamiliar to 'les Anglo-Saxons'. My hope has been to set in their particular context the armies that fought at Dien Bien Phu, which were shaped by their past; and also to offer snapshots from this 50-year-old campaign and battle that are accessible to readers who are not military specialists. The seriously middle-aged sometimes forget that several generations have now grown up in Britain who have had no connection with the military – who have never known a professional soldier and have never handled so much as a shotgun. I hope that readers with expert knowledge will be patient with the brief and simplified explanations of military matters; a clear picture of the physical realities seemed to demand an occasional pause to explain how the process actually worked, and the results when it did – or did not. Equally, I hope that these explanations are detailed enough to be useful without being so relentless that the general reader feels as if he has strayed into a lawnmower catalogue. For this reason many of the supporting facts and figures have been banished to the pages of notes at the end of the book.

The intellectual satisfactions of pursuing an interest in military history lie in tracing patterns and watching the play of one factor upon another – both at the level of tactics (the business of moving troops across a battlefield), and of strategy (that of moving armies around a map); but there are parallel dangers. Our admiration for the courage and endurance of the officers and rankers of combat units is easy, even automatic; our hasty judgements on their senior commanders are sometimes less valid. The French officers charged with conducting this campaign made serious mistakes and paid the price of disgrace, even of ridicule – historically, France has an ugly taste for scapegoats. In retirement some of them waged unattractive paper wars against one another, but to repeat their charges and counter-charges here would be barren. It was at one time fashionable, particularly in the United States, to sneer at the commanders of the French Expeditionary Corps; but this disdain usually sprang from sheer ignorance of the imbalance between their mission and their inadequate means.

It is surely absurd simply to dismiss these officers as incompetents; they were experienced professional soldiers, some of whom had shown great personal bravery on the battlefield. Christian de Castries, the fortress commander, has been lampooned by writers of more limited social experience as a dim aristocrat – even as a bunker-dwelling coward; but he was never seen that way by the iron-hard paratrooper Pierre Langlais, who shared his burden daily and who knew his combat record. On the basis of some of his correspondence René Cogny, the general commanding in North Vietnam, has been criticized for lack of moral courage; but this man had spent nearly two years in the hands of the Gestapo and in the concentration camps for his Resistance activities, emerging crippled for life. The commander-in-chief himself, Henri Navarre, has been accused of failing to see the dangers inherent in the Dien Bien Phu operation. In fact the record shows that he was fully alive to them, but that he shouldered his responsibility and made a calculated gamble in the face of many uncertainties.

Navarre was responsible for an entire theatre of operations, and had to juggle his strictly limited resources according to educated guesses about enemy capabilities, the wavering stamina of his own political masters and the uncertain temper of the Associated States. He was, in effect, playing on at least three chessboards at once; that he seems to have regarded his flesh and blood battalions purely as pawns may make him unattractive, but it does not allow us to call him blind. (The record also suggests that his subordinates' misgivings before the event were in fact rather more muted than some would later claim.) The French generals and staff colonels were not free agents; some approached the battle with foreboding, others with confidence, but all were the prisoners of circumstance. At that place, on that day, faced by difficulties which finally proved insurmountable, they failed, and many men died wretchedly – but to say 'better' men is surely the cheapest sort of jibe.

The armchair observer also runs the risk of becoming as brutalized, in his safely detached way, as the war-weary soldier. In one or two brief passages I have tried to break through that detachment by focusing on the flesh-and-bone realities behind familiar technical phrases. More generally, all we can do is remind ourselves – over the distance of half a world and 50 years – that the actors in this story were the products of their place and time, as we are of ours. A high proportion of them were volunteers, however robustly that word may sometimes have been defined, and we may assume that their reasons seemed good enough to them. It is one of the central human tragedies that war is not an aberration – it is what human beings do. Unlike the huge majority of the current generation in the West, the men on both sides at Dien Bien Phu did not live at a time or in places where they enjoyed the luxury of disregarding that fact; and we who are lifelong civilians have not earned the right to sit in judgement over them.

THE SOURCE NOTES TO THE chapters indicate the most important of the books and journals upon which I have relied, of which a few should be acknowledged specifically.

The major primary sources are the documents now lodged in the archives of the Service Historique de l'Armée de Terre (SHAT) and de l'Armée de l'Air, (SHAA) of which perhaps the most relevant are the records of message traffic. The destruction of the internal documents of Operational Group North-West at the fall of Dien Bien Phu is to some degree offset by the survival of its external exchanges of signals with Land Forces North Vietnam in Hanoi. Extensive study of this material – among very many other documentary sources from cabinet and general staff level down, including evidence presented to the 1954–5 Catroux commission of inquiry, thousands of military reports, scores of personal memoirs, journal articles and theses – formed the basis for Colonel Pierre Rocolle's *Pourquoi Dien Bien Phu?*, published in 1968 and now sadly out of print. Colonel Rocolle's archival research was supported by a programme of written questionnaires and by personal interviews with officers at every level, whose recollections were patiently collated, together with various correspondence which was made available to him.

Wherever possible, Colonel Rocolle compared this information with such material as had been released by the government foreign language publishing house of the Democratic Republic of Vietnam. The latter included various memoirs published by or in the name of General Vo Nguyen Giap; and the nearest thing to a Viet Minh official history of the battle, published in Hanoi in 1965 as *Contribution à l'histoire de Dien Bien Phu*, Fascicule No. 3 of the journal *Études vietnamiennes*. It would be naive to imagine that some of the published French accounts are not partial and self-serving, but at least we are protected by the Western tradition of free inquiry and competitive debate. In weighing accounts published by an Asian Communist government we have no such help; and this book is greatly in debt to Pierre Rocolle's balanced comparisons of French and Vietnamese sources. Rocolle's magisterial analysis, running to 600 pages of scrupulously sourced and annotated text, is the indispensible rod and staff for any student of the battle (although even this source is not infallible in every detail – as a soldier Rocolle was naturally less familiar with the Air Force).

I have also made extensive use of back numbers of the journal *Revue Historique des Armées*. Many of the contributors – usually serving or retired officers – have special personal knowledge of various aspects of the Indochina War and the battle of Dien Bien Phu, and their articles are annotated to the documentary sources in the archives of SHAT and SHAA. Other contributors are distinguished academics, who have cast their nets wider. This mass of material is a most valuable source for the specific facts and figures without which general accounts are sometimes hard to confirm or interpret.

Among the several more or less well-known general histories and personal accounts, the works by Bernard Fall still retain their vivid interest and are a mine of information. In this company Erwan Bergot has the unique claim of having fought throughout the battle as an officer of Foreign Legion paratroops, who later interviewed many paratroop and Legion officers, NCOs and men while researching various works. The much less well-known study of the artillery at Dien Bien Phu by General Henri de Brancion gives many important insights into an absolutely central aspect of the battle, and he too served alongside some of the key personalities. The books by René Bail are particularly useful for Air Force material and include aerial photographs. The most obvious value of the late Howard R. Simpson's published works lies in his extracts from US State Department message traffic of 1953–4, although as an eyewitness he brought to the whole subject a much wider and deeper personal knowledge.

For anyone trying to tell the story of the battle at battalion level, the destruction of unit war diaries has been a serious handicap. When some surviving members of these almost annihilated units returned from captivity, careful efforts were made to reconstruct the stories of their battalions at Dien Bien Phu, but inevitably these reconstructions are less than complete and sometimes contradictory. Men's memories of the relative timing of events in the confusion of battle are notoriously difficult to reconcile; in this case the number of surviving eyewitnesses was relatively small, and many interviews did not take place until months after the events – often, months of terrible hardship.

Comparison of the various sources reveals (unsurprisingly) a number of inconsistencies over the timing of particular episodes, sometimes by margins of 24 hours or more. Many actions took place by night and were only reported to FTNV later, and the sometimes arbitrary choice of recording events that took place over several hours as happening before or after midnight has led to many ambiguities. Where possible I have followed Rocolle's analysis based upon dated and timed signals traffic. When in doubt, I have suggested timings which seem to be supported logically by known chains of cause and effect; I have certainly made errors, but I hope that these have not distorted the broader picture too badly. Given these uncertainties, I make no apology for the use of such weasel phrases as 'probably', 'may have been' and 'roughly' – in the circumstances they are the only honest words.

The problem of producing accurate maps of a battlefield that was notoriously badly mapped at the time has bedevilled all commentators. The sketch maps which have been meticulously drawn for this book by John Richards are based on my comparisons of several versions, whose lateral measurements often differ. Where possible I have tried to confirm the scale lines against aerial photos, using the wingspan of a C-47 Dakota as my datum, but I make no exaggerated claims for their accuracy. Their purpose is simply to enable the reader to follow the actors in these events around the topography of the battlefield. Similarly, the outlines of the different strongpoints are only roughly indicated; in aerial photos the perimeter trenches do not stand out clearly against the shell-churned clay soil.

I WOULD LIKE TO ACKNOWLEDGE my debt to all those who have helped me during the preparation of this book; some of them gave generously of their time and expert knowledge, and others tracked down essential sources of information or lent photographs. In alphabetical order, they are: the eagle-eyed Sarah Barlow; Wayne Braby, of Hollywood, California; Dr Simon Chapman; Shirong Chen; Captain Dale Clarke; Ian Drury of the Orion Publishing Group, for his faith, patience, and extraordinary steadiness under fire; Simon Dunstan; ECPA, Fort d'Ivry, Paris (Adjudant Jean-Michel Villaume); Gerry Embleton; David Filsell; Christian Folini; Will Fowler, as so often; my editor at Weidenfeld & Nicolson, Penny Gardiner; Tim Hawkins; Tony Holmes; Hilary Hook; Jim Hooper; Lee Johnson; Kieran Lynch; Thamaz Naskidachvili; Teddy Neville, TRH Pictures; Ronald Pawly of Antwerp, Belgium; Martin Pegler, Royal Armouries, Leeds; Lieutenant Colonel T. E. Pollack, RAMC; Graham Scott; Ms Mavis Simpson, Ministry of Defence Library; Francois Vauvillier of Paris, for hospitality and informed advice; Flight Lieutenant David Wilson, RAF retd; Adjudant-Chef Johann Wallisch, late 2 BEP and 1 REP; and Dick Windrow.

I owe a special word of appreciation for the advice and encouragement of the late Howard R. Simpson, whom I knew far too briefly before his untimely death. He knew the ground and he knew the men, and few Americans can have equalled his knowledge of Vietnam over more than 20 years, beginning at the height of the French war.

I must also record my gratitude to my family and friends for their saintly patience over two years of unforgivably obsessive behaviour.

Finally, I would like to pay my grateful respects to three dead légionnaires, to whom I would have been proud – though nervous – to give copies of this book if the years had allowed: the late

Adjudant-Chef Charles Milassin (4 REI, RMLE, 2 REI)

Caporal-Chef Georges Gebhardt (2 BEP, 1 BEP)

Légionnaire Eric Morgan (2 REI, 4 REI, 6 REI).

M C W

RINGMER, SUSSEX, MAY 2003

PART ONE

1. *La Formule*

'*It is up to us to keep awake, and to refine continually an aggressive defence capable of breaking the assaults of these clear-headed fanatics.*'
General Raoul Salan

NA SAN, DECEMBER 1952

ON A CRISP, SUNNY WINTER'S day on a red earth hilltop in North Vietnam, a young Californian named Howard Simpson was reluctantly fishing around with borrowed chopsticks in a lunchtime bowl of *pho* soup, while trying to ignore the stench of torn-up corpses festooning the barbed wire a few yards away. Simpson, a stocky World War II veteran with a broad smile and thick glasses, was an information officer from the US Embassy in Saigon. Part of his job was to monitor the use that the French Expeditionary Corps was making of the generous flow of US aid provided through the Military Advisory Assistance Group installed in Vietnam two years previously. He had hitched a flight here from Hanoi on a C-47 full of ammunition, to gather facts and impressions after what was being presented as a particularly significant French victory over the Communist Viet Minh insurgents.

The French theory was that even in the roadless wilderness of this 'High Region' a strong air–ground base could be implanted and kept supplied by airlift alone – a concept for which the British 'Chindit' campaign in Burma in 1944 offered encouraging precedents. The Viet Minh had been born as elusive guerrilla bands; but for two years now, with Chinese help, they had been reinventing themselves as a conventional army, with

10,000-man divisions and light mobile artillery. Such forces are a great deal more unwieldy to move and supply than furtive packs of guerrillas, and the French Air Force could hope to track and harass their marches, robbing them of surprise. By using their American-supplied transport aircraft to create and sustain strong garrisons in the hills, complete with field artillery for defence and paratroop battalions for aggressive sorties, the French high command hoped if not to block, then at least to channel and hamper the cross-country movement of Giap's large regular formations, and to lure him into attacking them where they were strongest. Howard Simpson would be told that what had happened here at Na San seemed to vindicate that hope.

The garrison which had defended Na San over the previous few nights was a microcosm of the French Expeditionary Corps and its local allies. As he was jeeped across the camp Simpson saw French Colonial and Foreign Legion paratroopers, Legion infantry, North African riflemen, lowland Vietnamese from the Red River delta, and Thais recruited in the hills round about. Virtually all the officers were mainland Frenchmen or 'blackfeet' from France's North African colonies. On previous occasions Simpson had not received a particularly warm welcome from the French Army in the field. Here at Na San, however, most of the officers of the *Troupes Aéroportées d'Indochine* (TAPI) and the *Légion Étrangère* were happy to drink the *'Amerloque's'* whisky and let him look around; they had a story that deserved to be told.[1]

SINCE MID OCTOBER 1952 THE Viet Minh's military commander-in-chief, General Vo Nguyen Giap, had been leading three divisions of his best troops, trained and equipped by Communist China, deep into these Thai Highlands – the jumbled, forested hills of north-west Tonkin that straddled the border with Laos to the south. Until recently these sparsely populated highlands had played little part in France's six-year-old Indochina War; the cockpit of the fighting against General Giap's regulars had been the Red River delta, 100 miles away to the east. But after a first probe in October 1951, this last autumn Giap had opened a new front here in the High Region.

The tribal peoples of the border country had no love for Ho Chi Minh's Communist cause, and the French had never needed to guard these hills with more than a chain of tiny forts scattered along the ridges between the Red and Black rivers, mostly garrisoned by local recruits. There were no usable roads, and apart from jungle tracks the lines of communication to these remote posts had been maintained by air. Few had airstrips that would take anything larger than small bush aircraft, and any large-scale resupply or reinforcement had to be done by parachute. Since October 1952, these little garrisons had been swept aside by Giap's advance; French paratroopers had made sacrificial jumps to buy time for their retreat, and now the remaining defended islands in this green ocean had been pushed west of the Black River (*see Map 6*). Their anchor had been planted here, at Na San, where a dirt airstrip had been skinned with pierced steel plates to allow its use by the Air Force's C-47s, and an entrenched camp had been created in Giap's path with frantic haste. It was held by a mixed garrison of a dozen battalions, designated 'Operational Group Middle Black River' – GOMRN for short.

The defences of Na San were a series of dug-in positions surrounded with barbed wire and minefields, most of them manned by single companies of a hundred or so French troops, and arranged to occupy a rough ring of hilltops about 3 miles across that surrounded the airstrip cupped in the valley below. Inside this outer rampart GOMRN's commander – a dour, one-eyed paratroop colonel named Jean Gilles – had built a continuous inner ring of entrenched strongpoints around the airstrip, headquarters, medical aid post, stores depots, and artillery and heavy mortar positions (*see Map 2*). But not all the garrison had arrived, the defences had not been fully prepared, and most of the vital artillery was not yet in place when the first Viet Minh units reached the area in the third week of November. In keeping with their guerrilla tradition, they arrived unannounced.

STRONGPOINT PA8 IN THE NORTHERN face of the inner ring was held by only 110 men – 11th Company, III Battalion of the Foreign Legion's 5th Infantry Regiment – but it was exceptionally well built. Its commander, Captain Letestu, had served in the Maginot Line as a young ranker, and understood exactly how to lay out a defensive position; under his guidance his légionnaires had worked with a will, and their generous allocation of machine guns were well sited in sandbag 'blockhouses' pushed out to sweep the approaches to the wire (*see Map 3*).[2] All this fieldcraft and labour might have gone for nothing on the night of 23/24 November. With neither warning nor preparatory fire, a Viet Minh battalion infiltrated right up to the northern wire of PA8 under cover of some nervous movement by Thai troops, and at about 8pm they tried to rush it.[3] The only other officer, Lieutenant Durand, was killed at once, and Letestu led a small counter-attack force into a desperate hand-to-hand struggle with the two enemy platoons that had got into the trenches. The Viet Minh were finally killed or driven out at about 9.30pm, by which time 11th Company had already lost 15 men dead or disappeared and as many again seriously wounded.

Meanwhile heavy mortar fire was falling on the southern part of the position, heralding another attack. In the absence of French artillery, Captain Letestu got in radio contact with the Foreign Legion mortar company in the central area, and although no fire plans had yet been prepared Lieutenant Bart managed to bring down the fire of his ten weapons on the threatened sector and the gullies approaching it.[4] A company of 3rd Colonial Parachute Battalion from the central reserve was sent to reinforce PA8, arriving at about 11pm just in time to help hold off a dangerous attack; but Letestu was furious to overhear their commander Captain Guilleminot reporting that he had arrived to 'retake the strongpoint', and obliged him to get back on the radio and put the record straight. The wounded were now being cared for by the battalion medical officer Lieutenant Thomas, who with Sergeant Chief Rinaldi had disobeyed orders and crawled half a mile from the central camp to slip through the enemy ranks and the barbed wire.

The last attack came at about 12.30am; it was repulsed like the others, and a useful part was played by a 'PIM' – a Viet Minh prisoner long kept by the company as a tame porter. On his own initiative he replaced the wounded crew of one of the company's 60mm mortars and loaded and fired it by himself. The enemy finally fell back under cover of darkness, taking most of their casualties with them, but 64 corpses and five abandoned wounded were found around the strongpoint. Next morning Colonel Gilles – not a man much given to public praise – told Captain Letestu that he had saved Na San; he also ordered the officers of the other strongpoints to come and examine Letestu's 'magisterial' example of field fortification.[5]

GENERAL GIAP'S ATTEMPT TO BREAK in by infiltrating his first unit to arrive – a battalion from his oldest and most trusted Division 308 – was followed by a week's pause while he brought up the rest of his force and prepared for a major assault. The time was gratefully employed by Colonel Gilles, who received his 105mm howitzer batteries and his last parachute battalion.[6] He was ably seconded by Major Vaudrey, an officer with long experience of the Thai country who had been personally selected by the French commander-in-chief, General Salan. During the whole build-up phase at Na San, a C-47 Dakota landed every ten minutes for at least six hours a day (the airstrip was always closed by fog until about 11am each morning). In all some 3,000 tons of cargo were flown in, including 300 tons of barbed wire, and more than a hundred trucks and jeeps. These transported, amongst other loads, some 5,250 cubic yards of locally cut timber for the overhead cover of dug-in positions. Colonel Gilles insisted that these be dug deep, so that the garrison's weapons could be fired safely across the inside of the strongpoints as well as their approaches. Three days' rations were issued to the perimeter positions, and another five days' were stockpiled in the depots. Mule and pony trains were constantly climbing the hills to the strongpoints loaded with jerrycans of drinking water. Ammunition stocks were reckoned in 'fire units' – the amount reckoned necessary for each weapon for 12 hours' fighting; the Na San strongpoints received three fire units, the artillery two, and the central depots held the same amount again. In the command posts a great deal of work was done on plans for artillery and mortar fire support for the strong-points.

Under a full moon on the night of 30 November/1 December the storm broke, on PA22*bis* at the western edge of the outer ring of hills. This strong-point, held by a company from the 2nd Thai Battalion, was attacked in battalion strength, and despite supporting fire from the Legion mortars the Thais left their position and fell back to the airstrip after about 20 minutes.[7] The Thais were brave fighters when ranging their forested hills like the hunters they were; but they had neither the temperament nor the training to be expected to hold trenches under the fire of 120mm mortars and 75mm recoilless guns. If the enemy got a permanent grip on this hilltop the airstrip was doomed; the 2nd Foreign Parachute Battalion were alerted for a counter-attack to retake it, but first Colonel Gilles ordered a barrage. Under the sickly glow of parachute flares dropped by a circling Dakota called up from the far-off Delta airfields, the defenders could see the Viet Minh on the hilltop being ploughed under by a storm of explosive and flying steel. The heavy mortars continued to fire on them from 3.30am to 6am; and when one company of Legion paratroopers put in their counter-attack with the rising sun behind them, they retook the hill without difficulty.

The northern hill position at PA24 was a different matter. It was held by one company each of Thai and Moroccan infantry when it was assaulted by Giap's Regiment 102 'Ba Vi'; they stood off a mortar barrage and two 'human wave' assaults, but at about 3am the third charge overran the position. Paratroopers of the 3rd Colonial were chosen for the counter-attack at dawn, with two companies from 2nd Foreign Para and one from the II/6th Moroccan Rifles. The 'Ba Vi' Regiment resisted fiercely, however; they had dug in on the reverse slopes, and the fighting went on all day as the paras made successive rushes up the hill supported by artillery fire and diving aircraft. When the paratroopers finally retook the hill at about 4pm, after ten hours' fighting, they found a lieutenant and a handful of his Moroccans still holding out from the previous night. Orders from General Giap found on the body of a dead Viet Minh officer on 2 December would confirm the prime importance he had placed on taking and holding these two strongpoints, in order to install AA guns there and to bring down observed mortar fire on the airstrip.

THE NEXT NIGHT, 1/2 DECEMBER, Giap repeated the tactics that had already failed. Strongpoint PA21*bis* was an abrupt hilltop at the extreme south-west of the outer ring, held by Lieutenant Bonnet's 10th Company, III/5 REI – a sister company of Captain Letestu's 11th, whose example they had taken to heart. This position was the company's second: they had already spent three weeks digging in on another hill before, on 21 November, the cursing légionnaires had been transferred to this heavily wooded feature. They had put their backs into clearing and fortifying it, working on in the moonlight and encouraged by Bonnet's lavish wine issue; but this was a huge task for only a hundred men in ten days. Occasionally the Viet Minh could be seen and heard patrolling and clearing trees on the approaches.

At about 8.30pm on 1 December, under a glorious starry sky, sounds of movement prompted Bonnet to call down the first 105mm shells on to the avenues of approach; but the enemy continued a slow and cautious advance up to his wire, their arrival signalled by mine explosions which attracted the company's light mortars and machine guns. At 1.30am Viet Minh mortars and 75mm recoilless guns began to seek out the Legion weapon pits and blockhouses; a storm of automatic fire broke out on both sides, and survivors described to Howard Simpson how enemy sappers had pressed forward with almost suicidal courage to detonate charges to cut the barbed wire. The first massed rush was stopped and thrown back, and the camp's 105s raked the approaches to the strongpoint. The pressure persisted; Lieutenant Bonnet was killed trying to throw an enemy grenade back out of his trench, and Lieutenant Bachelier took command. A machine-gun crew and a 57mm RCL gunner both carried their weapons out of the shelter of blockhouses to get better fields of fire, and did great execution in an infantry fight which was raging at about 30 yards' range.[8] Lieutenant Bachelier, already wounded, was shot in the throat and died; the last officer, Lieutenant Blanquefort, took over the company.

At about 4am the attacks petered out, although harassing fire continued, to cover the enemy's grudging withdrawal. At 7am a misty sun came up, revealing the battlefield. One blockhouse had sustained eight direct hits without collapsing. The 9th Company came up in support, and patrols went out to gather up an extraordinary number of discarded weapons. Most unusually, the attackers had not been able to carry away their casualties; they left behind 350 dead and about 50 wounded. At a numerical advantage of at least ten to one, three Viet Minh battalions had been unable to submerge a single company of the Legion with artillery support.[9]

On that same night, over to the east on the jutting spine of a hill shaped like a lizard, an entire Legion battalion – III/3 REI, commanded by an eye-patched veteran of Syria and Tunisia, Major Favreau – held PA26 without difficulty during four distinct waves of attacks by at least three Viet Minh battalions.[10] The fighting lasted from 1.20am until 5.30am; once more the Viet Minh blew lanes in the wire, and attacked under the support of mortars of all calibres and 75mm recoilless guns which knocked out two blockhouses. Favreau reported that when the enemy fell back they left about 260 dead, but French casualties amounted to no more than six killed and 20 wounded.[11]

The early morning attacks of 2 December were the last made on Na San. Covered by Regiment 102 and their mortars and 75s, the other Viet Minh units made a general withdrawal over the next few days, eventually leaving only regional troops to keep a relaxed watch over the camp. The garrison sent out strong patrols for miles in several directions without hindrance – indeed, Simpson heard French officers voicing their frustration that they had not been able to catch up with the retreating enemy. GOMRN's defensive victory brought Colonel Gilles his brigadier general's stars, and a widely trumpeted confidence to the press releases authorized by staff officers of the Expeditionary Corps.

AT NA SAN THE CONCEPT OF THE *'base aéro-terrestre'* seemed to have been vindicated, and with this victory came the hope that the Expeditionary Corps had found at last the way to break a long deadlock. For years the two sides had seemed almost to be fighting two parallel wars: the French were the masters in the Delta lowlands, and the Viet Minh in the hills, forests and marshes. When either side ventured seriously on to the other's ground they lost the particular advantages of their structure. General Giap had employed the skills and mobility of the guerrilla to inflict a shocking defeat on the Expeditionary Corps in October 1950, when he caught two large columns strung out along a road through the jungle hills on the Chinese frontier. Encouraged to gamble by an apparent collapse of French morale, he had soon brought his brand-new divisions down into the Delta flatlands – where in spring 1951 they had been smashed into ruin by French artillery, fighter-bombers and tanks.

Giap had learned from this lesson, and in the Thai Highlands he had found a battlefield where French motorized troops could not follow. But the air–ground base could plant in the path of his divisions an airmobile microcosm of the Delta's heavy garrison troops, watched over by a tactical air force. It is unclear to what degree the very particular advantages that Colonel Gilles' men had enjoyed at Na San – and that might not be available on future battlefields – were discussed at French staff level; but the outcome of the battle was considered deeply by General Giap during the painful process of 'revolutionary self-criticism' that followed a defeat which had cost him at least three thousand casualties.

Viet Minh intelligence gathering – normally impressive – had been faulty on several points. Giap had underestimated both the numbers and the quality of the French garrison, failing to identify units correctly, and assuming that the long retreat many had made to reach Na San would have sapped their morale. Handicapped by the lack of surrounding higher ground for observation, he had believed that the defence had little depth to it, and that the separated hill strongpoints could be overrun one by one without interference; he had not appreciated the importance of the inner ring of strongpoints and their potential for launching counter-attacks. He understood that continued use of the airstrip was vital to the defence; but as long as he failed to take and hold an overlooking hill strongpoint it was safe from observation and fire. He had also overestimated the damage that his heavy mortars and recoilless 75s would do to French field positions.

The lessons that General Giap took away from Na San would not be forgotten when he next faced a major French entrenched camp. If he could not take and hold higher ground near by, for observation and supporting artillery, then he should avoid battle. It would be important to concentrate his troops in large numbers around this sort of target, and across its ground lines of supply and/or retreat. He had to plan for a prolonged battle, preparing his jumping-off positions patiently rather than committing his men to costly 'human wave' assaults too soon. Above all he needed heavier artillery – howitzers to lob shells over intervening hills on to targets beyond; and AA guns to destroy the defenders' vital 'air bridge'. All of this dictated the creation of reliable logistic support on a large scale to sustain his army in the field. He would have to build up food and ammunition stockpiles in advance, and maintain lines of resupply throughout what might be a longer battle than he had ever yet fought.[12]

NATIONAL STEREOTYPES ARE CRUDE but not always wholly wrong: in their embrace of the air–ground base concept, French staff officers were following an intellectual tradition that had long been prone to seduction by elegant theories. One example of the dangers of this approach had been the dazzling General Robert Nivelle, promoted chief of the French general staff in December 1916. His confident claims for his plans to break the stalemate on the Western Front – 'We have the formula...' – passed into the vocabulary of cynicism after his disastrous failure on the Chemin des Dames in April 1917 nearly ruined the French Army. It is tempting to wonder whether in 1953 any enthusiast in Saigon permitted himself the same phrase. If the severe General Gilles – now Commander, Airborne Troops Indochina - ever heard such a view expressed, his reply would have been biting. He was well aware of how thin a thread his victory had hung by, and of the large part played by General Giap's mistakes.

In a year's time and after various journeys Jean Gilles, 1st and 2nd Foreign Parachute, III/3rd Foreign Infantry, 2nd and 3rd Thai Battalions, Howard Simpson, and many other actors or observers at Na San would reassemble in the valley of Dien Bien Phu 65 miles to the west. They would be joined at that last valley by Vo Nguyen Giap, and Divisions 308, 312 and 316 of the Vietnamese People's Army.

2. The Three *Ky*

'The emperor's word stops at the village fence.'
Vietnamese proverb

FRENCH INDOCHINA – COMPRISING Vietnam, Cambodia and Laos – occupied the eastern half of the Indochinese peninsula, bordered by China to the north, the South China Sea to the east, and Burma and Thailand (Siam) to the west. Vietnam forms a shallow S-shape (in local imagery, that of two rice baskets slung at the ends of a pole) down the eastern littoral, facing the sea with landlocked Laos tucked behind its 'shoulders' and Cambodia behind its 'legs'. Collectively, the French colonial occupiers called the three countries the Indochinese Union from 1887 onwards. Vietnam was the main arena of the war fought by the French forces and the Communist national liberation movement – the Viet Minh, and its People's Army main force – between 1946 and 1954.

Vietnam measures some 1,000 miles from the Chinese border above the 23rd parallel in the north-west, south to Ca Mau Point. The populous, fertile delta of the Red River in North Vietnam – Bac Bo or Tonkin – measures about 350 miles from west to east; that of the Mekong in South Vietnam – Nam Bo or Cochinchina – some 150 miles. They are linked by the long, narrow waist of central Vietnam – Trung Bo or Annam – which at one point is only 31 miles wide. Vietnam's total land area is about 126,000 square miles, making it slightly larger than Italy.[1] Historically, the three parts of the country were collectively known as 'the Three *Ky*'.

Hills and mountains fill perhaps three-quarters of Vietnam; about one-third is over 4,900ft above sea level. Fifty years ago nearly half of Vietnam's surface was covered with tropical forest, still rich in animal life – tiger, panther, elephant, bear, wild boar, *gaur* buffalo, a few Asian rhinoceros, many types of deer, monkeys, birds, snakes and reptiles. There are innumerable species of insects, some of them dangerous; not only the wet lowlands but also the Annamese highlands swarm with the malarial anopheles mosquito. The highland vegetation ranges from patches of grassy savannah on the plateaux, and tall, razor-sharp elephant grass on the crests, to bamboo forest in the valleys; through various levels of subtropical and tropical forest choked with undergrowth and parasitic tree plants; to true primary jungle with bare, buttressed tree trunks rising to a triple canopy. There are pine woods in the Central Highlands, and mangrove swamps along the southern coastline. The character of the vegetation changes markedly with altitude over quite short distances.

Tonkin, the cockpit of the war against the Viet Minh, is geologically a southwards extension of Yunnan province in China. It is largely covered with hills and mountain ranges, running roughly from north-west to southeast, rising to about 10,300ft above sea level. These are divided principally by the parallel valleys of the Clear, Red and Black rivers (respectively the Song Lo, Song Hong and Song Da) and their tributaries. These highlands wall in the triangular Red River delta – hereafter, in the usage of the 1950s, simply 'the Delta'. This fertile rice-growing lowland of about 5,790 square miles contains Hanoi, the capital of Tonkin, and Haiphong, its main port, both on the Red River. With a population density of more than 1,000 per square mile, the Delta was one of the twin economic hearts of French Indochina, and its control was considered vital to French interests.

The mountain walls to the north of the Delta, stretching over the Chinese frontier, were called in the 1950s the 'Middle Region'; the Delta's western ramparts, straddling the Laotian border, were called either the 'High Region' or the 'Thai Highlands'. Here the mountains are pure primeval wilderness: steep, chaotically jumbled, punctuated by saw-toothed crests and plunging gorges, cloaked with luxuriant forest, they recede to the horizons in ridge after endless ridge. For several thousand-square miles between Lai Chau in the Thai Highlands and the Plain of Jars in northern Laos, mankind's brief history might never have happened. Airmen flying over these frightening mountain jungles might catch a momentary glimpse of a snaking silver river at the bottom of a canyon; but only in one or two tiny folds, hours apart, would they spot the vivid green patchwork of a few toy rice-fields – and thus the rare possibility of a dirt airstrip. Some French pilots deliberately left their parachutes behind, like old-time sailors who chose not to learn to swim so as to avoid prolonging the misery of drowning. It was in one of the few small river valleys through these mountains that the battle of Dien Bien Phu was fought.

The most striking geological features, particularly characteristic of Tonkin though also found to some extent further south, are the limestone buttes that the French called *'calcaires'*. The peaks left behind by eons of erosion, these karst formations jut abruptly from the landscape in pinnacles covered with scrub and trees, fissured and riddled with caves. During all Vietnam's wars these groups of natural towers have provided guerrillas with almost impregnable hiding places and vantage points for observation and ambush.

From Tonkin, the Truong Son (Annamite Cordillera) runs south unbroken down the western borders with Laos and Cambodia, behind a narrow strip of coastal lowlands. The mountains bulge out eastwards to meet the coast south of the ancient Annamese capital of Hue and just north of Tourane (now Da Nang) above the 16th parallel; thereafter they occupy virtually the whole of southern Annam down to the 11th parallel, forming the Central Highlands (known to the French as the 'High Plateaux'). This was the most sparsely inhabited and least explored region of southern Vietnam, its game-filled forests still home to primitive tribal peoples; in the late 1960s it would be the arena for some of America's most costly battles in her own Vietnam War.

South of the Central Highlands lie the paddy-fields of Cochinchina, with the capital and river port of Saigon – the southern seat of French government and commerce – cradled to its south by the multiple mouths of the great Mekong river. This delta wetland covers some 23,000 square miles, and is one of the great cultivated rice baskets of Asia, more reliable because not so prone to flooding as the Red River delta. Otherwise it resembles its counterpart at the northern end of the Annamese 'pole': as in Tonkin, the muddy flats are divided up by innumerable natural waterways and man-made irrigation canals, studded with patches of woodland and occasional hills. Between Saigon and the Cambodian border lies the Plaine des Joncs ('Plain of Reeds'), an immense waterlogged jigsaw puzzle of swampland, creeks, tussock islands and lush vegetation.

THE TROPICAL AND SUBTROPICAL climate of Vietnam is dominated by the north-east and south-west monsoons; but the length of the country, its mountain barriers and differences in altitude produce remarkably diverse weather. Broadly, the north-east monsoon between November and April brings cool, dry weather to the north, and the south-west monsoon between May and October brings rain and high humidity to the whole country. Tonkin and northern Annam – the scene of most conventional military operations from 1950 onwards, roughly north of the 18th parallel – have two main seasons, winter and summer, separated by a brief, hot, dry spring. The winter and spring last from November to April; low-lying Hanoi averages a pleasant 62°F, but in November–December the difference between early morning and afternoon can be from 40°F to 68°F. The temperature drops with altitude, and in the High Region night frosts are common. The highland winter begins chilly and dry, but in January– March the mornings, in particular, are often heavily overcast and there may be drizzling rain; even in dry weather the High Region is notorious for morning fog – 'crachin' – which interferes seriously with aircraft activity. The summer lasts from May to October, with heavy monsoon rains in the highlands, and in the Delta temperatures average around 86°F.[2]

THE HUMAN BATTLEFIELD WAS the product of a long and volatile history. The 20th-century states of Cambodia, Laos and Vietnam were defined by modern political frontiers which bore only an approximate relationship to the distribution of the peoples of Indochina. Of various origins, these groups had washed back and forth during more than 2,000 years which had left many strains mixed in a sort of ethnic archipelago along the inland borders of the peninsula. The prehistoric inhabitants of Vietnam were of Australo-Asiatic origin and probably arrived in successive waves from what is now Indonesia. These were gradually overlaid by Indianized conquerors from the west (Chams and Khmers), and by Chinese from the north. A Mongoloid people from Nam Viet in China moved south into the Red River delta in the 2nd century BC; and there, for about 1,000 years, the culture of China flourished – though her central government was periodically resisted. The imperial bureaucracy existed in uneasy parallel with a local feudal society; this Vietnamese people, a fusion of

Indonesian, Chinese and Thai stock, are thought to have formed a distinct ethnic group by AD 200 at latest. Under Chinese rule a Vietnamese national consciousness and language evolved, and the earliest historical epics sprang from attempted rebellions against China – notably that against the Han Dynasty led by the legendary Trung sisters in AD 39–43, which briefly achieved independence. Further risings in the 3rd and 6th centuries were crushed, and in AD 679 the Chinese named the country Annam, 'the pacified south'. This proved optimistic. With the collapse of the Tang Dynasty in the 10th century Vietnam rose again, and an independent monarchy owing China a formal allegiance was recognized in AD 968.

During the European medieval period the northern Vietnamese state was modelled internally on the Chinese system of administration by an educated mandarin class, its flourishing culture and religion incorporating both Confucian and Buddhist influences. Repeated wars were waged against the Chinese, Khmers and Chams, and in the 13th century three separate Mongolian invasions were all eventually repulsed. In 1407, during a period of civil war and Cham resurgence, the Ming Dynasty restored Chinese rule, this time governing with oppressive harshness and attempting to snuff out Vietnamese culture. Although independence was regained by the great guerrilla general Le Loi in 1428, this detested Chinese occupation became embedded in Vietnamese folk memory. The 16th and 17th centuries brought Portuguese and Dutch traders, firearms, and French missionaries. At about the time of the American and French Revolutions, the so-called Tay Son Rebellion spread from central Vietnam over the entire country, and expelled yet another Chinese invasion of the north. In 1802 the southern prince Nguyen Anh was enthroned in Hue as the Emperor Gia Long, unifying the whole of Vietnam.[3]

FRANCE'S INTEREST IN SOUTH-EAST Asia dated from a visit to Versailles in 1787 by the future Emperor Gia Long's small son, organized by the Jesuit missionary Bishop de Behaine. However, after her 18th-century defeats in North America and India, France's efforts to acquire a colonial empire were late and haphazard, and it was not until the third quarter of the 19th century that French troops landed on the Vietnamese coast. Thereafter, as in Africa, the tricolour was carried forward in fits and starts, as often by the initiative of obscure officers reacting to local events as in accordance with any plan from Paris. Colonialism was more controversial in France than in Britain, and was associated with particular political and commercial factions.

The initial excuse – as so often – was maltreatment of missionaries. After some false starts in 1858–9 French troops returned in 1861 to expand their control over eastern Cochinchina. Vietnam's military resources were archaic, and a defeat at Chi Hoa that year more or less ended conventional resistance. In 1862 the Emperor Tu Duc signed a treaty granting the invaders generous concessions. Although some Catholic and progressive groups favoured co-operation, the treaty aroused fury among both mandarin and peasant classes, and guerrilla resistance continued, which in turn gave the French excuses to seize more territory. A campaign in 1867 ended with Cochinchina declared a French colony and Cambodia a protectorate.

Imperial authority was effectively destroyed, and Tonkin became prey to the Co Ben – *pavillons noirs* or 'Black Flags' – a freebooting army of Chinese troops from Yunnan, Thai highlanders, and outright bandits – 'pirates' in the local term. In 1872–4 a French river squadron penetrated the Delta, but its commander was killed. Bloody anarchy ensued, with outbreaks by sectarian and anti-French militias, a pretender claiming the throne of Hue, and the Chinese-sponsored Black Flags raging unchecked. In 1882 a French expedition under Captain Rivière seized Hanoi, but his head and those of 30 of his men were later to be paraded around the countryside on Black Flag spears.

Following the death of the Emperor Tu Duc in 1883 the French manipulated the succession to install a puppet emperor and government in Hue. Between December 1883 and a Franco-Chinese treaty in April 1885 Admiral Courbet and General de Négrier led major expeditions against the pirates and Chinese regulars (the campaign that first brought the Foreign Legion to Indochina). In 1887 the French declared the foundation of the Indochinese Union, comprising Cochinchina, Annam, Tonkin and Cambodia, and Laos became a protectorate in 1893. At various dates thereafter the colonial or protectorate status of the different territories would be adjusted on paper, but the reality was French rule and sparse military occupation, alongside a continuing puppet monarchy and local mandarin administration. Although organized resistance died down from about 1895, skirmishing continued in various parts of the country for many years, inextricably muddled with simple banditry; the French had to mount periodic punitive columns into the wilder regions well into the 20th century.

After a thousand years of disputed independence, the patient defiance of foreign invaders was by now a defining self-image of the Vietnamese people, whose regional suspicions were far less important than their shared national identity. This clan solidarity is underlined by the fact that in the whole country there are even today only some 300 family names.[4]

AT THE TIME OF FRENCH CONQUEST the huge majority of the population still lived as their ancient ancestors had done: by growing rice in the fields around scattered, virtually self-sufficient villages sited near a water source. Vegetable gardens, Indochina's plentiful fish, and domestic pigs and poultry completed a healthy diet. Communications were primitive and travel rare, since trade was insignificant above an artisan level. In a tropical climate fields irrigated with river silt produce two rice crops annually; although these require intense labour in the planting and harvest seasons, the cycle allows a reasonably leisurely life for the rest of the year, and a water buffalo, a wooden plough and a rice flail were all the machinery a peasant needed. In devoutly Buddhist Cambodia and Laos the cultivation of more land than that required to feed a family, and the amassing of possessions, was actively discouraged. In Vietnam the predominant religion was a more relaxed Mahayana Buddhism, long diluted with elements of Taoism, Confucianism, local animism and ancestor worship into *Tam Giao*, 'the triple religion', whose observance was a matter of reassuring family and village ritual. Although each village had both a Buddhist pagoda and a shrine to the ancestral spirits, there was no powerful priestly caste to make stern demands; the tight-knit life of household and village was ordered along Confucian lines of respect for established hierarchy and practice.

The ultimate source of power in pre-colonial times was the emperor surrounded by his court of aristocratic tribal leaders; in practice its exercise was delegated to the mandarins, forming a pyramid of seniority from great ministers down to petty local governors. In almost all daily matters the local mandarins delegated in turn to the village council of elders. The council's decisions were transmitted to each head of household, which was the basic social, economic, political and religious unit – 'one fire, one lamp'.

A feature of Vietnamese life that was to be highly significant in the 1940s–50s was the tradition of parallel associations, coupled with an instinctive secrecy. The village had a mutual aid society into which people paid contributions towards the cost of funeral rituals. Many, especially in the flood-prone Delta, had an emergency relief fund, which stockpiled contributions of rice assessed according to a farmer's acreage. Artisans had their craft guilds, and enthusiasts for various pastimes and sports their own clubs. Individuals might be members of several associations simultaneously, but there was a culture of separation and secrecy between the parallel activities. In front of any but trusted intimates the very existence of a particular association might not be acknowledged, let alone the names of its real leaders. The habits of hidden identity, duplicity and ambiguous intentions were deeply ingrained; for the politically powerless, life had often depended upon concealment and misdirection. This was a society perfectly designed by history for supporting an underground guerrilla movement.[5]

In pre-colonial times the peasants were taxed, although usually at tolerable levels, by the mandarins, who were the active and visible agency of the imperial government. Entry to this civil service was by individual examination, but these educated families had inevitably developed into a more or less hereditary local aristocracy – though of different grades and widely differing levels of wealth. There was no commercial class of exploitative landowners or wealthy merchants in parallel to the mandarinate, which was a wholly conservative force. The imperial regime was autocratic, illiberal and arbitrary; there was no conception of individual rights, and punishments for incurring the wrath of the powerful were terrifying, but in a widely dispersed rural society few of the peasantry would actually attract such baleful attention.

TO SOME VIETNAMESE, ALMOST entirely limited to the small urban minority, French colonial rule brought improved infrastructure, some access to Western education and medicine, the protections of law and order, and – depending upon class – opportunities for either amassing wealth, or finding employment as labourers, craftsmen, servants and petty functionaries. To the vast rural majority, who had at least enjoyed a sustainable subsistence economy, it brought greedier bureaucrats enforcing alien regulations, a European settler plantocracy and Chinese entrepreneurs. Lured by the colonialists' money economy, there sprouted a new class of rapacious Vietnamese landowners, who soon learned all they needed to know about buying cheap, selling dear and keeping the primary producer powerless. This class identified its interests with the French and was despised by the old ruling families.

Salt, one of the few essentials that inland villagers could not get for themselves, became subject to a monopoly and very heavy taxation. The cultivation of opium as a cash crop was encouraged, producing profit for the merchants and the state but – since they could not eat poppies – leaving the producers vulnerable. Although the acreage of cultivated land and its rice yield increased greatly, the benefit went to the new stratum of middlemen rather than to the peasants, whose standard of living plummeted. Worst of all, moneylenders flourished; small plots of land passed from debt-ridden peasants into the swelling holdings of ever richer landlords, turning many small farmers into landless labourers, or wretched sharecroppers who fell into everlasting debt and had to give up the proceeds of between 40 and 60 per cent of their harvest. A regional differential emerged, with the larger land holdings and much of the wealth concentrated in Cochinchina, which was under more direct French administration.[6] The revenue produced by her colony did not greatly benefit France, however: although Indochina was a tariff-protected market for French goods, few could afford them, and the large profits extracted from Indochina's raw materials went only to a small number of French private companies, Chinese businessmen and rich Vietnamese landowners.[7]

For all the rhetoric about France's 'civilizing mission' there was still only one doctor for every 50,000 people, and 90 per cent illiteracy. The rural Vietnamese *nha que* might not have been able to read, but he did not need newspapers to tell him that his conditions of life were wretched. His village grandparents remembered life before the French – before the children went hungry and their fathers were buried alive in debt, before they were robbed and beaten by the arrogant new landlords. Their oral tradition was strong, passing down the old stories of legendary heroes and heroines who had risen against the Chinese and Mongolians. They were Asians: they bowed to the power that was, rather than courting disaster by romantic gestures of hopeless defiance. But the village was still a fortress in their minds; and they waited patiently behind its palisades and *chevaux-de-frise* of sharpened bamboo.

THE SIZE OF THE VIETNAMESE population in the mid 20th century is speculative, but in 1957 the total was estimated at 27 million, with perhaps 15 million in Tonkin and northern Annam, and 12 million in Cochinchina and southern Annam. Among these totals some 50 distinct ethnic groups could be identified, but about 80 per cent of the people were Vietnamese. The largest minority were the Chinese (Hoa), totalling perhaps half a million, with communities all over the country but predominantly in Cochinchina. As throughout East Asia, this Chinese diaspora tended to dominate commerce and some had become extremely rich, but they remained largely unassimilated. Their most visible centre was Cholon, the western quarter of greater Saigon. Alongside them in western Cochinchina there lived some 300,000 ethnic Cambodians or Khmer.[8]

The tides of history had left about 2 million people of the older ethnic groups in the central and northern hill country. The true *'montagnards'* were the dozens of tribes scattered through the otherwise unpopulated Central Highlands on both sides of the Cambodian border, probably numbering around 720,000. Historically despised and persecuted as savages, these 'Moi' had long memories of Vietnamese ill treatment. Until the early 19th century they were believed to be a sort of higher animal, with 8in tails; Annamese lowlanders regarded them with contempt and fear, and even in the 1950s ventured into their tiger-haunted hills only reluctantly.[9] While the more remote villages retained their vigour (some tribes had managed to avoid contact with the French until the 1930s), by 1950 many groups were in decline. Despite the efforts of enlightened French administrators to protect them, many were conscripted on to plantations as forced labourers. In 1950 the Viet Minh had as yet made only isolated inroads into this region, where their lowland origin made them unwelcome.

Equally suspicious of the 'Annamites' and thus of the Viet Minh were the tribal peoples who were found in Tonkin, distributed across the Chinese and Laotian border marches. The Thai linguistic group, about 700,000 strong, included the Black, White and Red Thai (so named from the characteristic dress of their women), the Nung, Tho and Lao; the Australo-Asiatic group, the *c.* 200,000 Muong and Khmu; and the Sino-Tibetan group, the *c.* 170,000 Lolo, Meo and Yao. These were mostly highlanders, although the Nung – noted for loyalty to the French – also occupied the coastal fringe from Ha Long Bay north to the Chinese frontier. The Tho were few in number, and their home range was lost to French influence when the Viet Minh overran the Middle Region along Route Coloniale 4 (RC4) in autumn 1950. Soon afterwards the ancestral hills of the Muong, around Hoa Binh south-west of the Delta, were also abandoned to the Communists.

The opium-growing Meo of the Thai Highlands, numbering perhaps 80,000, were known for their fierce independence, internal democracy, sexual freedom, sturdy indifference to evil spirits, massive silver necklaces, splendid dogs and 'dry' cultivation by slash-and-burn methods which steadily deforested the hills at their chosen altitudes of 3,000–6,000ft. The other main group in the High Region were the Thai, the aboriginal ancestors of both the Laotian and Siamese peoples, who had originally migrated south from Yunnan. Under the French the three traditional Thai 'kingdoms' had been united in a puppet Thai Federation headed by Deo Van Long, the elderly son of a 'Black Flag' leader of ferocious memory. The Black Thai shared the high hills with the Meo, the other Thai clans preferring lower altitudes and 'wet' rice cultivation.[10]

AS IN EVERY COLONIAL EMPIRE, it was the colonizers themselves who created the leadership of the independence movement, which first became visible in the years following the Great War. The missionary schools had already turned out an upper working class of literate foremen and clerks. The government then brought further education to the cities, and a tiny but growing class of Indochinese professionals and intellectuals emerged from the Chasseloup-Laubat and Albert Sarraut lycées. Some of these young men came from mandarin families that had never ceased nurturing their national heritage and brooding over the French ocupation; but many of them, educated entirely in French and so knowing more about the history of Alsace than of Annam, found themselves painfully uprooted from their own culture. Nevertheless, armed with their new diplomas and eager to embrace the wider possibilities revealed to them by their teachers, they strode forward into a Western tomorrow. They soon learned that tomorrow's doors were narrow and its ceilings low for a yellow man, even for a French-speaking graduate wearing a suit and tie.[11]

France has always trumpeted its enlightened lack of racism compared with the Anglo-Saxons, but the claim of universal republican fraternity does not stand up to much examination. True, France might not allow skin colour to stand in the way of the successful 'évolué' who pursued a flatteringly complete integration; but there is more to colour blindness than outward acceptance of a black parliamentary deputy or the exquisite Vietnamese wife of a colonial general – Britain, after all, smiled upon her cricket-playing Cambridge maharajahs. There are as many ugly words for 'wog' in French as in English, and the lower strata of colonial adminis-tration and commerce knew them all. An Indochinese might, by heroic application, gain a baccalaureate, and might even go on to secure a junior post in the administration; but he would be paid much less than his white colleagues, he would languish in his grade while inferior French candi-dates were promoted above him, and he would never be allowed past the doors of the clubs where they spent their weekends. If his professional ambitions were frustrated, he might have to find work as a commercial bookkeeper or lowly schoolteacher, inhabiting a shabby Franco-Asian limbo which denied him the full dignity of either world.[12]

It was in the educated class that anti-French resentment and access to international political theory collided. Aware of what they had lost as much as what they were being refused, these men and women began to explore the idea of nationalism; and before long this usually attracted the heavy-handed attentions of the Sûreté and colonial police. In pursuit of political education some of them travelled, to France and further afield; a pioneer among these, in 1911, was a 21-year-old ship's cook using the name Ba – one of dozens of aliases, of which the last would be Ho Chi Minh. In 1920 this patient, charismatic son of a poor Annamese mandarin, now named Nguyen Ai Quoc, was among the founding members of the French Communist Party, and by 1923 he was being trained by the Comintern (Communist International) in Moscow. In February 1930, by now based in China, he launched the Indochinese Communist Party (ICP).

Various nationalist groups carried out occasional inarticulate acts of defiance, assassinations and jailbreaks; but the first serious trouble came in 1930, when failed rice harvests and commercial recession reduced the poor to near desperation. In February the nationalist Viet Nam Quoc Dan Dang Party (VNQDD) fomented a violent mutiny by native Tirailleurs troops at Yen Bai, an up-country garrison on the Red River. The outbreak was put down with much bloodshed, and the VNQDD was largely destroyed. In May an internal Communist group led a more general peasant uprising around Vinh in Annam; many Frenchmen and Vietnamese officials were killed and a number of 'soviets' were proclaimed. This rebellion, too, was crushed with heavy loss of life and mass imprisonments; although full control was not regained for a year, the internal Communist leadership was destroyed, and survivors of both the VNQDD and the Communists fled into China.[13]

Working at different times from Hong Kong, Canton and Siam, Ho Chi Minh consolidated the internal and external groups, and the Indochinese Communist Party was fully recognized by the Comintern in April 1931. A thorough territorial and functional organization was worked out; and by 1932, despite the earlier losses, the ICP had some 1,500 members and tens of thousands of sympathizers in Vietnam. It was only one of many factions within the independence movement; but it was the best organized and disciplined, and offered the poor the most specific and attractive programme. In 1936, France's left-wing Popular Front government allowed some outlets for political activity; the ICP took advantage of this, entrenching and extending its organization under cover of various 'fronts'.

IN 1927, DURING THE CHAOTIC civil wars of the 'Warlord Period', the first Chinese Communist army had been born in a mutiny by General Chu Teh's 24th Division of the Kuomintang or Nationalist army. While Chiang Kai Shek's Nationalists and Chu Teh's and Mao Tse Tung's Communists struggled for advantage across the immense, ruined expanses of China, in the far north Japan invaded Manchuria in 1931, later launching strikes across the Chinese border proper. In 1936 Chiang Kai Shek was forced to agree to a united anti-Japanese front with the Communists, although this was always fragile. The following year saw an outright Japanese invasion of China; and one of the Nationalists' important supply lines was the Haiphong–Kunming railway through Tonkin.

The outbreak of World War II in Europe at first had little impact on French Indochina, beyond starving the small, outdated garrison of reinforcements and equipment, and prompting – in view of the Nazi–Soviet Pact – a clampdown on the Communist Party; but Germany's *Blitzkrieg* campaign of 10 May 1940 smashed the Low Countries, France and the British Expeditionary Force in six weeks, and on 22 June the French accepted Germany's armistice terms. While no formal alliance yet existed between Germany and Japan, in June 1940 the Japanese approached General Catroux, the French governor-general of Indochina, with a demand for the closure of the Haiphong–Kunming railway under Japanese supervision. Catroux had no option but to agree; he was relieved of his post by the new Vichy government of Marshal Pétain and replaced with Admiral Decoux, but France's humiliations were only beginning.

In September 1940 Japan – about to conclude the Tripartite Pact with Germany and Italy – demanded the use of Indochinese airfields, the installation of garrisons and free movement of troops through French territory. When Decoux hesitated, the Japanese attacked over Tonkin's northern border from China, defeating the Lang Son garrison and marching on Haiphong, where more men were landed; some 800 French troops died in this two-day clash. Admiral Decoux was forced to agree to Japanese demands and, unsurprisingly, further concessions were extracted as time went on. The French administration and garrisons were allowed to remain in place, responsible for domestic affairs only. This demonstration of French weakness encouraged a premature Communist rising in Cochinchina in November 1940, but it was quickly crushed. An opportunistic Siamese attempt to recover lost territory on the Mekong river led to fierce fighting in January 1941; Japan insisted on mediating, and in March five Cambodian and Laotian provinces were handed over to her ally, Siam.

By now the prestige and morale of the French in Indochina were seriously undermined; and when Japan went on to win her sweeping victories over American, British and Dutch forces a year later, the humiliation of the European colonialists at the hands of fellow Asians delivered an enormous boost to nationalist confidence and ambition. Despite Japan's bestial treatment of so many Asian civilians, millions of former colonial subjects within the 'Greater East Asian Co-Prosperity Sphere' accepted the propaganda of their Japanese 'elder brother' at face value.

IN CHINA, MEANWHILE, the united front broke down completely in January 1941; thereafter Nationalists and Communists simultaneously fought each other and – to some extent – the Japanese. From their southern havens, in territory governed by the Nationalists from their capital at Chongqing, Ho Chi Minh and his followers continued to pick their way delicately among the pitfalls and opportunities that surrounded them. Since China was destabilized by civil war, foreign invasion and the intricate conspiracies of a dozen competing interests, their true goals had to be concealed under shifting layers of opacity. Indochinese exiles of various political complexions gathered at Jingxi in Guangxi province – only 60 miles from Cao Bang in Tonkin – where in May 1941 they founded a broad nationalist organization under the title Viet Nam Doc Lap Dong Minh Hoi (roughly, 'League for the Independence of Vietnam'), later known simply as the Viet Minh. From its inception the Communists were a powerful element of this common front, which they planned to use as the instrument for ultimate Communist government in Vietnam; but it was obviously wise at this stage not to antagonize the Nationalist Chinese or, indeed, the other Allies. Ho Chi Minh later became a member of the Dong Minh Hoi, a provisional coalition government acceptable to the Nationalist Chinese, who provided it with limited facilities and supplies.[14]

One of Ho's most promising lieutenants was Vo Nguyen Giap, a 30-year-old Communist law graduate and schoolteacher with a passion for military history, who had evaded the French security round-up in 1939–40 and crossed into China in company with a long-time comrade, Pham Van Dong. The son, like Ho, of a poor mandarin of the second class, Giap came from Quang Binh province in the narrow waist of Annam. He had been a student activist, imprisoned for three years while still in his teens; and his young wife, held in Hanoi's Hoa Lo prison, would die there in 1943. Although he was a voracious reader of political and military theory, Giap's attachment to the cause was emotional as much as intellectual. Physically he was short and stocky, with a round face, thick springy hair, bright eyes, a broad, generously cut mouth, and a natural expression of good nature and animated enthusiasm.

This was the man Ho entrusted from 1941 with creating a guerrilla intelligence network in Cao Bang province just across the border. Giap successfully established hideouts in the hills and extended a web of agents down into the towns; so effective was this that the ICP were able to trade his intelligence 'product' for Nationalist Chinese concessions – though this commerce was undercut from late 1943 by the Chongqing representatives of a more widely connected Free French *maquis*. Moving between the Nationalist- and Communist-dominated zones, in 1942 Giap attended the Red Chinese guerrilla warfare school at Guangta, becoming an enthusiastic student of the writings of Mao Tse Tung. Back in Guangxi he persuaded his comrades to plan their future revolutionary campaign against the French entirely on the Communist Chinese model.

Volunteers for a politico-military organization were sought from across the border, and potential leaders were selected, indoctrinated and trained with great care. When ready, these cadres returned to set up safe refuges in Tonkin where, in their turn, they recruited and trained underground bands; in time these coalesced into larger groups, able to dominate limited areas. While a few oppressive Vietnamese officials and the occasional constable would be assassinated to give credibility to their promises, there were to be no premature trials of strength with the Japanese; at this stage their goal was to survive, grow, train, extend their clandestine influence and gather information. By the end of 1943 several hundred men and women had been trained at Liuzhou in Guangxi and in Tonkin, although only small numbers of weapons were obtained from the Chinese under the cover of the Dong Minh Hoi.

In September 1944 a conference approved the formation of armed 'propaganda brigades' – their mission was still predominantly to spread the word rather than to fight. In October, Ho Chi Minh – alone among the members of the self-proclaimed provisional government – finally went home, crossing into Thai Nguyen province and joining Giap's guerrillas in their mountain camps. In December the 1st Armed Propaganda Brigade was formed; the 31 picked men and three women reportedly had one light machine gun, 17 modern rifles, two revolvers, and 14 more venerable firearms. A few days later, for public relations purposes, the unit successfully captured two small French posts from local levies. In early 1945 propaganda brigades proliferated and spread out through the hills; their success in recruiting was remarkable, and by March bases had been established in six provinces of northern Tonkin, extending as far west as Lai Chau and as far south-east as Lang Son.

While French garrison towns had to be bypassed, interference from the Japanese was minimal. They had always left internal security to the Vichy authorities, and the Viet Minh had been careful to avoid Japanese troops. In 1944, fearing Allied landings, the Japanese actually encouraged some nationalist activity in Cochinchina in order to hamper any French plans. Spring 1945 saw the Allies on the Rhine and Germany's defeat imminent; Japan could no longer apply the leverage of Axis power over a compliant France. Early in March 1945, Japanese troops and artillery were redeployed around the main French garrisons; and on 9 March an ultimatum was delivered without warning – French troops were to be disarmed and personnel were to surrender to Japanese custody. Refusal was met with immediate attack and, after the inevitably brief resistance, with massacre and atrocity; in Saigon the senior military and civil prisoners, General Lemonnier and Resident Auphalle, were beheaded after being forced to dig their own graves. About 5,700 French and French-led troops of up-country garrisons had enough warning to avoid the coup, and General Alessandri gathered these men to fight their way out to the Chinese border. Around a core provided by the three battalions of the Foreign Legion's 5th Infantry Regiment (5 REI), the columns made an epic march of 51 days through the Thai Highlands, fighting a number of rearguard actions before reaching the safety – if not the welcome – of Nationalist China in the first days of May 1945. One of those actions was fought by the rearguard of the 5 REI at the remote airstrip of Dien Bien Phu, where 7th Company was led in a bayonet charge by its captain, Jules Gaucher, close to a hill called Him Lam.[15]

WITH FRENCH CONTROL REMOVED, the Viet Minh were presented with extraordinary opportunities: the Japanese openly handed over administration to the Vietnamese – in Annam and Tonkin to the hereditary emperor, Bao Dai, and in Cochinchina to the United Party, a ramshackle coalition of sectarian and Communist groups. These nominal authorities were no match for the well-organized and dedicated Communist cells, who exploited the situation energetically. As long as their troops were not attacked the Japanese made no real attempt to enforce internal security, and the Viet Minh were able to expand and intensify their activities unhindered, implanting 'propaganda brigades', 'people's committees' and 'liberation committees' throughout the border country of Tonkin and down into the Delta. While the best recruits were accepted for Giap's 'regular' or full-time mobile units, most were left in place as part-time local guerrillas or unarmed village supporters; planting a solid infrastructure of political agents and expanding control over the population was more important at this stage. Generally the Communist programme followed – with modifications for local conditions – Mao's 'Seven Fundamental Steps': to arouse and organize the people; achieve internal political unity; establish bases; equip bases; recover national strength; destroy enemy strength; and regain lost territories. The later steps were postponed for the time being; and the forging of 'internal political unity' was initially pursued by persuasion, with only selective recourse to shooting the uncooperative.

Secondly, and pricelessly, the intelligence-gathering network of the Free French mission at Chongqing was destroyed at a stroke, and the Viet Minh's monopoly of information from inside Vietnam was skilfully traded for Allied support. They agreed to recover downed Allied airmen; there was even some limited collaboration with clandestine French parties, and a legend about a pro-Japanese mandarin shot by a joint Viet Minh–French firing squad. Still posing as straightforward nationalist patriots, the Viet Minh established friendly contact with the US Office of Strategic Services (OSS, the forerunner of the CIA). This connection brought training teams and a limited supply of weapons and radios – benefits delivered directly, rather than routed via the Dong Minh Hoi provisional government. In April 1945 a conference chaired by Ho Chi Minh agreed to consolidate all armed revolutionary groups – now nominally some 5,000 strong, though only half, at most, were armed – into a Vietnam Liberation Army under Giap's operational command; and to merge the six liberated provinces into the 'Free Zone of the *Viet Bac*'. (Throughout the subsequent war against the French this mountainous region east of the Red River – the provinces of Cao Bang, Ha Giang, Tuyen Quang, Bac Kan, Thai Nguyen and Lang Son – was to be the safest redoubt of the Viet Minh.)

During the rains of May–August 1945 two OSS teams led by Majors Archimedes Patti and Allison Thomas worked directly with the Viet Minh at Tra Trao in Tuyen Quang province, training several hundred men, arming a smaller number and accompanying them on a few raids against Japanese posts. Sources differ about the number and scale of these actions, but clearly enough was being done to justify the OSS's support. Far more important than a few dozen Thompson guns, however, was the hope that these contacts could be parlayed into Allied recognition of a Communist-dominated Viet Minh as the legitimate representatives of the national liberation movement.

The arrival of the monsoon rains in spring caused a catastrophic famine in the Delta, where – in the absence of the French technicians – the flood control system failed. At least half a million Vietnamese starved to death, and the desperate poor were still dying on the pavements of Hanoi when, on 6 and 9 August, the USAAF dropped the atomic bombs on Hiroshima and Nagasaki. On 16 August the Japanese garrison in Vietnam officially handed over control of the country to the Bao Dai regime in the north and the United Party in the south. When the news spread, the people rose in a cathartic orgy of celebration and vengeance; French men and women and loyal Vietnamese were hunted through the rioting streets, spat upon, beaten, raped and killed. For the second time, and now to an unlimited extent, the Viet Minh were suddenly presented with a power vacuum.

HO CHI MINH AND HIS LIBERATION Committee moved with extraordinary speed and confidence. Inside Tonkin the Viet Minh political and military organization went into overdrive, rushing to establish its authority on the ground, while the Chinese-sponsored Dong Minh Hoi back in Guangxi was cut off from information and overtaken by events. All over the country Communist agents fomented or manipulated popular uprisings, of which their local committees claimed leadership as by right. There was ugly blood-letting as mobs took revenge on unpopular officials, landowners and moneylenders. In the south, Tran Van Giau, a Communist, seized the helm of the United Party, and guerrilla bands soon controlled the whole of Cochinchina except the home areas of the powerful Cao Dai and Hoa Hao sects.[16] In the north the guerrillas from the hills moved rapidly to take over the key towns and disarm the Japanese, their way prepared by agents in place; they also seized large quantities of French weapons which had been stored by the Japanese since the March coup.

On 25 August the powerless Emperor Bao Dai formally abdicated and invited Ho Chi Minh to form a government; on the 28th, Vo Nguyen Giap's troops entered Hanoi. There was no chance whatever that the few French administrators and soldiers emerging shakily from their prison camps would be able to reconstruct an administration. The nearest thing to a unified and disciplined force able to take control was Giap's Liberation Army – soon to be retitled the People's Army (Quan Doi Nhan Dan).

On 2 September 1945, as US aircraft flew over Ba Dinh Square in salute and America's local representatives smiled from the dais, Ho Chi Minh declared before a vast crowd the independence of the Democratic Republic of Vietnam. His speech quoted phrases from the US Declaration of Independence; he repudiated all French treaties, but emphasized Vietnamese friendship towards both Nationalist China and the USA. His hope was obviously to present the French with a *fait accompli* already approved, at least tacitly, by the Allies. The provisional government ostensibly included all shades of nationalist opinion, though the Communists were dominant; and General Vo Nguyen Giap was made not minister of defence but minister of the interior. News arrived that in Cochinchina the Communist Tran Van Giau had announced a separate provisional government, and envoys between Hanoi and Saigon concluded a loose agreement.

THE US GOVERNMENT HAD NEVER wished to restore the pre-war status quo in Indochina; and at the Potsdam Conference in July the Allies decided that in the first instance, while an ultimate solution was negotiated, Vietnam should be divided in two at the 16th parallel, with Nationalist Chinese troops taking the Japanese surrender in the north and the French returning to the south. Free French forces which had been preparing to take part in a campaign of liberation were not yet ready to move in any numbers, however, so in the meantime a British/Indian force from South-East Asia Command would occupy the south and disarm the Japanese. The de Gaulle government now installed in Paris was determined to restore French power over the whole country, but lack of troops in Asia forced it to accept this scheme. From 9 September some 150,000 Nationalist Chinese troops under General Lu Han began to move south into Tonkin, which they pillaged enthusiastically, despite the near starvation that they found there.[17]

Three days later the first few troops of Britain's 20th Indian Division landed at Saigon, with orders to disarm the Japanese, release internees and restore public order, but to remain neutral between local factions and the French. In fact its commander, Major General Gracey of the Indian Army, was sympathetic to Britain's fellow colonialists and allowed a French advance party to accompany his division. Martial law was declared and the carrying of arms forbidden, but Gracey's force was too small to exert effective control; he was therefore obliged to employ the surrendered Japanese, and also to rearm some released French troops of the 11th Colonial Infantry. Although many of the armed bands the British encountered were simple criminals, Tran Van Giau's Communists had been quick to emulate the Viet Minh programme, spreading out across the south to preach, recruit, tax, enforce and punish; they were particularly successful in the provinces of the far southern peninsula, the Trans-Bassac.[18] In late September there were bloody clashes in Saigon between French troops and Giau's Communists.

In early October 1945 advance units from General Leclerc's French 2nd Armoured Division began to land in Saigon, and shortly thereafter the British gratefully began a six-month process of handing Cochinchina back to the French. The energetic Leclerc and his fresh, well-equipped troops soon put Giau's mostly small and indifferently armed bands to flight; motorized columns fanned out all over southern Indochina, and by February 1946 some 30,000 French troops had achieved freedom of movement – though not the claimed 'pacification' – up to the 16th parallel. The hard core of Giau's surviving guerrillas returned to the forests and swamps; liaison with the Viet Minh in the north became much closer, and the independence of the southern Communists was virtually abandoned. Giau's treatment of the local population had been much harsher than that meted out by the northern Viet Minh, and influenced the Cao Dai and Hoa Hao sectarian communities to reach an eventual accommodation with the French. Giau was called north to Tonkin, taking many of his men with him to be amalgamated into the Viet Minh. Hanoi's grip over the southern revolutionaries was tightened by his replacement, Nguyen Binh – who was no less cruel a despot than Giau, but whose 'security' teams were rather more carefully targeted.

IN FARAWAY FRANCE ANOTHER change of leadership was also taking place: on 20 January 1946 General de Gaulle, frustrated by parliamentary squabbling, resigned from both the government and public life. Unlike Tran Van Giau, he was not to be replaced by another strong leader, but by a succession of indecisive coalition governments. De Gaulle's moral authority remained unique; he had played the resignation card before, and he probably anticipated a summons to resume the national leadership long before it eventually came in 1958. Nevertheless, throughout that period many Frenchmen would continue to draw comparisons between the weak, even squalid leadership of the Fourth Republic and that huge, eloquent silence at Colombey-les-Deux-Églises. One appointment made before his resignation would have lasting consequences, however: that of Admiral Thierry d'Argenlieu as French High Commissioner in Cochinchina.

This icily controlled former Carmelite arrived in November 1945, intent on fulfilling his wartime chief's stark instructions to restore French sovereignty over the whole of Vietnam, and deaf to arguments for exploring a compromise. His staff's grasp on local subtleties was limited; a purge of the former Vichy administration had replaced many old Asia hands with Gaullist successors selected more for political reliability than for knowledge of Indochina. A fresh eye was not invariably a blind one, however. The dashing General Leclerc, with no previous Asian soldiering behind him, had arrived full of confidence that order could be restored within a matter of weeks; but his experience on the ground soon changed his mind – as did personal meetings with Ho Chi Minh, and with seasoned French officials. Leclerc became convinced that genuine negotiations were the best outcome the French could hope for: they were facing not just a guerrilla army, but an entire people inspired by a national idea. Leaving Indochina early in 1947 to take up a post in North Africa, he advised the incoming High Commissioner, Émile Bollaert, to 'Negotiate – negotiate at any price'.[19] To most French soldiers, with colonial experience only during the last stage of Moroccan pacification in the mid 1930s, the problem and its solution seemed simpler. Still smarting from the army's recent humiliations, they were inclined to give short shrift to these Asian bandits who were defying France's historic title to Indochina.

Meanwhile, in the north, Ho Chi Minh was playing a long game of negotiating with the French while consolidating his position. The Dong Minh Hoi, dominated by the non-Communist nationalists of the VNQDD, had come trailing south in the wake of their Nationalist Chinese sponsors. Luckily for the Communists, the Chinese occupation army's medieval style extended to unashamed corruption. Collecting money and valuables, the Viet Minh bought General Lu Han's agreement not to interfere with their activities, and the VNQDD had only local successes in supplanting the Communists. The Chinese also sold Giap 32,000 captured Japanese weapons; but the newly improvised Viet Minh army was still too lightly armed and patchily trained to resist a determined French advance north led by Leclerc's armour, which seemed predictable once Lu Han's horde finally straggled home to China. Foreign support for the Democratic Republic was no more than verbal. America was now uneasily aware of the Communist core of the Viet Minh, and furious French protests over excessive encouragement of Ho Chi Minh led to the withdrawal of the OSS mission, while Chiang Kai Shek's attention was entirely focused on his resumed civil war against the Red Chinese.

Throughout 1946 Ho Chi Minh pursued negotiations; but since he was demanding recognition of a unified independent Vietnam under his own government, and the French were insisting on restoration of the colonial status quo, no positive outcome seemed likely. However, every month's delay gave the Communists more time to build up their army, to eliminate rival groups within the Viet Minh, and to deepen the people's support. The talks took place against a background of famine and a typhus epidemic in Tonkin during the winter of 1945–6, which the Viet Minh's agents eloquently blamed on the French. In February 1946 the French concluded an agreement with Chiang Kai Shek, but their concessions did not win them an immediate withdrawal of the Nationalist armies; the deciding factor was the lucrative opium harvest, from which the Chinese were determined to profit before they marched north. They did agree, however, that an advance party of French troops could return to Haiphong.

Although their first boats were fired upon by both the local Chinese garrison and the Viet Minh when they docked on 6 March, a ceasefire was soon agreed and French troops entered Hanoi on 16 March. March 1946 also saw a highly provisional agreement concluded between Ho Chi Minh and the French High Commissioner to Tonkin, Jean Sainteny, though this would need ratification by Paris: its main headings were limited self-government for Vietnam within the French Union, in return for the stationing of 25,000 French troops in strategic garrisons, mostly on the Chinese frontier and for five years only. France rushed troops into Tonkin through her steadily enlarged beachhead around Haiphong, and the Communist leaders had real difficulty in reconciling their followers to this compromise. Their basic argument was to appeal to Vietnam's age-old distrust of China, pointing out that Chinese occupations tended to last for a thousand years, and that five more years of the French were a small price to pay.

While Ho pursued negotiation, Giap was becoming convinced that war was inevitable – an attitude perhaps sharpened by his loss of face during unsuccessful personal meetings with Leclerc brokered by Jean Sainteny. (The aristocratic general could not take seriously Giap's pretensions to military rank; and the latter's manner when confronted by leaders of a world he genuinely admired seems to have been effusive rather than dignified.) At the Dalat Conference in April, d'Argenlieu's team back-tracked from what Ho believed had been agreed the previous month; throughout their dealings with the Viet Minh the French authorities treated them with disdain, never conceding that they were legitimate represen-tatives of their people. It was said of d'Argenlieu, a man of almost papal *froideur* and distance, that he reacted to the least contradiction with the expression of a gentleman suffering painful indigestion; and, with a few intelligent exceptions like Sainteny, his colleagues took their tone from him.[20] Convinced that only direct talks with Paris offered any hope of a settlement, at the end of May 1946 Ho Chi Minh and Pham Van Dong led a delegation to France as representatives of a newly created Popular Front government (the 'Lien Viet') . Immediately they had left, d'Argenlieu announced the foundation of an 'autonomous' Republic of Cochinchina, thus dismissing the Viet Minh's insistence on negotiating for the whole country.

In Ho's absence, Giap ordered the preparation of two military base areas: the main one in the Viet Bac of northern Tonkin, and another on less well-prepared ground below the southern edge of the Delta, in the coastal hills of Thanh Hoa, Nghe An and Ha Tien provinces. From the earliest days Giap had followed Mao's doctrine of differentiating between his 'regular' troops – full-time mobile units, with the best available men and weapons; 'regional' forces – less well-equipped troops, able to operate in their own areas when required; and 'village militia' – sympathizers who filled mostly non-combatant supporting roles. It was the regulars who were to use the base areas, and although two-thirds of them had been moved down to Hanoi and Haiphong, Giap still had perhaps 10,000 in the Viet Bac. Here the familiar forested hills, with their loyal population and countless hidden caves and valleys, would house the Viet Minh head-quarters, rest camps and training schools, hospitals, printing presses, stores and arsenals, workshops and factories. Here the training and equipping of the regulars was proceeding with the help of about 3,000 Japanese deserters and some Chinese. Here the former Japanese officer Major Saito ran an arms factory at Quang Ngai, while a larger one at Thai Nguyen was already turning out 50 rifles a day and a machine gun every week. Other ordnance workshops were set up in Annam and Cochinchina, while Viet Minh agents traded gold, opium and rice with gun runners in Siam, the Philippines and Hong Kong.[21]

After long delays the Fontainebleau Conference eventually opened in August 1946, dragging on until mid September before Ho's delegation accepted that it was a futile exercise. When they returned in October, however, Giap was able to report solid progress of his own. In May, Lu Han's Chinese troops had begun to pull back north with their looted opium. The French surged forward, trying to keep close behind them; but this was the wet season – the nimbler Viet Minh dug up the roads, wrecked the bridges, and moved across country on the heels of the Chinese. Long before the French could arrive in any town, Giap's men had taken over, briskly executing local authorities set up under Chinese protection by the Dong Minh Hoi. Giap exploited sporadic guerrilla outbreaks as the excuse to eliminate the last rival nationalist groups with French approval. The non-Communist leaders, tempted out of cover by the summoning of a constituent assembly, were quickly liquidated. The 'Viet Minh', originally and still ostensibly the title of a broad nationalist front, was from now on essentially synonymous with the Communist movement; and, having completed his ruthless 'police' task, Vo Nguyen Giap was named as the new government's minister of defence.

With a ceasefire still officially holding, and French and Viet Minh garrisons patrolling in uneasy proximity, the Viet Minh in fact controlled the whole of rural Tonkin and northern Annam, and less disciplined regional units sometimes ambushed French patrols and convoys to capture weapons. In Cochinchina they were forced to keep a lower profile; the French and their compliant Vietnamese regime were in overt control of the towns and roads although, as throughout the country, their real mastery extended no further than rifle range from the nearest troops.

The bristling hostility between the neighbouring French and Viet Minh troops in the Delta caused repeated incidents; and it was friction over Viet Minh control of the customs dock in Haiphong that finally provided the explosion for which the French seemed to hunger. On 20 November 1946 the French tried to seize a boat suspected of carrying contraband weapons; both sides opened fire, and as anti-French crowds poured into the streets the fighting escalated, with Viet Minh mortars being answered by French armoured vehicles. Although a brief ceasefire was agreed, the French commander-in-chief, General Valluy, ordered local commanders to take over the whole of Haiphong. It is claimed that the time limit given in the ultimatum had not yet run out when, on 23 November, the French Navy cruiser *Suffren* opened fire on the Chinese and Vietnamese quarters of the town with her main armament, supported by French artillery and aircraft. The death toll was reported to be heavy, with many more injured.[22] Intense street fighting followed, but by 28 November the French were in control of Haiphong.

Ho Chi Minh's government was still in Hanoi; but Giap now pulled all his regular battalions out of Haiphong and Hanoi and started them marching for the Viet Bac and South Delta Base, leaving only regional units in place. Some of these were ordered to merge back into the population of the Delta, but others were still patrolling Hanoi. On 19 December the French ordered them to disarm, but the following evening there was a general uprising in the capital. The French troops got enough warning to take up strong positions; their losses were much lighter than those suffered by the weakly armed Viet Minh regionals, and a French counter-attack on 21 December cleared the city of opposition. Ho Chi Minh finally left Hanoi for the safety of the Viet Bac; and the Indochina War had begun.

3. The Dirty War

'In all territorial species, without exception, possession of a territory lends enhanced energy to the proprietor... the challenger is almost invariably defeated, the intruder expelled. In part, there seems some mysterious flow of energy and resolve which invests a proprietor on his home grounds.'

Robert Ardrey, *The Territorial Imperative*

THE WAR THAT BEGAN AS HO Chi Minh's government faded back into the limestone caves of the Viet Bac was an additional burden on a traumatized nation. Since 1940 France had been invaded, shockingly defeated, divided, occupied and pillaged by foreigners; then reinvaded, fought over again by great armies, and finally liberated – very largely by foreigners. Her physical infrastructure, economy and administration were in tatters. From a population of some 42 million, she had suffered about 122,000 military dead and 335,000 wounded, and more than 1.4 million had been made prisoners of war; but battlefield losses were far surpassed by civilian casualties. Nearly half a million French civilian men, women and children had died as a direct result of the war – perhaps 70,000 of them killed deliberately by the German occupiers, but many more by Axis and Allied bombs and shells as what we now call 'collateral damage'.[1] Another 1.2 million had been sent as forced labourers to Germany, and vast numbers of others had been scattered and dispossessed as refugees from the battle zones. The end of the war left huge numbers facing hunger and destitution without the normal protections of civil society.

The mental scenery of the French people had also suffered terrible damage. Fundamental assumptions about their country and society had been revealed as self-protective myths, and countless personal relationships had failed under the weight of events. During the Occupation there had never been any shortage of anonymous 'crows' eager to assist the German security police by betraying their neighbours. The so-called 'purifications' that had accompanied the Liberation had seen at least 10,000 French men and women executed for proven or supposed wartime treacheries; but only about 1,500 of these killings had been sanctioned by any court of law, and some were undoubtedly opportunist lynchings motivated by personal or political hatred.[2]

Bitter political enmities both between and within Left and Right, and a succession of weak coalition governments (some of which included Communist ministers) denied the institutions of the Fourth Republic any more than grudging support from much of the electorate. Confronted and usually overmastered by great difficulties and contradictory demands, no fewer than 19 successive governments failed to secure a mandate for a realistic strategy in Indochina, to provide adequate military means, or to offer convincing political leadership. After the initial French reoccupation of Indochina in 1945–6 operations in the Far East had a low priority, and the Expeditionary Corps (CEFEO) was in constant competition for men and equipment with France's NATO forces in Germany – a competition which it usually lost. The financial cost of the war was a serious drain on an impoverished country that periodically faced balance of payments crises and bouts of industrial and social unrest.[3]

In 1947–50 the rhythm and intensity of operations appeared to most French citizens to be listless, and their interest in this colonial war was very limited. In the public forum only the extremes of Right and Left argued for and against the conflict; the loudest and most consistent voices came from the Left, relentlessly hostile to this 'sale guerre' – this 'dirty war' of colonial repression. Widespread public interest would be aroused only intermittently and briefly, usually by some atrocity, scandal or disaster. In October 1950 France responded with shocked dismay when thousands of men were wiped out on Route Coloniale 4 (RC4) along the

Chinese frontier with Tonkin, and a major tract of North Vietnam and huge amounts of matériel were abandoned to the enemy; but even this sensation was short-lived. The arrival of General de Lattre shortly afterwards encouraged a confidence which soon turned to complacency; with predictable journalistic judgement, the 'human interest' story of his son's death in action in May 1951 took pride of place over any strategic analysis.[4]

THE FIGHTING IN HANOI IN December 1946 was accompanied by Viet Minh risings all over the country, and most major towns were cut off. This success was brief, since these regionals were weak in firepower and were still largely organized only in separate companies of a hundred-odd men. In Tonkin and northern Annam General Valluy reacted vigorously, and mechanized columns struck out in all directions. Early in January 1947 the Hanoi–Haiphong corridor was secured; in February the Hue garrison was relieved; and during March most towns in the Delta and northern Annam were cleared, although Vinh – close to Giap's South Delta Base – remained troublesome. In Cochinchina increased guerrilla activity reduced the areas where the French could claim control, but it soon settled to a relatively tolerable level of insecurity.[5]

The Viet Minh areas of control ('liberated zones') held about 10 million of the population – perhaps 40 per cent of the total; but the level of that control varied widely from actual parallel administration to mere freedom of movement. During the years to come agents spread out from the Viet Bac to consolidate support: village committees and militias were formed, and indoctrination was aided by an energetic and popular literacy programme. The Viet Minh supported itself by collecting taxes – cash extortion in the towns and a rice levy in the villages – and organized rotas of labour to serve as porters in their clandestine logistic network, which enjoyed the freedom of the country by night. Villages provided hideouts and guides for guerrillas; and even those too young, old or infirm to work actively for the cause could carry messages, watch, listen, and report every useful detail of French activity. Where necessary the Viet Minh reinforced education and encouragement with carefully focused terror.

For the main force regulars in the Viet Bac and South Delta Base – the *Chu Luc* – 1947 was a year of defence as they prepared for a long, patient war. These strongholds – more or less remote, inaccessible to the French, cloaked by forest, and inhabited by a loyal population – provided Giap's regulars with safe havens. The Chu Luc still had only about 30,000 men, and shortage of weapons would prevent any quick growth. Most new equipment had to be bought on the open market and smuggled in through the French blockades; the Viet Minh small-arms factories could not achieve mass production and were more or less limited to a repair and replacement role. At this stage in the war hundreds of secret workshops fulfilled a real need by reloading discarded French cartridge cases. The Viet Minh's ordnance branch could nevertheless turn out simple weapons such as small mortars, mines and the hand grenades which actually played a larger part than rifles in the arsenal of the village guerrillas.

The constant and country-wide guerrilla war was left wholly to the clandestine regional troops who moved like fish through the ocean of the civil population; their total strength in 1947 was somewhere between 30,000 and 50,000, although very unevenly equipped. The whole of Vietnam was divided administratively into 14 Viet Minh regions each headed by a committee, with a commander and a senior commissar appointed by Ho Chi Minh and answerable to the Party's central organs. Nevertheless, it took years to perfect the central control and co-ordination of the regional forces.

FROM MARCH 1947 A NEW High Commissioner, Émile Bollaert, sought to construct local administration and ultimately a government from non-Communist Vietnamese leaders, offering an ill-defined and eventual form of independence within the French Union (the cosmetically retitled Empire) after a period of French tuition. This required Bollaert to maintain contacts with a wide range of groups, and caused friction between him and the French commander-in-chief, General Valluy.

In October, Cochinchina was ostensibly granted the status of a free state of the French Union under Prime Minister Nguyen Van Xuan, a French citizen and former French Army colonel. Valluy's hope of crushing insurgency in South Vietnam quickly proved vain; the great majority of his forces there were soon tied down in perhaps 500 small posts providing an illusory local security, and Viet Minh activity in the south, although on a relatively small scale, remained constant. Their main refuges in Cochinchina were the Plain of Reeds west of Saigon, Thu Dau Mot province,

Ba Ria on the coast, and the Trans-Bassac at the southern tip of Vietnam. The ruthless southern Viet Minh leader, Nguyen Binh, had inherited a complex situation from his predecessor, and devoted most of his resources to fighting the powerful sectarian militias – the Cao Dai in Tay Ninh province and the Hoa Hao of Can Tho on the Bassac river. Both these groups came to an accommodation with the French, and were allowed to carry arms in return for keeping their areas clear of Viet Minh.

Even in the supposedly pacified areas of Cochinchina and Annam the French military occupation was purely notional. Memoirs convey a Wild West frontier atmosphere, with European civilians and administrators routinely going armed with Sten guns, and never venturing far without exchanging the latest information on which villages and roads were safe and which should be avoided. In practical terms the French Army controlled only a shifting pattern of invisible islands in the human landscape. The spaces between were roamed not only by the Viet Minh but also by various other armed groups, only some of which had direct connections with either the Communists or the Franco-Vietnamese forces. The wartime activities of the French, Japanese, British, Americans, Nationalist Chinese and Siamese had scattered South-East Asia with weapons; and the vacuum following Japan's surrender was exploited by local warlords, drug smugglers, freebooting deserters, and the partisans and ragged militias of many groups and causes.

IN OCTOBER 1947, VALLUY OPENED a winter offensive in Tonkin with far fewer troops than he wanted, and his planned encirclement of the whole Viet Minh zone was tailored back to thrusts at some of the hard-core refuges. Operation 'Léa' began on 7 October, and combined ambitious attacks on the Viet Bac by road columns – up RC4 from Lang Son to Cao Bang, and from the Delta via Viet Tri to Tuyen Quang – with parachute drops on Cao Bang and the Viet Minh headquarters in Bac Kan, while another force sailed up the Clear River. In November this was extended into Operation 'Ceinture', an attempt to lay a noose around the Viet Minh's Thai Nguyen base area. Meanwhile, Operation 'Lison' sent other forces into the High Region between the Red and Black rivers, thrusting for Lao Cai on the northern frontier with China and Nghia Lo in the Thai Highlands.

At Bac Kan and Thai Nguyen parachute attacks narrowly failed to capture the Viet Minh leadership; but the Lang Son–Cao Bang road column was held up by constant ambushes, and the riverine force ran into physical obstacles and had to take to the fields for a much longer cross-country march than had been planned. The French inflicted heavy casualties, but these delays allowed the Viet Minh to evade and regroup. At the end of three months the French were back on the Chinese frontier from Lang Son to Cao Bang; with local help they had beaten the Viet Minh regionals badly in the Thai Highlands; but the Chu Luc regulars were still safe in the heartland of the Viet Bac, and had learned a great deal. So had the World War II veterans who officered the Expeditionary Corps – mostly about the difficulty of conducting conventional operations in South-East Asia.

The most significant factor of the physical environment, even more than the exhausting effect of the climate on European troops, was the primitive road network. Historically the geography of Indochina made waterways the most practical means of travel over any distance. The main arteries were rivers and canals, connected to the coastal routes between the two Vietnamese deltas by small ports for transhipment of cargo between sampans and junks. At the beginning of the 20th century the French had built a rudimentary single-track rail system linking Saigon with Hanoi, Haiphong and Kunming in southern China; but motor roads had been neglected. Although the colonialists had driven dirt roads between the main towns these were simply (in General Gazin's pleasing phrase) 'an instrument of administrative penetration, of which little more was demanded than to support tourists' cars and a few pick-up trucks'.[6]

Military movements in the wet season were hardly possible; valley floors turned into swamps, hillsides became spongy and treacherous, it was exhaustingly slow work to hack a path through water-gorged vegetation, and the swollen streams made both fording and boat movement dangerous. In 1947 there were still very few miles of asphalted road surface outside the main towns, and the monsoon turned most of the dirt roads into quagmires; in the hills they were often washed away or blocked by landslides, and in the deltas periodic flooding drowned them. In just two seasons of neglect the jungle could reclaim them completely, and neglect had been almost total since 1940.

Apart from a handful of major steel spans like Hanoi's Paul Doumer, the bridges and causeways crossing the innumerable water obstacles (some of them up to a thousand yards wide) were not built to take weights of more than about six tons – adequate for a jeep, but useless for heavy trucks and armoured vehicles.[7] The roads were generally narrow, often single-track with occasional passing places; and although the French made efforts to clear vegetation back from the edges of the road, bamboo and scrub grew a lot faster than the labour could be found to cut them. For most of their length many of the proudly named 'Routes Coloniales' and 'Routes Provinciales' were unsurfaced lanes perhaps 12ft wide; in highland valleys the arching bamboo turned them into tunnels, on the slopes the jungle scraped the sides of passing trucks, and in the mountains they crept precariously along ledges between sheer rock faces and yawning drops.

With local exceptions, movement off the roads was generally difficult to impossible for wheeled vehicles. In many areas the going was marginal even for tanks and half-tracks, which bogged down with maddening frequency; in large parts of the deltas only amphibious tractors could move across country with any ease, and even these were often halted by vege-tation clogging their tracks.[8] The earth was saturated to such a depth – for instance, to about 150ft in Haiphong – that even driving piles for major construction works was an uncertain business; it was said of the ground in the Delta that 'it barely believed itself to be ground at all'. Foundations sank, embankments dissolved, roads washed away, rail tracks slid peace-fully beneath the mud and airfield runways buckled.

The nature of French operations was dictated by these brute physical realities. This was not a European war, where both sides employed similar resources to meet similar needs in a neutral physical environment. The Viet Minh had very few European resources, and chose to fight a war which freed them from European needs; but the CEFEO was a European army transplanted to Asia. In Indochina success depended upon a mobility which everything conspired to frustrate. France's only real advantage lay in her heavy weapons, and – with the exception of a few riverine units – these depended on roads to bring them to the battlefield (indeed, artillery often had to be fired from the actual road surface). Their effective use was therefore limited to those areas where the road network was dense enough to carry them within range of the enemy's chosen fighting ground.

Generally these conditions existed only in certain areas of the Red River and Mekong deltas, and the People's Army became skilled in choosing their ground to deny the French this advantage.

Much of the road network was vulnerable not only to the ravages of the monsoon but also to constant enemy sabotage; some major bridges were blown up and rebuilt as many as seven times during the war. The part played by the French Army's engineers became so vital that it could be argued that on many occasions the other arms of service were present essentially to escort the sappers. Road-borne French operations had to be planned in anticipation of the obstacles to be faced and overcome by the engineers – frequently, dozens of them over relatively few miles. Vehicles were loaded with the necessary tools and materials to repair each specific breach, including prefabricated bridging sections cut to exactly the right size. On the narrow roads heavy trucks often could not pass one another, so the engineer parties were placed in the road columns in the sequence in which they would need to tackle each separate obstacle. If the operation were a dash into Viet Minh country where routes were physically intact, spearhead parties of paratroop sappers were sometimes air-dropped to seize vital bridges and remove any demolition charges and mines ahead of the road column.[9] Such movements were often carried out with admirable efficiency at the cost of huge physical effort; but they could succeed only where French firepower achieved at least local and temporary dominance of the terrain.

NO MAJOR OFFENSIVES WERE launched in 1948; many French troops enlisted during the last stages of World War II had been repatriated in 1947, and replacing them proved difficult. Those who were available were spread thinly across the country in small security detachments, robbing the Expeditionary Corps of the chance to maintain a mobile reserve. Meanwhile the French government became bogged down in attempts to find a political solution. There was lack of agreement over the most essential arena of operations: Tonkin, where the main enemy were lurking, or Cochinchina, the economic engine of the colony. Early in 1948 the pendulum swung towards the south, where the regional commander General Boyer de Latour concentrated – apart from a few profitless lunges into the Plain of Reeds – on a methodical policy of implanting small posts and launching modest local security operations. In both the Mekong and Red River deltas such sweeps achieved only fleeting results and were exhausting for the troops.

For much of the year the rice paddies were glue traps through which the mud-caked soldiers could make only ponderous progress. Half-blinded by the sun's glare off the putty-coloured water, they were all too aware that they presented easy targets. Most practical movement was limited to the narrow raised dykes between the fields, where the troops were visible from far away – and which their predictable passage made it worth the enemy's while to booby-trap. Small post garrisons in these regions were literally islanders – the water often lapped the very ramparts of a small patch of soggy earth rising at the junction of two causeways above the paddies. A long tour in one of these miniature forts felt like living at the intersection of two lines on a piece of graph paper, which stretched away for miles on all sides in a mesmerizingly repeated pattern. The difficulties of movement were multiplied in Cochinchina's million-acre Plain of Reeds, which began just 15 miles west of Saigon. In this waterlogged malarial chaos of spongy islands, swampland and scrub divided by countless waterways, most infantry and motorized movement was simply impossible, and only small boats or the CEFEO's few amphibious tracked vehicles could follow the Viet Minh into their lairs.

A RELENTLESS LEITMOTIV OF THIS war was the sabotage of roads – classically, with half-width 'piano key' ditches dug from alternate sides, like the closely spaced teeth of a zip fastener. No sooner had these been repaired laboriously than they were dug up again – an undramatic but wearyingly effective way for the lowest level of village guerrillas to do their bit for the cause. The innumerable little bridges and culverts spaced along the dykes and roads were destroyed again and again, and sometimes booby-trapped to catch the French engineers sent to repair them. The most constantly repeated task for the local sector troops was 'road-opening', the morning patrol along their assigned stretch to check for mines and overnight sabotage; inevitably, the work gangs of local villagers pressed into refilling the ditches would often be the same men who had dug them. The French reliance upon mobility made it essential to guard or regularly patrol almost limitless numbers of vulnerable points on the road network, thus making the simple totals of CEFEO manpower meaningless as a measure of combat availability.

Anti-vehicle mines were fashioned from unexploded French shells and bombs which had been courageously recovered and ingeniously re-fused; Viet Minh sappers also lifted and relaid French mines sown to protect forts. Anti-personnel booby-traps were rigged with grenades and tripwires or – simply but horribly – with *panji* stakes: bamboo or barbed iron spikes, often smeared with excrement, set in camouflaged pits just deep enough to ensure that the weight of a careless step would drive them right up through the foot and out the instep, producing a filthy, medieval wound. (The iron spikes were often set into blocks of wood, so that it took much time and pain even to free the impaled victim.) Losses from this type of opportunist warfare mounted steadily; for instance, over two relatively quiet years in Cochinchina the Foreign Legion's 2nd Infantry Regiment suffered 200 casualties. Prolonged search and pursuit operations – even if no serious combat resulted – had a cumulatively exhausting effect which left the troops worn out and their nerves jangling. All soldiers hate and fear mines, and feel them to be somehow 'unfair' – what defence is courage or skill against a hidden wire that without warning can stretch a man in the grass in a shambles of torn flesh and splintered bone? In the Delta, in the six months between September 1953 and February 1954, 75 per cent of all deaths and 56 per cent of wounds would be caused by mines.[10]

The tension of constant vigilance, and the frustration of losing friends dead and maimed at the hands of an enemy who seldom showed himself, provoked a brutality towards civilians which simply increased Viet Minh support, and so multiplied the risk next time. Security operations sent the troops sweeping, often for weeks at a time, through village after village. They knew the Viet Minh were there, because the sniping, mining and booby-trapping were habitual; almost every day they had to carry back one or two bloody figures hanging in nets from shoulder poles. They knew the villagers knew where the Viet Minh were, because without the villagers' knowledge the Viet Minh could not move, lie up or eat. They knew the Viet Minh would very seldom let themselves be surrounded and forced to fight it out, because the Viet Minh were far better informed than they were. It was these men who faced every day the classic dilemma of the counter-insurgency soldier: 'I know that this wooden-faced peasant who won't meet my eye and who is pretending not to understand me knows the man – perhaps is the man – who laid the booby-trap which killed my friend yesterday, or which will kill me tomorrow; so how long can I endure his refusal to give me an excuse to strike back?'

During this war both sides committed what are primly called 'excesses' – in plain language, they maltreated and murdered helpless civilians. The endlessly frustrating security sweeps gave the troops plentiful opportunity for banal pillage and rape; there was a good deal of casual killing on such excuses as curfew violation; and there is anecdotal evidence for outright massacres of the type which, in a later war, would make the name My Lai infamous. The presence of many locally recruited Vietnamese in the French ranks does not seem to have been much of an inhibition. Typically for a modern army maddened by the pinpricks of guerrilla warfare, the French tended to lash out in destructive brutalities; villages near the sites of Viet Minh attacks were burned down under a declared policy of collective punishment, and the careless use of massive firepower in inhabited areas was a convincing recruiting sergeant.[11] French intelligence officers – or their local counterparts, with their full knowledge – routinely tortured suspects under interrogation; typically this progressed from casual blows, to serious beatings with clubs or rifle butts, to 'water torture' and 'the thousand cuts'. After the formation of the Vietnamese National Army, government troops terrorized civilians as a matter of course, thus undermining the psychological war being waged for their allegiance by the Bao Dai regime.[12]

Given France's own recent experience of occupation, murder and atrocity, it is hard to understand how French officers – even setting aside all moral questions – could fail to grasp that this sort of behaviour was self-defeating. While angrily sensitive to media and diplomatic criticism, the French authorities seemed to have no answer more sophisticated than references to omelettes and broken eggs, coupled with a shrugging resignation over the historic cruelty of South-East Asia. That cruelty was real, and the Viet Minh, too, could be barbaric in their treatment of civilians; but often their brutality was more exactly focused than that of the security forces. In a world of sometimes anarchic insecurity, simple people who wanted nothing more than to till their fields in peace were put under intolerable pressure by soldiers of both sides who were supposedly fighting in their name, each demanding commitments which would inevitably expose the helpless to the vengeance of the other. That provoking such atrocities by the French was a conscious aspect of their programme of revolutionary war leaves an ugly stain on the moral claims of 'Uncle' Ho Chi Minh's movement.

IN AUTUMN 1948 GENERAL Valluy was replaced by General Blaizot, who favoured a military focus on Tonkin; but his planned operations against the Viet Minh heartlands were frustrated by lack of reinforcements and political indecision, and little was achieved.

Untroubled by major enemy offensives, the Viet Minh regular units had continued their consolidation in the Viet Bac and South Delta Base. The leadership concentrated on improving their communications and control throughout the country, while keeping the Expeditionary Corps dispersed and distracted by guerrilla warfare. In March, the Viet Minh reorganized Vietnam into six 'integrated zones' – usually shortened to 'interzones' *(Lien Khu)* – in which the political and military authorities were integrated under a single committee; within each zone similar integrated authorities were responsible for provinces, districts and villages. Interzone 1 was north-west Tonkin and Interzone 2 north-east Tonkin, divided by the Red River; the Delta itself was Interzone 3, Annam north of Hue was Interzone 4, southern Annam was Interzone 5, and Interzone 6 covered Cochinchina. Communications between the central command and the zones were mostly by radio, since movement between them involved long and dangerous journeys.

Travel was no less difficult for the CEFEO, which faced not only the monotonous frustration of road sabotage but also regular ambushes of both military and civilian traffic. All movement between towns was by escorted convoy, and travellers might have to wait days for one to assemble; every evening the roads were formally 'closed', and abandoned to the enemy during the hours of darkness. While certain areas in south and central Vietnam were always dangerous (perhaps most notoriously the 'street without joy' on RC1 between Hue and Quang Tri in the waist of Annam), major ambushes of military convoys were particularly typical of the Tonkin/China frontier zone. The remote one- or two-company French posts reimplanted in the Middle Region by Valluy's operations in autumn 1947 were isolated along Routes Coloniales 4, 3*bis* and 3, and linked only by supply convoys to which civilian traffic attached itself for protection. The whole Middle Region around these corridors was haunted by the enemy, but with a few famous exceptions the People's Army did not mount direct attacks on the posts. The little forts were more of a cumulative liability to the French than an obstacle to the Viet Minh: their garrisons could not control infiltration through the jungle hills, and their usefulness was outweighed by the haemorrhage of casualties that it cost merely to keep them supplied.

In the hills the single-track dirt lanes snaked in series of switchbacks and hairpins over thickly forested ridges and through sinister gorges, over-looked by *calcaires* – the abrupt limestone pinnacles, covered with scrub and trees, that jutted into the sky. This was an ambusher's heaven; in many places deployment off the roads was impossible even for tracked vehicles and extremely punishing for infantry. There were no alternative routes by which the French could outflank an ambush party, and any relief column was obliged to drive towards the scene of action from one or other end of the same road – to be blocked or ambushed in their turn.

The most notorious road was Route Coloniale 4, running inland from the Gulf of Tonkin and closely parallel to the Chinese frontier, which it followed from Tien Yen north-west for 147 miles all the way up to the major garrison at Cao Bang (*see Map 4*).[13] The forward depot for all supplies and personnel destined for the frontier forts was Lang Son, at the junction of RC4, RC1 from Hanoi, and the Ky Cong river. Although often sabotaged, the road was rarely ambushed south-east of Lang Son, but from there on the going became more difficult and dangerous. At Dong Dang the road passed within 750yds of the Chinese frontier; then it climbed over passes, through gorges and tunnels to a perilous stretch of mountain ledge, overlooking the Ky Cong river for several miles before dropping down to the wet flats around That Khe ('Seven Rivers') at Kilometre 67. Beyond this garrison the road climbed in hairpin bends up to Luong Phai Pass, where it entered a rocky gorge 650yds long. After plunging down again it entered another half-mile canyon through wooded cliffs, leading to the little cultivated valley of Dong Khe and its fort at Kilometre 91, surrounded by jutting conical *calcaires*. From there it climbed to Nguyen Kin Pass, through another tunnel, and then twisted down four miles of hairpin bends through the foothills surrounding Cao Bang. If its garrison had been American or British, Cao Bang would inevitably have been nicknamed 'Fort Apache'. Held by two battalions, Cao Bang lay in a wide loop at the confluence of the Hien and Bang Giang rivers, dominated from the north by the glowering mountains of China.

Manpower was too short for the use of two-man crews, and the French, Foreign Legion, African and Vietnamese truck drivers of the Train (Service Corps) made this journey alone in the baking cabs of their beaten-up old American GMCs. A shortage of tyres meant that few carried spare wheels, and the springs had usually been rewelded several times already; under constant traffic and sabotage the surface of RC4 deteriorated, and the ageing trucks suffered repeated breakdowns. For long hours at a time the drivers strained their eyes through dust clouds, mist or torrential rain to keep a safe interval from the truck ahead and to spot any obstacles on the road. They sawed their steering wheels from lock to lock on the hairpins, feeling through their whole bodies the traction of the wheels and the grip of the brakes on gradients, listening for a stutter in the note of their abused engines – on the narrowest sections the most trivial breakdown or mishap could halt the whole convoy for long, frightening hours. At the few designated stops the drivers refuelled from jerrycans, checked the engine, radiator, transmission and tyres, and often had to help load or unload before snatching a little sleep.

The Viet Minh were routinely alerted to approaching convoys – sometimes in specific detail – by their efficient spy network. The military vehicles, mixed with ramshackle and chronically overloaded native trucks and buses, were typically guarded by an escort of riflemen and a couple of light armoured vehicles, but the impossibility of overtaking on many stretches of the road robbed the latter of much of their value. An armoured car at the head of the convoy could give warning of a roadblock and hose the forest with machine-gun fire; but the Viet Minh soon became expert at letting the first vehicles through before halting the middle section of the convoy by destroying carefully selected vehicles ahead and behind. Armour at the tail of the convoy would thus be immobilized, and on a twisting road through tall cover the gunners could not see more than a few trucks ahead.

The Viet Minh varied the tactical details of each ambush to suit the terrain and target, though the range was seldom over 50yds. Some drivers were killed at the wheel by enemies who jumped on to their trucks unseen; sometimes an attacker would roll a grenade under the engine from the edge of the scrub. Sometimes just a few snipers opened fire, and convoys forced their way through for the cost of one or two dead and wounded. Sometimes hundreds of men attacked along several miles of road – the disembarked infantry escort had little chance against well-concealed automatic weapons and mortars. The trucks were emptied and burned, the wounded butchered and the dead stripped of arms and ammunition before the ambushers melted back into the wilderness.

AMBUSHES BEGAN SHORTLY AFTER the reoccupation of the road in October 1947. On 28 February 1948 a Legion company 'opening the road' between Dong Khe and Cao Bang took 22 dead and 33 wounded – about 40 per cent casualties – in a major ambush. After two ambushes in April the Frontier Zone was reinforced with two more battalions: the Algerian 21 BTA with headquarters at Cao Bang and the Foreign Legion's III/3 REI at Dong Khe. Security improved, at the cost of backbreaking exertions; every day infantry set out to march along the road, dropping off men at intervals to occupy or keep watch on the hilltops. The enemy response was audacious. A secondary road through the Ngan Song mountains, RC3*bis*, linked RC4 at Cao Bang with Phu Thong Hoa, a small post about 30 miles to the south-west. On the wet, misty night of 25 July 1948 this earth-walled fort, held by the hundred-strong 2nd Company, I/3 REI, was attacked by two Viet Minh battalions after a preparatory bombardment not just with mortars but with 75mm guns – an unprecedented event. After two hours' shelling, trumpets heralded 'human wave' assaults, which penetrated the fort, at one stage capturing three of the four blockhouses. The légionnaires held out all night in hand-to-hand fighting; after the enemy pulled back it still took three days for Lieutenant Colonel Simon's relief column to fight their way through the several co-ordinated ambushes along the Cao Bang road.[14]

This deliberate exercise to see whether Giap's regular infantry could take a French post by assault suggested the answer 'probably, with more men and artillery'; but it was not repeated soon. On RC4 they reverted to targeting convoys, 28 serious ambushes being carried out in 1948. In

February 1949, at Lao Cai, where the Red River crosses the Chinese border, the experiment was repeated, this time successfully, by five People's Army battalions with mortar support; the post was later reoccupied by paratroopers when the Viet Minh chose not to stand and fight. On RC4 the tempo of ambushes kept up in early 1949; and just before the rains came in late May another post – the key staging point of Dong Khe, with a strong North African garrison – was assaulted by four battalions with artillery and heavy mortars, and briefly captured before being retaken by paratroopers.

The climax came on 3 September 1949, when a westbound column of about 100 vehicles left That Khe for the two-hour drive to Dong Khe 16 miles away. Infantry pickets had been placed along the road, but the last eight miles up to Luong Phai Pass were narrow, twisting and uneven with hurriedly repaired 'piano keys'. On the left side of the road were rock faces, steep slopes of scree and heavy undergrowth; on the right, a thickly wooded ravine, with an unbroken chain of *calcaires* beyond it. The first 20 trucks reached Dong Khe, and after a gap, ten more – whose drivers reported coming under automatic fire; but they were the last. Beyond the crest of the pass the rest of the convoy was being ripped apart by machine-gun and mortar fire from unreachable crags. Three trucks exploded, blocking the road. From the head of the pass the escort half-tracks forced their way back, firing until they too were hit and set on fire, their crews killed. The infantry pickets on the hilltops were pinned down by the weight of fire, those on the road itself wiped out. Along the road hundreds of Viet Minh surged up from the bush in the eastern ravine and began to massacre and loot, soldiers and civilians alike. A Morane spotter plane radioed Dong Khe that the centre of the convoy was being destroyed and the road was cut in force near both ends. The next day, hacking their way through the flanking brush, infantry reoccupied the route hilltop by hilltop. At midday they reached the first of the 52 burnt-out vehicles; they found just four wounded men alive, among a mile and a half of blackened metal and shrivelled corpses.

Following this ambush, temporary security corridors for convoys had to be formed all along the road; groups of only ten or 12 vehicles were sent off from the various staging posts at ten-minute intervals, and spotter planes constantly circled overhead. Ambushes continued, but the losses to each were more limited. In 1950 it was decided to halt regular supply convoys at That Khe and to provision Dong Khe and Cao Bang by air. Troop convoys continued periodically, often coming under fire but always fighting their way through, though sometimes having to cover the last several miles on foot.

IN MARCH 1949, AFTER PROTRACTED negotiations, the less than eager Emperor Bao Dai was recognized as the 'head of state' of a nominally independent Vietnam. The kingdom of Laos achieved the same kind of status that July, and that of Cambodia in November, the whole being termed the Associated States of the French Union. The French naturally retained all powers over defence and foreign affairs, and Bao Dai was in any case reluctant to show uncompromising hostility to the Viet Minh, whom he believed might play a part in a future unified Vietnam which he vaguely hoped to construct. A succession of his ministers engaged in intricate games of chess with successive French high commissioners, for which the prizes were the greatest possible rewards of government coupled with its least burdensome responsibilities. There were only about 7,000 French civil administrators in the country, and apart from the security aspects the French did not greatly interfere with Bao Dai's regime and its traditional corrupt exploitation of the Vietnamese people.

In view of continuing disagreements between the civil administration and the military command, a study of French possibilities in Tonkin was made in spring 1949 by the Chief of the Defence Staff, General Revers; and his subsequent report was radical. In simple terms, he advocated abandoning all of North Vietnam except a rough quadrilateral around the Delta anchored on Haiphong, Hoa Binh, Viet Tri, Thai Nguyen and Mon Cai. On 26 August 1949 the contents of this top-secret document, with its huge military and political implications, were broadcast – by the Viet Minh radio station. The consequent scandal ('the Affair of the Generals') rocked Paris, Saigon and Hanoi for months, and stalled any decision on Revers' recommendations.

In March–July 1949, Giap committed some of his regular units to limited attacks on French communications and posts in the High and Middle regions, and in November–December to consolidating the Viet Minh's grip on territory around Hoa Binh, cutting the roads between the Delta and the Thai Highlands. Paratroopers of the French reserve had to jump into the hills to save a number of isolated garrisons. The winter 1948–9 campaign season nevertheless saw the Viet Minh in some difficulty. The new C-in-C, General Carpentier, delegated responsibility for the Delta to the ground forces commander in North Vietnam, General Alessandri – an old Tonkin hand – who concentrated with some success on a major campaign to cut off the supply of rice to the Viet Bac, while General Chanson achieved similar results in Cochinchina. Food shortage apparently became so serious that General Giap was even contemplating committing his regulars to a general and dangerously premature assault on the Delta. Giap was inclined to be headstrong, and had perhaps not fully grasped the importance that the Maoist guerrilla warfare doctrine placed on the distinction between the different phases of an escalating campaign.

In October 1949, however, the first great turning point of the war took place: a year of victories won by Mao Tse Tung's Communist armies over the Nationalist regime was crowned by the formal announcement of the foundation of the People's Republic of China. The 2nd Red Field Army reached the border of Tonkin, and in December and January some 30,000 defeated Nationalist troops crossed east of Lang Son (to be eventually repatriated to Formosa). The Viet Minh now had an immensely powerful ally across a common frontier, even if it was one still nominally guarded by French troops. On 18 January 1950 Communist China formally recognized Ho Chi Minh's government as the legitimate representatives of the Vietnamese people, and the Soviet Union followed suit on the 30th. To the outside world this new status put Ho Chi Minh on an entirely new diplomatic plane, and France had real fears that China would actually invade Tonkin.

Mao preferred to support his new allies as proxies, however; a military mission arrived in the Viet Bac in December 1949, Ho visited Beijing in April 1950, and during the years that followed China opened her arsenals and training camps to Giap's army. Mortars, anti-aircraft machine guns and light field guns soon allowed Giap to form heavy weapons companies within his infantry battalions, and his first artillery units; about 25,000 regional troops were promoted to regular status, and battalions began to coalesce into regiments, then into divisions. The importance of Chinese aid and training in this first great step towards transforming the Chu Luc from a guerrilla to a conventional army cannot be overstated, but is more logically summarized in Chapter 4.

THE FRAGILITY AND EXPENSE of France's hold on Cao Bang and the upper RC4 forts were undeniable; many smaller posts had already been abandoned when, in early September 1950, General Carpentier decided to evacuate Cao Bang itself. The withdrawal was scheduled for early October, just before the end of the rainy season; it was thought that the People's Army would not yet be ready for major operations. In the meantime, however, General Giap had moved at least 14 of his infantry battalions, newly equipped and trained by the Chinese, and three of artillery, into position along the frontier ridge.[15]

On 16 September 1950 French preparations were violently forestalled when the People's Army threw four or five battalions from Regiments 165 and 174 with artillery and mortar support against Dong Khe (*see Map 4*). Two companies of légionnaires – 5th and 6th from II/3 REI – put up desperate resistance, but this vital fort fell after two days, putting the People's Army astride RC4 well south of Cao Bang. The 1st Foreign Parachute Battalion (1 BEP) were dropped further south along the road at That Khe on the 18th, but over the next week they failed to fight their way up to Dong Khe. A column of 3,500 Moroccan and local troops was assembled at Lang Son under Colonel Le Page; they marched up to That Khe, and on 1 October they and 1 BEP started north together, with orders to retake Dong Khe.[16] On 3 October, Colonel Charton was ordered to leave Cao Bang and march south to meet them with his 1,500 légionnaires and Moroccans, in a column burdened by many civilian refugees.[17] What followed was, in the French term, a 'calvary'.

By the night of 3/4 October both columns were blocked, dislocated, and taking casualties; as the Viet Minh closed in around both ends of the narrow corridor through the forested hills ambushes and roadblocks became constant. Bad weather prevented air support from the dozen Bell P-63 Kingcobras which were the only available combat aircraft in Tonkin. The Charton column were forced to abandon their vehicles on the road and take to the hills to the west in hope of outflanking the blocking forces; the Le Page column did the same, aiming to rendezvous at a feature called

Hill 477. Both columns had to fight their way across the hills along faint jungle tracks; they became dispersed, and many men were simply lost in the forest. By the time Charton and Le Page managed to link up late on 7 October both commands had taken heavy casualties, were short of food, water and ammunition, and were carrying many wounded. Of the 500 from the Legion parachute battalion who jumped, just 130 men emerged from a breakthrough fight in the natural amphitheatre of Coc Xa; they had only escaped by clambering down the lianas shrouding a 75ft cliff with their wounded tied on their backs.

The commanders decided to divide the survivors into small parties to try to infiltrate through the jungle and the Viet Minh, reassembling at That Khe; half the 3rd Colonial Commando Parachute Battalion (3 BCCP) and a company of 1 BEP replacements were dropped at that post on 8 October to hold it against their arrival. The badly wounded were left behind with volunteer medics. Only about 300 men reached That Khe on the 9th and 10th, and the post was abandoned in some haste. The three weak companies of 3 BCCP and 1 BEP, reluctant to leave while survivors were still wandering in the jungle, formed the rearguard for the retreat; by 14 October almost all had been killed. In total only about 600 men of the two columns found their way back to French lines; of some 6,000 casualties suffered in 'the disaster of RC4', no fewer than 4,800 were listed as dead or missing. It was by far France's worst defeat of the war so far, and panic ensued.

French posts far from immediate threat were simply abandoned; these included the important frontier post of Lao Cai on the upper Red River, and Hoa Binh in the Muong hills west of the Delta, but the most notorious was Lang Son, where huge amounts of matériel were left for the enemy on 18 October.[18] The entire Middle Region was evacuated, leaving the Viet Minh in control of the Chinese frontier from the Red River to the sea above Mon Cai. The Delta seemed naked to attack, and there was open talk of abandoning Hanoi. General Boyer de Latour arrived in Tonkin on 23 November and took immediate steps to stop the rot, forming available troops into seven motorized brigades – 'Groupes Mobiles' – to defend the Delta. General Juin, Chief of the Defence Staff, also flew in to take stock of the situation in person.

This defeat had a stunning psychological impact on the CEFEO and the French colonists, and alarmed a large part of the French public. Then and for long afterwards 'RC4' occupied the same raw corner of the memory as that in which the World War II generation kept the fall of Singapore or Bataan in 1942. The generals had been out-thought, and the soldiers out-fought, apparently with almost contemptuous ease; the enemy, once disparaged, had shown himself to be lethally dangerous. A much quoted statistic was that during 1950 the losses of French regular officers in Indochina – about 140 – matched the annual output of the Army's St Cyr officer academy: the Viet Minh were killing them as fast as France could graduate them.

Apart from the casualties on RC4 and the shaming behaviour of some officers elsewhere, the jolt for the military mind came from the unsus-pected transformation of the Viet Minh from guerrillas into soldiers. Many had regarded them simply as glorified bandit gangs – destructive as ambushers and raiders but posing a limited threat to a real army. The career soldier believed that he was more than a match for them, 'if only those bastards would come out and fight'. It had never been imagined that they could confront a force of several battalions – including paratroopers and légionnaires – and annihilate them. The special vulnerability of the French columns, strung out in the jungle for all the world like Varus' legions in the ancient Teutoburg Forest, did not lessen the shock. Throughout modern military history guerrillas had been a parallel and essentially minor threat; they had sometimes been a serious distraction for regular armies – as in Spain in 1807–13, or Yugoslavia in 1941–4 – but were always secondary to the conventional operations that won or lost campaigns. For Asian guerrillas to confront and challenge major European forces was unheard of; the Indochina War had undergone a shift not just in degree but in nature, which would draw attention from far beyond Indochina and Paris.

On 26 November came news from elsewhere in Asia which seemed to throw an even more baleful light on the loss of north-east Tonkin. On 25 June 1950 the North Koreans had crossed the 38th parallel into the American-protected South, beginning a relentless advance which by the beginning of August had penned the South Korean Army and US troops into an enclave around the port of Pusan. The United Nations Security Council condemned the aggression, and US General Douglas MacArthur was appointed commander of the UN (predominantly US) forces which began to pour in from Japan. The North Koreans had lost the initiative by mid September, when MacArthur's audacious landings at Inchon behind their western flank began a counter-offensive which within a month drove them north again almost to the Chinese border. On 14 October, Chinese forces began crossing the frontier secretly to support the North Koreans; and on 25 November they launched a massive offensive, driving US troops before them. In the feverish days that followed it was easy to see the whole Western position in East Asia as menaced by some vast Chinese Communist master plan.

The news of the Chinese onslaught in Korea, only a month after the loss of the Tonkin/China border country to the Viet Minh, arrived in a Washington where ingrained hostility to French colonial policy in South-East Asia suddenly seemed a self-indulgent luxury. The United States had already formally recognized the Associated States of Vietnam, Cambodia and Laos; France's appeals for material and financial aid to defend them would not be refused. October/November 1950 was the second turning point of the Indochina War.

FOR ONCE PARIS WAS SHOCKED into decisive action, and on 6 December 1950 a new joint military commander-in-chief and high commissioner was appointed to replace both General Carpentier and Commissioner Pignon: General Jean de Lattre de Tassigny – French signatory of the German surrender in May 1945, former C-in-C Western European Land Forces, and one of France's most admired soldiers.[19] The immaculate and charismatic 61-year-old 'King Jean' arrived on 17 December with the unprecedented powers of a proconsul, and made the most of them; he was an autocratic but inspiring leader, and CEFEO morale soon began to recover. De Lattre cancelled all plans for evacuation and retreat, carried out a wholesale purge of staff officers, brought in many former members of his old 'Rhine and Danube' army, rushed reinforcements from Cochinchina and Annam to Tonkin, and announced to the Expeditionary Corps: 'Henceforward, I promise you that you will be *led!*'

While de Lattre gathered his available troops and vehicles into a motorized reserve to react to the expected threat to the Delta, his opponent played into his hands. Rapid expansion and continuing Chinese training and supplies would soon give Vo Nguyen Giap a regular force of between 45 and 60 infantry and 12 light artillery battalions, and their organization into regiments and divisions was under way. Over-impressed by the scope of his victory on RC4, Giap was deceived into believing that he had an opportunity to pass straight to the final stage of the Maoist plan for revolutionary war. He would telescope the 'mobile warfare' phase into the 'general offensive', and launch his regulars against the Delta in Operation 'Tran Hung Dao'.[20] In mid January 1951 parts of his newly equipped Divisions 308 and 312 burst out of the cover of the wooded Tam Dao hills north-west of Hanoi and, taking as their war-cry 'Ho Chi Minh in Hanoi for *Tet!*', tried to break into the Delta across the Red River near Vinh Yen (*see Map 5*).[21]

Two regiments from Division 308 crossed to the west bank of the river on the evening of 13 January; Groupe Mobile 3 from Vinh Yen reacted, but was enveloped and half destroyed. While its survivors pulled back under cover from artillery and aircraft dropping napalm, part of Division 312, which had crossed in hills higher up the Red River, also moved down the west bank.[22] By the night of the 14th three full regiments were installed in hills near Vinh Yen. De Lattre sent his deputy General Salan to Vinh Yen to counter-attack with Groupe Mobile 1 and the remains of GM 3 under cover of air support. Simultaneously he organized an airlift of reinforcements from elsewhere in Indochina to be formed into another Groupe Mobile in the field. Giap had a chance to exploit an opening east of Vinh Yen on the 15th, but missed it. On the 16th, de Lattre flew into the front lines in a Morane spotter plane and took charge of the operation; when his chief-of-staff protested by radio at the risk the C-in-C was taking he replied, superbly, 'Well then, come and get me out...'[23]

On the evening of 16 January both of Giap's divisions were committed to a massed assault; this was the first time that major units of the CEFEO had faced 'human wave' attacks, and they were astonished by the enemy's reckless courage. Savage fighting continued all night and into the 17th, but by the morning de Lattre had called up virtually every French combat aircraft in Indochina. He sent his last reserves forward under their cover, and by noon Giap had ordered a withdrawal. His casualties totalled at least 5,000, including about 500 taken prisoner. Giap's first true battle of manoeuvre had been a costly failure, but it had been a close-run thing for both generals; only de Lattre's unique authority had enabled him to gather reinforcements immediately, and even so his men were too few and too weakly motorized to exploit their victory by pursuing and destroying the retreating enemy.

Vinh Yen provided the Expeditionary Corps with a much-needed boost to morale, and sealed de Lattre's authority. He threw his energies into many initiatives to secure the French position in the Delta; he gathered as many troops as possible from static security duties for a strong mobile reserve; he tried to encourage the Vietnamese themselves into joining the fight against the Viet Minh, at the price of clashing with the French government over the necessary concessions; and he exerted himself to win support from the USA. There his rather theatrical style and his understanding of media relations, reminiscent of General MacArthur, earned him an excellent reception.[24]

Giap made two more attempts to break into the Delta before the next rains began, and both failed. The first was on the north-east sector, where parts of Divisions 308, 312 and 316 threatened Haiphong by attacks around Mao Khe and Dong Trieu on 29/30 March and 4/5 April. French reinforcements were slow to gather while small garrisons put up a desperate defence, but finally beat off the main effort by Division 316 with naval gunfire support; the Viet Minh left about 400 dead at Mao Khe alone, so total casualties probably exceeded 1,500 men.

The third attempt was more elaborate and dangerous, and fell on the south-east Delta defences behind the Day River in late May and early June. It took many weeks to move part of Giap's troops and their logistic support all the way around the Delta while Division 312 made distracting movements outside the northern and western defences, and the monsoon rains had started before the attack could be launched. The objectives were strongly Catholic areas around Ninh Binh and Nam Dinh (see Map 5), whose resistance to infiltration needed to be broken. The inexperienced Division 304 and the battered Division 308 made diversionary attacks towards Phu Ly and Ninh Binh; the main effort was by the new Division 320 towards Phat Diem, and one of its regiments had already infiltrated deeply to co-operate with the local regional Regiment 42 in attacking the French from the rear. Division 320 crossed the Day River on 30 May, but de Lattre quickly assembled eight motorized brigades, artillery and armour. Posts were lost and retaken in heavy fighting; the Catholic militia proved a match for the Viet Minh inside the defences, and riverine units finally cut Giap's rear lines across the Day. The People's Army made slow progress across the flooded paddy-fields under artillery and (when the weather allowed) air attack, and by 6 June the French held the initiative. Giap's disengagement and withdrawal between 10 and 18 June was a wretched ordeal, and his losses finally totalled about 9,000 dead and 1,000 captured.

In his first conventional campaign Vo Nguyen Giap had shown himself to be a general of limited talents. He had committed his main force before he or his staff were properly trained in the movement of large units or their handling in battle. He had exposed them in open terrain and by day, which favoured the heavier French firepower. He had broken several fundamental rules – notably on the Day River, by committing all his units and leaving himself without reserves to exploit success, to overcome a check, or to cover withdrawal. Since his only experience had been of brief hit-and-run attacks, he did not have much nervous stamina, and at Vinh Yen had broken off when persistence might have succeeded. He had not learned to balance caution against audacity, so he overdid both – failing to seize opportunities, and reinforcing failure. On the Day River he seems to have allowed the distinction between diversionary and main attacks to become as blurred in his own mind as it was supposed to be in his adversary's. His total losses since January were probably equivalent to two divisions – perhaps half of his main force infantry. He would be made to rehearse his errors in public self-criticism before the Party Central Committee, and at least one leading Party figure, Truong Chinh, would urge his dismissal. It is believed that even Ho Chi Minh's leadership was questioned, for his loyal support of Giap. Both survived, and another scapegoat was found – though an unconvincing one: the southern leader Nguyen Binh was blamed for urging the premature offensive against the Delta. Summoned to the Viet Bac, he was killed 'during an encounter with a French patrol' while on his way north.[25]

Giap's opponent had also suffered grievously, however. On the night of 29/30 May, during the defence of a hill position near Ninh Binh against Giap's Regiment 88, Lieutenant Bernard de Lattre of the 1er Chasseurs à Cheval had been killed at the head of his troopers.

ONE OF GENERAL DE LATTRE'S most ambitious projects was the construction of a chain of fixed defensive posts all round the edges of the Delta, intended to hamper Viet Minh infiltration and also to defend against the possibility of a conventional invasion by the Chinese Red Army. Later known as the De Lattre Line, this programme made extraordinary demands on the Expeditionary Corps' engineering resources.

The engineer corps ('le Génie') had been central to all French operations from the first, and faced in particularly acute forms the universal problem of lack of adequate means. High standards were achieved, however, largely through a combination of an entirely competent central command with the encouragement of local initiative. The intelligent use of local resources extended far beyond simply hiring Indochinese labourers: all kinds of shortages were met by tying into the CEFEO engineering effort a wide range of commercial firms across South-East Asia and the Pacific, from little 'cottage industry' workshops to large-scale manufacturers and transport fleets. These civilian suppliers would play an indispensable part in the construction of the Delta defences, which were an engineering epic.

On de Lattre's orders, within one year the CEFEO had to construct 1,200 separate concrete blockhouses proof against 155mm artillery, in clusters of between three and six for mutual fire support, grouped in 250 strongpoints along an arc of nearly 235 miles. These varied in size and design, but even the smallest pillboxes accommodated at least a section of ten men. Most had towers and casemates, some of them mounting old tank turrets; the largest were relatively elaborate, with generators, ventilation systems, and protected emplacements for attached artillery or armoured vehicles. In addition to these peripheral posts the Génie had to construct a double inner belt of defences to keep the enemy out of artillery range of the CEFEO's potential final redoubt – the harbour, base facilities and airfields at Haiphong; this was an arc 31 miles long, 22 miles outside the port. All these defences had to be linked by a network of new roads allowing rapid reinforcement from the centre, and capable of taking 30-ton tanks. At the same time, throughout Indochina, five airfields had to be built, enlarged or upgraded, complete with protected dispersal pens, workshops and living quarters.[26]

A galaxy of local workshops, large and small, were commissioned and funded; materials such as reinforcing bars were hunted down on the commercial market all over Asia; interchangeable prefabricated sections were designed, ordered, poured, delivered and assembled; the whole civilian truck fleet was hired to work alongside the military park and the railway; river boats carried about half the total cargoes, including a newly built fleet of armed barges manned by légionnaires.[27] Part of this was achieved while Giap's spring 1951 offensive fell upon the defenders of the Delta, disrupting every timetable and sometimes forcing engineers to fight in the front lines. The prospect of turning de Lattre's requirements into reality daunted many of his subordinates. There was a legend that spread throughout Indochina to the effect that one of his staff officers had stammered, 'But General, the cost! – and to garrison it would take everybody we have!: de Lattre is supposed to have replied: 'F*** the cost. As for the men, we'll put the real c***s down there.'[28]

GIAP'S FIRST MOVE AFTER THE END of the 1951 rains was cautious, but may be seen as the first hesitant step along the road to Dien Bien Phu. He decided to send Division 312 south-west across the middle Red River to attack Nghia Lo, a strategic French post in the hills between the Red and Black rivers which commanded important tracks through the Thai Highlands (*see Map 7*). Nghia Lo was assaulted on the night of 2/3 October, but the thousand French-officered Thai troops held out. General Salan dropped three parachute battalions around the fort, and by 10 October the Viet Minh troops were falling back to the Red River crossings at Yen Bai, weakened and now harassed by air attacks from France's newly acquired B-26 bombers. The successful relief of Nghia Lo was hailed as another significant French victory, vindicating a policy of maintaining isolated garrisons which could be reinforced by parachute if threatened. For two of the units involved – 8th Colonial and 2nd Foreign Parachute Battalions – this was not to be their only meeting with Division 312.[29]

Deeply affected by the death of his only son, de Lattre now faced another crushing blow: in early October 1951 he was diagnosed with advanced cancer of the hip. Nevertheless, he followed up his defensive victories of the spring by launching in November an ambitious thrust south-westwards from the Delta to recapture Hoa Binh, about 25 miles from the nearest secure base. This lost capital of the friendly Muong tribesmen was an important road and river junction; it was reached by

RC6, leading directly south-west from Hanoi like a bowstring through the hills, and by a wide northern loop of the Black River forming the arc of the bow (*see Map 5*). The shape of de Lattre's plan was reminiscent of conventional European operations in 1944–5, here fatally misapplied against a different sort of enemy. Operation 'Lotus' bore some similarity to 'Market Garden', the Allied airborne and armoured attempt to drive a narrow corridor deep into Holland in September 1944; but in de Lattre's creation of his corridor to Hoa Binh it was as if Montgomery's paratroopers and tanks had been fighting not the German occupiers, but the hostile and armed population of Holland.

On 15 November three parachute battalions jumped over Hoa Binh and captured it without difficulty; three Groupes Mobiles with additional tank support pushed down RC6 to join them, while strong naval units from Viet Tri forced the loop of the Black River. Giap refused a confrontation, pulling his troops back into the forest hills and patiently building them up for a battle of attrition on his own terms, along both the road and river lifelines. In December he was ready; and as Jean de Lattre de Tassigny finally departed from Indochina – to death from cancer within a few weeks, and a posthumous marshal's baton – Giap threw Division 304 into heavy attacks against French positions along the Black River. The following month Divisions 304, 308 and 312 closed in around Hoa Binh and RC6, while back in the Delta units from Divisions 316 and 320 infiltrated from north and south to harass the French rear areas. The De Lattre Line, such as it then was, did not appear to be much of a barrier.

De Lattre was replaced as C-in-C by his deputy in Tonkin, General Raoul Salan, an officer with a long background in colonial intelligence work. He was faced with an immediate crisis as enemy pressure threatened to cut off the five battalions holding Hoa Binh. On 12 January the last Black River convoy was turned back with heavy losses, and thereafter the People's Army could concentrate on RC6, held open by four French battalions dispersed between a number of posts. 'Chinese' Salan was an inscrutable old Asia hand, but it is hard to believe that the ant-scoured bones of the Charton and Le Page columns never figured in his dreams. In the second half of January 1952 he launched a major operation to force the Viet Minh back from RC6; it took 12 battalions, with air and heavy artillery support, 12 full days to fight their way the 25 miles to Hoa Binh by the 29th. Salan ordered the withdrawal of the garrison; but he only finished leap-frogging his units back down the highway to the shelter of the De Lattre Line in late February after costly running battles (Operation 'Arc en Ciel').

During the Hoa Binh campaign it was noticed that Viet Minh infantry tactics had become more sophisticated, that they were supported by cleverly concealed 75mm guns, and that heavy anti-aircraft machine guns were starting to challenge the French Air Force's freedom of the sky. Perhaps Giap's most significant success, however, was simply that his logistic organization had maintained three full divisions in action for three months, supplying them with food, ammunition and all other necessities by the labour of at least 150,000 porters; at this date his truck fleet – from captures on RC4, and the first Russo-Chinese supplies – is thought to have had only about 100 vehicles.

GENERAL SALAN SPENT THE monsoon months of 1952 on major security operations within the Delta, and Giap on building up his main force and assimilating an increasing flow of weapons from China. His regulars now totalled perhaps 110,000 troops, supported by heavy 120mm mortars and 75mm recoilless guns – both being transportable across country by human porters and pack animals. With the approach of the winter campaigning season he looked once more towards the Thai Highlands, where he saw the possibility of opening up a new front to disperse Salan's resources.

The Viet Minh controlled the upper Red River, but to the west the parallel Hoang Lien Song mountain range barred the way to the upper and middle Black River, and beyond it to the Thai country along the border with Laos. Although far from the Delta, these uplands were still dotted with small French garrisons, and the Viet Minh had had little success in enlisting the tribal inhabitants to the Communist cause.[30] Major operations on this north-west front could plant the necessary political infrastructure and regional units; and they would force the Expeditionary Corps to choose between abandoning the border and exposing northern Laos, or defending them. If the French accepted battle in the Thai Highlands they would be robbed of the advantages they enjoyed in the Delta. Far from their bases, at the end of roads cut by the enemy years since, they would find it extremely difficult to deploy artillery and impossible to bring up motorized troops, while the shortage of airfields in the High Region would make it hard for the Air Force to operate there in strength. In this terrain the People's Army, accustomed to movement across country and not dependent on motor transport, could manoeuvre with much greater confidence.

In September 1952, Giap concentrated his Divisions 308, 312 and 316 – at least 30,000 men – on the east bank of the Red River between Phu Tho and Yen Bai. Most movement was by night, and so skilled was their concealment that French air reconnaissance failed to detect more than vague signs of activity. Their objective was not identified until strong elements were well past the Red River in mid October. On the 15th two regiments of Division 312 surrounded a post at Gia Hoi; together with Independent Regiment 148, this force formed the northern prong of a triple advance (*see Map 6*). South of it were two regiments from Division 308, approaching Nghia Lo, and two more from 316. Elements of Giap's new artillery units were also present, with 75mm guns and 120mm mortars.[31]

On 16 October, General de Linarès – commanding Land Forces North Vietnam (FTNV) – reacted to the first, still unquantified threat to the key post of Nghia Lo by dropping Major Bigeard's 6th Colonial Parachute Battalion (6 BPC) at nearby Tu Le, where it took under command small local units. On the evening of the 17th, Nghia Lo was unexpectedly attacked by two regiments with heavy mortar and gunfire support; it fell the next morning, as bad weather kept French aircraft away. On the 19th, Bigeard sent a company to bring in the little garrison of Gia Hoi, and others made their way to Tu Le, where 6 BPC waited for them until the last possible moment. In the early hours of 20 October, Regiment 165 from Division 312 assaulted Tu Le but was beaten off. That afternoon 6 BPC and the other troops started a 40-mile retreat south-west through the mountains towards French positions on the Black River, with the Viet Minh bounding forward on their trail. Bigeard's rearguard held off a number of attacks, his companies leap-frogging one another on the narrow tracks as they covered each other's retreat. On 22 October, 6 BPC reached Franco-Vietnamese troops on the Black River; the Vietnamese battalion TD 56 held off Regiment 165 and a battalion of 209 while the refugees crossed. Bigeard's 6 BPC lost about 100 dead and missing, but had saved the small garrisons. The battalion had in fact been given up for lost, and were much praised and heavily decorated on their return to Hanoi. Pro-French partisans who had followed the route of 6 BPC and their pursuers found it lined at intervals with the severed heads of French casualties set on bamboo stakes.[32]

IN THE HIGH REGION THE BEST Viet Minh units – though not all of them – enjoyed an advantage over French troops, based on their long training in guerrilla fieldcraft and night movement. The terrain and vegetation gave the People's Army the choice of seeking or refusing combat, and when they did find themselves in danger it favoured their well-practised tactics of dispersal and later reassembly. In the enervating climate every task and movement required extra effort, and during CEFEO operations the European troops' progress across country was usually painfully slow. From the air the steep jumble of hills which cover highland Tonkin and northern Laos look like a tightly crumpled green blanket; there are few clear landmarks, and in the 1950s the maps were approximate, making navigation across country difficult. Once off the few rudimentary roads there were only sparse tracks linking tribal villages to their water sources and little patches of fields on the narrow valley floors; otherwise movement was just possible along animal trails, laboriously opened up by cutting paths with machetes. The bamboo in the valleys, the thick forest vegetation on the slopes and the tall elephant grass on the ridges cut speed and visibility to a minimum, and silent progress was impossible.

Although pack ponies or mules were sometimes available for the heavy weapons and radios, the French infantry usually had to carry all their own food, water and ammunition; bivouac gear was limited to a poncho, a blanket and sometimes a mosquito net, and rations were unsustaining. 'We lived on rubbish – fish heads and rice. We were parachuted in some food once, and we could see that the tins had been overpainted. A friend got hold of a tin and made a hole in it with his bayonet. A sort of green mist flew out. [I] scraped off this painted layer... [underneath] it said in French, "For Arab Troops, 1928".'[33] A fighting patrol in the hills might last a month before the column came in to replenish their ammunition – by which time their pallid skin was encrusted with filth and covered with ulcerated sores, the clothes and boots were rotting off them, and a good many were weak with malaria or dysentery. Early in an operation the jungle noises – screaming howler monkeys at first and last light, tigers coughing, large animals crashing away through the undergrowth, birdsong which sounded like anything but birds, bullfrogs croaking all night long – worked on the soldiers' nerves; some were constantly jumpy, but after weeks in the wilderness a man might become attuned to the forest and achieve a sort of inner silence.

Although many white soldiers have spoken of Vietnam's spell-binding beauty, the landscape concealed countless other enemies than the Viet Minh. The tigers of folklore were certainly heard but not often actually encountered; far more lethal were poisonous snakes, scorpions, centipedes and spiders, stinging insects, blood-sucking leeches, soldier ants, burrowing ticks, and microscopic parasites which could eat out a man's health for the rest of his life. Even inside a jungle fort's bunkhouse the big, fearless rats would bite through a sleeping soldier's boot to sink their teeth into his foot – the fate of men helplessly wounded and abandoned in the forest did not bear thinking about, and was the soldiers' worst fear. 'If you were really wounded badly, there was an old German saying, *"Magen Schuss, Kopf Schuss – ist Spritzer"* ("Belly shot, head shot – it's an overdose job"). They'd give you a shot of morphine – that was your lot... We had these collapsible ampoules and we used to stick them in a chap's cheek. You gave them an overdose if they'd got their legs blown off – you're 300km from anywhere – what are you going to do? The chap would be covered in ants in a moment...'[34]

Although only a minority of People's Army units were in fact raised from men born in the highlands, it was nevertheless believed that this was the Viet Minh's natural hunting range – a myth analogous to the exaggerated fear of Japanese jungle skills among Allied troops in 1942. Everyone seemed to have heard stories of platoons which had gone in and never returned, or from which one or two wild-eyed survivors had eventually staggered into some lonely post 'looking like Christ down from the cross'. The fate of French prisoners in Viet Minh hands was unknown but the subject of uneasy speculation; everyone, too, had heard tales of tortured corpses in the ashes of burnt-out forts and convoys. Some of these stories were true; as a general rule, however, the Viet Minh seem to have treated

French casualties more often with blank callousness than sadistic cruelty. Most wounded were either shot or stabbed out of hand, or simply left to die horribly where they lay. There was an arbitrary and unnerving quality to the enemy's treatment of prisoners. Executions in retaliation for French activities were sometimes announced; but on other occasions the French were told to collect a few wounded prisoners from a pre-arranged spot – presumably as a psychological ploy.[35]

ON 20 OCTOBER 1952, GENERAL de Linarès entrusted the defence of the middle Black River and Route Provinciale 41 to an Operational Group (designated GOMRN) commanded by a paratroop colonel, Jean Gilles. East of Tuan Giao the road was overlooked by a cluster of hills around a *'dakotable'* airstrip at Na San, and Colonel Gilles was ordered to prepare this position for defence. Although the French had no road links into the High Region, General Salan believed that a strong garrison, with artillery, could be planted and sustained far from the Delta by airlift alone; and Na San was to be the testing ground for this theory of the *'base aéro-terrestre'*.

Giap's Divisions 308, 312 and 316 were having some logistic difficulties; their ammunition expenditure had been heavy, and while few of the Thai population actively resisted them, it proved hard to gather enough rice or the tens of thousands of porters to carry it. A distraction which Salan created far to the north-east across the rear lines of the expedition would also cause Giap to pause, and it took five weeks for his divisions to reach Na San, some 45 miles from Nghia Lo. In the meantime a hasty airlift was preparing Na San to stand off a major attack.

Knowing that three of Giap's five infantry divisions were absent in the Thai country, Salan launched an ambitious thrust out of the north-west tip of the Delta, up RC2 and the Clear River to threaten the Viet Minh base areas around Phu Tho, Phu Doan and Tuyen Quang (*see Map 4*). Its objectives were to draw Giap back from the High Region by cutting his lines of supply and communication, and to destroy his stores depots. Operation 'Lorraine' opened on 29 October, and involved no fewer than 30,000 men in four motorized, one airborne, two armoured and two riverine groups, laboriously scraped together by stripping the Delta. Initially using two routes, they bridged the river at Trung Ha and Viet Tri and advanced in parallel, but by the time they got moving all surprise had been lost. In bad weather, and repeatedly blocked and ambushed by Viet Minh regional troops, it took them until 5 November to reach Phu Tho where the two columns linked; thereafter they advanced up a single, narrow road deep into enemy country. On 9 November some 2,350 paratroopers of Groupe Aéroporté 1 (1st and 2nd Foreign and 3rd Colonial Parachute Battalions) dropped over Phu Doan, meeting light resistance; the regional troops faded into the forests for the time being. The next day the armour reached the depot areas and spread out to find and destroy the enemy's stores. Although much had been spirited away and hidden before their arrival, fairly large amounts of matériel were located: 250 tons of munitions and 1,500 weapons, together with a surprise – four Molotova trucks (proof of Soviet as well as Chinese aid). Strong patrols were pushed out, the furthest getting to Phu Yen some 15 miles beyond Phu Doan, though never threatening Tuyen Quang.

'Lorraine' was sitting astride an important knot in the Viet Minh's road network; but they could not stay for ever, and Giap refused to rise to the bait. He did not turn his main force back from the Thai country, sending only two regular regiments north and leaving most of the fighting to the regional units. Meanwhile he ordered Divisions 304 and 320, then on the northern and southern edges of the Delta respectively, to infiltrate the De Lattre Line and keep the weakened French garrisons occupied. He correctly judged that the strain of supplying such a large, strung-out column would soon force its withdrawal; and on 13 November, Salan gave the order. Now the Viet Minh closed in again around the narrow corridor; and on 17 November regular Regiment 36 sprang a major ambush on Groupes Mobiles 1 and 4 at the Chan Muong Pass. The column was trapped all day, and suffered about 300 casualties. Shortly afterwards the other returned regular unit, Regiment 176, also cut the road; and there was further heavy fighting on the night 23/24 November before the column hacked its way back into the Delta. In all 'Lorraine' – its largest ever operation – had cost the CEFEO some 1,200 casualties. It had failed to influence Giap's strategy; it had not drawn significant regular units into combat; and although it had caused useful material damage, the depots destroyed were only capital, which could soon be made up by the Viet Minh's swelling flow of revenue from China.[36]

AS 'LORRAINE' FOUGHT ITS WAY home to face the damage wreaked
in the Delta during the absence of so many troops, Giap turned his
attention back to the Thai Highlands. Paratroopers were screening the
approaches to Na San, and slowly fell back in a series of delaying actions,
covering the retreat of small post garrisons. When the first attack was
made on Na San on the night of 23 November the defensive preparations
were incomplete, but 12 French, Legion, North African, Vietnamese and
Thai battalions had soon been flown in, supported by three artillery
batteries and a heavy mortar company.[37] Gilles' GOMRN had constructed
an outer ring of hilltop strongpoints, backed by a continuous inner ring
around the airstrip in the centre of the position (*see Map 2*). The dug-in
troops were protected by wire, minefields, and interlocking fields of fire; in
the central redoubt were the artillery and heavy mortars, and paratroop
battalions as a reserve for counter-attacks. However, when the Viet Minh
began to arrive most of the artillery had been temporarily withdrawn to
support Operation 'Lorraine'.

General Giap's intelligence was for once badly mistaken: he believed
that the garrison had only five weak infantry battalions. As already
described in detail in Chapter 1 above, a Viet Minh battalion attacked one
of the inner strongpoints after dark on 23 November; but although manned
by only one Legion company, this particularly strong position held out all
night with help from the heavy mortars. Foiled in this attempt to break
in by surprise, Giap spent the next week gathering his whole force for a
more prepared assault.[38] Gilles' garrison had its artillery back by the time
Giap committed units from all three of his divisions on the nights of
30 November/1 December and 1/2 December. Two of the French strongpoints were lost but soon recaptured, and two others held off all assaults;
French artillery support was notably effective. In all more than 1,000 enemy
dead were counted at Na San, so the total killed and wounded were
probably three times that many.

The Viet Minh pulled back from Na San over the next few days,
eventually leaving only small numbers to keep a passive watch over the
camp. Paratroopers made a number of aggressive sorties in strength during
December–February on RP41 and the Black River, reaching Co Noi and
Son La. The garrison was maintained for months, though some units
were rotated and only one parachute battalion remained by April.[39]

The theory of the 'air–ground base' seemed to have been vindicated, and Salan repeated the formula elsewhere.

GENERAL GIAP'S THREE DIVISIONS were still in the High Region threatening the Laotian border, although their losses and logistic difficulties would delay them for several months. The most practical invasion route through the Thai Highlands into north-west Laos lay along RP41 to Tuan Giao, thence to Dien Bien Phu in the valley of the Nam Youm, down it through the Massif des Calcaires range to Sop Nao, and south along the valley of the Nam Ou river. General Salan ordered the creation of two smaller air–ground bases at Lai Chau, and Sam Neua in Laos. He also ordered Dien Bien Phu to be held; but the local commander could spare only two companies, and these had to be withdrawn when threatened on 30 November. Nagged by the abandonment of this strategic position, the importance of which he noted in several documents, Salan at first planned to reoccupy it in January 1953, but never had the means to do so.[40]

While the CEFEO were distracted by attacks in the Delta, the 'waist' and Central Highlands of Annam, and by manoeuvres in the upper Song river valley, Giap prepared for a renewed thrust into Laos, planting advance food depots along the route. In February 1953 the French expected another attack on Na San; but this supposed blocking position was only guarded (by Regiment 102) and was bypassed when, early in April, Division 316 moved south towards Sam Neua (*see Map 6*). After some hesitation Salan decided that Sam Neua was indefensible and ordered the garrison to march south; many Laotian troops deserted, Division 316 caught up with the rest on the march, and few escaped.[41] At the same time Divisions 308 and 312 were also moving south by separate routes; Giap's true objective was unclear, and Salan faced difficult choices with limited means. Though barely defensible, the Laotian royal capital of Luang Prabang was reinforced to ten battalions, and by 30 April two regiments of Division 312 were outside the city.[42] Meanwhile another ten battalions had been planted in an air–ground base on the Plain of Jars to guard the approaches to Vientiane, and by 23 April this was surrounded by Divisions 308 and 316. These deployments put a huge strain on the inadequate French air transport fleet, and left the Delta vulnerable.[43] In the event, neither of these positions was assaulted; with the onset of the rains in mid May 1953 – and with their logistics hampered by active Meo partisan bands – the three People's Army divisions left Laos and returned to their normal staging areas in Tonkin.

Their foray into Laos had been valuable practice in the movement and supply of large formations over long distances during a period of several months. The army had achieved complete freedom of movement throughout northern Laos, and had planted food depots, a political infrastructure and regional guerrilla units, all for future exploitation. Although the pro-French Meos remained troublesome, after Giap's departure the weak Franco-Laotian troops of Land Forces Laos (FTL) were able to reoccupy only a few posts in the lower Nam Ou valley. In the Thai country the Viet Minh remained strong outside the immediate vicinity of French bases, and the powerful Independent Regiment 148 was firmly established at various points throughout the hills.

THE LONG MEMORANDUM which the C-in-C General Salan handed to his successor before his departure in May 1953 included a clear-sighted summary of the strategic position; but there were some truths too brutal to be put down on paper by a career soldier.

Throughout Vietnam, and particularly in the main cockpit of war in Tonkin, the Viet Minh enjoyed a unified commmand which maintained an agreed programme towards a single purpose. Their war aims could not have been simpler: to kill as many French as possible, to drive the foreigners off their soil acre by acre, and to suborn, terrorize or destroy their Vietnamese 'puppets'. Their methods for achieving this had proved sound, and successes had accumulated. They had sometimes stumbled over the timing of the next step up the ladder, but when they did so – even at great cost in lives – time was still on their side. They simply returned to their safe havens, rebuilt their strength, and went back a few steps to try again more cautiously, while the constant distractions of the nationwide guerrilla war kept the Expeditionary Corps dispersed and preoccupied. Their capabilities grew steadily greater: People's Army soldiers did not go home every two years, and the potential manpower pool was enormous, even allowing for the high proportion of the population whose labour was needed to keep the country fed. Each success improved morale, prestige and popular support, while defeats were accepted patiently as temporary setbacks in a thousand-year story, never shaking the faith in ultimate victory. From mid 1950 the Chinese were prepared to continue arming and training them more or less in pace with the growth of their numbers and needs; and where they were weak in particular material resources they simply found ways to do without them. After all, Viet Minh troops had never had them before; unlike those of a Frenchman who had fought alongside the US Army in Europe, the expectations of a former peasant farmer or forest guerrilla were not high. Seen from his perspective, the scale and quality of his unit's equipment were rising steadily; it took very severe deprivation indeed to reduce the morale of the *bo doi* to a level which destroyed his fighting potential.

By comparison, for much of the war the French were hampered by disunity between the military and civil authorities, and by a lack of any real continuity in strategic planning. Their home governments came and went, none of them able to pursue a coherent policy either for winning the war or for abandoning it, and in the face of soaring costs each one was less committed than the last. Every couple of years a new commander-in-chief arrived and appointed new regional commanders, each inheriting a disappointing situation from his predecessor, and each denied the scale of reinforcements needed to achieve any real transformation in the strategic balance. In time each announced his military priorities, according to his means and his staff's appreciation of the enemy's resources and intentions. These appreciations were of variable accuracy, but in any case the realities on the ground meant that the new programme seldom achieved any success beyond local tactical victories. The steady turnover of men through repatriation at the end of their tours, and a chronic shortage of experienced junior leaders, ensured that the combat readiness of the Expeditionary Corps was always uneven, while the prospect of creating effective Indochinese armies receded like a mirage. Total numbers of reliable fighting troops remained more or less static; recruitment was difficult in a France profoundly unenthusiastic about this war, and concentration of a mobile reserve for major initiatives was always hampered by the need to react to periodic regional threats throughout the peninsula.

While an increasing flow of American dollars, weapons, vehicles and aircraft in the early 1950s did improve the firepower and mobility of the CEFEO, they could not offset the fundamental disadvantages of a roadbound army facing a hill and forest army in a country which had few roads but a great many hills and forests. Always lacking the means to exploit his local victories, in time each general would gratefully go home himself to a comfortable NATO command, leaving to his successor a gloomy report, an army with static resources and sinking morale, and a 'pox map' whose areas of red kept creeping relentlessly outwards from the Viet Minh's irreducible heartlands.

BY THE SPRING OF 1953 the armies of both sides in this war had changed fundamentally from those which had first confronted one another in 1945–6. In each case the process and its outcome deserves some examination.

4. The People's Army

'The Apache never attack unless fully convinced of an easy victory. They will watch for days, scanning your every movement, observing your every act; taking exact note of your party and all its belongings. Let no one suppose that these assaults are made upon the spur of the moment by bands accidentally encountered.'

J. C. Cremony, *Life Among the Apaches* (1868)

THE VIET MINH'S AIMS, PURSUED in parallel, were the total independence of a unified Vietnam – Tonkin, Annam and Cochinchina – and the construction of a Communist state. Independence could be achieved only by the victory of the People's Army, but the Party's programme for the transformation of society was not subordinated to short-term military goals. The codes governing the conduct of the war were laid down by the Party; these authorized the use of terror and assassination, but sought to prevent any fatal alienation of the army from the people, and also served the long-term goal of politicizing the people along the Party's desired lines.[1]

This effort to politicize the population and to harness their support for a war of liberation is a separate story of great complexity, but it must be summarized briefly if the recruitment and motivation of the People's Army are to be understood. In December 1946 the active, armed membership of the

Viet Minh was limited to a few tens of thousands, and its hard-core popular support to a few provinces of Tonkin; there were also solid areas in Cochinchina, and various 'islands' in Annam, but all of these presented difficulties of communication and control. The creation of an effective nationwide network of Party activists to take local command had made great strides since March 1945; but an enormous task still remained, and under war conditions this would take years to complete. Each step along the way began in the hard-core areas and spread gradually outwards as increasing numbers of leadership personnel – cadres – were indoctrinated, trained, and dispersed throughout Vietnam.

The first step was the literacy programme, announced in September 1945; this was obviously vital if a population suffering 90 per cent illiteracy was to be mobilized by any means faster than individual word of mouth.[2] Instruction of all ages and both sexes was pursued with great energy, but as in all Viet Minh programmes the young were targeted particularly. New readers were tasked with teaching in turn their families, workmates and other associates. Generally the programme was eagerly accepted; those reluctant to attend lessons after a hard day's work were encouraged by peer pressure – for instance, red labels were displayed on houses to show how many illiterates remained within, and if these did not diminish in reasonable time social sanctions were applied. The reading matter provided was naturally chosen to further 'revolutionary consciousness', and literacy greatly accelerated the existing programme of spreading propaganda by direct contact.[3]

Propaganda was calculated to suit particular audiences, by agents who penetrated the many parallel associations which dominated Vietnamese life – everything from age-group societies and town-quarter associations, through veterans' and ex-pupils' groups, to cock-fighting or bird fanciers' clubs.[4] Urban students could stomach a rich diet of Marxist–Leninist indoctrination; rice farmers needed more roughage, and this was provided by the denunciation of local landlords and tax collectors. The promise of land reform – confiscation of large French and Vietnamese holdings, and collectivist redistribution – was one of the twin pillars of the Viet Minh's practical programme.

The other was straightforward nationalism: hatred and distrust of the French were preached at every level, and every hardship and misfortune suffered by the particular audience was blamed on the French and their local 'puppets'. The need for armed insurrection to reverse France's 'theft' of the Democratic Republic was constantly repeated, as was the Viet Minh's promise to provide the means for it. Many were sufficiently convinced by this core message alone. Captured guerrillas sometimes denied knowing what the Viet Minh was, but explained their sniping in simple terms: if the French were allowed to come back, so would the landlords and bureaucrats, who would take all the farmers' rice and demand back-dated rent and taxes.[5]

The doctrine preached by Viet Minh agents in innumerable meetings – from hidden forest camps, to rural schools, to locked rooms above city alleyways – was convincing to many partly because those who preached it were themselves sincerely convinced. As in so many 20th-century societies of wretchedly abused peasants, Communism served up in digestible forms had the appeal of a religion. It answered every question, and promised a decent future of social justice. Its priests were patient and articulate, and their sermons had a strong moral aspect: the revolution demanded hard work, thrift, self-sacrifice, loyalty, and respect for the rights of all comrades. There was even a confessional element: at every level, the public analysis of errors by means of individual self-criticism was expected, and the cadres set the example.

ASSUMING A GENERALLY RECEPTIVE local environment, the next step after propaganda was actual contact between armed groups and the peasantry, which – given the natural climate of suspicion – was obviously a delicate moment. Only after careful enquiry into local conditions and personalities would the advance members of an 'armed propaganda platoon' approach selected men in a particular village. A small network of basically sympathetic locals would be created before the main armed group showed themselves, and great care was taken not to frighten or offend the villagers. A code of 'Six Do's and Six Don'ts' was formalized by Ho Chi Minh on 5 April 1948, and further developed at later dates. The incomers must adapt sympathetically to local customs, even superstitions; help with the daily work; and offer instruction in literacy and hygiene. If remote from markets, villagers should be offered simple purchases of goods such as knives, salt, needles and thread, pens and paper.

The agents should tell happy, encouraging stories to spread the spirit of resistance; and should consistently show by example that the Viet Minh were serious, hard-working and disciplined men and women. They were never to damage the villagers' fields, houses or property; to offend against local customs and beliefs; to insist on buying or 'borrowing' anything the owners were unwilling to part with; to break their given word in any matter; to pursue village women; or to do or say anything to make the locals feel scorned.[6]

Once accepted, the agents identified the most reliable elements for a crash course in political education and commitment to the armed struggle; these in turn would become the cadres for local extension of the movement. Eventually the village would provide a small squad of part-time guerrillas. If conditions were ripe, a regional combat platoon might be sent in to organize an armed presence. These platoons would become, in General Giap's words, the drops of oil, which might slowly spread and coalesce until the area became chronically insecure for the authorities.[7]

From the earliest stages, Ho Chi Minh was aware of the obstacles raised by the ethnic distrust of the highland minorities (his 'Six Don'ts' specifically addressed this point). In the Thai Highlands, the normal sequence was unavoidably reversed: there it was Giap's regular combat units that arrived first, in 1951–2. However, they were accompanied by political teams to create a Viet Minh infrastructure; these were planted all over the hills, and outlasted the temporary presence of the regular troops. Notables were arrested and tried by 'people's courts'; those condemned as 'great traitors' were shot and their goods shared out among the villagers. The new administration made efforts to attract the younger generation; local customs were studied, various existing associations formally registered, and newly indoctrinated cadres appointed. Communist Party recruitment was pursued, though with careful filtering. The seeding of the hills with guerrillas began; trained by regular People's Army instructors, these formed an embryonic armed militia, which was eventually entrusted with small-scale ambushes and mine-laying[8] – although they faced serious resistance from pro-French Meo and Thai partisans organized by the French secret service (*see Chapter 6 below*).

While the High Region was an extreme case, progress everywhere was slow and uneven. In the Delta and on the coast of Annam the villagers were generally receptive; but townspeople were often sharply divided, and in Roman Catholic areas the Viet Minh were resisted from the pulpit and by armed force – strong militias were raised in the bishoprics of Bui Chu and Phat Diem on the Tonkin coast. Catholics were more scattered in Cochinchina, where the main popular resistance to the Communists was mounted by the Cao Dai and Hoa Hao sects.[9] Throughout the country and at every level of society there were, of course, some who remained stubbornly unreceptive; but in East Asian societies the rights of the individual weigh lightly against the demands of the group.

To the sincerely convinced, it was genuinely puzzling that some refused to support the movement for national liberation and social justice, which was of such transparent benefit. Persuasion was redoubled, in terms calculated to sway the particular individual depending upon his character and his standing in the community, and argument was accompanied by the coercion of peer pressure. To the fanatically determined, motive was unimportant: opposition to the Party had to be eliminated. Once a certain level of local commitment had been achieved, the few who still stood out against the many could be isolated as perverse, disloyal, probably willing tools of the oppressor. They were denounced publicly, and if they refused to admit their errors and rejoin society, then they were punished. However, although the cause justified all means to achieve it, terror was not to be gratuitous: it had to be explained as an act of justice against an enemy of the whole community.[10]

The Maoist handbook placed great emphasis on enlisting the willing support of the population, and Viet Minh agents seem often to have felt genuine identification with the villagers, even if tinged with superiority. Their 'people's courts' made a public show of due process, and sometimes even members of the hated landowner class were let off with a period of 're-education' and a heavy fine. Meanwhile, the political commissars and *Cong An* 'security' teams did not shrink from using exemplary terror when other means of persuasion failed, and this sometimes went beyond workaday shootings and even village-burnings. East Asia has a long history of demonic tortures, and the Communists did not shrink from inflicting imaginative medieval horrors on the stubbornly uncooperative and their helpless families to terrify France's local 'puppets' into submission.[11]

THE PEOPLE'S ARMY 135

THE MACHINERY BY WHICH the Viet Minh gradually came to control large numbers of the population reflected the age-old tradition of parallel associations. A new system of parallel hierarchies was formed, and the three main examples of these were pyramidal, with committees at various levels from village or town quarter up to centralized national direction, and integrated, in practice, by a series of (usually hidden) lateral links. The *Cu Quoc* was a 'national safety' organization, not overtly political and relying upon normal social pressures to ensure useful mass co-operation. The political *Lien Viet* or 'Unified Popular Front' embraced those of broad nationalist sympathies but various allegiances, including open anti-Communists, thus allowing the Party to keep track of both the useful and the dangerous. The Communist Party itself existed in parallel, secretly recruiting among the leadership of the other hierarchies; each province had a small centralized Party direction committee. Within the Viet Minh military organization all political officers and most combat commanders – though initially, not all – were Party members.

This intricate system ensured that the Party held the levers of control of a wide range of groups throughout Vietnamese society. It also enjoyed a flow of information from an enormous popular base, whose members were motivated by either Communist conviction or patriotic ideals; self-interest or simple fear. Through this machinery the programmes of political education and military mobilization were pursued in parallel. The slogans were 'The whole people in arms – each person a fighter, each village a fortress, each Party cell and resistance committee a general staff'.[12]

IN TERMS OF VIET MINH MILITARY activity, Vietnam was divided into three: 'liberated zones' or Viet Minh country; disputed zones, where the Franco-Vietnamese forces faced varying degrees of danger; and nominally pacified zones, where the French had a strong and permanent presence.[13] Despite these obvious practical differences, from March 1948 the territorial organization of the Viet Minh in 'Interzones' (described in Chapter 3 above) admitted no formal distinction between liberated, disputed or French zones.

In the liberated zones the Viet Minh's authority had gone unchallenged for years; here the Communists enforced their own laws, provided administration and public services, and presided over a collectivist economy.

Here, too, the People's Army had its headquarters, base camps, training schools, hospitals, factories and depots, all hidden in the wilderness – or, in parts of Annam, ingeniously concealed in and below the numerous villages. The CEFEO raided these regions by parachute or amphibious craft, but their penetrations were too shallow and brief to have any lasting effect. The Viet Minh withdrew, dispersed, slowed the French by sabotage and ambush, and reassembled to attack them as they pulled back.

In the disputed zones French units were based in the midst of the civilian population; in their immediate vicinity the Viet Minh remained hidden, their political agents working to increase their control. Guerrillas carried out sabotage, death squads assassinated officials, a vast network of eyes and ears gathered intelligence, while tax collectors harvested cash and produce. Open resistance only occurred in villages where French troops rarely ventured. Here the Viet Minh created self-defence militias to guard valuable depots and way stations for full-time combat units passing through the area.

The boundaries between 'disputed' and supposedly 'pacified' zones were fluid and porous. Widely spaced outposts marked out lines which the Franco-Vietnamese forces seldom crossed; but these could not prevent 'osmosis' between neighbouring zones.[14] Supplies of weapons, munitions and other matériel passed nightly from the exterior to the interior of the Delta, a thousand infiltrations by messengers and agents kept the separated Viet Minh forces in Tonkin in mutual contact, and whole regular and regional combat units were rotated between disputed zones and safe Viet Minh country near by.

THE BIRTH OF THE PEOPLE'S ARMY is dated to 22 December 1944, when Ho Chi Minh signed the directive creating the first Armed Propaganda Brigade of the Vietnamese Liberation Army. The title People's Army *(Quan Doi Nhan Dan)* was adopted after 'liberation' was considered to have been formally achieved – that is, the proclamation of the Democratic Republic in September 1945 gave their armed force, in Viet Minh eyes, the status of the national army of a sovereign state. Its organization was pyramidal, in three upwards levels – from popular, to regional, to regular – with the lower two each serving the one above. Members of either might be ordered to support an operation by the next level up; and each was recruited from the most promising members of the level below.

At the lowest level of the pyramid were the popular forces, *Tu Ve*, comprising both the *Dan Quan* and the *Dan Quan Du Kich*. The *Dan Quan* embraced the whole unarmed population – men, women, children, old people – to contribute according to their abilities as guides, messengers, spies, look-outs, builders of hideouts, and above all as the Viet Minh's logistic manpower. They provided the coolies who were called up periodically to clear tracks for the combat units, to carry their food and other supplies, and to spirit away their wounded and dead (the immediate removal of casualties from the battlefield to thwart French intelligence was standard procedure at every level). The combat units of the regional and regular troops depended absolutely on this logistic support.

Within this organization the *Du Kich*, selected from among the able-bodied men, provided the village guerrillas and self-defence militias. They were very lightly armed, typically having machetes, a few grenades and/or home-made mines, and only handfuls of old Japanese or French rifles or pistols. The village *(Xa)* formed a squad of a dozen or more, who might have only two or three firearms between them; a group of neighbouring villages, a platoon *(Lien Xa)* of perhaps 50 men, which might boast one light machine gun. They almost never formed units as large as companies *(Dai Doi)*, and their leaders were locally elected. In disputed zones their ability to exist depended upon total integration within their village community, and for most of the time they followed their normal lives. Occasionally they were assembled for clandestine instruction; less often, they were authorized to carry out some strictly limited act of sabotage, terror or guerrilla raiding. In villages under direct French occupation a shadow of the same organization was created, biding its time in secrecy. In the liberated zones the militia could operate freely as the Viet Minh's basic level of security and enforcement. The military value of the *Du Kich* was thus extremely variable.[15]

The heart of the guerrilla method was patience and singleness of purpose, enforced by a discipline that became tighter as the years passed and Viet Minh central control was perfected. In the disputed zones the enemy was never to be confronted unless he was greatly outnumbered. Progress was by gradual increments: two or three men with machetes could butcher a careless rural constable and take his pistol; half a dozen men with machetes, pistols and a couple of grenades could flush a pair of night watchmen out of their flimsy timber watchtower and take their rifles; a dozen men with rifles and an improvised mine could ambush a truck on a back road and capture a light machine gun and a case of ammunition. Their prizes were hidden with great ingenuity, and they faded back into the anonymous mass of peasants. The Viet Minh command very occasionally ordered assembly of 'concentrated' guerrilla units *(Du Kich Tap Trung)* for longer periods of activity if there was particular local need, or in order to make selections for the regional troops.

THE NEXT LEVEL UP, AND THE most important for much of the war across most of the country, were the regional troops *(Bo Dai Dia Phuong)*. Their task was to pursue the guerrilla war within their region, under central control of the People's Army. They were not to defend ground unless to inflict casualties as they fell back, but were to snap up any vulnerable French force when opportunity offered. They were to develop and recruit from the popular forces, and to co-ordinate activity with regular units which might temporarily be passing through or operating in their region. Their part always involved 'preparing the battlefield' with hideouts, guides and porters; it might demand the mounting of major diversionary attacks, which were sometimes sacrificial; and it always exposed them to vigorous French reaction, persisting after the regulars had left the area. Apart from the major Tonkin campaigns of the Chu Luc in 1950–54, these regionals bore the main weight of the entire war.

The regional troops were full-time soldiers, operating only in the disputed areas and based in hidden camps. Where the terrain did not provide suitable cover they lay up in groups of isolated villages, surrounded by an outer belt of villages where look-outs were posted to provide warning of French activity. The regionals were recruited from the best young men among the village guerrillas; they were fed, clothed and equipped, but not paid (before 1958 no regional or regular troops received wages).[16] Each district formed a local company; administratively this was part of a battalion and sometimes of a regiment, but these seldom operated together as tactical units. In addition, each province had a 'mobile battalion' – an actual tactical unit – for more wide-ranging operations under control of the provincial command *(Tinh Doi Bo)*. The mobile battalion had an HQ element, three rifle companies, and a support company with some mortars and machine guns (often Japanese) and perhaps an engineer platoon. In liberated and disputed Tonkin (Lien Khu 1, 2 and 3) the total regional strength was about 35 battalions in March 1952, rising to 52 by March 1954; of these totals, 14 and 23 battalions respectively were based inside the Delta (Lien Khu 3), the remainder in the regions outside the De Lattre Line. (By comparison, Lien Khu 5 in southern Annam had only six and 13 battalions respectively at those dates.)[17]

Although the officers of regional troops were periodically summoned for training courses in the Viet Bac, the district companies and regional battalions were of variable quality. At first they were only lightly armed, since theft or capture from the Franco-Vietnamese forces were their only way of supplementing their original Japanese stocks; but from 1950 they increasingly received French arms handed down from the regulars who were being re-equipped by China with Communist bloc weapons. In addition to relatively poor equipment, most Tonkin regionals also led dangerous and uncomfortable lives. Unlike the regulars they seldom enjoyed periods of rest in the liberated zones, and they had to be constantly on the look-out for French security sweeps. Nevertheless, the best of them were formidable enemies – particularly the three-battalion Regiments 42, 46 and 50, permanently based inside the Delta along with about a dozen separate battalions.

Mao's tactical doctrine served them well: 'Exploit the enemy's weakness, flee from his strengths. When he advances, retreat; when he retreats, advance and harass him; when he camps, surround and harass him; never face him when he wants you to.' As throughout the People's Army, the regionals took enormous pains over camouflage and concealed movement, of which the Viet Minh were masters throughout the war. They were faithfully supported by a dense civilian population devoted to their welfare in a terrain entirely familiar to them. By 1953 those who had survived were expert in concealment, evasion and guerrilla tactics; they very seldom allowed themselves to get trapped, or took on an enemy they could not beat.[18]

The Delta was one vast disputed zone, where between 3,000 and 4,000 villages were dispersed over more than 5,000 square miles of paddy-fields. A French 'pox map' of June 1953 shows each Viet Minh-controlled village by a dot; in the south-eastern third of the triangle they cluster so thickly that the map seems to be printed with a *pointilliste* screen.[19] In the countryside the CEFEO, overstretched by the need to provide permanent guards for towns, roads, railways and airfields, could only plant forts at wide intervals. Within the 'useful Delta' – and not counting the actual De Lattre Line perimeter – the number of these posts reached 917 by 1954. Most were weakly protected with brick or even earth walls, and their towers and pillboxes varied greatly in strength; many had only – in the insouciant French phrase – '*un blockhaus de fortune*', and the enormous demands of the De Lattre Line allowed only about 80 of them to be rebuilt in concrete.[20]

By the last years of the war, when the Delta regionals had received some heavy weapons and were supported by infiltrated regular units, a smooth routine had been perfected for attacks on rural posts. For days beforehand scouts watched and noted, so the commander could plan his attack with full knowledge of the fort's layout, garrison and routine; often the assault parties were rehearsed on detailed mock-ups of the post's defences. Arriving after nightfall, the attackers dug one or two approach trenches up to the barbed wire surrounding the walls, and brought up their heavy weapons – mortars, perhaps 57mm recoilless guns, and machine guns – to knock out the blockhouses and radio aerials and sweep the embrasures and parapets. When all was ready, carefully practised sapper teams blew lanes in the wire, the heavy weapons opened fire and the assault parties went in. The small garrison could do nothing but shut themselves up inside the pillboxes and pray for daylight. They could call in supporting fire from artillery several miles away if their radio still worked; but often the nearby posts were also being attacked, with at least enough firepower to keep artillery crews away from their open gunpits. Even if the post did manage to alert the sector commander, about all he could do before morning was to send aircraft to drop parachute flares over the desperate little battle. There was no chance of sending a relief column before dawn: their routes were obvious, and the Viet Minh mined them and set ambushes in up to battalion strength. If the artillery could not intervene effectively, then it was all up for the garrison once the grenades and machine-gun ammunition ran out.[21]

Most Delta villages were only visited by occasional local patrols, whose approach was visible from far off and whose movement easy to hamper; but in the aftermath of such an attack French sector forces would sweep the neighbourhood in search of the Viet Minh responsible. Large numbers of troops were needed to put a *bouclage* around a sufficiently large area; the preparations were nearly always betrayed in advance, and cordons were rarely so tight that the enemy could not slip away by an unwatched route on at least the first night of an operation. The process of 'sweeping' was painfully slow; by definition, it moved at the pace of a walking man – and a man walking through paddy-fields. The usual formula was reckoned to be 'one village = one battalion = half a day'.

Each village offered remarkable possibilities for concealment – and defence, on the rare occasions when the Viet Minh were forced to stand and fight. Typically it was surrounded by a tall, thick palisade and bristling bamboo *chevaux-de-frise* – barricades made by lashing X-shapes of sharpened stakes side by side in long, densely interwoven hedges. Most had inner ditches filled with water, and these moated ramparts were pierced by only a few narrow gateways. Inside, the soldiers were sucked into a labyrinth of lanes and alleys between blank walls. There were many little fenced or hedged gardens, occasional big shade trees, and the maze of lanes was often confused further by clay ponds maintained for house repairs. The soldiers, quickly separated into small parties, were often deep inside a sort of spiderweb before they had even grasped the general layout of the village.

If the Viet Minh had dug themselves in, machine-gun positions were concealed around the edges of the village and roofed over with timber and earth cover. The alleys were sown with mines, the houses with booby-traps, and from hides dug underneath them groups of Viet Minh would charge out at the last moment in murderous short-range counter-attacks. Even after they engaged the troops, prepared systems of underground tunnels – sometimes with 'siphon' entrances below water level in the banks of streams and canals – often enabled them to slip away.[22]

Despite frequent security operations the hard-core regional units were never eliminated, and large French forces were tied down for mediocre returns. Of ten major operations in the Delta in 1951–4, the smallest employed eight battalions, the largest 20, and the average investment was 15. The shortest of these operations lasted five days, the longest 35 days, and the average was 14. As for the gains and losses, two examples of operations which made large claims of success will suffice. Operations 'Citron/Mandarine' in September/October 1951 around Song Tra Ly and the Bamboo Canal lasted 13 days, and needed 17 battalions; the French claimed 1,150 Viet Minh killed and 'many' prisoners, and suffered 127 dead, 363 wounded, and 28 missing. The month-long Operation 'Bretagne' in December 1952 tied down 18 battalions; it claimed the destruction of two regular battalions from Divisions 304 and 320, and the recovery of a battalion's-worth of weapons. It is certain that French losses were 61 dead, 386 wounded, and the extraordinary figure of 121 missing – in all, the equivalent of a small battalion. The great majority of operations cost far fewer casualties but recorded negligible results, and in many cases the identification of all Vietnamese dead as 'Viet Minh' was naturally suspect.[23]

AN IMPRESSION OF REGIONAL troops under the more relaxed circumstances of Cochinchina is provided by the respected English travel writer (and former Army intelligence officer) Norman Lewis. In spring 1950 Lewis was able, without much difficulty, to find contacts in Saigon who eventually led him to a hidden Viet Minh camp in the Plain of Reeds. He describes good camouflage and physical security, on a swamp island approachable only by waterways which were easily guarded and mined. Whenever French aircraft appeared, a whistle signal produced absolute stillness, and standing orders forbade the guerrillas from opening fire. Discipline was excellent, and enforced by public criticism. The atmosphere in this mixed-sex unit was puritanical; food was simple but plentiful, and standards of hygiene first class. Officers did not use rank titles but were addressed, like all other comrades, as 'Brother'. A rigid daily routine included sessions of physical training and indoctrination lectures, with time set aside for teaching literacy and spreading propaganda in the nearby villages. This unit's primary task was reconnaissance; its personnel spread out over an assigned sector in shifts which covered 24 hours a day, reporting all French and Vietnamese government troop movements in scrupulous detail, and this intelligence was then passed back up the line by radio for collation at a regional headquarters.

Lewis was able to witness a night attack on a weak Vietnamese government post. The garrison surrendered – as the attackers had expected – after receiving a few mortar bombs, and he was struck by the formalized nature of the action. It seemed to be accepted that outnumbered soldiers would usually concede after a few shots to save face, and that the prisoners would join the People's Army after a process of 're-education'. This relatively humane policy was obviously intelligent: their aim was to encourage their countrymen to change sides, not to give them reasons for resisting to the last. (There were, however, many instances of merciless revenge being taken against Vietnamese captured while fighting in the ranks of CEFEO units.) The group Lewis visited were holding prisoner a Sudeten German légionnaire, whose wounds had been simply dressed and who told Lewis that his captors were treating him decently, though he was afraid what his eventual fate might be.[24]

SUCH HIGH STANDARDS WERE not attained over night. Throughout Vietnam as a whole, even central operational control of the regionals was not achieved without local rivalries, factional struggles, the jealous clash of personal ambitions, enemy infiltration and treachery. The Viet Minh had to harness a hydra-headed movement for independence which had evolved during long years of chaos under self-proclaimed or locally elected leaders of many political colours (or none). Nevertheless, this inherent disunity eventually yielded to the imposition of Party discipline, enforced initially by appeals to patriotism and offers of support, but ultimately by the gun.

The transition from regional guerrilla chieftain to People's Army officer was not one which every Viet Minh leader managed to make. Thanks to the researches of General Raymond Boissau, we know something of the evolution of a small independent unit active in 1946–7 north-west of Saigon. At that time it went by various names (in typical Vietnamese fashion): ostensibly it was the 'Tay Ninh Mobile Company'; administratively it was *Dai Doi 52*, a dispersed company of regiment *Chi Doi 57*; it was also *Bo Doi Luu Dong 1* ('Mobile Unit 1'); but to its members it was simply *Bo Doi Hoang Tho* ('Hoang Tho's Unit').

Hoang Tho (predictably, an alias – he was born Nam Tho) was a dynamic young man, formerly a chief scout in a Saigon Catholic organization, but now a convinced nationalist. When the terrifying Nguyen Binh was sent to take over the Viet Minh network in Cochinchina after General Leclerc's victories in early 1946, his eye fell on Hoang Tho – who, though not a Communist, was the energetic leader of a group of about 30 volunteers. From time to time this platoon would serve as Nguyen Binh's bodyguard; it also took part in his campaign of terror against the southern sectarians, and in minor ambushes against the Franco-Vietnamese security forces. On 5 October 1946, Nguyen Binh personally authorized Hoang Tho to form his unit into company DD 52, with a zone of activity around Go Dau Ha and Tran Bang on Route Coloniale 1 between Saigon and Tay Ninh, the Cao Dai sectarian capital (*see Map 1*). The young man was able to repay his commander's trust in the most direct way: on 13 November it was Hoang Tho who saved Nguyen Binh's life during an assassination attempt by Cao Dai agents at the Binh Hoa pagoda.

Hoang Tho's unit fought a succession of small-scale actions against sectarians and the French alike. An ambush on a plantation pay truck allowed him to make judicious gifts to other commanders, and he received more weapons in return; in December 1946 his three small squads held three light machine guns, four sub-machine guns and 25 rifles. Sometimes he linked up temporarily with other units, sometimes he played a lone hand. On 7 May 1947 an ambush on plantation traffic, escorted by two armoured cars of the 5e Cuirassiers and local infantry, left one scout car blazing and seven soldiers and 11 civilians dead; it brought him a Japanese light machine gun, a Sten and seven rifles – but cost him eight dead. The loss of a third of his men did not deter Hoang Tho; by that June the unit had five armed squads each with an LMG, SMGs and rifles. His attacks on small militia-posts and road convoys became more ambitious; in one action on 20 August 1947 he killed five Europeans and 40 Cambodians of the Bataillon de Marche de Cochinchine, took 25 prisoners, and captured his first two mortars. This exploit earned him the People's Army Military Medal 1st Class, but sparked a quarrel with another leader which had to go to Nguyen Binh for arbitration. Although Hoang Tho was becoming famous throughout Zone 7, his privileged relationship with Nguyen Binh was making him patient enemies.

He was also ambitious. That September he raided a Michelin plantation, kidnapped 450 civilians, selected 80 young men for his unit, and applied to form a second company; Nguyen Binh agreed, and sent his fiery protégé 100 more trained fighters. In January 1948 the enlarged Hoang Tho Unit was sent south to the coastal region of Ba Ria, where the Viet Minh were taking worrying losses. During their journey they ran straight into a French airborne operation, 'Têta'; coolly Hoang Tho fought his way clear, his men capturing a Thompson gun, eight rifles, and enough of 2 BCCP's discarded canopies to give every man a dashing scarf of parachute nylon. After some harder fights in the following weeks, the unit returned to its old hunting ground during the rainy season of spring 1948.

By May 1949 the slow process of amalgamating small units of variable size into larger ones modelled on the regulars in Tonkin had given birth to *Bo Doi 303* – the members' own name for a battalion-sized unit officially designated *Trung Doan Chu Luc Luu Dong Khu 7* ('Regular Mobile Regiment/Zone 7') – commanded by Hoang Tho. His old unit now formed Company 2719; Co 2720 was a unit from the Plain of Reeds, Co 2721 was raised from former Binh Xuyen gangsters, and Co 2723 provided the headquarters element. Yet the fiercely independent nationalist Hoang Tho was uneasy in this new command: his old deputy and political commissar were both posted away, most of the new commissars came from Tonkin or Annam, and he seems to have been outspoken in his resentment of the more intrusive system of Communist Party control then being installed at every level. The battalion was sent for three months' working-up north of Cap St Jacques, after which it was posted to the Binh My area north of Tan Uyen; but soon after its arrival, Hoang Tho was summoned before his old protector Nguyen Binh and relieved of his command.

The former leader of guerrilla ambushes was appointed to the staff of Zone 8 and given responsibility for transport and supplies. One day he got violently drunk, smashed up his office furniture and set fire to it. He was arrested, his head was shaved, and he was imprisoned at Rach Gia on the remote north-west coast of the Trans-Bassac wetlands. From this point on Hoang Tho disappears from the record.[25]

THE ACHIEVEMENT OF A HIGH level of guerrilla skills, equipment and central co-ordination could force a stalemate upon an occupying conventional army, and could win local victories; but it could not bring about national liberation. It was only a step in Mao Tse Tung's programme for conducting revolutionary war, as studied by General Giap. The theoretical stages of such a war are never absolutely clear-cut in practice, and their relative duration varies according to local conditions, but they remain a useful guide to the progress of events.

Assuming that the political preparation has been successful, the first stage of military activity is the 'guerrilla' phase. The objective is simple survival, while gaining support among the population; retreating to inaccessible areas to establish safe bases, the guerrillas must create channels for the supply of arms, food and other necessities. Their fighting bands must remain mobile, evading pursuit while they persuade the population to conceal them and to provide warning and tangible support. They must launch pinprick attacks to capture weapons and ammunition and to win prestige, but they must fight no major engagements against the security forces. If threatened they must disperse, reassembling when the immediate danger has passed. This guerrilla phase is the critically vulnerable period, on both the physical and psychological planes. In Tonkin it lasted from 1946 until early 1950, and it continued in Annam and Cochinchina in parallel with the next stage in Tonkin.

The boundary between the 'guerrilla' and the 'protracted' phases is often imperceptible to the enemy, since guerrilla activity continues; but in the meantime a sizeable main or 'regular' force is being formed. This becomes possible only when reliable lines of supply have been secured, and when consistent popular support over large areas has reached a significant level. Guerrillas can be said to have entered the protracted phase when their bases have proved secure against most foreseeable threats, and when they have achieved a balance of military profit and loss that is sustainable in the longer term. In Indochina this phase started roughly when Chinese aid began in 1950.

The classic Maoist progression of phases was not, in fact, followed in Indochina. Its pattern was heavily distorted following Giap's victory on RC4 in October 1950, when he attempted to move directly to the fourth stage of 'general offensive' early in 1951, ignoring the third or 'mobile' phase.

During the 'mobile' phase the insurgents practise long-distance movement by large units of their new regular force, which must prove itself capable of manoeuvring and sustaining itself away from its safe havens, perhaps among a less supportive population. These movements oblige the security forces to react, dispersing their reserves. While the insurgent main force may thus seize the initiative, it must still avoid pitched battle unless it enjoys very superior odds. It now has a new vulnerability to match its new strengths: it needs lines of communication and supply leading back to its bases. This phase in Indochina began in autumn 1951 when Giap, sobered by his costly defeats in the Delta, returned to the classic progression, making his first expedition into the Thai Highlands and probing at Nghia Lo. It continued until the rains of spring 1953 brought him back to his base areas from his second thrust through the High Country into northern Laos.

The mobile phase is the dress rehearsal for the final trial of strength, the 'general offensive'. Having assembled, trained, equipped, and practised handling a large regular force capable of confronting the enemy in conventional operations, the leaders of the insurgency must pick the most promising time and place to accept pitched battle. In Indochina this phase would open in early winter 1953.[26]

INSURGENTS CANNOT PROGRESS to the third and fourth phases without building a regular force. This top level of the People's Army was already in existence at the outbreak of war in December 1946, but its combat strength was restricted to some 30,000 men. The limitations of acquiring weapons by capture and overseas purchase prevented any rapid growth before 1950, although strength was maintained by periodic selections from the best regional units. The great majority of the regular force – the *Chu Luc* – remained in the safe Viet Bac provinces and the South Delta Base, although independent regular battalions and regiments *(Trung Doan Doc Lap)* were created elsewhere.

By April 1949 the Chu Luc had 32 regular battalions, at a time when the regionals totalled 137.[27] Between autumn 1949 and autumn 1950 the number of regular units would roughly double when the first Chinese aid allowed a mass transfer of 25,000 regionals. In May 1950 the Party announced that all males between the ages of 16 and 55 in Tonkin and Annam were liable for conscription to serve the cause, and this was extended to Cochinchina in mid 1952. By June 1951, at the time of the Day River campaign, the regulars counted about 110,000 men in 117 battalions while the regionals had correspondingly declined to 37 battalions. By spring 1953 the regulars had risen to some 125,000 men, and the regionals to 75,000 (the popular forces reportedly numbered about 150,000 at this stage). A CIA report of May 1954 lists total Viet Minh infantry units throughout Indochina at 111 regular but only 40-plus regional battalions, with a total strength of about 185,000 men. The decline in regional units was presumably due to Giap's call-up in the winter of 1953/4 of another 25,000 reinforcements for the regular units committed to the Dien Bien Phu campaign (*see Chapter 8*).[28]

The Chinese Communist victory of October 1949 made possible a rapid expansion of Giap's regular force, and despite the visceral distrust of China which Vietnamese inherit from birth the new relationship was irresistible. It roughly coincided with Giap's creation of his first formation larger than a regiment: the quasi-division Regimental Group 308, in August 1949. Regiment 308 had been his first multi-battalion unit, formed in January 1947, and he now added to it Regiments 88 and 102. Routine contact with the 2nd Red Army began in December 1949, and in April 1950 an assistance pact was signed in Beijing. Deliveries of small arms and heavy weapons – mortars, light artillery and anti-aircraft machine guns – began almost immediately, and training was offered inside China. At Ho Chi Minh's request a Chinese military mission crossed into the Viet Bac in August 1950: some 330 officers and men led by a veteran of the Long March of 1934–5, General Wei Guo Qing.[29] At the same time a flow of Vietnamese began in the other direction; between May and September 1950 some 20,000 men were trained, armed and equipped in southern Chinese camps.[30] The first units were Regimental Group (soon to be Division) 308, and Regiments 174 and 209. By the time Giap unleashed his attacks along RC4 that October he had two-plus regular divisions ready for combat, and several battalions of light artillery.

A 'division' can mean a formation of almost any size between 8,000 and 20,000 men; in this case Giap accepted the Chinese model, itself copied from the Soviet Army's 'triangular' plan – three regiments, each of three battalions, each of three companies, plus command and specialist elements at each level. The division was standardized in 1953 at three regiments each of 2,850, giving about 7,200 actual riflemen in the nine infantry battalions of a division of 9,600 men.[31]

The classic People's Army regular infantry division, as it had evolved by 1953, was commanded by a staff with direct control over a signal company, a headquarters protection company, an intelligence *(Trinh Sat)* company, an engineer company, a transport company (initially, short of motor vehicles and including pack animals and porters), and an anti-aircraft battalion with up to 18 heavy machine guns of 12.7mm (0.50in) calibre. At different times some but not all divisions seem to have had an integral artillery battalion with heavy mortars and 75mm guns, others just a divisional heavy weapons company. These units were only gradually formed within infantry divisions because the weapons were needed for the parallel formation of the special artillery force, Heavy Division 351 (*see below*). Each of the division's three infantry regiments had its HQ staff; signals, protection, and intelligence companies; a recruit reception/ training company; and a heavy weapons company, with four or six 75mm guns and/or 120mm heavy mortars. Each of the regiment's three battalions had three rifle companies, and a heavy weapons company with eight 81mm/82mm mortars, three 75mm recoilless guns and three bazookas. Belt-fed machine guns do not seem to have figured at battalion level, and the scale of light machine guns seems to have been surprisingly low.[32] (It should be noted, however, that in heavy support weapons the People's Army infantry unit was now superior to the French.) This standard organization came about only slowly and unevenly, as the arrival of weapons allowed support elements to be added to pure infantry units.[33]

Orders of battle of the divisions will be found in Appendix 4 at the end of this book, but since their titles will recur during the story of the battle of Dien Bien Phu their basic identities should be listed here, in the order in which they were officially formed:[34]

Division 304 'Nam Dinh' (*Regiments 9, 57, 66*). Formed in January 1950 in the South Delta Base, it was commanded by General Hoang Minh Thao, a former warrant officer of French Colonial troops, 34 years old in 1953, who had first trained in China shortly after 1945; he may have been replaced in November 1953 by General Hoang Sam. Its units were normally based in the Tuyen Quang area of the Viet Bac.

Division 308 'Viet Bac' (*Regiments 36, 88, 102*). Formed in China in August 1950 from pre-existing Regimental Group 308; the commander, General Vuong Thua Vu, was aged 40 in 1953, the son of immigrants from Yunnan, China. A political officer, he also headed an officers' training programme. Raised from Hanoi and its surroundings, the division was normally based in the Thai Nguyen area of the Viet Bac. At every stage of its development from battalion to division, '308' was always Giap's most trusted force.[35]

Major units of these two divisions were ready for deployment in October 1950.

Division 312 'Ben Tre' (Regiments 141, 165, 209). Formed late in October 1950; later also named *'Chien Tang'*, 'Victorious', possibly after Dien Bien Phu? The commander was Colonel, later General Le Trung Tan, the former deputy CO, age unknown; he may have been replaced in 1953 by General Hoang Cam. Normally based around Thai Nguyen, the division was in action by January 1951, at Vinh Yen.

Division 316 'Bien Hoa' (Regiments 98, 174, 176). Formed in February– March 1951, this division included many men from the tribal minorities of the Middle Region – Tho, Nung, and Yao; the commander was General Le Quang Ba, age unknown, who had been a chief-of-staff and held a territorial command – he reportedly directed operations on RC4 in October 1950. The division was in action at Mao Khe by the beginning of April 1951, and was normally based around Thai Nguyen.

Division 320 'Dong Bang' (Regiments 48, 52, 64). Formed in the South Delta Base from January 1951, it included many recruits from the Delta itself; its commander, General Van Tien Dung, was a former weaver. It remained based south of the Delta.

Division 325 (Regiments 18, 95, 101). Formed officially in March 1951, but perhaps only administratively, from independent units around Thua Thien in northern Annam. The only division formed outside Tonkin; its commander was General Tran Quy Ha. It was not operational as a division until at least summer 1952, and perhaps a good deal later.

Between October 1951 and the end of 1952, with the frontier now completely under Viet Minh control, some 10,000 officers and 40,000 men were sent into China for training.[36] At the beginning of the winter 1953/4 campaign morale was considered good in all divisions, though slight doubts were expressed about the 'highland' Division 316. Readiness was best in Division 308, but satisfactory in 304, 312 and 325; training standards were lower in 316 and 320.[37]

Heavy Division 351 (Regiments 45, 675, 367, 237, 151) embraced the People's Army technical troops – all the artillery, and most of the engineers. It was commanded by General Vu Hien, formerly deputy chief of the general staff, then deputy commander of Lien Khu 3; he was the artillery chief on the general staff from 1950 to April 1952.

The original Viet Bac Artillery Group was formed as early as June 1946, with 40-plus mostly light guns of diverse origins, from French 25mm and 37mm cannon to French and Japanese 75mm field and mountain guns. The concentration of the bulk of the artillery into a single administrative command, following Soviet and Chinese models, made sense. The People's Army had relatively few men who were sufficiently educated for the technical tasks involved, and from the end of 1950 these were gathered together to pass through various courses at Chinese artillery training camps at Jingxi and Longzhou in Guangxi province. Their first new guns were reportedly US light 75mm pack howitzers captured from the Chinese Nationalists ('pack' meaning that they could be taken apart into several assemblies for transport over difficult terrain). Units from Division 351 were apparently attached to infantry divisions during the 1951/2 and 1952/3 winter campaigns in the Thai Highlands. In 1953 the Chinese supplied the division with US 105mm howitzers (probably 48 of them in all), supposedly captured in Korea during 1950–51, but at least some of them probably more elderly examples from the former Nationalist inventory.[38] Chinese generosity with these and other American-made weapons also made sense: the Chinese People's Liberation Army was equipped with Soviet types, and would be unable to obtain continuing supplies of ammunition and spare parts for the US guns, while the Viet Minh, fighting a partly US-equipped French Army, would have the chance to acquire them on the battlefield.

Finally, outside the divisional system, a number of independent regular units were based in Tonkin. Among others, these included Regiment 148, associated with the High Region; 246, guarding the Viet Minh headquarters; 35, a large recruit reception and training regiment; Battalion 905, a commando/assassination unit; and a general staff reconnaissance battalion of five companies which operated in small cells.[39]

In his appreciation of the People's Army made in July 1953 the French commander-in-chief, General Navarre, believed that after having grown steadily over several years the Chu Luc had more or less reached the limit of its potential size. At that time the Viet Minh held about 60 per cent of the country, but only about 44 per cent of the population, and of these some 90 per cent were peasants and fishermen and thus unlikely officer material. Pursuing the war obliged the People's Army to seek constant replacements for casualties; but beyond a certain point they could not weaken the young male population without threatening the production of the food needed for the growing army, and the provision of coolies to carry it. Among the better educated class the Chu Luc was also in competition for men with the Viet Minh's arms factories and the political teams that maintained the Party's grip on the population. The key to this problem was escalating Chinese aid, which would enable General Giap to improve the armament and equipment of enough existing regional units in Annam and Cochinchina to field, in effect, the equivalent of two more regular divisions during 1954–5.[40]

AFTER AN INITIAL SHIPMENT OF some 1,500 tons the flow of Chinese munitions and other supplies to the Viet Minh took some time to hit its stride, and was hampered by China's simultaneous war in Korea. During the first half of 1952, only 250 tons were provided each month; by the end of that year the monthly rate was 450 tons; in early 1953, 900 tons; by June 1953, 2,000 tons; and in 1954, 4,000 tons per month.[41] The two main routes of entry were by road and river to Lao Cai in north-west Tonkin, and by road and rail from Nanning to Pingxiang, just over the border from Lang Son in the north-east.

The logistic system of the enlarged People's Army – the business of moving food, ammunition and other necessities from the depots to the troops, wherever they were operating – remained primitive. This was inevitable given the poor roads and shortage of motor vehicles; the Chinese did begin to supply Russian trucks at some point, but although the transport park had reportedly reached between 600 and 800 vehicles by late 1953 its size in earlier years is unclear and seems to have been modest. The divisions had no 'train' to carry what they needed to sustain operations in the disputed zones or *'les grands vides'* – the wilderness of the High Region and Laos; and such operations depended almost entirely upon human porters. This system proved effective, but slow, and the need to prepare for major movements well in advance made it hard for Giap to vary his plans 'on the hoof'. Such preparations were also hard to conceal from the French Second Bureau's intelligence gatherers, who were aware of the ration scales, and were thus able to work out the numbers of troops involved.[42]

Vegetables, fish and sometimes meat were eaten with the staple food of rice when in camp, but for soldiers on the march a little salt or perhaps *nuoc mam* fish sauce had to be sufficient flavouring. Each soldier typically carried his rice in a sausage-shaped cloth roll around the waist or shoulder, holding anything from four to ten days' rations at a maximum daily scale of 24oz for a rifleman; in emergencies, of course, the Viet Minh could survive on a good deal less.[43] The normal rhythm of marching was three or four nightly stages of about 20 miles followed by a day or two of rest, then another three or four stages; on forced marches they could cover the ground perhaps half as fast again.

During the mobile phase of the war, when regular troops were on operations for several weeks at a time, a chain of rice and ammunition depots had to be set up in advance and kept topped up regularly. Any campaign preparations thus required advance mobilization of Dan Quan popular forces to form columns of coolies to plant the depots and keep them resupplied, and also to clear and maintain the surfaces of rudimentary tracks. A regular formation moving without advance depots could not cover more than ten daily/nightly stages even if accompanied by a porter column, limiting its radius of operation to about 200 miles. Each 10,000-man division needed 50,000 porters. These men and women, conscripted in relays along a division's route of march, were not intended to be absent from their villages for more than ten to 14 days, thus giving them seven carrying days plus the time it took to assemble and return home.[44]

BY 1953 THE ARMAMENT OF General Giap's infantry had made huge progress since 1943–4, when he had negotiated with French officers for a couple of hundred old carbines with which to fight the Japanese. In summer 1945 the captured weapons of the Japanese, and of the disarmed French garrison, brought Giap's total arsenal to 35,000 rifles, 1,350 light and medium machine guns, 200 mortars, 40-plus small cannon and half a dozen field guns.[45] The French weapons – securing ammunition for which would be easier in the long term – were issued mostly to the regular units, the regionals receiving the Japanese. By the end of 1945 the further purchases of Japanese arms from the Nationalist Chinese had brought the totals up to about 60,000 rifles and 3,000 machine guns.

The Viet Minh's own factories, set up with the help of renegade Japanese soldiers, were unable to build bolt-action rifles from scratch, but by the end of 1946 they had manufactured thousands of copies of the much simpler Sten sub-machine gun. In October 1946 an engineer named Tran Dai Nghia was appointed chief of the Viet Minh ordnance department, and had the metal-working machinery from the Haiphong factory of the Caron company stripped out and carried away into the Viet Bac. The first bazooka was made in January 1947; the following year 60mm and 81mm mortars went into production, and in 1950 a clandestine factory made the first of the SKZ 75mm recoilless guns.[46]

The agreement signed with the Communist Chinese on 1 April 1950 brought large shipments of weapons, totalling some 40,000 to 50,000 rifles, up to 200 light and 100 medium machine guns, perhaps 100 mortars including some heavy 120mm Russian weapons, and modest numbers of Czech-made bazookas and recoilless guns. The first units re-equipped included Regiments 9, 98 and 246 – the latter being the HQ guard force for the Viet Minh leadership, which had some anti-aircraft weapons.[47] In November 1950 the enormous booty captured at Lang Son was more than sufficient to equip the equivalent of an entire division with French weapons (*see Chapter 3, note 18*). During 1951 and 1952 China provided a total of about 58,000 rifles with 10 million rounds of ammunition, 5,200 machine guns, 600-plus mortars, perhaps 170 Czech recoilless guns, at least 35 field guns of 75mm calibre with about 10,000 shells, and 50 light anti-aircraft guns.[48]

By late 1953 most riflemen among the *bo doi* who had not been issued with captured examples of the standard French MAS36 seem to have received Chinese- or Czech-made 7.92mm Mauser bolt-action rifles taken by Mao's armies from the Nationalists. When Giap's Division 308 paraded through Hanoi in October 1954 they were carrying Mausers, and since these showcase troops had been given clean new uniforms and packs for the occasion we may assume that the Mauser was still well enough regarded. It was longer and heavier than the MAS36, so should have been marginally more accurate – though its kicking recoil must have been painful for slightly built Vietnamese. In fact, the outcome of battles never depends on such notional differences between weapons. They may be significant to a marksman lying on the firing range, but not in the panting scramble of a night-time encounter battle, where all that matters is how accurately a man can snap-shoot at a fleeting target half seen in the glow of a parachute flare.

A higher proportion of Viet Minh than French infantry – perhaps three in every ten – were equipped with sub-machine guns. Some had captured French 9mm MAT49s, but most seem to have carried the 7.62mm Chinese Type 50.[49] Its rapid rate of fire gave inexperienced troops confidence, and partly compensated for its inaccuracy; the short effective range of only about 50yds forced the 'burp-gunner' to close with his enemy rapidly, encouraging aggressive tactics. The necessary accompaniment was the hand grenade, of which vast numbers were made and used by the Viet Minh. By 1953 the regulars were normally issued with Chinese-made 'stick' grenades, so called because the explosive head was mounted on a wooden handle for easy throwing.

Apart from captured examples of the standard French FM24/29, and a few US Browning Automatic Rifles and British Brens taken from the Vietnamese National Army and Franco-Vietnamese partisans, the standard infantry platoon light machine gun was the 7.92mm Czech Zb26 or Zb30 – an excellent magazine-fed weapon which in the 1930s had been the original parent design for the Bren, and which took the same ammunition as the standard Mauser rifle.

The Viet Minh made widespread use of mortars from the earliest days of the war. The standard 60mm and 81mm calibres of these simple weapons – little more than a steel tube and a baseplate – could be carried by three men. They gave guerrilla units their first 'indirect fire' weapons – that is, they could lob bombs at a high angle from behind cover, rather than having to be set up within line of sight of the enemy. Although guerrilla units still had some French 50mm grenade-launchers and 60mm light mortars, by 1953 the regulars normally used only the 81/82mm, which had a useful range of up to 2,000yds, and fired 7.7lb high explosive bombs as fast as the crew could drop them down the muzzle – up to 15 shots a minute. In smaller numbers, the divisional and regimental heavy weapons companies had received the much more destructive Soviet 120mm mortar; this had to be dragged on a half-ton wheeled carriage, but it gave the infantry their own 'pocket artillery'.[50]

One weapon issued to the heavy companies of Viet Minh regular units but not to their French opponents was the bazooka, but since accounts use this loosely as a generic term it is hard to identify the exact models. The true bazooka – the original US 2.36in anti-tank rocket launcher – had been supplied to the USSR in 1942 and widely copied ever since. Many are seen in photos of captured Viet Minh weapons, including the original US model with its big wooden understock, but later models and larger calibres were also in regular use, against blockhouses as often as against French armoured vehicles.[51] Shoulder-fired 57mm recoilless guns – copied from the US M18, or actual captured examples from Korea – were used for the same tactical tasks as the bazooka. The generic term for recoilless guns was *Sung Khong Ziat* (SKZ). This seems to have embraced a number of 75mm or even heavier models, dragged on two-wheeled carriages, that were issued to infantry heavy weapons companies.[52]

GROUP PHOTOGRAPHS OF VIET Minh from the late 1940s show a motley mixture of city and country civilian costume with military styles. Village popular forces wore their black, dark brown or blue *cao ao* and *cai quan* 'pyjamas' in local variations. Regional troops strove for a more military appearance, in shirts, slacks and sometimes even sidecaps of khaki, drab green, grey or blue; civilian felt fedoras often served the role of bush hats, and a few units acquired Japanese steel helmets. By 1953 the regulars were uniformed, from home factories, Chinese-stocks or French captures, but there was no real uniformity: khaki, light grey-green, drab and dark green garments were all worn. The norm was a cotton military-style shirt, baggy slacks (often rolled up in wet weather), and in cold conditions a quilted jacket or sleeveless vest (these latter usually dark green Chinese items). The neat, light-coloured Chinese-style tunics buttoning to the throat, displayed by units marching into Hanoi after the ceasefire in 1954, were issued for the occasion and were not widely worn in the field except by senior officers and commissars. The soldiers wore either sandals, often made from old motor tyres; or a wide range of canvas and rubber '*baskets*', i.e. basketball boots – copied from the French soldier's tropical *pataugas*. Their personal equipment – belts, pouches and packs – was as assorted as the clothing, ranging from old French leather issue to fabric Chinese locally made copies.

The most distinctive item worn by the *bo doi* was his headgear: a dish-shaped sun helmet of woven cane and palm fibre, covered with drab-coloured cloth and a string net for attaching camouflage. (Famously, troops on the march were reported wearing panels of wire netting on their packs; at each suitable halt the soldier changed the foliage camouflage on his own helmet and on the wire mesh of the man in front, to ensure that it was always fresh and matched the surroundings.) The other common headgear, popular particularly among officers and commissars, was the *casque colonial* or solar topi, made of cork or pressed fibre covered with cloth; this – like a holstered pistol and a map case – carried a definite cachet of authority. Badges were seldom worn in the field, apart from the occasional display on solar topis of the Viet Minh's yellow star on a red ground.[53]

THE INCREASING SIZE OF THE regular force from 1950 presented the Viet Minh with the problem of providing enough qualified officers and junior leaders. In 1945–6 the movement had attracted many of the educated élite – colonial officials, intellectuals, employees of French companies – encouraged by the declaration of the Democratic Republic and its apparent de facto recognition by the French. The test of actual war sorted those who were suited to the military calling from those who were not. Thereafter officers had to be found in the ranks; the best young men were not selected from the start for a methodical training in leadership, but were chosen for NCO and officer courses once they had proved themselves as common soldiers. Short but frequent, these courses were held in camps in the liberated zones, where Giap had created the first schools as early as May 1945. From 1950 others were opened inside China, with mostly Chinese instructors. One major training centre was established at Minho, near Kunming in Yunnan province, housing six separate training battalions – two for engineers, and one each for officer candidates, artillerymen, infantrymen and machine gunners; each could handle 400 pupils at a time. There was a joint staff college at Szumao in Yunnan, and other schools at Kaiyuan and Tsaopa.[54]

After weapons, munitions, radios and training in their use, the professional education of Vietnamese officers was China's most vital contribution to the transformation of General Giap's guerrillas into an army. Beyond a certain basic level, the leadership skills demanded of the commanders of these distinct types of organization are quite different. A guerrilla leader – like the unfortunate Hoang Tho, described above – needs charisma, the tactical instinct to be able to lay an ambush and withdraw safely, and practical local knowledge; a military commander needs theoretical education in staff duties. The unglamorous skills of the staff officer make the difference between, on the one hand, deciding on the need to move men from one valley to another; and on the other, foreseeing and organizing every detail of their route, itinerary, equipment, feeding and shelter, so that they arrive in the right place, on time, and ready to fight for an objective which is suitable to their equipment and training. Staff work is the systematic management of paperwork that turns ideas into reality, and is absolutely central to any military enterprise.

After they returned from schools in China, the honing of staff officers and commanders was pursued without respite, by conferences, demonstrations and study courses. Regular officers were also transferred for spells with the regionals in order to gain combat experience. While the People's Army leadership cadres were solid, their military knowledge was essentially practical rather than theoretical; Giap himself would admit that they lacked a general education and abstract understanding of military affairs, science and technology. These weaknesses were found at every level, and despite Vietnamese denials it seems most unlikely that the People's Army could have carried out the large-scale operations of winter 1953/4 without Chinese and/or other foreign Communist advisers on at least the divisional staffs.[55]

The most characteristic method of identifying and correcting errors was the process of 'self-criticism' after any operation. At every level, from the infantry company to the senior staff, thorough debriefings were held during which all ranks were expected to analyse their own and their comrades' performance publicly. Juniors were encouraged to identify the mistakes of their seniors. These long meetings, punctuated by applause and murmurs of disapproval, were an important reinforcement of the subordination of the individual to the cause. For common soldiers, admission of error brought 'absolution' – the forgiveness of the group; repeated faults were punished by ostracism or, ultimately, dismissal. Mutual critiques among senior personnel were certainly taken seriously, as confirmed by a radioed report of a Party Central Committee inquest on the spring 1951 defeats, intercepted on 27 June 1951 by the SDECE listening station at Dalat.[56] The Communist jargon in which the minutes of such meetings were recorded is numbing, but they are not without interest; this is a later example:

> We have fallen into subjectivism, in underestimating the enemy and in letting ourselves get carried away by the easy early success of this campaign... Rightist tendencies betray a backwards and unproletarian ideology, in opposition to the spirit of our party and our army; they prevent our army from accomplishing its tasks and constitute our worst enemy at the ideological level. Usually they manifest themselves in two tendencies. Firstly, they make us hesitate, dreading hardships and difficulties, death, losses, the wearing out [of our resources] and fatigue... Secondly, subjectivism can lead to underestimating the enemy and falling into self-importance, leading to a superficial bureaucratism. Apparently one shows much ardour, having the air of not fearing the enemy at all; in fact, there is a rightist and negative tendency that refuses to face the extreme cruelty and ferocity of the enemy, which dulls our hatred of the enemy and robs us of vigilance...[57]

(In Party language a courageous enemy was always 'ferocious', and even his inanimate weapons were 'cruel'.) The apparent illogic of using 'subjectivist' and 'rightest' tendencies to mean, at one and the same time, both loss of nerve and overconfidence becomes understandable if we equate both terms with 'following individual judgement and emotions rather than obeying Party orders without question'. On the one hand, such passages confirm a determination to learn from mistakes without hiding behind rank; on the other, they fail to make allowance for human fallibility. What this meant in practice was famously spelt out by a tough Algerian NCO after Dien Bien Phu. Interviewed by Bernard Fall, Abderrahman ben Salem recalled that as he was marched off strongpoint 'Gabrielle' by his captors his way was blocked by a hideously wounded but still living *bo doi*; the Viet Minh officer or commissar in charge told him to step on the man and keep moving – the casualty had already fulfilled his duty to the People's Army.[58]

A combination of the political doctrine of unquestioning obedience, the limited and rigidly schematic training of combat officers, the novelty of literacy, and the importance of 'face' in an East Asian culture, often prevented field commanders from taking the right decisions in fluid situations. No engagement, even a simple ambush, was undertaken without precise written orders and plans. (In an army most of whose officers were only recently trained, and thus more obedient than confident, the habit of carrying every order in writing was a precious gift to French intelligence officers, who often found valuable documents on the dead or prisoners.) As in the programme of political indoctrination, the essential training method was endless repetition of a limited number of lessons. During Division 308's training for attacking fortified positions in the autumn of 1953 the troops were rehearsed on terrain where all features of typical French outposts were reconstructed. Attacks were practised over several days: eight or even ten times at company level, and then repeated by whole battalions and regiments.

These minutely detailed rehearsals often paid dividends in battle, but allowed very limited scope for individual initiative. Confronted by something unforeseen Viet Minh commanders usually hesitated, not daring to modify plans without seeking higher authority. This often led to a halt or even a retreat when a bolder response would have brought success. The People's Army were not unaware of this fault, and documents captured after the Hoa Binh campaign in 1951–2 include criticism of junior leaders for acting 'like machines stripped of all intelligence'.[59]

THE PART PLAYED BY THE political commissars – *Can Bo* – at every level of the People's Army was considered central. Unit leadership was collective, and in some circumstances the political officer's voice ultimately carried more weight than that of the combat commander. These were former teachers or students, selected for their complete political reliability from among dedicated members of the Communist Party. Their tasks were to indoctrinate, explain, inspire, reassure, rebuke and, if necessary, denounce. They instructed in Marxist–Leninist thought; interpreted events for the soldiers according to the Party line; kept up morale by praise and encouragement; supervised relations between the troops and local civilians – but also monitored the officers and men through a system of internal informers. They tried to follow the Chinese model of internal surveillance: each platoon was divided for tactical purposes into teams of three men *(Tam Tam Che)*, and one of these soldiers – whose identity was kept secret – was also supposed to be a Party member, tasked with both encouraging and spying on his comrades. In some units this was almost literally achieved: although applicants to join the Party were carefully screened, in early 1953 one division of 8,400 men had 2,050 Party members.[60]

From the few (inevitably censored) accounts we have of life in the ranks of the People's Army, an impression of genuine admiration for the commissar usually emerges. In ideal, at least, they were respected as intellectuals who chose to share the hardship and danger of life in the hills alongside the simple peasants.[61] The system of integrated politico-military command is so alien to Western thought that we tend to judge it by its most notorious historical examples – particularly, the murderous idiocies inflicted on the Soviet Red Army under Stalin. In the service of a cynical or deranged dictatorship the pernicious effects of political interference on combat decisions, and of informers on unit morale, seem axiomatic. In the Asian context this need not necessarily be so, and in the early 1950s Viet Minh commissars and combat officers often seem to have worked together positively. The surveillance aspect may also have appeared less divisive to members of a group-oriented Asian 'shame' culture, very different from the individualist Western tradition.

Accounts from the ranks reveal simple men whose world view was formed entirely by their and their families' immediate experience. Since that experience was coloured by oppression and hardship over generations, it is hardly surprising that they were convinced by the Party's propaganda. In the simplest terms, they were believers; and they would prove the strength of their belief on the battlefield of Dien Bien Phu. The counter-propaganda pointed to the terrorist methods which the Viet Minh certainly employed, and to the quite large numbers of soldiers – even including some commissars – who deserted and allowed themselves to be 'turned'. It sought to dehumanize the People's Army as an undifferentiated mass: ant-like, brainwashed, fanatic, even 'slaves'; but that army's soldiers fought from genuine conviction, often heroically, and the relationships between its rankers and between them and their leaders were in most respects recognizable to any Western soldier.

The French were unnerved by the sacrificial courage of Viet Minh frontal attacks; but so were German officers by British and French assaults on the Western Front in 1914–18. To some, the *bo doi*'s willingness to die for his cause had to be explained away by brainwashing, terror, drink or drugs; to admit that it was born fundamentally out of love of country, and the hope of freedom and a decent life, would have been too disturbing.

The analogy should not be pushed too far, of course, and there were certainly many cultural differences between the People's Army and the Expeditionary Corps. The Viet Minh followed one doctrine which the French found almost shocking: reinforcements were seldom risked in order to rescue hard-pressed units, which were usually abandoned to break free or perish on their own. This cool insistence that each unit 'do or die' often foiled French efforts to divert Viet Minh movements. By contrast, People's Army attacks on isolated French units were routinely planned to draw any relief columns into devastating ambushes along the few and predictable approach routes. They could count upon the French to react according to Western expectations: some attempt had to be made to rescue surrounded comrades who were in danger of being overrun. Acknowledging no such obligation, Giap and his commanders enjoyed a greater freedom of response to the fortunes of battle.

Another difference in attitude was a natural consequence of the youth of this recently self-invented army. The reports of several French officers captured at Dien Bien Phu mention one naive aspect of the behaviour of their captors. Intensely proud of their achievements, but still in awe of French professional military skills, some betrayed a need for an open show of respect from the defeated enemy, as if craving their approval. This was particularly noticeable in the interrogation of artillery officers, during which the boastful captors revealed a surprising amount of information to their prisoners.[62]

AS THE RAINS OF MAY 1953 brought operations to a close, the regulars of the Chu Luc looked forward to a season of rest, regrouping and training, while their leaders planned the next winter campaign starting in October. The first phase of that dry season would see logistic and tactical preparations, while the Trinh Sat scout units spread out for several weeks to gather information about the Expeditionary Corps' deployments. Each division's reconnaissance company was divided into 27 three-man teams. Each team was trained in special skills: some were simple scouts who located, counted, and noted routines; others spied out and interpreted the features of defensive positions; some traced French movements; some got close enough to eavesdrop on conversations or infiltrated to steal documents; some even provoked desertions or captured prisoners for questioning. When Giap's intelligence staff had collated every scrap of information, he could present to the Central Committee his operational recommendations for the coming season.

Whatever these might be, Giap could have confidence in the resolve of his regular troops. The People's Army *bo doi* was ignorant of the world, fed and equipped only to a very basic level, and unpaid. He would have to walk for many hundreds of miles through the roughest terrain, sheltered only by the forest and always hunted by an enemy who had more destructive weapons. He had infrequent (if any) contact with his family, and if he fell sick or was wounded he could only hope for the most rudimentary care. But he had confidence in his leaders; and he was fighting in his own country, for his own country – for a future that he believed in.

The average soldier of the Expeditionary Corps waiting for him in the Delta generally had rather better equipment, and more of it; he was supported by heavy artillery, tanks and fighter-bombers, and if he was wounded there was some chance of his reaching first-class medical care. He had little faith in his generals; he was fighting for his *copains* and his battalion. He might suspect that he was on the wrong side of the world, and he certainly knew that back home only his family gave a damn. Statistically, of course, it was unlikely that he was even a Frenchman.

5. The Expeditionary Corps

'The failure of members of the Expeditionary Corps to adapt to the natural and human conditions of Indochina often appeared to be the essential element in France's overall failure.'
Professor Michel Bodin

TO UNDERSTAND THE NATURE of the army that France sent to confront the Viet Minh, it is necessary to take a brief look at earlier generations, and a rather closer one at the events of World War II. The French garrison in Indochina in 1940 was shaped by a military system that differed fundamentally from that of the British Empire or United States.[1] The French home army – *l'Armée Métropolitaine* – was the conscripted youth of the nation fulfilling two years of compulsory service under the leadership of professional officers and senior NCOs. Its mission was to defend the national territory against Germany; the young soldiers of what was known as 'the contingent' were seldom shipped overseas – French voters being unwilling to see their conscripted sons sent to some disease-ridden outpost for the sake of controversial colonial interests.

The North African possessions were garrisoned by *l'Armée d'Afrique* (Army of Africa). This included both white regiments – *Zouaves* infantry and *Chasseurs d'Afrique* cavalry – drawn by a combination of conscription and voluntary enlistment from the settler communities; and locally recruited native regiments of *Tirailleurs* infantry and *Spahis* cavalry. The largest European infantry element was provided by the volunteer *Légion Étrangère*

(Foreign Legion). Units of the Army of Africa had been deployed further afield during campaigns of colonial conquest, and in mainland France during the wars against Germany. The Legion had provided 'marching' units for both the conquest and policing of Indochina, which by 1940 had been consolidated in permanent garrisons as the 5th Foreign Infantry Regiment (5 REI).

The colonies in black Africa, Asia and elsewhere were largely the responsibility of the *Troupes Coloniales*, a distinct organization tracing its origins to 17th-century naval companies and still sporting the anchor as its badge. The history of *'La Coloniale'* was highly complex; at various dates units also served in France and North Africa, incorporating both conscripts and volunteers.[2] By 1940 the Colonial forces abroad consisted of French volunteers serving alongside locally recruited native Tirailleurs led by white Colonial cadres. A feature of La Coloniale was the amalgamation of units of white and native troops together within *Régiments d'Infanterie Coloniale* (RIC) and *d'Artillerie Coloniale* (RAC).

Historically, relations between the officer corps of the Metropolitan Army and the African and Colonial units had been somewhat chilly. The former considered the latter to be, relatively speaking, social and professional roughnecks, but they were lured to volunteer for colonial postings by the undeniably better opportunities for action, medals and promotion; for their part, colonial officers dismissed the home establishment as snobbish and professionally rigid. Any such antique prejudices which survived the shared agony of the Great War were swept away – as were most practical distinctions between these organizations – in the chaos of World War II. But the traumatic events of the years 1940–44 would create their own deeper divisions, which gave the French Army of 1945 its unique character.

UNDER THE TERMS OF THE ARMISTICE which followed the French collapse in June 1940, the Third Republic was replaced with the Vichy regime led by Marshal Pétain, governing unoccupied southern France. Vichy France was permitted a weakly equipped home army of 100,000 men, *'l'Armée de l'Armistice'*. More importantly, she was allowed to retain her colonial garrisons – predominantly l'Armée d'Afrique in French North Africa.

These events confronted the professional officer corps with painful dilemmas, and in 1940–41 it was possible for patriotic Frenchmen to choose any one of several paths. For a minority, the escape to Britain of the obscure General Charles de Gaulle with a handful of troops to raise the splendid but tiny flag of Free France was the only encouragement they needed to find ways of carrying on the fight. For most, however, the choices were harder: however bitter the defeat, the army seemed to owe legitimate obedience to the Pétain government, and the need to maintain discipline and preserve what was left of the national territory was paramount. Limited co-operation with Germany might hasten the release of nearly 1.5 million French prisoners of war. The Armistice was ostensibly just that, not a finally negotiated settlement; both duty and prudence argued for taking a long view. Britain, after all, seemed doomed, and was seen by many as no friend to France.[3]

The second fault line was opened by Operation 'Torch' in November 1942 – the Anglo-US landings in Morocco and Algeria. The 'Anglo-Saxons' counted on persuading the French in North Africa to join the Allied cause. Armed resistance to the landings was brief, if locally fierce. Some French officers had been privy to 'Torch' in advance, but many were resentful, and the longer-term agenda of the Allied powers was regarded with suspicion. By this stage the Gaullist force serving with the British 8th Army had grown in size and prestige; it had attracted new troops from African garrisons led by General Philippe 'Leclerc' (de Hautcloque), and was celebrated for its resistance at Bir Hakeim under General Pierre Koenig in May–June 1942. Nevertheless, de Gaulle was an unpopular figure among many officers who had obeyed the Armistice in 1940, and who rejected his followers' assumed monopoly of patriotic virtue. His leadership of the Free French was challenged not only by President Roosevelt but also among his fellow Frenchmen. However, news of the German occupation of Vichy France on 27 November (and of the unresisted disbandment of the Army of the Armistice) rendered futile any further manoeuvring by French leaders in North Africa in search of a 'third way' between armed resistance to and outright collaboration with the Allies.

A major obstacle for de Gaulle was American willingness to negotiate with the Vichy High Commissioner, Admiral Darlan; this was removed by his assassination on 20 December. Thereafter the pliable General Henri Giraud – a popular old Africa hand, but no intellectual giant – was favoured by Roosevelt, putting Winston Churchill in the unenviable position of broker between the president and de Gaulle. Although the French camp was still riven by intrigues and enmities, the logic of their situation was inescapable: the Army of Africa must seize its opportunity to get back into the war on the right side if it was to earn a place in Allied councils planning the liberation of France itself. Haltingly, piecemeal, but with instances of great heroism, its outdated and weakly armed units began to confront the battle-hardened Wehrmacht.

Following the Axis surrender in Tunisia in May 1943, l'Armée d'Afrique – swollen by mobilization of the local European and African populations and by a stream of escapers from the mainland – began a massive programme of reorganization, and re-equipment by the United States. Any hope, however, for an early reconciliation between 'old' and 'new' Free French was doomed; General Leclerc's brigade insisted on marching in the victory parade of 20 May with the British contingent rather than the Army of Africa.[4] Mutual hostility led to obstructiveness, and de Gaulle's success in securing Giraud's resignation as co-chairman of the French National Liberation Committee in September 1943, and finally as French C-in-C Africa in April 1944, did nothing to heal the rift between their followers. General Koenig's enlarged 1st Free French Division retained its British connections for some time, and was somewhat cold-shouldered by the mainly African Army commanders of General Alphonse Juin's French Expeditionary Corps (CEF), which it was eventually sent to join in Italy in spring 1944.

The other formations of the CEF, which fought – extremely well – in Italy from late 1943 until summer 1944, were essentially the old Army of Africa. General Leclerc was given command of the single French division to be landed in Normandy alongside the Allied armies in summer 1944. This new 2nd Armoured Division, composed of units from both 'traditions', would be allowed the honour of entering Paris first in August 1944; but even there it was noticed that some units pointedly omitted the Gaullist Cross of Lorraine from the divisional insignia painted on their vehicles.[5] General Jean de Lattre de Tassigny's 1st French Army, which landed in the South of France in the same month and later fought in Alsace, was essentially the CEF plus other 'post-1942' Free French units. By the end of the war the shared experience of fighting for the liberation of the homeland had to some extent eased the relationship between the 'Gaullists' and 'Giraudists', but it had not erased their differences (for instance, Leclerc refused to serve under de Lattre). With the war once more being fought on French soil, however, other fissures had become more immediately threatening.

THE TASKS FACING GENERAL DE Gaulle on his return to a ruined and divided France, over which huge Allied and German armies were still fighting, would have overwhelmed any man with less than his monumental self-belief. His status as president of a provisional government was self-assumed and nominal; he had yet to impose his authority over a wide range of armed Resistance groups, some springing from mutually hostile political traditions, which had come into being in various regions of the country at different stages of the Occupation. While continuing to be completely dependent on the material aid of allies who had yet to recognize his legitimacy, he planned to unify this diverse manpower into an enlarged French Army, whose presence among the victors would give him the weight to frustrate any Anglo-Saxon policies which he believed to threaten France's national interests.

At the beginning of 1944 a unifying agency had ostensibly been created by the internal Resistance – the *Conseil National de la Résistance* (CNR) – but this lacked true unity of purpose or strategy. The most controllable Resistance network from the Gaullist viewpoint was *l'Armée Secrète* (AS), which was in direct contact with de Gaulle's London headquarters. The ex-soldiers of *l'Organisation de Résistance de l'Armée* (ORA), born in the south from the former Army of the Armistice, were apolitical but tended to identify with the 'Giraudists' in Algiers. By contrast, the *Francs-tireurs et Partisans Francais* (FTPF), strongest in the north, were the armed wing of the National Front, which had direct Communist Party links with Moscow and a very definite agenda of its own.[6]

In February 1944, de Gaulle announced the creation of the *Forces Francaises de l'Intérieur* (FFI) under General Koenig's leadership, beginning a programme to impose unity on the Resistance and to claim authority over the whole national liberation effort for his London government in exile; and as soon as significant Free French forces had landed in the south, de Gaulle returned to France and began to prosecute his claim. His supporters kept repeating the assertion that de Gaulle's provisional government was the only legitimate French authority, and the forces which answered to its Council of National Defence the sole legitimate bearers of arms. This claim was at first resisted by many, including powerful *maquis* leaders of unquestioned patriotism; nevertheless, the Gaullists began to turn this poker-player's bluff into reality.

In August, with Paris liberated and a French army ashore in the south, Free French forces were authorized to take under command, and recruit from, all local FFI groups, thus bringing these under regular military authority. In October all armed groups were declared disbanded. France had an army, one and indivisible; all who wished to bear arms against Germany should join it and submit to its authority; any armed group which continued to hold itself apart was a legitimate object of suspicion. The most dangerous of these groups was, of course, the strong Communist Resistance, which could point to a relatively impressive record under the Occupation; but eventually even they came grudgingly into the fold.

Having achieved at least an appearance of national unity, de Gaulle's government threw itself into creating the new field army. Hundreds of thousands of young conscripts, FFI volunteers and older reservists had to be assembled, equipped and hastily trained; the records of former officers claiming either regular or *maquis* ranks had to be examined, the undesirable weeded out and the qualified given appropriate duties. Some FFI units were incorporated into regular regiments and divisions more or less *en bloc*, while others were broken up and their assorted manpower used to create new units with regular leadership. Turning a mixture of white and African combat veterans, idealistic or merely bewildered youths, older ex-soldiers, foreign refugees, former *maquisards* and political activists into a mechanized army fit to face the Wehrmacht was an immense task that was only partially achieved. Nevertheless, by VE-Day in May 1945 the French Army had some 1.3 million men under arms, with eight divisions in the line and 11 others being formed or planned.[7]

Since the autumn of 1944 two divisions had been intended to take part in the Allied reconquest of South-East Asia from the Japanese; and although the atomic bombs relieved them of this role in August 1945, de Gaulle's government remained determined to reoccupy France's lost colonies.

THE INITIAL COMMITMENT OF French troops to the reconquest of Indochina in 1945–6 was about 50,000 men. A crisis of manpower faced the *Corps Expéditionnaire Francais en Extrême-Orient* (CEFEO) during 1947, when wartime enlistees were repatriated at the end of their tour just as serious campaigning began in Tonkin. The expedients which France adopted to meet this need soon gave her Far East Expeditionary Corps the remarkably varied character that it displayed for the rest of the conflict, resembling some ancient Roman field army with a spine of legions supported by a colourful range of multinational auxiliaries.

By late 1948 reinforcements brought the total to just over 100,000, and the following year it approached 150,000. In late 1951 General de Lattre managed to raise overall strength above 190,000 by French reinforcement and local recruiting; but in summer 1952 it actually fell to about 174,000, and remained at roughly this level for the last two years of the war.[8] In 1953 the breakdown of regular ground troops in the CEFEO (excluding the Vietnamese National Army) was roughly 52,000 Frenchmen, 30,000 North Africans, 19,000 Foreign Legion, 18,000 West Africans, and 53,000 Vietnamese; to these were added some 55,400 local auxiliaries in attached or autonomous units – a total of perhaps 228,000. These figures – for the whole of Vietnam, Cambodia and Laos – invite comparison with the roughly half-million US personnel deployed in the late 1960s in South Vietnam alone. Frenchmen represented less than a quarter of the total, although virtually all the leadership; and about half the fighting men facing the Viet Minh in French uniform were Indochinese. In that year the CEFEO had about 90 infantry battalions, 20 artillery and eight engineer battalions.[9]

THE FIRST REGULAR FRENCH troops to land at Saigon on 12 September 1945 alongside the leading elements of the British General Gracey's 20th Indian Division belonged to the so-called Light Intervention Corps (CLI) – soon renamed the 5th Colonial Infantry Regiment – which had been training with the British in Ceylon. In October a 'marching group' of General Leclerc's 2nd Armoured Division began to arrive from France. These, and various other small units such as Navy commandos and French SAS paratroopers, were joined during November 1945 – February 1946 by the 9th and 3rd Colonial Infantry Divisions. The rank and file of the newly redesignated Colonial Infantry Regiments forming these divisions were mainly young FFI soldiers recruited in 1944–5, who had joined up for the duration of World War II. Had the enemy still been Japanese, their deployment to Asia would have been unremarkable; in this new situation their contracts of service were altered with a fairly arbitrary hand.

The officers and senior NCOs who led the CEFEO in 1945–6 included 1940 Gaullists; African Army, CEF and 1st Army men blooded in Tunisia, Italy and Alsace in 1943–5; veterans of 1939–40 and the Armistice Army; and former Resistance fighters. Throughout the Indochina War the mixed character of the officer corps remained unchanged – and so, to an unusual degree, did its individual members. By 1953–4 many were into their third tour of duty, some in their sixth or seventh year in Indochina. There was, of course, a progressive dilution with subalterns newly graduated from the military academies; but because of the parallel demands of NATO and Indochina, and also the high rate of casualties they suffered, these young sub-lieutenants were never numerous enough to replace the older men by a systematic, generational process. Thus, by 1953–4 the overall shortage meant not only that many battalions had little more than half the number of officers they needed; but also that many of the company officers were older than was desirable for soldiers fighting an exhausting tropical war. In that year the average age of captains was $38\frac{1}{2}$ and of lieutenants nearly 33; moreover, a large number of both officers and NCOs posted to the infantry were 'substitutes', originally trained in other arms of service.[10]

Because of the speed with which the CEFEO was shipped out after World War II, a proportion of its officers – including some of the most effective – were 'wartime' men in a particular sense. Junior officers of courage and energy had been promoted very rapidly to lead the vastly expanded wartime armies of civilians in uniform, and some of them had been given significant commands more or less on the battlefield. The need for combat officers in Indochina had saved a proportion of these men from post-war demobilization, preserving within the CEFEO cultural differences between pre-war staff-trained professionals and wartime 'brawlers', which sometimes had negative consequences.

ONE OF THE CENTRAL characteristics of the CEFEO from about 1948 was that the rank and file were composed entirely of volunteers. It was legally and politically impossible for French governments to deploy conscripts to Indochina, a Colonial rather than a Metropolitan posting. France's commitment to provide NATO with a large contingent in Germany absorbed the majority of the conscript Metropolitan Army, whose overall size had to be cut sharply immediately after World War II because of financial constraints. The second and consequent defining characteristic of the CEFEO was its poverty in trained manpower and in every other necessity, since it had to compete with NATO for every man, gun, truck and litre of petrol.

A few Metropolitan infantry regiments did send 'marching battalions' to the Far East in 1946–9, but these were formed from individual volunteers.[11] After October 1951 individual conscripts could also choose to volunteer for the Far East expressly for service in non-combatant roles outside 'zones of active operations'. However, throughout the war the overwhelming majority of the specifically French units in Indochina (as opposed to Foreign Legion and African) were Colonial, with specially organized Metropolitan regiments providing many of the armoured, artillery, engineer, signal, logistic and other specialist assets – and all of them formed from volunteers enlisted for fixed terms of service.

Most Frenchmen of military age had seen enough of war to last them a lifetime, and few felt any personal attachment to the overseas empire. The French media paid very little attention to events in Indochina; and the powerful Communist Party and other voices on the Left waged a damaging campaign of propaganda, a campaign in which Viet Minh agents living in France played an intelligent part. Opposition to the war was pursued at every level, from parliamentary obstruction of the means to fight it, to actual sabotage by trades unionists of equipment bound for the Far East. At various times mobs abused embarking troops; it was felt necessary to omit from the official gazette citations for gallantry decorations won in Indochina, and to announce that blood donated by the public would not be used for transfusing Indochina casualties. It was in this environment that the army had to try to attract volunteers.

Frenchmen who did volunteer for the ranks of the Metropolitan Army or La Coloniale did so in the knowledge that they were almost certain to be shipped to Indochina for an operational tour of two years (officially – in practice this was often extended to 27 or 30 months). Some – including many Bretons, Corsicans, and *'pieds noirs'* from Algeria – were simply following family or local traditions of colonial military service. Some were veterans who had found that army life suited them, or whom the fortunes of war had left without home or family ties. Some were genuine patriots who believed in their duty to the French Empire, and others were passionate anti-Communists. A great many were simply hungry: a significant proportion came from the traditional areas of high unemployment in northern and eastern France. The average age of the CEFEO was notably higher than that of the Metropolitan Army 'contingent'; in 1951 it was around 28, and it rose during the next three years. Most career NCOs came from rural backgrounds, and countrymen still outnumbered city boys in the ranks. The volunteer status of the rankers after 1948 narrowed the social base, and average educational standards declined.[12]

THE WAGES OF ALL RANKS WERE low – a private received the same as an agricultural labourer in France, and a captain the same as a non-graduate French employee of the Tonkin coal mines. The cost of living in Indochina was high, and got higher the further up-country one travelled; in Saigon a beer might cost 7 piastres, but at Luang Prabang, 1,500 miles up the Mekong, the same weak brew was priced at 24 piastres – when a French private's daily pay was about 19 piastres.[13] The exchange rate for the piastre was maintained at the artificially high level of 17 francs, so soldiers received too little local currency for their nominal French pay; in 1950 the black-market rate was anything between 40 and 20 per cent of the official rate. A widespread racket developed by which those in a position to accumulate large amounts in black-market piastres smuggled them out of the country and made huge profits by reconverting them at the official rate. Such opportunities led to chronic corruption, including the selling of military supplies to middlemen acting for the Viet Minh.[14]

Despite the dangers and discomforts of tropical soldiering, at the end of their first tour some regulars signed up for one or a whole series of extensions; by the end of the war a few had served eight years in Indochina. Seen from a café table on some balmy evening amid the exotic delights of Saigon or Hanoi, surrounded by mates with enough back pay to fund at least a few days' happy oblivion, the thought of France sometimes failed to entice. Civilian employment back home meant a building site or a dirt-poor smallholding, while garrison life in Europe meant boredom, spit-and-polish and bureaucratic penny-pinching. Many of those veterans who did volunteer for extended tours naturally provided the hard core of seasoned NCOs on which the CEFEO depended; and even privates were often able to secure transfers to more desirable units and postings when they re-enlisted.

The CEFEO suffered from a constant shortage of experienced junior officers and NCOs to train, guide and motivate its new intakes. Its multi-national nature, and its weakness in Metropolitan support and service units, saw combat battalions repeatedly stripped of experienced cadres for non-European units, and of the most skilled men for transfer to specialist roles. This haemorrhage of real competence was bandaged over by the French practice of selecting promising recruits for junior NCO courses straight from basic training. This meant that many young corporals and even sergeants arrived with their units theoretically qualified, but without the necessary experience or authority to lead their men effectively.

ALTHOUGH SOME COMPLETE units were shipped to and from the Far East during the war, most regiments were permanently based in Indochina and periodically received batches of replacements for their time-expired personnel. This is perhaps the place for a brief explanation of the basic military family tree, with the caveat that under war conditions unit strengths in the field were often well below official establishment, and commands often held by men of more junior rank than officially prescribed.

The fundamental numbered and titled building block of the French Army's infantry was the regiment, a full colonel's command with a strength of roughly 3,000 all ranks. This was the soldier's 'tribe', distinguished by a badge and sometimes by the coloured lanyards which recorded recognition of collective valour in the World Wars. During at least the first half of the war a regiment – e.g. the Legion's 2nd Foreign Infantry, 2 REI – normally had responsibility for a large 'sector' of countryside. It was usually made up of a headquarters with administrative and logistic elements, and three combat battalions – e.g. I/, II/ and III/2 REI – each led by a lieutenant colonel or major, and numbering in practice anything from 500 to 850 men. The battalion-sized organization is what is usually meant by the word 'unit'.

Particularly from 1951 onwards, many infantry battalions were removed from the geographical sector organization and given a mobile 'intervention' role as part of the CEFEO's general reserve, typically forming part of a brigade-sized *Groupe Mobile* (GM). In such cases the battalion's connections with regimental headquarters would become entirely bureaucratic, and its everyday existence became the responsibility of the Group headquarters. The other two infantry units with which it was brigaded in the GM were very rarely sister battalions of its own regiment, and were often of different nationalities.

French and African infantry were often organized in separate *Bataillons de Marche*, 'marching battalions' – temporary units assembled from men of a regiment whose parent depot remained in Europe or Africa. In some cases, including most airborne troops, there was no regimental level of identity at all, and the numbered battalion – e.g. 6th Colonial Parachute Battalion, 6 BPC – was the basic autonomous unit. The battalion was in any case the soldier's military 'village', the largest group whose important personalities he might know by name and sight. Each battalion was usually divided into a headquarters and support company incorporating administrative, logistic, transport, signal and medical teams, plus a small central pool of mortars and machine guns; and either three or four numbered rifle companies.

Each rifle company, of perhaps 150 to 200 men, was commanded by a captain or an experienced lieutenant in his 30s. The company had a small headquarters including (theoretically) at least one other officer and several senior NCOs, with a radio link to battalion HQ and a handful of heavy weapons; and three rifle platoons each of between 30 and 45 men. The platoon – the usual focus of a soldier's identification and loyalty – was supposed to be led by a young lieutenant or sub-lieutenant, but in practice command was very often held by a senior sergeant. The platoon's communications with company HQ depended – when in static positions – on laying wire to connect field telephones, and at all other times on runners carrying messages. Sergeants also led the three sections or squads, each of ten to a dozen soldiers, which together made up the platoon. Each section had one light machine gun; the NCOs (and in parachute units, the most experienced privates) carried sub-machine guns or light carbines, the rest of the men rifles, and each of them a few hand grenades.

The section were the soldier's closest comrades – his *copains*, mates or buddies; he marched, fought, ate and slept beside them, and came to know them as well as he had known his childhood brothers. It would be absurd to imagine that every soldier likes and trusts all the men in his squad; nevertheless, every serious study of individual motivation among combat soldiers confirms that the key to a man's behaviour in battle is his feeling of mutual dependence and obligation towards these immediate comrades. Today many veterans of serious and prolonged combat are not embarrassed to use the word love. This unique sense of unselfish fellowship forged in shared ordeals is the principal reward of soldiering, and its rupture by the death of friends is the most painful price.

THE COURSES OF ABOUT FOUR weeks which many replacements attended at a Pre-Colonial Instruction Centre at Camp de Caïs near Fréjus were often barely relevant to actual combat conditions in the Far East. During the crisis of spring 1951 the overall length of basic training between enlistment and embarkation was cut from four to two months or even less. The great majority of meaningful training had to be accomplished 'on the job' after a man joined his unit in Indochina, and patterns of deployment often hampered this. Effective training can be given, and combat readiness maintained, only when a battalion is kept together under the eyes of its officers and senior NCOs, so that men become accustomed to their leaders and to operating as teams, and can absorb the whole unit's cumulative experience and ethos. Until 1951 particularly, far too many of the CEFEO's units were dispersed in penny packets as static sector troops, providing (notional) security for towns, roads, waterways, fixed defensive zones such as the De Lattre Line, and – to a much smaller extent – for the rural population. This dispersal meant that single companies, platoons, and sometimes even sections spent much of their time physically separated from their units, with a consequent loss of morale and efficiency.

The Viet Minh forced this pattern on the French by their constant campaign of guerrilla harassment. Although the thousands of small blockhouses and watchtowers scattered along the roads and rivers were manned by the lowest-quality troops and local militias, larger outposts were manned in company strength by reaction units of the Colonial, Foreign Legion and African infantry which supplied the bulk of the CEFEO's fighting strength. From 1951 all commanders-in-chief attempted to replace these static garrisons with Indochinese troops, to allow the assembly of a reserve of high-quality intervention units with which to confront the People's Army main force in Tonkin. These efforts were only intermittently successful.

The intervention forces of the general reserve were provided largely by two types of formation: the parachute battalions (of which more below), assembled into brigade-sized *Groupes Aéroportés* (GAP); and the motorized Groupes Mobiles. In 1951, in the aftermath of the RC4 disaster, General de Lattre ordered the widespread expansion of these mixed-arms brigades based on the model of the US Army Combat Command or Regimental Combat Team. Typically each Groupe Mobile comprised a tactical headquarters, under a full colonel; three battalions of infantry – normally at least one Colonial or Foreign Legion, to stiffen two North African, West African, or Indochinese units – carried in trucks with, less often, some armoured half-tracks; a battalion ('*groupe*') of towed artillery, normally with a dozen 105mm howitzers; a squadron of a dozen or so armoured cars and/or Stuart tanks; and integral engineer, signal, medical and other service elements, the whole totalling between 3,000 and 3,500 men in some 250 vehicles. For particular operations other units might be attached temporarily, including local irregulars for scouting.

In 1953 only seven GMs were available, but at various times 17 of these nominally self-sufficient brigades were operational. They proved their worth from de Lattre's earliest defensive battles around the Delta in spring 1951: they could move swiftly along 'interior lines' to bolster threatened perimeter sectors; they threw cordons around suspect areas during security sweeps; they were assembled in divisional strength (three brigades) for thrusts along major highways into the enemy's rear areas. However, 250 trucks are still 250 trucks, whether you call them a Mobile Group or a traffic jam. The narrow, easily sabotaged roads and the many vulnerable bridges allowed the Viet Minh to slow down and ambush the GMs like all other road traffic, despite their integral engineer companies. In the worst terrain they were forced to advance essentially on a 'one-vehicle front', which made it difficult to bring their armour and artillery into action. Most of the fighting had to be done by their disembarked infantry, on ground chosen by the enemy. In the final stage of the war the vulnerability of these brigades was demonstrated once and for all by the destruction of GM 100 on Route Coloniale 19 in the Central Highlands in June 1954.

ALTHOUGH THE US MILITARY Assistance Advisory Group (MAAG) was installed in Saigon by August 1950, it was not until mid 1951 that General de Lattre's passionate advocacy convinced America that the Korean and Indochina Wars and Britain's Malayan Emergency were parallel campaigns in the same struggle against expansionist Asian Communism. In consequence, the Expeditionary Corps began to receive more significant US material and financial assistance.[15] Until then it was a beggar's war, fought on the cheap with hand-me-downs and improvisations; France's flow of US Lend-Lease supplies had been switched off immediately the war in Europe ended. American interest in the French military had begun and ended with its contribution to the guard on the Iron Curtain, and any diversion of post-war US aid to fight a colonial war in Indochina – even so much as a spare propeller for a US-built aircraft – had provoked protests and the threat of sanctions.

In the late 1940s and early 1950s French feelings towards the USA were in most respects already as tortuous as they are today (though 'France's mission to counterbalance American hegemony' was not yet a commonplace assumption among the *bien-pensants*). France had been liberated by the 'Anglo-Saxons', predominantly by the Americans; but natural gratitude did not go deep among the governing classes. To acknowledge the inferiority implicit in the Liberation was unbearable; just as certain Frenchmen would never really forgive Britain for not doing the 'reasonable' thing and surrendering alongside France in 1940, so they would never forgive America for having to liberate them. Like de Gaulle, France's traditional leadership class 'had a certain idea' of their country, an idea for which their overseas empire was an important buttress. The tricolour had been planted in the Far East in a long-ago time of plausible French greatness, and they bitterly resented America's openly anti-colonialist agenda. They knew that America was the only possible source of the material help they needed to fight this war; but they distrusted her motives, resented the attached conditions, and detested any interference in their use of the aid she provided.

THE MOST STRIKING PHYSICAL evidence of the CEFEO's poverty in 1945–51 was its miscellaneous array of clothing and equipment. Before the belated general issue of their own olive-green fatigues, French troops fought the early years of the war in an assortment of British, US, French and locally made garments.[16] Personal equipment – packs and belt kit – was as diverse, ranging from French leather sets of Great War origin to 1940s British and US webbing, supplemented with many locally procured expedients of 'artisan manufacture'. This gypsy miscellany of sandy khaki and jungle-green, topped off with a milliner's catalogue of solar topis, sidecaps, berets, bush hats and steel helmets, may not have mattered; the lack of uniformity in weapons certainly did.

The most common infantry weapon throughout the war was the standard French MAS36 7.5mm rifle, a light and handy bolt-action weapon (i.e. after each shot the user had to work a bolt-like lever at the breech to eject the empty cartridge case and feed another round up from the magazine into the chamber). It was not particularly robust, lacked a safety catch, and had only a five-round magazine, but it was adequately efficient. As in most armies since 1916, the tactics of each squad of ten to a dozen infantrymen revolved around a light machine gun: with a two- or three-man team, the section's LMG provided a 'base of fire' while the other men manoeuvred with rifles and grenades, each element leap-frogging the other. The squad LMG (*fusil-mitrailleur* or 'automatic rifle') was thus the vital weapon, and in the CEFEO it was the sturdy, reliable, magazine-fed 7.5mm FM24/29. It was conventional for the squad leader – and in parachute units, up to half the squad – to carry a fully automatic sub-machine gun, firing pistol ammunition in bursts. The French 9mm MAT49 SMG was not widely issued until the second half of the war, and before its appearance in quantity the usual junior leaders' weapons were the British 9mm Sten gun or the US 0.45in Thompson. In fact, however, during 1945–51 the CEFEO were obliged to use a wildly mixed armoury of French, American, British, Chinese, even captured German and Japanese small arms. All required different ammunition, which made logistics a nightmare – one can easily imagine the lively curiosity felt by a surrounded unit as they tore open their air-dropped ammunition boxes. At one time the Expeditionary Corps and its local auxiliaries were carrying small arms of at least ten different calibres.[17]

Although most of the foreign types were steadily transferred to second-line troops as standardized French models became more plentiful, this took several years. Sergeant Janos Kemencei – one of fewer than 50 survivors of the 1st Foreign Parachute Battalion from the October 1950 RC4 battles – recalled that when the unit arrived in Indochina in November 1948 his ten-man section were issued one FM24/29 light machine gun, five MAS38 7.65mm machine pistols (a lightly built police weapon), and four CR39s – an uncomfortable version of the MAS36 rifle with a hollow, folding, aluminium butt. By March 1949 all the rifles and all but one of the machine pistols had failed, the latter mostly through swollen or burst barrels. In their place these paratroopers of a crack intervention unit had received six rifles of 1915 vintage.[18] These relics of Verdun were so awkwardly long that during combat jumps they had to be dropped separately, the paratroopers having to locate them on the drop zone before they could defend themselves. With only three-round magazines and no ammunition feeder clips, the légionnaires had to load the rounds singly. In 1950 the section received excellent German MP40 sub-machine guns, but with ill-matched British 9mm ammunition – a combination which caused repeated stoppages and accidental discharges.[19]

The shortage of heavy support weapons in infantry units had serious operational consequences in the early years. The scarcity of modern belt-fed US Browning 0.30in machine guns reduced the French to issuing infantry and even paratroop companies with 'fortress' machine guns, stripped from the casemates of the Maginot Line or the hulls of old tanks and 'jury rigged' to tripod mounts – an unconvincing contrivance fed by a big clockwork drum clamped to one side.[20] A battalion was lucky if it had ten rifle-calibre machine guns (two per rifle company and two more with headquarters), and the same number of mortars, of which six or even eight were often light 60mm tubes rather than the standard 81mm – less than half the number of heavy weapons provided to contemporary US Army battalions. Ammunition sometimes came from stocks dating back to the 1930s which had not been packed to resist the tropical damp.

By late 1953 the increased flow of US material and financial aid had improved the lot of the infantry considerably.[21] The CEFEO had standardized on the MAS36 rifle, MAT49 sub-machine gun, FM24/29 light and US 0.30in medium machine guns.[22] Battalion headquarters might also receive a couple of US M2 0.50in heavy machine guns, and had at least four 81mm mortars. Some independent support companies were forming with the French super-heavy 120mm (4.2in) mortar. The US M18 57mm 'recoilless rifle' was on issue to infantry company headquarters; and the even more powerful M20 75mm RCL was becoming available in small numbers to support units. These recoilless guns, particularly useful for their flat trajectory fire in direct support of infantry, also had special drawbacks.[23] Finally, the support elements of some infantry battalions had received a few flame-throwers.

THE PROVISION FROM 1952 of newer US transport and combat vehicles was also extremely welcome; in 1945–51 the CEFEO's chaotic 'lucky dip' of war-weary trucks and armoured vehicles of several nationalities had been bedevilled by breakdowns due to age and poor maintenance in punishing tropical conditions. One central problem was that apart from arms and munitions, the provision of logistic support for what was officially 'the maintenance of order in colonial territories' was the responsibility not of the Ministry of War but of the Military Affairs Directorate (DAM) of the Ministry for Overseas Affairs (FOM – *Ministère de la France d'Outre-Mer*). This bureaucracy lacked the means and the experience to fulfil what became an overwhelming task, involving 50,000–60,000 separate types of item, with budgetary regulations preventing the FOM placing orders for more than one financial year ahead. The annual budgetary vote was subject to parliamentary obstruction, and the whole process to bureaucratic lethargy. The FOM had to search the commercial marketplace for suppliers quite independently of – and sometimes even in competition with – the Ministry of War. French industry, painfully rebuilding itself after 1945, preferred to seek civilian rather than military orders, and was often hobbled by political strikes. Shipping capacity was scarce, weatherproof packing careless, and dockyards at both ends of the voyage clogged. The inevitable consequences were wasteful duplication, poor quality control and endless delays.[24]

However, by 1953 the CEFEO had standardized on US types for 80 per cent of its vehicles; large numbers of newer GMC and Dodge trucks replaced the ramshackle veterans of World War II, and many of the original museum gallery of armoured cars were replaced with the US M8

Greyhound. The M24 Chaffee light tank was available in some numbers to the specialized *Sous-Groupements Blindés*, though the tall, narrow-tracked old M5A1 Stuart was still operating with the Groupes Mobiles.

THE HUMAN ELEMENT OF THE CEFEO was often as ill prepared as the mechanical. Troops sent out from France and her African colonies had difficulty adapting to Indochina.[25] Few had any knowledge of the country beyond the half-remembered banalities of their school textbooks, and the reality was bewildering. As they approached their landfall most of their information was gleaned from the anecdotes of the few old hands returning for a second tour – highly coloured, but of questionable survival value.

Partly acclimatized to tropical heat during the latter stages of their voyage via Suez and the Indian Ocean aboard the *Pasteur, Athos II* or *Île de France*, the new drafts destined for Cochinchina were still shocked by the blanket of steamy dampness and faecal stink which closed around them during the final approach up the Saigon river. To Europeans the oven heat of the dry season was exhausting, but high humidity – the sensation of trying to drag warm, damp cotton wool into their lungs – was the most enfeebling factor. Given the wide variations in temperature and humidity between north and south Vietnam, coastal lowlands and inland hills, the process of acclimatization should have been – but seldom was – repeated if units were transferred over long distances. Soldiers rushed 750 miles from the Mekong Delta to the hills of Tonkin in spring faced a drop of 20°F; and those who were moved even from the Red River delta up into the foggy Thai Highlands in winter were shocked by the difference between a balmy 60°F and a hard night-time frost – rheumatism and influenza were common.

Malaria was a constant threat despite the provision of Atabrine tablets, and other endemic diseases included cholera, bush typhus, dengue fever and smallpox. In the wet season constantly damp clothing chafed under the pressure of web equipment and packs; consequently all kinds of skin diseases flourished, the smallest cuts, sores or stings remaining stubbornly unhealed and often becoming ulcerated. Veterans gave the weeping skin disorders the generic name of 'bul-bul', and could tell a sufferer at a distance by the way he walked.[26]

Gastric problems were more or less universal. The immediate response to the tropical heat was to drink – anything cool, and in great quantities. In a country where human excrement was the normal agricultural manure the local water was a *'bouillon de culture'*; despite repeated official warnings about the risks of cholera and amoebic dysentery, drinking untreated water still accounted for 40 per cent of all medical cases in Indochina. Safe soft drinks were hard to find, and expensive – a packet of cigarettes and one orangeade cost a West African soldier his whole daily wage – so most of the troops (including many Muslims) drank alcohol, in a climate where even beer could be dangerous. Excessive drinking led to brawling and indiscipline, illness, and habitual alcoholism.

Many troops on static duties – always the majority – found it difficult to cope with the tropical rhythm of life. When not on actual operations, work was done early in the morning and the afternoon was given over to a siesta, but in some regions the unvarying temperature made sleeping exhaustingly difficult. At the height of the hot, dry season just before the spring rains broke, the temperature in the lowlands reduced even the natives to utter lethargy. Whenever they could get away with it, the troops stripped off their heavy, chafing fatigue clothing and leather boots and went about in shorts or sarongs and sandals. In small garrisons, often commanded by a young NCO far from supervision, casually unsoldierly habits might be the first step down a slippery path. A smell of burning caramel hanging in the air might hint that the troops were 'going native' to an alarming degree; a jaundiced yellow complexion and an oily smudge on the left forefinger betrayed over-indulgence in opium, in whose gentle embrace the long, empty hours drifted by like blue smoke. In isolated posts soldiers might degenerate through boredom and loneliness into a demoralized slackness that could be fatal in a war zone. The surrounding rice-fields and bamboo thickets might seem peaceful, the villagers undisturbed; but nothing was ever certain – potentially, almost the whole of Vietnam was 'Apache country'. More than one batch of newly arrived replacements were heavily ambushed in the heart of the Delta while making their first train journey from the Haiphong docks to Hanoi.

THE SOLDIERS' INITIAL ENCOUNTERS with the people of Indochina were usually memorable. Fifty years ago, long before TV brought the whole world into their homes, the average Frenchman or German – let alone a Berber or Senegalese – was entirely ignorant about the Far East. Some had a vague idea that the 'Annamites' (as the French called all Vietnamese) were pagan savages who lazed amid dirt, and few had any mental picture of the landscape beyond dim expectations of palm trees. Men shipped directly to Tonkin were sometimes mesmerized before they landed by the dreamlike spectacle of Ha Long Bay, with its 3,000 impossible islands rising in wooded pinnacles from a pearly sea like fantastic Chinese scroll paintings. When they ventured out of the transit barracks for their first glimpse beyond the curtain, they were astonished by the swarming streets of Saigon or Hanoi. Around city centres resembling French provincial towns the pagodas, dragons, gongs and incense of timeless Asia pressed in, and throngs of slight, graceful people conducted their unguessable affairs in the open streets. Amidst an incomprehensible sing-song of voices and a hundred other exotic sounds, sights and smells the soldiers wandered, gaping and exclaiming – particularly at the exquisite young women gliding past in their elegant costumes.[27] Some Europeans in Vietnam came to appreciate a natural delicacy, good humour and courtesy which made other races seem coarse. After a spell in Vietnam, Cambodia, or the ultimate Buddhist languor of Laos the impact of this refined culture, set in the extraordinary natural beauty of many regions of Indochina, bewitched some of them for a lifetime with a baffled, unrequited love which they called the *mal jaune* – 'yellow fever'.[28] Tragically, they were often clumsy suitors.

Throughout the war the official line was that the enemy were little more than marauding bandits – *'pirates vulgaires'* was a traditional term – and that French soldiers were protecting grateful colonial subjects from looting, murder, and (paradoxically, given this dismissive analysis) the threat of Communist slavery. In the city centres soldiers were surrounded by transplanted features of French life, and serviced by Vietnamese and Chinese who had acquired the language, outward trappings, and sometimes even the Roman Catholic faith of the colonisers.[29] Out in the countryside the 'otherness' of the Vietnamese was much more striking.

Frenchmen despatched to tiny garrisons, either of French Army sector troops or – particularly – of Indochinese led by only a handful of whites, were thrown into the company of the local villagers. At first both sides might be suspicious; but relationships grew through simple daily need into mutual toleration and even genuine affection. The instinctive racism of the common soldiers seems to have rubbed away easily enough with actual daily contact. Like Roman garrisons on some far-flung Celtic frontier, each fort had a cluster of native homes near by; if the troops were mainly Vietnamese their families normally lived with them, creating a ready-made community. The villagers seized any opportunity for lucrative trade and services: laundry and tailoring, labour and portering, the sale of food, drink and other small comforts, and more or less discreet prostitution.[30] These relationships of negotiable affection were not always fleeting: there was a long tradition of taking a *congai*, a semi-permanent mistress installed near by in quarters where an off-duty soldier could enjoy some domestic comforts – including, not infrequently, the joys of fatherhood.

The villagers living close to a French post felt protected by the presence of an established and familiar garrison – protected as much from ill-treatment by Vietnamese officials and by strange soldiers passing through as from the Viet Minh; and the garrison needed the villagers if daily life was to be supportable. If a unit remained in one place for long the walls between the military and civilian worlds might become distinctly porous. The comings and goings of Vietnamese around the posts soon became commonplace and unquestioned – and security from Viet Minh scrutiny utterly impossible. On the relatively rare occasions when French posts were directly assaulted, it is not surprising to read that the Viet Minh regional units were briefed on detailed models of the fort layout. The sudden, eerie emptiness of the nearest village was an infallible sign of an impending attack.

SINCE THE FIRST 19TH-CENTURY colonial campaigns local coolies had been used to carry all heavy loads, even the knapsacks of soldiers 'on column', and this tradition persisted; many photographs show Vietnamese carrying ammunition, stretchers, even radios. In fact these porters were usually 'PIMs' – 'interned military prisoners' – who enjoyed an ambiguous status. Viet Minh suspects among the civilian population were turned over after interrogation to take their chances at the hands of the Vietnamese government. By contrast, PIMs were enemies captured under arms who were accorded a semblance of prisoner-of-war status under the Geneva

Convention. Some were held in camps open for International Red Cross inspection; but many were simply retained by the unit which had captured them, for employment as labourers and porters.[31] After long periods with a French unit its PIMs might come to identify with their captors, and hardly needed serious guarding. In Vietnamese culture there was no indelible shame in changing sides after a reasonable interval, and many PIMs eventually chose to join the French as active combatants.[32]

There was also widespread local enlistment of armed auxiliaries quite separate from the recruiting of Indochinese regulars and official militias. From the earliest days of the war almost every unit had its band of lightly armed *supplétifs*, usually run by a resourceful French NCO. These varied from simple interpreters and scouts, to mercenaries, half-tamed dacoits and 'turned' Viet Minh prisoners, who might be allowed free rein to counter local insurgent activity with few questions asked. The shortage of Frenchmen able to speak local languages and of French-speaking rural Vietnamese put too much unsupervised power into these often unscrupulous hands, with results that may easily be imagined.

Contacts between CEFEO personnel and rural Indochinese (other than their own camp followers) were hampered by cultural as well as linguistic incomprehension. Soldiers uninstructed in local beliefs could unwittingly cause great resentment. For instance, a European's most natural response to the delightful village children was to hand out sweets, ruffle their hair, and perhaps compliment their parents. Nobody had told the soldiers that to touch an infant's head was to damn it to lifelong bad luck, or that to praise its beauty attracted the vengeance of envious spirits. The Vietnamese bore their diluted form of Buddhism lightly, but in devout Cambodia intricate taboos surrounded the *bonze* monks. In Laos it was believed that cruelty was proportional to physical size; given the reputation of the Japanese, the approach of European or West African troops was greeted with stark terror and the panic evacuation of villages – easily misinterpreted as showing guilty knowledge.

Centuries of oppression had embedded in the Indochinese peasant a fear of risking the anger of the powerful when questioned. A patrol commander sweeping a sector after some Viet Minh attack would interrogate a village elder, who would answer 'yes' to every direct question.[33] Forced to communicate either in a pidgin-French in which neither soldier nor peasant was fluent, or through a single interpreter whom he might not entirely trust, the Frenchman, angered by the apparent idiocy or dishonesty of the answers, might lose his temper, shout or punch – and a swaggering Vietnamese *supplétif* might do a great deal worse. At the least the elder lost face in front of his people, and France and Bao Dai had made another bitter enemy. Similarly, resentment over a public outburst of anger or ridicule directed at an incompetent Vietnamese militiaman might fester into active treachery, with serious consequences.

The distrust of civilians which is inseparable from any guerrilla war was most noticeable in the airborne and motorized intervention battalions, which were often shifted over long distances at short notice. These military fire brigades had little opportunity to build a relationship with local populations. Apart from the local recruits in their own ranks, they encountered very few Indochinese on relaxed terms; their whole tours were spent in combat against the Viet Minh, or in trying to find them and bring them to battle.

THE FRENCH CIVIL ADMINISTRATION and their Vietnamese counterparts, local Asian magnates, and commercial concerns such as the rubber, timber, tea, coffee and mining industries all employed an assortment of local militias on security duties. Many were little more than watchmen whose fate might serve as a warning bell of local Viet Minh activity. The chains of flimsy little rustic watchtowers – *miradors* – in which they shut themselves up at night offered no serious deterrence to guerrilla bands, and were sometimes a tempting source for an elderly carbine or a couple of Japanese grenades. Other groups, usually those employed by commercial interests, were well armed and ruthless, providing a heavy stick alongside the carrots which often changed hands as part of the private arrangements between businessmen (French as well as Chinese) and the local Viet Minh. These gangs were often provided by local warlords who used their ostensible status as a cover for protection rackets.

The most powerful armed groups outside the direct control of the CEFEO were the militias of the Cao Dai and Hoa Hao religious sects based in Tay Ninh and Chau Doc provinces respectively.[34] These movements were only concerned to guard their local autonomy, and fought either the authorities or the Viet Minh when it suited them. Some outright criminal gangs were enlisted in the French cause; the most flagrant were the Binh Xuyen of greater Saigon, whose warlord 'General' Le Van Vien was given immunity to profit from drugs, prostitution and gambling as police chief of Cholon in return for his persecution of the local Viet Minh.[35] (This accommodation did not prevent a constant drizzle of grenade attacks on cafés, clubs and cinemas frequented by the French, and almost nightly flurries of mortar bombs fired into the eastern quarters of the city from across the river.)[36] Throughout the war there was a considerable overlap between political and criminal violence and corruption, as several French intelligence agencies and various local groups pursued their own agendas, sometimes co-operating, sometimes competing. This shadow world owed as much to gangsterism as it did to intelligence operations; a lot of people made a great deal of money, a lot of others were murdered, and a lot of information and supplies found their way to the Viet Minh.[37]

IN A MORE CONVENTIONAL military context, the CEFEO sought local recruitment from the earliest months of the reconquest; today it is little appreciated that the war as a whole, and the battle of Dien Bien Phu itself, were far from being clear-cut confrontations between Europeans and Indochinese, but involved significant numbers of Vietnamese fighting under French command.

The auxiliary gangs of *supplétifs militaires* which accreted around most units were formalized as the war went on as numbered companies (CSM), and some were assembled into larger units or attached to Groupes Mobiles. The most formidable of these small units were various 'commandos' that included large numbers of recycled Viet Minh; these took a relentlessly active role, gathering intelligence for the Second Bureau and waging a harsh counter-guerrilla war of infiltration and raiding. Some remarkable French NCOs and junior officers risked their lives to lead the commandos, and names such as Bergerol, Barrès, Vandenberghe, Romary and Rusconi became famous in the CEFEO; they achieved extraordinary results at the cost of extraordinary risks, and more than one would die at the hands of assassins.

In parallel with these ad hoc initiatives there was, from the first, widespread enlistment of *'autochtones'* into regular units of the CEFEO; they were always a necessary supplement to French manpower, and later their recruitment was encouraged as a visible sign of popular support for the Bao Dai regime. By early 1951 the number of Vietnamese regulars was quoted as about 41,500, or roughly 25 per cent of the total manpower of the Expeditionary Corps. The Colonial Infantry, with its long tradition of mixed-race units, led the way; locally raised companies and later battalions were incorporated into the RICs, and a number of regiments became pre-dominantly Indochinese.[38] La Coloniale also provided the cadres for most of the separate local battalions which were raised from such ethnic groups as Khmer mercenaries and highland tribes; these 'Far East Marching Battalions' (BMEOs) were most numerous in Cochinchina and Annam, but also existed in Tonkin.

The word 'local' hints at one complication of this policy – a funda-mental difference in attitudes to soldiering between European and Asian troops. Accustomed to daily care by their womenfolk, and understand-ably nervous about their families' safety, the local men were usually reluctant to serve far from home. In many cases of unit movements the CEFEO had to factor in plans for moving the soldiers' families and building them a new village at the end of the march.

THERE HAD BEEN LANGUID discussion about the formation of a separate Vietnamese national army since 1948, but its real midwife was General de Lattre, who understood that only a genuine mobilization of the Vietnamese people against the Viet Minh offered any hope of success. If they remained militarily and psychologically passive, the CEFEO could not win; but if an efficient Vietnamese army could be created to take over the defensive and local security tasks, then the bulk of the Expeditionary Corps would be freed to pursue an aggressive war of movement. Success in the longer term might stiffen the resolve of the Associated States to the point where France could reduce her military commitment to a sustainable level. De Lattre was also well aware that the United States regarded the creation of a viable Vietnamese army as a condition of their providing the guns and gold upon which the CEFEO depended.

On 14 July 1951 the *Armée Nationale Vietnamienne* (ANV) was offi-cially born and general mobilization was announced. At first the numbers actually conscripted were modest, since it would take time to provide them with officers. To coincide with the decree, de Lattre made a widely reported speech to the Vietnamese graduating class of the Lycée Chasseloup-Laubat at Saigon, appealing to the educated youth of the country to enlist in the national struggle against Communism. He spoke with unprecedented bluntness: 'Be men! If you are Communists, then join the Viet Minh – there are some good people there, fighting well for a bad cause. But if you are patriots, then fight for your country, because this is *your* war... France can only fight it for you if you fight with her.' His uneasy audience responded with only polite applause.[39]

An officers' academy and regional schools were established, as was a skeleton general staff; and an embryo Vietnamese Navy and Air Force, all controlled and largely manned by French officers. Professional instruction of Vietnamese cadres was unconvincingly hasty; by the end of 1951 about 800 Vietnamese officers were already claimed to be serving with some 35 infantry battalions and 29 other units. These totalled about 63,600 men, equal to an addition of roughly one-third of the paper strength of the CEFEO; and during 1952 this figure doubled.[40] Most of the already existing locally raised units were now taken into the ANV.[41] Moreover, de Lattre ordered that many French regiments should incorporate at least one Indochinese company in every battalion for on-the-job training under French leadership.

This *'jaunissement'* did not apply to African units, but it was carried out in Metropolitan and Colonial regiments, including the parachute battalions. The Foreign Legion infantry regiments, suspicious of any threat to their *esprit de corps*, grouped the Vietnamese companies in separate battalions. Despite all misgivings, the quality of these troops was generally fairly good if they were given positive leadership by the parent unit; local recruits seem to have felt real pride at serving with prestigious regiments. Many French officers did not rate the Vietnamese peasant highly as a fighting man (ironically, given the successes of the Viet Minh). In pre-1951 Colonial units a noticeable proportion of the NCOs were ethnic Khmers or minority tribesmen, who had a tougher reputation; it was from this pool of experience that the few pre-1951 Indochinese officers had emerged.[42] Some commanders of parent units assigned their least valued French officers and NCOs to lead the Indochinese companies; others recognized their potential if properly instructed and motivated, and were rewarded with loyalty and effort – the Vietnamese troops' agility was praised, although their steadiness under fire was felt to be rather fragile. In late 1952 and early 1953 these Vietnamese sub-units were split off from their parents to be formed into numbered infantry battalions – *Tieu Doan* (TD) – of the ANV; and by the end of 1953 the ANV claimed a strength of over 160,000 men.[43] In the test to come, however, the ANV's main weakness lay not in those formerly attached units with a background of French leadership and example, but in the majority of entirely new battalions. In practice, ANV units would display the whole spectrum of behaviour from admirable to pitiful, depending largely upon the accident of their leadership; but collectively, there is no denying that they were an extremely brittle instrument.

The conscripts who had been unable to avoid the draft were unwilling, bewildered, scared or resentful; in the South many young men fled to the safer ranks of the sectarian militias. A proportion of recruits were completely unfit for military service – and some, inevitably, were Viet Minh agents.[44] Desertions and mass refusals to leave home provinces were rife. Although instructed by seasoned Colonial NCOs and provided with a few French advisers, the units of new recruits were led mostly by inexperienced NCOs plucked from their own ranks for brief training and superficial indoctrination; and for reasons of 'face' – as well as the drain on French manpower – the French cadres were often withdrawn far too soon.[45]

The ANV reflected the society from which it was raised, so rank was valued as the door to personal privilege rather than to responsibility, discipline was harsh and arbitrary, corruption was endemic, and initiative and devotion to duty were rare. In 1953, some 60 students about to take their final exams at the Hanoi medical faculty were told that those who passed would become army doctors; 40 immediately abandoned their studies and applied for a long dentistry course.[46] Anyone whose family could raise 50,000 piastres could bribe his way out of the net altogether; and too many sons of the wealthy who did volunteer for officers' school had the connections to ensure that graduation led to positions of profit rather than the front line.[47] Many of the new officers despised and neglected their peasant soldiers, while illiteracy blocked the advancement of most of the best Indochinese junior leaders from pre-1951 Colonial units. Although US weapons were provided specifically for the ANV, these were often diverted to units in which the French commanders had more confidence.[48]

One initiative trumpeted by the ANV was the creation of 'light' infantry battalions – *Tieu Doan Kinh Quan* (TDKQ) – for security and pacification duties. These 625-man units (contrasting with the 820 of a French model line battalion) were officered entirely by Vietnamese. They were supposed to be trained to a high standard in both guerrilla tactics and the psychological warfare doctrine of 'hearts and minds'; the much abused term 'commandos' was even bandied about. Their mission was to settle into disputed areas, win the support of villagers by propaganda, medical aid and practical everyday help, and root out the local Viet Minh.[49] Raising and equipping TDKQs promised to be less costly in time and matériel than conventional battalions, and as something very like this scheme had worked in the Philippines, the US mission approved of the plan. Special training schools were set up throughout Vietnam; the first conscripts arrived for an intensive three-month course at Quang Yen, the main northern camp, in April 1953, and this programme was supposed to provide 40,000 men for TDKQs – a significant part of the ANV's total strength – by the end of that year.[50] It was planned that by the end of 1954 no fewer than 108 TDKQs would have been raised, and another 27 early in 1955 (though it is hard to imagine where all the officers were supposed to come from).

In practice the TDKQs turned out to be almost useless. Their training, both for battle and for winning over the peasantry, was superficial, and their officers were unskilled and poorly motivated. It was the Viet Minh who took the hearts-and-minds doctrine seriously, since it was potentially a dangerous threat, and they made a point of targeting the green TDKQs wherever they took the field. The result was a series of bloody defeats, panic flights and mass desertions, which destroyed both the morale of the TDKQs and any hope of their gaining prestige among the population. Poor leadership and training were, of course, only the symptom, not the cause of the failure of these and other ANV units. One is inescapably reminded of the furious question posed during America's programme of 'Vietnamization' at the end of the 1960s: 'Why can't *our* gooks fight like *their* gooks?' Bao Dai's army failed to command the loyalty of Vietnamese peasants because disinterested service and civic honesty were almost unknown in the Vietnamese governing classes who should have led them, and because the Viet Minh promised them a better future.[51]

IN THE CENTRAL HIGHLANDS there was some local militia conscription for a *Garde Montagnarde*. Like Americans after them, some Frenchmen found the way of life pursued in the tribal longhouses particularly appealing. Typically of independent highlanders the world over, it seemed more relaxed and sensual than that of the lowlanders, and much of communal life and ritual revolved around feasting and alcohol.[52] The *montagnards* belonged to a number of distinct groups, but many were great hunters with the crossbow, the lance, and the razor-sharp 18in *coupe-coupe*. However, in their culture a violent death was regarded as a spiritual disaster requiring long and expensive funerary rituals. Given these beliefs, and their wariness of all Vietnamese, one must suspect coercion when one reads that several former Far East Marching Battalions recruited among such tribes as the Rhadés, Jarais and Sedangs were integrated into the ANV from 1951 in at least eight numbered *Bataillons Montagnards*.[53]

Many of the larger and more cohesive tribal communities of the High Region of north-west Tonkin were directly threatened by the Viet Minh and, being free of the Annamese *montagnards'* particular sensibilities, were therefore more enthusiastic allies. They not only scouted for the French, and fielded large counter-guerrilla bands with French arms, instruction and leadership; they also enlisted in formed regular units to defend their territory – for instance, two battalions of Muongs from the hills around Hoa Binh distinguished themselves with Colonel Vanuxem's Groupe Mobile 3 in several pitched battles. The most numerous peoples in the immediate vicinity of Dien Bien Phu were Black Thai, Lao, and opium-growing Meo; many Thai auxiliary companies would join the garrison, as well as two full Thai battalions.[54]

THE FRENCH UNION FORCE which would fight at Dien Bien Phu presented in microcosm the same military goulash as the Expeditionary Corps itself. The spearhead, as always, would be provided by the *Troupes Aéroportées d'Indochine* (TAPI). Indochina was the paratrooper's war par excellence – indeed, it was the only war after 1945 to see large-scale parachute insertions of several thousand troops at a time, as well as numerous smaller drops by single battalions.

The paratroop units were a self-conscious élite. Like all airborne soldiers, they cultivated a mystique that attracted highly motivated volunteers, and the nature of their training weeded out any who were not fit, brave and aggressive. A higher than usual proportion of the rank and file were serving second or subsequent tours in Indochina. Their leaders were almost universally of a high calibre; battalion commanders, many company commanders and senior NCOs had seen action during World War II. The nature of the paratroopers' missions soon exposed any junior leaders who lacked the necessary energy, initiative and endurance, and such men did not last long. The relationship between officers and enlisted ranks was much closer than in some other French units; a proportion of officers came from modest social backgrounds, and leaders with a reputation as *baroudeurs* – 'brawlers' – were particularly admired. As throughout the CEFEO, proven officers shouldered responsibilities beyond those normal for their ranks – battalions were sometimes led by captains, and most companies by lieutenants.

The parachute battalions were virtually the only units that could carry the war to the enemy by achieving surprise. Installed at the main airbases in north and south Vietnam, their mobility made them the chosen intervention units of the general reserve, and consequently they were committed to a very punishing tempo of operations. It was not unusual for a battalion to be in the field for two months at a time, followed by perhaps two weeks' break to rest and make up numbers before the next operation. A brief summary of the war diary of the 2nd Foreign Parachute Battalion (2 BEP) in the year before they fought at Dien Bien Phu provides a typical example of the para's war.

In November–December 1952 the battalion fought in the defence of Na San (*see Chapter 1 above*). Flown back to their base at Hanoi–Bach Mai on 26 February 1953, from 9 March to 11 April they were on counter-insurgency operations in the Delta. Five days later they were flown to the Plain of Jars in Laos, where the entrenched camp was threatened by two Viet Minh divisions. Returning to Hanoi in early July, on the 17th they made a battalion jump at Loc Binh behind enemy lines on RC4 as part of Operation 'Hirondelle' – an airborne raid on supply dumps around Lang Son. Loc Binh was the halfway point on the withdrawal route for the two Colonial battalions dropped at Lang Son; the Legion paratroopers repaired and held a vital river crossing until the retreating assault force reached them and passed through on 18 July. They then formed the rearguard during a 20-mile forced march in the full heat of the summer sun – a march which cost the battalion deaths from heat exhaustion. Picked up by trucks on the night of 19 July, they were driven to the coast and extracted by sea; the men's average weight loss over four days was 11 pounds.[55]

After ten days' rest 2 BEP returned to Hanoi in mid August 1953, and from 28 August to 15 September they carried out counter-insurgency sweeps in the Delta, suffering casualties to mines, booby-traps and snipers. Between 22 September and 12 October they took part in Operation 'Brochet' around Nam Dinh in the southern Delta – a major combined arms operation involving 18 battalions. They were in the field again in mid December, before the offensive into Laos by Giap's Division 325 saw them rushed on 27 December to Seno, where they operated with Groupe Mobile 2 until 10 January 1954 (see Chapter 8 below). Two days later they were flown to Saigon, and on to Nha Trang; from 20 to 29 January they took part in Operation 'Aréthuse', the amphibious landing around Tuy Hoa in Annam which opened General Navarre's 'Atlante' offensive. On 30 January the battalion were trucked to Pleiku in the Central Highlands, and operated in the parched terrain between An Khe, Dak Doa and Plei Bon until 17 March. Recalled to Hanoi, the 2nd Foreign Parachute Battalion was dropped into besieged Dien Bien Phu between 9 and 12 April 1954.

This pace of operations is comparable to some episodes in World War II, but in Western armies today it would be regarded as intolerably demanding. The best analysis of combat fatigue – the process by which an infantry-man's finite stock of courage and resilience drains away – suggests a limit of between 200 and 240 days in the front line.[56] Since the paratroopers of TAPI kept up this kind of rhythm for years, we can at least say that by autumn 1953 some of them were battle-proven to a point which threat-ened to tip over into fatigue. However, their self-belief and combat skills were of a high order, and because they had 'the habit of victory' they often achieved impressive successes. The Viet Minh took their presence on any battlefield very seriously, keeping careful track of their deployments and even of the careers of individual officers. There was a price to pay, however: these often high-risk operations led to a similarly high, and occasionally catastrophic, rate of casualties.

The paratroopers could be dropped anywhere in Indochina; but if they were inserted deep in Viet Minh territory there was no way to extract them from the jungle hills other than by long, perilous marches on foot to the nearest French post with an airstrip or a truckable road.[57] The paratroopers marched lighter and faster than any other French units and were often as agile as the People's Army; but they were generally isolated, outnumbered, and forced to carry every bullet, biscuit and stretcher themselves, usually over punishing terrain. If a net of enemy units could be drawn around their route of withdrawal, such a retreat could become a nightmare punctuated by ambushes, forced dispersal in the jungle, even the abandonment of wounded with heroic medical orderlies. The worst ordeals of Britain's World War II Chindits in Japanese-occupied Burma were repeated in the Tonkinese highlands ten years later.

IN 1953 THERE WERE FOUR types of parachute unit: Metropolitan (RCP), Colonial (BPC), Foreign (BEP), and Vietnamese (BPVN). In practical terms they differed only in details of formal uniform and of ethnic composition. (In March 1951 General de Lattre had ordered all Metropolitan and Colonial paratroopers to wear the red beret as a mark of unity; previously a mixture of royal blue, maroon and black berets had reflected a lineage divided between the pre-World War II Air Force, British-sponsored wartime French SAS battalions, and post-1942 formations.) The Metropolitan and Colonial units were composed of French and Vietnamese volunteers, the two Foreign battalions of volunteers of all nationalities. The usual organization was a single headquarters company ('command and support', or CCS), plus four rifle companies; since 1951 the official ratio had been two Indochinese rifle companies in each Colonial, and one in each Metropolitan and Foreign battalion. In spring 1952 the official establishment of a Colonial para battalion was 22 French officers, 81 French and 17 Vietnamese senior NCOs, 344 French and 388 Vietnamese junior NCOs and men, giving a total of 852 all ranks of whom 405 were Vietnamese.[58]

In practice all battalions had to keep up their strength by local recruiting, and Indochinese paratroopers typically made up between 30 and 50 per cent of unit personnel. When Groupe Aéroporté 1 jumped over Dien Bien Phu on 20 November 1953, Major Bigeard's 6th Colonial Parachute Battalion (6 BPC) would count some 200 Vietnamese among its 651 men; while the 'jaunissement' of Major Bréchignac's nominally Metropolitan French 2nd Battalion, 1st Parachute Light Infantry (II/1 RCP) had reached no fewer than 420 out of 827 men by that month. Even the Legion's 1 BEP, supposedly limited to one native company out of four, jumped at Dien Bien Phu with 336 Vietnamese out of a total of 653 men.[59]

Officers joined Metropolitan or Colonial units irrespective of their original branch, and within the 'paratroop family' they moved freely from one battalion to another at need. (This did not apply to the Foreign battalions, which by 1953 drew almost all their officers exclusively from the Legion.) Some commanders were colourful 'hands on' leaders who stamped their strong personalities on every aspect of their battalions' activities; for instance, the 6 BPC was universally known as the 'Bataillon Bigeard', and its remarkable commander was criticized by some for running his unit like a medieval *condottiere*. Others were less highly visible, trusting their capable teams of company commanders to do their jobs without too much supervision. This was the case in the Foreign battalions; although newly raised for this war, they had the Legion's long history and traditions to underpin their culture, while the Colonial units had a more diffuse background.

All the parachute units had the strengths and the weaknesses of their special role. In French terms they were 'supple' and had 'punch' – they were fit, fast-moving, versatile and lethal, and command and control was flexible due to a generous scale of radio sets (68, against the norm of 44 in infantry battalions; this allowed their issue at platoon level). Like all airborne units, however, their scale of support weapons was modest: normally two 60mm light mortars, one 0.30in machine gun and a 57mm 'recoilless rifle' for each rifle company, and in the HQ company two machine guns and four 81mm mortars.[60]

The only ANV combat unit which fought at Dien Bien Phu was the *5e Bataillon de Parachutistes Vietnamiens*, 5 BPVN or – as such units were always called in a phonetic version of their Vietnamese title – 'the 5th *Bawouan*'. Raised as a very visible part of the French programme to create a viable Armée Nationale Vietnamienne, the *bawouans* had been formed by splitting off the Vietnamese elements of mixed units once they were judged to be seasoned enough for an independent existence. Brigaded alongside French para battalions, they were probably the best of the ANV units, since by definition the personnel were more highly motivated, and they retained a large French cadre from their parent units.

PARATROOPERS COULD SEIZE an objective; but consolidating and holding positions demanded 'heavy' infantry, and that meant the Foreign Legion. With nearly 20,000 men in Indochina at its peak strength in early 1952, the *Légion Étrangère* provided some 35 per cent of European manpower and the majority of European infantry throughout the war. The years 1946–54 would see the Legion grow to its largest ever size, more than 30,000 men; and in Indochina the corps supported four infantry regiments each of three (briefly, four) battalions, a light armoured cavalry regiment with two detached amphibious tractor battalions, two parachute battalions, and numerous independent specialist companies.

Legion infantry had a reputation as slightly ponderous but rock-solid troops: in the words of the novelist Nicolas Freeling, 'old-fashioned soldiers – stomachs, beards, hung around with grenades and canteens full of vino'. The belief that their ranks were largely filled with German ex-Wehrmacht and Waffen-SS veterans recruited straight from French prison camps with few questions asked lent them a sinister glamour in the eyes of journalists. This legend had been more credible in 1945–50, but by 1953 the majority of the original post-war enlistees had departed after serving their five-year contracts, and it was only among senior NCOs that Wehrmacht veterans were found in any concentrated numbers – though these very capable soldiers certainly underpinned the overall quality of many units. Perhaps 50 per cent of the légionnaires in Indochina were still Germans, but their average age was only 20–23, and Legion commanders often lamented the lack of military experience, training, and even of physical fitness among the later intakes.[61]

The remainder were of dozens of other nationalities; the Legion tried to limit the proportion of Frenchmen in any unit to perhaps 10 per cent. The aftermath of the Liberation had given some Frenchmen pressing reasons to leave the country: some enlisted as 'Belgians' or 'Swiss' –

although no serious obstacles were put in the way of Frenchmen with dubious records, and Legion service earned a number of former Miliciens and LVF men a clean slate.[62] There were only a handful of légionnaires from the English-speaking countries.[63] The aftermath of General de Lattre's reforms had left each Legion infantry battalion with one Indochinese company, as in the BEPs.[64] The Legion had been particularly sensitive about the process of *'jaunissement'*; only those who had passed through basic training at the corps' depot at Sidi bel Abbès in Algeria were considered to be 'true légionnaires', and Indochinese recruits were not permitted to wear the traditional white képi with formal uniform, being issued a white beret instead.

The Expeditionary Corps' hunger for men in 1951 cut the légionnaires' pre-embarkation training in North Africa to just six weeks; they were barely taught to understand French orders, march and shoot, and although their battlefield discipline was always impressive their tactical skills depended very largely upon on-the-job training after they reached their units. Before 1951 the dispersal of battalions in isolated company-sized garrisons, and the constant creaming-off of skilled men for non-regimental duties, degraded standards; in some units the numbers of officers and (to a lesser extent) of experienced NCOs were reduced to dangerous levels. While a battalion's field strength sometimes slipped to about 500, the Legion was careful to maintain strong depots for NCO training and rotation of tired men. The units that had seen service as complete battalions with the Groupes Mobiles in Tonkin since 1951 had regained much of the strength, discipline and morale which post garrison duty had tended to leech away. The Legion was at its best in large-scale conventional operations when officers and senior NCOs could supervise junior leaders, encourage combat skills, and nurture the unique Legion culture of discipline, self-sufficiency and *esprit de corps*, expressed in the last resort as a willingness to 'do a Camerone' – to fight to the last.[65]

While disenchanted légionnaires had always been prone to desertion, and a good many took their leave during the long journey out to Asia, Indochina itself offered few opportunities for white men on the run to melt into the background. There were a handful of confirmed cases of desertion to the enemy; a very few men seem to have actively helped the People's Army and even fought alongside them, but white deserters were usually regarded by the Communists with great suspicion and most were subsequently executed.[66]

TO BRITISH EYES FRANCE'S North African troops, who by 1953 provided the Expeditionary Corps with some 30,000 men, are reminiscent of the old Indian Army, and the Armée d'Afrique did share the latter's introverted character, if never its autonomy.[67] The Algerian and Moroccan *Tirailleurs* (literally 'skirmishers', usually translated as Riflemen) were volunteers mostly recruited in the Berber villages of the Atlas, Kabylie and Aurés mountains. Physically and mentally hardy, they were drawn from a warrior-clan culture of raiding and blood-feud; military service brought them status, good pay by their own impoverished standards and, after discharge, valuable privileges. Regiments benefited from regional loyalties over several generations, and the style of command was paternalistic; officers maintained contact with the local administration at home and were expected to be helpful over the soldiers' domestic concerns. Special arrangements were made to respect Muslim needs in such matters as rations and regimental imams. In the Italian campaign of 1943–4 several divisions built around Tirailleurs and the smaller units (Tabors) of Moroccan Goumiers had proved reliable and aggressive, though brutal towards civilians. France's eventual status as a victor earned Muslim respect – success was a proof of her *baraka*, the spiritual force that is earned by superior qualities. Despite the shock caused by the massacre of Algerians around Sétif in May 1945, there was a general belief that Algeria's wartime contribution must soon bring the reward of constitutional reforms.[68]

A new enlistment drive in the late 1940s enjoyed a good response, bringing in many valuable World War II veterans whose morale was initially high. Perhaps four-fifths of the battalion officers were French, and the minority of *officiers musulmans* seldom rose above captain's rank; many of the senior NCOs were also French, as were some specialist enlisted men. Very few North African recruits were literate, but French was the language of instruction and discipline.[69] Because of the men's illiteracy their training by the French cadres involved close personal instruction in small groups, which fostered the bonds between leaders and led; it also put a premium on the quality of those leaders. The Algerians were comfortable in a patriarchal system, and willingly gave their loyalty to brave and humane Frenchmen who respected their ways; but when trusted leaders fell in battle they often became confused and dispirited.

The first battalions sent to Indochina in 1947 were relieved as complete units after their tour; but thereafter battalions usually remained in the Far East for the duration, kept up to strength by successive drafts of replacements, and the increasing pressure on manpower saw the introduction of conscripts to the ranks. These units were usually designated 'marching battalions', and were raised from regiments which remained in North Africa or Germany.[70] The Muslim soldiers found the climate exhausting, the landscape of swamp or forest oppressive and Asiatic culture unsympathetic. Tirailleurs units were therefore unsuitable for the local security role unless closely supervised; they, too, were at their best when serving with the Groupes Mobiles. The constant drain of casualties, carefully targeted anti-colonialist propaganda, and a series of defeats which suggested that France was losing her *baraka* all caused declining morale in units which, from about 1951, no longer boasted many World War II veterans. It was reckoned that North African soldiers needed between one and two years of service before they were ready to enter combat; but by 1953 men with less than six months in uniform were being shipped out to Indochina.

Algeria was a French colony – indeed, it was claimed to be a part of 'France overseas', an obvious constitutional fiction sustained by parliamentary representation in Paris. Morocco, however, was a protectorate with a reigning royal house; complete independence was in prospect (it would come in 1956), and Moroccan sensibilities had to be respected. For Moroccan Tirailleurs the terms of service and retirement were notably good, and there was greater overt respect for the native officers and senior NCOs, whose career prospects were better than in the Algerian regiments. The Franco-Moroccan units traced a tenuous lineage to the old pre-French Shereefian army of the sultanate, and were not seen as an alien institution imposed by a colonizer. There was never any element of conscription, and the flow of volunteers was steady; in Morocco the warrior tradition was particularly strong and French power was respected. In the Expeditionary Corps the Moroccans generally had a higher reputation for dash and reliability than the Algerians; a decline in quality towards the end of the war was due to some of the same strains as those suffered by Algerian units, aggravated by nationalist and religious outrage at France's recent exile of their sultan in the course of Morocco's struggle for independence.

THE LEAST EFFECTIVE TROOPS in the Expeditionary Corps – probably because the worst led and the worst treated – were the West Africans of the so-called *Tirailleurs Sénégalais* (in fact, recruited all over French West and Equatorial Africa). Historically these were part of the Colonial establishment rather than the Armée d'Afrique.[71] Their deployment – almost entirely in small, static garrisons, particularly in the De Lattre Line defences – aggravated their worst qualities while denying them the chance to show what they were capable of. These volunteers from a mixture of forest and savannah tribes arrived in Indochina as if to a strange planet. They suffered physically and psychologically from the unfamiliar climate and terrain, particularly in the wetlands; they were not only prone to all kinds of diseases, but mentally vulnerable to a wide range of terrifying superstitions inflamed by these alien surroundings. They found Asian culture baffling, and were themselves regarded with horror by local populations. Alcoholism, mental breakdown, and consequent murders and suicides were all too common. Despite these handicaps the African Tirailleurs were generally cheerful and willing when they first arrived, ambitious to return home with the honoured status of victorious warriors. As time passed they came to resent their very low pay, their lowest priority for every necessity and reward, and their treatment – not so much by French officers as by the low-quality NCOs too often assigned to them. The shortage of cadres throughout the CEFEO brought into the Senegalese battalions some Frenchmen who should never have been posted to African units and whose dull-witted racism did great damage. The Africans looked to their French leaders to take the place of their village chiefs as paternal figures answering their worries, caring for their own and their distant families' needs, and providing brave and encouraging leadership in battle. What they often got instead was neglect, the most menial and demoralizing tasks, stupid abuse, and abysmal examples of slack soldiering; consequently very few re-enlisted for a second tour. Although their fieldcraft was generally poor, on the rare occasions when they met the People's Army in pitched battle a few African units did distinguish themselves.[72]

ON 19 MAY 1953, LIEUTENANT General Henri Navarre, the latest Frenchman to shoulder command of this uniquely diverse army, stepped from a Constellation airliner into the stunning heat and humidity of Saigon's Tan Son Nhut airfield, and gazed down at the waiting crowd of white, khaki and gold as the trumpets sang out the first thrilling notes of 'La Marseillaise', and the guard of honour crashed to attention.

6. The Air-Conditioned General

*'I have a very strong feeling of responsibility
for Dien Bien Phu. I have no feeling of guilt.'*
General Henri Navarre, *interviewed by Pierre Charpy, 1963*

IN MAY 1953, HENRI NAVARRE was two months short of his 55th birthday. The son of a professor of Greek at Toulouse University, he had entered St Cyr at the age of 18 in 1916, and survived 15 months with a dragoon unit on the Western Front before the Armistice. After occupation duties in Germany he served for two years in Syria with a Spahi regiment. He graduated from staff college, then spent four years in Morocco during the last campaigns of pacification.

The next stage in his career was perhaps the key to it: he spent eight years with French Army Intelligence, working on the German desk from 1937 to 1940. He served most of World War II in intelligence work, some of it in France and some as chief of General Weygand's Second Bureau in Algeria. However, the last six months of the war did take him to the front lines, as commander of the 3rd Moroccan Spahis – a light armoured regiment – during the final advance into Germany. Colonel Navarre rose quickly thereafter, and commands alternated with senior staff appointments; he was an aide to General Koenig, French C-in-C Germany, and was chief-of-staff to General Juin when the latter was NATO commander of Allied Forces Central Europe. Command of a territorial division in Algeria in 1948–9 brought him his brigadier general's stars, and in 1950 he was given the 5th Armoured Division in Germany.

Lieutenant General Navarre thus had no experience of Asian warfare when he accepted the post of Commander-in-Chief Far East in May 1953, but he brought shining qualities to the job. He was intellectually brilliant, with an air of calm authority; an exacting superior, he nevertheless left men alone to get on with their duties once he had defined them. He was energetic and fearless in travelling back and forth between the remotest corners of Indochina to see conditions for himself and, once briefed to his satisfaction, was quick to take decisions. His NATO experience had fitted him for dealing with political cant and evasion, and his long background in intelligence for sifting information and keeping his own counsel. Indeed, the habit of secrecy was ingrained; Navarre kept himself socially aloof, moving only in the smallest circle of loyal colleagues. Navarre neither projected nor attracted warmth – the more passionate Major General Cogny would later refer to him as a freezing, 'air-conditioned general' and as a disconcerting 'electronic computer'. He was accused of approaching military operations as an intellectual exercise, and of calculating acceptable levels of casualties with cold logic. This quality is certainly unattractive; but it has been shared by many of history's most successful generals, including Napoleon.

Navarre was trim and elegant, his silver hair brushed back above dark brows, hooded eyes and high cheekbones. He had a quality of stillness; he was said to be a cat lover, and the word 'feline' keeps cropping up in descriptions by those who met him.[1]

THE MISSION DEFINED TO Navarre when he was appointed to the Indochina command on 7 May 1953 by Prime Minister René Mayer was not to destroy the Viet Minh or to win the war: it was to create the conditions for an 'honourable way out' – to achieve a position of military advantage that would allow France to negotiate a favourable peace. The political class was suffering one of its more feverish episodes, and the Mayer cabinet fell just three days after Navarre's arrival in Saigon. For more than a month thereafter France was without a government as several candidates manoeuvred for power. One who came close to securing the necessary votes was Pierre Mendès-France, who attracted support from the centre as well as the Left. Although Mendès-France's appeal lay in his perceived competence to tackle the country's chronic financial problems, one passage in an interview published in *L'Express* in the third week of May was also significant: 'A fact that we have long been forced to admit is that a military victory [in Indochina] is impossible. The only possible outcome will thus be by negotiation. Our situation for negotiating was better last year than it is now; and it is probably better now than it will be next year...'[2]

After nearly seven years of war a pessimistic lassitude among the French people and their politicians – one can hardly speak of leaders – was unsurprising. Parliamentary voting patterns were manipulated for short-term party and personal advantage, but there was an overall feeling that the war could no longer be regarded in primitive terms of defending the national interest. The political class was tipping in favour of a negotiated ceasefire; some parties and factions turned their faces against formal negotiations, yet all but the most diehard nationalists accepted that these must eventually take place. The government faced many other urgent challenges: inflamed relations with Morocco and Tunisia, and financial, industrial and social turmoil at home. Six months later, on the very day of the reoccupation of Dien Bien Phu, a poll published in *Le Monde* showed only 15 per cent supporting vigorous French pursuit of the war. The rest favoured either a negotiated withdrawal or a shifting of the burden to the United Nations, or simply declared their lack of interest in the Indochina problem. Within the armed forces there were many who yearned for an end to the huge expense and to what they saw as a distraction from their proper tasks – this was a time of heated arguments over a future European Defence Community.

WHILE THE FOURTH REPUBLIC was demonstrating some of its inherent vices, General Navarre shuttled between Saigon and Hanoi; he was briefed by his predecessor, formally taking over from General Salan on 28 May. The 'Généchef' did not retain many of Salan's senior subordinates. Before leaving France he had picked General Fernand Gambiez as his chief-of-staff and Air Force General Pierre Bodet as his deputy. On arrival, one of his first appointments was the commander of Land Forces North Vietnam (FTNV). This was the most important command in Indochina; FTNV had some 119,000 French and Vietnamese troops, plus most of the French naval and air assets, in order to confront the People's Army main force. The general holding this command would in theory enjoy a wide freedom to conduct his own operations within the strategic guidelines laid down by General Navarre; and the choice fell on the 48-year-old Brigadier General René Cogny, who put up another star when he accepted.

In every army artillery officers are regarded by the Foot and Horse as slightly worrying intellectuals, and Cogny had a particularly distinguished academic record. The son of a police sergeant, he had won a scholarship to high school, leaving the prestigious École Polytechnique not only as an engineering graduate but holding a diploma in political science and a doctorate in law. This brawny 6ft 4in gunner was far from being simply a book soldier, however; captured by the Wehrmacht in June 1940, he had escaped in May 1941 and made his way south to join the Armistice Army – and the underground ORA resistance. In 1943 Major Cogny was arrested by the Gestapo and thrown into Fresnes prison for interrogation; it was six months before they spat him out into Buchenwald concentration camp. After another 18 months in Buchenwald and Dora he emerged in April 1945 as a tottering skeleton; eight years later his massive frame had filled out again, but he walked with a stick for the rest of his life.

When his health recovered he was given an infantry regimental command near Paris in 1946–7; a subsequent posting to the War Ministry brought political experience, and was followed by a senior appointment on the staff of General de Lattre, with whom he travelled to Indochina in late 1950. It was said that he caught from 'King Jean' a taste for shows of military pomp (Cogny was nicknamed 'Coco the Siren' from his liking for shrilling motorcycle outriders); he certainly became familiar with the press, and was accustomed to massaging them for his notoriously indiscreet chief. After de Lattre's departure Cogny commanded one of the four territorial divisions in Tonkin, based at Hai Duong. By the time Navarre offered him FTNV he knew the Expeditionary Corps, the enemy and the Delta well; indeed, he was so utterly focused on this French heartland that he would call himself 'Delta Man'. Ruggedly handsome, outgoing and volatile, Cogny attracted affection and loyalty. He was popular with soldiers, with women, and with journalists; but beneath the charm and passion he was extremely sensitive to criticism, and he tended to brood on real or imagined injuries.[3]

ON 26 JUNE A NEW FRENCH cabinet headed by the elderly, decent, but pedestrian Joseph Laniel was finally sworn in; it retained several members of the previous administration, and its collective view of France's war aims was unchanged.[4] Laniel's posture on Indochina was an assurance of working towards a general negotiated peace in Asia while still avoiding any commitment to direct overtures to the Viet Minh. Voices on both sides of the Atlantic were arguing a connection – through Communist Chinese sponsorship – between Indochina and Korea, where the Pan Mun Jon talks had resumed in early April 1953 after an interruption (and where a long-awaited armistice would be signed on 27 July). Some saw this as a hopeful portent for Indochina, and suggested that the death of Stalin in March offered hope that the USSR would not raise impossible obstacles to any general settlement.

WHILE GOVERNMENT OPINION remained divided over what political concessions to offer them, there was general agreement over the absolute necessity of rallying the Associated States of Vietnam, Cambodia and Laos into an effective alliance. On 3 July 1953 the Laniel government made a solemn declaration of intent, whose main architect seems to have been Paul Reynaud, the deputy prime minister with special responsibility for Indochinese affairs. Stripped of its sonorous courtesies about brotherhood-in-arms and maturing institutions, the declaration stated that the time had come to adjust the 1949 treaties defining the status of the Associated States within the French Union, in order to 'perfect their independence and sovereignty'. Those 'competencies' which France had up to now retained to herself under 'the perilous circumstances of war' were now to be transferred to the Associated States. Meetings would take place with each of the three governments to address questions in the economic, financial, judicial, military and political spheres, in order to safeguard the legitimate interests of each of the parties (with a clear implication that those of France herself would carry considerable weight).

It was transparent that in return for full sovereignty, France was demanding that the Associated States make the war against Communist subversion their own, as responsible members of a mutual defence alliance rather than merely as recipients of French military protection.[5] There must be real movement towards reversing the French and Indochinese roles, until the Associated States were fighting the Communists with French help rather than the other way round. Apart from eventually reducing France's crippling military commitment to a sustainable level, and giving her some answer to international accusations of waging a colonialist war, this scenario offered some hope of separating nationalist from outright Communist sentiment among the Indochinese populations.

THIS TRANSFORMATION WAS also central to the proposals which the C-in-C Far East presented to the joint chiefs-of-staff and the National Defence Committee in Paris in late July; these outlined what would become known as the 'Navarre Plan'. Two separate documents were addressed to the chiefs-of-staff, one devoted to the conduct of operations in 1953–4, the other to the development of the Armée Nationale Vietnamienne.[6] These were broadly endorsed by the chiefs-of-staff before Navarre presented his plan in person to a meeting of the National Defence Committee on 24 July. The core of Navarre's appreciation was that a major increase in the size and effectiveness of the ANV, to take over the static defence and local security roles within both the 'secure' and the 'disputed' zones, offered the only chance of concentrating French troops into a sufficiently enlarged *corps de bataille* to take on the People's Army main force in Tonkin.

The ultimate objective was to recapture at least some of the Viet Bac, but this could not be contemplated until a much larger mobile reserve had been created. It would take time to erode the advantage which the People's Army enjoyed, in having actually or potentially seven 10,000-man main force divisions (five infantry, one artillery, and units equivalent to at least a sixth infantry division in South Vietnam) which were almost wholly free of the territorial security burden distracting the CEFEO. The French strategic reserve – currently standing at seven 3,000-man motorized brigades (Groupes Mobiles), and two smaller airborne brigades (Groupes Aéroportés) – could not be built up to the strength necessary for major offensive operations before summer 1954 at the earliest. This could only be achieved by augmenting the ANV; diverting existing French manpower from post garrisons to the mobile reserve; and despatching new reinforcements from France and North Africa. Given these assets, and provided there was no major escalation of Chinese supplies to the People's Army, Navarre envisaged his mobile reserve achieving a balance with Giap's Chu Luc by spring 1954, and surpassing it by the end of the year. Until then a defensive strategy in Tonkin was unavoidable; the Expeditionary

Corps simply had to hang on grimly and hope – in the expressive French phrase – to 'weather the cape' of winter 1953/4. General Navarre did not minimize the probable hardships of that winter voyage.

The C-in-C quantified the necessary enlargement of the ANV as from about 165,000 to 217,000 men during 1954; this would allow not only the replacement of most French garrisons, but also the formation of several purely Vietnamese Groupes Mobiles – at first to acquire the necessary combat skills, and later to take over the task of providing 'fire brigades' within their zones of responsibility. In time the deployment of major ANV units in a joint offensive, to gain confidence and prestige, would be necessary.[7] The 'Vietnamization' of garrisons within the disputed zones would free – in the Delta alone – more than 82,000 French and French-led troops.[8] From France, Navarre requested 12 additional battalions and significant increases in Air Force and Navy strengths. These demands were thoroughly unwelcome to the Army and Air Force chiefs-of-staff, Generals Blanc and Léchères, who were concerned with the difficult tasks of fulfilling French obligations to NATO and the needs of garrisoning North Africa. (Navarre would not receive more than part of his requested reinforcements; it would be late November before he received a formal reply from the National Defence Committee, which told him to do the best he could with what they could spare him.)[9]

Turning to operational questions, Navarre naturally reserved his decisions until the enemy's intentions for the coming campaign season became clearer. The situation in South Vietnam was essentially a stable guerrilla war; although the enemy's regional units in Cochinchina and southern Annam maintained liaison with the Viet Bac there seemed to be no prospect of movement by large regular units south to this front. The threats against which Navarre must defend were a major campaign of infiltration in the Delta, probably co-ordinated with assaults on its perimeter; a repetition of the previous winter's thrust through the Thai Highlands into northern Laos; or a westwards strike from Annam into Middle Laos, to reach the alluring prize of Savannakhet on the Mekong river – the great water highway which gave access to the whole peninsula (*see Map 1*). The question of the C-in-C's exact responsibility for defending Laos seems to have brought out the instinctive evasiveness of his political masters during the meeting of 24 July.

It was clear that the Viet Minh had a long-term aim of invading Laos and planting a Communist regime there; they regarded the whole Indochinese peninsula as potentially a single military and political battlefield. Their early attempts to infiltrate had met with little success among the devoutly Buddhist Laotians, upon whom the French colonial yoke rested lightly. In a step towards overcoming this hostility the old Indochinese Communist Party had ostensibly split into three national parties in 1951, the Laotian branch taking the name Pathet Lao; their guerrillas ('issarak'), led by Prince Souvanouvong, were active mainly in the north-eastern province of Sam Neua. The French attitude towards limited Communist infiltration of Laos had become less relaxed in winter 1952/3 when Giap launched his full-scale invasion of the north through the Thai Highlands, which had left behind regional units and busy political teams when it eventually receded in May.

The political argument for defending Laos was obvious. Although it had only been a unified kingdom since August 1946, King Sisavong Vong was a loyal ally of France; he had been the first Indochinese leader to sign the French Union treaty in July 1949, and gave a prompt and positive response to the declaration of 3 July 1953. How such a defence could be conducted in practice, however, was much less clear. With a scattered and generally pacifist population of only about 3 million, there was little prospect of Laos raising an effective army herself. The road network was even less developed than in highland Tonkin, and the terrain made military movements extremely difficult. The French chiefs-of-staff advised that only the most limited forces be put in place to oppose any Viet Minh invasion, and urged that such a threat should be countered mainly at the diplomatic level.

At the meeting of 24 July, General Navarre expressed grave doubt about his ability to defend Laos. He judged that the loss of its northern region would have political rather than immediately disastrous military consequences, although that would not be true for long. No government decision seems to have been taken; Marc Jacquet, Secretary of State for Relations with the Associated States, would later claim that the choice of whether or not he should defend Laos was left up to Navarre.[10] In the absence of specific instructions from Paris, Navarre and Commissioner General Maurice Dejean took for granted France's responsibility to defend her fellow signatory of the new treaty of association (which would be formally concluded on 22 October 1953). On 6 February 1954, when People's Army Division 308 was apparently menacing Luang Prabang for a second time, Defence Minister René Pleven – on the point of flying out to Indochina – would tell the National Defence Committee that Navarre was specifically asking if his mission still included the defence of Laos. Although opinions at this meeting seem to have been expressed in deliberately vague terms, it was apparently agreed that priority should be given to safeguarding the French troops rather than Laos.[11] The withdrawal of Division 308 by the time he arrived saved Pleven from giving Navarre any clear strategic instructions.

This abject evasion of cabinet responsibility was typical of France's failure, over nearly seven years, to construct a coherent political machinery for directing the Indochina War; one might logically look to a 'National Defence Committee' for such direction, but one would be disappointed. While Prime Minister Laniel held ultimate authority, he had delegated to his deputy Paul Reynaud responsibility for Indochinese affairs. The Finance Ministry were necessarily involved in the budgetary decisions, and the War Ministry in most aspects of the Expeditionary Corps; yet as already mentioned in Chapter 5, its logistic support, for what was still officially 'the maintenance of order in colonial territories', was the responsibility of the Military Affairs Directorate of the Ministry for Overseas Affairs. Marc Jacquet was the minister responsible for relations with the three Associated States, but Foreign Minister Georges Bidault for all other international aspects. No effective co-ordination was achieved at cabinet level until the creation of a Restricted War Committee – which did not take place until 11 March 1954, just two days before the first attack on Dien Bien Phu.[12]

Within Indochina the official remit of Commissioner General Dejean included responsibility for defence and security, and as military commander General Navarre was subordinate to Dejean. The Commissioner General's theoretical authority was, of course, ignored in practice; he kept the C-in-C informed on political matters, leaving the general to formulate strategy while he himself wrestled with the innumerable problems of the Associated States – for which he was answerable, in his turn, to Secretary Jacquet in Paris. This whole tortuous web of responsibilities offered politicians and bureaucrats limitless opportunities to distance themselves from the consequences of their mistakes or indecision.

RETURNING FROM PARIS TO Saigon in August, General Navarre could not wait for a response to his request for reinforcements before beginning to put his plan into effect. He had to plan alternative deployments based on constantly changing assessments of where Giap would strike his main blow when the monsoon ended. During the next three months a constant flow of intelligence – aerial photographs, radio intercepts, captured documents, prisoner interrogations, the reports of agents and counter-guerrilla units – would be compared, collated and balanced in Hanoi and Saigon, and almost from one week to the next different staff officers claimed to discern patterns which threatened first the Delta, then the High Region, then the Delta once more. Protecting the Delta was an absolute necessity, and Major General Cogny, commander of Land Forces North Vietnam, was hypnotized by this responsibility. In 1951 he had worked closely with General de Lattre; he had spent his whole Indochina service in the Delta, and he and his staff had inherited his old chief's preoccupation. They regarded the base areas of Hanoi and Haiphong, linked by the frequently ambushed 50-mile corridor of RC5 and the railway, as France's essential redoubt, through which much of the Expeditionary Corps would have to retreat in the case of ultimate disaster. At a less apocalyptic level, this had long been René Cogny's turf: he had fought the Viet Minh for this ground for two years, and he was determined not to lose it now through a dissipation of effort towards what he regarded as secondary missions. Finally, it could not be ignored that most journalists were based in Hanoi, and that any setback in the Delta would receive more alarming coverage than events elsewhere.

The nature of the threat had changed since the heroic winter season of 1950/1, when de Lattre had beaten off Giap's first overconfident offensive. The People's Army would never repeat that particular mistake; but they did not have to launch massed frontal attacks in order to inflict heavy damage in the Delta. The 250 forts of the De Lattre Line formed an illusory barrier through whose gaps dispersed parties of Viet Minh infiltrated every night – not only messengers, political teams and supply columns, but whole combat units. In rotation, elements of the regular divisions were sent into the Delta to co-operate with the independent units – Regiments 42, 46 and 50 – which were permanently dispersed between the thousands of scattered villages of Lien Khu 3. In the autumn and early winter of 1952 several battalions from Divisions 304 and 320 had slipped in to cause havoc while many French units were absent on Operation 'Lorraine'; and it could happen again this winter. The hundreds of security posts were as scattered as the villages, and there was a limit to the amount of territory that the Groupes Mobiles could cover at any one time. A widely dispersed campaign of night-time attacks and ambushes on many small forts and roads simultaneously – especially if co-ordinated with large-scale assaults on selected sections of the De Lattre Line – could soon slice off whole groups of villages, cutting roads, dislocating the French reaction forces, and isolating new areas for attack.[13]

The rainy summer saw the usual indecisive security operations inside the Delta; but in late August and early September intelligence reported that no fewer than four of Giap's regular divisions were hovering just two or three days' march outside the northern and southern reaches of the De Lattre Line. It was known that their summer training programme had included much practice for assaults on fortified positions; that resupply depots were being filled both north and south of the Delta, and that routes between the two fronts were being improved. Perhaps most alarming, given the Viet Minh's known pattern of lengthy reconnaissance of the target of any planned attack, the Second Bureau believed that they had identified scout units from Divisions 304, 308 and 312 inside the Delta, as well as a special general staff reconnaissance battalion. It was suggested that November was the time of greatest danger: in previous years enemy regulars had infiltrated during that month to help collect the Delta's rice harvest, which was a vital factor in the logistics of the Chu Luc.

In the face of this threat General Cogny was insistent that he should be given all available reserves to defend the Delta, and Navarre's refusal led to heated exchanges. The C-in-C judged that the wider game was still too uncertain for him to gamble on a single number. One broad principle on which both could agree – though each had his own ideas about its translation into practice – was that it was desirable to take the initiative. Navarre strongly believed that fighting People's Army regulars outside the Delta, before they could complete their preparations for an attack, would be of much more benefit to Cogny's defence than simply deploying more brigades inside to wait passively on Giap's convenience. Despite his natural instinct to take the war to the enemy, however, such *chevauchées* had a very mixed history in Tonkin, and Navarre had no wish to fall into the trap which had sprung shut on General de Lattre in November 1951 and very nearly on General Salan a year later. He believed neither in trying to capture and hold ground at the end of vulnerable cross-country corridors, as at Hoa Binh; nor in risking precious brigades on deep raids for questionable returns, as in Operation Lorraine.

While the Généchef had been absent in France he had allowed Cogny to launch a limited airborne hit-and-run operation against reported People's Army stores depots around Lang Son at the junction of RC4 and RC1 (*see Map 5*). This Operation 'Hirondelle', meticulously planned to minimize the risk of the paratroopers getting cut off, went ahead on 17 July. Some 2,000 men jumped: Major Bigeard's 6th Colonial and Captain Tourret's 8th Shock Battalion close to the caves where the caches were reported, and Major Bloch's 2nd Foreign behind them at Loc Binh on RC4, to hold open their route of retreat. The Colonial paratroopers met only light opposition from regional troops; they photographed the Chinese weapons and ammunition crates, laid their demolition charges and got out, force marching down RC4 towards Groupe Mobile 5 which was punching up from the coast to meet them. Three days later they were back at their barracks, tired but triumphant.

This brief raid to destroy a fairly modest amount of Viet Minh matériel was of no strategic value; but it demonstrated that if an airborne *coup de main* was planned with sufficient secrecy, it could get men on to the ground in Viet Minh country before the People's Army could react. The spies busy around the Hanoi barracks and airfields could always tell when *les bérets rouges* were about to launch a big operation. Apart from the hints overheard in the local cafés and brothels, the drain on the air transport fleet meant that civilian DC-3s had to be requisitioned, and the Dakotas in airline livery were highly noticeable as they practised formation flying in shaky 'vics' of three. But 'Hirondelle' proved that the specific destination of even a jump by a full brigade could not necessarily be reported to the Viet Minh in time to throw a noose around the objective. In November 1953 this would be a significant factor.

IN LATE SUMMER 1953, NAVARRE was planning his own kind of operation to relieve the pressure outside the Delta – in the jargon of the day, to 'aerate' it; but while he did so he had to keep one eye on the Laotian border country. The old practice of trying to hold a scattering of small permanent posts weakly garrisoned by low-quality sector troops was completely discredited; Navarre would counter any invasion by planting in its path a small number of strategically located 'air–ground bases' on the model of Na San, held for only limited periods by strong units from the general reserve.

Some commentators have made heavy weather of the distinction between the offensive and defensive tasks of the *base aéro-terrestre*; but the whole point of the concept was that it embraced both, with the emphasis shifting as circumstances dictated. General Cogny would claim – much later – that his initial enthusiasm for the plan to reoccupy Dien Bien Phu had been on the understanding that it would be little more than a lightly held temporary base for local guerrilla and patrol activity, rather than a defensive jungle fortress; but the documentary record does not support him.[14]

The idea of the 'airhead' was to establish, around a suitable airstrip, what was essentially a logistic base, like those created in March 1944 behind Japanese lines in Burma by General Wingate's British and Indian 'Chindit' brigades and Colonel Cochrane's USAAF Air Commando. Depending upon enemy reactions, this 'hedgehog', sustained by its air bridge and protected by strong defences including artillery, could play the simultaneous roles of a refuge and resupply base, and a jumping-off point for offensive operations against the enemy's lines of communication. Following the defensive battle at Na San the paratroopers based there had made several deep penetrations through the Thai Highlands in winter 1952/3. In a region where the number of practical routes for large-scale military movement was strictly limited, an advance in strength by the People's Army regulars could in theory be channelled and harassed by a pattern of such bases. Air transport would allow them to be inserted, 'inflated', 'deflated', or withdrawn as the campaign evolved. In the fog of war all operation plans are necessarily provisional; but the flexibility of this concept seems to have seduced some officers, who overestimated the freedom that it would give them to react creatively to later events.

An objection to the theory later voiced by Cogny's chief-of-staff, the paratrooper Colonel Dominique Bastiani, has made something of a career for itself through its neat quotability: 'In this country you cannot bar [the enemy from taking] a direction. That is a European notion without value here. The Viet goes where he likes – he's proved that well enough in the Delta.' Giap's advance into Laos in April obviously supported this view; but the *base aéro-terrestre* was never imagined to be a Maginot Line – its supposed strength lay in its versatility, and the danger it thus posed if left in the enemy's rear. General Cogny, in an interview with a correspondent of the United Press agency in January 1954, would declare: 'I look forward to a Viet Minh assault. Certainly, their artillery will be bothersome for a while, but we will silence it. Since Giap is unable to move into Laos in force through fear of an obstacle rising up behind him, he finds himself forced to attack.'[15]

In the hills of the High Region the number of potential sites for such bases was limited (*see Map 6*). The French still held the Thai tribal capital of Lai Chau, but its dramatic topography made it difficult both to reinforce on a large scale and to defend. Na San was still garrisoned with Thai and Algerian troops; but continuing Viet Minh works to improve their road access from Yen Bai to the Son La plateau threatened to outflank it, and the weak surveillance force to which the People's Army presence around Na San had now been reduced raised the question of who was actually tying down whom. Better placed than either of these was Dien Bien Phu on Route Provinciale 41 close to the Laotian border, where an old airstrip had good potential for improvement. The valley of the Nam Youm in which it stood had been abandoned to the Viet Minh during their November 1952 advance, but General Salan had repeatedly urged its reoccupation when circumstances permitted. Deep within Laos itself, either Luang Prabang or the Plain of Jars were possible candidates; the latter was a potentially good position, though too far south-east to protect the northern capital. Luang Prabang itself was not practical; nestling among high peaks in a little valley, its mediocre airstrip was separated from the town by an unbridged river, and to protect both would take 16 battalions, occupying crests far out from the valley floor.[16]

On balance, the best option appeared to be the withdrawal of the Na San garrison, which threatened to become irrelevant, for redeployment elsewhere; the eventual but not immediate reoccupation of Dien Bien Phu if the People's Army made determined moves towards the High Region;

and the maintenance of Lai Chau for the time being, although it would have to be evacuated if menaced. General Cogny was eager to recover the garrison from Na San; he agreed with Navarre that Lai Chau had a limited future, and that Dien Bien Phu would make a much better site.[17]

THE ESTABLISHMENT OF A stronghold in the Thai Highlands was desirable for a second reason: to provide an anchor for the Thai and Meo tribal partisans who had been operating successfully against the Viet Minh for two years. Their expansion had been promised by General Navarre to their controller, Lieutenant Colonel Roger Trinquier, as another step towards freeing up regular troops for mobile operations.

This programme of taking the war to the enemy by turning his own tactics against him had long been discussed, but was put in hand systematically only during General de Lattre's reign in 1951.[18] Organized by the Action Service of the SDECE, it planted small French teams with the tribal minorities – mainly the Nung along the Chinese frontier and the Thai and Meo astride the Laotian border. Appealing to the independent sentiments of the highlanders, who had enjoyed a tactfully unobtrusive French colonial administration, a handful of adventurous French volunteers created a veritable *maquis* to infiltrate, reconnoitre, ambush, sabotage and harass the enemy throughout the nominally Viet Minh-controlled hills. Given the blanket title Composite Airborne Commando Group (GCMA) in 1952 – retitled Composite Intervention Group (GMI) from December 1953 – these bands grew to something between 3,000 and 5,000 men in Tonkin, and claimed perhaps three times that many in the whole of Indochina.[19] Despite their light armament (mostly British World War II small arms), the partisans – with their expert knowledge of the trackless hills, and their warrior culture – achieved some remarkable results, creating genuine 'safe areas' where the writ of the Communists no longer ran, and tying down thousands of enemy troops. A few uniformed *montagnard* officers helped lead the programme; specially trained mixed-race commando teams were occasionally parachuted in to carry out specific operations, and from June 1953 selected partisans were flown out for training courses at Ty Wan on Cap St Jacques.

However, the French investment in this counter-guerrilla war was too modest and too late. It was unpopular with conventionally minded commanders, who resented its creaming-off of outstanding NCOs and some airlift capacity, but with an earlier start and greater resources it might have achieved a good deal more. The partisans had no ideological motive: Communism was a meaningless abstraction, and their energy seems to have sprung from the most basic territorial feelings.[20] Their example was potentially more dangerous for the Viet Minh than that of the regular ANV's reluctant conscripts. So seriously did the enemy take their activities that in June 1952 the Viet Minh were obliged to invite the direct support of the Chinese People's Liberation Army, which sent a division across the border into Vietnam and spent three months suppressing partisans on the right bank of the Red River around Lao Cai.[21]

This shadowy parallel war was fought without mercy by either side; heads were taken by tribesmen and Viet Minh alike, and the commissars declared the partisans and their French leaders to be 'pirates', taking prisoners only for questioning before execution. The few French personnel on the ground were men of extraordinary courage and character. Young NCOs led groups up to a thousand strong, living and fighting among the partisans for many months at a time at the mercy of fragile radio links, their only direct contact the occasional Beaver light aircraft lurching down on to a makeshift airstrip. They spoke the highlanders' languages, ate their food, shared the risks of their spartan lives and in some cases married their chieftains' daughters. Some Frenchmen adopted their silver-buttoned dark clothing and turbans in order to blend in. (The Meo, in particular, could make a striking spectacle, their pony-mounted warriors wearing massive necklaces of bar silver as well as slung Sten guns, and accompanied by the handsome white dogs for which they were renowned.) While the Frenchmen brought modern weapons and radios, they learned as much about guerrilla fieldcraft from their hosts as they taught them.

The GCMA would prove their ability to co-ordinate partisan activity with conventional operations during the French withdrawal from Na San in August 1953. Some 3,500 Meos had dominated the Long He and Co Tonh hills between Son La and Dien Bien Phu from May 1953, led by Captain Hébert and a few NCOs in territorial bands codenamed 'Colibri', 'Calamar' and 'Aiglon' (another guerrilla zone, 'Cardamome', was created in the hills north of Lai Chau, but its partisans took no part in this operation). Airlifting out the garrison of Na San, even though the base was not closely invested in August, was potentially a very risky operation. Although reduced since the winter and spring, the garrison still numbered four infantry battalions with two artillery batteries and the Legion heavy mortar company.[22] 'Disengagement under fire' is one of the most dangerous manoeuvres soldiers can attempt: if the enemy close in on a perimeter, then no matter how carefully its defenders are progressively thinned out and pulled back, there will come a point when they run the risk of the rearguard being overrun, and the bulk of the retreating force being cut down before they can escape. The principle applied just as acutely to men crowding round Dakotas on a Tonkinese airstrip as to a British battalion stumbling down a ridge on the old North-West Frontier.

The Na San airlift was set to begin on 5 August; an attempt was made to mislead the Viet Minh by leaking a rumour that two parachute battalions were coming to reinforce the base, and by landing Dakotas virtually empty – only a single company of 3 BPC was in fact flown in. On the night of 3/4 August Captain Hébert came down from the hills, drove a weak enemy force out of Son La, and cut a 12-mile stretch of RP41 between Na San and Dien Bien Phu. Son La was the rear base for the Viet Minh regiment 88, then keeping watch on Na San; elements fell back on Son La, were allowed to reoccupy it, and were then boxed up in the town by the partisans. That night some of Hébert's Meos slipped into Na San and took over the most vital blockhouses from the garrison troops, while others took up positions on dominating hills and put out long-range patrols, holding up the approach of other troops from the south. From dawn on 5 August one Dakota would land at Na San on average every six minutes, and on the 8th and 9th there would be 444 air movements (more than at Paris–Orly and Le Bourget). Bad weather caused a worrying interruption on the 10th; but the evacuation, including the families of the Thai troops – though without much of the heavy equipment – was completed on the 12th without enemy interference. This success greatly increased French confidence in the air–ground base concept; considerable doubts had hung over the withdrawal phase, and it had been feared that at least one rearguard battalion might have to stay behind and take their slim chances in the jungle with the partisans. With the value of his GCMA forces proven, Lieutenant Colonel Trinquier looked forward to their rapid expansion.[23]

IN THE SECOND HALF OF AUGUST, General Navarre was primarily concerned with the four People's Army divisions threatening the Delta, and with no signs of an enemy move towards Laos he hesitated to commit a large part of his airborne reserve to an immediate reoccupation of Dien Bien Phu.[24] During September it was reported that a regular regiment from Division 316 were engaged against the GCMA partisans in the valley of the Song river between Na San and Dien Bien Phu, but this gave no reason to suppose that Laos was in imminent danger. On 19 September, Navarre wrote in a general instruction that the threat to northern Laos seemed 'provisionally reduced', and that the Delta seemed likely to be the site of battle.[25] (He apparently saw no need to divert troops to help the *maquis* on the upper Song Ma; after all, they were simply fulfilling their planned purpose of dying usefully in the place of Frenchmen.) Concentrating his reserves to 'aerate' the southern Delta defences, Navarre planned a major thrust to disable one of Giap's regular formations: Division 320, which was reported to be lying up in the forests near Phu Nho Quan, 12½ miles outside the De Lattre Line.

This Operation 'Mouette' was launched on 15 October. It was not a raid, but an attempt to fix and destroy a major element of the Chu Luc before Giap could deploy it as part of a co-ordinated offensive against the Delta. The immediate objective was a crossroads at Lai Cac on the Viet Minh route towards Thanh Hoa in the South Delta Base, but Navarre masked his intentions. French intelligence officers were perfectly well aware that the CEFEO were under constant scrutiny, and often used this knowledge to plant disinformation; on this occasion they successfully deceived the enemy with false indications of a planned landing on the coast near Thanh Hoa. Seven Groupes Mobiles were committed to the various phases of 'Mouette', alongside amphibious and riverine units, paratroopers of Groupe Aéroporté 1, and Chaffee tanks of the Groupements Blindés. A temporary forward base at Lai Cac was established by Group A, composed of GMs 2 and 3 under command of a dashing cavalry officer, Colonel Christian de Castries. Together with the paratroop General Gilles and 8th Parachute Shock Battalion, and part of Colonel Vanuxem's Group B, they stood off heavy attacks on the night of 18 October. Over the following two weeks both Groups (including GM 4 and the paratroopers of II/1 RCP) pushed a series of columns out through the surrounding territory; there were a number of severe engagements – particularly on 2 November at Yen Mong – with units of Division 320, which suffered significant losses. The French claimed more than 1,000 enemy killed, 2,500 wounded, and 182 captured along with 500 infantry weapons, plus 100 bazookas and recoilless guns and 3,000 mines.[26] If accurate, these figures represented about one-third of the division destroyed. The final French withdrawal inside the Delta (Operation 'Goeland') took place on the night of 6/7 November, without major interference. French losses totalled 113 killed including seven officers, 505 wounded including 22 officers, and 151 missing (about 40 per cent of the casualties were Vietnamese).

Despite this apparent success, however, General Navarre drew one pessimistic lesson: the inefficiency of the bulk of the Expeditionary Corps' infantry by late 1953. He would later declare before General Catroux's commission of inquiry into Dien Bien Phu that 'a few parachute battalions remained the only units of superior value. Frankly, "Mouette" demonstrated – in the opinion of Generals Cogny, Gilles and myself – that if we sent our infantry, given its present quality, outside the (six-mile) radius within which it enjoyed artillery support, then if it encountered Viet Minh infantry, it would be beaten.' This discouraging judgement naturally increased the appeal of entrenched camps such as the *bases aéroterrestres*: well dug in behind fixed defences and strongly supported by artillery and aircraft, the infantry were still confident of repulsing massed attacks, as they had proved at Na San. General Navarre's deposition continued: 'We were absolutely convinced of our superiority in defensive fortified positions; that was considered in Indochina as a dogma, and we were absolutely persuaded that a fortified position could hold out easily at odds of three to four against. The Viet Minh had never taken important fortified positions – I do not speak here of surprise night attacks on posts...'.[27]

WHILE OPERATION 'MOUETTE' was still in progress, the volume of intelligence reports drawing Navarre's attention back to the High Region suddenly increased. Division 316 specialized in highland operations; now the Second Bureau staffs of both Navarre and Cogny were learning from radio intercepts that other units of this formation were being warned for a march to join its Regiment 176 on the upper reaches of the Song Ma, and that these could arrive between 7 and 11 December. The pace of work on the access roads to the forward depot at Tuan Giao was increasing, and a regular engineer battalion had been identified; enemy reconnaissance patrols were active around Lai Chau; and a new infantry battalion was operating between Lao Cai and Lai Chau (*see Map 7*). This might be simply a major effort to wipe out the GCMA counter-guerrillas, but it looked like something more ambitious. General Navarre did not dare to wait until the strategic murk cleared; Na San had been abandoned, Lai Chau was indefensible against People's Army regulars, and as part of his overall strategy he could no longer put off installing his new air–ground base to protect Laos. Setting up a functioning airfield and defences solid enough to stand off attacks by a regular division would take time, and during the second half of October the practicalities were studied by the staffs in Saigon and Hanoi. The need to dust off this particular contingency plan, among many, came as no surprise; such an operation had been discussed in principle since the early summer, and mentioned in passing both at the 24 July meeting of the National Defence Committee and in Directive No. 563 issued the following day by Navarre's staff in Saigon.[28]

On 2 November 1953 the C-in-C's Directive No. 852 ordered preparations for an airborne assault to reoccupy Dien Bien Phu. The operation was to be put in hand by FTNV, and carried out at some date between 15 and 20 November, so as to secure the objective while the elements of Regiments 176 and 148 already in the area were absorbed in hunting down partisans, and before the rest of Division 316 could arrive.[29] Another factor was the economic value of the Nam Youm valley around Dien Bien Phu, the most important cultivated area in the High Region; its annual rice harvest of 2,000 tons could feed two People's Army divisions for a month, and must be denied them. The valley was also an important collection centre for the Meos' opium, with a yearly value to the Viet Minh of about 1 million US dollars – money to be spent on the open market to meet the needs that China could not satisfy, such as an assured flow of ammunition and spare parts for captured US weapons.[30]

NAVARRE'S DEPUTY CHIEF-OF-STAFF/Operations, Colonel Louis Berteil, conveyed the C-in-C's orders to General Cogny in Hanoi on 3 November. In the retrospective mythology of Dien Bien Phu, Berteil was assigned the role of a conceited and short-sighted military bureaucrat; DBP was said to stand for *'du Berteil pur'* – 'typical Berteil'. This may be an unjust judgement on an officer whose lofty and pompous manner made him unpopular. It stretches belief that a cool perfectionist such as Navarre would have tolerated in this post of close trust a man who was not intelligent and hard working. Berteil also had personal experience of combat: in Italy he had led a Tirailleur battalion with some distinction, and in Tonkin both GM 7 and (admittedly at a quiet period) the Na San garrison. He was certainly an enthusiast for the air–ground base idea; but it seems unconvincing that he would have been able to insert into the plan for Dien Bien Phu any fatal weakness which was not already innate. No documents earlier than this date raising objections to the idea of reoccupying Dien Bien Phu have been found in the archives.[31]

On 4 November, General Cogny's three principal subordinates at Land Forces North Vietnam put their opinions in writing: Colonel Bastiani, FTNV Chief-of-Staff; Lieutenant Colonel Denef, Deputy Chief-of-Staff/Operations; and Lieutenant Colonel Multrier, Deputy Chief-of-Staff/Logistics. These memoranda from 'Delta Man's' loyal lieutenants predictably recorded the writers' worries about the defence of the Delta if the bulk of the airborne reserves and a major airlift effort were devoted to the creation of another air–ground base in the High Region. At this date FTNV were preoccupied by the threat of at least a three-division offensive hanging over the Delta; Operation 'Mouette' was raging astride their southern ramparts, similar external spoiling operations were under discussion, and the fate of Laos was far from the forefront of their minds. There is some confusion over whether the inherent long-term risks of the operation – as opposed to its utility – were even mentioned in these documents. Colonel Bastiani, in the context of resisting the diversion of resources away from the Delta, did make the remark that 'the Viet goes where he likes', as quoted above; one source suggests that he voiced a rather starker warning about the risks, but does so in slightly ambiguous terms.[32]

Cogny sent his response to Navarre on 6 November. He recognized the political importance of a base in the Thai country, and the strategic importance of defending Laos; said that he and his staff naturally attached higher priority to the defence of the Delta; and added that if troops were going to be diverted from FTNV to Dien Bien Phu then he was going to need reinforcements to safeguard the Delta. On 9 November he repeated this last request.[33]

On 11 November, General Cogny and his staff held another meeting with Colonel Berteil to discuss what had now been christened Operation 'Castor'. Also present were the commander of Airborne Troops Indochina, Brigadier General Jean Gilles; and from the Air Force, Brigadier General Jean Dechaux, commander of Tactical Air Group/North (GATAC/Nord), and Colonel Jean-Louis Nicot, commanding the Indochina air transport group (S/GMMTA). The authors of the memoranda mentioned above now repeated their arguments in person.

The planning for 'Castor' was complicated by the fact that the paratroopers would be expected to seize a 'hot DZ' – a drop zone close to and perhaps occupied by enemy troops. It was known that the village of Muong Thanh (the Thai name for Dien Bien Phu) was the base for Battalion 910 of Independent Regiment 148; and that a second regular battalion was also somewhere near by. The plan for 'Castor' evolved over time, but crystallized into jumps by two full airborne brigades. Two parachute battalions of Lieutenant Colonel Fourcade's GAP 1 would be dropped directly on Dien Bien Phu, to be joined a few hours later by the third, together with 75mm recoilless guns of the Marching Battalion, 35th Parachute Light Artillery Regiment (GM/35 RALP), and sappers of the 17th Parachute Engineer Battalion (17 BGP) to repair the airstrip. The following day all three battalions of Lieutenant Colonel Langlais' GAP 2 would be dropped to reinforce the lodgement.

The gruff, one-eyed General Gilles, designated to command 'Castor' in person because of his experience gained at Na San, put his views to the meeting bluntly. He was no more enthusiastic about dropping his men down the enemy's throat than any paratrooper would be. Even assuming that the first lift went smoothly, and surprise and overwhelming numbers secured the DZ, he still had vivid recollections of the enemy night attack on Na San on 23 November 1952, before that base was properly organized – the attack which only Captain Letestu's heroic légionnaires had kept off the airfield. He had no intention of risking his paras without artillery support and time to dig in before the enemy reacted in force. It was agreed that the timetable for getting the airstrip into condition to receive heavy equipment should be halved from the ten or 12 days originally envisaged, and that greater priority should be given to flying in field artillery. (The following day, Berteil would give Navarre's assurance to Gilles that he and one parachute brigade would be flown out as soon as conventional infantry – envisaged at this date as including the withdrawn Lai Chau garrison – could replace them. Gilles was always suspicious of operations which might misuse his paratroopers, whose sheer quality tempted commanders to commit them to missions beyond the realistic grasp of such light troops.)

General Dechaux's main concern was the safety of his transport planes. He also warned that providing fighter support would be difficult, because without belly-tanks the realistic limit of action for F8F Bearcats flying from the Delta bases was Tuan Giao; the only aircraft which could operate beyond that were B-26 bombers and some Navy types. The weather would also be a major factor, since it was often completely different over the Delta airfields and the High Region; morning fog in the hills was a constant problem, and the Army must not expect uninterrupted air support.[34] General Dechaux's contributions were not entirely negative, however: he suggested that if a few fighters could be based on the Plain of Jars and (when the airstrip was reopened) at Dien Bien Phu itself, a modest number of sorties could still be flown when bad weather closed in the Delta bases but not the High Region.

Colonel Berteil had calculated, on the basis of experience at Na San, that the daily need for supplies flown in by the C-47 Dakota transports would be 80 tons. Colonel Nicot admitted that this figure was within the limits of possibility for his three squadrons, provided that no other impossible calls were made upon them at the same time. He emphasized that this figure must not be increased; and he, too, insisted on the importance of protecting the airstrip from enemy fire.

In short, this meeting seems to have been a typical pre-operation conference between the representatives of various commands confronting a challenging mission together, each trying to ensure that his own people had the most straightforward possible task and the greatest possible insurance. No one raised any objections to the broad concept of the plan, only to the narrow details of its execution. On 12 November General Cogny gave Generals Dechaux and Gilles their orders. One longs for the brutal clarity insisted upon by the British Army: Bernard Fall quotes Cogny's instruction that the defensive system should be 'designed to ensure the protection of the airfield to the exclusion of any system aimed at creating a belt of strongpoints around the airfield'.[35] Without a more detailed context it seems unsafe to build upon this odd phrasing (as Fall seems to do) an argument for Cogny's envisaging only a light and temporary occupation at this stage. The commander of FTNV was perfectly aware that the bulk of Division 316 was on the move towards the High Region, and that a major purpose of the airhead was to shield Laos from invasion; he could hardly have doubted that Dien Bien Phu was indeed intended to be a repeat of Na San.

On the same day Cogny gave Colonel Berteil a letter for Navarre summarizing his conclusions from the meeting, and outlining the preparations then in hand. He repeated FTNV's lack of enthusiasm for Operation 'Castor', while recognizing the political and strategic aspects at Navarre's level of responsibility, 'which are... of no relevance to the territory which you have confided to me'. Nevertheless, he assured the C-in-C that 'opinions founded upon often partial views will in no case interfere with the intellectual discipline of all concerned'. Perhaps we may assume that this serpentine Gallicism translates as, 'We have our own reasons for disliking this operation, but you can count on us to do a professional job.' Once more, the probable fate – as opposed to the utility – of 'Castor' went unquestioned by a commander who had supported it some months earlier. This was despite the fact that by 1953 many senior officers had acquired a defensive habit of committing to paper their reservations about, or their exaggerated requirements for, operations that they were ordered to carry out, in the apparent hope of warding off any blame in the case of failure. On 13 November, General Cogny sent Lieutenant Colonel Trancart, commanding at Lai Chau, instructions to plan for withdrawal upon receipt of further orders, but to keep this secret.[36] On 14 November, Navarre issued instructions to Cogny for Operation 'Castor'; these summarized his political and strategic aims, and the immediate purpose of establishing an airhead to form a land link with forces in northern Laos and to provide support for Lai Chau until the latter was evacuated. These orders were also sent to Colonel Boucher de Crèvecoeur, commander of Land Forces Laos (FTL); Dien Bien Phu lay only eight miles north of the Laotian border, and FTL were ordered to move four battalions north in order to liaise with the future air–ground base. De Crèvecoeur had only 11 battalions at his disposal on this very secondary front, of which nine were Laotian units of delicate morale; they were divided between Muong Sai, Luang Prabang and the Plain of Jars (*see Map 8*). He could only hope to push columns north up the Nam Pak and Nam Ou rivers as far as the lost fort of Muong Khoua at their confluence, and would have to eject the Viet Minh lurking in that area before a link with Dien Bien Phu could be attempted. The terrain made for desperately slow movement, and it would be 3 December before the Na San veteran Major Vaudrey recaptured Muong Khoua; even then his rear was still threatened from Muong Ngoi further south in the eastern valley, which FTL troops would not retake until 9 December.[37]

IN HANOI ON 17 NOVEMBER, General Navarre held a briefing in carefully vague terms for Commissioner General Dejean, the visiting Secretary Jacquet, and the Vietnamese Prime Minister, Nguyen Van Tam.[38] An hour later he chaired a final meeting for senior staff, at which he asked for opinions. 'Castor's' tactical and technical weaknesses were pointed out once more by Generals Gilles and Dechaux, and by Brigadier General René Masson, General Cogny's deputy at FTNV. Hanoi could hardly pretend now that the troop levels involved in 'Castor' would put the defence of the Delta in serious doubt; since the memoranda of 4 November, Operation 'Mouette' had reduced the threat from the south considerably, and radio intelligence reported that Viet Minh scout units had been ordered to pull out of the Delta and return to their divisional bases. Neither Dechaux nor Nicot questioned the possibility of maintaining the air bridge, though they rehearsed once again their concerns about the weather, the distance of 185 miles from the Delta bases, the need for a fireproof defensive perimeter on the ground, and the strain on the air transport fleet. On this last point, General Navarre had already authorized General Lauzin, commanding Far East Air Forces (FAEO), to requisition civilian aircraft to ease the pressure during the insertion phase of 'Castor'.[39]

General Gilles was still unhappy about the 'hot DZ': his men would be scattered during the drop, unable to regroup or get their heavy weapons into action quickly. If the rumoured second enemy battalion arrived fast things could get very serious; indeed, they could become disastrous, if other regional battalions turned up within 48 hours before his paras had a chance to entrench themselves. These doubts were slightly soothed by intelligence reports that Battalion 910 was certainly at Dien Bien Phu, but dispersed, and that other units were between 20 and 50 miles from the valley; only three companies were in a position to move rapidly to the aid of Battalion 910. The meeting was – once more – entirely concerned with the 'how' of the airborne insertion and its immediate risks, rather than with 'whether or not'; no predictions of long-term doom are recorded as having been made by anyone present. The conclusion was that 'Castor' had to go in fast, and under conditions of maximum security.[40]

General Navarre confirmed his orders: 'Castor' was set for Friday 20 November if weather conditions permitted. For security reasons General Gilles' detailed operation orders would not be distributed or the aircrew briefed until the morning of the 20th. Many of the aircraft and paratroopers would only return from operations in the southern part of the Delta shortly before the 20th; they would be gathered at Hanoi–Gia Lam and Hanoi–Bach Mai on the pretext of a forthcoming operation in the northern sector, and in some cases the mechanics would have to work through the night while the paratroopers snatched a few hours' sleep. Only battalion commanders would be given the plan on the evening of the 19th; the soldiers would be told just to take warm clothing for a highland operation. Pilots and paratroopers alike were used to being briefed at very short notice. Everyone knew his job; they had been fighting this war for a long time.

PART TWO

7. Castor

'At Na San I spent six months of my life like a rat. Use me in the open air.'
General Gilles *to General Cogny, 22 November 1953*

THE IMPORTANCE OF DIEN BIEN Phu can be seen from the briefest glance at an air navigation chart of North Vietnam. The monotonous brown crumples of the Thai Highlands are broken by only three tiny slivers of green: Nghia Lo, Na San, and Dien Bien Phu. South of that valley the brown is unbroken until the eye reaches the green ivy-leaf shape of the Plain of Jars nearly 120 miles into Laos.

Dien Bien Phu is not a true Vietnamese place name but a designation; it means 'big frontier administrative centre'. About a third of the way down a valley roughly 11 miles long, a central village straddled the Nam Youm river; this was actually known by the Thai name of Muong Thanh.[1] Route Provinciale 41 from Tuan Giao hooked in from the north-east, flanking the river, but this 'highway' had never been motorable south of the valley. An old horse track named after the 19th-century pioneer Auguste Pavie came in from due north, leading from Lai Chau. Dien Bien Phu was the focus of up to a hundred hamlets with a total population of 10,000–15,000; most of the tiny villages scattered over the valley floor and the surrounding slopes were occupied by the Black Thai clan (*see Map 9*). With the highest rainfall of any valley in these hills – averaging 59in in the wet season, about half again the figure for the other highland valleys – it was the most important rice-growing area in the High Region. It had also been a mainstay of the French government's opium monopoly, and thus the station for a junior district officer, whose bungalow mouldered quietly among a handful of other brick buildings on the eastern hill which would soon become notorious as 'Eliane 2'. The mosaics of aerial photos provided by the Bearcats of Captain Moulin's 80th Overseas Reconnaissance Flight (EROM 80) showed Muong Thanh itself to be a neat little township of more than a hundred substantial timber houses laid out along dirt streets on both banks of the river. Built on head-high platforms raised on sturdy tree-trunk pillars, under steep-pitched roofs thatched with rice straw, they were surrounded by vegetable plots and pens where chickens and black pigs scratched, and shaded by many trees including thick copses of mango, breadfruit, citrus and areca palm.[2] Since the withdrawal of the French a year previously the villagers had found themselves hosts to a People's Army regular battalion – at first from Divisions 312 and 316, but since May from the more familiar Independent Regiment 148, raised in the High Region. The people of the valley had long ago learned to be pragmatists, and concerned themselves with their crops and water buffaloes. They were unexcited when, at about 6.30am on the dim early morning of Friday 20 November 1953, they heard the hum of an aircraft circling slowly above the mist.

THE C-47 (NO. 76356 'SEIGNEURS-INDIA' from Transport Squadron 2/64) was equipped as a radio command post, and among its passengers were three generals: Gilles of the paratroopers, Dechaux of the Air Force's Tactical Air Group/North, and the C-in-C's deputy General Bodet, to whom General Navarre had delegated the last-minute judgement of the weather conditions. The aircraft circled slowly above the *crachin*; and at around 7am the rising sun began to burn off the fog. About 20 minutes later one of the operators radioed Hanoi: 'Castor' was 'execute'.

The tired aircrews of Transport Squadrons 2/62 'Franche-Comté', 1/64 'Béarn' and 2/64 'Anjou' had been roused at 5am, and were briefed by Colonel Nicot 50 minutes later. The paratroopers would ride to battle in the Douglas C-47, the military version of the DC-3 airliner of the 1930s, known to the French by its wartime British name of 'Dakota'. Nicot's transport command was shorter of trained crews than of aircraft, even though the USA provided the machines and France the men to fly them. A week before 'Castor', Nicot had had only 52 crews for a fleet of 69 Dakotas. Today – by drafting in a few spare crews from a new fourth squadron who were waiting for their aircraft to arrive, and by leading the mission himself with some of his staff – Nicot (call-sign 'Texas') would put 65 Dakotas into the air. These were enough to lift only two parachute battalions, with 24 soldiers and a jump-master crammed into each aircraft. Major Fourcaut of GT 2/62 ('Yellow Leader') would lead 33 planes from Hanoi–Bach Mai – 23 from his own squadron and ten from Major Clayeux's GT 2/64. Major Martinet of GT 1/64 ('Red Leader') would lead 32 from Hanoi–Gia Lam – 24 of his own, plus eight from GT 2/64. The distance from Hanoi to Dien Bien Phu was 185 miles; after a lengthy forming-up process above the airfields, flying time was estimated at just over 1 hour 16 minutes, at an altitude of 2,900ft.

The paratroopers had been up since 4am, were briefed at 6am and, loaded with their gear, began to waddle up the steps into the aircraft half an hour later. They had been sitting uncomfortably in the rudimentary canvas and tubing seats along the fuselage sides for an hour and a half before the engines began to start up, some of them catching up on their sleep, their faces resting on crossed arms on top of their chest-mounted reserve packs. Most gazed into space, withdrawn into their private thoughts: no matter how seasoned, a soldier is never unaffected by pre-battle fears, and the need to make a parachute jump before even entering battle multiplies them. The junior officers and NCOs at least had practical concerns to occupy their minds. The newest men were tormented by the fear of showing fear and of letting down their comrades. The experienced soldiers at the peak of readiness felt a jumpy impatience to get into action, some of them even a confident hunger to get stuck into the enemy. The oldest hands, coming close to the bottom of their well of courage, were haunted by images of mutilation or helpless abandonment. It is probable that none were actually afraid of death itself – soldiers have more immediate terrors to cope with.[3]

Battle would at least free them from the physical discomfort of the gear which confined them. They wore American steel helmets, and assorted sweaters under baggy camouflage jump uniforms with bulging pockets. They were trussed helplessly by the heavy web strapping of main and reserve parachute packs on back and chest, and burdened by a bulging knapsack on the front of their thighs, a folding-butt sub-machine gun or rifle, and extra packs of ammunition for the machine guns and mortars.

The ideal paratrooper is not a tall man; even so, the slightly built Vietnamese who made up a proportion of these battalions looked as if they were being swallowed alive by their mass of impedimenta. For this vital first wave, who had to seize the drop zones against active resistance and hold them for the later lifts, General Gilles had selected his best units: Major Marcel Bigeard's 6th Colonial Parachute Battalion (6 BPC), 651 strong today, from the barracks at Bach Mai; and Major Jean Bréchignac's 2nd Battalion, 1st Parachute Light Infantry Regiment (II/1 RCP), which embarked 569 all ranks at Gia Lam.

The Parachute Chasseurs of II/1 RCP moved to a rhythm set by 'Brèche', their commander for nearly a year: modest, solid, utterly professional. Despite its title the unit was no different in composition from the Colonials; raised at Quimper, it had sailed from Marseille in November 1952 as the 10th Colonial Parachute Battalion, and had been retitled on arrival in Saigon purely for traditional reasons, to keep the name of Free France's original parachute regiment alive in Indochina. Since then it had been employed in the High Region around Na San and on the Plain of Jars, and in late August had dropped on the 'street without joy' north of Hue for Operation 'Camargue'. In September the unit had been back in Laos, operating from the air–ground base at Seno; and in October it had fought in Navarre's Operation 'Mouette' around Lai Cac, returning to Hanoi only a few days before 'Castor'. This battalion did not segregate its Vietnamese into separate companies but spread them throughout the unit.

In 6th Colonial the Vietnamese were grouped separately in 3rd and 4th Companies. The paras of the 'Bataillon Bigeard' took their tone very consciously from their hard-driving leader; in an army not noted for training runs they cultivated physical fitness, and a slightly monkish air of austerity – the Legion para officer Erwan Bergot would call them 'puritans, who would die clean-shaven'.[4] The 37-year-old Marcel Bigeard was tall, hawk-nosed, with an Oriental droop to his eyelids; he radiated confidence, healthy energy, and a fierce battlefield intelligence. He led from the front but never carried a personal weapon, believing that his job was to lead his men to exactly where they needed to be, and then to co-ordinate the combat over field radios. Bigeard was one of those rare officers with an instinctive eye for ground: when he looked at a map he did not just absorb facts, he saw a three-dimensional landscape with men moving across it in various alternative patterns. Most valuably of all, he had a knack for putting himself inside the heads of the enemy and asking himself what he would do in their place.

The son of a poor railwayman from Toul, Bigeard had been an infantry warrant officer when he went into the bag in June 1940. He escaped and managed to reach Gaullist forces in West Africa; and in summer 1944 he was parachuted into the Ariège to work with the *maquis*. He ended the war with the temporary rank of major (although he had never officially passed for lieutenant); with several decorations, including Britain's prestigious Distinguished Service Order; and with the radio call-sign by which he was known ever afterwards – 'Bruno'. He had landed in Saigon in 1945 as a captain in the 23rd Colonial Infantry, and the following year volunteered for service in the High Region with Thai auxiliaries. He returned for his second tour in October 1948 as a paratroop company commander with 3 BCCP, and by 1950 he was back in the High Region leading the 3rd Thai Battalion. For his third tour, from July 1952, Major Bigeard brought out to Tonkin his newly raised 6 BPC. Since then he had led them at Tu Le in October 1952 (after which he enraged some contemporaries by putting every one of his surviving men up for a Croix de Guerre); from Na San into the hills around Co Noi during the exploitation phase of December–January; and in Operation 'Hirondelle', the hit-and-run jump over Lang Son. Bigeard was opinionated, rather humourless, and ambitious for his own and his unit's reputation – photographers were always welcome at 6 BPC, provided they could keep up. Some contemporaries found him hard to tolerate, but nobody ever questioned that he was a born combat leader who knew the Thai Highlands as well as any man in the Expeditionary Corps.

AT 8.15AM COLONEL NICOT'S plane led the first 'vic' of three C-47s down the runway, the others following at 20-second intervals, and by 9.15am all had closed up in formation and were droning west on a heading of 280° for the High Region. By the time the yellow-nosed Dakotas of GT 2/62, carrying Bigeard's men and 52 sappers from the 17th Parachute Engineers, arrived over the Nam Youm valley at around 10.30am the air was clearing, but a low ceiling of broken clouds would complicate the drop. Stray shafts of sunlight gilded the grey paddy-fields, where tiny figures could be seen scattering. The smoke from the village fires rose

238 THE LAST VALLEY

almost vertically – there would be no bone-breaking crosswind on the drop zones. 'Yellow Leader' circled in from the south and began his run for drop zone 'Natacha' at 2,500ft, throttling back to 105mph for the jump.

'Stand up!... Hook up!' – the ungainly figures lurched against one another on the unsteady aluminium deck, snapping the spring hooks of their webbing static lines over the cable running down the fuselage roof and jerking to make sure they were secure. *'Equipment check!'* – each man focused on the parachute pack of the man in front, particularly the vital static line attachment and its pull-out panel, now held closed round the edges by breakable pack-thread laced through brass eyelets. *'Red light!'* – the icy blast and deafening noise through the opened cargo door were disorienting, but the wide-eyed paratroopers were in the grip of their training. *'Green light!'* – at 10.35am the buzzers sounded, and the jump-masters slapped the stick leaders on the shoulder and screamed *'GO!'* – for a couple of seconds the door was suddenly empty until the next laden figure shuffled frantically forward, and the next, and the next... The growing bundles of static lines whipped and slapped from the top corners of the doors, and in the Dakotas' wake the first lines of canopies blossomed and swayed. The American T7 parachutes were 'canopy first' rigs; their vicious opening shock left 6 BPC little time to worry about the quality of the packing.[5]

Drop zone Natacha was about 200yds north-west of the village, and the thick clumps of trees around the houses made it easy to spot; about 300yds east of it lay the edge of the old earth airstrip (*see Map 9*). Natacha was a rectangle 1,300yds from south to north by 450yds wide, apparently surfaced mostly with rice-fields lying fallow, divided by overgrown dykes; a small stream crossed it, and there was thick brush at the southern end. About half a mile to the south-east of the village lay the northern margin of drop zone 'Simone', of roughly similar size, where the red-nosed aircraft of GT 1/64 were due to drop Bréchignac's II/1 RCP simultaneously, along with an advance party from the 35th Parachute Light Artillery group (but not the guns and crews, which were coming with the second lift). The 6th Colonial were to take the village; II/1 Chasseurs were to locate and protect Lieutenant Colonel Alain Fourcade's Groupe Aéroporté 1 command team, who would jump with them, and then seal off any enemy flight from the village towards the south of the valley.

The first hint that the briefing might have been out of date came during the 2½ minutes that it took 6 BPC to rock gently down to earth: some of the little figures below were running not away from, but towards the drop zone, and were firing into the sky. The paratroopers' eyes were drawn down towards them by a chilling sight – one of their comrades plunging to his death beneath the flapping muddle of both his main and reserve canopies – as they heard the crack of bullets splitting the air around them. But a man falling at about 16ft a second is not an easy target; it was a fluke shot which blew out the brains of the battalion's medical officer Captain Raymond on this, his first combat jump.

French intelligence had reported that the headquarters of Independent Regiment 148 was in Muong Thanh; the paras hoped to capture the officers and documents of this first-class regular unit, veterans of Na San and cornerstone of the whole Viet Minh implantation in the High Region. Three of its four battalions – 900, 920 and 930 – were absent; the RHQ and Battalion 910 were at home. What the briefing had not mentioned was the simultaneous presence, resting and training in this peaceful valley, of Heavy Weapons Company 226 from Battalion 920, and a detached company from Artillery Regiment 675, both with mortars and recoilless guns; and a regular infantry company from Regiment 48, Division 320. On this brightening morning two People's Army companies were out on a training exercise near the airstrip, and some of their heavy weapons were set up ready for action on DZ Natacha.

When the last few seconds of their half-mile fall confronted the paratroopers with the 'green rush' that ends all such journeys, they discovered that the aerial photographs had also been deceptive: much of smooth-looking Natacha turned out to be covered with tall grass which reduced visibility to a few feet. The plan had called for Lieutenant de Wilde's 4th Company to cover the drop zone from interference from the north, and Trapp's 2nd Company the west side, while Le Page's 1st and Magnillat's 3rd, with Bigeard's HQ and Lieutenant Allaire's mortars, faced the village from the south-east corner of the drop zone. This plan had optimistically presupposed a tight drop, quick regrouping, and no enemy interference; but 6 BPC were now scattered along a corridor nearly two miles long, with Lieutenant de Wilde far to the north at the foot of the wooded hill which would later be christened 'Gabrielle'. Le Page was close to the village, Magnillat somewhere up the airstrip, but Trapp was wandering far off to the north-west, and Bigeard's command and support group was half a mile too far west.

After the bruisingly hard landings, inescapable with 1940s vintage parachutes, Bigeard's troopers, alone or in small muddled groups, struggled free of their harness, unpacked their weapons and tried to find their leaders and companies. Some blundered into face-to-face encounters with the enemy in thick cover, and hesitated fatally – Viet Minh corpses were later found to be wearing capes made from old camouflage parachute material. At Bach Mai airfield some dangerous fool had muddled up the issue of the company-coloured smoke grenades that served as beacons for regrouping. Heavy mortar fire fell among one group who, looking for radio aerials above the grass, mistakenly rallied on what turned out to be the flag-bedecked recent grave of a Thai chieftain. Bigeard fumed over the radio net, but 13 of the sets had been smashed on landing, and the mortars and their ammunition were lost. Facing a force potentially equal in number and stronger in heavy weapons, Bigeard and his men would have to improvise under fire and would need every ounce of their initiative and aggression to survive. One blessing was that as soon as the collapsing parachutes sank below the tall grass, the Viet Minh were as confused as the French by this lethal game of hide-and-seek.

Obeying the old rule of moving back in the opposite direction to the course of the aircraft, the paras began to coalesce, each chance-found group fighting its own series of small battles until they could find an ad hoc company to link up with. By about 11am 'Bruno' had most of his 1st Company under his hand at the south of the drop zone and had engaged the enemy in the village. The 4th Company were still struggling south towards the sound of gunfire; the 3rd were fighting on the airstrip; Hervé Trapp reported his 2nd Company two-thirds intact in a screen off to the west, but taking flank fire from machine guns and recoilless guns. (Trapp's appeal for mortar support brought just three rounds that Allaire had managed to find for his single tube – the lieutenant was not amused when a poker-faced private advised him to let it cool down now.) By 12.15pm a circling spotter plane was acting as a radio relay, and when Bigeard at last managed to call in air strikes by B-26 Invaders of Bomber Squadron 1/25 'Tunisie' some enemy positions were silenced.

Le Page's 1st Company met fierce resistance from the north-east of the village, where Battalion 910's HQ company had turned houses into machine-gun redoubts and fought to cover the retreat southwards of Regiment 148's command staff. Some time after 3pm an attempt to flank these positions by 3rd Company became pinned down under heavy fire. More air strikes were called in, and the centre of the village went up in flames. Bigeard moved his command post forward with Le Page, into the northern houses. The battalion's 81mm mortar teams at last found some ammunition and brought down fire on to the southern escape route. The 1st and 3rd Companies fought their way forwards, house by house and alley by alley. The village was falling; but despite air strikes, the prize of the enemy regimental staff had slipped away to the south-west.

Down beyond DZ Simone on the east bank of the river, Bréchignac's Chasseurs never got into action. They had been dropped late; the low ceiling had caused delays as Dakotas circled for their chance to go in below the clouds, and some crews were inexperienced at this sort of formation flying. The battalion had been dropped south of the drop zone and were badly scattered amid paddies and scrub-covered hillocks. Even at the accepted rate of five seconds per man out the door, it still took a stick of 24 paratroopers two minutes to leave a Dakota; and at 105mph, that was long enough to spread them over three miles. It took II/1 RCP some time to link up with the GAP 1 brigade staff – Lieutenant Colonel Fourcade was not thanked for having pressed ahead on his own. Further handicapped by unreliable radio links with 6th Colonial, the Chasseurs did not manage to lay a solid cordon across the thick belt of trees and undergrowth down the banks of the river, through which many of the enemy escaped to the south. On finally coming up to the village the frustrated II/1 RCP were diverted east, and took up a position on the low, terraced hill that was crowned by the 'governor's house'.

When the Dakotas returned to Hanoi, 41 of them were refuelled and at 11.30am began loading up for the second lift. Thirty carried GAP 1's third and strongest unit, Major Jean Souquet's 1st Colonial Parachute Battalion; of its total of 911 men (of whom 413 were Vietnamese), 722 all ranks were available for this jump. Since arriving for their second tour in June 1953, 1st Colonial had fought on the Plain of Jars, and had returned to Hanoi only the previous day from operations in the south of the Delta. Seven of the other Dakotas carried Major Millot and the rest of his group from the 35th Parachute Light Artillery, with their eight 75mm 'recoil-less rifles' and 40 rounds per gun. This was a very new unit, formed at Tarbes from conscripts who had volunteered for a two-year overseas tour, plus some Colonials, and virtually untrained Vietnamese drafted in when they reached Hanoi. They had been in Vietnam for less than two weeks, and still lacked much necessary equipment, especially maps; a thick bundle of aerial photos had simply been thrust into one officer's hands at the foot of the aircraft steps. The rest of the lift would be taken up by the medics of the 1st Parachute Surgical Team (1 ACP).

The second wave jumped at about 3.50pm over Natacha, by now held firmly by Bigeard's 6 BPC; they landed without incident, and some of the recoilless guns were able to get off a few shots in support of 1 BPC as they mopped up the last resistance north-west of the village. At about 4pm two H-19 helicopters came flipping in from Lai Chau, carrying one HF and two VHF radio transmitters, which would allow Air Force Captain Pierre Lorillon's forward control team to make contact with the aircraft and the parachute units; when they left they took the seriously wounded with them. Considering those first few moments on Natacha, the bill was modest. From the 2,650 men on the ground by nightfall, 15 had been killed, ten of them from Bigeard's battalion; 34 were wounded, and 13 suffered jump injuries. The Viet Minh had left behind 115 uniformed dead and four wounded prisoners; about 40 small arms, 20,000 rounds of ammunition, and the documents of Battalion 910 and Company 226 were recovered as well. They had also abandoned some of the officers' black leather jackets, which would be appreciated that night by shivering radio operators working late on the link with Hanoi. It was hardly – in the words of Lieutenant Robin, an historically minded gunner – the sack of the Summer Palace.[6]

Cargo aircraft began dropping the first heavy stores over drop zone 'Octavie' on the west bank south-west of the village; at this early stage men and cargo would be dropped on separate DZs for safety. Some pilots from GT 2/62 were also tasked with precautionary night missions, circling the valley with loads of 'Luciole' ('Firefly') parachute flares in case the enemy mounted an immediate counter-attack. As evening approached the sky filled with clouds, heralding the mist that would cover the valley all night; as soon as the sun went down the temperature sank to a teeth-chattering 41°F. Drained by their day, the paratroopers tried to dig in as best they could with their small folding entrenching spades; 1st Colonial took the northern quadrant, II/1 Chasseurs the east, and 6th Colonial the south and west. There were few lights and an almost complete silence; all fires had to be extinguished before dark.

The paras had stuffed the pockets of their baggy camouflage uniforms with ammunition, field dressings, cigarettes, chocolate and perhaps a flask of rum. Once he had got rid of his burden of machine-gun or mortar ammunition, then apart from his personal weapon, belt pouches and canteen, a rifleman carried only an entrenching tool and his 'airborne musette'. This was a modestly sized webbing pack into which he stuffed a rainproofed tent section/poncho, blanket, mosquito net, change of underwear, washing kit, two combat rations and as many grenades as he could lay his hands on. For the first few nights and misty mornings the paras shivered in their shallow foxholes wrapped in everything they had, including bundled nylon parachute canopies to keep off the damp. Their meals came from combat ration packs: supper that night was hastily warmed soup, canned tuna or sardines, hard biscuits, malt tablets or mints, and strong coffee – usually fortified with a slug from the pocket flask. The only other food available, as they dug in and carried out their first local patrols, would be rice and the occasional chicken or pig 'liberated' or bartered from the Thai villagers who filtered back once the shooting stopped. More substantial rations would be dropped a few days later, though taking a low priority behind picks, shovels, wheelbarrows and barbed wire; the early drops would feature a depressingly unvarying diet   of canned *mouton aux haricots*.[7]

IN SAIGON, GENERAL NAVARRE spent much of 20 November with a high-ranking visitor from Paris. Admiral Cabanier was the assistant general secretary to the National Defence Committee, and he brought unwelcome news: the formal decision of the committee's meeting on 13 November was that Navarre could not have more than a part of the reinforcements he had requested in July as a necessary condition for executing his strategic plans. The reason given was a general overstretching of all French military resources in Europe, North Africa and Indochina; the details were addressed in writing, but there was another question that the cabinet had thought best to convey by a senior officer in person. Two months after the conclusion of the Korean armistice, sinologists had become excited by a Radio Beijing broadcast on 14 September suggesting that a negotiated armistice in Indochina, too, was not impossible – the first ever hint of Chinese willingness to compromise in South-East Asia.[8] Did Navarre believe that the CEFEO had achieved a military balance that was relatively good enough to make negotiations with the Viet Minh desirable?

In July, at the government's instruction, the C-in-C had presented a medium-term plan carefully costed in terms of the military means required to pursue it; with some evasion over those means, the government had encouraged him to proceed with its execution; now, four months later, when he was fully committed, the means were being reduced and he was being asked if it was all really necessary after all. A general of Navarre's experience cannot have been surprised by these reminders of the highly perishable nature of political resolve – politicians operate on far shorter timescales than generals must. Navarre told Cabanier that he certainly did not think the moment opportune: it would be months before the results of the winter campaign season could be judged. The Viet Minh's intentions were still obscure; and the central question of the potential of the Vietnamese National Army would not be tested until Navarre's planned operations in Annam began in January. To make tentative political advances to the Viet Minh at this stage would merely encourage them to redouble their military effort.[9]

AT 8AM THE NEXT MORNING, 21 November, the first battalion of GAP 2 was dropped over the valley. The Legion's 1st Foreign Parachute Battalion (1 BEP) jumped with 653 all ranks, of whom 336 were Vietnamese, and were directed to the hillocks to the north which would later become strongpoint 'Anne-Marie 1 and 2'.

The decision in 1948 to form two Foreign Legion parachute battalions had been controversial. Both the Legion and the Airborne Troops cultivated a fiercely exclusive *esprit de corps*; and the speed and agility that were central to the role of the paratroop units were not felt to be natural to the Legion, who were more *genre rouleau compresseur* – 'steamroller types'. Such doubts had evaporated with experience, and 1 and 2 BEP, formed in North Africa, had disembarked at Haiphong and Saigon in November 1948 and February 1949 respectively. Most of the original officers were from the Metropolitan or Colonial paras; a number of the rankers were former World War II paratroopers with combat experience in several armies, and a high proportion had already completed a first Indochina tour with infantry or mechanized units. For nearly two years 1 BEP operated effectively all over Tonkin before, in mid September 1950, Major Segrétain's battalion had jumped at That Khe on RC4 in reaction to the fall of nearby Dong Khe to the People's Army (*see Map 4*). From 1 October they had spearheaded 'Bayard', the column led by Lieutenant Colonel Le Page up RC4 to meet Lieutenant Colonel Charton's garrison withdrawing from Cao Bang. In a disastrous series of engagements with overwhelming enemy forces the battalion was ambushed, broken up, driven into the hills and finally annihilated; the largest group of survivors to find their way out of the jungle numbered 29 men, led by Captain Jeanpierre.[10]

The unit was rebuilt in March 1951 with drafts from North Africa formed around a spine provided by 2 BEP; it was back in action that month, and in the years since had proved itself worthy of its predecessors. The légionnaire-paras saw a lot of action during the Hoa Binh campaign, jumped over Phu Doan in Operation 'Lorraine', helped defend Na San, and in the past year had been flown all over Indochina. They came to Dien Bien Phu from the frustrating Operation 'Brochet' around Nam Dinh and the Bamboo Canal in the southern Delta, which by 11 October had cost the unit 96 casualties for an enemy body count of ten. Major Maurice Guiraud was a solid officer of the old Legion type, backed by some outstanding company commanders. The Legion liked its small comforts, and the style of the battalion was not so self-denying as 6 BPC; it was said of them that while just as quick to throw themselves into desperate combats, the légionnaires would get up earlier than anyone else to make sure they had their hot coffee before they got themselves killed.[11]

With 1 BEP came the operation commander, the 49-year-old General Gilles, who was determined to see the ground for himself at the earliest opportunity; as always, he removed his glass eye and tucked it into a pocket of his jump smock before leaping out into the buffeting slipstream with the other members of his Airborne Divisional Command Element. His landing was uneventful, and he bundled up his canopy and lugged it off the DZ like any private. The GAP 2 brigade commander, Lieutenant Colonel Pierre Langlais, was not so lucky; he broke his left ankle on the drop zone – one of five such almost inevitable casualties – and had to be flown out again the next day on a light aircraft, furious, and cursing with his usual freedom; he was afraid that he would miss the whole operation.[12]

That afternoon at 1.05pm the next lift arrived: 8 BPC dropped on Natacha, 656 strong, and moved into the central area. Raised at Hanoi in February 1951 as the 8th Colonial, this battalion too had seen a relentless round of operations in Tonkin (their battle honours included heavy fighting on RC6 during the withdrawal from Hoa Binh in February 1952). That September the then commander of TAPI, Colonel de Bollardière, who was a supporter of the GCMA partisan programme, authorized the unit's withdrawal from the general reserve; retitled 8th Parachute Commando Group (8 GCP), it spent three months at the GCMA special warfare school on Cap St Jacques. The plan was for the battalion to operate in dispersed 'commandos' in direct support of the highland *maquis* behind enemy lines; but when General Gilles took over TAPI he demanded its return to the airborne reserve. It was back in action in Cochinchina and Annam the next spring, and in August 1953 became the 8th Parachute Shock Battalion (8 BPC) – once more a Colonial para unit conventional in everything but its title and the superior jungle-craft of many of its men.[13] Like II/1 RCP, the battalion was only just back from operations in the southern Delta against Division 320. Since January 1953 it had been commanded by Captain Pierre Tourret, formerly Major Bigeard's adjutant in 6 BPC and a veteran of Tu Le, who had thoroughly absorbed that unit's ethos. Tourret was a dark, slightly built 33-year-old with a face already lined; he was known for his scrupulous sense of duty and a warmth and care for each of his men which tormented him when they fell. A rock in battle, in private he would seek reassurance from a chaplain.

Sharing the 8th Shock's central position for the time being were the two 75mm recoilless gun batteries of GM/35 RALP, and now they had to manhandle their 175lb weapons more than a mile – the only vehicles on the ground at this point were bicycles. The gunners got some local help to carry in the 1,000 rounds – 12 tons – of ammunition parachuted on DZ Octavie that day; each individual shell weighed 26lbs, or for simple comparison, about as much as five volumes of the *Encyclopaedia Britannica*. They also had to dig themselves firing positions, always difficult for the RCLs: their low tripod mounts, manufactured for machine guns, meant that their shallow pits could give little protection, and their fierce back-blast of flame meant that they could not be fired at a steep angle.[14] The special characteristics of the recoilless guns were new to many infantry officers. The gunners' Major Millot had to explain to General Gilles – who had given him fire tasks in support of the paratroopers on the perimeter – that his flat-shooting weapons were not suitable, his men were not trained, and he was not provided with the necessary plotting apparatus to lob shells safely over the heads of friendly troops at long range. This made Gilles even more anxious to get some howitzers into the valley. He took some comfort from the arrival that day of the 1st Foreign Parachute Heavy Mortar Company (1 CEPML), made up of Legion paras led by the gunner Lieutenant Molinier transferred from GM/35 RALP. This newly raised unit had eight 120mm mortars, which were almost as effective as howitzers at shorter ranges.[15]

The day's heavy cargo drops on Octavie saw the first appearance of C-119 Packet heavy transports – 'Flying Boxcars'. These big, square-bodied, twin-engined freighters had a six-ton payload which could be delivered out of wide rear doors between the twin tail booms. At this time the French Air Force had only five in Indochina, though the USAF would lend more over the next few months. As with the C-47 Dakotas, the limiting factor was not American generosity but French aircrews. Although 15 French crews had been trained on the C-119 in Germany and the Philippines, and 15 Packets would have arrived by the end of December, by then there were still only five crews available in Indochina.

The C-119s' first load for Dien Bien Phu today was a small bulldozer and its separated blade, rigged on pallets for parachuting by two Packets. The vehicle was dropped by Captain Soulat, the senior C-119 pilot; somehow it slipped free of its harness in mid-air and fell to earth like a six-ton bomb, burying itself deep in the paddy to the admiring applause of watching soldiers. Lieutenant Magnat dropped the dozer blade safely, but it was useless by itself; it would be 23 November before Soulat successfully delivered another bulldozer and the engineers could get down to serious work on the earth airstrip, where many of the paratroopers had been toiling with their shovels. The runway had not merely been neglected: the Viet Minh had dug an estimated 1,200 holes all over it.[16]

The airspace above the valley was already the arena for a crowded aerial circus orchestrated by Captain Lorillon's forward air control team. Over the surrounding hills the combat aircraft circled and dipped – tubby Bearcat fighters, elegant B-26 attack bombers, even occasional sorties by the Navy's handful of huge four-engined Privateers. In the first two days about 190 tons of cargo were dropped by the C-47s and C-119s, including in the latter case huge ton-weight bales of barbed wire, which were dropped without parachutes; bounding wildly around the DZ after a fall of about 600ft at more than 100mph, these killed more than one unfortunate day-dreamer. Priority was given to tools and materials for work on the airfield and the first basic defensive positions, and also to ammunition in large quantities. General Gilles was everywhere, but his mind was in the hills.

BY THE MORNING OF 22 November a long enough section of the airstrip had been repaired for the first Beaver bush plane from Hanoi to bump down safely at around 10.30am. A few hours later Major Baup and Lieutenant Camoin landed in No. 106, the first of three Morane 500 spotters from Major Robert Durand's 21st Artillery Air Observation Squadron (21 GAOA), based at Lai Chau since the 18th; soon there would be an average of six of them here, acting as the garrison's eyes. The Morane 500 'Criquet' was a familiar and welcome sight in the muggy skies of Indochina. It was war booty; like the Junkers Ju52 which had been the mainstay of the transport fleet in 1945–51, it was a Luftwaffe veteran turned out on production lines that France had taken as part of her reparations in 1945. The Morane was in fact the Fieseler Fi156 *Storch*, a stalky-legged aerial insect with broad, high-shouldered wings and an angular 'greenhouse' cockpit giving excellent downwards vision. It could loiter in the air just above stalling speed; in a high headwind observers on the ground could swear that it was hanging stationary. However, it had a small engine and thus a low 'ceiling'; the Morane could not climb higher than 4,900ft above sea level at most. At Dien Bien Phu the airstrip was at 1,560ft, and some of the surrounding hills topped 3,900ft. In this relatively thin air the little spotter – loaded with two men and three radios – would thresh its way down the runway for several hundred yards before unsticking, and pilots had to search for thermals to lift them quickly to a safe altitude.

The same morning the second parachute brigade was completed when the Vietnamese National Army's 5 BPVN was dropped into the valley. This unit's French 'parent' had been the 3rd Colonial Parachute Battalion, which was disbanded in August 1953 when the *'cinquième bawouan'* was formed. The ex-3 BPC commanding officer was Major Bouvery; Frenchmen also provided 11 others of the 38 officers, 58 of the 109 senior NCOs, and 67 of the 818 corporals and privates.[17] All the company commanders were French, although Lieutenant Pham Van Phu would lead 2nd Company from January. In its brief three-month career so far the unit had seen action in Operation 'Brochet' in the southern Delta alongside 1 BEP and 1 BPC.

With the Vietnamese paras jumped Colonel Bastiani from General Cogny's staff, to relieve the load on General Gilles – whose wider responsibilities as commander of Airborne Troops Indochina still applied – although Gilles would remain in the valley until a permanent replacement commander had arrived. Beneath another canopy in the same 'stick' floated Brigitte Friang, a remarkable and uniquely respected woman reporter for the magazine *Indochine Sud-Est Asiatique*. A survivor of the wartime Resistance and Ravensbruck concentration camp, she qualified for her para wings ('bicycle badge') in Indochina and would make six combat jumps in all – a year previously she had made one of them with Bigeard's 6 BPC at Tu Le.[18]

Colonel Bastiani found Gilles buzzing around the valley on a little airborne motor-scooter; other officers had managed to scrounge pushbikes or Thai ponies. Scrub was being cleared and burned, picks and shovels rose and fell in clouds of yellow dust, wire was being strung, cook-fires were alight, and companies and platoons were slouching along the tracks – or smoking sardonically as lieutenants cursed over rudimentary maps and awkward sheafs of aerial photos. Occasionally a *crack-whooosh!* and a cloud of dust rose from the airborne gunners' position as they fired a ranging shot from an RCL; clanking and hammering echoed from the airfield where the parachute engineers were making a start on laying the first few loads of PSP – pierced steel plates. By now 4,560 men in camouflage fatigues were burrowing themselves into the hillocks around the valley, and there was still no sign of any enemy reaction.

That afternoon General Cogny arrived in person, sharing a Beaver with another load of bicycles. He found Gilles surrounded by the purposeful bustle of a successful operation, and congratulated him. Cogny was in an excellent mood; the Paris newspapers were full of excited reports fed to their correspondents by FTNV's assiduous press officers. After the briefings and introductions, General Gilles stepped aside for a private word with his towering commander, and asked when he could be relieved: he had hated being tied down at Na San, and wanted to get out of this valley and back to somewhere where he could keep track of all his para battalions. Cogny promised him a replacement in a matter of days. 'Cyclops' Gilles owed the CEFEO nothing, and the doctors said that his heart was starting to show signs of trouble; he would be back in France by early March.[19]

WHILE THE WORK ON THE airstrip continued, on 22, 23 and 24 November the paratroopers also sent strong patrols out into the hills in all directions to feel for the enemy's presence; but there were no signs of the rapid intervention feared by General Gilles. The sorties were successful in their second objective, to make contact with pro-French Thai partisan bands. However, these were not the guerrillas led from Na San by Captain Hébert's GCMA teams: many of those were already dead.

Lieutenant Colonel Trinquier's vision – nourished by what he had understood to be the outcome of discussions with Generals Navarre and Alessandri – had been that the GCMA, having proved themselves at Na San, would receive an immediate increase in resources; and that a French airborne occupation of Dien Bien Phu would be mounted while the enemy were still off-balance. Anchored on a supply base and bastion with heavy firepower and a *'dakotable'* airstrip, multiplying partisan bands could provide in their turn a valuable outer screen for scouting and ambushing the enemy's approach routes.

Whatever the basis of Trinquier's belief in Navarre's endorsement of such a plan, when he returned from Paris in August the C-in-C, as already described, had still been in two minds about the imminence of the Viet Minh threat to the Laotian border and the relative priority he should give to reoccupying Dien Bien Phu. The evidence of People's Army activity around the Delta soon drew his eyes eastwards, and over the following weeks he and Cogny committed their reserves to Operation 'Mouette'. The funds Trinquier believed he had been promised for expanding his *maquis* were instead allocated to raising 24 Thai Auxiliary Light Companies (CSLT) based on Lai Chau. Unlike Trinquier's self-sufficient and local guerrillas, led by their own chiefs and supported by their villages,

these new companies were hired, uniformed, but woefully trained imita-
tions of regular infantry under the control of Thai 'sector' command rather
than of GCMA. Captain Hébert's Meo partisans, having revealed their
potential to the enemy, were now on their own.

During late August 1953 the People's Army reacted violently to the
partisan blockade of RP41 and the valley of the Song river, which ran
parallel to and a few miles west of the highway; in these chaotic hills they
represented the only possible routes for an advance in strength into the
High Region from the south-east (*see Map 7*). On 20–21 August, Sergeant
Chief Chatel's 'Colibri' band repulsed attacks in a narrow pass by a regional
and a regular battalion. In early September soldiers from Division 316
tried once again to break through in the Song valley. Chatel switched units
to join Sergeant Chief Maljean with 'Aiglon', holding villages along the
river; meanwhile Sergeant Chief Schneider's 'Calamar' guarded the hills
separating the two axes of advance, and over at Thuan Chau on RP41
'Colibri' was now led by Sergeant Chiefs Pallot and Ansidéi. With very
occasional support from B-26 missions, the partisans managed to hold
their ground in intermittent fighting throughout September and October.

By the beginning of November strong elements of Regiment 176 had
arrived in the hills, and assembled – complete with the 120mm mortars and
recoilless guns of a heavy weapons company – for a two-pronged attack
north-westwards up both the highway and the river. The hopelessly
outgunned partisans took heavy casualties, and were forced to fall back
through the hills at the end of the first week of November, fighting stubbornly in retreat and accompanied by fleeing villagers. They had held the
Viet Minh for three months; but on 20 November – the day of the airborne
assault on Dien Bien Phu – Captain Hébert ordered his surviving guerrillas to bury their weapons and disperse to find what safety they could.

Perhaps a hundred of them chose to filter through the hills to join Hébert
at Dien Bien Phu, arriving from 28 November.[20] The French NCOs were
also advised to make for the camp, but after 22 November Hébert was
unable to raise them by radio as he made overflights in a spotter aircraft.
He learned later that Maljean and Ansidéi had been captured near Thuan
Chau (astonishingly, they would survive Viet Minh captivity). Chatel and
Schneider, choosing to make for familiar territory around Lai Chau, were
also caught; their captors hanged them. The fifth NCO, Pallot, was never

heard of again.[21] By the first day of Operation 'Castor', the *maquis* which Trinquier had hoped to develop until it could challenge the Viet Minh's freedom to operate north of Dien Bien Phu had been fatally weakened – and with it one of the ostensible justifications for the airborne operation.[22]

THE TWIN OPERATION TO 'CASTOR' had been born on 13 November when General Cogny had issued secret orders to prepare the evacuation of Lai Chau, some 50 miles north of Dien Bien Phu. The capital of the French-sponsored Thai Federation headed by the elderly chief Deo Van Long, this little town had been isolated for two years. Now threatened by People's Army Independent Regiment 148 and Regiment 176 from Division 316, Lai Chau was overlooked at the bottom of a deep, narrow gorge that would allow enemy machine guns to fire downwards at planes using the airstrip. It was indefensible against even a modest attack; and since a failed attempt to defend it would send out the worst possible signal, it had long been decided to withdraw Lieutenant Colonel Trancart's garrison, and transfer the nominal seat of the Thai Federation to a reoccupied Dien Bien Phu. Operation 'Pollux' had two parallel aspects: the air evacuation of Deo Van Long's government and the French regular troops via Dien Bien Phu; and the cross-country withdrawal of the Thai auxiliary units and associated guerrilla bands – the latter were expected to remain active in the hills between the two positions. The first phase went fairly smoothly; preparations for the second seem to have been hurried and optimistic.[23]

On 23 November, the fourth day of 'Castor', General Gilles sent Bréchignac's II/1 RCP north up the Pavie Track to meet a first battalion-strong column from Lai Chau; Brigitte Friang accompanied them. These 700 men were led by Reserve Captain Bordier, Deo Van Long's Eurasian son-in-law; they had left Lai Chau as early as 15 November, and had encountered several ambushes as they slogged along the rudimentary track through steep hills for a week and more. Nevertheless, they had fought their way through in reasonably good order, and met up with the paratroopers at Ban Na Ten some five miles north of Dien Bien Phu. The next day they marched into the camp to join the garrison, with flags flying (French and Thai – not Vietnamese), led by their officers riding mountain ponies.[24]

LATE ON THE MORNING OF 25 November, just six days after Bigeard's first paratroopers had jumped over Natacha, Captain Hentgès' Dakota from GT 2/62 rolled to a safe halt on the cleared and filled airstrip amid clouds of orange-ochre dust. From this moment Dien Bien Phu was an operational airbase, codenamed 'Torri Rouge' by the Air Force. From the makeshift control tower built from a dismantled village house a permanent detachment of Air Force personnel, equipped with VHF and MF radio beacons and a full suite of communications, would operate the *Poste Contrôle des Interventions Aériennes* (PCIA), controlling – in direct liaison with GATAC/Nord at Hanoi – all transport and combat missions destined for Dien Bien Phu. It would take another month to finish laying the nearly 23,000 plates of PSP in a reinforcing strip 1,260yds long by 32yds wide down the centre of the runway, to complete the hard-standing 'parkings', to clear the old storm drains and install goose-neck lamps for night landings. Nevertheless, from 25 November the 'air bridge' was open for the men, materials and supplies to transform a defended drop zone into a *base aéro-terrestre*.[25] Just a week later, on 1 December, Dien Bien Phu would receive its own flight of six Bearcats of Major Jacques Guérin's Fighter Squadron 1/22 'Saintonge' (GC 1/22), which would be based in sandbagged dispersal pens just south of the runway, surrounded by tents and underground burrows for their pilots, mechanics and armourers.

On the same day that 'Torri Rouge' accepted its first Dakota, the FTNV Second Bureau sent a message to General Navarre's staff in Saigon. They had learned from radio intercepts and other intelligence sources that People's Army Division 308 'Viet Bac' was following close behind Division 316 'Bien Hoa' on the roads towards the Red River. From the same staging areas in the triangle Phu Tho–Yen Bai–Thai Nguyen, Division 304 'Nam Dinh' (less its Regiment 66) would get on the march on 26 November, probably for the upper Black River; and both Division 312 and Heavy Division 351 were also preparing to move. Engineers had received orders to prepare ferries to take 6,000 troops per night across the Red River at Yen Bai, starting on 3 December.[26]

All over the High Region and beyond, the first of the battles of Dien Bien Phu was about to begin, and it was the Air Force that would have to fight it for the French.

8. Torricelli and the Front Supply Commission

'The results that we obtained were far from negligible, [and] comparable to those which the Americans had achieved in Korea. We estimate that the progress of the Viet Minh divisions was delayed. But in my view there was absolutely no possibility that it could be interrupted.'

Air Force General Lauzin, *before the 1955 Commission of Inquiry*

WAS IT OPERATION 'CASTOR' that persuaded the People's Army to deploy most of their regular divisions to the High Region during winter 1953/4, or had the intention existed before the French reoccupation of Dien Bien Phu? By 20 November General Giap had committed only Division 316 to the Laotian border country, and had warned Division 308 to be ready to follow; so he already intended to fight there to some degree, but not necessarily in great strength. Although he was still considering his options, there were strong reasons why he should find the idea of a campaign in the north-west attractive.[1]

The main lines for military activity were laid down at meetings of the Party Central Committee, which were normally initiated by Ho Chi Minh or General Giap. The committee had met in late September to consider Giap's report on the options for the coming campaign season, which presented a choice between two broad approaches. Firstly, the People's

Army could concentrate the bulk of its units to guard against a French offensive out of the Delta perhaps towards the Viet Bac; if this occurred, then after defeating it in the fringe of the hills the main force divisions could either counter-attack in the Delta or disperse elsewhere according to circumstances. However, to pursue combat in the Delta flatlands themselves would favour the CEFEO. The alternative was to attack in regions where the French were weaker and conditions favoured the People's Army, while at the same time intensifying the guerrilla campaign throughout the country, thus forcing the enemy to disperse their reserves and reducing their ability to launch their own initiatives.

If the second approach were adopted, then another offensive into Laos might this time win the tantalizing strategic prize of a grip on the upper Mekong river. The leak from the French National Defence Committee published in *France-Observateur* on 30 July (*see Chapter 6, note 10*) might have encouraged a hope that the CEFEO would not defend Laos in strength. More immediately, there was a real need to counter the activities of the GCMA partisans in the border country before they did any further damage; and this was linked with another consideration. In the first week of September a Party conference had been held for the representatives of different ethnic minorities, both those established in the liberated zones and those designated as the leaders of zones not yet liberated; to lend its decisions credibility the Viet Minh needed military success in the High Region and northern Laos. A confident move in that direction would also have a useful impact on the National Assembly, which was due to meet in the first week of December to vote through an important new land reform programme for the liberated zones – the first such sitting in seven years.

It is interesting that Giap seemed as apprehensive as General Cogny about the Delta, where each believed that his opponent enjoyed an advantage. Giap would later write that the Navarre Plan, whose broad outline was clear to him, presented the Viet Minh with 'new and serious difficulties'. Giap knew that the Franco-Vietnamese forces were engaged on a major programme of enlargement, which was a worrying prospect for the following winter 1954/5; and he overestimated existing French strength in the Delta. During autumn 1953 Giap had to keep his options open in case of a major French initiative, preparing his units and his logistics for both Delta and High Region campaigns; whichever proved to be the main focus of activity that winter, some troops and supplies would still need to be sent to the other front. In the meantime preparatory work on various different routes and supply depots continued, as did training in attacks on fortified positions; this all sent mixed signals to French intelligence gatherers.

After his bitter lessons in 1951 Giap never forgot the Viet Minh's fundamental principle of engagement: 'Attack with a sure blow, advance at a steady pace. If we are sure to win, fight to the end; if not, resolutely refuse combat.' Rightly or wrongly, Giap did not believe that he had a sufficient margin of superiority to justify a major campaign against the Delta that year. When the Central Committee meetings ended in early October the decision had been reached to take the initiative in the High Region that winter, while co-ordinating secondary operations throughout the country – including the Central Highlands of Annam – in order to disperse French reserves.[2] But on 15 October, Navarre's Operation 'Mouette' burst out of the fog of a neat deception plan and rampaged towards the South Delta Base, and by the time it ended on 7 November it had given Giap renewed reasons for wariness. If the French launched another sortie from the north of the Delta, no doubt that too could be contained; but if several regular divisions had to be devoted to keeping General Cogny's brigades in their Delta 'box', then planned operations towards Laos would be delayed. Orders went out to the regional troops that they would have to wear down any such French thrusts with their own resources; the Chu Luc would not get involved unless the French penetrated more than nine miles into the liberated zones. Only Division 320, which would not be marching for the High Region under any circumstances, was ordered to 'profit from any chances to wipe out enemy forces'. Even though based near by, south of the Delta, Division 304 was not to get drawn in – the Second Bureau report of 25 November would misinterpret its mission.

On 15 November the bulk of Division 316, most of whose Regiment 176 were already crushing Captain Hébert's partisans in the upper Song river valley and whose route depots had been prepared, was ordered to leave its staging area north-west of Thanh Hoa in the South Delta Base and march up the Song into the Thai Highlands. On 19 November, in a forest camp in Thai Nguyen province, the principal military leaders of the Viet Minh from all over the peninsula gathered to receive a general staff briefing on operations and logistics over the next several months. The north-west campaign was to involve either two or possibly three divisions – initially 316 and 308 – depending upon developments; Division 312 was to remain for the time being around Phu Tho on the Red River to guard against French thrusts, but might also march for the High Region if that threat receded. The news of Operation 'Castor' on 20 November arrived while the conference still had three days to run.

THE FRENCH SEIZURE OF DIEN Bien Phu might therefore seem to have demanded of General Giap only minor adjustment and acceleration of strategic plans which had already been made – two of his divisions were already under orders for the High Region.[3] Nevertheless, there is no reason to believe that immediately he received word of 'Castor', Giap seized upon the prospect of gambling most of his manoeuvre force in a once-for-all trial of strength and endurance hundreds of miles from his own rear bases.

At first he had no idea of French intentions at Dien Bien Phu: was this a temporary incursion? If he reacted strongly, would they reinforce the airhead into a powerful entrenched camp like Na San, or withdraw – and if so, to where – the Plain of Jars? The first signs of an answer quickly appeared in the French and foreign press, partly due to the inexperience of some Army press officers and partly to General Cogny's unfortunate habit of confiding in newspapermen. FTNV seem to have become euphoric when their fears for Operation 'Castor' proved groundless; in this champagne mood the press began to report that an entrenched camp like Na San would be established at Dien Bien Phu, in a long-term commitment to provide the focus for a powerful Thai partisan movement. Cogny himself was quoted as saying that 'if he could, he would have transported Na San *en bloc* to Dien Bien Phu'. A more damaging indiscretion was a series of reports of Division 316's progress towards the High Region; these could only be based on radio intercepts, and the Viet Minh changed their code for operational traffic, frustrating French intelligence for several important days.[4]

It is possible that shortly after 'Castor' Giap may also have received encouraging news about the limits on the reinforcements that Navarre could expect from France during the winter, thus easing his fears of further thrusts out from the Delta. On 21 November a copy of the long-delayed official response of the National Defence Committee to the C-in-C's requests submitted in late July was sent to Secretary Jacquet by the permanent secretary to the committee, a civil servant named Mons. This may have been among the many documents leaked to the French Communist Party (and thus almost certainly to an Eastern bloc embassy) by two well-placed senior functionaries of the permanent secretariat, R. Labrusse and R. Turpin. It is therefore credible that the flavour certainly, and in some cases perhaps the verbatim proceedings, of French government discussions at the highest level became known to the Viet Minh.[5]

It is safe to assume that General Giap was kept informed of developments and Viet Minh intentions in the political dimension. On 26 November, during talks at Bermuda, a Soviet delegation suggested a four-power conference between the USA, USSR, Britain and France to discuss a range of concerns including South-East Asia; the French response was positive, and on 6 January Prime Minister Laniel would formally announce in parliament that delegates were to convene in Berlin on 25 January. President Ho himself hinted in an interview on 28 November that a negotiated settlement was possible.[6] Although it would be another three months before the date of what would prove to be the ultimate conference, at Geneva, was publicly agreed, it must already have been clear to Giap that a momentum towards negotiation was being created. This did not, of course, reduce the pressure on him, but increased it: the importance of a military triumph to the Viet Minh's relative advantage in such talks could not be overstated.

Despite these encouragements to pick up the gauntlet at Dien Bien Phu, Giap must have had deeply rooted misgivings. He had been entrusted with complete freedom to lead the People's Army on the understanding that he would never attack until he was sure of winning. The self-taught former schoolmaster, painfully snubbed long ago by General Leclerc, was a lifelong admirer of France's military institutions; since that humiliating meeting he had achieved victories to be proud of, but only under special circumstances which he had been careful to shape. Giap had broken Mao's golden rule in the Delta in winter/spring 1951, at terrible cost, and he had resolved never again to underestimate his enemy or to fight on France's chosen ground – receiving a painful *aide-mémoire* at Na San in December 1952. Yet now he faced once again the prospect of meeting in conventional battle a professional Western army led by products of some of the finest military academies in the world.

The techniques of guerrilla warfare could not prevail now; this would be no campaign of hit-and-run, ambush and evasion. The People's Army had never successfully assaulted a fortified French position held by more than two companies. Indeed, they had very seldom fought actions which lasted more than a single night; if Giap accepted battle at Dien Bien Phu this would be their first experience of sustained fighting – of taking ground, and holding on to it in pitched battle – since the dreadful precedents of Vinh Yen and the Day River in 1951. The young and improvised People's Army had since received more and better weapons – but so had the CEFEO, whose educated personnel were far better grounded and trained in their use than the *bo doi*.

Even to bring his army to the battlefield would involve marching them – and dragging their artillery – at least 300 miles through the hills from the Viet Bac and South Delta base areas; and Giap's supply lines from the Chinese frontier would eventually extend over 500 miles, along a network of rudimentary roads which in many places still had to be excavated from the jungle and landslides which had virtually reclaimed them during years of neglect. The Viet Minh would have to assemble and carry over that distance every piece of equipment, every bullet, every bowl of rice for an army of perhaps 50,000 men; and they would have to keep these vulnerable lines of communication open to supply that army, in a mountain wilderness, during a major positional battle which might last many weeks.

A single division striking across country for a limited objective could sustain itself with a few days' rice rations carried by the soldiers themselves; mortars and 75mm guns could be carried by ponies, even by porter teams with shoulder poles. When Giap announced to the Thai Nguyen conference in late November that two or perhaps two and a half divisions would operate in the High Region that winter, he was almost validating the French intelligence estimate of the limit on his logistic capability – the estimate upon which Navarre's staff rested their own plans for Dien Bien Phu. But a major expansion of Giap's original ambitions for the north-west front would entail a vast logistic programme involving motorized transport – hundreds of trucks travelling along hundreds of miles of roads. The forces committed to Dien Bien Phu would have to risk becoming, in a sense, an imitation Expeditionary Corps. They faced giving up their traditional advantages of concealment and fast cross-country movement, while handing the French their own traditional weapon of ambush – for the French had an air force, and the sky would be their 'jungle'.

Giap did not take long agonizing over his choices; he would later claim that he took the final decision to commit his army to Dien Bien Phu in the first days of December.[7]

THE VIET MINH TROOPS WHO would fight at Dien Bien Phu were put on the march over a period of about a month, from late November to late December 1953. During this period work on the approach roads was pushed ahead, but the only combat troops in the Thai Highlands were two battalions of Regiment 176 from Division 316, Independent Regiment 148, and regional units. Some of these were deployed in the hills south of Dien Bien Phu to prevent contact between the airhead and French troops in northern Laos.

Around 17 December, the seven remaining infantry battalions of Division 316, together with Artillery Battalion 980, arrived in the area of Dien Bien Phu, some of them delayed by destroying the Lai Chau auxiliaries on their way (*see Chapter 9*); they would be deployed east of the valley. At the end of the month Division 308 also began filtering into the hills to the north. Engineer Regiment 151 from Heavy Division 351 had marched at the end of November to carry out urgent road work on RP41 between Son La and Tuan Giao. By 22 December enough had been achieved for the division's artillery to begin its journey, the last of its separated convoys crossing the Black River on 4 January.[8] From 23 December, French intelligence calculated from the known scale of rice rations that depots around Tuan Giao were already supporting a force of at least 32,000 combatants and 16,000 service troops. By 24 December, Giap had discounted the danger of a French raid towards the Viet Bac, and ordered Division 312 to join him from Phu Tho. It would take 15 days for them to march from the Red River at Yen Bai to Dien Bien Phu, where they would settle into camps to the north-east of the valley from mid January.[9]

The People's Army battalions regularly covered up to 20 miles each day, moving off the tracks into forest cover to sleep. If they marched all night they could cover up to 30 miles, since they did not have to worry about concealment from the air. The majority of People's Army infantry were recruited from the peasants and townsmen of the Delta flatlands; these young men – 18 to 20 years of age, with officers only in their mid 20s – had no more natural affinity with the forested highlands than did the French, and initially had just as much difficulty adapting. In the jungle they suffered from malaria, dysentery, typhoid and general exhaustion like any paratrooper; they had to be urged on by the constant encouragement of their commissars, and they kept up their spirits by singing marching songs, like any German légionnaire. Colonel Bui Tin, then a 27-year-old battalion commander, described the hardships of long marches through difficult terrain in the early 1950s:

> Our men died in many ways. They lost their way, they fell from high bridges... venomous snakebites often meant instant death. Tree falls during typhoons crushed them in their hammocks. Flash floods were very dangerous. There were fevers, malaria, even tiger attacks. The small jungle leeches attached themselves during the night, so a man would awake weakened and covered with his own blood... We took what precautions we could. General Giap issued special orders on hygiene... Drinking water was to be boiled. The troops were to use clean socks after washing their feet in warm water and salt. They should have hot rice with adequate meat and vegetables at least once a day, and sleep at least six hours every night... uniforms [were ordered to be] changed every two or three days.[10]

On 5 January 1954, General Giap himself and his general staff arrived at the site of an advanced HQ close to a waterfall in a glen of the Muong Phang hills, about nine miles north of Dien Bien Phu. During the following weeks a bomb-proof cave system would be prepared for Giap's battle headquarters and linked with communications networks. (The captured General de Castries would be taken there in May; he confirmed that it had some 300yds of underground galleries, protected by a massive thickness of rock overhead.) On the day of his arrival Giap signalled Regiment 57 from Division 304 to join his army by forced march from Phu Tho; Colonel Hoang Khai Tien's three battalions arrived exhausted on 23–24 January after a ten-day, 200-mile marathon, to be deployed south of Dien Bien Phu.[11]

Since the same division's Regiment 66 was still south of the Delta, that left only its Regiment 9 to cover the Thai Nguyen base area. By now the battered Division 320 had been ordered to infiltrate into the Delta from the south; and further south still, Giap was holding Division 325 (Regiments 18, 95 and 101, Artillery Battalion 888) for another task entirely. The shape of the People's Army deployments for the winter campaign season was now complete: the great majority of the regular manoeuvre force and all the artillery was committed to the north-west front.

THIS BRISK ITINERARY CONVEYS little of the challenge which the Viet Minh faced in turning General Giap's movement orders into reality. It was not simply a question of marching unprecedented numbers of infantry and porters with huge quantities of supplies over hundreds of miles, on difficult dirt tracks through jungle hills and across many water obstacles. The transport of their field and anti-aircraft guns (and well over a thousand tons of ammunition for these alone) across some 500 miles of North Vietnam would be impossible without using their recently acquired fleet of at least 600 Russian Molotova 2½-ton trucks. This confronted the Viet Minh with exactly the same problems of mobility as faced by the French since the beginning of the war – and under a sky ruled by enemy aircraft whose effectiveness the Viet Minh tended, if anything, to exaggerate.

Between spring and autumn 1953 General Giap had invested some 2 million man-days of labour in opening up neglected roads and improving them to take motor traffic; but much remained to be done, particularly on the final stretches of RP41 between Son La and Dien Bien Phu. Obviously vulnerable bottlenecks had to be duplicated in advance with bypass sections. The main flow had to be fed by an intricate arterial system of smaller tracks travelled by snake-like columns of porters, trains of pack animals and horse-drawn wooden sledges. Waterways had to be integrated into the overall plan, using sampans and rafts – in particular, bulk rice supplies from China had to be rafted down the Black River, and from mid December they were unloaded at Lai Chau and broken down into small loads for overland transport down the Pavie Track.

The sparse road network and the north-west to south-east grain of the mountain ranges and rivers meant that the main supply route was shaped like a huge fish-hook (*see Map 7*). It led from the Chinese border at Lao

Cai, about 80 miles south-east following the upper Red River, to the major crossing at Yen Bai; here the route was also joined from the east and south by roads from Tuyen Quang, Thai Nguyen and Phu Tho. From Yen Bai the route turned roughly south-west across the slant of the mountains and rivers. A series of tracks climbed about 4,000ft, snaking up past Nghia Lo to the 9,800ft crest of the Sa Phin massif before dropping down again to the Black River at Ta Khoa. This stretch, collectively dignified with the title of RP13*bis*, was only about 50 miles as the crow flies but at least twice that long on the ground. The tracks had returned to a state of nature, and a huge effort was now needed to clear and link them, widen and in some places reinforce them to take motor traffic, and to bridge or ford the many watercourses that cut them.

This work had to be extended on the west bank to a junction at Co Noi, where the route joined the hardly less neglected RP41. This road was an extension of RC6 coming up from Hoa Binh via Moc Chau; Giap's supply route followed it for about 80 miles north-westwards up the eastern flank of the Son La plateau, passing Na San, through Son La and the Meo (Pha Din) Pass, to Tuan Giao, which would become the main rear depot for Dien Bien Phu. The last stretch, where RP41 (or '41*bis*') from Tuan Giao hooked south-west again to Dien Bien Phu, was among the hardest; it had to be more or less rebuilt from scratch, and its serpentine course covered up to 50 miles. Initially everything had to be carried by porters from Tuan Giao to Dien Bien Phu, but by 15 January the improved roads reached the immediate vicinity of the valley, and thereafter a truck shuttle operated as far as the tracks were practicable. Around the valley itself an almost complete circuit totalling at least 18 miles of entirely new, concealed tracks then had to be built through the forested hills, with bypasses and tributaries, to allow the guns and 120mm mortars of the Heavy Division to be installed in fighting positions and the infantry to circulate around their assigned sectors.

When the Viet Minh engineers and labour gangs had finished their work, French intelligence calculated that a priority convoy could travel the 500 miles of unsurfaced road from the Chinese border to Dien Bien Phu in about seven days.[12]

DURING THE LAST WEEK OF November and the first half of December, General Cogny bombarded the C-in-C with alternative plans for thrusts out of the Delta – to Phu Doan once more, to Thai Nguyen, even to Yen Bai. Navarre rejected all these schemes, which were impossibly greedy of troops; indeed, it has been suggested that Cogny's true motive was not only to create some fresh air around his Delta defences, but also to provide visible employment for the reserves he had been given in the summer, before Navarre could be tempted to send them elsewhere.[13]

On 29 November Navarre and Cogny flew in to inspect progress at Dien Bien Phu. On the 30th, Cogny issued his Directive No. 739 defining the tasks of the garrison. These were to guarantee freedom of movement for a radius of at least five miles around the airfield; to gather intelligence from as far out as possible; and – when ordered – to support the withdrawal of the remainder of the troops from Lai Chau. The defensive aspect of the airhead was now spelled out: it was to be held 'without thought of withdrawal'. Nevertheless, the garrison was also to deploy 'at least half its strength' on external operations to the north and east, to inflict losses on the approaching enemy and slow their advance. The contradiction between preparing serious field defences to safeguard the airfield while simultaneously sending half the 5,000-man garrison out into the hills was not addressed. General Cogny was still hoping that active operations could be pursued in the triangle Dien Bien Phu–Lai Chau–Tuan Giao.[14]

Since receiving the report that Division 308 was to join 316 in the border country, General Navarre had not shared this sanguine view. On 3 December he issued clear instructions to Cogny. He had decided to accept battle in the north-west, centred on Dien Bien Phu, which was to be held at all costs. Lai Chau was to be evacuated as soon as the threat to it exceeded the capability of the force still stationed there. Ground communications with Lai Chau to the north and Muong Khoua to the south were to be maintained as long as possible. Navarre even sketched a scenario of the battle to come, based on Giap's logistic difficulties so far from home. He expected the enemy's 'movement phase' to take several weeks. On arrival in the region his 'approach and reconnaissance phase' would last from six to ten days. This would be followed by the 'assault phase', lasting several days and inevitably ending in failure.[15]

The following day, 4 December, the FTNV Second Bureau warned

General Cogny that a regiment from Division 316 was already threatening to get between Lai Chau and Dien Bien Phu, and that other units were on the move between Tuan Giao and Dien Bien Phu. General Navarre's doubts about Lai Chau's survival prospects had been vindicated, but not his estimate of Giap's 'movement phase': the People's Army was advancing with unexpected speed.[16]

APART FROM THE ENGINEER regiment from the Heavy Division, some other troops were used as labourers: even the veteran infantry of Regiment 88 from Division 308 were pressed into service on RP41 in January, replaced the following month by 5,000 raw recruits from Depot Regiment 77. However, the ox's share of the task of creating and maintaining the roads fell to civilian labourers – coolies, or in Viet Minh parlance *Dan Cong* – working only with the simplest hand tools and baskets. It was on their backs, too, that a proportion of the supplies finally arrived, though not as much as has sometimes been supposed.[17]

The total numbers of labourers gathered along RP13*bis*, RP41 and right to the very rim of the valley – for road building, on-going maintenance and repair of bomb damage, digging the artillery's gun positions, and portage of supplies during both the three-month preparatory phase and the eight-week battle itself – can never be known. However, the numbers were certainly (and crucially) much higher than the French staff had expected. Based on experience, the French had estimated that the total impressed labour force in the High Region could not exceed about 20,000 – enough to support a campaign by two, or at most two and a half divisions.[18] Their intelligence reports on the progress of Giap's army during the winter tended to draw only vague distinctions between military and civilian labourers; but they suggested that by 13 March there were present in the vicinity of Dien Bien Phu, in addition to 49,500 People's Army combatants, some 31,500 'logistic support personnel' plus 23,000 other support troops and personnel spread along the supply lines – the terms and figures are those quoted by Bernard Fall.[19] Pierre Rocolle suggests that civilian labourers immediately supporting Giap's army may have numbered 35,000 on 13 March, but that later collation of Second Bureau intelligence gave a variable figure of between 50,000 and 75,000 during the battle – at least twice the numbers of People's Army infantry.[20]

General Giap would write that 'hundreds of thousands of Dan Cong, women as well as men, surmounted perils and difficulties and spent more than 3 million work days'.[21] At least 100,000 people giving a month's labour each would certainly be credible, since the first week of December saw the Viet Minh announce an unprecedented measure. On 6 December an order of general mobilization was broadcast; under the direction of commissars of the Front Supply Commission, men and women were pressed into service in their scores of thousands, allocated to gangs on specific sections of the supply route, and assigned their tasks. The commission was given the authority to commandeer human labour, vehicles and draft animals; a countrywide campaign was announced, under the slogan 'Everything for the Front, Everything for Victory!'

The leadership also recognized that such real hardships must be sweetened; and general mobilization was carefully associated in Party propaganda with a land reform programme voted through the National Assembly on 4 December under the slogan 'The Land to the Peasants'. Until then the Viet Minh had handled the small rural landowners within the 'disputed zones' with some restraint; they needed to maximize support for the revolution, and had dealt harshly only with notorious bloodsuckers. Now the Viet Minh gambled that enthusiasm among the masses for the promise of land redistribution would outweigh the enmity of the 'landed proprietor class', whose property rights were abolished and whose holdings were to be divided among those who worked the soil.[22]

The results produced by this general mobilization of labour were remarkable, and French accounts inevitably use metaphors comparing the massed Dan Cong to swarming ants. The clearing, widening and re-inforcement of earth tracks to take motor traffic and towed artillery were followed by the stationing of groups of repair workers and porters along RP13*bis* and RP41 to keep the convoys moving. The route was divided into eight main sections, their limits coinciding with major obstacles such as watercourses, bridged ravines or vulnerable passes, where checkpoints were set up. The truck convoys did not travel the whole route: columns of 30 or 40 Molotovas were assigned to each section, and when these (or water traffic) reached the checkpoints gangs of porters unloaded them and reloaded the cargoes on to the vehicles allocated to the next section.

Some natural obstacles and bomb-damaged stretches required carrying the loads by human muscle-power over considerable distances of very difficult ground. Here hundreds of porters were gathered, with makeshift shoulder pads and bamboo carrying rigs, or the famous strengthened bicycles used as two-wheeled trolleys. A bicycle could carry up to 200lbs of rice in sacks. One man with a bamboo back frame could carry a mortar baseplate, two a gun wheel; there are photographs of four-man teams carrying the barrels and the breech blocks of 75mm Japanese mountain guns up forested hillsides slung from two shoulder poles. The casualties from accidents, sickness and air attack among the Dan Cong are unrecorded but were certainly heavy (among the ordnance dropped by French aircraft were the latest American anti-personnel bombs which spread lethal clouds of small steel splinters).[23] The coolies were publicly lauded as heroes, but the Viet Minh could give them little practical care; a handful of medical students were scattered along the roads at sector checkpoints, but their resources were minimal.

Huge numbers of man-hours were also devoted to camouflaging the route wherever possible. Along some stretches the treetops were actually lashed together over the road to make tunnels, and many log bridges were built just below the surface of rivers and streams. The cargo vehicles were thickly covered with camouflage, replaced at regular intervals to ensure that they always matched the foliage through which the trucks were passing. Road gangs brushed away the marks of tracks as soon as a convoy had passed them. On some stretches – notably the high slopes flanking RP41 between Son La and Tuan Giao, where forest was largely replaced by elephant grass – overhead concealment was not feasible. Here motor traffic was essentially limited to the hours of darkness and morning fog, which hid them from the only French aircraft that regularly operated by night – the Navy's long-range Privateer bombers. By day and night, shifts of look-outs were posted in treetops or on heights with whistles and jangling triangles to warn of the approach of aircraft. At night, during their long tours of the High Region (up RP41, then right around the Chinese borders via Lao Cai and Cao Bang), the Privateer crews would see lines of truck headlights crawling across a hillside all wink out within a few seconds, long before they could reach the target. The aircraft sentries' task was fairly simple: any plane they heard approaching was obviously hostile, and since the French had no jets in Indochina all aircraft could be heard well before they arrived.[24]

THE OPERATIONS OF GENERAL Dechaux's Tactical Air Group/ North – call-sign 'Torricelli' – were dictated by the available airfields. While there were a number of auxiliary airstrips on which the smaller machines could put down in an emergency, entire squadrons with their personnel, stores and workshops for a regular programme of war missions demanded much more elaborate facilities. Tonkin had only three airbases that could support major operations: Hanoi–Gia Lam, Hanoi–Bach Mai and Haiphong–Cat Bi. A fourth *'dakotable'* airfield at Do Son south-east of Haiphong was devoted entirely to maintenance and repair of the C-47 fleet (*see Map 5*). In northern Laos the situation was far worse. The airfield at Luang Prabang was marginal; although troops were sometimes flown in there, it was useless as a base for large-scale operations. Only a rough fighter strip had been prepared at Xieng Khouang on the Plain of Jars, about 136 miles due south of Dien Bien Phu. Some 80 miles south-west of the valley an emergency airstrip on the little plateau of Muong Sai had been extended to take Dakotas by the end of 1953, but again, facilities were rudimentary as they were at Muong Nam Bac also (*see Map 8*). In winter 1953/4 the main concrete runway at Cat Bi was under repair and only half its width could be used; the secondary runway suffered rapid wear and tear under the constant traffic, with a consequent reduction in the frequency of take-offs and landings.[25]

For most of the war in Indochina the French Air Force combat squadrons were handicapped not only by a shortage of aircraft, but by the unsuitability of many of them for long-range ground-attack missions. Like the Army, the Air Force had muddled its way through the years 1946–51 with a motley collection of hand-me-downs which were all that impoverished France could provide. By late 1953 the situation had improved, but to an extent the French were still taking what they could get rather than acquiring the best tools for the job. The total numbers of combat aircraft available to GATAC/Nord have been variously recorded; the number of planes which can actually be put into the sky on any particular day always falls short of an air force's theoretical total of machines, due to routine maintenance, mechanical breakdowns and – crucially – the number of aircrew available to fly them. Each of Dechaux's fighter squadrons normally had four or five spare machines to keep their serviceable strength up to about 16. However, they had no spare pilots; the Allied norm for squadron aircrews was one-and-a-half times the number of aircraft, but Dechaux's units were lucky if they had a one-to-one ratio and often fell below this figure, leaving aircraft sitting idle.

During the period November 1953 to May 1954 GATAC/Nord had a theoretical total of 40 Grumman F8F-1 Bearcat single-seat, single-engined fighter-bombers divided between two squadrons, GC 1/22 'Saintonge' and 2/22 'Languedoc'. These were normally based at Hanoi–Bach Mai but with detached flights sometimes operating from Dien Bien Phu and Xieng Khouang. Developed just too late to see action in World War II, the Bearcat was a robust US Navy fighter designed to withstand the rigours of carrier operations. It was a burly-looking machine which seemed to stand aggressively tiptoed on its tall undercarriage, with the 'bubble' cockpit canopy peering down from behind its fat, barrel-shaped radial engine. The F8F mounted four wing guns, and in practice the French usually flew with an underwing load of either two 500lb bombs or napalm tanks; each wing also had launch rails for two 5in unguided rockets. This load gave the Bearcat a serious punch as a ground-attack aircraft; but it had two problems, both stemming from the fact that it had not been designed as a low-altitude fighter-bomber but as an interceptor. The Bearcat was a highly manoeuvrable sprinter, able to get up to high altitude quickly and out-turn enemy fighters in high-speed dogfights. It did not 'fly itself'; it was a highly strung thoroughbred, not a forgiving workhorse. The pilot who made a momentary misjudgement could easily lose control and needed plenty of air beneath him to recover – a luxury he would not enjoy on low-level missions over the hills of North Vietnam.

The Bearcat's other drawback was its relatively short range. Unlike the naval fighters from the carrier *Arromanches*, Air Force Bearcats were not provided with external belly-tanks for extended range. Depending upon speed and altitude, their flight endurance was no more than $2\frac{1}{2}$ hours; at a speed of just over 300mph they had a maximum round-trip range of 750 miles, and a good deal less when fully loaded with ordnance and flying low. Since the distance from Hanoi to Dien Bien Phu was 185 miles, and they had to come down to low level and burn up fuel once they reached the High Region, the Bearcat pilots had relatively little 'loiter time' to search out targets and attack them.[26]

Two bomber squadrons, GB 1/19 'Gascogne' and 1/25 'Tunisie', were based mainly at Haiphong–Cat Bi with some use of the Hanoi airfields. They were equipped with American B-26 twin-engined attack bombers (the Douglas Invader, previously designated A-26 – not the wartime Martin B-26 Marauder). This was an elegant-looking, streamlined machine with a tall tailfin and two big radial engines hunched close to the slim nose, where the crew of three – pilot, navigator-bombardier, flight engineer – were clustered. The first 25 Invaders had arrived in Indochina in January 1951, and the US provided a second batch of 22 on 26 January and 16 February 1954, raising each squadron to a theoretical strength of 20. By 13 March the two squadrons in fact had a total of only 34 aircraft on strength, and the shortage of aircrews meant that the number actually available for missions still averaged only 11 bombers per squadron. The B-26 had a flight endurance of 5½ hours, so could reach any target in the Thai Highlands; its round-trip time between Cat Bi and Dien Bien Phu was only about 2 hours 20 minutes, giving as much 'loiter' in the target area as the crew needed. The theoretical maximum bombload was 8,000lbs or 3½ tons, but in practice this was never carried. The levels of training and operational skills in the bomber squadrons in 1953/4 were frankly sub-standard; and the absence of an overall bomber commander, with authority over the whole force and the ability to represent it on the staff of GATAC/Nord, was a serious weakness.[27]

'Torricelli' thus had a practical maximum of 40 to 50 Air Force combat aircraft available for operations on any one day. To these were added the valuable resources of the Aéronautique Navale ('Aéronavale'), mostly based on the carrier *Arromanches* in the Gulf of Tonkin.[28] Her air group comprised a fighter-bomber and a dive-bomber squadron; and although not strong in numbers, the Navy crews were excellent – the demands on carrier pilots ensure particularly high levels of flying expertise, precision and nerve. On average, both of the two carrier squadrons would put a maximum of two flights each of six aircraft over the High Region on any one day before and during the battle.

Flotille 11 (11F), call-sign 'Savart', had single-engined, single-seat Grumman F6F-5 Hellcats. Dating from 1943, the F6F was the most battle proven of the Grumman Aircraft series of '-cat' carrier fighters; it was an ugly, chunky, squared-off scrapper, famous for its ability to soak up punishment. Apart from its six wing guns it could carry a maximum 2,000lb load of bombs and rockets, and unlike the Bearcat it was a steady little truck when flown on ground-attack missions. With a belly-tank it had an endurance of three hours at a speed of 270mph carrying two 500lb bombs, giving a maximum round-trip range of 840 miles. Hellcats could operate over the High Region, but the fuel gauge often gave reason for unease during the last evening stage of long return flights to the carrier in Ha Long Bay, especially in dirty weather.

The *Arromanches'* dive-bombers were the Curtiss SB2C-5 Helldivers of Flotille 3 (3F), call-sign 'Ganga'. This two-seat, single-engined type was also a US Navy veteran from 1943, and the most successful ship-killer of the Pacific War; but it was never loved – flyers claimed that its designation SB2C stood for 'Son-of-a-Bitch 2nd Class'. It had a maximum range of 1,100 miles and a top speed of 290mph, but its bombload of 1,000lbs was unimpressive. Pilots found it tricky to fly – underpowered, overweight, treacherous at low landing speeds, and with uncertain air brakes which made it hard to hold it straight in a dive. Its French Navy crews were first class, but it was not the ideal aircraft for bombing pinpoint targets a good deal smaller than a ship's deck.

The final contribution by the Aéronavale was the most immediately imposing: Flotille 28, call-sign 'César', a small squadron of Convair PB4-Y2 Privateers – the only four-engined heavy bombers in Indochina. Previously based at Saigon, 28F sent first three, then six of its eight Privateers up to Haiphong–Cat Bi, where they operated from November to May. Since there were never more than five crews this was the maximum number of aircraft available for operations, but the tireless sailors put in more flying hours than anyone else in Indochina; one Privateer crew logged four sorties, totalling 13 hours, during one 24-hour period – two of them by night. The Privateer was a US Navy ocean patrol bomber re-engineered from the wartime B-24 Liberator. In this naval form it had lost its twin tailplane and acquired a huge single fin; its slim, high-shouldered wings supported a bull-nosed, slab-sided fuselage as elegant as a line of railway freight wagons, barnacled with turrets and blisters. Cruising at about 145mph, it had a range of more than 1,500 miles and could stay in the air for 11 hours, so it could reach any target in Indochina. The Privateers had been fitted with the excellent Norden bombsight; they usually carried loads of

6,000–8,000lbs, 2½ to 3½ tons, bombing from altitudes of between 10,000 and 13,500ft above sea level – the engines of this maritime version were set up for medium-altitude efficiency.[29]

THE AIR EFFORT AGAINST the Viet Minh supply routes was directed from General Dechaux's GATAC/Nord headquarters in Hanoi. This was physically close to General Cogny's FTNV in the Citadel, and their respective Second and Third Bureau staffs (Intelligence and Operations) were in daily contact. Liaison worked well enough in normal times; but the pace and urgency of events in winter 1953 and particularly spring 1954 were not normal, and the system quickly revealed its central weakness: the lack of a single chain of command enforcing a consistent doctrine. Real efficiency demanded a true joint Army/Air Force staff: a single team able to weigh the competing demands which came in from ground troops throughout Tonkin, to monitor events and to react quickly, with full authority and in full knowledge of all relevant factors. Although the creation of such a staff had been discussed since winter 1952/3 it still did not exist.

General Navarre demanded its establishment on 7 January 1954, and at first rejected the short-term compromise of an exchange of liaison officers; but when General Cogny stressed the technical difficulties he did not insist. It was not until 23 March 1954 that General Cogny created a *Centre de Co-ordination des Feux* (CCF – Fire Control Co-ordination Centre), which was a joint committee of FTNV and GATAC/Nord staff officers meeting twice each day to consider the latest intelligence and to decide on the following day's air operations.[30]

The 'battle of the roads' was directed from the GATAC/Nord operations room; this was small, understaffed, and had at its disposal too few radio frequencies, which soon became swamped on busy days. Crucially, it lacked the means to follow and control aircraft once they were in flight. If the original briefed target of a mission proved not to be feasible, then aircraft could not be redirected to the most urgent alternative.

From the beginning of Operation 'Castor', General Navarre insisted that the Air Force give priority to attacks on the enemy lines of supply, and he reiterated this demand in orders of 26 November, 3 December, 6 January, 21 January and 25 February.[31] But the C-in-C's orders could not silence demands for support from troops in action elsewhere; Hanoi could not ignore these, and consequently the already inadequate strength of GATAC/Nord was spread too widely for decisive success in any one task. This dispersion of effort is confirmed by simple arithmetic. A 'sortie' in this context means a single mission flown by a single aircraft – one raid by a formation of three bombers counted as three sorties.

Between 20 November and 1 March, during virtually the whole air battle against the Front Supply Commission, the fighter-bombers flew 669 sorties against the lines of supply, but 1,583 sorties against targets in the Delta.[32] The B-26s flew 483 sorties against the lines of supply, and 141 against Delta targets. The average sorties per month per available B-26 are reported as 20 in November, 13 in December, 17 in January, and 14 in February, during between 30 and 41 flying hours per month. Averages are obviously deceptive, and by definition individual crews must have logged higher figures. The weather was also a factor, being particularly bad over the High Region in mid January and again at the beginning of February. Overall, however, this average figure of roughly one $2\frac{1}{2}$-hour sortie every two days seems to fall rather short of the all-out effort for which General Navarre was calling. (For comparison, the norm for Free French crews flying Marauder bombers with the Allied tactical air forces in 1944 was 20 to 25 missions a month, over 100 to 125 flying hours.)[33]

Direct comparison between the work rate of the B-26 squadrons and the naval Privateers is unjust, since the mission endurance of the latter was so much longer; however, it is perhaps worth noting that in January each crew of 28F's Haiphong detachment averaged 19 sorties over 72 flying hours. Their Norden bombsight also allowed the Privateers to drop their loads a good deal more accurately than the B-26s. But even though the Navy crews flew more hours per month than the Air Force, carried roughly twice the bombload, and dropped it with greater precision, there were only five of them, so the results of their contribution were marginal. The essential problem was too few bombs on too many targets.

Targets for these missions were scattered along the whole supply route from the Viet Bac to Tuan Giao and beyond, but priority was given to RP13*bis* and RP41, between the Red River crossing at Yen Bai and Dien Bien Phu (*see Map 7*). Over this stretch 20 main targets were identified and codenamed, and another three on RP41 east of the Co Noi junction.

About half were major potential choke points; the others were hit mainly to disperse the Viet Minh road repair effort. During the three-month 'battle of the roads' a total of about 568 tons of bombs were dropped on these 23 targets.[34] To put that figure in context: in the winter of 1940/41, while still in its weak and unsophisticated infancy, RAF Bomber Command routinely dropped that much in two nights' raids by about 300 aircraft with half the bombload of the B-26 – that is, their figures *pro rata* were nine times better than French results.

One of GATAC/Nord's highest priorities was the Co Noi junction where RP13*bis* linked with RP41, codenamed 'Mercure'. The first raids took place on 13 December; 39 sorties were flown, dropping only 52 tons of bombs.[35] The route was cut and the Viet Minh had to build a bypass of about 300yds, but the main road was open again by 25 December. A second raid by 23 aircraft dropped just 23 tons of bombs; only light damage resulted, and the route was repaired by the next day. Later raids on 'Mercure' dropped a total of about 50 tons over some 20 days, causing only brief interruption to the flow of supplies through the junction. Other strategic targets escaped as lightly: 'Mimosa' and 'Mandarin', at either end of the Meo Pass, were attacked by a total of 58 sorties dropping 135 tons of bombs, which had only temporary effects on motor traffic.[36]

WHILE THE AIR CAMPAIGN continued in north-west Tonkin, General Giap obliged General Navarre to turn part of his attention further south. All sources seem to agree that during December, Giap's hope was to have his army prepared to launch an attack on Dien Bien Phu in the last week of January. He could not commit himself finally until the logistic situation was clearer; but in the meantime he could execute a planned diversion-ary operation, which might bring benefits whatever his final decision over the Dien Bien Phu timetable. In Christmas week 1953 the People's Army struck south-westwards from around Vinh in Annam into central Laos, through the mountains of the Annamite Cordillera and across the narrow waist of the country towards the Mekong river (*see Map 1*).

Seven battalions, mainly from Regiment 66 of Division 304 and Regiment 101 of Division 325, infiltrated through the mountains by dis-persed routes; the weak and scattered garrisons were taken by surprise, and the French fell back in some confusion. By 26 December the People's

Army had captured Thakhek on the Mekong – much to the consternation of the French press. General Navarre was spreading a little wintry cheer at Dien Bien Phu over Christmas (*see Chapter 9*); he flew directly to Seno, an airfield near Savannakhet about 60 miles south of Thakhek, which offered the only platform for French action. The C-in-C quelled the panic, dismissed the ineffectual General Bourgund, and summoned reinforcements from Tonkin. These included General Gilles with five French and ANV parachute battalions – among them Bigeard's 6 BPC, Bréchignac's II/1 RCP and Souquet's 1 BPC, pulled out of Dien Bien Phu to rejoin the strategic reserve a couple of weeks earlier.[37]

When the People's Army failed to press their apparent advantage Bigeard and Bréchignac struck out from Seno on 5 January, attacking the Viet Minh at Ban Som Hong and killing at least 400 in two days' hard fighting. This Viet Minh force depended entirely on porters for its logistics, and its advance this far was surprising; it was soon forced into a fighting withdrawal, and Thakhek was retaken on 20 January. Nevertheless, it inflicted bloody losses on Groupe Mobile 2 during this retreat, and would remain an elusive threat throughout February and March, tying down GMs 1 and 2 and Laotian units in brutal terrain.[38]

WHILE DEALING WITH THIS brief but noisy alarm, General Navarre was simultaneously having to digest unwelcome information from Tonkin. Neither Navarre nor Cogny had access to detailed statistics on the progress of the air campaign; they were given only overall figures, and reports of the difficulties faced by the Air Force. By the beginning of January, however, the C-in-C was certainly aware that the results of GATAC/Nord's campaign were seriously disappointing. Giap's units and supplies were building up steadily around Dien Bien Phu in numbers which he had not anticipated – already at least 32,000 troops. The People's Army were dominating the hills north and east of the valley, stifling any ambitious sorties by the garrison; and the hope of supporting a large Thai *maquis* in the region had already proved vain.

Navarre was still committed to giving battle at Dien Bien Phu, which was fulfilling at least part of its strategic purpose. He believed that it could frustrate any major invasion of northern Laos, and that it was an '*abcès de fixation*', attracting to itself large enemy forces which were thus unavailable to threaten the Delta or Navarre's planned operations in Annam. On 27 December he sent a curt telegram to Cogny in response to 'Delta Man's' continual urging of major pre-emptive operations: 'You should consider that within your overall responsibility for the Delta and the High Region, the latter – and particularly the defence of Dien Bien Phu – must have priority. The Delta is currently only your second priority, and for me it is the fourth – after Dien Bien Phu, central Laos and Operation "Atlante". I may have to take some troops away from the Delta, and you may have to take some risks...'[39]

Nevertheless, as a prudent commander he had to prepare for any number of contingencies simultaneously; and there was no contradiction in his orders to Cogny on 29 December to examine – in absolute secrecy – two alternative plans for the Dien Bien Phu garrison to break out overland if the need arose (operations codenamed 'Ariane' and 'Xénophon'). This Directive No. 178 was followed by a personal letter on 31 December: 'One must face the fact that the battle may not go in our favour... either if the defences are dislocated by very powerful attacks mounted with modern resources employed for the first time; or if Dien Bien Phu is smothered, the enemy succeeding in preventing our use of the airstrip either by artillery or AA guns.'[40]

The reference to Giap's possible 'modern resources' reveals that General Navarre was already having to consider that the air–ground base might face weapons which had not figured in his staff's calculations – a suspicion which became firmer over the following days. The exact dating and weight of the various intelligence reports is not transparent; but by 1 January, when Navarre wrote to Secretary Jacquet, he certainly suspected that Heavy Division 351 was trucking 37mm anti-aircraft guns, and probably heavy artillery, towards Dien Bien Phu:

> Two weeks ago I would have put the chances of victory at 100 per cent – Dien Bien Phu is a very good defensive position... I have assembled there a strong force of infantry and artillery, equivalent to a heavy division. I have given command to a senior officer of whose energy I am certain... Battle has been accepted on terrain of our choosing and under the best conditions, against an enemy of whose resources we were aware up to about 15 December. But during the past two weeks serious

intelligence informs us of the arrival of new resources (37mm AA guns, perhaps heavy artillery and motorized equipment); and if these really exist, and the enemy succeeds in getting them into action, then I can no longer guarantee success with certainty.[41]

The sombre tone of Navarre's letter – echoed in his end-of-year report to Paris – should perhaps not be taken wholly at face value. Any information he chose to share with politicians was certainly calculated to create a desired response, and the C-in-C was also enlisting Jacquet's support for a request for more bombers and transport aircraft. As always, Dien Bien Phu was just one of the pieces on Navarre's board, and he apparently remained confident about his longer game. On 3 January the US Ambassador Donald Heath, reporting to John Foster Dulles' State Department on one of his regular meetings with Navarre, quoted the Généchef as declaring that even the loss of Dien Bien Phu or of ten battalions of his *corps de bataille* would not prevent him pressing on to eventual victory.[42]

The existence of Giap's 105mm howitzers had been known since well before 'Castor'; but the 37mm AA guns, and the national effort to provide the roads over which hundreds of trucks could move both types of guns and their ammunition so far from the Viet Bac, were a revelation. General Cogny certainly reported the movement of two battalions of 105s on 6 January and this was confirmed by aerial photos on the 9th.[43]

General Cogny would send Navarre the requested appreciation of 'Ariane' and 'Xénophon' on 21 January. He considered any break-out plan 'a solution of despair... a quasi-impossibility', inviting disaster at the hands of the Viet Minh forces that were believed to be in place around Dien Bien Phu.[44] Bernard Fall quotes from the internal FTNV staff memoranda which lay behind this conclusion: any break out would involve the sacrifice of most of the best units in order to cut a way free for the worst, and would have to be supported by resources from all over the peninsula if it were not to become a hopeless retreat. A verbal shrug by Cogny's chief-of-staff Colonel Bastiani revealed an attitude at FTNV which the Dien Bien Phu garrison would not have found reassuring: 'In any case, it will have to be the Commander-in-Chief's battle. Presumably he must have foreseen the necessary requirements before getting himself into this kind of hornet's nest.'[45]

GENERALS AIM TO WIN THEIR reputations by offensives; and the battle which the C-in-C certainly regarded as his own now opened on 20 January among the dunes, marshes and lagoons of the southern Annamese coast. Some commentators have criticized Navarre for proceeding with Operation 'Atlante' in view of the clouds gathering around Dien Bien Phu, but this is surely unrealistic. The two operations were on completely different scales, involving different troops against different enemies, on widely separated and different types of battlefield, with different objectives. Most of the assets which Navarre had carefully assembled for 'Atlante' would not have been usable in the High Region, even if it had been practicable to transfer and sustain them there at short notice.

The grip of the Viet Minh's Fifth Integrated Zone (Lien Khu 5) on the difficult coastal terrain of southern Annam dated from 1946, and had never seriously been threatened by French operations. The 'fish' were about 30,000 fighting men, including 12 regular and six good regional battalions, swimming at ease in the 'ocean' of a population perhaps 2 million strong, in many hundreds of villages densely planted throughout an area of nearly 10,000 square miles. The aim of Operation 'Atlante' was nothing less than to destroy or drive out the Viet Minh and establish the authority of the Bao Dai government, over an area stretching about 230 miles from south of Tourane (Da Nang) down to north of Nha Trang, and some 40 miles inland into the plateaux of the Central Highlands (see Map 1).

This offensive was to provide the Armée Nationale Vietnamienne with its first serious test in major, sustained operations. It was the only way to create on the ground the politico-military situation that Paris needed, and General Navarre attached so much importance to it that he had 'decided to subordinate to it the conduct of the whole Indochina campaign during the first half of 1954'.[46] The mass of the ANV were never going to win their spurs in North Vietnam; and it would be remarkable if Navarre had not already understood that the future negotiations which the government favoured must inevitably raise the question of partition. Territorially, Tonkin might well be a lost cause; but South Vietnam might have a future in association with France, and it was the ANV who would have to learn to defend it.

'Atlante' was planned as a six-month offensive unfolding in three phases, the numbers of troops committed increasing with each phase as they penetrated deeper and spread out. The first, Operation 'Aréthuse', would open with landings on the coast around Tuy Hoa and last from three to four weeks, involving 25 infantry and three artillery battalions with supporting troops. At the beginning of March they would be reinforced for 'Axelle', to 34 infantry and five artillery battalions; this phase was to last six to eight weeks. Finally, in May, 45 infantry and eight artillery battalions would undertake Operation 'Attila', envisaged as lasting for another two months. In sheer numbers, then, 'Atlante' dwarfed Navarre's commitment to the High Region.

The great majority of these troops would be Vietnamese, supported by French spearhead and specialist units. For the initial phase 21 ANV infantry battalions would be committed, including 12 brigaded in four ANV Groupes Mobiles supported by two French motorized brigades.[47] For the final phase in early summer these would be reinforced by one more ANV and three French Groupes Mobiles, and the TDKQ light battalions committed would increase from six to 12.[48] French paratroopers and naval commandos would also be available for specific missions; the infantry would enjoy strong armoured, amphibious and naval support, and the whole resources of the Air Force's GATAC/Centre and GATAC/Sud. Inevitably, the services of some of Colonel Nicot's transport squadrons would also be needed – the air supply programme for Dien Bien Phu was noticeably affected in late January and February.

The initial landings and advance around Tuy Hoa proceeded without any serious problems, but also without decisive clashes. The Viet Minh made the French and ANV pay dearly for the first villages, then followed their familiar pattern: behind sacrificial rearguards which slowed the pursuit and caused a steady drain of casualties, they faded back into the marshes and hills. As the weeks dragged on and the troops spread out, the numbers of casualties crept up; the countryside was thick with mines, booby-traps and snipers, and as the lines of communication to the coast became stretched and individual units more isolated, the serious ambushes began.

General Giap had been taken by surprise; he had planned that Lien Khu 5 should mount diversionary attacks to coincide with his first attempt on Dien Bien Phu, which he may still have hoped to unleash on 25 January. Nevertheless, he did not react hastily; the regions had long understood that this winter they could not count upon any assistance from the Chu Luc. (The exception was Division 320, which had been ordered in late December to filter through the De Lattre Line from the south and help the local independent regiments to turn up the pressure inside the Delta. The usual cycle of attacks on posts and ambushes had been escalating, usefully aggravating General Cogny's immediate concerns, and on 21 January a major ambush on the Vietnamese Groupe Mobile 31 virtually destroyed one of its battalions.) While the regional units resisting 'Atlante' settled in for the type of evasive delaying campaign that they understood so well, other Viet Minh units drew off some of their opponents by attacking unexpectedly in the High Plateaux, where some 16,000 regulars and regionals had been awaiting orders to go on to the offensive.[49] The only major French asset in the triangle Kon Tum–Pleiku–An Khe was GM 100, which now began a six-month ordeal of zig-zagging back and forth along RC14 and RC19 through the baking, scrub-covered hills, while the Viet Minh pulled its strings to lead it into a long series of costly ambushes. On 27/28 January the town of Kon Tum was menaced; it was abandoned on 5 February, shortly after the visiting French junior defence minister Alain de Chevigné had publicly declared that it would be defended to the last.[50] The Viet Minh then advanced on Pleiku, which, if they took it, would give them a base for operations all over the Central Highlands. Pleiku had to be supplied entirely by air, thus adding to the strain on Colonel Nicot's Dakotas. The Viet Minh then moved to threaten An Khe. Reinforcements had to be rushed into the hills in the most exhausting weeks of the dry season; some – including the Legion paratroopers of 2 BEP – had to stay there until mid March, and the second phase of 'Atlante' had to be postponed for two weeks. Giap's 'raid' by Division 308 from Dien Bien Phu towards Luang Prabang in early February (*see below*) would be another urgent drain on the French reserves during these weeks.

On 25 February the preamble to General Navarre's directive for operations in March and April included the claim that the first phase of the offensive had been successfully achieved – more or less...[51] In fact 'Atlante' would never recover its momentum, and 'Attila' would remain in the realms of the might-have-been.[52] Depite the huge resources invested in it the offensive simply leaked away into stagnancy; and by late March the behaviour of many ANV units had shocked even Navarre into questioning the central role of 'Vietnamization' in his strategic plan. On 26 March he admitted in a letter to General Paul Ely, now Chief of the Defence Staff: 'It is now clear that, however sceptical I was when Monsieur Pleven asked my opinion on the possibility of the Vietnamese relieving us in the short term, I was still too optimistic. They are incapable of doing anything serious for several years yet...'[53]

LOOKING BACK ON THE CAMPAIGN, General Fay, Chief of the Air Staff, would write: 'It would have brought better results if we had consistently concentrated the maximum of bombs on one or two points and ensured the almost permanent cutting of the route at these points by harassing the repair work.'

In fact, in early January General Navarre had ordered a change of tactics to concentrate GATAC/Nord's resources on Tuan Giao, where intelligence reports confirmed the accumulation of stores and where aerial photos identified general areas of activity. Operation 'Bazard' followed on 8, 9 and 11 January: a total of 98 tons of bombs were dropped, causing visible secondary explosions and fires. But the Viet Minh had years of practice in safeguarding their stockpiles from air attack, and at Tuan Giao the depots were dispersed over several dozen square kilometres of forest. Those seen around Phu Doan during Operation 'Lorraine' were described by Lieutenant Ferrandi: 'Each package corresponded to the resupply for not more than one company; but it included, in never more than one cubic metre's space, everything that the company needed – small arms ammunition, mortar bombs and rations. Tens of these packages were carefully isolated and perfectly camouflaged.'[54] To destroy a significant proportion of supply dumps protected with such intelligence would have taken saturation raids dropping thousands of bombs; and 'Torricelli' could not dream of mounting such operations.

Even those bombers which were available were not employed for mass effect; the great majority of missions were flown by formations of three aircraft or fewer.[55] Following a visit of inspection in February, General Fay reported: 'Bombers are currently employed as if they were fighters, not for massed action... A study should be made of grouping the bombers under a single commander, for use against targets which justify massed action.' This recommendation was not followed up with any force until 9 April, when General Navarre demanded from General Ely the despatch of an expert bomber leader from France.[56]

The final reason for 'Torricelli's' failure to cut the arteries of Giap's Front Supply Commission was simply that the Air Force bomber crews were poorly trained. Bombing is a highly technical skill, which had been neglected for several years. The need to form the B-26 squadrons from 1951 had been met by reassigning transport crews whose training in their new role had been patchy at best. A good deal of discussion went on about the best ways of attacking the supply routes: whether at one spot or many; whether from 8,000 or 2,000ft; whether by bombing the hillside above a road to cause a landslide, or the slope below to undercut it. There was some use of radar-fused bombs to produce air bursts, but these became unpopular after an accidental mid-air explosion destroyed two B-26s. Whatever the technique chosen, however, a report subsequently compiled for the C-in-C during May is blunt:

> The examination of aerial photographs shows that the bombing was scattered. There was no concentration on the targets; the terrain all around was cratered in an almost uniform manner... The bombing campaign suffered from lack of leadership: the young squadron commanders, without experience of [aerial] bombardment, were ignorant of its principles. There were no massed formations, not even of six aircraft; the bombs were released together on the order of the lead bombardier... The bomber pilots, coming from transport units, lack aggression and are too accustomed to the safety of flying over our own lines.[57]

THE DIFFERENCE IN SAFETY between the skies over the Delta and the liberated zones was well known to the Air Force. The dividing line was often the Ba Vi hills south-west of Son Tay, and pilots who were suspected of too many convenient engine problems early in a mission were called 'Ba Vi experts'. But while the Air Force had encountered anti-aircraft machine-gun fire increasingly over the past two years, the most vulnerable points along Giap's lines of communication were now protected by more dangerous concentrations than most pilots had ever experienced. These might be found at any choke point or frequently attacked stretch of road, particularly around the river crossings. During 1953 the number of aircraft hit had increased fivefold over 1952 figures, to a total of 255 including ten shot down; but after Operation 'Castor' AA fire became more the norm than the exception. Between 24 November and 8 December alone, of 51 fighter-bomber sorties 45 were hit and one was shot down, along with two spotter planes. During the rest of December, of 367 sorties against the Viet Minh road system by Air Force and Navy aircraft – the great majority of them by Bearcats – 49 aircraft reported hits; and from Christmas onwards an increasing number of sorties had to be diverted to the specific task of locating and suppressing the AA guns.[58] General Lauzin's report on operations over the whole month of December noted that increasingly active and accurate flak had hit 53 aircraft in all, of which three were high-flying Privateers; the immediate consequence was the loss of 470 precious flying hours. Many pilots reported 20mm fire, and others 37mm or 40mm; General Lauzin gave the latter no credence in December, but by 15 January General Cogny did, and mentioned them to the US Consul Paul Sturm.

The carrier pilots from *Arromanches* played a full part in these interdiction missions, at constant risk and with little to show for their dedication. Lieutenant Commander de Castelbajac's Hellcats of *11e Flotille de Chasse Embarquée* usually flew in patrols of only two aircraft, each pair succeeding one another over the target zones, which embraced the whole enemy supply route from Tuyen Quang to Dien Bien Phu. Since only a pair of fighter-bombers could attack together it is not surprising that they usually had to report their results as 'not observed' or 'uncertain'. Labour gangs and marching troops were sometimes bombed and strafed, but they quickly scattered into the cover of the forest, and any damage to the roads was usually repaired overnight.

On 5 December patrol 'Savart Blue' (Lieutenant Robin and Petty Officer Andriès) were flying a routine 'mission of assault and reconnaissance' (MAR) over RC2 between Phu Tho and Tuyen Quang, armed with parachute-retarded anti-personnel bombs (*see Map 7*). South of Cho Chu, Robin was killed when his '11F-30' was shot down in flames – the Aéronavale's first loss in this tour. On 11 December, Hellcat '11F-16' flown by the squadron's *'pacha'*, Castelbajac, was hit by 12.7mm fire while on a mission south of Thanh Son. Two days later 'Savart Green' (Lieutenant Commander

Lespinas and Petty Officer Michon) were both hit by AA fire while attacking large parties of troops and labourers near Thach Thanh. On 9 January four Hellcats led by the CO attacked targets at Tuan Giao from 150ft; Lieutenant Commander Doe de Maindreville's aircraft was hit over 'Melchior', a stretch of RP41 just east of the village, and several AA emplacements were spotted south of the road between Tuan Giao and Dien Bien Phu. On 23 January, Lieutenant de Torcy's Hellcat was hit just behind his seat while attacking target 'Vautour' immediately west of Tuan Giao; and on the 25th, Petty Officer Michon was hit once again over 'Melchior'.

At this point the *Arromanches* shifted station southwards to Tourane (Da Nang), where for some days her aircraft flew in support of Operation 'Atlante'. Between 11 and 28 February she was absent on a voyage to Hong Kong dockyards, but her air group continued operations from the Delta bases, now concentrating on attacks in the immediate area of Dien Bien Phu as the French attempted to locate and knock out Giap's artillery emplacements. Although the suspected targets were marked for them by artillery smoke shells or Morane spotters, the results continued to be 'not observed'; increasingly heavy AA machine-gun fire was encountered around Dien Bien Phu, and one damaged Hellcat had to force land on the airstrip on 26 February. The flak continued to grow in intensity at the beginning of March, but attempts to find and suppress its sources were as frustrating as ever.[59]

It should not be forgotten that flak was not the only hazard faced by the fighter-bomber pilots. Navigation is always challenging for the pilot of a single-seater, and these barely mapped mountains, so short of landmarks, were often cloaked by dramatic weather with little warning. On 7 February, three Bearcats from GC 2/22 flown by Captain Rapinet, Lieutenant Jouvenel and Sergeant Sahraoui were on a mission over the Laotian border when they ran into appalling conditions – 'eight-eighths' cloud and turbulence at 3,000ft. Only the young Algerian, Sergeant Ali Sahraoui, managed to find his lonely way back to Haiphong–Cat Bi: his two companions both flew into mountainsides.[60]

DESPITE ALL THEIR HANDICAPS, the effort by GATAC/Nord's aircrews did have an effect on the flow of matériel to Giap's assembling army. By concentrating on hillside sections of the road they aggravated the difficulties of the repair gangs, even though these usually managed to fill or bypass all but the largest craters within a couple of days by felling trees and moving large volumes of earth. After Dien Bien Phu fell the captured Major Nicolas, commander of I/4 Moroccan Rifles, was able to watch the process:

> There were many holes in the road, but we saw 250 or 300 coolies
> emerge from the woods with picks, shovels and baskets. They quickly
> set to work to repair the damage. One episode struck me particularly:
> they called for volunteers to neutralize an unexploded bomb with a long
> delay fuse. More than ten men raised their hands; one very slightly built
> man slipped into the bomb crater and tied a rope to the tail fins. The
> team dragged it out and rolled it into the woods, where we heard it
> go up about half an hour later...[61]

The stretch of RP41 north-west of Co Noi became extremely crowded during late December and January, when it was shared by marching troops of Divisions 308 and 312, artillery and supply columns (the *bo doi* apparently greeted the sight of the towed 105mm guns with astonished delight, calling the trucks 'mothers pulling young ones').[62] French intelligence intercepted radio traffic which suggested that the Viet Minh were experiencing real difficulties. General Giap's planned schedule for opening the attack on Dien Bien Phu in late January depended entirely on the arrival of sufficient men and supplies and the installation of his artillery. He would later write that he monitored the movements of rations and ammunition on a daily basis; the Front Supply Commission reported to him by telephone at 6am each morning, and he kept a constantly updated graph beside his desk so that he could check the previous night's figures. After one night of heavy rain when not a single ton of rice moved on the road, he laid his operational tasks aside for several days and devoted himself to the logistic problems.

An officer of Division 312 recalled that in the period 25 January to early March the arrival of rations was very uneven, to the extent that many men fell sick. His unit was about three miles forward of the nearest depots, up rudimentary jungle paths. They lacked tobacco, meat and vegetables, and received only 'sticky' rice which they found difficult to cook properly – when it arrived at all. Most companies had to organize groups of foragers to gather what wild food they could find in the jungle, giving each man a daily allowance of 7oz of greenstuff from extremely mixed sources. Little by little the situation improved, and by mid March they were receiving regular rations of salt meat, soya sprouts and tobacco; thereafter, throughout the battle, there was no shortage of food.[63]

IT IS UNCLEAR EXACTLY WHEN General Giap accepted that his original timetable for attacking Dien Bien Phu on 25 January had been too optimistic, but he confronted the problem in the middle of that month. His scouts had been observing and mapping the camp and identifying its defending units since 25 December. Most of his infantry were probably present, but that did not mean that they were ready: approach trenches – an essential feature of Viet Minh assault tactics – had not been dug close to the French positions. A series of new tracks through the hills to make possible the emplacement of his heavy guns was not completed until 15–20 January. Given that Division 312 would soon be reduced to eating leaves, it is not surprising that Giap was dissatisfied with the state of his forward depots. The Front Military Committee met to consider the options on 14 January. Some favoured attacking without delay, since the 25th would coincide with the opening of the four-power conference in Berlin, and a Viet Minh initiative would have an excellent propaganda effect. Others argued that the People's Army should stick to the slow, methodical approach that had served them well.

The official Viet Minh account dates the decision to postpone as 18 January, citing as reasons 'imperfect' preparations, and French reinforcement of Dien Bien Phu. This may refer to the creation of the northern strongpoint 'Gabrielle' in early January; to the simultaneous construction of protected dispersal pens for Bearcat fighters, which confirmed the French intention to base aircraft there permanently; and to the appearance of Dien Bien Phu's tanks (*see Chapter 9*).[64]

The arguments for postponement may have been supported by Giap's 'fraternal' advisers. French wounded repatriated after the battle reported seeing a number of Europeans with the People's Army, either East Germans or Russians, and one of the former was apparently important enough to be surrounded by staff officers and bodyguards. Another, thought to be a

Russian, interrogated German légionnaires at length. The Chinese, however, were by far the most numerous foreign advisers. It is generally believed that two or three senior People's Liberation Army officers were attached to each of Giap's divisions; but the part played by the military mission at his headquarters – about 20 officers, led by General Li Cheng Hu – remains cloudy. The Second Bureau reported that a Chinese and a Russian military mission were present in the rear areas near Dien Bien Phu in January.[65] This is a subject of great sensitivity, given the historic suspicion of China and the enormous pride that the Democratic Republic of Vietnam takes in the victories of 1954. While freely acknowledging the debts owed to the Communist Chinese example and to material aid, any direct Chinese involvement has always been denied. It is difficult to imagine, however, that the advice of senior officers installed by the Viet Minh's supplier, armourer and trainer could have been ignored at a moment when the People's Army was undertaking by far its most ambitious operation.

The infantry went grumbling back to their holding camps in the forest, and Giap ordered large supplies of picks and shovels. Those artillery batteries which had already been emplaced with such hard labour were also pulled back; a member of Division 312 would write: 'We were nearly at the end of our toil when the order came... the arms which had ached to get them up [7 miles] of slopes now had to bring them all down again.' The officers and men were unhappy at being stood down after preparing themselves mentally for an attack on 25 January.[66] At a command conference on 7 February, General Giap explained to his subordinates that a rushed attack would have been foolishly 'adventurous'. Its postponement would allow the siege army to ensure supremacy of numbers and firepower; February and early March would be devoted to perfecting preparations for a long-term campaign, and they were to institute various security measures the better to protect the army from French artillery and aircraft.[67]

THE IMMEDIATE EVIDENCE OF Giap's determination to dilute French reserves in Tonkin while he completed his preparations was an order that uprooted Division 308 from their hidden camps around Dien Bien Phu, and sent them marching south towards Luang Prabang in Laos. The division moved on 27 January, so the need for logistic preparations would tend to support a date around mid January for Giap's decision. It was accompanied by Independent Regiment 148, and Battalion 970 from Division 316's Regiment 176 – all units recruited from highlanders, in contrast to 308's Delta farmers enlisted around Hanoi and Vinh Phuc province.

How seriously General Giap intended this detached force actually to reach the Laotian royal capital is questionable, but it could in any case do much useful work on the way. The siege ring around Dien Bien Phu was vulnerable from the south, where partisans were active and the skilled jungle soldier Major Vaudrey was fighting Viet Minh regionals in the Nam Ou river valley. On 21 January, Generals Navarre and Cogny had discussed the possibility of Giap continuing to fix Dien Bien Phu by limited attacks while also sending some of his force down into Laos. They had considered how to react to this scenario, and by 25 January Colonel de Crèvecoeur's small Land Forces Laos command had been unconvincingly reinforced by flying the 2nd and 3rd Thai Battalions from Dien Bien Phu to the airstrip at Muong Sai.

By 1 February the People's Army had already captured the strategic post of Muong Khoua (*see Map 8*), inflicting serious losses on II/2 REI (Crèvecoeur's best unit) and the 2nd Laotian Light Infantry Battalion. Division 308 was obliged to halt at the confluence of the rivers Nam Ou and Nam Pak in order to gather rafts and sampans to transport them across, and to bring up the heavy weapons and supplies which the leading infantry had outpaced. Here at last the French Air Force were able to blunt their progress, by attacks on their line of march and on the river traffic.

Regiment 148 and elements of Division 308, including its integral artillery battalion, were ordered to prepare for an attack on the important post at Muong Sai, a thrust in which the other regular units would follow them. However, despite French fears for the Laotian king's capital which reverberated as far away as Paris, only two regional battalions probed further south towards Luang Prabang. On 13 February, Major Souquet's 1 BPC were dropped to reinforce Muong Sai in their third operational jump since 20 November; by the time the first four battalions of Division 308 could hope to reach the post it would be defended by six battalions, and GATAC/Nord was already flying protective sorties.[68] The troops of Groupe Mobile 7 were flown into Luang Prabang, bringing the total garrison to nine battalions. There was no further major movement until the night of

20/21 February – when all the Viet Minh units turned about and headed north again. From mid February it had been clear that any further advance would meet serious resistance, tying down an important part of Giap's army in its turn.[69]

The garlands thrown or denied to Giap's raid into north-west Laos by later commentators depended upon their view of its objective. If it was ever intended to capture Luang Prabang or even the airfield at Muong Sai then it was a complete failure, frustrated by a prompt and effective French response. If its ambitions were limited to destroying the hope of a productive overland link between Dien Bien Phu and Laos, cowing the border partisans and distracting French reserves, then it was a success. Rather more damaging was its demonstration that Dien Bien Phu could not, after all, threaten the rear lines of any Viet Minh invasion of Laos: Division 308's expedition was blocked largely by troops from elsewhere in Indochina, and while it was taking place the remaining People's Army units around the valley were frustrating all the garrison's attempts at long-range sorties.

ON 18 FEBRUARY THE FOUR-POWER delegations in Berlin announced that a wider conference at foreign minister level would be convened in Geneva on 26 April, to discuss outstanding issues over both Korea and Indochina. This time Communist China would be represented; and although not a formal participant, it was understood that a Viet Minh delegation would be present under Chinese sponsorship. It was obvious that the announcement of the conference would have immediate and far-reaching effects on the conduct of the campaign. At Geneva the positions and tactics adopted by the French, the Viet Minh and all other parties would be dictated by the military map of Vietnam as it existed on 26 April. The importance to each side of a decisive victory was impossible to overstate. This knowledge must have been central to General Giap's decision to abandon the advance on Luang Prabang, since Laos was now merely a distraction from the arena in which he had a chance of winning incalculable political prizes.[70]

The French stance at Geneva as foreseen by Prime Minister Laniel and Foreign Minister Bidault might be cautious; but no one could doubt that if senior figures such as Paul Reynaud and Marc Jacquet got anywhere near a Viet Minh delegation they would negotiate seriously. When he returned to Paris from his tour of inspection on 27 February, Defence Minister Pleven was still hostile to direct negotiations. He sent General Navarre a copy of his report, which stressed that news of face-to-face discussions between France and the Viet Minh would be seen as treachery by the Vietnamese National Army, whose already dubious morale would collapse. The fear of a French scuttle would present them with good reasons to curry favour with their prospective Communist masters, opening the floodgates to mutiny and assassination – Pleven used the phrase 'one risks the Sicilian Vespers'.[71] Pleven's view was that France must go to Geneva armed with the best military situation possible; but he did not shrink from considering the implications of a partition of Vietnam on the Korean model somewhere between the 16th and 18th parallels, and he predicted that China would not veto such a solution provided that the Viet Minh got Tonkin and northern Annam.

General Navarre had never had any illusions about the fragility of France's political will, but now it was explicit. The coming battle for Dien Bien Phu would be regarded by both sides as a test of endurance and will-power for the highest prize, and all sane military judgements of cost and benefit would be abandoned. There are few worse missions that soldiers can face than being sent to fight for a political symbol; and in later years Navarre would always argue that it was the government's announcement of the Geneva conference on 18 February that sealed the doom of Dien Bien Phu.

DURING DIVISION 308'S RAID to the south, the siege army continued the back-breaking work of emplacing the artillery of Heavy Division 351 as it arrived during January and February. There seems to be no evidence that any of its successive convoys were damaged or even seriously delayed by French air power during their whole journey from the Viet Bac. In the face of modern Western disbelief, General Giap had harnessed one of Asia's few great strengths: her massed numbers, mobilized and organized to a single purpose. Now, in choosing how to emplace the artillery that this epic had delivered to him, Giap once again put his trust in the Viet Minh's particular experience rather than looking to Western models. This would be his first large-scale attempt to introduce a wholly new element to the Viet Minh's methods of warfare; all the more reason, then, to cling to the tactics that had served him best over the past seven years. What the People's Army understood was concealment, and surprise attack from short range.

Conventionally, artillerymen place their guns in the temporary concealment of folds in the landscape, free to turn their aim towards an enemy wherever he appears; and after a few shots their instinct is to move them, to avoid the return fire which will surely come soon. Such movements, in almost trackless terrain and under French-ruled skies, would be hugely difficult and dangerous; so Giap installed his guns not on the outer slopes of the valley, but in special casemates – in effect, caves – sunk into the forward slopes of the hills facing Dien Bien Phu. Faced with the twin threats of the Air Force and the camp's own artillery, he gave priority to avoiding the first. In theory it was suicidal: to emplace guns on the forward rather than the reverse slopes opened them to destruction by the counter-battery fire of the French artillery as soon as they were seen – at the latest, as soon as they fired or moved to switch targets. Giap's artillery officers were only recently trained to a fairly rudimentary standard; but his scouts would spend at least ten weeks observing and mapping every detail of the camp below them. If Giap took this gamble, then he would be able to give his batteries the simplest possible task – to fire by direct observation at only one or two stationary targets each, never moving to engage in a complex fire plan. Since they would not even have to traverse to fire in several directions, they could be installed in very narrow, heavily protected emplacements with only the muzzle exposed behind a camouflaged gunport.

Tunnels were dug into the slopes under cover of night by large gangs of labourers, and revetted with heavy logs. The soldiers and coolies were supervised by camouflage experts to ensure that the surrounding undergrowth was disturbed as little as possible and carefully replaced before dawn to hide any raw earth – the People's Army were deeply concerned by the danger of air attack. The guns were then dragged off the tracks and up the hillsides; once they had been manhandled backwards into the casemates, the entrances were almost blocked with logs and earth spoil consolidated with wicker gabion work.[72] In May the French artillery commander Colonel Vaillant was shown 105mm positions by his proud captors. From the front, the narrow port looked like an inverted 'L'; to bring the gun into position it was manhandled sideways and forwards to fire out the vertical slot, then withdrawn backwards and sideways behind the partial front wall – the whole process was rather reminiscent of 'running up' the cannons of an old sailing warship. The camouflage was checked daily and continually renewed with fresh foliage; it would be moved aside immediately before the gun fired so as to avoid scorching. The camouflage made the guns invisible from the air, and when they began intermittent ranging shots from 31 January a gun could be located only if its muzzle flash was seen – and if the observer could fix that point on a monotonously unvarying jungle hillside. (Concealment was extended to the airwaves: the People's Army were well aware of French radio interception skills, and all the artillery positions were patiently linked with field telephone cables so that they could maintain radio silence.) Vaillant reported seeing batteries of three or four guns, but also a number of isolated pieces, and all beneath at least 13ft of overhead earth cover.[73]

Although a Chinese influence has been argued plausibly, the description of these positions also recalls some of those constructed with such lethal brilliance by the Japanese on Pacific islands such as Peleliu and Okinawa in 1944–5. It is tempting to wonder what became of those officers and soldiers from the Japanese 38th Army who are known to have assisted the Viet Minh in their earliest post-war days.

Apart from the casemates themselves the siege army also dug and camouflaged ammunition stores, crew shelters, command and observation posts. This achievement argues a heavy use of labourers, and in fact it had been known to the Second Bureau in October 1953 that Heavy Division 351 allocated no fewer than 1,100 men to each battery of 75mm guns including 217 per gun, of whom 118 were porters.[74] The 105mm howitzers were divided into two groups, one emplaced in the upper Nam Youm valley north-east of what would become 'Béatrice', and the other due north of the valley in the area where the Pavie Track climbed the slopes of the Muong Phang plateau.

The time needed to manhandle a gun from the nearest track to its battery position – with block and tackle, drag ropes, levers and chocks – had been calculated at three nights. The half-ton 75mm guns were not too difficult to move, since they could be broken down into 11 loads and carried along the ridge tops. The 105s, each weighing just under two tons and not designed for 'pack' transport, in fact took seven nights each. The future General Tran Do, then a member of Division 312, was among the infantry pressed into helping with this *keo phao* or cannon-pulling:

> Each night, at the hour when the freezing fog came down the hills into the valley, groups of men arrived on the road... The [six-mile] track was so narrow that if a slight deviation of the wheels had taken place the gun would have fallen into a deep ravine. The newly opened track was soon an ankle-deep bog. With our sweat and muscles we replaced the trucks to haul the artillery into position... We ate only rice – sometimes undercooked or overdone... the kitchens had to be smokeless by day and sparkless by night. To climb a slope, hundreds of men crept in front of the gun, tugging on long ropes, pulling it up inch by inch. On the crest the winch was creaking, helping to prevent it slipping... It was much harder descending the slope... The gun was all the heavier, the track full of twists and turns... Steering and chocking were the work of artillerymen, while the infantry worked with ropes and windlass. Whole nights were spent toiling by torchlight to move a gun 500 or 1,000 metres.[75]

Tran Do claims that French spotter planes did locate the teams' passage by daylight due to the withering and disarrangement of foliage camouflage, and that combat aircraft strafed and bombed them. The only such recorded success seems to have been on 23 January, when a group of men around several guns were spotted and attacked from the air, and later shelled.[76] He states that by night the French artillery was very active and sometimes caused many casualties, particularly by the lethal splinters from tree bursts; when they came under fire there was nothing the hauling teams could do but throw themselves flat, still clinging to their drag ropes, and hope for the best. The Viet Minh made a national hero of a soldier named To Vinh Dien, who threw his body as a living wedge under the wheel of a slipping gun.

The hasty return of Division 308 at the end of February coincided with accelerated preparations for attack, and the flow of munitions and supplies to Tuan Giao increased in the first days of March. A Viet Minh source again quotes the officer from Division 312: 'Our division received the new task of constructing communication paths – [18 miles] in three directions, and [13ft] wide, for artillery towing vehicles... They had to be camouflaged from the air... the more progress we made, the more difficult it got – there was a lack of big shovels, saws, crowbars, rock drills, axes and sledge-hammers. We crossed streams [50yds] wide, attacked rock walls, cleared huge old trees...' [77]

THE EXACT NUMBER OF ARTILLERY pieces deployed by the People's Army at Dien Bien Phu is still the subject of some disagreement. In October 1953 the first report by the Second Bureau of Giap's acquisition of 105mm guns had mentioned a possible figure of three battalions each of 12 pieces. In January 1954 another report gave the field strength of Heavy Division 351 as Regiment 45 (24 × 105mm); Regiment 675 (18 × 75mm, of which 12 × Japanese mountain guns and 6 × US pack howitzers; plus 20 × 120mm mortars); Regiment 237 – whose presence at Dien Bien Phu was unconfirmed – (30 × mortars, of 82mm and/or 120mm); and Anti-Aircraft Regiment 367 (approximately 100 × 12.7mm heavy machine guns, plus at least 36 × 37mm cannon).[78]

These and other estimates are discussed in Appendix 4 at the end of this book; however, on balance it seems safe to assume that Giap in fact opened the battle with 36 × 105mm howitzers, probably 24 × 75mm mountain guns/howitzers, 50 × 120mm mortars, plus perhaps 60 × 75mm heavy recoilless guns with the infantry support companies. These numbers would be reduced by breakdown and enemy action, but the exact figures are perhaps unimportant: the Viet Minh would certainly outnumber the French in weapons of 75mm and above by between two and three to one, but it was their concealment that was always the decisive factor.

As for the anti-aircraft artillery, General Navarre's letter to Secretary Jacquet on 1 January shows that he was aware by that date that the enemy had 37mm guns; and General Cogny's conversation with Paul Sturm before 15 January said that pilots had come under large-calibre fire over the lines of supply. It still seems unclear whether or not any had arrived at Dien Bien Phu by the time Giap cancelled the planned 25 January attack. On 3 March further Second Bureau reports informed Navarre that a column of heavy weapons had been seen on the Tonkin side of the Chinese frontier on 23 February. These were hidden under tarpaulins, but from their shape they were believed to be either 37mm AA guns, 152mm heavy artillery, or even Russian armoured vehicles. Their identity would remain uncertain for some time, but labour gangs were working ahead of them to widen the roads, and particularly the corners, to take vehicles with a turning circle of 52ft; it was this that finally convinced French intelligence that these were in fact anti-aircraft guns. Were these the heavy guns of AA Regiment 367, following the machine guns and light cannon already en route or installed; or were they a second unit?[79]

Although some commentators believe that a second 37mm regiment in addition to Regiment 367 was sent to Dien Bien Phu, and have suggested that up to 80 × 37mm guns were present, hard evidence for more than 36 actually being deployed there seems to be elusive. It is as logical to guess that any second 37mm regiment might have been dispersed along the lines of supply. The 37mm ammunition stock at the start of the battle is believed to have been 44,000 rounds, which would not seem to support more than 36 guns (although other convoys might, of course, have eluded French surveillance).[80]

Ammunition stocks for the field guns by mid March stood at somewhere between 8,800 and 10,400 rounds for the 105s, plus about 5,000 rounds for the 75mm guns. Figures of 21,000 mortar bombs are quoted, of which 3,000 were for the heavy 120mm weapons. A further 200 tons of ammunition were expected shortly, with two tons of medical supplies.[81] Although the mortar ammunition figures are surprisingly low, and surely cannot be comprehensive, the often expressed French fear that General Giap would 'rob them of their battle' at Dien Bien Phu by flinching from a general assault seemed increasingly ill founded.

GENERAL GIAP REMAINED preoccupied by the enemy's firepower and monopoly of the air, but was also concerned to brace his officers and men for their first-ever sustained positional battle. On 22 February he confronted his subordinates once again with the implications of uninterrupted fighting through the monsoon:

> If the campaign is prolonged into the rainy season the construction of field works will be difficult, and our troops will suffer from the wet. But we are on the slopes, where we can dig drains; the enemy down on the plain will find his works flooded and destroyed without respite. Our

opponents have more to fear from the rains than we do... We will have difficulty in resupplying. But we have good engineer units stretched out behind us, which will repair any destroyed roads; if the trucks cannot get through, then our porters will bring up rations and ammunition; and we always have the river traffic. If things come to the worst, then the revolutionary spirit of our troops will allow them to endure all hardships and privations... We are going to suffer casualties in this battle. Our victory will be bought at the cost of bloodshed – all revolutionary victories have to be paid for with sacrifices...[82]

On 25 February, a confident General Navarre issued a general directive. Major enemy movements seemed to have been blocked by air–ground bases at Dien Bien Phu, Muong Sai, Luang Prabang, Seno and Pleiku, and holding these was the key to future offensive exploitation. He would accept and win a battle at Dien Bien Phu; he would assemble in the Delta an airborne brigade to reinforce it if necessary, and the camp was to be strengthened in men, munitions and supplies. The Air Force was to give priority to supporting Dien Bien Phu and to harassing Division 308 during its return march north (of which he had been informed on 23 February). Navarre's strategic enthusiasm for air–ground bases was as undented as his outward faith in a victory at Dien Bien Phu. So far the CEFEO had 'weathered the cape' of the winter campaign season without suffering any major defeat at the hands of the Chu Luc (whatever its other disappointments), and the air–ground bases seemed to be succeeding in channelling the enemy's offensives into unimportant wildernesses – 'les grands vides'.[83]

General Cogny was, as usual, hypnotized by the defence of the Delta; he had received intelligence warnings of a major Viet Minh effort against the Hanoi–Haiphong railway in mid March by units from Bac Ninh province, and appealed to Navarre for another three or four battalions. He was refused them; instead he could use the paratroopers of GAP 1, returning from Laos.[84] Instructed by Navarre to plan how best to exploit a Viet Minh retreat from Dien Bien Phu following the enemy's failed assault or avoidance of battle there altogether, he responded on 27 February in terms which we may by now consider predictable: by urging a strike north out of the Delta to enemy base areas around Lang Son.

By the end of February, Navarre was receiving intelligence reports that Division 308 had returned from Laos and was in position west of Dien Bien Phu. Orders had been issued to Viet Minh commanders throughout the country for operations in June and July. They were also instructed to step up conscription of new troops; and to put men on the road for Dien Bien Phu – from as far away as Lien Khu 5 in southern Annam – as casualty replacements for the siege army. China had been asked to supply more vehicles, arms and ammunition. Early in March heavy Viet Minh radio traffic suggested that preparations for an attack were nearly complete.[85]

The strain on Colonel Nicot's transport fleet during the build-up of men and matériel at Dien Bien Phu had increased steadily – the garrison now numbered about 10,000 men in 12 infantry and two-plus artillery battalions; and it was noticeable that the AA fire was becoming bolder and more accurate. Captain Soulat, commanding the handful of French crews for the big C-119 Packet transports, made a strongly worded request for more cover: his 'Flying Boxcars' were having to fly straight and level at 1,500ft to parachute their loads, while the B-26s – many of which had a murderous battery of machine guns in the nose – continued to bomb tranquilly from 12,000ft. It was agreed that the B-26s would dive down in attempts to suppress the AA fire immediately before the C-119s made their runs. Flak over the valley, however, was not the only danger faced by the transport fleet.

A month previously, on the night of 1/2 February, a disturbing incident had taken place at Do Son airfield on the coast south of Haiphong. A Viet Minh commando team had crawled up a sewage pipe from the sea and penetrated this Dakota repair and maintenance base; before they were driven off, leaving four dead behind them, they had destroyed four C-47s, shot up the officers' mess, and burned a fuel depot. Far East Air Forces had become paranoid about security, but apparently to no great avail. Now, on the night of 3/4 March, commandos got past the barbed wire and sentries at the key operational base of Hanoi–Gia Lam; they reached the hard-standing where aircraft were parked, and blew up five Dakotas and five requisitioned civil aircraft. On 6/7 March a similar attack was made on Haiphong–Cat Bi; and although the paras of Bigeard's 6 BPC from their nearby barracks killed all but one of the Viet Minh, four B-26 bombers and five Morane 500 spotters were still destroyed.

THE PEOPLE'S ARMY WERE digging growing networks of approach trenches close to Dien Bien Phu's perimeter strongpoints, and Colonel de Castries, the camp commander, was convinced an attack was imminent. On 11 March, General Cogny replied that his Second Bureau reports of enemy ammunition movements indicated a probable date of 13–14 March. There was a resumption of the sporadic harassing fire from Viet Minh artillery, which had begun at the end of January but had tapered off after 20 February. An accumulation of intelligence suggested that the Tuan Giao depots expected to issue food rations for 52,000 men during March and April.[86]

Such totals have been quoted carelessly elsewhere to exaggerate General Giap's advantage; in sheer numbers of men he outnumbered the Dien Bien Phu garrison by five to one, but the proportion of those who were combat infantry was much lower. In the hills surrounding the valley he had assembled 28 infantry battalions; at full strength each should have had about 800 all ranks, giving a total of around 22,400 men.[87] The average strength of the 12 French battalions was rather lower, but in infantry Giap barely had the superiority of three to one that is reckoned to be the minimum an attacker needs to overcome the inherent advantages enjoyed by a dug-in defender.

His heavy artillery was untried, and locked into an experimental deployment which would be terribly difficult to change if it proved a failure. He had only marginally adequate supplies of ammunition; he had no armour, no air force, not even steel helmets for his men. This would be his army's first attempt to sustain a pitched battle over a matter of weeks – against the army whose fathers had endured at Verdun for ten months, and won. 'If we are sure to win, fight to the end; if not, resolutely refuse combat.' Vo Nguyen Giap was not an 'air-conditioned' general; we are surely permitted to imagine that in his cave near the waterfall in the Muong Phang hills he sat late into the night, poring over his maps of Dien Bien Phu and wondering just exactly what kind of enemy he faced.

9. GONO

'The general feeling was that Dien Bien Phu was very solid, that the Viet Minh knew it and would not dare unleash a general assault. Doubtless they would continue their harassments, sound out various strongpoints, even try to take them – but in the opinion of the troops there was no possibility of a general and sustained action.'

General de Castries, *in his report to the 1955 Commission of Inquiry*

ON 30 NOVEMBER 1953 TWO officers met on the staircase of the Hotel Métropole in Hanoi. Both veterans serving their third tours in Indochina, they knew and respected each other, although they were utterly different personalities. The next six months would see their lives entwined for ever.

One, hobbling on the plastered ankle that he had broken at Dien Bien Phu ten days before when he jumped at the head of the 2nd Airborne Brigade, was a gaunt, wiry, 44-year-old paratrooper with a closely cropped skull, big ears, and a razor-slash mouth which was almost invariably clamped round a cigarette. Lieutenant Colonel Pierre Langlais was a Breton from the poor, rock-bound north-west of France, a region with a long tradition of providing recruits for both the Navy and the Army – and of stubborn resistance to the arrogance of Paris. Langlais was a grown-up whisky drinker, famous for his sulphurous temper. When he graduated from the officers' academy at St Cyr in the early 1930s he had chosen the most uncomfortable posting the French Army had to offer – the Saharan camel companies, where a subaltern spent lonely months at a time ranging the world's most desolate wilderness with only his native *méharistes* and a couple of French NCOs for company. From the African Army he had passed into the CEF to fight in Italy, and thence into de Lattre's 1st Army in Alsace and Germany. After the war Langlais had shipped out to Indochina as a battalion commander with the 9th Colonial Infantry Division, taking part in the house-to-house fighting in Hanoi in winter 1946. His second tour, from 1949, had brought service on the Chinese frontier, in Annam and Laos. Back in France, he qualified as a paratrooper and in October 1951 took command of a half-brigade of Colonial battalions (1 DBCCP) in training as replacements for Indochina. He returned to the Far East for the third time in June 1953 to command GAP 2.[1]

The man Langlais ran into on the hotel staircase had just been appointed as his next commanding officer. Tall and debonair, with silver-grey hair and heavy black eyebrows over a parrot's beak of a nose, he, too, walked with a slight limp – in his case, a permanent reminder of old wounds which obliged him to use a shooting stick. Although Colonel Christian Marie Ferdinand de la Croix de Castries was, at 51, seven years older than Langlais, they felt themselves to be contemporaries since they had both been in Indochina since the start in 1946. Colonel de Castries' background was pure French military aristocracy; the family tree included a marshal, an admiral and nine generals. Yet when he reached the age of 20 just after World War I, the young blade had perversely chosen to enlist in the ranks of the cavalry, putting up with the hard knocks of barrack-room and stable for three years. He was a sergeant in the 16th Dragoons (in which regiment also served a Lieutenant Henri Navarre) when, in 1925, he was selected for the Saumur cavalry school as an officer candidate. After graduating he clearly felt that he had earned the sweets of privilege. The very model of a fashionable cavalry subaltern, he held a place in the national equestrian championship team for 12 years, and for amusement flew aircraft, gambled himself into debt, and made a string of scandalous conquests among society ladies.

During the 'Phoney War' of 1939–40, Castries volunteered for the Corps Francs, and distinguished himself with these raiding parties which stalked no-man's-land on the Sarre front. When the *Blitzkrieg* overwhelmed France in June 1940 he and 60 men held off a German battalion for three days. Wounded and taken prisoner, he made four escape attempts before he tunnelled out of Oflag IVD camp in Silesia in 1941 and made his way across Germany, France and Spain to join the Free French in Africa. Castries was wounded a second time in Italy, but recovered to lead a light armoured squadron in Colonel Navarre's 3rd Moroccan Spahis during the final advance into Germany, and distinguished himself at the capture of Karlsruhe.

In 1946 he led a Spahis squadron in Cochinchina during General Leclerc's first campaign; he was not without vanity, and his trademarks were the handsome scarlet sidecap of the Spahis and a matching silk scarf. After a course at the War College he returned in 1951 to a sector command in the Delta under de Lattre. This brought him a growing reputation as an audacious fighting commander, more medals and mentions in despatches – and, while leading from the front in a jeep, an encounter with a Viet Minh mine which smashed both his legs. After convalescing from this third wound he was appointed to a staff job at Supreme Headquarters Allied Powers Europe, and despite his injuries actually returned to competitive riding in 1952. When his old *patron* Navarre succeeded to the supreme command in Indochina Castries volunteered for a third tour, leading a Groupe Mobile in the Delta as a full colonel.

When Navarre had to pick a man of sufficient experience and rank for what was in effect a divisional command at Dien Bien Phu, he had few options. The size of the force justified a general officer, but the best generals were in important appointments from which they could not be spared. At the next level down – colonels who were considered *'généralisable'* – only two names presented themselves: Paul Vanuxem, a legendary infantryman, who had only just taken up a vital sector command in the southern Delta; and Christian de Castries, who had done well with a two-brigade force at Lai Cac during Operation 'Mouette' only a month previously. The emphasis of 'Castor' was on the supposedly offensive mission of the garrison, who were not foreseen as getting shut up in a tight perimeter, but as manoeuvring freely all around the flat valley floor. Navarre had little hesitation in choosing the dashing cavalryman, and General Cogny had no objections. Castries would arrive at Dien Bien Phu to take over from General Gilles on 7 December, on which date his command would officially be named Operational Group North-West – in its French abbreviation, GONO.[2] In the brief interim he would survive yet another adventure: on 4 December he, his private secretary Mlle Paule Bourgeade and his artillery colleague Colonel Piroth had a narrow escape when Viet Minh commandos raided their divisional headquarters at Thai Binh in the southern Delta.[3]

A COMMANDER TASKED WITH defending a position has two main options when planning how to use his forces. The Roman army historian Derek Williams has likened the extremes of these doctrines to the oyster and the peach.[4] The 'oyster' commits the bulk of the defenders to an outer shell of perimeter positions, dispersed between them according to a judgement of where the main attacks will fall. The perimeter may hold off the attackers for a long time, but if they manage to break through, then the soft interior, and the rear of the defensive perimeter, are at their mercy. The 'peach' defence spreads a relatively thin membrane around the outer edges to slow and weaken the attackers, but holds back most of its best assets in a central reserve. It accepts that attackers will break into the interior, though hopefully weakened by the resistance of the perimeter, and gambles on being able to destroy them by concentrating powerful reserves for a counter-attack when the direction of the threat has revealed itself. Choosing an effective balance between these approaches, governed by the ground and the available troops, is one of the fundamental skills of military command, whether the defenders are a company holding a hilltop or an entire army guarding a national frontier.

The first choice the commander must make is how far out from the essential centre – at Dien Bien Phu, the airfield – a perimeter can be held. A small garrison can hold only a small perimeter, but they can hold it 'shoulder to shoulder', and their concentrated fire should be deadly to assaulting infantry. However, if the perimeter is too small the enemy can get close enough to fire into the essential centre without having to assault the perimeter. If a breakthrough does occur, there is no depth in the defence to buy time, and the enemy's rush may overrun the centre before the defenders can move to counter it. If the perimeter is too large, the troops holding it are spread too thinly to prevent the attackers breaking through at some point, and the distance between them and the reserves in the centre is too great for them to be reinforced in time.

General Cogny's orders called for the garrison to maintain free movement out to a radius of five miles from the airstrip; so the balance chosen at Dien Bien Phu tended towards the 'oyster'. Legion and North African infantry would form an outer shell, while two agile paratroop battalions, supported by artillery and heavy mortars, would provide a central reserve. In an order on 19 December, Colonel de Castries defined the role of the battalion localities around the perimeter as to hold out by their own resources augmented by supporting artillery fire, and to make local counter-attacks to recover any temporarily lost strongpoints, until counter-attacks by the central reserve were mounted.[5]

THE INFANTRY ORIGINALLY envisaged as occupying Dien Bien Phu were half the airborne assault force – GAP 2 – to provide the offensive agility, with the troops that were going to be withdrawn from Lai Chau as static defenders. These were two Indochinese battalions – the ANV's *Tieu Doan* 301 and the CEFEO's 2nd Thai Battalion – and a Moroccan light infantry unit, the 2nd Tabor of Goumiers; they would be flown into Dien Bien Phu by 10 December. At an early stage in the planning it was decided to add the infantry and artillery of a full Groupe Mobile: GM 9, strong in légionnaires and led by a renowned combat officer, would be flown into the valley by 20 December. A more realistic judgement of the potential of the Lai Chau troops, and developments in the High Region during the first days of 'Castor', quickly persuaded Generals Navarre and Cogny to add a second Groupe Mobile – GM 6 – and to reinforce the garrison steadily to about 10,000 men by the end of December, including 12 infantry battalions. Four of these were units of the Foreign Legion.

The 2nd Foreign Infantry Regiment had been formed in 1945 as the Foreign Legion Marching Regiment/Far East, originally intended for operations against the Japanese, and was the first Legion unit to land in Indochina. After operating around Tourane (Da Nang) its 1st Battalion (I/2 REI) had moved up to Tonkin in December 1946. Among its many subsequent combats, this unit had fought on RC6 during the battles of disengagement from Hoa Binh in early 1952.

The 3rd Foreign Infantry bore the traditions and the many decorations of the legendary World War I and World War II Foreign Legion Marching Regiments (RMLE); it had come up from Cochinchina to Tonkin in 1947, to be dispersed in posts close to the Chinese border. The 3rd Battalion was wiped out in the retreat of Colonel Charton's column from Cao Bang in October 1950. Re-raised around a draft from the 1st Foreign Infantry, III/3 REI served with Groupe Mobile 4, and in winter 1952/3 paid some of the regiment's debt to the People's Army in the successful defence of the Na San airhead. At Dien Bien Phu, III/3 REI would come under the sector command of Lieutenant Colonel André Lalande, CO of both 3 REI and Groupe Mobile 6, to which the battalion would belong administratively. Lalande was a former artilleryman who had graduated top of his class at the War College in 1946, after a fine World War II combat career with a unit that was regarded as something special even within the Legion – the 13e Demi-Brigade.

Formed in 1939 too late for a planned expedition to aid Finland against the Soviet invasion, 13 DBLE had been sent into battle in spring 1940 against the German Wehrmacht at Narvik in Norway, alongside British and Free Polish troops. Withdrawn to Britain almost simultaneously with the fall of France, a sizeable proportion of its men rallied to General de Gaulle when he raised the flag of the Free French in June 1940; 13 DBLE were, indeed, virtually his only infantry in those first desperate months. The regiment had fought a long and at first a lonely war, trailing like a military orphan at the heels of the British. In 1941 the 13th fought the Italians in Eritrea and soon afterwards, in a bitter episode, Vichy French troops – even fellow légionnaires, of 6 REI – in the Levant. In North Africa it served with the British 8th Army, and counted among its battle honours General Koenig's defence of Bir Hakeim and the attack at El Alamein, where the regimental commander, Lieutenant Colonel Amilakvari, had fallen at the head of his men. It fought in Italy in 1944, before landing in the South of France and driving north into the savage winter campaign in Alsace as part of the new 1st Motorized Infantry Division. There was always bad feeling between the original Gaullist units and those who had obeyed the terms of the 1940 Armistice; 13 DBLE were fiercely proud of their record as the first defenders of the flame of Free France, and even in 1954 they still contrived to wear a khaki beret recalling the years of desert exile when they had been clothed by the British. Since 1946 the regiment had fought all over Indochina; in 1948 another much admired CO, Lieutenant Colonel Alain de Sairigné, had been killed in action. The 3rd

Battalion had served in the Delta in 1951, and both I/ and III/13 DBLE fought in the Hoa Binh battles of 1951/2. In 1953 both units formed the backbone of Groupe Mobile 9, commanded by 13 DBLE's regimental commander, Lieutenant Colonel Jules Gaucher. A burly, hard-drinking veteran of years of jungle fighting, with a nose like an axe-blade and a mouth like its cut, the 48-year-old Gaucher had been in Indochina since 1940. His legend had grown since he fought the Japanese in this very valley in April 1945 (it now included much more recent fist fights in Hanoi bars, as well as more conventional engagements).[6] Gaucher commanded huge respect and confidence; he was 'the Old Man', a fighting Legion officer of the old school, dedicated to his men and his corps rather than to the furtherance of his career.

The final Legion units were the 1st and 2nd Foreign Composite Heavy Mortar Companies (1 and 2 CMMLE), raised from légionnaires of 3 and 5 REI respectively. Each had eight 120mm tubes; the 1st Foreign Parachute Heavy Mortar Company (1 CEPML), which had remained in the valley since jumping in on the second day of 'Castor', would scrounge an extra four.

ONE MOROCCAN AND THREE Algerian battalions would fight at Dien Bien Phu; between them these units had long experience of combat in most parts of Indochina, as both sector security troops and mobile intervention units.

The 2nd Battalion, 1st Algerian Rifle Regiment (II/1 RTA), raised in the Blida area of the department of Algiers, had landed in Tonkin in September 1949 as part of the Groupe Mobile Nord-Africain (GMNA – retitled GM 1 in October 1950), and took part in all that brigade's operations in the Delta, central Annam and the Thai Highlands. It fought in the victorious pitched battles of Vinh Yen and the Day River in early 1951; the following winter the unit saw action at Cho Ben and on RC6 during the Hoa Binh campaign. The Tirailleurs were later flown into the Na San airhead, where they stayed from November 1952 until late spring 1953. After a few months with GM 3 from August 1953 the battalion was flown into Dien Bien Phu in mid December to form part of the new Groupe Mobile 6. This record is deceptive, however. The men in the ranks of II/1 RTA in winter 1953 were mostly young, some with only four months' service, and they were seriously under-officered: instead of the 18 theoretically necessary for an efficient battalion, they had ten, of whom only five were infantrymen by training.[7]

The 3rd Battalion, 3rd Algerian Rifles (III/3 RTA) was raised at Bône in the department of Constantine, and landed in Tonkin in December 1949; they were posted at first to the north-east (Tien Yen, That Khe). In May 1950 the battalion went south to Cochinchina for security operations in the Viet Minh stronghold of Thu Dau Mot province north of Saigon; then into Cambodia, and later to central Annam. As a unit of the general reserve from November 1952, III/3 RTA served with Groupe Mobile 7 in Tonkin; but during 1953 they were shifted back and forth all over Indochina. In the five months before it was flown into Dien Bien Phu as the third battalion of GM 9 the unit had had only ten days of rest, and it was unquestionably too tired to be considered wholly reliable.

The 5th Battalion, 7th Algerian Rifles (V/7 RTA), was also recruited among the tough Berber highlanders of the Constantinois. Formed from occupation troops in Germany, it landed at Haiphong in May 1951 and thereafter spent its whole service as a local sector battalion with the Delta security forces until posted to join GM 6 in Dien Bien Phu in December 1953. The Legion officer Erwan Bergot states that V/7 RTA still had a fair number of long-service veterans in the ranks.[8]

The 1st Battalion, 4th Moroccan Rifles (I/4 RTM) was shipped to Tonkin at the end of 1950, arriving at the height of the crisis following the Viet Minh triumph on RC4. In the early days of General de Lattre's reign the unit served with GM 4. It stayed in Tonkin throughout its service; after the Hoa Binh/RC 6 battles of winter 1951/2 it took part in several major operations within the Delta, winning a citation in Army orders for an attack on a fortified village near Nam Dinh. In winter 1952, GM 4 took part in Operation 'Lorraine'. In 1953 the battalion was transferred to GM 7, seeing more action in the south of the Delta before being selected for Dien Bien Phu. Early in its stay it would earn respect for determined road-opening operations between the main camp and the far southern location codenamed 'Isabelle'.

Moroccan gunners also served in the mixed-race III/10 RAC and 11/IV/4 RAC. The only black African combat unit at Dien Bien Phu was the artillery battalion II/4 RAC. Here they were to serve under circumstances which brought out the best in them: devotion to good leaders, a cheerful willingness in their work, and – particularly remarked upon – an admirable steadiness under enemy artillery fire.

A TOTAL OF 11 AUXILIARY COMPANIES of the Thai Mobile Partisan Group (GMPT), patched together from the survivors of the retreat from Lai Chau (see below), would be dispersed between the various strong-points at Dien Bien Phu, together with two Thai regular battalions. Both the latter had previously served with the experimental Groupe Mobile Vietnamien, behaving well as light infantry skirmishers but far less reliably in defence of dug-in positions at Na San.

The 2e Bataillon Thai (BT 2) dated back to mid 1947, when it was raised from Black Thais and Nungs in the Hoang Lien Song mountains; it had fought well there around Lao Cai, but one company had been roughly handled by Giap's Regiment 141, at Na San exactly a year before 'Castor'. Now led by a Legion officer, Major Maurice Chenel, the Thais had suffered declining morale since they were driven out of their own hills; nevertheless, they were assigned to the central reserve at Dien Bien Phu.

The 3e Bataillon Thai had been formed in 1949. At one time led by Marcel Bigeard, it operated around Phu Yen and Son La, earning an Army citation for its conduct on the Black River in spring 1951; but again, since the end of 1952 its home region had been occupied by the Viet Minh. The Thais' morale during Operation 'Mouette', when serving with GM 4 near Yen Lai, was questionable; they were badly shaken when they suffered 100 casualties in an ambush. The Thais apparently showed little fight, and the Viet Minh contemptuously sent some unwounded prisoners stumbling back to the French, stripped naked.[9] Major Léopold Thimonier's battalion had a most beautiful badge – a pair of crossed silver native war-hammers, banded and spiked, with a scarlet python coiling around the shafts; but they seemed to have lost their stomach for this war. Colonel de Castries asked for the replacement of both Thai battalions with better units from the Delta, but General Cogny felt unable to oblige him.[10]

COLONEL DE CASTRIES' ABILITY to manoeuvre his central reserves anywhere in the defended area was paramount; and to add punch to this effort the former cavalry commander requested, early in December, that a tank squadron be flown in. In a minor epic of ingenuity and sweat codenamed Operation 'Rondelle II', ten M24 Chaffees were each stripped down into 180 components, flown into the camp, and reassembled. The skilled work was done by just 25 men of Lieutenant Bugeat's 2nd Platoon, 5th Foreign Legion Medium Repair Company (2/5 CMRLE) on a makeshift open-air production line beside the airstrip, plagued by blowing dust and equipped only with a heavy lifting rig borrowed from the artillery. Airlifting each 18-ton tank took six Dakota sorties and two by British Bristol 170 freighters requisitioned from the commercial airline Société Indochinoise de Ravitaillement; the latter, with their six-ton capacity and clam-shell nose doors, were the only aircraft which could take the Chaffee's hull (and, indeed, most of the trucks which also had to be flown in).[11] The légionnaires achieved the extraordinary rate of one tank reassembled every two days; although the first did not arrive until 18 December a platoon of three 'bisons' was ready for operations by Christmas Day, and all ten by 15 January. The squadron commander was the popular 24-year-old Captain Yves Hervouët of the 1er Régiment de Chasseurs à Cheval (1 RCC), who arrived with his left arm in a sling after a recent accident; his mixed crews came from that unit and the Régiment d'Infanterie Coloniale du Maroc (RICM), and the squadron was designated 3e Escadron (de Marche), 1 RCC.

WHILE THE ARRIVAL OF THE FIRST Dakota on 25 November started the construction of the camp's central facilities, the various battalion localities forming the perimeter would only be definitively established on various dates from 15 December onward. It will be less confusing, however, to describe them as the coherent system which they had become by February. The simultaneous expeditions by the paratroopers into the surrounding hills, which took place in parallel with the construction of the defences, are described later in this chapter.

The heart of GONO was placed south of the airstrip and the newly bridged Hong Lu stream, tucked to the west of the serpentine loops of the Nam Youm in the area where the village of Muong Thanh had stood (*see Map 11*). Here, in the area codenamed 'Claudine' extending west from the river astride a stretch of the Pavie Track, there grew up between December 1953 and February 1954 a cramped town of tents, roofed dug-outs, sandbag pens and earthen berms, jammed together on every available square yard of ochre dust. Immediately south of the airfield the paratroopers of Captain Tourret's 8th Shock were dug in (after the first few days of the battle in March they would be moved slightly north-east to occupy a new strong-point, 'Epervier', created on the old 'Dominique 4' between the southern end of the runway and the river). South of their trenches and rudimentary shelters was a large depot area with stores dumps of every kind, workshops and transport parks, power generators, and the water purification plant on the river-bank.[12] East of this area, in a sluggish curl of the river, were the underground hospital and the little cemetery.

South of the depots of the Commissariat were the three large dug-out command posts of the garrison and its constituent brigades. Colonel de Castries' GONO HQ resembled a large buried Nissen hut, with a central corridor flanked by dimly lit compartments, their raw walls screened with rattan mats. Along one side were the Second Bureau (intelligence), a briefing room, offices for Colonels de Castries and Piroth, the artillery fire control HQ ('PC Feux'), and an office for Lieutenant Colonel Trancart, commanding the northern sector; facing them were hutches for the air control HQ and various staff and secretariat. Here a secure teletype and Z13 UHF radio link between Castries and General Cogny's HQ in Hanoi was maintained throughout the battle; they would talk at least twice a day. Beside the main HQ to the west was Lieutenant Colonel Gaucher's similar GM 9 command post; east of it, on a hummock on the other side of the roadway, that of Lieutenant Colonel Langlais' GAP 2. Near the HQs the engineers scooped out hull-down positions to protect seven of the garrison's ten tanks.

Straddling the Pavie Track north-west of the headquarters were the large circular gunpits for part of the artillery force – the 105mm howitzers from III/10 RAC and a 155mm battery from IV/4 RAC. One battery of 105s from II/4 RAC was placed in Dominique 3 east of the river, and the other two in Dominique 4 east of the southern end of the airstrip. The 120mm mortars of the three Legion heavy companies were initially divided between these two artillery areas, but some platoons would soon be dispersed to Dominique 2 and Gabrielle. Immediately south of the row of headquarters, GAP 2's other reserve paratroop battalion – 1 BEP (Major Guiraud) – dug their trenches.

Around and among these major landmarks of the earth and canvas metropolis, scores of humbler dwellings would be burrowed by home-steaders from a variety of support and service units – signallers, mechanics, electricians, military policemen, drivers, storekeepers and cooks. Soon the once lush valley floor looked from the air like a chaotically crowded yellow slum – veiled with wind-blown dust, plumed with smoke from field stoves and trash fires, spider-webbed with dusty tracks, cheerfully flagged with drying laundry by day, treacherous by night with forgotten slit trenches and temporary wire barricades. The dwellings of the military *bourgeoisie* sprouted thickets of radio aerials; they were also linked by countless telephone cables, some of them buried, some strung between the occasional tree trunks which were spared the axe to support them.

Further still to the south, a safe distance from the nerve centre, Sub-lieutenant Léonard and his logistics troops of the Service du Matériel established the enormous ammunition dump. Here too were conveniently sited prisoner-of-war compounds where the PIM labour pool lived under the most casual of guards; more than 2,400 of these prisoners of ambiguous status would be flown in as labourers.

Around this denuded central area the green valley floor stretched away, covered with grass and light brush, seamed with dykes, hedge lines and streams. To the north, west and south paddy-fields alternated with stretches of heavy undergrowth and trees, studded with occasional Thai hamlets of stilted huts; on the eastern river-bank the valley was closed in by a line of low, scrub-covered hills; and beyond, around the whole compass, steep, thickly forested ranges receded to the horizon – the nearest rising about 2,300ft above the valley floor.

Given the size of the valley – some 11 miles long north to south, by three miles wide – it was obviously impossible to construct a continuous line of outer defences: at the accepted rate of one battalion per 1,500yds that would have taken 50 battalions, not 12. The defences were prepared as a series of defended localities ('centres of resistance', CRs) identified by codenames, each comprising several numbered strongpoints sited for mutual defence by the interlocking of their fields of fire. These localities and strongpoints were of irregular sizes and shapes dictated by the ground. Among the lessons of Na San had been that the People's Army were skilled at infiltrating between strongpoints that were sited too far apart; and that if these were held by isolated companies, they could be overrun too easily.

The enemy had to be held far enough away from the airfield to prevent their interfering with its use by machine-gun and mortar fire; and the defenders on the east flank obviously had to hold the nearest hilltops (*see Map 14*). Averaging about 130ft above the valley floor, and mostly covered with trees and thick brush – as were those which faced and in some cases overlooked them – these hill features were only about a quarter of a mile across the Nam Youm from the main camp area. The battalion localities planned for the north-east flank, codenamed 'Dominique' and incorporating two hills about 130 and 230ft high, were assigned to the Algerian riflemen of Captain Jean Garandeau's III/3 RTA. The gap between Dominique 1 and Dominique 2 would be covered by an artillery battery in location Dominique 3 on the eastern river-bank flats behind them.

The high Dominiques overlooked the hilltops of 'Eliane' to the south-east, which would be held by the Moroccans of Major Jean Nicolas's I/4 RTM. East of the tallest, the 130ft Eliane 2, were two other features which were not taken into the perimeter: to the north Mont Fictif ('Phoney'), crowned by a fake French position visited by daily patrols; and to the south Mont Chauve ('Baldy'), which was linked to the lower slope of Eliane 2 by a saddle. Behind these eastern ramparts two bridges crossed the lazy brown water of the Nam Youm – about 30yds wide – to link the central camp with the east bank defences: an original wooden span to the south, and a British prefabricated steel and plank Bailey bridge to the north. The defensive positions of the two Moroccan sapper companies from the 31st Engineer Battalion (31 BG) were dug into the east bank flats of Dominique 3 and Eliane 3.

In the level terrain of rice paddies and scrub stretching away to the north and west of the central camp there were no hill features on which to anchor the perimeter. The west side of the airstrip was protected by a series of positions codenamed 'Huguette', entrusted to légionnaires of Major Clémencon's I/2 REI with support from three CSLTs – Thai Light Auxiliary Companies (*see Maps 12 and 13*). The south-western arc of the central camp would be guarded by the 'Claudines' – only vaguely defined from the camp itself – held by Major de Brinon's (later, Major Coutant's) I/13 DBLE, with two more Thai companies (*see Map 11*). The furthest defenders to the west would be Sergeant Chief Comte with a lonely little group from 414 CSLT at 'Francoise' – a sort of 'doorbell' about 500yds out in the paddies, where this western flank was covered by a long 'wave-breaker' barbed wire entanglement.

The north and north-west of the airfield would be covered by 'Anne-Marie', a very widely dispersed series of four strongpoints held by the Thais of Major Thimonier's BT 3, and supported by the fire of a platoon of mortars from 2 CMMLE in Claudine. Anne-Marie 3 sat at the northern end of the runway, with Anne-Marie 4 in the brush about 600yds west of it. About 750yds north of Anne-Marie 4, Anne-Maries 1 and 2 crowned the twin hillocks of a crescent-shaped feature rising from the paddies (*see Map 12*).

Even with Legion mortars to stiffen them the Thais did not inspire huge confidence; and the all-important bastion blocking access to the valley from the north where the Pavie Track emerged from the hills would be 'Gabrielle', a substantial, boat-shaped feature rising some 180ft above the rice-fields and scrubland about a mile and a quarter north of the end of the airstrip. This was confided to the Algerian riflemen of V/7 RTA, flown in from the northern Delta on Christmas Day under the command of Major Roland de Mecquenem. The battalion was reinforced by 416 CSLT and – more solidly – by the four 120mm mortars of Lieutenant Clerget's platoon of 2 CMMLE.[13]

Guarding the north-eastern access to the valley between the Nam Youm and RP41 was another isolated hilltop location variously known as Him Lam, Hill 506 and 'Béatrice' (*see Map 12*). Just under a mile north of the northern edge of Dominique, this was surrounded by thick scrub and butted into the edge of the forest proper, which cloaked the hills of equal height immediately to its north and south. This vital outwork, control-ling the enemy's approaches to the left flank of Dominique and the right of Gabrielle, was to be held by perhaps the most highly regarded infantry unit in the garrison: the légionnaires of Major Paul Pégot's III/13 DBLE.

Finally, completely isolated far away to the south, lay 'Isabelle' (Ban Hong Cum), occupied from 16 December (*see Maps 9 and 19*). This was a supposedly self-sufficient satellite of the main camp which straddled a wide, marshy loop of the Nam Youm a good 3½ miles down the valley. Its garrison had three tasks: to guard a secondary airstrip; to house two 105mm batteries providing artillery support for the hill strongholds along the east of the main camp, whose outer faces could not easily be covered by howitzers inside the valley; and to launch, if necessary, counter-attacks against enemy units threatening the southern face of the main camp. For this reason Lieutenant Préaud's platoon of three tanks would be based at Isabelle, together with the Algerians of Captain Pierre Jeancenelle's II/1 RTA and the légionnaires of Major Henri Grand d'Esnon's III/3 REI. All these were on the west bank; across a hastily built bridge, an isolated strongpoint east of the river would be held by Lieutenant Wieme's 431 and 432 CSLTs.[14] Since the whole locality was only some 750yds wide, conditions were miserably cramped. Command of Isabelle was held by 3 REI's veteran Lieutenant Colonel Lalande. A patrol base codenamed 'Marcelle' was established about halfway up RP41 towards the main camp, and held by 434 CSLT under Sergeant Chief Cante until 14 March; on that date they had to be withdrawn to Isabelle, and joined Wieme's other companies in the swampy trenches of Isabelle 5.

The command responsibilities of the senior officers did not exactly conform to their previous Groupes Mobiles: Gaucher of GM 9 was entrusted with the defence of the 'central sector' – the whole perimeter to the north-east and east (Béatrice, Dominique and Eliane), and also the western edge of the central camp (Huguette, and such fighting positions as Claudine then possessed). In the north and north-west, Gabrielle and Anne-Marie were under the command of Lieutenant Colonel Trancart, formerly CO of the Lai Chau garrison. From an early stage in the defence these theoretical divisions would become practically irrelevant; as will be seen, units from all over the main camp were sent wherever they were needed.

TYPICALLY, A BATTALION locality or 'centre of resistance' consisted of a number of strongpoints each surrounded by its own trenches and wire entanglements; only on Gabrielle's large hilltop did a battalion have a single clear-cut perimeter of continuous trenches. The defences surrounded a central core, where dug-outs protected the command post (CP) with its radios, the medical aid post and a few other positions, and where the HQ company's 81mm mortars were planted in open pits. At a couple of carefully chosen points on the perimeter, log and sandbag 'blockhouses' holding 0.50in heavy machine guns were usually pushed slightly forward from the trenches to command the most important approaches.

The localities were typically divided into company strongpoints; each had one or more blockhouses, usually sited at protruding angles of the trench system, where the company's 0.30in machine guns and 57mm recoilless gun were positioned to pour enfilading fire along the faces of the strongpoint. A short zig-zag of ditch linked advanced machine-gun bunkers with the perimeter trench (and when the time came, a veteran officer would know enough to station a man with a haversack full of grenades by the MG blockhouse entrance, facing back towards the main position). The shoulder-fired light machine guns were not covered over, but left in the open air of the trenches so that they could be shifted as the occasion demanded. Near the company CP the two 60mm mortars were dug in. Men with rifle grenade launchers were often posted here too; and wise officers, however meagre their manpower, kept a small reserve of riflemen – *grenadiers-voltigeurs*, in French parlance – close to their CP for immediate counter-attacks to choke off any enemy penetration.

Some machine guns were emplaced opposite slanting lanes – not obvious to frontal attackers – through the barbed wire and minefields which were laid in outer defensive belts. Supposedly at least 80yds out from the manned positions (the range of a People's Army bazooka), these belts were fairly thin due to shortages of wire and particularly of mines – which also prevented the laying of adequate internal barriers to seal off one strong-point from another within some battalion localities.[15] The reader should not imagine the huge entanglements seen in some Great War photographs. The purpose of the wire was to stop an enemy rush for long enough to make its front ranks helpless targets, and to channel it into the sights of the machine guns; it was usually strung from iron pickets and wooden stakes in a series of interlocking 'cattle fences' at about thigh height. At a few points the conventional anti-personnel mines had been thickened up a little with electrically triggered 'command detonated' charges, and drums of napalm buried at the tops of convenient slopes. The defended locations were criss-crossed with internal communication trenches, and the battalion command posts were linked to company CP bunkers by field telephone cables strung along the side walls of the trenches.[16]

THE CONSTRUCTION OF THESE perimeter strongholds was left to the troops who would hold them. The 11 officers and 300 overworked Moroccan sappers of Major André Sudrat's 31st Engineer Battalion – flown in on 4 and 21 December – were normally fully occupied with plating the airstrip, building bridges, and constructing the central facilities, though infantry units were sometimes sent small specialist teams and labour gangs of PIMs. Labour was a constant problem: to dig in properly a battalion needed about two months (it took a platoon five days just to build one weapons blockhouse with adequate protection). Throughout the winter the relative priority given to fortification work was subject to constantly changing orders, and before mid February the paratroopers and infantry had to give precedence to sorties and patrols which left inadequate time to work on their positions.

The first step in fortifying a locality was felling and saving any timber and clearing off the scrub. How far out the undergrowth should be cut was a matter of opinion; Colonel de Castries ordered that wide fields of fire be cleared all around, but some officers – such as Major de Mecquenem on Gabrielle – believed that shaving the positions allowed the nearby Viet Minh scouts too good a view of the defensive preparations.[17] On most positions the degree of clearance was governed more by the available time and manpower than by fine tactical judgements, but the majority were more or less shaven bare. While the felling and clearing was still being done, unit commanders had to plan the layout of the defences – not easy, when the lines of sight were still obscured; and there was unlikely to be time to correct any mistakes or open up any overlooked 'dead angles' once the digging had been done. Some officers were no doubt better than others at planning defences, though the basic theory was well understood. Old hands even built fake 'blockhouses' to draw enemy infantry into planned killing fields, making sure to visit them regularly so that the watchers would have no reason for suspicion.

Once the brush had been cleared the trenches were dug easily enough; these were not the major subterranean highways of the old Western Front, but simple shoulder-deep ditches with low parapets of thrown-up spoil, a yard wide at most and zig-zagging every few yards to protect the inhabitants from any lengthways sweep of blast or bullets. In most cases, however, the construction of the protective dug-outs and blockhouses suffered from a lack of man-hours, of urgency, of expertise and of suitable materials. Before late December the emphasis remained on the camp's offensive role, and the need for field fortifications capable of resisting prolonged assaults was not acknowledged. Most of the French units had few (if any) officers or men with experience of facing serious artillery fire; up to now the troops' experience of enemy heavy weapons had been limited to mortars, bazookas, recoilless guns, and a few old Japanese 75mm mountain guns.

The high command's knowledge that the enemy had 105mm howitzers, and was attempting to deploy them to Dien Bien Phu, was not translated into general orders until 26 December when – prompted by a Christmas inspection by General Navarre – Colonel de Castries distributed specifications from Colonel Legendre, General Cogny's chief engineer, for overhead cover proof against field artillery.[18] Some unit officers did give priority to such protection; notable in this regard were Major de Mecquenem on Gabrielle, and Lieutenant Colonel Lalande – the former gunner – at Isabelle, while a few ex-Wehrmacht NCOs set a good example on other Legion positions. However, most commanders were handicapped not only by the French Army's culture of distaste for serious digging, and by a lack of skilled hands to do the work, but also by a chronic shortage of building materials.

The standard norms for such protection had been understood since the Great War: preventing a shell from penetrating required at least 3ft of tightly packed earth between two layers of heavy logs at least 6in thick, with sturdy props no more than 6ft apart, and all – crucially – beneath a hardened 'bursting layer' of stone rubble, concrete, or sheet metal, to detonate impact-fused shells as far above the dug-out as possible. The valley of Dien Bien Phu offered no source of quarry stone; there was simply no provision for a programme of concrete pouring; and even when the valley and its immediate surroundings were stripped of trees the local timber supply was quite inadequate. Without a hard bursting layer a dug-out roof needed a good 6ft of packed earth and logs. Major Sudrat estimated that in addition to locally available materials, the engineer stores needed for building shelters and weapons positions for 12 battalions totalled about 34,000 tons. This represented at least 12,000 sorties by Indochina's entire air transport fleet – a fantastic five-month airlift devoted to nothing but building materials. The competitive pressure on airlift capacity governed everything in the valley.

The engineering stores that the garrison actually received amounted to only about 4,000 tons in total – three-quarters of it barbed wire, but including such specific essentials as 500-plus tons of PSP for the airfield, bridging components and five small bulldozers. Actual building materials amounted to just 130 tons of sawn timber and 20 tons of 'elephant iron' – heavy corrugated metal arches (Lieutenant Colonel Lalande's demand for iron rails to make bursting layers was refused).[19] Priority was given to the main headquarters and communications centre, the hospital and the water purification plant. Otherwise all construction relied upon some 2,200 tons of local timber, from dismantled villages or felled by parties sent as deep into the forest fringe as could be risked; and upon the soldier's traditional stand-by – earth shovelled into sandbags, and into any other containers left over from unpacked stores.[20] The hilltop localities in the north were well wooded; those to the east, less so; and trees on the plain quickly disappeared, with the central positions taking priority over the western strongpoints of Huguette and Claudine. The units which arrived latest found that the best materials had already been taken.

To this problem, as to so many others, the garrison was simply expected to apply 'System D' – the troops' innate talent for improvisation and scrounging. Competition between the units, encouraged by cash prizes, was sometimes energetic to the point of larceny, but the overall result was inevitably patchy. The positions of the Legion battalions and V/7 RTA were reasonably solid; those of the other North Africans and the paratroopers, less so; and those of the Thai units, useless – some shelter roofs were made of thick branches or even bamboo set several inches apart, the gaps disguised with sandbags. Many trenches were rudimentary, particularly those for circulation rather than defence; and most telephone cables were too shallowly buried – an often overlooked point which would later have dire consequences. Lieutenant Le Boudec of 6 BPC recalled that the Tirailleurs aligned their trenches too regularly; and that the eastern hilltop positions were too weak in men for perimeters to be extended to include the 'military crests' – those points some way below the physical crest from which the bases of the slopes could be brought under fire.[21]

EVEN BEFORE GENERAL GILLES' paratroopers had landed at Dien Bien Phu, Operation 'Pollux' – the withdrawal of the Lai Chau garrison to the valley – was being planned. The first cross-country column under Captain

Bordier (perhaps significantly, a member of Deo Van Long's family) left only two days after Cogny's supposedly secret orders reached Lieutenant Colonel Trancart on 13 November, and was successful in fighting its way down the Pavie Track through a series of ambushes, to a rendezvous with II/1 RCP on 23 November.[22] The air evacuation via Dien Bien Phu of Deo Van Long's government and household and the Franco-Vietnamese regular troops was achieved without difficulty by 10 December, although it involved the destruction of quantities of heavy equipment and supplies.[23] The withdrawal on foot of the Thai auxiliary units would be a great deal bloodier, and ominously instructive.

Very little warning was given, and the order to evacuate the immediate area of Lai Chau found the auxiliaries widely dispersed; their hasty assembly prevented many necessary preparations. Some 2,100 Thais and 37 Europeans of what was collectively termed the Thai Mobile Partisan Group (GMPT) left in relays between 5 and 11 December. General Cogny had envisaged a guerrilla resistance to the advancing Division 316; but these Thai Light Auxiliary Companies were not tribal guerrillas clinging to their own hills, they were imitation regular infantry – badly trained, lightly armed and hardly disciplined. There were four main parties each of several companies, commanded by Lieutenants Ulpat, Guillermit and Wieme and Sergeant Blanc. Each company was about 110 strong, and there were something over 20 companies in all; some were accompanied by their families and pack ponies for their belongings.[24] The Thais were badly shaken by the order to leave Lai Chau to the mercy of the Communists and large-scale desertions began almost at once.

The fate of most of the auxilaries can never be known; they simply disappeared, during a ten-day nightmare which unfolded beneath the dark shroud of the forest canopy. Division 316 reached Lai Chau on 12 December, far earlier than expected, and immediately put savage pressure on Lieutenant Guillermit's lightly armed rearguard; some elements outflanked the refugees in the forest and got ahead of them to cut the Pavie Track. Although the Thai columns received warnings from spotter aircraft, some air-drops of food, water and ammunition, and a few helicopter casualty evacuation sorties, over the next ten days they were broken up, forced off the tracks, and hunted to their deaths in separate parties dispersed over some 6,000 square miles of punishing hill and jungle terrain. The true *maquis* who remained in the area to guide and screen the retreat were unable to bring much help; and two regiments of Division 316 – 174 and 176 – were themselves made up of Tho tribesmen from the north-east Delta who were comfortable in hill country and spoke a Thai dialect.

Some of the fleeing groups were wiped out in major ambushes; some were worn away by relentless, wolfish pursuit; others seem to have sold their lives dearly in heroic but unrecorded last stands.[25] As during the earlier battles of Captain Hébert's GCMA partisans, the leadership shown by very junior French soldiers was extraordinary. Some isolated survivors were spotted from the air and picked up by helicopter; others were seen, but disappeared before they could reach a rendezvous. Of the larger groups only Lieutenant Wieme's three companies managed to reach Dien Bien Phu more or less together, by detouring far to the east.[26] The last couple of companies straggled into the valley on 22 December.[27]

The total losses can only be guessed, but one source puts the survivors who reached Dien Bien Phu by 20 December at fewer than 200 all ranks – that is, GMPT had suffered 90 per cent killed and missing.[28] The American information officer Howard Simpson saw one of the exhausted parties from Lai Chau arrive, and described a Thai officer haranguing French officers of the garrison for 'betraying' his people; he also noted the Frenchmen's air of embarrassed resentment, as if the disaster that the Thais had suffered might somehow be contagious.[29] The future value of the Thai companies to the entrenched camp seemed dubious.

IT WAS THIS OPERATION 'POLLUX' that brought into sharp focus the central question of GONO's potential for aggressive sorties outside the valley. From the first days General Gilles had sent his paratroopers up into the surrounding hills in battalion strength, to feel out any Viet Minh presence. On 23 November, Bigeard's fast-marching 6 BPC had pushed 12 miles south-east to the confluence of the Nam Youm and Nam Noua rivers.[30] Bréchignac's II/1 RCP had been given a similar mission to the north, up the Pavie Track to Ban Na Ten to meet Captain Bordier's first lucky column from Lai Chau.[31]

In the first days of December a more ambitious expedition set out to the north-east. Half of the jungle-wise 8 BPC, operating in four separate 'commandos' each with an attached scout platoon from 12th Company of the 3rd Thai Battalion, were to contact a Meo guerrilla band; they were then to push on in an attempt to reconnoitre the important Viet Minh roadhead of Tuan Giao, no less than 50 miles by track from Dien Bien Phu (*see Map 7*). The country north of the valley was extremely challenging even for these specially bush-trained paratroopers: the paths that led up and down steep slopes were little more than faint game tracks through a chaos of fallen trees, entangling vines, thorny undergrowth, thick elephant grass and impenetrable stands of bamboo, cut by steep, boulder-strewn stream-beds.

Leaving on 4 December, Captain Tourret's men hacked their way into the 6,000ft Pha Thong range, contacting friendly tribesmen and encountering no resistance. The next day, after covering an impressive 20 miles, they rendezvoused with a Morane from Dien Bien Phu bringing silver to pay the partisans and more maps. For another week they struggled on through difficult terrain without meeting the enemy; but on 11 December, already badly fatigued, they received orders to turn back and make for the village of Muong Pon to link up with another column of paratroopers.[32]

Meanwhile, also on 4 December, Major Souquet's 1 BPC with attached troops from II/1 RCP had pushed north-east up RP41 (*see Map 12*). Three miles out, just short of Ban Him Lam village, the dirt road led through a narrow defile between wooded hills. Advancing confidently, the lead company reported signs of the enemy's passage, and then immediately came under heavy mortar and automatic fire. The point platoon was wiped out; the rest took up positions for all-round defence, and stood off an infantry charge which got to within hand-to-hand range. Over the noise of firing could be heard amplified propaganda appeals to Vietnamese paratroopers in the ranks. Then the rest of the column arrived, as did artillery support fire, and 1 BPC extricated itself at a cost of 14 dead and 26 wounded. Almost invariably the Viet Minh managed to carry their wounded and dead away before they could be counted, but on this occasion a few corpses were recovered and searched. They were not the regionals who had been expected: documents found in their quilted mountain jackets identified them as regulars from Battalion 888, Regiment 176 of Division 316 'Bien Hoa'.

That same day Generals Cogny and Gilles decided that despite its distance from the camp, Hill 506 above Ban Him Lam would have to be taken into the defence plan (on 10 December it would formally be codenamed 'Béatrice'). Gilles, as gloomy as ever, did not like the look of Hill 781 looming a mile and a half to the south-east, but it could not possibly be occupied – it was too far out, and covered with thick jungle. The artilleryman Cogny was confident that French howitzers and air power could neutralize it. On 7 December another powerful sortie up RP41 by 1 BEP, 6 and 8 BPC with fighter cover got four miles past Hill 506 to Ban Na Loi, sharply repulsing an enemy attack, while behind them trucks brought up fortification materials for III/13 DBLE's new strong-point; and on the 9th the patrolling paratroopers drove off an attempted ambush by Regiment 176, thanks to artillery and air cover.[33]

This was the last operation by Lieutenant Colonel Fourcade's Groupe Aéroporté 1. The infantry battalions of the long-term garrison were now beginning to arrive, and by 12 December Bigeard's 6 BPC, followed by Bréchignac's II/1 RCP and finally by Souquet's 1 BPC, had each assembled by the dusty airstrip with full packs to be flown out to Hanoi. With the arrival of his replacement, Colonel de Castries, on the 7th, General Gilles gratefully departed the next day. Over a farewell drink he seemed embar-rassed to have to tell the officers of GAP 2 that their battalions would be remaining in the valley for some weeks – the mere thought of paratroop-ers being expected to dig in and hold ground, rather than taking it, made him uneasy.[34]

WITH COLONEL DE CASTRIES had returned GAP 2's commander, Lieutenant Colonel Langlais, hobbling on his plastered ankle but furiously determined not to let it slow him down (during his first days in the valley he rode around on a Thai pony). The burden of external operations now fell entirely upon his brigade; and his first mission was to rescue the refugees from Lai Chau, whose desperate situation was now emerging. In particular, by 10 December it was known that Sergeant Blanc's group of perhaps 200 men, with many civilian dependants, were surrounded at the village of Muong Pon, some 11 miles up the Pavie Track.

Captain Tourret was to lead the remainder of his 8th Shock Battalion up RP41, and then to strike west through the jungle; the other half of his unit, already deep in the hills, were radioed to abandon their mission towards Tuan Giao and also make their way back to Muong Pon. At dawn on 11 December, 1 BEP and 5 BPVN began their advance up the Pavie Track. The 1 BEP's leading company got only 300yds beyond the forward French positions at the hill which was soon to become Gabrielle before they ran into resistance; Lieutenant Roux was surprised by the number of enemy sub-machine guns, and noticed the faster rate of fire of these Russian or Chinese 'burp guns'.[35]

Under shellfire from two batteries of howitzers detailed to support the operation from the north of the valley, the People's Army eventually broke contact and the column pressed on; but Langlais had to order them to leave the track and climb the ridge to the east, cutting their way through heavy jungle with machetes.[36] Visibility was reduced to a few paces, and progress to perhaps 200yds an hour; every 15 minutes the point men had to be relieved – shaking and gasping for breath, with the sweat pouring off their livid faces, tormented by thorn cuts, mosquito bites and leeches. By nightfall the paratroopers still had at least seven miles to go; they bivouacked on high ground, and a brief mortar attack during the night was silenced by an artillery mission.

They got moving again in the chill darkness at 4am on the 12th, clambering up and down thousand-foot slopes along a saw-toothed ridge covered in elephant grass which stood taller than their heads; this made for dreadfully airless conditions and when the sun got up they suffered badly from thirst, though a few veterans copied the PIMs and cut pieces off young banana trees to suck for moisture. In the afternoon Tourret's companies from 8 BPC, who had fought their way through their own ambush, seem to have joined up.[37] Hobbling along with his arms round the shoulders of two paratroopers, Langlais kept the column marching for 36 hours with only the briefest halts, in a delirium of fatigue. From dawn on 13 December they could hear firing from Muong Pon. It dwindled, as the paratroopers slashed their way frantically forward; and when they were less than a mile from the village it died away altogether. A spotter plane reported that resistance had ceased and the village was in flames. At noon the lead scouts reached the deserted ruins of Muong Pon, smouldering silently amid the blood-stained trash of battle.[38]

While the exhausted paratroopers bivouacked, the rest of the 8th Shock 'commandos' – diverted from the Tuan Giao mission – linked up with them, together with some tribal guerrillas, after an agonizing three-day forced march across the grain of the high ridges. The enemy were now close around Langlais' brigade, installing heavy weapons unseen by either aircraft or patrols; and as GAP 2 were making their return march on the afternoon of the 14th, with the units taking turns to pass through one another's rearguards, they came under lethal fire. Heights had to be taken by infantry rushes, supported by some 400 rounds of artillery fire; with great labour one of the two howitzer batteries had been towed about three miles north from Anne-Marie up on to the Pavie Track to improve its accurate range. A napalm strike by a patrol of B-26s was finally needed to cut 5 BPVN free, but they were so mingled with the enemy in thick cover that some of the paratroopers, too, perished horribly in the flames. The brigade's padre, the heavily bearded Father Chevalier, presided over the hasty burial of the dead (a scene later immortalized in a much-published photograph) before the column got under way again. The leap-frogging retreat to Dien Bien Phu was a 36-hour running fight, but thanks to a circling Morane 1 BEP's artillery observer Captain Clairfond was able to direct shellfire with some accuracy to keep the Viet Minh from pressing too close on the rearguard.[39] The reeling paratroopers pushed on through the night of 14/15 December; Lieutenant Roux nearly went astray in the pitch dark of a bamboo thicket, but luckily some of his légionnaires had broken bits of phosphorescent wood off rotting logs while passing through a damp gorge and tied them to their packs like friendly glow-worms.[40]

Back in camp at last, the debriefing gave food for thought on the high command's concept of offensive operations striking out from the valley to dominate the terrain. Between them 1 BEP and 5 BPVN had suffered 47 dead and missing and 69 wounded; and none of the three battalions had achieved its objective.

AS IF TO DISPROVE THIS GRIM lesson, on 15 December the C-in-C issued preparatory orders for another major sortie. If the enemy were already dominating the hills to the north and east, Lieutenant Colonel Langlais was to exploit the relative freedom to manoeuvre to the south by effecting a link with troops coming up from Laos. GAP 2's part in this exercise – which seemed to have little military purpose beyond a demonstration that contact between GONO and Colonel de Crèvecoeur's Land Forces Laos was possible – would be codenamed 'Régate', and would begin on 21 December. It would involve the paratroopers in a 30-mile march through the exhausting terrain of the Massif des Calcaires on the Laotian border towards a rendezvous at Sop Nao (*see Map 8*). Meanwhile Major Vaudrey of FTL was to lead three battalions of Moroccan Goumiers, légionnaires and local troops northwards via Muong Sai and Muong Khoua (Operation 'Ardèche').[41] Vaudrey would have by far the harder task: he had to cover about 120 miles in all, fighting his way through some 1,500 Viet Minh regional troops haunting the river valleys which were the only practical route. On 19 December, General Cogny, anxious that this operation should have some lasting value beyond its 'public relations' impact, asked Colonel de Crèvecoeur to leave at least two of his battalions at Sop Nao following the rendezvous, to act as a satellite to Dien Bien Phu and a jumping-off point for further parachuted reinforcements if necessary. Crèvecoeur refused, and Navarre backed him: he would be unable to maintain and supply his men at Sop Nao, where they risked getting encircled. On 23 December the two columns met at Sop Nao; Colonel de Castries had been flown down in a Morane, and a number of journalists and photographers were lifted in by helicopter to record the event. Among the press was Brigitte Friang (who had arrived, characteristically, by parachute); she noted the badly worn condition of Major Vaudrey's troops. Weak with fever and dysentery, they had not only been harried on the march by Pathet Lao guerrillas but had had a hard fight with a battalion from Independent Regiment 148 at Muong Khoua. Shortly after Vaudrey's and Langlais' symbolic handshake had been photographed the press and VIPs were flown out, and the exhausted troops parted to begin their journeys home. Langlais led his paras on a different route from the one they had followed south: they had avoided the enemy once, and he did not wish to tempt fate. They found no local guides, and had to keep to the crests among the stifling elephant grass, with only a circling Morane to watch over them.[42]

THE C-IN-C HAD ANNOUNCED that he would spend Christmas 1953 with GONO, and preparations were made to celebrate the season in style. For the 10,910 men stationed at Dien Bien Phu, Christmas started with a bang on 24 December when the sappers blew up the 'governor's house' on Eliane 2, providing some precious stone debris for bunker roofs (the cellar would become an unusually strong command post). German légionnaires decorated a huge skeletal tree outside Lieutenant Colonel Gaucher's command post using paper garlands painted with mercurochrome, cotton wool, vehicle lights, and bits of multicoloured parachute cloth. The explosive theme of Christmas Eve continued when an ambitious mortar-man of 1 CEPML, fiddling with a candle and what he thought was an empty shell case, started a major fire which caused some alarm during the landing of General Navarre's Dakota. A great deal of the valley's alcohol reserve was deployed and heroically expended over the next 24 hours.

In the Continental tradition, the celebration took place on Christmas Eve. Colonel de Castries was in his element as the host of a feast for the Généchef held in a huge tent erected outside the main HQ, assisted by his private secretary Paule Bourgeade, a brave and cheerful 28-year-old who had been with the Army in Indochina for five years.[43] Officers were still arriving almost daily, and a happy chatter of whatever-happened-to and do-you-remember-when soon rose above the clink of glasses as they sought out old friends and made new ones. The junior ranks were, of course, quite ignorant of their part in the staff's broader plans; until now Dien Bien Phu had been just one more posting of uncertain duration. If the unusually lavish flow of kit from the normally parsimonious rear echelons had not already convinced them, then the C-in-C's decision to spend Christmas in the valley told the soldiers unmistakably that they were an important weapon in his armoury.

Although this was his third visit, most had never seen him before, and he was a coolly impressive figure.[44] Even his name helped: 'Henri Navarre' was ridiculously close to that of France's most attractive king – as if a British general had been christened 'Henry Agincourt', or an American 'Washington Lee'.[45] After they had worked their way through to the brandy under a blue haze of cigarette smoke, the young officers invited to the feast from each battalion might have welcomed an uplifting speech along the lines of 'We few, we happy few, we band of brothers...'; but they did not get one. The chess player Navarre was a more sophisticated man than Montgomery or Patton, but he had none of their instinct for putting heart into his troops. His visit would soon be cut short by news of the attack into central Laos.

Lieutenant Colonel Gaucher of the Legion avoided as much of the fuss as he decently could, sending the limping Captain Capeyron of I/13 DBLE to represent him in the reception party: Capeyron's impressive moustache and obvious recent wounds were felt to be suitably *'folklorique'*. Personally, the colonel preferred to start Christmas by drinking and singing German carols with III/13 DBLE on Béatrice.[46]

RETURNING ONLY ON THE 25th from their slog into Laos and back, the paratroopers of GAP 2 enjoyed a belated Christmas dinner on 26 December: fresh cold cuts, roast beef with fried potatoes, French cheeses, gateaux, good wines, even champagne. They made the most of it – one recalled that the feast lasted about six hours.[47] Although their alleged contents nominally reflected national preference – tinned *choucroute* or *cassoulet* instead of bully beef or pork-and-beans – there was nothing special about the tinned rations provided for CEFEO troops on operations; but the French Army maintained its tradition of eating and drinking as well as circumstances would permit and the cooks could devise. Makeshift unit canteens sold beer when they could get it flown in, but in any case rough red wine – *pinard* – was standard daily issue. Officers' mess dugouts put cooked meat and vegetables on their ammo-box tables, and the air bridge from Hanoi kept them supplied with cheese, drinkable wine, aperitifs, and usually a bottle of something mellower as a *digestif*. The North Africans had a taste for couscous, harissa sauce, and mint for their tea; the Vietnamese, for pork, 'sticky' rice, noodles, and their infamous *nuoc mam* fermented fish sauce. Fresh vegetables were appreciated when they could be provided. On special occasions the cooks made an effort to boost morale – Christmas was celebrated hard, particularly by the Legion, and the North Africans occasionally enjoyed a *méchoui* feast with a spit-roasted lamb.[48]

The storage and distribution of most everyday equipment and consumables in the valley was the responsibility of the *Antenne Intendance* ('service team') in the main depot area of the camp, manned by an 'exploitation battalion'. Amid islands of stacked crates, this had a familiar layout of tented or dug-out stores for rations and clothing, with a sort of military supermarket (*économat*), a bakery producing fresh bread, cold chambers, even pens and a slaughterhouse for fresh meat. Every morning, in an echo of French domestic ritual, vehicles from each unit would bring the quartermasters; each would haggle with the duty officer over lists and chits, and then proceed about his morning marketing, with a dozen or so NCOs and men circulating behind him to do the heavy lifting. The stockpiles were as varied as the multi-racial crowds of bustling 'shoppers': tinned meat and fish from France, Madagascar, Australia and Argentina, conserves of every kind, Antilles rum, Tonkinese vegetables and rice from Cochinchina.[49]

IMMEDIATELY AFTER CHRISTMAS, GAP 2 was reduced to two battalions when 5 BPVN were flown out, but the infantry were strengthened by the arrival of the Algerian V/7 RTA. The garrison made no major sorties over the next week, but a steady series of encounters with enemy patrols and probes confirmed that the People's Army was growing in confidence. This was shockingly demonstrated on 28 December when Castries' chief-of-staff, the conscientious Lieutenant Colonel Guth, took a jeep and drove up to scout the hill north of the Anne-Marie strongpoints which would shortly become home to V/7 RTA under the codename Gabrielle. Guth was ambushed, and died in a hail of sub-machine-gun fire. The next day a force from III/13 DBLE carrying out a road-opening patrol up RP41 from Béatrice ran into resistance. On the 30th a local sortie southwards from Isabelle came under fire at Ban Cang, about three miles from the perimeter.

On 6 January a more ambitious operation was attempted by 8th Shock, once more sent out north-eastwards towards Tuan Giao, but it ended in fiasco. Led by Thai guides from the local hamlets, Captain Tourret passed Béatrice before taking to the hills to avoid the enemy-held village of Ban Na Loi. By the afternoon it was clear that the guides were completely lost, and on the morning of the 7th Tourret's paratroopers found themselves back on RP41 a little way north of Ban Na Loi. Coming under fire, they charged, suffering five men wounded; with their presence revealed they had no option but to fall back on Dien Bien Phu. At Ban Na Loi they were pinned down by heavy shooting and mortar fire, and had to call in air cover. A Morane guided patrol 'Savart Red' – two Hellcats flown by Lieutenant Commanders de Castelbajac and Campredon – to the roadblock, and under their bombing and strafing the paras managed to slip past; however, it was 8 January before they got back to the camp.[50]

On 12 January it was the turn of Lieutenant Colonel Langlais' other battalion, the Legion paratroopers. The area to the east of Isabelle was vulnerable to Viet Minh activity, and 1 BEP were sent to reconnoitre a series of villages. Leaving the main camp at 4am they reached Ban Phu at 9am, Ban Co Hen at 10am, and Ban Lung Con an hour later; all these villages were found to be abandoned and burned out. At about 1.30pm Lieutenant Martin's 3rd Company reached Ban Huoi Phuc, still only about two miles from Isabelle. While he was standing taking a compass bearing 'Lulu' Martin was fired upon and hit in the hand; this was the signal for heavy small-arms fire from the surrounding paddy-fields and from a hillock about 400yds ahead. This feature was silenced by the 57mm RCLs, while 2nd and 3rd Companies deployed to clear the paddy-fields.

At this point the battalion came under accurate mortar fire; Major Verguet, the second-in-command, had a miraculous escape when one bomb landed less than 6ft from him, yet its fragments killed Sub-lieutenant Nenert and wounded Sub-lieutenant Thibout about 30yds away. The other listed casualties from this mortaring interested the US observer Howard Simpson, whose brief was partly to monitor Vietnamese troops: 1st Company – Légionnaire Pittak killed, volunteers Than Trong Phong and Pham Van Vinh wounded; 4th Company – Adjudant Martin, Corporal Chief Zivkovic, Corporal Do Van Kinh, Légionnaires Larensac, Mlekusch, Ahlgrin, volunteers Nguyen Van Mui, Nguyen Van Ngai and Do Van Phong all wounded. (This confirms that Vietnamese were serving throughout the Legion battalion rather than being grouped in a 'Compagnie Indochinoise'.)[51]

The most serious casualties were picked up by a helicopter from Dien Bien Phu and the battalion started to withdraw northwards. When they neared the camp perimeter they came under fire yet again, this time apparently from Viet Minh who were lying in ambush for a simultaneous patrol by Thai partisans. It was 11.40pm before the paratroopers got back to Claudine; Lieutenant Colonel Langlais' welcome was a rebuke for making too much noise coming in. The 1 BEP had suffered five dead including one officer, and no fewer than 33 wounded including five officers. They had confirmed the enemy's presence, counted 16 Viet Minh dead on the ground, and brought back one wounded prisoner: a thin reward for such a price.[52]

IN MID JANUARY THE GARRISON had one positive piece of news to gossip about: after long argument at staff level, a Mobile Field Brothel (BMC) was flown into the camp and placed under the care of the medical officer of I/2 REI. (The staff were Indochinese; a second, North African BMC would follow.) There was no shortage of willing hands to build the women suitable quarters; although the wide dispersal of the French units around the valley meant that very few men outside Claudine and Huguette would actually have any opportunity to visit them, just knowing that they were there was a cheering thought. For the first couple of weeks, that knowledge had to suffice: none of the combat units had much leisure for female companionship.[53]

On 18 January, General Cogny warned Colonel de Castries that the latest radio intercepts suggested the imminence of a major enemy attack; urgent requests were being passed for completion of ammunition stocks at Tuan Giao, and Division 316 was pressing its Regiment 98 to deliver reports on the surveillance of the camp by the 20th.[54] On the 19th, Castries issued orders to his unit commanders for the forthcoming 'battle of annihilation'. As we have seen, it proved a false alarm. Enemy patrol activity continued – an outpost of III/3 RTA east of Dominique mysteriously disappeared on the 30th; but the next substantial intelligence to arrive revealed that Division 308 had left the hills around the camp and was marching south for Laos. On 1 February, General Cogny visited the camp to discuss the new situation created by Giap's now confirmed thrust towards Luang Prabang.

Cogny visited 19 times between 22 November and 12 March, and he was often accompanied by other senior Army and Air Force officers. While many of these obviously had legitimate reasons for inspecting progress at Dien Bien Phu, the impressive growth of the camp also became something of a tourist attraction for others who could pull rank or talk their way on to a Dakota. Colonel de Castries and his officers often found themselves distracted from their duties by the need to extend hospitality, conduct tours, and smile while they answered repetitive questions from generals, politicians, their staffs and entourages, and even more irrelevant guests, both French and foreign. Oddly, the first to arrive (in a Beaver, as early as 24 November) was the British military representative General Edward Spears, whose whole career since the Great War had centred on

Franco-British liaison; a later visitor would be the writer and novelist Graham Greene.[55] The routine for such visits became well worn, although it was naturally adjusted according to the visitor's rank and influence. Greeted at the airstrip by a guard of honour (usually supplied by the Legion, decked out in white képis and colourful *fourragères* citation lanyards), the VIPs would be jeeped to the GONO HQ for a carefully graded map-board briefing by Colonel de Castries. The visitors would then be driven (by Castries in person, if sufficiently important) to inspect one of the battalion localities – usually the highest, Dominique 2 on its red laterite hilltop; they might also be treated to a flame-thrower demonstration by a bored squad of Legion pioneers. There would be speeches, perhaps the presentation of decorations, and always a first-class lunch with good wines before the beaming visitors were helped on to their Dakota by 4pm for an early return to Hanoi. Unit officers loathed these pointless interruptions, and 1 BEP tried to discourage them by serving any visitors refreshments from combat ration packs. In the more monotonous periods, however, especially down at Isabelle, the novelty of turning out an honour guard (in return for the usual discreet gift of a few bottles) made a welcome break.[56]

The military and political VIPs were accompanied by journalists, both French and foreign; these usually flew out again after a cursory tour, but one group stayed in the valley – a handful of reporters, photographers and cameramen of the French Army's Information and Press Service. Not all of them would survive the battle and its aftermath.[57]

AMONG THE VISITORS TREATED with the greatest seriousness were the US military delegations, and the need for diplomacy was the greater due to a foolish lapse of communication between Paris and Saigon. One condition of the massively increased American financial aid agreed in September 1953 was the right of the US mission to receive more detailed briefings from French commanders, and for their advice to be sought; but inexplicably, Foreign Minister Bidault's agreement to this was not communicated to General Navarre.[58] This privilege was exercised fully by Lieutenant General John W. ('Iron Mike') O'Daniel, who was soon to replace Major General Thomas Trapnell at the head of the US Military Assistance Advisory Group in Saigon. A bull-necked veteran whose nickname spoke for itself, O'Daniel had shown little patience with the sinuous insincerities of French officers, from Navarre downwards, and had freely expressed his views on the conduct of the war and his suggestions for US participation in the ANV training programme. His opinions did not always demonstrate a sure grasp of local realities; but in any case, Paris's failure to inform Navarre in advance of the advisory concessions made to the Pentagon guaranteed that the two generals' conversations would be offensive on the one side and icily reserved on the other. Early in February 1954 the US ambassador felt moved to cable Washington to warn of the undesirable consequences of 'Iron Mike's' free habit of speech on subjects about which he was less than fully informed.

General Trapnell, a survivor of the defence of Bataan, made two visits of inspection to Dien Bien Phu on 29 November and 19 December; and on 2 February, General O'Daniel led a large group of American officers to the valley. After this visit O'Daniel reported in less dismissive terms than previously; neither he, nor any other US officer, put in writing any fundamental misgivings about the Dien Bien Phu plan or the position itself.[59]

TO AMERICAN VISITORS THE immediate impression created by this spacious panorama of bustling military activity must have been reassuring. Against a constant background of droning C-47s landing and taking off, thousands of men were at work – unloading and stacking stores, digging and building, hauling timber, filling sandbags, raising tents, stringing barbed wire and telephone cables, uncrating equipment of all kinds – while US-supplied jeeps and trucks busily criss-crossed the valley floor under clouds of dust.

It is to 1 BEP's medical officer, Lieutenant Rondy, that we owe a number of rare colour photographs. Spring days could be pleasant in the High Region; by noon the warm sun shone from an intensely blue sky dotted with fluffy white clouds, and men stripped off their shirts to sunbathe as they worked. In the sunlight the vivid green hills did not look threatening and the valley seemed large and bright. As the sun waned the horizon turned pink, the golden valley darkened to orange-red, and the hills to a louring purple. The brief dusk brought a sharp drop in temperature, and in the last light men stared at the black walls overlooking their suddenly shrunken fortress as they bundled on their warmest clothes. The generals and their guests, of course, had always flown out long before the chill struck.

Although the occasional figure riding a Thai pony in preference to a bicycle added a touch of romance, from any distance these troops looked like GIs; most of them wore baggy olive fatigues, sand-khaki shirts or drab sweaters, completed – for those heading out on patrol – with webbing harness and American helmets. The radios, the jerrycans and ammunition boxes, even the picks and shovels, were American; many of the officers carried US carbines and Colt pistols; the machine guns in the strongpoints were Brownings; and the support platoons had familiar 81mm mortars and the elegant-looking M18 'recoilless rifles', like big bazookas on tripod mounts.

From the neck up, however, the labouring troops would have been more eye-catching to the passing military tourists. Most of them wore raffish, floppy brimmed 'cowboy'-style bush hats, but specks of colour in the olive mass lent an exotic air: the French Army, like the British, advertised its cherished 'tribal' differences by means of special headgear, usually sported when out of the line by officers and NCOs at least. In the North African Rifles the junior leaders wore pale blue sidecaps set off with yellow or green details, while the rank and file had tightly wrapped off-white turbans. The smart black sidecaps of the Colonial Artillery were trimmed with scarlet and proudly bore the gold anchor badge of 'la Coloniale'. The Foreign Legion had introduced a practical green and red sidecap during World War II; but it was never universally popular, and even when they were stripped for labouring in the sun some légionnaires still preferred the cherished white-covered képi of folklore. For the tank crews and many others the standard field headgear was a pale sand-khaki beret, often with unit-colour ribbons hanging from the nape, while the Air Force pilots favoured baseball caps *à l'Américain*. In the heat of the day brief sand-khaki shorts and canvas and rubber basketball boots – the Expeditionary Corps' beloved 'paddlers' – gave an insouciant, beach-party look.

The paratroopers were set apart by their multicoloured camouflage uniforms, more prized as a sign of élite status than a strictly necessary battledress. At the turn of 1953/4 the Troupes Aéroportées d'Indochine were in the course of a re-equipment which added to their already motley appearance. Some had received new French streaky camouflage uniforms, covered with baggy pockets on every surface; others still wore World War II US jungle jackets sharply spotted in green and brown, and British Denison smocks or thin 'sausage-skin' windproofs camouflaged with large panels of softly contrasting shades. Their headgear was equally varied. Most paratroopers were distinguished by the proud red beret; the Legion paras, never willing to be confused with lesser breeds, sported an entirely unofficial version in dark green. The different battalions also had various field headgear made up from camouflage material: the 8th Shock favoured peaked field caps with neck flaps, and a couple of little 'cigarette' pockets on the front, while the légionnaires of the *'Bep'* preferred camouflage bush hats.

If they had already spent any time in Indochina the US visitors would not have found particularly remarkable the many Arab and Berber faces, or the gleaming West Africans piling the cardboard shell tubes in the gunpits – colonial Tirailleurs were a common sight around Saigon and Hanoi. One thing they might have noted, as they were conducted smoothly around a carefully pre-planned circuit before their excellent lunch, were the numbers of slightly built Vietnamese soldiers in the ranks, looking like boys in their oversized fatigues. Although 5 BPVN had been pulled out on 26 January to rejoin the reserves in Hanoi, there were still about 2,500 Thai tribal soldiers and auxiliaries in the valley. As already noted, even in the nominally French paratroop battalions anything between a third and half of the corporals and privates were locally recruited, and many Vietnamese were to be found in the ranks of French and Legion units of all arms and services. In the battle to come, more Vietnamese than Frenchmen would be killed wearing French uniform.[60]

AT THE TURN OF JANUARY/February the officers and soldiers of GONO, who had been pumped up to meet the major attack that they had been warned to expect on 25 January, were suffering from as great a sense of anti-climax as the *bo doi* in the surrounding hills. General Navarre was groping for a sense of Giap's intentions in northern Laos: was the thrust by Division 308 merely a raid, or the first sign of a serious shifting of balance? If Giap had real hopes for Luang Prabang then he would have to send more of his troops south; at least a second division – probably 312 – would be slipping away from Dien Bien Phu and following 308, leaving the highland soldiers of Division 316 to keep contact with the garrison. If this happened then Dien Bien Phu's relative importance and vulnerability would lessen. On 2 February, the C-in-C asked General Cogny (and through him,

Castries) for their views on reducing the garrison from its current 12 battalions to nine, or even six, in case he needed to fly some of them down to Luang Prabang or the Plain of Jars. General Cogny – who believed that the presence of even two Viet Minh divisions prohibited any weakening of GONO – ordered Colonel de Castries to probe vigorously to identify the enemy units in the hills, and the sorties sent out from the camp in the first half of February had this as part of their objective.[61]

AFTER A VISIT TO DIEN BIEN Phu on 26 January, General Blanc, Chief of the Defence Staff, held a meeting in Saigon with General Ely, Army Chief-of-Staff (who was soon to replace him); General Fay, Air Force Chief-of-Staff; Defence Minister Pleven, and Secretary de Chevigné. It took place on 10 February, at a time when all were preoccupied by the unknown implications of Division 308's move into Laos. General Blanc made no secret of his lack of belief in a military solution in Indochina, and particularly not in Tonkin; he had a fixed opinion that the CEFEO should withdraw to South Vietnam. At this meeting he expressed the view that GONO would be swamped (literally) by the monsoon rains by 15 April; for that reason it should be withdrawn, or at least halved in strength, in order to return men, matériel and airlift capacity to the resources of the strategic reserve. He did not believe that the Viet Minh would oblige Navarre by engaging in a battle of annihilation: 'To pretend we are going to destroy the enemy main force is a delusion... We believed we could draw three of the best Viet Minh divisions into a battle of destruction. In practice, the enemy has fixed an important part of our troops, and it is he who is manipulating us.' Like the critics at FTNV in November, he doubted Dien Bien Phu's utility, but not, apparently, its survivability.[62]

At the 10 February meeting General Fay supported General Blanc's argument, specifically because of his fears that air transport in and out of the valley would become impractical during the rainy season. Fay visited Dien Bien Phu himself with René Pleven on 19 February, and it has been said that when asked his opinion he advised General Navarre to pull GONO out, because it was 'done for'; but he did not elaborate. Since at this date all eyes were on Giap's threat to Laos, his comment can hardly have been a serious prediction of a major attack and defeat at Dien Bien Phu.[63] However, at a meeting with Navarre on 26 February, the Air Force general was reassured by a new report from Colonel de Castries showing that although monsoon flooding might affect parts of Claudine, Huguette and the low-lying Dominiques, the airfield itself was not threatened. He still advised Navarre to lighten the garrison, however, and declared that with a maximum effort the transport fleet could lift out six or seven battalions in two nights.[64]

When Division 308 moved into Laos at the beginning of February, perhaps as the spearhead for a larger force, Navarre had indeed envisaged transferring half the garrison from Dien Bien Phu to that front; but by 26 February he knew that the Viet Minh had turned back. He would later state that he understood General Fay to be urging such a transfer only if Giap committed a second division to Laos; Fay would claim that he advised withdrawal in any case, irrespective of the size of the threat to Luang Prabang. Nowhere in this tangle do we find General Fay predicting military disaster for GONO, but only difficulties in maintaining the air bridge during the monsoon rains. He did not address the immense cost, difficulty and danger to the Army of trying to withdraw the garrison at this stage – any more than did later commentators, notably Bernard Fall. General Ely would write in his memoirs that in February 1954 'there could be no thought of evacuating [Dien Bien Phu], and nobody suggested it... General Blanc... who was never a supporter of our presence in North Vietnam, stressed its solidity. The most worried was General Fay... who believed that the airstrip... might not stand up to the rains.'[65]

It is clear that in February, even after the announcement of the Geneva conference, if any of these senior officers envisaged any serious danger to Dien Bien Phu *from direct enemy action*, then they failed to record their alarm in writing.

ON 31 JANUARY AN OPERATION by GAP 2 with additional companies from BT 2 and III/13 DBLE attempted to reach and destroy enemy gun batteries suspected on Hill 633, less than a mile north of Gabrielle. The Thais came under heavy machine-gun fire, and reacted slackly; by the time paratroopers managed to cover their retreat they had lost 17 killed. The dead were abandoned in the forest, which was bad for the unit's already shaky morale. One of them was Lieutenant Negre, who had been carrying a copy of the latest 1/25,000 map of the area, only recently provided by

Hanoi. This was of no great help to the French (*see Chapter 10*); but it showed the People's Army both the current state of French knowledge about their positions and details of the camp's layout.[66]

Well before dawn on 6 February, Lieutenant Colonel Langlais led his paratroopers (1 BEP, 8 BPC), I/4 RTM, BT 2, Legion flame-thrower teams and a demolition platoon from 31 BG towards Hill 781, 2½ miles due east of the camp (*see Map 9*). The operational objective was to hit enemy artillery emplacements which they expected to find on the reverse slopes of this feature. The force pushed up RP41 as far as Ban Him Lam village some 300yds east of Béatrice; leaving 1 BEP there to secure the withdrawal route, Langlais turned off to the south-east. At about 11am, after eight hours' tiring but unopposed struggle through the forest, I/4 RTM reached the top of Hill 781. No artillery positions were found on the reverse slopes; but at 1pm, as the force moved west to investigate the forward slopes, it suddenly came under heavy fire followed by infantry attacks. Both French and Moroccan personnel fought impressively, taking and holding high ground; but the flank was endangered when BT 2 began to fold up. After a whole afternoon's fighting, at 6.20pm Langlais ordered all units to fall back to Ban Him Lam.

It was not until 3am the next morning that the force got back into camp; it had lost more than 90 dead, including three officers and 12 sergeants, and I/4 RTM alone had suffered 56 dead, wounded and missing. The gains had been nil; it was clear that there was no significant weakening of the siege ring, but definite unit identifications could not be made. In the early days of GONO's sorties into the hills the typical fire fights had been patrol clashes with enemy units who had sprung opportunist ambushes. Now, French troops were running into solidly dug-in opponents in carefully camouflaged trenches, supported by machine guns, recoilless guns and mortars emplaced, protected and concealed for the long term.[67]

On 9 February it was the turn of the Legion infantry. A mixed force from I/13 DBLE, I/2 REI, a company from I/4 RTM and another from BT 2 pushed out from the Huguettes westwards towards the village of Ban Hong Lech Cang, about 2½ miles due west of the camp. There the leading platoon surprised a group of soldiers whom they took for Vietnamese paratroopers, until they opened fire: this People's Army unit had acquired French paratroopers' camouflage uniforms. The fight lasted for four hours and came to hand-to-hand contact; the French had to call up rein-forcements, and in the end the cost was seven dead and 21 wounded.[68]

ON 10 FEBRUARY, GENERAL Navarre pressed GONO once more for confirmation of the enemy units still in contact. Over several days Lieutenant Colonel Langlais mounted and led another major operation to fix, destroy and identify enemy infantry both north and south of Béatrice, and to find artillery positions in the hills east of Dominique. After a night of heavy artillery and mortar preparation, the forces committed to a pre-dawn advance up RP41 on the first day were 1 BEP and a company of 8 BPC, three companies of III/3 RTA, plus three companies of III/3 REI brought up the night before from Isabelle. Lieutenant Bergot says that after weeks in their dull and inhospitable swamp the légionnaires welcomed a chance to come up to the main camp, which was almost like 'a night in town' for them. There were sappers with demolition charges, pioneers with flame-throwers, tanks, and a company of Thai auxiliaries. A company of V/7 RTA came across from Gabrielle and two companies of III/13 DBLE from Béatrice, while BT 3 made a co-ordinated but separate push north-west from Anne-Marie. This was clearly the largest commit-ment GONO had yet made to offensive operations.

The objective is identified by Bernard Fall as Hill 674, described as some 1,200yds east of Gabrielle; in the same general area, perhaps 1,500yds north of Béatrice, were Hills 701 and 561 (*see Map 9*). René Bail couples these with a series of hills to the south-east of RP41, notably the notorious Hill 781 about 2½ miles east of Dominique. The operation lasted at least two days, and may have continued for four.[69] The first day saw a series of violent encounter battles against well dug-in and camouflaged enemy positions, and little progress was made. On either the first day or second morning the Tirailleurs of V/7 RTA were pinned down at Hill 674 despite artillery support; some shells fell short and caused Algerian casualties.

The second day saw more movement, and support by napalm strikes from B-26s of GB 1/25 'Tunisie'. Bergot describes III/3 REI advancing on the left, separated by some hundreds of yards from the paratroopers and III/3 RTA on their right; he seems to place III/3 REI north of Béatrice and 1 BEP well south of it facing the features around Hill 781. Confusingly, Bail describes engagements by 1 BEP and III/13 DBLE around Hills 674,

561 and 701, all of which were north of Béatrice. The details hardly matter, since the hills were meaningless as physical objectives and could not be occupied even when they were captured; their significance lies in the type of encounter that took place on them.

In the heat of the day Langlais' troops struggled up and down forested slopes thick with undergrowth and lianas, and through the blackened aftermath of the napalm strikes. There, above a bed of ash and glowing sparks which powdered up around the men's boots, only the leaves had burned off; the brief petrol fires left dried-out but still tangled branches and skeletal bushes that gave no cover but made a lot of noise as the troops forced their way through. The légionnaires of III/3 REI finally reached one crest only to walk into machine-gun fire grazing up the far slope, followed by an uphill rush by swarms of infantry; as they fell back they were raked by machine-gun and mortar fire from a neighbouring height. Lieutenant Bergot describes how 1 BEP ran into brilliantly concealed trenches and weapons bunkers north-west of Hill 781. They came under heavy fire from short range, then the Viet Minh charged them from hidden shelters only yards away in the thick brush. The 4th Company's much admired commander Captain Cabiro was badly wounded in the legs; his paras counter-attacked to rescue him, but lost four men in the attempt before Sub-lieutenant Boisbouvier finally managed to drag him in.

Although several features proved to be simply unclimbable the *bo doi* were driven off a number of hills, where solidly constructed and expertly camouflaged positions were cleared with flame-throwers and showers of grenades. They were studied hastily before the sappers blew them up; one observation post on Hill 674, linked with many field telephone lines, particularly impressed the légionnaires of III/13 DBLE. They went on to assault Hill 561 under covering fire from 1 BEP on Hill 674, but had to fall back under heavy machine-gun fire which not even artillery shoots and Bearcat strikes could silence. Eventually all units were ordered to withdraw and regroup so that the tanks could shepherd them home. It transpired that BT 3's probe north-west of Anne-Marie had been completely blocked well short of their objective. The cost of the whole operation was 13 dead and 98 seriously wounded; three Thais were listed as deserters. As always, most People's Army casualties and weapons had been removed before they could be counted.

The casualties suffered by GONO between 20 November and 15 February now totalled 32 officers, 96 NCOs and 836 corporals and privates. This represented something like 10 per cent of the officers and 8 per cent of the enlisted men in the garrison: the equivalent of a strong battalion, plus the officers from a second. At a time when supplying GONO, let alone reinforcing it, had lost its priority to the benefit of the units in northern Laos, this level of losses for such limited gains could not be sustained. On 17 February, General Cogny signalled Colonel de Castries that in future sorties were to be limited to light reconnaissance patrols in order to reduce casualties.[70]

That date marked the close of GONO's attempts to mount external operations; Dien Bien Phu's supposed offensive capability had been proved to be illusory. Far from being able to interfere with the rear lines of People's Army operations into Laos, GONO could no longer push out multi-battalion sorties with artillery and air cover to points within three miles of its own perimeter with any confidence.

THE RATE OF CASUALTIES suffered during the winter sorties from Dien Bien Phu raises the question of the camp's medical facilities. These had been planned on the basis of experience at Na San where, during five days of heavy fighting by a force comparable to that at Dien Bien Phu, the casualties had included some 600 wounded, or about 1.6 per cent of the garrison per combat day. The *Antenne Chirurgicale Mobile* (Mobile Surgical Team) at Na San had 120 'beds', and managed to cope with the flow of wounded because air evacuation was interrupted only on one day. The estimate arrived at for Dien Bien Phu was 3 per cent casualties per combat day; it was decided not only to provide two medical units, but to multiply the capacity to three-and-a-half times that at Na San, or 424 'beds' in total. But only 40 of these were bunks in the underground hospital, the others being simply spaces set aside for about 150 stretcher-cots there and in various HQ dug-outs, 60 at strong-point Isabelle, and the rest scattered between the various battalion aid posts.

The 1st Parachute Surgical Team (1 ACP) had jumped with 1 BPC in the second wave on 20 November and were fully functional the next morning. Each *Antenne Chirurgicale Parachutable* consisted of ten men, including one surgeon and seven orderlies trained as operating theatre, anaesthetic, sterilization and intensive care nurses. With its initial equipment and supplies an ACP could triage at least 80 casualties and operate on 20 emergency cases. The team remained at Dien Bien Phu until 21 December, when they were withdrawn and relieved by the 29th Mobile Surgical Team.[71]

This slightly larger 29 ACM, led by Major Dr Paul Grauwin, was flown in by Dakota. The ACMs had been designed to operate with a brigade group, and normally consisted of 13 men including two surgeons and three aides, with a mobile operating theatre complete with X-ray facility. Like the airborne team, its mission was to triage the wounded, stabilizing them for evacuation or operating on urgent cases. (These were reassuringly rare: of 1,190 wounded and sick admitted to the hospital up to 12 March, only 23 needed operations on the spot – well within the unit's capability.) A second team, 44 ACM led by Dr Jacques Gindrey, joined the 29th at Dien Bien Phu in February; and these two units staffed the underground hospital established next to the HQ complex (*see Map 11*). This had dug-out compartments linked by tunnels – a sterilization room, an X-ray room, an operating theatre measuring 12ft by 9ft with walls and ceiling lined with white material, and an intensive care room; further 'wards' were dug off a central corridor.[72]

Between them the teams had the use of two Dodge ambulances and three jeeps, plus one H-19 (Sikorski S-55) helicopter with a capacity of four or five cases for lifting casualties out of rough terrain where the ambulances could not reach them. At least one *'evasan'* ('casevac') Dakota, with a capacity of 20 stretcher cases, was permanently based at the camp's airstrip to make daily flights to Hanoi. A back-up ACM was also established at Muong Sai in Laos, to stabilize and evacuate any cases who were helicoptered there from Dien Bien Phu.[73]

However, everything depended on continual evacuation flights, and not everyone was confident on this score. On 19 January the then-senior MO in the camp, Captain Dr Rives, reported to Castries that the number of actual hospital beds available was 'beneath comment'.[74] Visiting the hospital on 18 February, the Army's Surgeon General Jeansotte was also unimpressed by the number of beds, and by the quality of the dug-outs' overhead cover. He said to Dr Grauwin: 'What if you have 300 wounded?...

If there's a big scrap here, my friend, it will set you back 40 years, and you won't be able to cope with it by yourself."[75]

On 28 February two Bearcats of Major Jacques Guérin's flight from GC 1/22 'Saintonge' collided on the airstrip and one pilot, Sergeant Perfetti, lapsed into a coma from a fractured skull. Dr Grauwin decided that the only chance to save him was to ignore normal evacuation to Hanoi and to fly him directly to the general hospital at Saigon. Taking off in the late afternoon, the Dakota made a five-hour flight down the whole length of Vietnam, while the flight nurse struggled to keep the patient alive through repeated changes of altitude and pressure – adjusting his drips and oxygen, constantly taking his blood pressure, and injecting heart stimulants. When the C-47 landed at Saigon–Tan Son Nhut after 3am the next morning the nurse's clothes were soaked with sweat despite the cold night air. Before flying back to Hanoi later on the 29th she rang the hospital for news; Paul Perfetti was stable but still comatose (he would die ten days later without regaining consciousness). On that morning the flight nurse believed that this had been the most difficult mission of her career. Her name was Geneviève de Galard.[76]

THE ONLY ASPECT OF GONO'S original *raison d'être* that remained credible was its defensive strength. Whatever its offensive failures, Dien Bien Phu was still by far the most formidable fortress that the People's Army had ever faced, a rock upon which Giap's divisions could smash themselves to ruin. Colonel de Castries' strongest weapon to achieve this was his Colonial Artillery; and at this point we must return to the early days of 'Castor' for a brief examination of GONO's iron fist.

10. Zulu Kilo

'I will carry my cross, whatever happens.'
Colonel Charles Piroth *in conversation with Major Guy Hourcabie, February 1954*

A CENTRAL FACTOR IN THE whole air–ground base concept was its provision with a powerful artillery. The eight 75mm recoilless guns from the 35th Parachute Light Artillery dropped on 21 November, but never intended as part of the long-term garrison's assets, were flown out on 26–27 December. The first field artillery support was provided by two 105mm howitzers flown in by Bristol freighters as soon as the airstrip was opened on 25 November, and two more were landed on the 29th. These guns were manned for the first six weeks by the Autonomous Laotian Artillery Battery (BAAL), an unimpressive stop-gap unit who were pulled out in their turn on 17 January 1954; so were their ancient guns, whose worn-out barrels had an accurate range of not much more than one mile instead of six.[1]

On 7 December a senior artillery officer, Colonel Charles Piroth, had arrived with Colonel de Castries' staff, but his initial appointment was simply as Castries' deputy; at that time the garrison's artillery was planned as a single battalion. Although Piroth would become the senior gunner of, in effect, a whole division, he was not provided with a staff suitable for that task. He had to contrive a team to meet the growing scope of his responsibility – largely from the HQ Battery of II/4 RAC, when that second artillery battalion was flown in after Christmas.

The 47-year-old Piroth was a bear-like figure with a friendly, open face; the most immediately obvious thing about him was the empty left sleeve tucked into his belt. A respected veteran of the Italian campaign, he was now serving his third Indochina tour. He had come to South Vietnam with General Leclerc as a major commanding a battalion; but during the early years of the war at least half the French artillerymen in Indochina had been pressed into service as infantry for lack of suitable targets for their guns.[2] Piroth's unit was responsible for pacifying the seething countryside around Thu Dau Mot north of Saigon. In sodden, heavily wooded terrain and without proper training, Piroth had to reinvent himself and his gunners as counter-insurgency infantrymen; but he proved a popular commander, both brave and thoughtful.

On 17 December 1946 he was leading a battery which fell into an ambush, and was hit badly, high in the left arm. Hastily bandaged, he continued to exercise command; by the time he let himself be evacuated to Saigon his wound was already dangerous. Astonishingly, the surgeon had no anaesthetic; Piroth was conscious throughout the amputation, bearing it stoically. After recovery in France he was serving his second tour when, in December 1950, General de Lattre arrived like a whirlwind to take over supreme command in the aftermath of the RC4 disaster. To cut out the cancer of defeatism in the CEFEO, de Lattre dismissed many officers without much concern for individual guilt or merit. Piroth had been an innocent victim of this purge, and it still rankled painfully.[3]

The camp's permanent artillery force was progressively flown into the valley between 6 December and 14 January: first the Moroccans of Major Alliou's 3rd Battalion, 10th Colonial Artillery Regiment (III/10 RAC), the organic artillery unit of Groupe Mobile 9; and later the West Africans of Major Hourcabie's 2nd Battalion, 4th Colonial Artillery (II/4 RAC), formally attached to GM 6. Each unit comprised a headquarters and three four-gun batteries of American HM2 105mm howitzers. During December a central fire control HQ (*PC Feux* – 'Fires Command Post') was set up next to Piroth's office in Colonel de Castries' subterranean headquarters, with communications links both to his units and to Colonel de Winter, the FTNV artillery chief at General Cogny's Hanoi headquarters; its call-sign was 'Zulu Kilo'.

Piroth's 24 howitzers were reinforced between 26 and 28 December with four heavier, longer-ranging 155mm HM1 pieces of Captain Déal's 11th Battery, 4th Battalion, 4th Colonial Artillery (11/IV/4 RAC). Their mission would be counter-battery fire against enemy artillery, and any other long-range targets designated by the PC Feux; the fire of the 155s would not be available on call to infantry battalions. Reporting to headquarters while Christmas decorations were still to be seen, the officers of this battery were startled to be ordered to dig in at once.[4]

The 105s of III/10 RAC had been ready for action since 10 December, emplaced in Claudine with their dug-in command post close to that of Groupe Mobile 9; the 155mm battery was near by, and became operational on 30 December. The II/4 RAC, which arrived in two halves in late December and mid January, were placed further north, between the southern end of the airfield and the Nam Youm on the flats codenamed Dominique 4, with one battery (the 4th) pushed out east of the river in Dominique 3 (*see Map 11*). There would be a certain amount of switching back and forth between some battery positions during January and February; and on 24 December and 5 January the 8th and 9th Batteries, III/10 RAC would be towed all the way down to Isabelle under command of Captain Libier, leaving just four 105mm batteries in the central camp.[5] (Since the Viet Minh artillery was being dug into the hillsides without much possibility of switching its assigned targets, these movements caused concern to the People's Army, whose scouts were given the priority task of checking daily on the French gun positions.)

PREPARING THE ARTILLERY TO fulfil its tasks was a lengthy and complicated procedure. Readers misled by the simplicities of war films may not realize that artillerymen do not usually wait until a target presents itself before aiming at it. This is termed 'direct fire'; but since at least 1915 the science of gunnery has been overwhelmingly concerned with 'indirect fire' – the delivery of shells to targets beyond direct observation from the gun position, and often separated from it by intervening high ground and/or friendly troops. This technique involves the painstaking preparation of a complex 'fire plan' for pre-registered 'shoots'. Target areas must be identified on the map, and calculations of angle, range, height of intervening ground, atmospheric conditions and many other variables have to be reconciled. This series of calculations produces solutions – final settings for the gun's angles of aim, the propellant charge in the shell case, and the fuse in the nose of the shell itself.

Today these fire-control solutions are produced by laptop computers; in

1953 it was a slower process involving maps spread on a plotting table, the manipulation of calculators resembling slide rules, and cross-referencing long columns of figures from printed tables.[6] Each of the solutions was identified by a name/number code, and registered by the battery officers, the fire control HQ, and other links in the chain of liaison between the gunners and the infantry units that they were to support.[7] When fire was needed on that spot in future this abbreviated code order would bring it down with the shortest possible delay. Producing these plans for the all-round defence of a valley measuring about 11 × 3 miles involved hundreds of different potential targets. 'Counter-preparation', 'halting' and 'caging' fires had to be planned for every strongpoint – on all possible routes of approach and attack, on the forming-up areas where the enemy would mass for assaults, and on any vantage points where he might emplace his own supporting guns and mortars.

THE PROCESS OF PRE-REGISTERING targets for indirect fire and the progressive correction of aim when the shooting started depended upon accurate location of targets. Training and experience made it easy enough in theory for Colonel Piroth's officers to prepare shoots for the immediate defence of the strongpoints, provided that they had accurate maps; but this was their first problem. When the first two howitzers had arrived to supplement the paratroopers' RCLs in late November, Major Millot of GM/35 RALP had been seriously worried by the quality of maps available, and this would remain a central concern throughout the battle. The problem was perhaps symptomatic of a general carelessness over detail which had become normal in a poverty-stricken army reduced for many years to 'muddling through'.

The only map provided for the artillery was to 1/100,000 scale – half the scale of a standard British Ordnance Survey map, and showing only 1km to 1cm on paper (roughly one mile to three-quarters of an inch). This was a hopelessly inadequate scale for plotting accurate shoots in the hills; worse, the map also showed a good deal of blank white space around Dien Bien Phu, and lacked many spot heights for hilltops and crests. The exasperated General Gilles got a survey team sent to the valley in December; but the conditions in which they had to work – accompanying infantry through thick cover on missions which often became encounter battles – prevented them from collecting serious amounts of data. Still, Navarre's artillery chief General Pennacchioni was led to hope for a 1/25,000 map at the beginning of January. In fact it did not arrive until the end of that month, and then only with the proviso from Major Privat, chief of the Cartographic Service, that they could not guarantee its accuracy and that 'the artillery would certainly detect errors which it was not currently possible to resolve'. Parts of this masterpiece lacked contour lines, and the northern section – the direction of enemy approach – was simply an unimproved mechanical enlargement of the old 1/100,000 version.[8]

Even this map was distributed in small numbers only. The fire control HQ and Colonel de Castries' staff had to rely heavily upon painstakingly assembled mosaics of aerial photographs; these were taken daily by reconnaissance Bearcats, processed by the FTNV Second Bureau at the Hanoi Citadel, and flown (later, parachuted) back into Dien Bien Phu the next day. To these were added every scrap of information gleaned from ground observation posts (OPs), local spotting flights, patrol reports, and Captain Hébert's Meo guerrillas. Simple transparent grids were issued instead of maps; these were overlaid on particular aerial photos and used to signal locations by reference to the numbered squares. These packs of photos and grids even had to be carried by the forward observation officers (FOOs) – the artillery liaison teams sent out into the jungle with parachute units during their major sorties.[9] Aerial photos had serious limitations: they were normally vertical, and so flattened out all contour detail; and the Bearcats of EROM 80 were at the mercy of the mountain weather, in a region where the mornings were always foggy.

Fire support for infantry in the field was the responsibility of the FOOs. These artillery officers and NCOs were attached to the command posts of the infantry battalions, usually in pairs, one making observations and the other handling the radio traffic. Their unwieldy two-part SCR609 radio sets, which had to be slung from bamboo poles and carried by PIMs, were far from ideal when the FOOs had to *'nomadise'* around the hills with their battalions, and could not be used on the move. Despite the shortage of suitable equipment, however, a combination of talent, courage and improvisation would provide the infantry with a generally high standard of artillery liaison throughout the battle. But the central task confronting Colonel Piroth and his PC Feux was not the familiar mission of infantry support, but the unfamiliar one of locating and silencing their People's Army counterparts.

THE MAXIMUM RANGE OF THE 105mm – the same weapon as their own – was 6.8 miles; that of the Japanese 75mm mountain gun was five miles, and of the US M3A1 75mm pack howitzer slightly more. Finding the enemy batteries was not simply a matter of drawing circles on a map, however. It would be conventional for Giap to place his artillery on the reverse or outer slopes of the Dien Bien Phu bowl, hidden from the French by a crest line from which his observers could correct the fall of shot; but mountainous terrain imposes its own limitations. Such was the steepness of the surrounding crests that howitzers placed on the reverse slopes, even well short of their theoretical maximum range, would have to shoot at such high angles of elevation to clear the intervening ridges that the area of their fall of shot would be limited. Irrespective of Giap's calculation of the air/artillery threats, the consensus among the French artillery officers was that in order to present a comprehensive threat to Dien Bien Phu the guns would have to be placed on the inner slopes of the valley. Some commentators have implied that Giap's choice came as a surprise, but Colonel Piroth's judgement was shared by a number of visiting VIPs: the ex-gunner General Cogny, his artillery chief Colonel de Winter, and Navarre's inspector of artillery General Pennacchioni. They were also receptive – at first – to Colonel Piroth's loudly expressed confidence that the Viet Minh artillery was therefore doomed.[10]

Piroth seems to have been in two minds over whether he had as many guns as he needed; but he never expressed any doubt over his ability to silence Giap's artillery. At various times he assured his colleagues that, first, the Viet Minh would be unable to transport their alleged 105mm guns across North Vietnam under skies ruled by the Air Force; second, if they did get them to Dien Bien Phu and into action, his guns would smash them; and third, that even if some did keep firing, the People's Army would be unable to keep them supplied with enough ammunition to do real harm. At first he was convinced that as soon as the Viet Minh started building emplacements on the forward slopes they would be spotted; later, when the difficulty of locating them became clear, he remained confident that as soon as the enemy guns betrayed their positions by opening fire they could be destroyed. During a visit on 17 December by Navarre, Cogny and Air Force General Lauzin, Piroth accompanied them to strongpoint Béatrice with Colonels de Castries and Gaucher. Seeing how this isolated hill overlooked the whole camp, Navarre expressed concern for GONO if it should fall to the enemy, only to be reassured by Piroth: 'General, no Viet cannon will be able to fire three rounds before being destroyed by my artillery.' 'Perhaps,' replied Navarre; 'but this won't be like Na San.'[11]

It seems that many officers and men of GONO who had never seen Na San were indeed under the impression that this battle, if it came, would be essentially a repeat of that classic defence on a larger field. Those who had been there – the légionnaires of III/3 REI and 1 BEP, some of the Legion mortar men, the Algerians of II/1 RTA, perhaps above all the two Thai battalions – needed only the evidence of their eyes to undeceive them. Na San had been half the size of Dien Bien Phu, though defended by the same number of battalions. Its airstrip had been closely surrounded and masked by a cluster of hills, all of them occupied by the garrison. Inside the ring of hilltop strongpoints an unbroken second perimeter of fighting positions had been constructed, blocking the enemy's infiltration between the hills and thus his opportunity to surround and isolate individual strongpoints. From this central redoubt, close behind the hill features, counter-attacks could be thrown out in any direction and over short distances. The most obvious difference of all was that outside Na San's ramparts the terrain was level or even sloped away; although woodland and scrub had offered cover to the attackers, the defences were at no point overlooked from higher ground.

The senior ranks, with access to intelligence reports, were also aware of the differences in both kind and scale which the People's Army presented at Dien Bien Phu. As far as was known, Na San had been attacked by a maximum of 18 infantry battalions, after inadequate logistic preparation which limited their endurance – they simply had not had the ammunition to keep up a pitched battle for long once their initial assault rushes had failed. They had been supported only by the fire of 120mm mortars and a modest number of 75mm guns; and the latter had been flat-trajectory recoilless weapons, whose line of sight and fire to the airstrip was blocked by the surrounding hills. To vary an analogy famously used by

Ho Chi Minh to describe Dien Bien Phu, at Na San the Viet Minh had been sitting around the brim of a hat looking up at the crown, while at Dien Bien Phu they were sitting round the rim of a bowl looking down into it. At Na San, finally, they had had neither 105mm howitzers nor 37mm AA guns.[12]

WITH 155MM HOWITZERS PIROTH'S artillery had a range of nine miles – long enough to reach any targets that he could locate. Ground observation posts were initially set up on Béatrice looking east, on Gabrielle facing north, on Anne-Marie and Claudine covering the west, and at the camp's main headquarters. These were simply sandbagged perches built on the highest available points, where artillery officers and NCOs under the leadership of Lieutenant Claude Verzat manned large tripod-mounted, range-finding binoculars. From these and other perimeter vantage points, rotas of observers spent endless hours scanning the surrounding hills for signs of any sort of activity, and passing reports to the staff for collation with the aerial photographs. Each infantry battalion had its own FOO team, and six more were held in general reserve; all contributed to the cumulative study of the landscape and its surveillance for signs of the enemy. These ground OPs had their obvious limitations, however, and the main burden of target location and correction of aim would have to be carried by airborne observers in Morane 500s. The task faced by these officers should perhaps be put into perspective.

Since the beginning of the war the absence of enemy artillery had inevitably led commanders to neglect the specialist art of artillery target intelligence (SRA) and, in the absence of helicopters, to divert these versatile short take-off aircraft to general reconnaissance and liaison duties. At Dien Bien Phu the old disciplines would have to be relearned by the four crews provided for the half-dozen Moranes of Lieutenant Asselinau's flight from 21 GAOA based on the airstrip. Given the poor quality of the maps, they too would have to rely mainly upon the aerial photos, which came up from Hanoi daily with possible recent developments highlighted in grease pencil.[13]

The procedure was for an artillery observer to cram himself into the rear seat of a Morane (likened by Lieutenant Pierre Camoin to the back of a Citroën 2CV), with his lap full of maps, aerial photos and code books.

During his turbulent flight – in a cockpit from which the door was normally removed – he had to act as navigator for the pilot and as spotter and fire controller for ground troops, artillery and air strikes, manipulating not just his paperwork and binoculars but also three different radios. To control air strikes he was linked to the pilot's VHF set; for liaison with the guns he had an SCR609 set mounted behind his head, tuned to an overcrowded artillery frequency which he could not adjust in flight; and for contact with infantry he had to carry an SCR300 man-pack set jammed beside his leg. Using these radios required him to juggle three separate sets of earphones and microphones, in a snake's delight of tangled cables. In his role as target spotter, he had to peer down at the unbroken vegetation in the hope of noticing some man-made sign of activity. If he saw something he had to keep it fixed in view while the pilot dipped and turned, and then try to mark it – by leaning out and dropping a coloured smoke grenade by hand, above an anonymous spot in a sea of monotonous greenery, with virtually no landmarks to act as datum points for his eye or his radio commentary.[14]

The results obtained by the spotter aircraft were extremely frustrating; possible targets were seldom located, and the fire unleashed on them had no verifiable results. One day in late December, Colonel Piroth went up to see for himself; with the radios pulled out of Major Baup's Morane, the burly colonel managed to crawl into the rear, kneeling behind Lieutenant Camoin's seat. After a reluctant take-off the little plane wavered off to the east, and Camoin pointed out a minute clearing which he had noticed on an earlier mission, about six miles from the Elianes. Piroth was convinced; and on 30 December, when the 155mm battery was ready for action, this was the target he chose.

The gun captain easily got the right line; but although succeeding salvoes 'for effect' dropped shells short of, beyond, and finally all round the target, Piroth and his officers – watching from the roof of the 155mm battery HQ – were unable to confirm any direct hits. The target was tiny, and some detail of the modelling of the slope seemed to be defying the accuracy of the howitzer (this was, of course, not the natural topography but the overhang of a deeply dug casemate). Colonel Piroth's mood became increasingly pensive; and the 155s were not employed again until 16 January.[15]

The frustration of 'Zulu Kilo' at their inability to prove the location of the enemy gun positions or to catch the artillery on the move was shared by the Bearcat photo-reconnaissance pilots of EROM 80, who took great risks to secure the evidence. On 23 January, Lieutenant Bigay, infuriated by the lack of results from more cautious tactics, disobeyed orders and flew a complete circuit of the hills surrounding Dien Bien Phu at top speed and 150ft altitude. He brought his F8F home riddled with bullet holes, and his CO Captain Moulin was obliged to 'soap his head' for the record; but his film showed unmistakable images of gun positions being constructed. Bigay's courage was wasted, however; it was 48 hours before the interpreters at FTNV released the photos to the B-26 bomber squadrons, by which time their interest was purely historical – the artillery positions had vanished back into the unvarying green carpet.[16]

ATTEMPTS WERE MADE TO lure the enemy guns into firing and revealing themselves by night. A typical mission took place on 23 January, when Lieutenant Junquet of 5/II/4 RAC was sent with a single 105mm and a Chaffee tank south-east of Eliane 3, to simulate the fire of an entire battery on to a stretch of RP41 north-east of Béatrice. Every five minutes the gun fired a salvo of eight or 12 shots, thickened up by the tank's 75mm cannon. After the fourth salvo a single flurry of mortar bombs fell around their position, causing no damage but letting them know that the People's Army had seen through the ruse.[17]

From 31 January or 1 February occasional harassing or ranging shells fell on the camp by daylight, usually in the late afternoon. These were identified – from the debris and from unexploded duds – as the old Japanese 75mm Type 94 mountain guns which the Viet Minh had long been known to possess. On 3 February the Viet Minh artillery celebrated *Tet*, the lunar New Year, with an unprecedented half-hour bombardment. The French guns fired back, the Air Force was called in, and Captain Hervouët's 'bisons' rolled up on to the hills; in all 1,650 shells and 158 bombs were expended. The GONO staff were convinced that they had destroyed several enemy guns; but most of their targets had probably been dummies. Years later Colonel Bui Tin would state that the initial emplacement plan called for three neighbouring casemates to be dug for each gun, so that it could be shifted after firing. This idea was abandoned because of the huge labour involved, and because French counter-fire proved less accurate than had been feared. Instead, dummy casemates were constructed, where charges could be set off to draw French fire on to the false muzzle flashes. The colonel claimed that most apparent Viet Minh artillery fire at this time was trickery, and that many more mortar bombs were fired than 75mm shells.[18]

On 5 February, Lieutenant Verzat, in an OP on Eliane 2, heard the sound of gunfire to the east and the rushing passage of shells through the air immediately above him. Turning, he saw two or three dark geysers of earth erupting on the airfield, and a few moments later he was sure he spotted a muzzle flash on a green hillside. The telephone and radio nets were clogged with excited chatter, and it was some time before Verzat got the 155mm shoot he requested. Fifteen rounds fell around the target, and there was no more incoming fire. By 6pm, when Colonel Piroth joined him, Verzat had tentatively identified half a dozen firing slits. The 155s thundered again, but without observable results. Eventually Major Hourcabie at fire control HQ called up a pair of Chaffees, which clanked up the hill to join the watch. One tank gunner saw a flash, and with his flat-firing, high-velocity 75mm cannon he 'posted one right through the letter-box', visibly causing a brief fire inside.

Discussing this rare success in private, Piroth and Hourcabie agreed that their only real chance of hitting the pinpoint targets of concealed enemy positions now lay with flat-trajectory guns rather than lobbing howitzers. Calling up the few tanks to the exact positions where they were needed for this job would always take too long; the sole option was for Piroth to ask FTNV for 75mm RCLs and crews to take positions on Dominique and Eliane. He asked, but he did not get them: the only unit which might have supplied them – GM/35 RALP – was by now committed to operations in Laos.[19]

APART FROM THE COUNTER-BATTERY problem, Piroth was depressed by his gunners' relative failure to give accurate fire support to the sorties into the hills mounted by the infantry. His FOO teams had difficulty in bringing down fire in thick jungle without good maps; during the operation in the area of Hill 781 on 6 February shells dropped on Major Nicolas's I/4 RTM, killing several Tirailleurs, and Piroth felt impelled to make a

1 ABOVE Dien Bien Phu, December 1953: Generals Navarre (left) and Gilles. (This, and all other photographs unless otherwise credited, are courtesy ECPA. For fuller captions to photographs, see pp.29–39.)

2 BELOW LEFT General Vo Nguyen Giap, photographed at Dien Bien Phu in 1984. (TRH Pictures)

3 BELOW RIGHT Colonel Christian de Castries, commanding officer of GONO, in his command post at Dien Bien Phu.

4 ABOVE Operation 'Castor', 20 November 1953: a paratrooper from 1st Airborne Brigade (GAP 1) organizes his kit on drop zone Natacha.

5 BELOW LEFT 20 November: Vietnamese paratroopers of II/1 RCP march up from DZ Simone to the village of Muong Thanh.

6 BELOW RIGHT 24 November: Captain Bordier's first column of Thai auxiliaries from Lai Chau arrive at Dien Bien Phu.

7 ABOVE 20 November: paratroopers of Major Bigeard's 6 BPC bring in one of their dead from DZ Natacha.

8 ABOVE RIGHT Evening, 20 November: paras of 6 BPC load their wounded on to a Sikorsky S-55 helicopter from Muong Sai.

9 BELOW A 120mm mortar of 1 CEPML – dropped on 21 November – fires a ranging shot.

10 ABOVE LEFT Midnight mass, 24 December 1953: Lieutenant Colonel Jules Gaucher (left), Colonel de Castries and Lieutenant General Navarre.

11 ABOVE RIGHT GONO's first artillery commander, Colonel Charles Piroth.

12 BELOW A paratroop unit commanders' conference in Lieutenant Colonel Langlais' command post: (left to right) Captain Botella, Major Bigeard, Captain Tourret, Langlais, and Major de Seguin-Pazzis.

3 ABOVE Lieutenant Colonel Pierre Langlais

14 ABOVE Major Marcel Bigeard

5 BELOW Major Jean Bréchignac

16 BELOW Captain Yves Hervouët

17 ABOVE The central valley, early December 1953, looking roughly north-west to south-east from above the southern end of the runway; see Map 14. (A) Baldy and Phoney; (B) Eliane 2; (C) the 'horseshoe' of the Nam Youm; (D) Muong Thanh, its houses hidden in the trees; (E) Japanese drainage ditch; (F) Pavie Track.

18 BELOW Paratroopers help unload a truck body from a requisitioned Bristol 170 heavy transport.

19 ABOVE The central camp in early March, from much the same angle as the photo opposite but slightly further south. See Map 11 – the Bailey bridge is just off the left side of the photo. (A) Eliane 2; (B) wooden bridge; (C) Eliane 11; (D) aircraft dispersal pens; (E) 105mm artillery; (F) 155mm artillery; (G) headquarters area; (H) ammunition dump.

20 BELOW 19 February 1954: Colonel de Castries drives Defence Minister René Pleven and Major General René Cogny on a tour of the camp.

21 ABOVE The typical appearance of one of the hill strongpoints on the east or north-east face of the camp.

22 BELOW One of the 105mm howitzers of II/4 RAC in its large circular gunpit, open to enemy shell and mortar fire.

23 ABOVE Early 1954: armourers load a 500lb bomb under the wing of an F8F-1 Bearcat of squadron GC 1/22 'Saintonge' on the airfield at Dien Bien Phu.

24 BELOW December 1953: Foreign Legion mechanics reassemble the Chaffee tanks beside the runway at Dien Bien Phu.

25 ABOVE The tank 'Auerstaedt' of Lieutenant Préaud's platoon at Isabelle, camouflaged with streaks of mud. (Photo Henri Préaud, courtesy Simon Dunstan)

26 BELOW Photographed in 1996, Warrant Officer Carette's tank 'Bazeilles', abandoned on the summit of Eliane 2 in the early hours of 1 April 1954. (Photo Kieran Lynch)

27 ABOVE 14 December 1953: Vietnamese paratroopers in action in thick cover during GAP 2's return from the failed sortie to Muong Pon.

28 BELOW Paras of 1 BEP take cover in the paddy-fields during one of the road-opening missions southward to Isabelle in late March.

29 ABOVE LEFT   Captain Cabiro, commanding 4th Company, 1 BEP, photographed during one of the sorties into the hills to the north during December 1953.

30 ABOVE RIGHT   The terrain of the High Region: a river cutting through the hills between Lai Chau and Tuan Giao. (Photo Kieran Lynch)

31 BELOW   Paratroop casualties being treated for fragment wounds by a unit MO (left – probably Lieutenant Patrice de Carfort of 8 BPC) on one of the eastern hill positions.

32 ABOVE A fuel depot burns after being hit by shellfire, seen from the main headquarters area; note the iron roof arches of the buried bunkers, and the radio aerials at right.

33 BELOW LEFT A youthful Viet Minh prisoner is marched into the camp after an engagement on the eastern hills.

34 BELOW RIGHT Paratroopers try to improve their trenches east of the airstrip, apparently in Dominique 4 or Epervier. After rain the rattan sacks became slippery, and did not pack into a solid parapet like hessian sandbags.

35 ABOVE Third week of March 1954: a shell bursts beside the airstrip as a casualty evacuation Dakota taxies after landing, its hastily applied red crosses no protection from the Viet Minh artillery.

36 BELOW 17 March: after waiting under cover of the drainage ditch, wounded soldiers crowd around the doors of a 'casevac' Dakota during its brief halt at the north end of the runway.

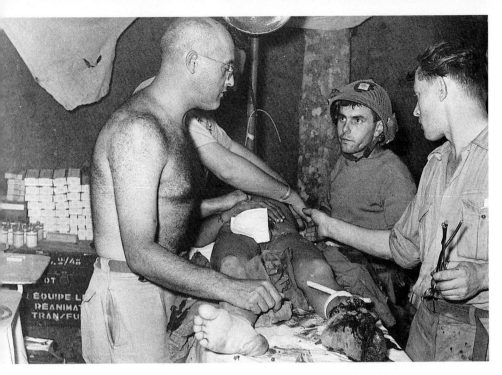

37 ABOVE In the underground hospital, Dr Paul Grauwin (left) examines a casualty who has had his foot partially blown off.

38 BELOW Operation 'Condor', late April: légionnaires of II/2 REI and Laotian troops halt in the jungle during the march of Lieutenant Colonel Godard's column up the Nam Ou valley in an attempt to link up with the besieged garrison of Dien Bien Phu.

39 ABOVE Aerial photo of Isabelle shortly before the end of the battle; see Map 19. The tiny white spots are discarded parachutes; the web of pale lines, Regiment 57's approach trenches.

40 BELOW The victors: on 14 October 1954, a propaganda section from Division 308 clap and sing in the streets of Hanoi. (USIA, courtesy Howard R. Simpson)

public apology. This was partly the responsibility of infantry officers, however: the artillery shoot had followed the agreed timetable, but delayed progress by the infantry had not been reported to the fire-control headquarters.[20]

Piroth was also naggingly aware that in any eventual duel with the enemy his own crews would be at serious risk, particularly from mortar fire. The 'all azimuths' position for a 105mm gun covered more than 750sq ft, for a 155mm it was twice that size, and since the howitzers were required to fire in all directions they could not be provided with any overhead cover at all. The gun barrel could be mechanically traversed on its carriage through 45°; any greater change of aim involved the crew picking up the ends of the heavy steel trail legs and carrying them round the edge of the circular pit like sailors turning a capstan, pivoting the 1.8-ton howitzer on its wheeled axle. This meant that the shoulder-deep pit had to be about 30ft across for a 105mm, and 50ft for the bigger 155mm.

Trenches looped out from the pits, leading to the four-gun batteries' reserve ammunition dumps and the dug-out command posts and crew shelters. The crews released from stand-by could use their time to raise the edge of their pits with a parapet of earth-filled sandbags, shell-packing tubes and boxes to give some solidity and sideways protection from blast and splinters; the lips of pits and trenches were also stiffened with empty brass shell cases driven into the ground. To protect the crews when not in action, and the ammunition stacked for their immediate use, caves were dug into the gunpit walls at intervals; some were roofed with the same improvised materials as were used for parapets, and the quality of such cover varied widely. Few positions were as well prepared as those for 5th Battery, II/4 RAC, whose Warrant Officer Jullian – one of the few World War II veterans – managed to lay hands on some teak logs and had iron clamps fashioned from old ammunition boxes; his battery would suffer fewer casualties than the others.[21] Among most of the gunners, as among the infantry, there was no real appreciation of the danger of serious counter-fire by enemy artillery. The Viet Minh's few previous revelations of their 75mm guns had not concentrated on silencing French artillery but on direct support for their assault troops.

Communications between the batteries, their battalion HQs and the PC

Feux were by both radio and field telephone, but when the battle started in earnest the telephone cables were often broken. Finding the breaks and mending them, often under fire, was a time-consuming and dangerous job, so for long periods the gunners relied upon radio conversations – to which the enemy could and did listen in. The People's Army artillery, which relied upon field telephones, avoided this insecurity.

ON 18 FEBRUARY, COLONEL Piroth was present when the visiting Generals Navarre and Cogny and Colonel Berteil studied a sketch captured on a prisoner, which seemed to show the layout for one of the Viet Minh's buried gun casemates. They were impressed; and Berteil remarked to Piroth that if it were accurate, then his counter-battery programme was in trouble – should he not consider providing overhead cover for his guns? Piroth apparently dismissed this with the assurance that he had discussed the point with Castries; but in fact such a plan was impossible. If his guns could not fire at all angles of the compass he would need at least twice as many to cover the whole perimeter, and roofing them in would have involved fantastic amounts of materials and labour, and specialist skills which were not available to him. The captured sketch was all very well; but for the enemy to build such casemates for his whole artillery on the facing slopes would be a major construction project, which Piroth still refused to believe could be achieved without being located from the air.[22]

Nobody present seems to have suggested that the work might already have been completed, yet this was the subject of press speculation. On 16 February, Robert Guillain reported in Le Monde that the Viet Minh had built positions, not on the reverse but on the forward slopes, 'right under our noses... without our seeing it'. He went on to add (correctly) that in Korea such threats had been neutralized by the USAF's saturation air attacks; but that at Dien Bien Phu the weakness of the French air effort put the outcome in doubt. Guillain had been unimpressed by watching what he called 'imitation' air strikes by single pairs of fighter-bombers.[23]

Claude Verzat now joined Major Le Gurun's team in the fire-control HQ, with responsibility for developing a 1/50,000 intelligence map. The lieutenant spent hours each day peering through a stereoscopic viewer at the latest aerial photos, alternating with trips up to the OP on the roof and discussions with the Morane crews. He became the lord of the multicoloured drawing pins, and the map slowly blossomed with marks for slit trenches, new lengths of track, possible mortar, anti-aircraft and artillery positions; but 'possible' was the operative word. During January much of the French shelling had been limited to unobserved shoots, by night, on tentatively identified target areas. There is some evidence that this almost blind harassment did achieve results; but the deeply buried artillery casemates did not figure among these successes.[24]

DURING FEBRUARY, GONO's loss of air transport priority to the benefit of Laos, and consequent worries over ammunition stocks, greatly reduced such shoots. The increased size of GONO, and thus of its daily requirements for simple subsistence, had slowed the build-up of munition stockpiles since December. The air supply programme was dogged by bad weather in January, when a constant low cloud ceiling prevented many missions, and on the 14th, 15th, 17th and 18th air activity was totally suspended. Even so, by 25 January, the date when the enemy assault was first anticipated, the camp's depots held about nine days' supply of all provisions, and between five and seven 'units of fire' – supposed daily combat needs – for all weapons.

During that month the newly supplied C-47s for the fourth transport squadron – Major de Saint-Marc's GT 2/63 'Sénégal' – had been arriving in batches, and its crews, who had been gaining experience by flying with the other units, were progressively gathered. All the Dakota crews were becoming tired, and many airmen were down with malaria, dysentery and various fevers; at the end of January there should theoretically have been 108 crews in Indochina, but in fact there were only 78, of which only 60 were operational. During the month 15 new crews had arrived, but they needed training in local conditions.[25]

In the first days of February visibility over the hill country was poor; it was usually within tolerable limits during the rest of the month, but between 25 February and 13 March the sky above the Delta bases was changeable, with many interruptions by the low *crachin*.[26] In the period from 1 February to 13 March, when Dien Bien Phu was expending ammunition during sorties and artillery shoots but was in competition with Laos and Annam for resupply capacity, the average daily tonnage delivered to the valley fell by 46 per cent from the figures achieved between 26

November and 31 January. The foreseen needs of the other fronts were to some extent allowed for and GONO registered much reduced requirements, but the average of 90 tons per day delivered was still 22 per cent below its needs. (More details will be found in Appendix 3.)

Bad visibility over the valley itself was extremely dangerous: the sky was often crowded with aircraft at medium and low altitude, stacked at different heights while the ground controllers tried to orchestrate an orderly progression of parachute or landing runs down through the murk. There was no radar equipment either on the ground or in the aircraft, and once he arrived at holding point 'Yankee' at the south end of the valley a pilot in thick cloud had very little idea of his relative position. On 6 January a C-119 Packet made the first attempt to parachute supplies over the airstrip at Isabelle, which proved exciting: the freighter had to make a north-to-south pass, ending in a violent eastwards bank to clear the *calcaires* at the southern end of the valley.[27]

One trick for accurate dropping through the low slabs of stratus cloud was tried out with great success by GT 2/64 on 6 December, and often repeated thereafter. In radio contact with a command aircraft, a team on the ground would send a bright red weather balloon up on a long line from the forward edge of the drop zone, until it appeared out of the top of the cloud; since there was no wind on cloudy days this served as an accurate marker, and excellent results were obtained.[28] Aircraft followed the radio beacons to 'Torri Rouge' at first light, and the shuttle sometimes continued as late as 9pm at night; on some days the Dakotas and C-119s would achieve up to 60 missions. During January and February the handful of C-119 crews bore a great part of the daily burden, often flying two missions daily. The crews trained to fly the C-119 were not even permanently assigned to the 'Détachement Packet', however; at times of need they might be summoned back to their original squadrons to fly Dakotas, leaving even more of the invaluable C-119s – which soon outnumbered the available crews – standing idle at Haiphong–Cat Bi.

The French use of C-119s in Indochina became the most visible example of American CIA assistance to the Expeditionary Corps. The French Air Force first acquired six C-119s on loan from the USAF following an appeal by Prime Minister René Mayer to Secretary of State Dulles in April 1953. At that time supplying General Salan's air–ground base on the Plain of Jars was placing enormous strain on the transport fleet, and larger aircraft than Dakotas were needed to carry armour and artillery.[29] The Eisenhower administration agreed to lend the aircraft, but not US military aircrews. While the first 12 French crews were under instruction in Germany and at Clark Air Force Base in the Philippines, the US government arranged a contract for American civilian crews to fly the Packets.

These men were provided by Civil Air Transport (CAT), ostensibly a commercial airline based in Formosa and headed by former USAAF General Claire L. Chennault, leader of the wartime 'Flying Tigers' volunteers who had fought with the Nationalist Chinese. In fact, in August 1950 CAT had been secretly purchased by the Central Intelligence Agency; while it continued its commercial activities it would also provide an air transport capability for the CIA in Asia (CAT was the direct ancestor of Air America). Operation 'Squaw' was launched with remarkable speed and efficiency: after three days' intensive training by 483rd Troop Carrier Wing the CAT pilots flew six C-119s in French markings from Clark AFB to Hanoi–Gia Lam on 5 May 1953, accompanied by USAF ground crews in civilian clothes. They flew missions over Indochina between 6 May and 16 July, when they left the country.

At the time of 'Castor' the Expeditionary Corps still had five of the loaned Packets and five French crews in country, but the increased pressure on S/GMMTA led to a request for a second American operation. Under the serial codename 'Ironage', another 12 C-119s were loaned from 5 December 1953, to be flown by French pilots (who were not, in fact, available in sufficient numbers) but maintained by USAF personnel; a second batch of 12 aircraft would be supplied the following March. In January 1954, 21 CAT pilots were trained on the C-119 at Ashiya AFB, Japan, in readiness for 'Squaw II'. On 3 March a three-month contract was signed between CAT and the French government for the provision of 12 two-man crews, to fly C-119s loaned and maintained by the USAF on logistic support duties, specifically excluding combat missions or the carrying of bombs or napalm. The CAT personnel arrived at Haiphong–Cat Bi from 9 March, quickly setting up a comfortable 'hotel' and sharing an operations building with the French Air Force 'Détachement Packet' led by Captain Soulat. They would begin drops over Dien Bien Phu on 12 March.[30]

IN PUBLIC CHARLES PIROTH maintained to the end his confidence that the enemy's guns could not escape him once they opened fire in earnest. During General Blanc's visit on 26 January, Piroth had reassured him: 'If I get 30 minutes' warning, my counter-battery will be effective.' Privately, the artillery commander was gnawed by his responsibility. In early December he had been surrounded by old colleagues from his previous posting at Nam Dinh, but with the growth of the garrison staff he became a more isolated figure at mess meals. During February the artillery's failure to silence sporadic harassing fire led to a good deal of criticism, particularly by a clique which formed around the acid-tongued Lieutenant Colonel Keller, the GONO chief-of-staff flown in to replace the dead Colonel Guth. While Castries' other senior officers joined regular evening bridge sessions, Piroth tended to return alone to his HQ to worry away at fire plans late into the night. He was a man with inner wounds to match his visible mutilation.[31]

During the first week of March, General Cogny ordered a review of the relative status of the two artilleries at Dien Bien Phu, given the latest intelligence reports on enemy ammunition shipments to Tuan Giao. Colonel de Winter's memorandum, which reached the general's desk on 9 March, stated the opinion that the enemy artillery was as numerous as the French; had better observation; and was already in a position to deliver about 33 shells per minute for five hours continuously, over the whole area of the central headquarters, the artillery and heavy mortar positions, and the part of Isabelle where the other two batteries were emplaced. The original report bears, in Cogny's handwriting and initialled, the comment 'Why was this study not made earlier?'[32]

ON 2 MARCH 1954 A FINAL artillery asset arrived: a platoon of four quadruple Browning M2 0.50in heavy machine-gun mounts from the under-employed Colonial Far East Anti-Aircraft Battalion (GAACEO), commanded by Lieutenant Paul Redon. Their provision was reportedly at the suggestion of the American Major Vaughn, who had seen these terrifying 'meat grinders' at work in the ground role in Korea. Their practical rate of fire of 2,000 rounds per minute – 500lbs weight of metal – would clearly be valuable, but the artillery were puzzled over how to deploy them. To drag their one-ton trailers up and mount them on hilltops on the perimeter, directly facing probable routes of Viet Minh attack over fields of fire clear of friendly troops, would have meant complex terracing work for which there was now neither the time nor the materials. It was finally decided to install the 'quad-50s' in the positions of 8th Shock around the south of the airstrip, with the trailers raised on quickly constructed ramps to lift the guns above the heads of the Vietnamese paras of Lieutenant Desmons' 4th Company. The guns were to be used largely for indirect fire, like artillery pieces – firing 'blind' on pre-registered killing zones and correcting the fall of shot by means of tracer ammunition. With artillery help Redon and Warrant Officer Lemeur drew up range tables for elevation; around the ramps they staked out the directions for the various shoots with triangles cut from ammunition boxes and cardboard signs marked with the necessary elevation angles.[33]

IF THE MORANES COULD NOT find the enemy artillery, during this first week of March they had no difficulty in spotting signs of infantry activity. Routine water and firewood parties from the more isolated perimeter strongpoints had been forced to evolve into large-scale operations. Each morning revealed new trenches creeping through the scrub and forest towards the northern localities, and both artillery and strong infantry sorties were tasked with destroying them. The infantry raids often led to heavy skirmishing, however, adding to the rising list of casualties.

On 4 March a mixed force of Thais from BT 3 and Algerians from V/7 RTA pushed up from Anne-Marie and Gabrielle to dislodge a Viet Minh force entrenched on Hill 633 barely a thousand yards north of the latter; the sortie failed, and was forced to withdraw with significant casualties. The following day 1 BEP tried once more to 'aerate' Béatrice, which now seemed to be embraced by trenches on three sides; they ran into new diggings between Gabrielle and Béatrice. On 6 March, General Cogny again warned Castries about risking heavy losses on such sorties – every indicator pointed towards a general attack on Dien Bien Phu in the middle of the month.

On 11 March, Lieutenant Colonel Langlais led what proved to be the last major sortie by GAP 2; the objective was Hill 555, just two miles from the centre of the camp and overlooking Béatrice, where the Viet Minh were now digging approach trenches even in daylight.[34] The troops loathed these missions for their pointlessness: they inflicted and suffered a few casualties, filled in enemy trenches and fell back, and the next night the Viet Minh dug them out again. In perfect weather, Captain Pichelin led his 2nd Company, 8 BPC, up RP41 supported by the usual pair of tanks; off to the south they could see Bearcats wheeling and diving, and smoke rising from the jungle ridges. On reaching the new Viet Minh trench works the paratroopers drove off the sappers and, guarded by their advanced platoon, shovelled the earth back, seeded with a few anti-personnel mines. Before long Sergeant Chief Marty's advanced screen came under attack, and the 2nd Company soon had a hard fight on their hands. Enemy machine-gun and mortar fire raked Pichelin's men from the heights south of the road, and *bo doi* poured forward through thick cover. It soon came to hand-to-hand fighting of a particular savagery – many of Pichelin's men were Khmers, brought up to hate the 'Annamites' from boyhood. The two-hour fight involved machetes, but also tanks, artillery, and finally aircraft before Pichelin could disengage and carry his dead and wounded home.[35]

For their part, 1 BEP were advancing through heavy cover when their point men stumbled into trenches full of silent enemy infantry, who seemed just as surprised by the encounter. Some prisoners were taken, but when the *bo doi* did react the Legion paratroopers, too, faced a stiff fighting withdrawal under infantry and mortar attack. The twice-wounded Lieutenant Jacques Molinier, 1 BEP's artillery liaison that day, had to call down fire perilously close to his own position before the rearguard could disengage.[36]

Late on the afternoon of the 11th individual enemy guns fired on the airfield; this marked the end of a relative pause since 20 February. Parked on the earth strip flanking the runway on the west was Lieutenant Magnat's C-119 Packet No. 546, which had force landed the day before with engine trouble. (This was a frequent problem with the C-119 – on this occasion Magnat had had to dump into the jungle six tons of petrol destined for the camp in order to get his plane over the last ridges on one engine.) The huge silver freighter made a tempting target, and the enemy gunner's discipline was as impressive as his skill. It took him just three shots to score a direct hit, and then he stopped, although other aircraft were parked close by. The C-119 tipped on to its nose with its twin tails rearing against the sky, and burned fiercely for hours. The 150ft cloud ceiling over the Delta airfields kept the clear sky over Dien Bien Phu empty that day; but the Bearcats based on the airstrip took off, strafed the hills more or less at random, and landed back. French counter-battery fire was blind and ineffective, and enemy shells continued to fall sporadically for some hours.[37]

On the morning of the 11th the usual trench-filling patrol from Béatrice to the south side of RP41 had led to a skirmish in which Lieutenant Bedeaux had been mortally wounded; III/13 DBLE were so short of officers that his 11th Company had to be taken over at short notice by Lieutenant Turpin, sent up from the regiment's 1st Battalion in Claudine. Late that afternoon Turpin was trying to get a clear idea of his position on Béatrice 3, the south-east hillock overlooking the road (see Map 15). There was no other officer, and Sergeant Chief Fels did the honours: 11th Company had only 11 senior NCOs, 11 corporals, and 85 légionnaires.[38] Turpin met his NCO platoon commanders and carried out the usual evening checks, setting the schedules for sentries, local patrols and listening posts outside the wire. He studied the fire plan left by his predecessor for 105mm and 120mm mortar shoots, and the battalion's own 81mm tubes; he familiarized himself with the minefield maps, and the position of the drums of napalm wired and ready at the top of some slopes. He made a round of his trenches, letting his new légionnaires get a good look at him, chatting with the sentries, sweeping the surroundings with binoculars; he noted with satisfaction that the long western slope in front of his wire seemed particularly well covered. Eventually Turpin retired to the little sandbag command post, but he was not asleep when a légionnaire roused him with word of noises from the hills beyond RP41. He called for two illuminating rounds from the battalion mortars; there was nothing to be seen, but shortly after the parachute flares burned out the clinking of picks and shovels was heard again.

The first morning light of 12 March revealed that an extraordinary amount of trenching had been completed south of Turpin's position under cover of darkness. The tightening of a similar noose around Gabrielle was confirmed when a strong patrol south towards the camp from V/7 RTA, including flame-thrower teams, lost one dead and ten wounded at the abandoned village of Ban Khe Phai, and a company mission to the north led by Lieutenant Moreau found trenches within 200yds of the perimeter.

That day General Cogny made his last visit to Dien Bien Phu, his C-47 taxiing up a runway now flanked to the west by several scorched wrecks. To an intermittent background mutter of enemy mortar fire, Cogny visited the Legion's positions on Béatrice. From that vantage point he watched as 4th Company of Tourret's 8th Shock assaulted the enemy approach trenches on a nearby hill. This time, with artillery and air support, the paratroopers were successful; but they encountered only one Viet Minh platoon, and driving them off cost Lieutenant Desmons five dead and ten wounded. The 4th Company of 1 BEP (now led by Lieutenant Domigo) did rather better, capturing a large number of weapons including two machine guns and a 75mm RCL. Simultaneous sorties by Algerians and Thais made little progress, however, even when supported by Bearcats dropping napalm.

As Cogny's Dakota prepared to take off in the late afternoon an artillery salvo fell near by, hurling shards of PSP into the air, wrecking two Moranes, and sending the farewell party diving for cover. There was no mistaking the teeth-jarring thump of these heavy shells: these were 105s, not antique Japanese 75s. When Castries returned to his HQ after seeing Cogny off, his Second Bureau chief Captain Jacques Noël passed him an intelligence report that commissars had been telling local villagers to clear out of the valley by noon the next day, Saturday 13 March: the implication was obvious.[39]

IT IS PERHAPS AT THIS POINT in the story of Dien Bien Phu that hindsight can be at its most deceptive. Remarkable as it now seems, it must be emphasized that on the eve of battle the mood of many regimental officers and men was optimistic. The widow of Lieutenant Colonel Gaucher later made a number of his letters available to the historian Colonel Pierre Rocolle. During the frustrating winter months their mood was variable, reflecting boredom and an old soldier's cynicism toward the high command and particularly the politicians; but as the battle drew nearer they became more positive. On 19 February, during René Pleven's visit, the minister asked Gaucher if he was concerned about the potential of the enemy artillery; he replied, 'In that case, we'll fight them as we did at Verdun.'

On 22 February, Jules Gaucher wrote to his wife:

For now, the Viets leave us almost in peace. This is a decisive period, because they are starting to withdraw from Laos. Will they go back to the Delta, or come back here? One has to ask oneself if the Viets are really going to attack us. We have created such a defensive system that it would really be a big mouthful to swallow, and that gives pause to the gentlemen opposite, who have already countermanded the order to attack [on 25 January]. But I still believe that for the sake of prestige they'll have to come, though we are already causing them heavy loss with our artillery and aircraft.

On 5 March the colonel contemplated the prospect of battle without fear: 'Things are still calm, but they tell us that a brawl is coming soon. Is it true? It's true they must wish to do something spectacular before Geneva. But I believe that if they do, they'll break their teeth.'[40]

General Navarre was prepared to take steps to postpone the battle if his commanders on the ground thought it wise; but they did not. On 4 March the C-in-C accompanied General Cogny to Dien Bien Phu, and during a meeting with Colonel de Castries he suggested reinforcing the camp with two or three more battalions. His explanation to the subsequent commission of inquiry was as follows:

We knew that the Viet Minh planned an attack around 15 March. We believed that there was a limit on the time that their main force could fight in the High Region during the monsoon rains, which they had always previously avoided doing. The rains were due to begin on about 15 May, so we needed to gain some time. I had it in mind to send two or three extra battalions to Dien Bien Phu – paratroopers or others – so as to present the Viet Minh commander with a new problem... [The Viet Minh] never launch an attack without the most careful study of the objective. I thought that by putting another two or three battalions in – perhaps creating a new defended locality on each flank – I could delay the opening of his attack by two or three weeks... I was probably deluding myself, but I mention it to show that I was uneasy.

Colonel de Castries agreed that it would be possible, but was unenthusiastic. He was not convinced that shoehorning another three battalions into his already crowded camp was wise, and would prefer to have them on call as reinforcements if he needed them later. His response is under-standable: how could worthwhile new strongpoints be built in time, and how could Colonel Nicot's Dakotas supply a garrison suddenly raised from 12 to 15 battalions? General Cogny, naturally, was not eager to tie down yet more of his reserves in Dien Bien Phu, and cited the difficulties of air transport. He apparently urged the undesirability of making the trap less attractive to the intended prey: they must not let the Viet Minh change their minds – they had a great defensive victory in their grasp.[41]

Captain Yves Rocolle was one of the staff officers who accompanied Cogny on his last flight to Dien Bien Phu on 12 March, and he passed his first-hand impressions to his brother Pierre; they simply confirm what many other accounts repeat. The officers and men of GONO had been waiting impatiently for their trial of strength for three months, and despite every frustrated sortie, every disappointment by the artillery, every evidence of the enemy's strength and skill, they still believed that they faced a hard but winnable battle. Repeatedly one reads phrases such as 'a prefabricated battlefield', and 'just pray the Viet doesn't rob us of our battle'.[42] Whatever the language of the bitter post-mortems, before the evening of 13 March most of the troops and many of their officers clearly saw Dien Bien not as a 'toilet bowl' *(cuvette)* in which they had been trapped, but as a carefully designed killing ground where they could destroy the enemy when he at last came out to fight them. They did not see the valley floor as an arena dominated by the enemy; they saw only the battalion strongpoints planted on the high ground. They were profes-sionals, and the Viet Minh were amateurs; and to dismiss this simply as blind arrogance is to misunderstand.

From their basic training self-belief is bred into all professional soldiers, and reinforced by every possible means throughout their careers. Men can endure battle because of their bond with their comrades; but what enables them to go into battle in the first place is faith in success – in the victory of the group, even though reason warns that not all of them will live to see it. At least half the garrison's infantry – certainly the paratroopers and légionnaires, but also some of the North Africans – were battle-hardened professionals, each of them convinced of the superiority of his own battalion. They were about to 'exercise their calling': to show one another, and 'the Viet', how well they could practise the trade which gave them their identity and self-worth. They did not need the interest or support of civilians, from whose mental world they were long separated; they found their strength in their tribal legends, the trust of admired leaders and the close company of comrades – the only men on earth whose opinion mattered to them. The *Le Monde* correspondent Robert Guillain, whose reports of his visit in February show no great gullibility, wrote that the words on everyone's lips were, 'We're going to show them!' All ranks, from the *deuxième classe* to the colonel, saw Dien Bien Phu as the place where Giap was going to give them a long-awaited chance to smash his regular divisions.[43]

EXPERIENCE HAD TAUGHT that the People's Army preferred to open their attacks while there was still enough afternoon light to correct the fall of their preparatory mortar fire, but late enough that the French had no time to call in air support before dark. Before dinner on the evening of 12 March 1954, Colonel Christian de Castries briefed his senior officers: 'Gentlemen, it's tomorrow, at 5pm.'[44]

11. Béatrice and Gabrielle

'The command echelon has not behaved
sensationally well under bombardment...'
Colonel de Castries *to General Cogny, 22 March*

THE MORNING OF 13 MARCH dawned dull and overcast, painting the valley in shades of slate grey. Some night-time damage was visible on the runway, where broken steel plates were sticking up like fangs, and engineer welding teams went out to repair them. Artillery fire was blamed for this, but it seems that Viet Minh sappers had infiltrated to place charges. These repairs would be repeated continually every day that the runway was in use; the individual plates of PSP could not simply be unfastened and replaced – if damaged, the grid had to be cut and rewelded.[1]

On the parking strip beside the runway a civilian Curtiss C-46 Commando freighter of the Blue Eagle line, which had been stranded by engine trouble, was almost ready to take off; but soon after the mechanics began running up the first engine, at some time between 8.30am and 9am, a shell landed on the steel plating with a noise like a hammer hitting a gong. Up on Dominique 2, Lieutenant Bergot's Legion mortar platoon turned to watch, and Sergeant Chief Maillard – called 'Babar' for his long nose and earlobes – gloomily offered a bet that the pilot would not get off before the enemy artillery found his range. His Italian comrade Sergeant Rol would not take it: the spectacle of the burning C-119 on the 11th had been merely interesting, but this was different – half a mile west of them they were watching Frenchmen struggling for their lives. A second shell landed, closer; the Commando's second engine started up; then a third explosion right beside the plane veiled the nose in dirt and smoke. When it cleared the paratroopers could see the crew scrambling clear, one of them obviously wounded. More shells fell all around the C-46; it did not catch fire, but soon lurched to one side and lay like a broken toy (*see Map 13*). In the weeks to come the abandoned wreck halfway up the west side of the runway would become a familiar landmark.[2]

Nobody had told the rank and file that the first assault was expected for 5pm that afternoon, but as the day wore on they soon picked up the tense mood of their officers, whose orders for every kind of preparation were given with testy impatience. The regular morning road-opening operation from the main camp up to Béatrice, today entrusted to BT 2 with tank support, came under heavy fire and had to call in fighter-bombers with napalm.[3]

From about 9am sporadic shelling of the airfield by 105s continued throughout the morning and early afternoon, and several aircraft were hit. During the morning two Dakota pilots from GT 2/64 'Anjou', Captains Defendini and Jeanson, had to pick their moments carefully to sprint from the shelter trenches to their parked aircraft amid a hail of fragments, racing them down the runway and into the air between blossoming shellbursts. Captain Amanou of GT 1/64 'Béarn' landed his C-47 'Boeufs Novembre-Hotel' only to see it riddled; that afternoon his squadron mate Lieutenant Cinquin's 'Novembre-Quebec' suffered the same fate on the emergency airstrip down at Isabelle.[4]

Most of the nine Bearcat fighters then at Dien Bien Phu were stuck in their sandbagged dispersal pens all morning by untimely technical problems: either dirt or water had somehow got into their fuel systems. Although the mechanics had worked all night they had not yet managed to clear more than two F8Fs, and others were damaged by shell fragments during the 13th.[5] The two serviceable fighters, flown by Sergeants de Somow and Barteau, each flew five missions that day, and others came up from the Delta; and at about 3.30pm one of the latter was shot down by heavy machine-gun fire north of Béatrice. This seems to have been the closest to the valley that the People's Army had yet unveiled AA batteries.

The first 37mm AA guns reportedly opened fire slightly later, in time to greet a formation of eight C-119 transports with sinister groups of black smoke puffs. The 37mm fired automatically but not continuously; it was loaded with a succession of five-round clips, and depending on the skill of the crew it could fire about 80 rounds per minute in a rapping cadence: *one-two-three-four-five, one-two-three-four-five...* With the barrel raised to an angle of 65° it had an accurate range of 9,400ft; thereafter the shells wandered across the sky, but were still lethal until they self-destructed at 14,400ft. A photo from later in the battle shows the results of a single 1½lb fragmentation shell on the flimsy aluminium structure of an aircraft: a Navy pilot of Flotille 11, Petty Officer Goizet, is being 'chaired' by his grinning comrades after nursing his Hellcat back to Haiphong on 9 April with a hole in the wing that a man could climb through.[6]

On this occasion five C-119s with mixed French-US crews and one manned by an American CAT crew pressed on, the latter taking some damage; the American crews of Nos 137 and 581 turned back. On returning to Haiphong–Cat Bi the CAT airmen pointed out that their contracts did not cover war missions under fire; Captain Soulat had to call back several trained French crews who had returned to their Dakota squadrons. (After some reflection the Americans decided that they would, after all, fly their next mission – the French pilots had lost a night's sleep for nothing.)

At 4pm 'Torri Rouge' radioed that Dien Bien Phu was closed to air traffic. The Army press men André Lebon and Jean Martinoff had hitched a ride on the last C-47 to get down; shortly afterwards both were hit and Martinoff killed by shellfire as they photographed the final destruction of a damaged Dakota.[7]

Three two-plane Hellcat patrols arrived over Dien Bien Phu and attempted to silence the flak. This was extremely difficult; heavy machine guns and 20mm cannon hardly had to expose themselves through their camouflage to fire, and although the long-barrelled 37mm had to be free to track its targets the emplacement was only a few yards square – the size of a small suburban lawn. 'Savart Red' (Lieutenant Commander Doe de Maindreville and Lieutenant Commander Villedieu de Torcy) suffered from bad radio reception, but each dropped two 500lb bombs on supposed AA positions; 'Savart Green' and 'Savart Yellow', unable to get any target information at all from the ground controller, dived on the same targets before all six Hellcats turned for the Delta once more.

The *Arromanches* was steaming off the Norways Islands in Ha Long Bay, at the limit of the fighters' range, and the weather turned dirty as night fell; Captain Patou radioed for the Hellcats to put down at

Haiphong–Cat Bi rather than trying to find the carrier in the dark with rapidly emptying tanks. Even this was dangerous enough: there was a ceiling of just 300ft, and in the thick clouds above the base at least 20 aircraft were trying to get into the circuit. The controller's radio channel was swamped with calls, and some pilots were flying low over the town in an attempt to find the airfield by following familiar street lighting. One of the C-119s did a 'touch-and-go' with engines screaming as the pilot realized he had landed too far down the runway; another managed to get down by 'pancaking' his big cargo plane like a fighter; a Privateer made a forced landing, and two B-26s collided in mid-air. The harassed controller routed the Hellcats in a wide sweep out over Ha Long Bay, which now resembled a dark, low-ceilinged cellar full of stone pillars. Lieutenant Commander de Torcy lost his leader in the murk, but managed to get down with his tanks almost dry. The wreckage of Maindreville's '11F-23' was spotted next morning on the summit of the Isle of Marvels.[8]

ON BÉATRICE THE MORNING OF the 13th revealed that a four-man listening post had disappeared during the night (they had probably been snatched, but the Legion listed them as deserters just in case). On Béatrice 3, Sergeant Chief Fels reported to Lieutenant Turpin that he could see Viet Minh look-outs in trenches across RP41 to the south; substantial earthworks were also identifiable to the north of Béatrice 1. Lieutenant Colonel Gaucher drove up during the morning; Major Pégot told him that his légionnaires were tired and tense. Sergeant Kubiak of 9th Company recalled that the officers hovered around all day giving constant orders, checking everything repeatedly; it was clear that they knew an attack was coming. Lieutenant Riondel, signals officer of III/10 RAC, drove up to check last-minute details of the fire plans with the strongpoint's artillery observer Captain Riès and to see that the FOO had enough radio batteries. The men got on with the familiar jobs – packing down loose sandbags, digging niches for grenades under the trench parapets, cleaning their weapons, filling magazines, stacking ammunition in the machine-gun blockhouses, checking the radio links. Cold rations were distributed in the trenches – the cooks, too, were busy at their fighting stations. At about 4pm Captain Pardi, the battalion's cheerful adjutant, telephoned the company command posts to confirm stand-to in an hour.

Occasional shells or mortar bombs had fallen on the position during the early part of the day, and five men were wounded. When things quietened down in the afternoon a jeep was ordered up to fetch them to the main hospital, but three of them refused, declaring that they could still fill magazines for their mates. The other two stretchers were loaded across the jeep; as it buzzed down the road to the camp it passed within a hundred yards of the nearest enemy approach trenches, in complete silence. The weather had cleared and the sky was bright; in the distance to the east a pair of Bearcats could be seen diving and wheeling over the jungle hills.

Shortly before 5pm, légionnaires on Béatrice 3 reported enemy infantry coming over the crests to the south and moving down the slopes through the trees and scrub to the trenches at the foot of the hill. Through binoculars Sergeant Chief Fels could make out machine guns, mortars and SKZ recoilless guns being manhandled forward. Soon the whole hillside seemed to be moving; this was a force of several battalions. As the *bo doi* filed into the trenches and covered shelters beyond the road Fels could see them clearly – their light green uniforms, dish-shaped palm-leaf helmets, even the fixed bayonets winking on their rifles.

At 5.05pm, Major Pégot told his FOO Captain Riès to radio Major Le Gurun's fire-control HQ and ask for 'counter-preparation' (CPO) artillery shoots on the enemy assembly trenches. At 5.18pm, Lieutenant Bergot's heavy mortar platoon on Dominique 2 recorded a signal from Lieutenant Lépinay in the PC Feux, calling for one of the prepared shoots: 'CPO Béatrice 321, 8 rounds per minute'. As the Legion mortarmen adjusted their sights, the world went mad. As in every battle, eyewitnesses differ over the exact moment when the first shot was fired; but it was long enough after 5pm for one or two officers to remark that the official briefing had been wrong, when the full weight of General Giap's artillery fell on Dien Bien Phu for the first time. The effect was stunning, both physically and psychologically.[9]

SERGEANT CHIEF MOUTY OF 6th Battery, II/4 RAC was checking a manual at the repair depot when he heard a sort of drum-roll from the east, quickly drowned out by a whistling rush through the air above him, and ear-splitting explosions from the headquarters area just to the south where a cluster of dirty grey-brown fountains spouted high into the air.

Mouty's driver raced back to the battery position through a numbing storm of sound, blinding flashes, boiling dust, and the constant rattle and ping of flying stones and metal splinters.

On the east bank of the river Mouty's battalion commander, Major Knecht, was visiting his 4th Battery when the air split above them. He and Lieutenant Brunbrouck looked at one another without needing to speak – this was not ranging fire, but the real barrage. Knecht hurtled his jeep back over the bridge to his battalion HQ, where Captain Combes told him that Béatrice was already under heavy fire but their own batteries had not been hit yet. Watching the clouds of smoke and dust rising over Claudine, Sub-lieutenant Pencréac'h, a commissioned veteran of the Italian campaign, remarked that it reminded him of the Garigliano in 1944 – but on that occasion the barrage had been outgoing.

Shells were falling all over the central area, around the headquarters, on the artillery positions, on the airfield, on Béatrice, Gabrielle and Dominique, and on Isabelle far to the south. The runway was erupting in volcanoes of earth and shredded steel plates; two Bearcats were destroyed in their pens, the makeshift control tower was badly damaged and the VHF radio beacon was destroyed.[10] Up on Dominique 2, the carefully prepared fire-support mission of Erwan Bergot's Legion mortars was destroyed in half a minute; the mortar pits, crew and ammunition shelters disappeared under a deluge of shellfire – Corporal Drescher and his four légionnaires, torn to pieces by a direct hit in their weapon pit, may have been the first men killed by the bombardment.[11]

The most clichéd but accurate metaphor for the sound of incoming shells in flight is that of an old-fashioned steam express train rushing past a few feet away. Depending on their distance, speed and angle, shells tunnelling through the air make slightly different noises, so a heavy barrage weaves itself into a bewildering cacophony of sounds; but the rushing always ends the same way, with a thunderclap detonation – *sscchhiiiii... boom!* Hollywood's microphones fail to convey either the sharpness or the loudness of battlefield explosions; and the visual effects normally used to simulate shellfire – with plastic bags of petrol and aluminium silicate – are equally misleading. In reality the eye usually registers a shellburst as an instantaneous orange-yellow flash inside a dark, leaping fountain of mixed smoke and pulverized earth, sometimes studded and fringed with large pieces of slower-moving debris. The bigger, heavier chunks of earth and stones thrown up by the explosion fall near by first; the smaller debris, blown much higher, comes pattering and clinking down for a considerable time afterwards and over a wider area.

The instantaneous pressure wave from the explosion moves outwards at supersonic speed – this is the expanding ring effect seen fleetingly in, for example, aerial footage showing the explosion of 'sticks' of bombs. It is followed after a slight but appreciable interval by a blast wind – the bulk flow of hot gases, fragments and ground debris away from the explosion. People in the target area experience the pressure wave as a sharp squeezing sensation in the chest, and its shock is also felt through the ground underfoot; this shuddering of the earth is powerful enough to make those sheltering in trenches fear (justifiably) that they are about to be buried alive, and those who are lying flat feel themselves being shrugged violently into the air. These sensations are accompanied by stupefying noise, and under heavy and persistent fire all the physical senses are overwhelmed. Completely impotent to affect their chances of survival, soldiers find sustained shelling and mortaring the worst ordeal of battle; those experiencing it often become temporarily unhinged, losing all muscular control (including of the bladder and sphincter) and the capacity for any rational thought beyond 'Oh please God no...' These effects are particularly marked among men exposed to shellfire for the first time – as were the great majority at Dien Bien Phu. Although these physical and mental reactions are quite involuntary, the fear is rational: in modern warfare it is shells and mortar bombs that cause the great majority of casualties.

In that minority of cases when men suffer a virtually direct hit from artillery the result is complete destruction of the body: 'The shell hit him. I'm telling you, it blew him to tiny little bits... a booted foot, a section of the human cranium, a bunch of fingers, a bit of clothing... it was simply a matter of *little, tiny bits.*'[12] To be a witness to this utter physical annihilation – perhaps of a friend – is particularly shocking; it abruptly tears away a number of necessary self-protective illusions all at once. When a body has been blown up, the spinal column – surprisingly resilient – often survives; after a shell has fallen among a group of men, counting the remaining spines is sometimes the simplest way to determine the number of dead.

Most injuries, however, occur further out from the site of the explosion.

Blast injuries to the human body are categorized as primary, secondary and tertiary. The first is the direct effect of the pressure wave; the second, the effect of projectiles and debris carried by the blast wind; the third, the result of the body being thrown through the air and smashing into the ground or other obstacles.

The most obvious sign of primary injury is rupture of the eardrums, which may occur when air pressure rises to anything between 5 and 15 pounds per square inch; war memoirs offer many instances of men killed by blast who appear peacefully asleep apart from tell-tale bleeding from the ears. The lethal internal damage caused by pressures of 50psi and upwards do not present dramatic outward signs (though shellfire casualties typically suffer multiple injuries). It is the gas-containing organs which sustain immediate and often fatal damage from the pressure wave: the lungs and occasionally the colon suffer catastrophic injury from the instantaneous compression effect of the blast. Large blood-filled cavities are formed in the spongy alveoli of the lung, and fatal air embolisms are released into the arterial system; less often, the bowels may rupture, as – in a few cases – may the spleen and liver.[13]

Secondary injuries will be more obviously dramatic. When a shell bursts the steel case breaks up into fragments of all shapes and sizes, from tiny beads to twisted chunks weighing several pounds. These – together with stones, pieces of weapons and equipment, and even large bone fragments from casualties nearer the blast – whirl outwards from the centre at different speeds. The effects of being struck by shell fragments (usually, though incorrectly called 'shrapnel') vary as widely as the size and speed of the metal shards. Sometimes a man is unaware that he has been pierced by a small splinter until somebody else points out the bloodstained hole in his clothing. Larger fragments, cartwheeling unevenly through the air edged with jagged blades and hooks, can dismember and disembowel.[14]

In many cases the evidence confronting an eyewitness is all too vivid. In others the immediate reaction is one of simple puzzlement: blast and steel can play such extreme games with the human form that the observer does not understand what he is looking at. When some random physical reference point suddenly jerks the whole image into a comprehensible pattern, the shock of recognition may be appalling. The results of massive destruction – the ruined hulk of a torso, the crimson rack of ribs, the glistening entrails; limbs ripped away and scattered, a severed head – have a charnelhouse squalor that denies all human dignity. On chilly evenings at Dien Bien Phu the warm, gaping body cavities steamed visibly, and the opened-up bowels gave off a stink of faeces.

IN THE CENTRE OF THE CAMP, Lieutenant Colonel Langlais was taking an open-air shower under a pierced fuel drum when the first shells burst close by. The paratrooper had not been exposed to fire like this since the Black Forest in 1945, and it galvanized him into immediate action. He dashed, naked, to his GAP 2 headquarters and tried to telephone his battalion commanders, Major Guiraud and Captain Tourret; but the lines had been cut.[15] The storm of steel and explosive was searching out the headquarters bunkers as priority targets. The accuracy of General Vu Hien's gunners was hardly surprising: for two months and more the patient scouts in the fringes of the forest had been watching the camp grow like a giant sand-table model spread out below them, and courageous teams had been slipping down under cover of darkness to reconnoitre the most valuable targets from closer range. At least 300 of the 1,400-odd radio sets in the camp needed external aerials, and these 'aiming stakes' clustered thickly and obviously above the main command posts.[16]

In the various HQ bunkers the staff were bewildered by the weight and accuracy of an enemy artillery in which they had only partly believed. Even in these, the strongest positions in the camp, the earth juddered and shook all round them as if the bunkers were suspended in jelly rather than dug into solid ground; maps fluttered on the walls, dust cascaded down from the ceilings, and light bulbs swung wildly. In his GM 9 headquarters Lieutenant Colonel Gaucher and his chief-of-staff Major Vadot craned over the radio operators' shoulders, trying to form a picture of what was happening to the battalions on Béatrice and Gabrielle. During the afternoon Gaucher had been writing to his wife: 'We are on the alert, and we are surrounded so tightly by the Viets that it seems they do wish to attack us. Yesterday and today we had serious scraps and alas, I have [lost? word missing] my sixth officer from a single battalion. It's tough. The terrain is being showered with shells... Aircraft are burning. Still, the long wait is over, and we hope that if all goes well...' – the letter breaks off in the middle of this sentence.[17]

In the nearby airborne brigade HQ, Langlais – call-sign 'Gars Pierre' ('Boy Peter') – managed to make radio contact with his unit commanders; Guiraud ('Maurice') and Tourret ('Pierrot') reported that their paratroopers were not yet under heavy fire. In the hospital a little way north of Langlais' dug-out, Dr Grauwin timed the shells falling at a rate of 60 each minute. At about 5.30pm the GAP 2 command post received a direct hit which buried Langlais and seven other men under earth, broken timbers, torn sandbags and rattan matting, but none was seriously injured. Immediately afterwards a second shell – perhaps from the same gun, dedicated to the destruction of this one target – came straight through the wrecked roof; it failed to explode.[18]

As on every evening, when the barrage started the gunner Lieutenant Verzat had been up in the observation post on the roof of the main HQ with some Morane pilots. He ran down to his post in the PC Feux; others, more reluctant or fascinated, became victims of their own curiosity. Down in the fire-control HQ Claude Verzat became aware that a noticeable minority of the enemy shells were not detonating – he half felt, half heard them thump into the ground near by, but there was no immediate explosion.[19]

Up on the slope of Dominique 2, shrouded in red dust and dark smoke under a continuing storm of shells, the deafened survivors of Bergot's 120mm mortar platoon were trying to come to the aid of their fellow légionnaires on Béatrice. After a few salvoes the hilltop was rocked by an unimaginable explosion which tore a huge crater: a direct hit on a dump of 5,000 mortar bombs. Within five minutes of opening fire four of the six mortars were out of action, and all communications were lost. The platoon continued to fire on their last known targets (a PIM volunteer helped crew one of the remaining tubes); their ordeal would continue for four hours, and cost 12 dead, three badly wounded and many more minor injuries out of a strength of 36 men.[20]

SHELLS FELL STEADILY ON THE artillery positions, both in Claudine and down at Isabelle, sending deadly fragments lashing across the open pits. Despite heavy casualties the gunners forsook their shelters, and the pre-registered shoots began; the young battery officers clung to routine to calm themselves and their men under the disorienting shock of their first bombardment. The fire orders passed down the line from the PC Feux to the battalion HQs, to the battery commanders, to the two-gun section commanders, and finally to the NCO gun captains. Major Alliou of III/10 RAC was responsible for supporting Béatrice, and to a gunner officer the infantry who counted upon his protection had absolute priority. In his shuddering command post Alliou, Lieutenants Bensa and Lépinay shouted down their radio and telephone handsets, trying to keep contact with the battery commanders and with the FOOs on Béatrice.[21]

Counter-battery fire on the Viet Minh artillery was entrusted to Captain Déal's four 155s of 11th Battery, IV/4 RAC. Under cover of night on 12 March three of these had been towed forward to pits east of the river in location Eliane 10, less open to enemy observation; but the morning of the 13th had dawned too soon for the fourth piece to join them in this safer position, and Sergeant Chief Pierrel's howitzer was still in the old battery location at Claudine. When the 155s got into action Pierrel received his fire orders from Lieutenant Constantin in the new position; the latter had to juggle firing solutions for both the old and new positions, 750yds apart. The late move to Eliane 10 had not been spotted by the Viet Minh, and consequently Robert Pierrel's position received all the enemy fire intended for the whole battery. The Moroccan 155 gunners were tireless that night, firing not only on the targets tentatively identified in the previous weeks but on new co-ordinates passed to the fire-control HQ by observers watching for gun flashes on the hills to the east; but the enemy's fire never faltered significantly.

Colonel Piroth had told his young officers: 'Don't worry, *mes petits*, the Viet will have to fire ranging shots. The moment that happens, the Moranes will all take off, and five minutes later there will be no more Viet artillery.' But there had been no need for ranging shots that evening; the Viet Minh had been firing them for six weeks past, and by careful reconnaissance noting the exact range and angle of the one or two specific targets assigned to each one of their guns for direct fire. As darkness fell on 13 March most of the Moranes were smouldering matchwood on the airfield; and the counter-battery fire was unable to silence Viet Minh guns dug into deep, narrow hillside casemates under several yards of solid overhead cover.[22]

JUST UNDER A MILE FROM the most northerly positions of Dominique, battalion location Béatrice was a feature on the north side of RP41 where the road left the north-east corner of the valley and headed east for Tuan Giao. It rose about 60ft above the dirt road, its three distinct hillocks separated by roughly T-shaped gulleys (*see Map 15*). The slopes had been cleared of most undergrowth, though patches remained, particularly in the gulleys. The feature was surrounded by thick scrub and forest to the west, north and east, and was overlooked by a hill of similar height immediately to the north; facing it on the southern side of the road rose another ridge, also heavily wooded.

Four separate strongpoints were held by the companies of III/13 DBLE. Béatrice 1, the long, narrow northern hilltop was held by 9th Company commanded by Lieutenant Carrière. The south-east feature nearest to the road, Béatrice 3, was occupied by 11th Company, newly taken over by Lieutenant Turpin. This was separated by the main north–south gulley – part-way up which a jeep track had been driven – from the larger western hilltop. The northern height of the latter, Béatrice 4, accommodated 12th Company (Captain Lemoine), the small battalion HQ Company (Command and Support, CCS – Lieutenant Madelain), and the battalion command post (CP – Major Pégot). Slightly south and east on the same hill was a lower feature, Béatrice 2, held by 10th Company (Captain Nicolas).[23]

The III/13 was regarded as a particularly solid unit, and had given proof of it only weeks before arriving at Dien Bien Phu: during Operation 'Mouette' one of its companies had held out all night against the assaults of a Viet Minh battalion. Its CO, Major Paul Pégot, could be trusted to fight stubbornly – indeed, to *'faire Camerone'* if need be; some believed that he had asked for this command in order to get himself killed honourably. (In early 1953 his wife, sailing out to join him at the end of his previous tour, had mysteriously disappeared overboard by night.) But III/13 DBLE was numerically weak: it had a ration strength of 517, but according to Major Vadot, its former CO, on 13 March there were fewer than 450 men on Béatrice. An officer and 20 men were detached as Colonel de Castries' HQ guard; another officer and a large platoon of candidate NCOs were also in the main camp; and about ten sick and wounded were in Dr Grauwin's hospital – a total of at least 80 absentees. Significantly, the battalion was so short of officers that each company had only one.[24]

The People's Army, too, considered Béatrice to be an extremely strong position, and had taken considerable pains to prepare for its capture. A member of Division 312 wrote that 'our officers had made reconnaissance patrols each night, noting each belt of wire, each fold of ground, trying to find weak points. Some of the information that was gathered seemed too imprecise, and the plans had to be reworked.' In the main position either Béatrice or Gabrielle were the obvious first choices for the assault phase: they were the furthest from French support, the nearest to the Viet Minh's direction of approach, and they barred the way to any concentration of People's Army artillery and AA guns closer to the airfield. Capturing Béatrice would knock a whole corner out of the camp's integrated defensive plan, exposing the flanks of both Gabrielle and Dominique.

In the days beforehand the People's Army had steadily tightened their encirclement of the hill, and on the night of 11/12 March infantry had occupied features to its north and south-east. The main earthworks were east–west parallel trenches along the ridges, from which approach trenches branched off towards Béatrice 1 and 3, the latter cutting the dirt surface of RP41. The purpose of digging and occupying these parallels, perhaps 200yds from the defensive barbed wire, was to emplace mortars and RCLs, and to provide jumping-off points for the assault infantry. From the approach trenches, which had been pushed forward as far as possible, final assault trenches would be dug during the preparatory artillery barrage until they reached the barbed wire itself.

People's Army tactics called for attacks concentrated on a narrow front – perhaps only 100yds. The whole defensive position would be treated to prolonged bombardment; then selected short sectors of the perimeter would be worked over by artillery, mortars and RCLs, before columns of infantry – ten or 20 times as strong as the defenders of that sector – surged forward from the ends of the newly dug assault trenches. Once an initial breach had been made, following waves of infantry would enlarge it and spread out sideways, clearing the defenders' trenches progressively. At Béatrice the plan seems to have been to hit the three hilltops with separate but converging attacks by two of the three regiments of Division 312 – seasoned units which had fought Legion paratroopers and infantry at Na San. Regiment 141 would attack Béatrice 1 from the north-east, then move through to hit Béatrice 2 and 4; meanwhile Regiment 209 would attack

Béatrice 3 from the south. If they followed normal practice and each committed two of its three battalions to the attack, the People's Army would enjoy a paper superiority of four to one; but in fact, if they were at full strength then each of those battalions was nearly twice the size of III/13 DBLE. The assault would be prepared and supported by two batteries of 105mm guns, backed by 75s and 120mm mortars; the barrage was scheduled for 5.10pm, and the assault for 6.30pm – about 15 minutes after sunset. Diversionary attacks would be made on Gabrielle and Dominique, and there may have been an intention for commandos to infiltrate the main camp and try to disrupt the French artillery.

At about 3pm on 13 March, Regiments 141 and 209 – inspired by an order of the day from President Ho Chi Minh – left their forming-up areas in thick forest and moved forward to their jumping-off points. By this time three trenches had already been pushed to within about 50yds of the wire, hidden by scrub; and one of the RCL positions was within 100yds of Béatrice 1.[25]

THE FIRST SHELLS OF THE bombardment fell on Béatrice shortly before 5.20pm, at the same time as that on the rest of the camp, and as shockingly violent. It continued uninterrupted for nearly two hours; the enemy sappers dug their assault trenches forward under cover of its impact and of the thick cloud of smoke and dust which soon hung over the hilltops, flickering with explosions. All over the strongpoints the heavy shells ploughed up the earth, collapsed dug-outs, filled trenches, wrecked weapons, killed and maimed many of the defenders, deafening and stupefying the rest. From the Viet Minh assembly trenches mortars and RCLs added their more selective fire, working their way steadily around the visible command posts, weapon blockhouses and shelters. Shellfire tore up the field telephone cables, leaving the separated companies cut off from information, warnings and orders. Behind the murk of battle the sinking sun glowed dimly, and the air was filled with a choking mixture of dust and acrid cordite fumes.

By about 6.15pm Regiment 141 had pushed two trenches forward to the edge of the wire on Béatrice 1, and in the first moments of dusk sappers crawled forward to breach it with 'bangalore torpedoes' – long bamboo tubes filled with explosive which could cut a path through the entanglements. Under fire from Carrière's 9th Company, it took them 15 minutes to breach the belt; opening one path needed 18 separate charges, and the sacrifice of an unknown number of lives.[26] On Béatrice 3, Lieutenant Turpin's 11th Company were also braving the murderous hail of steel to man their parapets, firing flares and raking the dimly seen approach of Regiment 209.

Through his liaison officer Captain Riès, Major Pégot was calling for artillery support, and was getting some on the pre-registered approaches; but down in the valley the bombardment was causing chaos and communications were poor. It was commonplace that due to the 'closing in' of the ionosphere radio reception faded badly for an hour before sunset and after sunrise, and the SCR609 sets of the artillery FOOs at Dien Bien Phu were particularly vulnerable to this. Adjusting the fire from general areas on to the specific assault lanes that were now revealing themselves was difficult, and the dispersion of the shells prevented them causing enough casualties to stop the People's Army coming 'over the top'. Béatrice was also supposed to enjoy the support of Lieutenant Clerget's 120mm mortar platoon on neighbouring Gabrielle, but his position too was being smothered by the enemy barrage.

Statements of survivors vary widely over the timing of specific events during the night of 13/14 March. Everyone involved, on the hill or in the valley, was under severe stress, and in these conditions the perception of the passage of time is notoriously unreliable; the message logs in the command posts did not survive to confirm later recollections, even if they were ever completed. The following sequence can only be approximate; it is drawn principally from the account of Lieutenant Turpin.[27]

Everyone agrees that it was about 6.30pm – just as the infantry assault hit the perimeter of Béatrice 1 – when III/13's battalion command post was destroyed by a series of direct hits. Major Pégot, his adjutant Captain Pardi and Lieutenant Pungier were killed outright and the FOO Captain Riès wounded and knocked unconscious; the command radio sets were destroyed. The battalion was headless and cut off from its artillery. At about the same time Lieutenant Turpin, whose company on Béatrice 3 had been taking casualties from shellfire, was wounded in the head and neck and passed out.

In the GM 9 headquarters Lieutenant Colonel Gaucher's staff lost contact with Béatrice for some minutes, until a wavering German voice came through the static, and the unknown légionnaire on an unidentified radio set reported '*C'est tout le monde mort – Alles tot!*' Contact was then lost once more. Normal procedure in such cases was to try to contact individual company commanders; after some time Gaucher seems to have reached Captain Nicolas of 10th Company on Béatrice 2, who made his way up to the wrecked CP and discovered the bodies of the staff about half an hour after Pégot's death. On the north-eastern and south-eastern strongpoints both 9th and 11th Companies were now under heavy attack. Lieutenant Carrière of the 9th was killed when a shell smashed his CP; Captain Nicolas had left an NCO in charge of the 10th as he made for the battalion CP, Sergeant Chief Fels had taken over the 11th from the unconscious Turpin, and Captain Lemoine of the 12th on Béatrice 4 was also temporarily out of action – the only company now commanded by an officer was Lieutenant Madelain's CCS.

Simultaneously, the first enemy infiltrations of their wire heralded perhaps five hours of diversionary attacks on V/7 RTA at Gabrielle; these were serious enough to capture some positions temporarily and cause perhaps 20 casualties, and to stop the Algerians from providing supporting fire for Béatrice. At about 7pm the bombardment of Béatrice 3 slackened and infantry assaults began; Turpin came to, got his wounds roughly bandaged, and resumed leadership of 11th Company's resistance just as the Viet Minh sappers were breaching his wire. Cut off except for intermittent radio contact with 9th Company (now being led by Sergeant Chief Bleyer and Sergeant Kubiak), Turpin was wounded a second time about fifteen minutes later. At some point after 7pm Captain Riès recovered consciousness on Béatrice 4, and tried to re-establish contact with the artillery; French shells were falling intermittently around the enemy assault columns, particularly on Regiment 209 advancing from the south, but these shoots were uncorrected. Captain Riès' SCR609 radio was still working, so he got help to lug it over the shell-torn hilltop to another dugout and installed it next to an SCR300 tuned to the infantry net. In this way he could pick up at least a fragmentary commentary by the companies on the progress of the fighting, and try to pass up-to-date fire orders down to Major Alliou's III/10 RAC headquarters at Claudine.

Captain Riès' requests remained calm – 'Resume Zulu Kilo 411, one hundred north... Down fifty... Resume blocking fires...' – but increased both in frequency and in their proximity to the French positions on Béatrice. In the artillery battalion HQ Lieutenants Bensa and Lépinay and Warrant Officer Guiglia divided the tasks between the 105s and 120mm mortars, but soon II/4 RAC also had to join the orchestra. Viet Minh shells fell murderously around the battery positions, and the CP of Lieutenant Lyot's 5th Battery was knocked out. At 6th Battery, Lieutenant Jean-Marie Moreau saw a fireball rise from his No. 3 pit, from which a blood-boltered African NCO staggered, roaring with pain: two shells had fallen right on the 105, destroying it, decapitating Sergeant Chief Scarpellini, killing one other man and wounding the rest of the crew. The gun crews – and the telephone linemen, who had to grope their way through the darkness and dust to find and splice the cuts in the lines – were virtually the only men in the main camp who were still out in the open air, and they paid for it with heavy casualties. Two other howitzers were knocked out by damage to their oil-filled recoil cylinders which could not be repaired until the morning.[28]

The transmissions from Captain Riès requested shoots first on the III/13's barbed wire, and then actually inside the position. Accuracy was now even more critical, and Major Alliou needed access to the infantry net too; his bunker was only yards from that of Lieutenant Colonel Gaucher's GM 9, but nobody had bothered to lay a telephone line between them. At shortly after 7.30pm he sent Lieutenant Lépinay running across through a communication trench; but when the subaltern stumbled into the GM 9 command post he found a scene of confusion and horror.

LIEUTENANT COLONEL GAUCHER could not get a grip on the battle via his tenuous radio links with company commanders: a replacement for Pégot had to be appointed quickly, either one of the surviving officers of III/13 or one of Gaucher's staff – and if the latter, then a way had to be found to get him up to Béatrice with functioning radios. Gaucher called into his office his chief-of-staff Major Vadot, Major Martinelli, and two aides, Lieutenants Bailly and Bretteville. As they crowded into the small cubicle, Vadot sat on Gaucher's bunk in the corner. At some time after 7.30pm a shell hit and penetrated the bunker's ventilation shaft, struck a roof pillar and exploded. Vadot was deafened and cut about but not seriously wounded; Martinelli was, and the two subalterns were killed, one of them decapitated. Jules Gaucher was still alive, but with both his arms torn off, his legs mangled, and his chest opened. When Father Trinquand reached him he was conscious, and asked the chaplain to wipe his face and give him a drink. An ambulance jeep took him through the continuing shellfire to the hospital, but he died almost at once. At 7.50pm Lieutenant Colonel Langlais received a telephone call from Castries telling him of Gaucher's death and ordering him to take over command of the central sector at once.[29] Langlais passed command of his own brigade to his second-in-command, Major Hubert de Seguin-Pazzis, and clambered into the roaring darkness outside. As the paratroop officer ran the few yards from his own wrecked bunker to the shattered GM 9 headquarters, a hot shock wave slapped his face and he saw a huge red and yellow fireball billowing up into the night sky – the enemy had scored a direct hit on the aviation fuel and napalm dump.

With Gaucher and three of his immediate staff gone, such plans as he had for supporting Béatrice were not put into action – for instance, planned heavy mortar shoots which awaited Gaucher's executive order were seriously delayed.[30] The command staff of GONO were disorganized by a bombardment beyond their nightmares; Colonel de Castries recorded 300 shells falling in the immediate vicinity of his HQ alone. GONO's internal communications were in tatters and their contingency plans were overtaken by events, minute by shocking minute; now they were demoralized – semi-paralysed – by the loss of an officer who had seemed a rock of invincibility. Unlike the gunners, the unfortunate staff officers had nothing to do except sit in their shell-rocked dug-outs and listen over the radios to the death rattles of a battalion of the Legion.

THE BATTLE FOR BÉATRICE 3 was reaching its climax. The enemy infantry were lit up by a stream of parachute flares dropped by a circling 'Luciole' C-47 which had arrived from the Delta, and 11th Company's remaining machine gunners under Sergeant Bartoli, and Lieutenant Madelain's 81mm battalion mortars, exacted a terrible price from the assault columns, particularly when the enemy exposed themselves to attack a false blockhouse erected as bait at the south-east tip of the company defences. Nevertheless, Sergeant Chief Schweiger's 1st and Sergeant Aubertin's 3rd Platoons were almost wiped out; the switches for the command-detonated mines and napalm tanks were buried in the wrecked company CP; and by perhaps 8.30pm Turpin had only about 25 men of Sergeant Chief Keil's 2nd and Sergeant Rosier's 4th Platoons still able to fight.

His deputy Sergeant Chief Fels reported hearing a shouted order from Béatrice 2 that 11th Company should fall back there to join 10th Company; this would mean crossing the main gulley – about 100yds wide, under heavy fire, and intermittently illuminated by the flares of the 'Luciole' Dakota. Somehow they managed it, carrying as many of their wounded as they could, but the effort of struggling across nearly reduced the wounded Lieutenant Turpin to helplessness by the time he reached the south-west hillock. It was only then that he found out that the battalion staff were dead and about two-thirds of the unit were casualties; his handful of survivors joined the HQ, 10th and 12th Companies in the trenches of Béatrice 2 and 4. Over on Béatrice 1 the remnant of 9th Company were still firing.

Some time between 9pm and 10pm the enemy assaults slackened in the face of this bitter resistance and of renewed salvoes of French mortar and artillery fire. The opportunity was seized to take more ammunition forward and regroup the remaining defenders, but soon afterwards Sergeant Kubiak radioed from the northern hillock that his positions had been penetrated, and he could see the Viet Minh swarming over abandoned Béatrice 3.[31] Colonel Piroth released the four 155mm howitzers from counter-battery work to fire in support of Béatrice, but without significant results. There are widely conflicting timings for the final fall of Béatrice 1 after a period of confused fighting by separated groups of légionnaires. Sergeant Kubiak led a party of survivors off the position into heavy cover, where they managed to evade the enemy in the darkness, finally making their way down to Dominique some time after midnight.[32] Meanwhile, Herbert Bleyer – a veteran of Germany's wartime '*Grossdeutschland*' Division – led other members of 9th Company in a break out through the gulleys to join the defenders of Béatrice 2 and 4.

Assaults on this final position, apparently by both Regiments 141 and 209 from the directions of Béatrice 1 and 3, resumed some time around 11pm. At that time Major Vadot at GM 9 headquarters made brief radio contact with the CCS's Lieutenant Madelain and 12th Company's Captain

Lemoine on Béatrice 4; the former reported that he had about 30 men left, the latter that there was fighting all around his command post. Lemoine was killed shortly afterwards; for a while one of his well-sited machine guns caused huge casualties among the attackers until they dragged up an RCL and destroyed the blockhouse at point-blank range. Waves of infantry grenaded and shot their way forwards and sideways through the trenches, blasting the remaining shelters and barricades with bazookas. The defence was dislocated by multiple breakthroughs; of the officers only Captain Nicolas and Lieutenant Madelain seem to have been still in condition to exercise command, but small groups of légionnaires, totalling perhaps 100, continued to sell their lives dearly in isolated actions.

After taking great losses among their junior leaders and weapons crews the attackers, too, were suffering from poor co-ordination; it became an NCOs' battle on both sides, with the outcome of a score of little local fights depending upon the initiative and courage of individuals. A People's Army veteran described how his company exploited forward with neither heavy weapon support nor radio contact from regiment or battalion; the company's two machine guns were destroyed, and the *bo doi* used every fold in the ground for cover before they rushed a succession of trench corners with grenades and sub-machine guns, marking cleared block-houses with flags as they worked their way deeper into the position.[33]

Under these circumstances it is impossible to establish when 'organized' resistance ceased. Lieutenant Bergot states that although 10th Company's radio operator, Légionnaire Bonte, could not receive from GM 9 HQ, his fragmentary transmissions were sometimes picked up; and that one of these, misheard and logged shortly after 1.15am, misled Castries into believing that the fighting was over, whereas some squads continued to resist for perhaps another hour and a half. The artillery historian General de Brancion does not specify the exact time when Captain Riès radioed III/10 RAC with the final message that every artilleryman hopes he will never hear: 'It's all over – the Viets are here. Fire upon my position. Out.'

Memoirs agree that after the fall of the position all shelling ceased, and a great silence fell over the valley. Shocked and bemused, men came out of their shelters and gazed north at the eerie glow of flares amid the cloud of smoke and dust which hung over Béatrice. They had been preparing for months; they had not been caught by surprise; yet 'Le Vieux' Gaucher was dead, a crack battalion of the Legion had been steamrollered flat, and the artillery, the tanks, the paratroop reserve, and the Air Force had been unable to do a thing about it. At 2.25am on 14 March, Colonel de Castries reported via the secure teletype link to General Cogny's HQ in Hanoi that Lieutenant Colonel Gaucher was dead; that nothing had been heard officially from III/13 DBLE since 12.15am, but that traffic overheard since then on the battalion's internal net suggested that Béatrice must be assumed lost.

DOWN IN THE CENTRAL FIRE-CONTROL HQ, Lieutenant Verzat shut off his mind from the chaos and demoralization all around him and doggedly took down dozens of reports of muzzle flashes to the east from the observers on the hilltop Dominiques and Elianes. By about midnight he reported that he at last had enough information for the artillery to lay on some serious counter-battery fire, and the 155s were switched back from direct support to the control of the PC Feux. Captain Déal made a dangerous journey through the bombardment to collect detailed target co-ordinates for his battery; but it was first light before he got them, and by then it was too late.

From the Air Force control post, Major Guérin asked the PC Feux for targets for an incoming flight of Privateer heavy bombers; Verzat gave him the new co-ordinates of batteries revealed during the night, and in the first grey light he went up into the rooftop OP to watch the bombs fall. Shortly afterwards the same batteries opened fire again briefly, as if in defiance.

ON 14 MARCH THE SUN ROSE at 6.18am, but did not pierce a heavy grey mist which soon turned to drizzle. In the central camp men emerged from their shelters into the ghostly quiet, and stood about listlessly, gazing at the aftermath of the bombardment. Everywhere the earth was pocked with craters, pale in the middle and darkly crusted round the rim; here and there a grey unexploded shell stuck out of the earth. Torn-open shelters exposed the almost shameful remains of their flimsy roofs. Men tried to get fires going to heat coffee as they made a cheerless breakfast of cold combat rations. A mass of debris was scattered all over the churned earth like some squalid municipal rubbish dump – smashed equipment of every kind, burnt-out vehicles, broken timber, ripped matting and burst sand-bags, discarded shell cases, boxes, tin cans, occasional bloody rags, the mysterious bits of paper which seem to proliferate on every battlefield, all punctuated by rain puddles and displaced curls of barbed wire. There was a smell of petrol and charring, and sluggish trails of smoke still rose here and there, dwarfed by the black cloud rising from the fuel depot.

Sergeant Prosper Dupuis of 9th Battery, III/10 RAC went to check his two GMC trucks in their shelters – open trenches with inclined access ramps; he knew that they would soon be needed to fetch ammunition after the heavy consumption of the night, and to his surprised relief the 'Jimmies' were intact. While Dupuis was checking them Colonel Piroth startled him by appearing on the trench lip, and asked about casualties in his battery. The one-armed commander then wandered off through the artillery lines to 6th Battery, II/4 RAC, where he gazed silently at the poncho-covered corpses of Scarpellini's crew before visiting the battalion command post. As always, he was fatherly and encouraging, but he seemed to be affected by the demoralized mood of his gunners rather than lifting it.

A group of légionnaires dug out the remains of the GM 9 command post, wrapping bodies in ponchos and carrying them up to the morgue behind the hospital. The morgue was an open square dug-out filled with plank coffins; in the early morning of the 14th it was full, and between the hole and the nearby barbed wire fence about 100 corpses lay jumbled together in the rain, on stretchers or on the bare ground. The surgeons, Drs Grauwin and Gindrey, had been operating non-stop all night. From the start of the bombardment the field telephone had never stopped jangling, calling for ambulances which were soon overwhelmed. Within hours every corner of the hospital had been crammed with wounded, many of them waiting on stretchers for urgent attention to major trauma amid the stench of blood, vomit, and voided bladders and bowels. Around 150 casualties had been admitted during the night, and at one stage Grauwin had protested that the battalion aid posts were sending him all their wounded rather than attempting to treat them; but he had soon learned that they, too, were overflowing – some ambulance drivers had even risked the long journey all the way up from Isabelle. That night the two surgical teams had operated on ten 'abdominals', ten chest wounds, two 'cranials', 15 fractured limbs, and 14 amputations; they had urgently requested that Hanoi provide another surgical team, as well as supplies of plasma and antibiotics.[34]

SOON AFTER 6.30AM ON THE 14th, look-outs at Dominique saw a figure reeling towards them through the mist, trailing bloody bandages; he proved to be Lieutenant Turpin, briefly commander of 11th Company, III/13 DBLE. He had staggered out of the aid post on Béatrice 4 in the early hours of the morning to find the strongpoint overrun and the last individual combats taking place all around him. He tried to make his way off the hill in the darkness and confusion; the enemy assault units were pulled back soon after their victory, but Turpin was eventually captured by one of the follow-up search teams which were combing the strongpoint for anything useful. Taken before a commissar – to whom he did not reveal his rank – Turpin was questioned briefly before being told that the People's Army were going to blow up the position. He was given two safe conduct passes, and a written message to deliver to Colonel de Castries, before being guided off the hill and set on his way down RP41 towards Dominique.[35]

When the news reached GONO headquarters, Captain Noël of the Second Bureau drove up to fetch Turpin in a jeep and took him for medical treatment. The letter for Castries proved to be from the general commanding Division 312, proposing a truce between 8.30am and noon so that the French could collect some of their wounded from Béatrice. Colonel de Castries signalled Hanoi; he spoke to General Cogny shortly before 7am, and in Navarre's absence from Saigon the request was passed to his chief-of-staff General Gambiez, who agreed to it. This temporary ceasefire would become a matter of some controversy. The events are beyond dispute, and it seems unusual that a divisional general in such a highly centralized chain of command would make the offer without the highest authority; yet the Viet Minh would later deny that the episode took place, asking dismissively what motive they could possibly have had.

One possibility suggested by past Viet Minh tactics is that it distracted the French from an immediate attempt to recapture Béatrice. Clearly, General Giap had never intended to hold the captured ground; the assault troops had been pulled off the hill, and Lieutenant Turpin reported more than one *bo doi* as saying that it was to be blown up or bombarded. Once the French had been deprived of it, and artillery observers had been installed on this valuable vantage point, why should the People's Army wish to swap places with the French, getting tied down on a position whose defences had been wrecked and that would be vulnerable to artillery and air attack? All the same, any attempted French reoccupation would have to be resisted. An immediate defensive fight for this ground would prevent Giap from moving some of his artillery to the west, and would use up valuable ammunition – both being obstacles to his planned attack on Gabrielle the next night.[36]

Many of the camp's garrison had never doubted that a counter-attack would be launched; this was, after all, the 'standard operating procedure' that had proved successful at Na San. At command level, however, it was far from an automatic choice. An immediate intervention during the night had been impossible: French troops, unlike the Viet Minh, were not trained for night manoeuvres (a crucial failure); and to send the paratroopers and Captain Hervouët's tanks blundering into unknown enemy forces in the dark would have been to risk bloody disaster. When Castries spoke to Cogny shortly before 7am about the truce offer he was evasive about any plans for a counter-attack, and it is easy to imagine the arguments against such an attempt: even if it succeeded, how were the new defenders to repair the ruined positions for defence, and how were they to be sustained in the long term?

Shortly before 9am the senior medical officer, Captain Le Damany, and 13 DBLE's chaplain Father Trinquand led a small party up to Béatrice in three vehicles under the Red Cross flag; the NCOs included Bleyer and Kubiak from 9th Company. In an unnerving silence they approached the hill, to be met by a small reception party; they noticed that III/13th's jeep was still parked incongruously unharmed at the foot of the track. They were allowed to search the strongpoints, where more than a hundred dead légionnaires lay unburied in the muggy heat beneath busy clouds of blue flies; all Viet Minh casualties had been removed. A small number of seriously wounded men were handed over, and the party returned to the hospital.

When the escapees to Dominique were accounted for, the final butcher's bill for III/13 DBLE totalled about 125 killed; 200-plus captured (most of them wounded – and a Viet Minh report on their condition mentioned the disoriented state typical of prolonged bombardment); one officer and either eight or 14 others badly wounded and handed back; and about 111 NCOs and men escaped. Two officers and 192 men answered the roll call, but at least 80 of these had not been on Béatrice during the battle. The survivors fit for service were posted to the GM 9 HQ company in Claudine (CCS, 11th and 12th Companies) or to I/2 REI in Huguette (9th and 10th Companies).[37]

THE DRIZZLE TURNED INTO A persistent rain – unexpected this early in the season.[38] Under the weeping sky men all over the camp were at work on thickening dug-out roofs, deepening existing trenches and digging new communications links, and splicing and reburying telephone cables (these were now strung along new grooves cut into trench walls at hip height, so that linemen could find the breaks easily in the dark by touch without 'going over the top'). Everywhere men foraged for ammunition boxes, timbers, sandbags, anything to build up overhead cover; the iron cases in which the separate charges for the 155mm shells were supplied were particularly prized as the basis for 'bursting layers'. Only the foolish left their positions unguarded against opportunist scavengers; and it was noticed that for the first time almost everyone was wearing his steel helmet. [39]

Although heavy transports were unable to fly in due to the runway damage and the bad weather, Major Devoucoux, the CO of 53 Liaison Flight, landed a Beaver bush aircraft at about 8am with the urgent medical supplies requested by Dr Grauwin. It did not take off empty: among the four seriously wounded men flown out was Lieutenant Turpin, and with them went Paule Bourgeade, whom Castries bundled into the aircraft despite her protests.[40] She had behaved bravely during the bombardment, and her presence in the headquarters had helped some officers keep control of themselves. Soon after midday the end of the truce brought the first shots of an intermittent enemy artillery and mortar fire on the headquarters and gun lines of Claudine, and the airfield dispersal pens, which lasted much of the afternoon.

The previous evening's shelling had wrecked all but one of the Moranes on the airstrip, but some time after noon Lieutenants Péria and Le Coz took off in the last machine to search the hills and valleys north of Gabrielle under the low cloud ceiling. After the weeks of frustration, Péria could hardly believe his eyes when, through a veil of rain, he suddenly saw below him a perfect target – three trucks were towing field guns across a patch of rice paddies. The banks at each end of the fields were being cut to let them pass, and gangs were rebuilding them immediately to hide the route taken. Péria managed to call in a 155mm shoot; within a few minutes all three trucks were burning, the guns seemed damaged – and the black puffs of 37mm cannon fire reminded the pilot that the sky no longer belonged to the French. The 105s had been moving westwards, and risking them in daylight argued that their mission was urgent; clearly, Gabrielle was in imminent danger.[41]

IN THE EARLY AFTERNOON, AS shells continued to fall on the airfield, two Bearcat pilots of GC 1/22 'Saintonge' – Sergeant Chief de Somow and Sergeant Barteau – were ordered by the air controller to take off and napalm troop concentrations in the hills around Gabrielle. They made a hair-raising take-off, timing the fall of shells and then slamming their throttles forward to race down the runway, dodging between the shellholes.

It is questionable how much this – and every other mission by Bearcats and Hellcats over Dien Bien Phu – could actually hope to achieve. On 14 March the low cloud over the valley and dirty weather in the Delta prevented reconnaissance flights apart from the single Morane mission, and the value of the ground OPs for fixing targets is doubtful. Notwithstanding Péria and Le Coz's isolated triumph, the Viet Minh's expertise and discipline in concealed movement and camouflage in wooded terrain was normally decisive. Even if a target was spotted – and it was likely to be fleeting – then dropping bombs accurately from the underwing shackles of a fighter aircraft demanded a lot more specialized training and practice than many of the pilots in Vietnam had yet received. There was no bombsight: the pilots had to learn by trial and error the correct moment to trip the release switch at various heights and angles of approach – usually their technical aids were limited to grease-pencil lines on the cockpit windshields.

A diving attack had the advantage that the whole aircraft was aimed directly at the target and the released bombs would continue in the line of the dive; but this tactic also kept the aircraft steady in the AA gunners' sights for a dangerously long time. Low-level approaches were more demanding of a pilot's accuracy, but made it harder for the gunners to track the aircraft and limited the time that it was visible between the treetops – it was always a trade-off. Another factor in the choice of height and angle, which was always tricky in narrow valleys, was the real danger of damage to aircraft from overflying the explosion of their own bombs, which had a considerable radius of blast and fragments. Napalm – tanks of jellied petrol – was sometimes devastating but was inherently inaccurate. The tanks could flip and tumble in the air, and their trajectory was less predictable than that of bombs. It was also relatively ineffective against targets in woodland, especially if the forest was damp (as it was on 14 March): igniting on contact, the blazing jelly coated the nearest trees but did not spread far, and soon burned out.

When they had used up their ordnance Somow and Barteau were instructed not to try to land back at Dien Bien Phu, but to fly to Xieng Khouang on the Plain of Jars in north-east Laos – a flight of 136 miles for which they had no maps. In the late afternoon heavy clouds built up over the border mountains, they became hopelessly lost, and their fuel situation soon became critical. Eventually their radio appeals were heard at Vientiane – a full 236 miles from Dien Bien Phu – by a renowned Dakota pilot, Captain 'Baron' de Fontanges, who happened to be manning the radio in the little rustic control tower while enjoying an evening beer under a coolie-powered fan. His friend Lieutenant Commander Babot, commanding a flight of Aéronavale Grumman Goose amphibians on the river, took over the job of guiding the Bearcats in. As they landed one engine ran dry and the fighter slammed down on the runway, bursting a tyre; the other Bearcat coughed into silence as it taxied. On 15 March the two young NCOs flew to Xieng Khouang to join their squadron mates transferred from Haiphong under Major Pierrot, and flew missions over Dien Bien Phu for the next eight days.

Three other Bearcats managed to get out of Dien Bien Phu on the 14th – flown by Lieutenant Parisot and Sergeants Bruand and Fouché – but the remainder were all destroyed by shellfire during that day. 'Torri Rouge' had lost its local air support capability.[42]

COLONEL DE CASTRIES FACED the crisis without as much help from his staff as he had a right to expect. His chief-of-staff Lieutenant Colonel Keller suffered a nervous breakdown. Colonel Piroth was sunk in guilty depression, Langlais was venting his tension with savage outbursts of temper and several other officers were suffering from plunging morale. It was predictable that the enemy would resume their assaults that night, and the logical target was Gabrielle. Castries had two immediate priorities: he needed a fresh battalion to replace III/13 DBLE, and replenishment for his artillery ammunition. The single night of 13/14 March had used up nearly a third of the camp's total stocks: 6,300 rounds of 105mm, averaging 260 rounds per gun – and representing 63 Dakota loads.

Despite the bad weather, Hanoi responded to GONO's appeals with parachute drops on the afternoon of the 14th. Locating the valley accurately from above the rain-clouds was demanding, since the VHF beacon at 'Torri Rouge' had been destroyed; the shorter-range MF beacon could only be picked up from a maximum of 20 miles away by aircraft flying at around 9,500ft, and was much more vulnerable to interference from electrical activity in storm clouds.[43]

Lieutenant Colonel Langlais hoped that the replacement battalion would be Bigeard's 6 BPC; what he got was 5 BPVN, whose command had been taken over since their last visit to the valley by Captain André Botella, a 40-year-old 'blackfoot' from Algeria. Botella had been parachuted into Brittany with the SAS in summer 1944 to operate with the *maquis*; badly wounded in the leg and surrounded by Germans in the Forest of Duault, he had made his men abandon him. Miraculously rescued and hidden, he had later requalified as a paratrooper; ten years later, nobody in TAPI had to make allowances for either his age or his old wound.[44]

At 2.45pm on 14 March, Botella's unit jumped from only 600ft, giving them about 30 seconds in the air. All three drop zones were used in order to split the enemy's fire; the HQ and 1st Companies had casualties on the ground before the paratroopers moved off the DZs to reassemble and make their way towards the Elianes. It took them until 6pm to get there, after which they had to dig in under steady rain and shell and mortar fire, mostly on an unprepared slope of Eliane 4. They had few tools apart from their little entrenching spades, and some men were reduced to scraping rifle pits under fire with their helmets. Captain Botella was greeted by Langlais with the blunt admission that the brigade commander would have preferred to see Bigeard's men instead of this Vietnamese unit which he frankly distrusted.

In Hanoi, General Navarre reached Cogny's FTNV headquarters around 6pm on 14 March after flying straight from a brief conference with Colonel de Crèvecoeur at Seno in Laos. When the C-in-C had been briefed on the latest reports he did not question Castries' dispositions; a counter-attack on Béatrice seemed impossible, and intelligence suggested that an urgent threat was hanging over Gabrielle.

THE PREVIOUS DAY, MAJOR DE Mecquenem had estimated Viet Minh strength in the immediate area of Gabrielle to be three battalions with mortar support. His V/7 RTA had suffered sporadic shelling during the 13th; among the casualties had been the MO, Lieutenant Chauveau – whose replacement, Dr Deschelotte, had been wounded himself only hours after arriving. Major de Mecquenem had been due to be relieved at the end of his tour, and his appointed replacement Major Kah had been assisting him for several days.[45] Roland de Mecquenem was of a similar physical type to General Navarre: slim, neat, narrow-featured, with bright blue eyes above high cheekbones, and receding light brown hair. Some officers of North African units made a point of swashbuckling display, wearing virile beards, desert scarves and *kachabias,* and encouraging their men with bursts of Arabic vulgarity; the aristocratic Mecquenem – a former member of General Ely's staff with the Standing Group in Washington DC – was the antithesis of this *type folklorique.* His uniform was issue fatigues and a sand-khaki beret; his manner was quiet, dry and calm, his eyes missed nothing, and he demanded absolute discipline and professional dedication (indeed, his subalterns nicknamed him 'Von Meckenheim').

The V/7 RTA was stronger in all ranks than the unlucky III/13 DBLE whose fate they had watched, appalled, the previous night: on 13 March the battalion had 877 men on strength including 14 officers.[46] Despite the general reduction in length of service found among the Tirailleurs by this date, V/7 RTA reportedly still had a fair number of 12-year men – veterans of Italy, where the battalion had won a citation.[47] Typical of these was Sergeant Chief Abderrahman ben Salem, 3rd Platoon leader in Captain Narbey's 1st Company; he had been recovering from a wound in Hanoi, but sneaked on to a plane to get back to Dien Bien Phu when he heard that battle was imminent.[48] The battalion was newly re-equipped, and had four days' worth of rations and ammunition stockpiled. After long generations of neighbouring service the Tirailleurs regarded the Legion with a respectful rivalry. As the afternoon hours of 14 March ticked away, their officers were confident; they knew that III/13 DBLE had been under-strength, particularly in officers, and believed that they had not had the time and materials to dig in properly – V/7 RTA were not, and they had.

The battalion had taken great pains to fortify Gabrielle, and had won the cash prize offered for the best positions. The hill had been completely forested, and its clearance had provided plenty of timber for making solid shelters; the trunks of ironwood trees *(lim)* were used to roof and revet the main positions, and their thick boughs furnished the other block-houses. Snapshots of the 2nd Company's command post and a 0.50in MG blockhouse show them deeply dug in and roofed with half a dozen layers of logs topped and sandwiched with several courses of sandbags, the entrance and firing slit edged with thick vertical trunk sections.[49]

The hill lay north to south and measured about 600yds long by 250 wide; the crest stood some 180ft above the paddy-fields, rising to 200ft at the northern end. This uniquely unified battalion location allowed a con-tinuous double perimeter trench and wire system giving easy and safe circulation, the two linked by frequent zig-zag communication trenches *(see Map 16)*. In this long rectangle, each company had a quarter sector: at the north-west, 1st Company (Captain Narbey, Sub-lieutenant Roux); north-east, 4th (Lieutenant Moreau, Sub-lieutenant Chassin); south-east, 3rd (Captain Gendre, Lieutenant Monneau); and south-west, 2nd (Lieu-tenant Antoine Botella, Sub-lieutenant Fox).[50] The company COs and their deputies occupied separate command posts in each case, for security. The machine guns and 57mm RCLs, in large, strong blockhouses, had been pushed forward to the military crest and emplaced to sweep the lower slopes of the hill, which were steepest on the north. There was also a 'dorsal' trench along the spine of Gabrielle; and at the junctions of all com-munication trenches *chevaux-de-frise* of timber and thick barbed wire could be dropped, to seal off any lost sections of the outer defensive line at will.[51]

The battalion CP was on the eastern edge of the central ridge; opposite this on the far side of the dorsal trench were the medical aid post and a signals bunker. A little way south of it was the officers' mess dug-out, which Major de Mecquenem had fitted out as a secondary command post with its own radio. The central crest was held by Captain Suzineau's HQ Company (CCS), with its 81mm mortar platoon. The company included a counter-attack reserve of some 40 men, including pioneer flame-thrower teams, led by the intelligence officer Lieutenant Sanselme and a particularly resourceful French NCO, Sergeant Chief Rouzic (who had enlisted when fortune deserted his former employer, a gangster boss named 'Crazy Pete'). Also on the hilltop were 416 CSLT, a company of Thai *supplétifs*. Here too were the pits for Lieutenant Clerget's 120mm mortars of the Legion's 2 CMMLE; this platoon originally had four tubes, but one had been knocked out by shellfire on the night of 13/14 March, and a second mysteriously exploded, killing its five-man crew on the day of the 14th.[52]

During the day Sergeant Lemanouric, the assistant to the FOO Lieutenant Georges Collin, spotted men installing what seemed to be a command post with radio aerials on Hill 674 to the north. He obtained permission to use Clerget's two mortars, which drove the enemy soldiers out of sight but could not seem to bring down the blockhouse. At about 3pm the Second Bureau informed Mecquenem that Gabrielle was certainly about to be attacked. Assisted by Major Kah, the battalion commander made his final dispositions: extra ammunition was issued, the PIMs were sent back to the main camp, a hot meal was to be served at 5pm, and stand-to was to be half an hour later. At the last minute a jeep arrived carrying – for lack of yet another replacement doctor – Sergeant Chief Soldati, a Czech légionnaire who had been a medical student in Austria; he settled into the aid post with obvious competence. Lieutenant Collin had all the approaches exactly zeroed, and from 5pm he began to bring down fire on the probable enemy assembly areas. Infuriatingly, the usual sunset fading of reception over his SCR609 was particularly bad on this stormy afternoon, but he was able to use Lieutenant Clerget's powerful SCR608 set as a relay station. Major Kah had arranged for continuous cover after dark by 'Luciole' aircraft from Hanoi; each parachute flare burned for four minutes, and the Dakota carried 60, giving each aircraft four hours' loiter time over the battlefield.

GENERAL GIAP'S PLAN OF ATTACK for Gabrielle seems to have been a repetition of the formula which had won him Béatrice.[53] He entrusted its execution to the commander of his oldest and most battle-proven formation, Division 308 'Viet Bac' – the 40-year-old Yunnanese political and training expert General Vuong Thua Vu. The hill – which Viet Minh propaganda officers announced had been christened *Doc Lap* ('Independence' – or alternatively, 'Loneliness') – rose more steeply than Béatrice, and its immediate approaches were flatter and less overgrown, which greatly added to the risks of digging approach and final assault trenches. Since 6 March the division had been preparing assembly trenches astride the Pavie Track and mortar and RCL positions on the hills north of Gabrielle; on 11 March work had started on Hills 633 and 701 to the north-east and east, and from the 13th on Hills 527 and 536 to the west (*see Maps 9 and 12*). Preparations were also made to cut off Gabrielle from the central camp: strong positions were created at the abandoned village of Ban Khe Phai about 750yds to the south-west, giving a field of fire over the Pavie Track, and at the point about the same distance again to the south where it crossed a creek.

The assault infantry would be Regiment 88 'Tam Dao' from Division 308, attacking from the north; and from the south-east, Regiment 165 'Dong Trieu' attached from Division 312 – a unit which had been held in reserve the previous night. Regiment 102 'Ba Vi' of Division 308 seem also to have been tasked with investing Gabrielle from the west and south. Artillery preparation would start at 6pm, 20 minutes before sunset; it would be carried out by one battery of 105mm howitzers perhaps two miles to the north, supported by large numbers of 120mm mortars, mostly emplaced in gulleys to the north. Giap's memoirs mention a delay in shifting guns from east to west due to the heavy rain on the 14th. During the course of the night, from about 3.30am, another two batteries of 105s to the north-east would add their fire; but when the barrage opened at about 6pm not all the artillery was in place, so only Regiment 88 was able to proceed with its advance trenching on schedule.[54]

The barrage fell on the hilltop from 6pm, and Captain Gendre reported 15 to 20 shells per minute in his sector. In their strong shelters the Tirailleurs endured the deafening noise and concussion stoically until about 7.45pm. In the full darkness shortly before 8pm the intensity and focus of the fire on the CPs and blockhouses increased, from mortars, RCLs, machine guns and perhaps even 37mm AA guns firing in the ground role; 4th Company's positions suffered severely. 1st and 4th Companies reported infantry movement visible through the smoke and dust on the northern slopes; they manned their parapets, taking increasing casualties from a bombardment which became more localized but did not cease when the infantry assaults began.

The battalions of Regiment 88 followed the usual tactics: first sappers ran forward with bangalores to cut the wire; then the officers' whistles shrilled, and massed columns of infantry with plentiful automatic weapons and grenades came surging up from the assault trenches, interspersed with 'death volunteers' carrying satchel charges for the French machine-gun posts. Shouting their war-cries – *'Doc lap! Tien lien!'* – the front ranks loomed into the sickly yellowish-green glow of the parachute flares, with an impression of moving masses in the darkness behind them as they pressed forward. The Algerians waited until they had clear targets, their NCOs moving along the trenches reminding them not to shoot too high as the enemy came up the slopes; then came the order, and the release they had longed for while they had to cower under the shellfire with no way of fighting back. Rifle fire, machine guns, RCL shells and mortar bombs tore lanes through the crowded masses in the perimeter wire.

Down in Claudine the artillery responded with the pre-planned shoots, the 105s firing at a high angle with low-charge shells so as to clear the hilltop and drop them on the northern slopes; the far-off batteries in Isabelle were unable to risk this, and were allotted safer targets on the eastern flank and in the rear assembly areas. The quad-50s at Dominique 4 had also been tasked with supporting Gabrielle; although 3,000yds was near their extreme range, their arcing streams of tracer dropping on to the southern slopes discouraged any attack from that quarter. From his observation post Georges Collin was satisfied to see shells falling on the middle and lower slopes behind the 'forward edge of battle', to rob the leading assault wave of the impetus of reinforcements. The Viet Minh counter-battery fire was also accurate, however, and more French gunners died that night in their unprotected positions (they had a sinister nickname for the scything shell fragments – *coup de serpe*, 'the billhook'). Early in the duel four were killed outright when a gun of 5th Battery, II/4 RAC was knocked out; later the 105 of Sergeant Loubet of 9th Battery, III/10 RAC was damaged by fragments and some of the crew killed, but replacements stepped forward and it was able to resume firing.[55]

The fighting on the 4th and 1st Company fronts ebbed and flowed for several hours, with growing losses on both sides. The main enemy effort was at the junction of these company sectors, and some time around 10pm Major de Mecquenem had to commit Lieutenant Sanselme's reserve platoon and flame-throwers when 3rd Platoon, 1st Company fell silent. The reserve, led by Sergeant Chief Rouzic, found that a knocked-out radio was to blame. Under continual shelling and infantry assaults such a mishap could leave a company both physically and mentally isolated and prone to confusion; in this case Sergeant Chief Abderrahman had a firm grip, but he was glad of temporary reinforcement to help stabilize his perimeter – a task that Rouzic's gang would perform several times that night in the northern sectors.

The pressure soon built up again, however; the barbed wire was festooned with corpses and wounded, which hampered the Viet Minh advance but also made it difficult for the Algerians to track their movements. In time 4th Company began to weaken; casualties were heavy, and its blockhouses were taking a merciless battering.[56] The clay soil of the hill dug and packed well; but hours of violent vibrations would eventually shake apart even the thickest roof of earth and timber to the point where a lucky shell or mortar bomb could penetrate. Rows of still figures now lay beside Sergeant Chief Soldati's aid post, where about 30 wounded were waiting their turn for treatment.

At about 2.30am there was a sudden complete lull in the Viet Minh artillery fire and infantry assaults; after six hours' fighting Regiment 88 seemed to be spent, and Mecquenem radioed GONO that his companies had the situation in hand. He conferred with his company commanders, had more ammunition and rations distributed, and took stock. The 2nd and 3rd Companies in the southern sectors were completely solid; 1st in the north-west had taken moderate casualties; but 4th in the north-east was in bad shape, and the battalion's 81mm mortars had been knocked out. Mecquenem knew that this was only a pause, and requested 'counter-preparation' shoots on the enemy assembly areas (his captors would later tell Major Le Gurun that these had seriously disrupted the advance of reinforcements).

After eight hours in action and under fire themselves, Piroth's gunners were also approaching exhaustion. As their ready-use ammunition was used up they had to make longer and longer trips to carry more forward; they were dazed by the constant thunder of their own discharges and enemy shellfire, and by the relentless yammering of Lieutenant Redon's quadruple 0.50in mounts near the gunpits of 5th and 6th Batteries, II/4 RAC. When the 6th Battery's barrels actually began to glow in the dark Lieutenant Jean-Marie Moreau had to slacken off from 'maximum cadence' fire (six shots per minute for the 105s, three for the 155s).[57] As for the artillery commander himself, he seems to have begun the night at least outwardly confident that the flashes located on 13/14 March would allow his 155mm howitzers (all four together now, since Pierrel's gun had been brought forward to Eliane 10 during the day) to do serious harm to the enemy batteries. However, as the hours wore on it became clear that Captain Déal's guns were having no significant effect, and they were switched from counter-battery to direct fire support for Gabrielle.

From this point on Piroth seems to have loosened his grip, leaving moment to moment decisions in the fire-control HQ to Major Le Gurun, Captain L'Hostis and Lieutenant Verzat. He may still have been pinning his hopes on the People's Army running short of ammunition; on the previous night each artillery battalion HQ had tried to keep a record of the number of enemy shells fired, making chalk ticks for every detonation. On the morning of the 14th Lieutenant Verzat had arrived at a total estimate of 3,000 rounds fired – at least one-third of the enemy's estimated stockpile.[58]

THE RESPITE LASTED ABOUT an hour, but at around 3.30am the barrage reopened with even greater ferocity than before. Two more 105mm batteries had now joined in; delay-fused shells were used, ensuring deep penetration before they exploded, and the 120mm mortar fire was also heavier than ever. At about this time 3rd Company's Captain Gendre warned that the enemy were listening in to the SCR300 radio traffic, and the battalion net shifted to the little SCR536 'handie-talkies' used at platoon level. It appears that Regiment 165 had finally pushed their assault trenches deep into the wire guarding 3rd Company's south-east sector, and these fresh troops stormed forward with the usual reckless courage while the regrouped Regiment 88 renewed their pressure from the north. This was now applied by the infiltration of small groups rather than en masse: individual companies exploited every local success to work their way forwards without waiting for their comrades to catch up on their flanks. These tactics soon achieved penetrations into 1st and 4th

Companies' lines, spreading uncertainty among the Algerians. Lieutenants Collin and Clerget found it increasingly difficult to bring down effective artillery fire on Regiment 88: once the attackers began spreading out inside the first line of trenches only airburst shells were truly effective, and there was a natural reluctance to unleash such an indiscriminate weapon above ground where defenders and attackers were mixed. Captain Gendre was still holding off Regiment 165 in the south-east, but Major de Mecquenem had to throw every man he could scrape together into the second line of defence in the northern sectors.

At about 4.30am, Georges Collin was arguing over the radio with Captain Combes down in II/4 RAC headquarters about the use of VT-fused airbursts; Lieutenant Clerget had just reported that his last two 120mm mortars had been destroyed, and from 4th Company, Moreau was appealing for reserves to engage a new sap that was being dug into his positions with extraordinary speed. Lieutenant Sanselme had just left the battalion CP to take Rouzic's rapidly dwindling platoon forward once more when two shells in quick succession penetrated the dug-out. It was presumably thanks to its ironwood roof that the result was less catastrophic than in Gaucher's and Pégot's CPs the night before, but it was bad enough. Every officer in the bunker was wounded; Major de Mecquenem lost consciousness for perhaps two hours, Major Kah had a leg blown off, and the command radios were destroyed.

In the trench outside, Sanselme was badly wounded in both thighs; when he dragged himself over the crest to Soldati's aid post he found that it, too, had been destroyed and Soldati killed with many of his patients. Sanselme lay on his back in the mud with a pocket torch clamped in his mouth, trying to arrange the rags of flesh in more or less the right places as he dusted them with sulpha powder and bound them together with field dressings. Sergeant Chief Rouzic found him there; Sanselme sent him on to 4th Company, and Rouzic disappeared up the dorsal trench with his sub-machine gun in his fist and a spare canister of flame-thrower fuel on his back.

When Lieutenant Sanselme dragged himself to the back-up CP he found Georges Collin on the radio to II/4 RAC headquarters, but only semi-conscious; he was telling Captain Combes that he could no longer function as FOO, and that the artillery should fire on his position. Combes refused, and managed to establish independent contact with Lieutenant Clerget; since the latter no longer had any mortars he and his few surviving légionnaires had been fighting as infantry with Lieutenant Botella's 2nd Company. He now took over from Collin as artillery observer; years later men would remember the unshakably calm transmissions of the Spanish légionnaire who acted as his radio operator. Mecquenem was made as comfortable as possible in a corner, but command of the battalion was taken by Captain Gendre of 3rd Company, who also came up to the secondary CP and got in radio contact with GONO. Colonel de Castries told him that if he could hold on until first light a relief force from the main camp would punch through to him.

Some time after 5am the first hint of grey could be seen on the horizon; the enemy fire had not slackened, and 1st Company reported deep penetrations. The tireless Rouzic and his flame-throwers headed north again, but by 6am the enemy had all but submerged 4th Company – one source claims that Lieutenant Moreau himself called for artillery fire on his own position, but he may have been dead by then.[59] Airbursts did explode over the northern sector, however, causing Algerian casualties – the price of slowing the advance of Regiment 88 as they continued to work their way west and south along the trenches. In the south-east Regiment 165 had been making slow but steady progress into 3rd Company's first line; this suddenly gave way at around 7am, and the survivors fell back as the enemy took the company CP. At about the same time Regiment 88 finally took the northern crest, and a 25-year-old sergeant named Tran Ngoc Doan was credited with planting the flag on the ruined battalion command post.

Antoine Botella's 2nd Company were still in control of their sector; part of 3rd Company were fighting in their second line and around the back-up CP, alongside men of Suzineau's HQ Company, Rouzik and his last seven Tirailleurs, and Thais of 416 CSLT. Isolated groups of Tirailleurs were still holding out in 1st Company's sector under Sergeant Chief Abderrahman and Sergeant Noureddine; but Captain Narbey was dead and Sub-lieutenant Roux wounded (he managed to roll himself into cover and crawl hundreds of yards off the hill, to be rescued on 16 March).[60]

At some time around 7am, Captain Gendre's radio operator picked up transmissions from Major Guiraud of the 1st Foreign Parachute Battalion. By 7.30am the sun was well up; and in the paddy-fields to the south of

Gabrielle, perhaps three-quarters of a mile from where he crouched, Gendre's binoculars showed him the turtle shapes of Chaffee tanks, clusters of little dark figures, and the muddy fountains of exploding shells around the stream crossing south of Ban Khe Phai (*see Map 12*).

THE GONO STAFF HAD BEEN following closely the progress of the fighting on Gabrielle; and by about 5am the deteriorating situation made Castries decide to mount a counter-attack 'to try to retake Gabrielle or at least to recover the survivors'. A certain imprecision over the relative weight given to these two verbs fuelled later controversy.[61] Castries delegated the operational details of the attack to Lieutenant Colonel Langlais, as commander of the whole central sector; and Langlais gave the leadership of the operation to Major de Seguin-Pazzis, who had taken over command of Langlais' GAP 2 the previous night.[62]

These two units – 1 BEP and 8 BPC – were those earmarked to carry out counter-attacks; but in the uncertainty which now reigned Langlais was unwilling to commit them in strength. Over to the east units of Divisions 312 and 316 were probing at Dominique 1 and Dominique 5 that night, and he was not yet satisfied that these were no more than diversions.[63] At about the same time as he informed Seguin-Pazzis of the imminent counter-attack – though not of its exact mission – Langlais contacted Major Guiraud directly and told him to assemble just two companies of his 1 BEP to move at short notice. Between 5am and 5.30am various reports from V/7 RTA apparently gave Langlais the impression that two good companies with tank support might be able to restore the situation on Gabrielle. At that hour he may well have been right – other officers both on and off the hill believed so.

Confusion over the chain of command was apparent from the first. The official commander of the northern sector – Gabrielle and Anne-Marie – was still the taciturn Lieutenant Colonel Trancart, who knew the ground well, but for some reason his opinion was never sought. At about 5.15am Maurice Guiraud reported directly to Langlais, to be told that Seguin-Pazzis was in fact in command; Guiraud insisted that he needed to get moving at once, since sunrise was only an hour away and he had to cover some two miles, much of it in the open.

Hubert de Seguin-Pazzis was preparing orders for a critical operation, dumped in his lap only moments before. This pipe-smoking 40-year-old cavalryman, with the long face and trim moustache of a caricature English gentleman (and the same ideals of loyalty and discretion), was an intelligent and courageous officer who had volunteered for the Colonial paratroops. There was nothing of cavalry languor about his soldiering; but proper operation orders would take some time to complete, since he had only fragmentary and often contradictory reports from Gendre, Antoine Botella and Clerget to give him a picture of the situation on Gabrielle. Maurice Guiraud, a fellow St Cyrien and a paratrooper since 1943, saw only the grey glow on the horizon and the open paddy-fields stretching northwards: and he led his men up towards the airfield without waiting for the operation orders. Lieutenants Péria and Le Coz were warned for a mission to shadow the attack from the air in the last Morane; but as soon as French troop movements south of the airstrip attracted the attention of the enemy they drew more shells – and Dien Bien Phu's last aircraft went up in flames.[64]

At perhaps 6.30am the Legion paratroopers reached the area of the stream crossing (a floating bridge) south of Ban Khe Phai, as the slight glow of sunrise through the grey drizzle revealed the billiard-table nakedness of the rice-fields to the north (*see Map 12*). Here Guiraud was joined by Captain Hervouët and the other six tanks of Warrant Officer Carette's 1st and Sergeant Chief Guntz's 2nd Platoons; and, rather later, by Major de Seguin-Pazzis in a jeep, with orders based on increasingly worrying radio messages from Gabrielle to GONO HQ. These suggested that reinforcement by two companies would now be insufficient, and that a complete fresh battalion would have to relieve the mauled V/7 RTA if the paratroopers and tanks could break in. The decision had been taken by Langlais – perhaps at about 5.30am, and after Guiraud had left him – to add 5 BPVN to the operation.[65]

Lieutenant Colonel Langlais' explanation for this puzzling decision, both at the time and in his memoir, was that he was concerned to keep 8th Shock – his best remaining battalion – under his hand as a final reserve for unforeseen developments. The clear implication is that he was still worried about threats to the vital eastern hill strongpoints, which had been mortared and probed by the Viet Minh during the night. The choice of 5 BPVN was questioned by Seguin-Pazzis; but Langlais' response was brusque, and orders were sent to Captain Botella. His Vietnamese paratroops had only landed 14 hours earlier; since then they had marched a couple of miles lugging their equipment, and had dug in on the rain-soaked hillside of Eliane 4 to spend a sleepless night, under sporadic shellfire. Now, about 45 minutes before sunrise, they were roused and sent off to cross the unfamiliar, shell-churned width of the camp, stumbling into trenches and barbed-wire barricades in the dark. To the north they could see the glow of flares and flash of shellbursts on Gabrielle; they knew this was their destination, but the briefing and orders received by André Botella were less than detailed.

It took the battalion about an hour to reach the airstrip; they had been promised guides, but did not get them. Since the sun was now up, 5 BPVN could only proceed further under the eyes of the enemy artillery by taking (more or less in single file) to the old Japanese drainage ditch which ran up the east side of the runway, and then crossing Anne-Marie to follow the Legion paratroopers to Ban Khe Phai. Constantly chivvied by their officers and NCOs, it would still take them until at least 7.30am before even the head of the strung-out battalion – led by Captain Gaven's 3rd Company – could catch up with Guiraud and the tanks.

AT LEAST A BATTALION – presumably of Regiment 102 from Division 308 – were holding trenches covering the ford, and were strongly dug in with support weapons in the village of Ban Khe Phai, about 750yds beyond it and to the west. This obvious bottleneck for any counter-attack had been registered by Viet Minh guns and mortars and was under easy surveillance. The BEP companies and tanks had halted south of the ford at about 6.30am while the officers conferred. Seguin-Pazzis' orders were to fight his way on to Gabrielle and install 5 BPVN, but there was no sign of that unit. Major Guiraud and Captain Hervouët were both in sporadic contact with Captain Gendre on Gabrielle, but the latter's radio was fading in and out, and beyond appeals for the relief force to hurry they could learn little. At some time around 7am, with his small force under enemy fire, Seguin-Pazzis received a second set of orders from GONO: his mission was now to 'recover survivors'.

On Gabrielle, Captain Gendre overheard at least part of this transmission through the whistling static of his dying radio. The wounded

Major de Mecquenem later recalled Gendre quoting this message to him, though without specifying if it came from Langlais in person. Earlier radio traffic had made clear to Gendre that the relief force was stalled by enemy resistance; he now took the latest message to mean that all hope of retaking the hill had been abandoned, and that Guiraud would be attempting only a brief link-up to escort the surviving Tirailleurs to safety. The Algerians were now locked in muddled fighting in several isolated groups and Gendre was unable to co-ordinate a single movement; he passed the word via those radios that were still functioning that each group should prepare to fight its way off Gabrielle through 2nd Company's positions at the south-west.

Down at the ford, Guiraud was unable to wait any longer for 5 BPVN, and attacked across the stream with close support from the tanks. Sub-lieutenant Boisbouvier of Lieutenant Domigo's 4th Company led the way across, exploiting west up the bank as Lieutenant Bertrand's platoon followed, then Lieutenant Martin's 3rd Company. Norbert Domigo got a bullet through his leg; Lieutenant Desmaizières remembered him standing in the open under fire with his trousers down, bellowing with frustration, as the MO Lieutenant Rondy hastily dressed the wound. Viet Minh artillery was now dropping shells all around the crossing, and in the claggy mud of the paddies the bursts went straight upwards like a copse of black poplar trees. The tanks silenced a heavy weapon firing from a hillock to the west; then the 'bisons' and Legion paras pushed on fast, charging and finally clearing the strongly held village of Ban Khe Phai.

There were perhaps 600yds to go to the foot of Gabrielle. Corrected by enemy observers on the heights, shells were falling thickly, and Sergeant Chief Guntz was killed in the turret of his tank 'Smolensk'. Now, at around 7.30am, GONO radioed Major de Seguin-Pazzis yet a third set of orders, based on his report of the successful breakthrough at Ban Khe Phai: he should push on to Gabrielle, but the ultimate decision of whether to reinforce or merely recover the survivors was left up to him. There was still no sign of 5 BPVN; and while he was considering this unhelpful advice, the choice was taken out of his hands by the Algerian Tirailleurs.

Still under the impression that the relief force's orders were simply to cover their retreat, Captain Gendre ordered the survivors of V/7 RTA to withdraw. The exact timing is, as always, uncertain; it seems that while Lieutenant Antoine Botella of 2nd Company was still radioing GONO for the tanks to advance, confident that the hill could be held if reinforced (an opinion shared by Suzineau of the HQ Company), some of his company were already leaving their positions at perhaps 7.45am, and 3rd Company followed from about 8am. Other survivors continued to fight on the hilltop; Major de Mecquenem was captured while trying vainly to fetch men from 2nd Company to go to the aid of the last Tirailleurs of 1st, holding out under Sergeants Abderrahman and Nourredine. Major Guiraud could clearly see Viet Minh infantry swarming all over the hilltop before 8.30am when, while still some way from the slopes, his paratroopers were joined on the Pavie Track by four officers and about 150 Tirailleurs and légionnaires: most of 2nd Company, some of 3rd, and a few stragglers from the others. A handful of Lieutenant Clerget's mortarmen fought their way clear through 3rd Company's sector, led by Légionnaires Putsch and Zimmerman with a light machine gun apiece; Clerget himself went back to get batteries for his precious radio, and was captured. The survivors had only escaped at last through a protective corridor of 105mm shells organized over the radio between Clerget and Captain Combes of II/4 RAC. Gabrielle was officially recorded as falling at 9am, but there are persistent claims that Blockhouse 3 kept firing for as much as four hours afterwards.[66]

Meanwhile, the leading elements of 5 BPVN were finally coming up under the continuing enemy shellfire. Although the unit contained many veterans of the old 3 BPC, all were receiving their baptism of artillery – and in open paddy-fields. The battalion stalled when the point company reached the ford below Ban Khe Phai; André Botella got them moving again, and 3rd, HQ and part of 2nd Company pressed on to catch up with 1 BEP a few hundred yards short of Gabrielle. However, about halfway back down the strung-out 2nd Company one Vietnamese subaltern froze on the spot, and behind him the rest of his company and the whole of 1st and 4th.[67]

While trying to find Guiraud or Seguin-Pazzis to get up-to-date orders, André Botella was passed by tanks heading south loaded with wounded Algerian survivors; he noticed their blood streaming down from the engine decks. He was told that it was all over and to pull his unit back; the paratroopers, Tirailleurs and tanks had to run the gauntlet of heavy and accurate shellfire for at least a mile, but by 9am they were back within the cover of the Huguettes. At about the same time the fall of Gabrielle was reported to General Cogny in Hanoi; and the enemy artillery resumed a widespread harassing fire on the camp.

Lieutenant Bergot reckoned the losses of V/7 RTA at some 540 dead or disappeared, including three officers, and about 220 captured, most of them wounded; he numbers the escapees at 114, apparently referring only to those fit for further service, who were transferred to Isabelle. Other estimates of the Algerian casualties differ widely, but these do not affect the essential facts: that within 36 hours a second battalion had been reduced to one company of shaky survivors; that a second northern strong-point had been lost, giving the enemy artillery observers and AA gunners greatly improved positions, and leaving only one – the much weaker Anne-Marie – still in French hands on this whole front; and that the planned counter-attack had failed in confusion.[68] The cost of the counter-attack to 1 BEP was nine dead and 46 wounded – perhaps 20 per cent of those engaged.[69]

One of the episodes of the battle which passed into folklore from the pages of Jules Roy and Bernard Fall was the 'purging' of 5 BPVN. It was reported that Captain Botella, heartsick at the failure of two of his companies to cross the ford during the counter-attack, disarmed a significant though unspecified number of Vietnamese officers, NCOs and men. Depending upon the version, Botella either told 'hundreds' of them to get out of his sight, after which they simply lurked around the safest holes in the river-bank as internal deserters (Roy and Fall); or alternatively, that he employed them thereafter as coolies to carry ammunition and supplies (Rocolle).[70] Such stories were certainly recorded by French debriefers as early as May 1954; yet when questioned later by Erwan Bergot, André Botella denied that anything of the sort took place. He claimed that he had simply told his company commanders to avoid in future using the more fragile elements for the hardest tasks. He added that there were only about 20 real absentees, all young and recently joined, among a battalion with many three- and four-year veterans from 3 BPC; and that all later slipped back into the ranks of their own accord. Captain Botella pointed out that 5 BPVN could hardly have fulfilled the many combat missions with which it was entrusted between 18 March and 7 May if it had been nearly halved in strength after its first action.[71]

WHEN MAJOR GUIRAUD GOT his 1 BEP companies back to the camp he was in a mood of frustration and dread. It was not only that hard-core units of the CEFEO had suffered their most summary defeat since October 1950; it was the fact that – in Guiraud's belief, and not his alone – the hill could have been saved. If the handling of the Gabrielle counter-attack was anything to go by, then Dien Bien Phu was doomed, and within days.[72] Missions of this difficulty simply could not be improvised at short notice.

French officers knew that at Na San morning counter-attacks had retaken positions lost the previous night, and they seem to have assumed that conditions would be similar at Dien Bien Phu – but at Gabrielle the counter-attack had to cover a much greater distance of open ground, and under artillery fire that was never encountered at Na San. The general outline of counter-attacks by GAP 2 and the Chaffees had certainly been discussed, and the paratroopers and tank crews had crossed the valley together several times during their earlier sorties to 'aerate' the northern strongpoints. But these had not simulated the conditions that would be encountered when trying to retake lost hills – not even in daylight, let alone before dawn. The degree to which such missions had been practised before 13 March as paper exercises on the map, let alone with troops on the ground, is a matter of disagreement; but Pierre Rocolle could find no convincing record of realistic rehearsals, and General Cogny's later claim to have discussed such tactical details thoroughly on 12 March is not supported.[73]

Lieutenant Colonel Langlais had been given new and vastly greater responsibilities only on the night of 13/14 March, taking up a burden for which he had received little preparation. Langlais was a combat para-trooper, at heart still a regimental officer whose instinctive response to setbacks was to attack with whatever men he had, seeking to dominate the immediate situation by audacity and aggression; it was said of him that he did not bring a 'nuanced' approach to solving problems.[74] These qualities would serve GONO spectacularly in the weeks to come; but at 5.30am on 15 March, Pierre Langlais had not yet settled into his new role. Nevertheless, he was already the most energetic subordinate in Colonel de Castries' headquarters. Among those few whose rank fitted them to act as, in effect, Castries' operations chief, Langlais' combat record made him the automatic choice; the only realistic alternative, Lieutenant Colonel Lalande, was three miles away in Isabelle. And an officer of iron will was certainly needed in Dien Bien Phu following the fall of Gabrielle.

MORALE PLUMBED A NEW LOW on 15 March, as tired and shocked staff officers brooded over the implications of the Viet Minh's successes. The chief-of-staff, Lieutenant Colonel Keller, had now completely collapsed, and spent his remaining days at Dien Bien Phu in the deepest dug-out wearing a steel helmet. His breakdown was only the most obvious of several instances of psychological frailty that Castries reported discreetly to Hanoi. A letter of 21 March from General Navarre to Marshal Juin reported:

> There was a certain drop in morale due to the surprise of finding themselves facing much worse conditions than they had expected... The command echelon had been too confident, and there was a tendency for their mood to swing from one extreme to the other... That is why I am going to send two lieutenant colonels – volunteers, and 'pumped up' – to assist and eventually to replace the tired chaps from Castries' staff. He himself still seems to be in good form.[75]

Lieutenant colonels flown in over the next few days included Ducruix, to replace Keller as Castries' chief-of-staff; Lemeunier, to take over command of GM 9; Vaillant, the new artillery commander; and Voinot, who took over the western sector defences.[76]

Colonel de Castries may have seemed 'in good form' on 21 March, but certainly not on the 15th or for some days afterwards. His reports to Hanoi – where General Navarre had joined Cogny – forecast a rapid fall of the central camp; if Giap kept up this intensity of attacks for a few more successive nights the outcome was inescapable. General Cogny tried to rally Castries' spirits, and promised him reinforcement by Bigeard's parachute battalion the next day, but he was a great deal less confident than his words: it would be alleged that he spoke in gloomy and self-excusing terms to journalists (neither for the first nor the last time).

Whatever the truth of this, Cogny certainly expressed his pessimism in a message to Navarre dated that day, even though the C-in-C was currently in the same building; their relationship seems already to have broken down, and memoranda were being written with at least one eye on the future record. It is probably unsurprising that the whole weight of this document bore not on the fate of GONO, but on the implications for Cogny's continued defence of the Delta. Since January, Cogny's troops had been forced to react to a greatly increased tempo of road ambushes and attacks on posts; now he predicted the most damaging political and psychological consequences on the civilian population – and, above all, on the fragile ANV units – following a collapse at Dien Bien Phu. In this and a second signal the next day he suggested that in such an event the People's Army would be able to bring a complete regular division back to the Delta within 12 days. He demanded at least three more Groupes Mobiles from the general reserve, even though he knew that Navarre was fully committed to Operation 'Atlante' in Annam, whose second phase ('Axelle') was now under way around Qui Nhon.

Navarre's true judgement of Dien Bien Phu's chances is unclear; in a private conversation he seems to have been pessimistic.[77] Nevertheless, when he shared his views with General Ely he could see no other solution than to defend Dien Bien Phu, and did not believe defeat was inevitable, pointing out that the central redoubt would be a good deal harder to capture than its outworks. On 14 March he had already ordered GONO's reinforcement with Major Bigeard's 6 BPC (they could not be dropped before the 16th, as the available Dakotas were all needed to replenish the camp's ammunition). Now he ordered the speedier return to Tonkin of Bréchignac's II/1 RCP; as already mentioned, since their sorties from Dien Bien Phu before Christmas both these battalions had been heavily engaged in central Laos.[78] (Once again, it is worth emphasizing that the French paratroopers maintained a pace of combat operations that would be regarded today as fantastic in any circumstances other than the last-ditch defence of the home country.)

Despite this commitment to reinforce Dien Bien Phu, it was with Navarre's explicit approval that, on 16 March, Commissioner General Dejean sent a telegram to Secretary Jacquet in Paris suggesting that the government beat the media to the punch by promoting a massaged version of the 'worst case scenario'. This was judged to be premature, but would be disseminated seven weeks later; Navarre's detailed suggestions for this statement make interesting reading today, when we are all more aware of the dark arts of the 'spin doctor'.[79]

NO MEMBER OF COLONEL de Castries' staff was more gripped by despondency than Charles Piroth. During the night of 14/15 March he wandered from one dug-out office to the next, apologizing for the failure of his counter-battery plan; his friend Lieutenant Colonel Trancart recalled him saying, with tears in his eyes, that he was completely dishonoured. A loud confrontation with Pierre Langlais – whose temper was shorter than ever after 36 sleepless hours of uninterrupted defeats, and whose own failed counter-attack was scalding him – was overheard by Major Guérin and Captain L'Hostis. The paratrooper was tactless at the best of times, and his choice of words on this occasion was lacerating. The one-armed artilleryman had tormented himself with his failure since the evening of the 13th – Castries had already asked a chaplain to keep an eye on him; now he took his shame to the privacy of his quarters. At some time on 15 March, Piroth took a grenade in his one hand, pulled the pin with his teeth, and clutched it to his chest.

Colonel de Castries decided for reasons of morale to try to keep Colonel Piroth's suicide a secret, and he was buried in his own dug-out by Dr Le Damany and Fathers Heinrich and Trinquand. Over the next couple of days various alibis were floated both in the camp and in the radio traffic to Hanoi to explain his absence; his death was eventually reported as due to enemy action, and a replacement was officially requested only on 20 March (when the officer in question was already on his way). Rumours of the truth nevertheless circulated quickly, and were confirmed a few days later when air-dropped copies of Le Monde carried the story (the paper's source is unknown). This attempted deception might appear futile, but is understandable given the frail state of morale after the fall of Gabrielle; besides, Charles Piroth was a likeable man who had several old friends at Dien Bien Phu.

There were some who condemned his choice as desertion under fire rather than an honourable expiation for failure. Others simply found it incongruous: a paratroop officer visiting what was left of Lieutenant Bergot's mortar platoon on Eliane 4 remarked that if everyone who was responsible for the mess they were in chose to take that way out, then Dien Bien Phu was soon going to be pretty damned empty – and Paris, too.[80]

12. Gars Pierre and Torri Rouge

'Langlais is an admirable lad as a fighter,
but he's... I won't say difficult to command –
but he forms many opinions which are
subject to revision...'
General Cogny *before the Commission of Inquiry, 10 October 1954*

THE SKY ABOVE THE HIGH REGION remained overcast on 15 March, and due to the continued lack of a VHF beacon resupply flights again had difficulty in finding their way. Only 12½ tons of cargo would be dropped that day, a derisory fraction of the previous night's ammunition expenditure. The 105s alone had fired about 10,000 shells – two-thirds of their remaining stock – and the four quad-50 crews about 40,000 rounds. The ten remaining guns of II/4 RAC had fired nearly 600 rounds each – in one night each gun had fired away six complete Dakota loads. That morning Lieutenant Moreau of 6th Battery noticed something he had never seen before: the paint had burnt off the barrels of his howitzers, showing bare steel.[1]

There was some air support activity, and during the day seven Bearcats of GC 2/22 flew missions over Dien Bien Phu. One, piloted by Sergeant Ali Sahraoui – the sole survivor of the mission of 7 February – was hit by AA fire and crashed in the hills; no parachute was seen. The Air Force sorties were followed by three patrols of Hellcats from Flotille 11, and by Helldivers of 3F. 'Savart Blue' (Lieutenant Commander Lespinas and Petty Officer Violot) were told to bomb an artillery emplacement north of the airfield marked by a smoke shell. Lespinas dropped his two 500lb bombs, but his Hellcat '11F-8' was then immediately hit, blazing up in mid-air and crashing 400yds north of the objective. Many in the camp saw his fiery death, and some came to attention and saluted: on that wretched morning the fighter pilots seemed to be their only friends.[2]

Everything depended upon the enemy's plans for the next night, which rested in turn upon the state of Giap's assault units after two nights of sacrificial attacks. No detailed casualty figures have been published by the People's Army, and French estimates vary. Captain Gendre reported that when he withdrew from the south-west corner of Gabrielle to join 1 BEP on the Pavie Track he passed over an unbroken carpet of enemy dead, killed by French artillery fire – presumably from Regiment 102 'Ba Vi'. After the fall of Gabrielle, French aerial reconnaissance produced a suggested figure of 1,000 dead on the field, which by conventional calculation would give up to a further 2,000 wounded. There is no way of knowing at what stage in the Viet Minh's clearance of the battlefield the reconnaissance flight took place, but since the weather probably delayed it until after noon, the actual figure may therefore have been higher. A conservative estimate of the cost of capturing Béatrice would be about half these figures; so we can risk a guess of at least 1,500 killed and 3,000 wounded over 13–15 March – the total can hardly have been much less than 5,000 casualties. This represents an average of perhaps 25 per cent each from the two divisions committed – 15 per cent of Giap's whole infantry force then present. French commentators claim higher figures, and this estimate is deliberately cautious.[3]

Captain Noël's intelligence cell included a radio intercept team under Sergeant Bertin Dubois; during 15 March enemy traffic revealed both urgent calls for replacements and ammunition to be sent up from Tuan Giao, and also one side of a conversation in which a unit commander sought, but was refused, permission to attack Anne-Marie.[4] This vital reprieve on the night of 15/16 March was not general knowledge, however, and certainly not to the garrison of Anne-Marie.

About a mile south-west of Gabrielle and three-quarters of a mile north-west of the northern end of the runway, a low crescent-shaped hill open to the north rose from the paddies (*see Map 12*). On the lowest slope of its south-west corner was the hamlet of Ban Kheo; and on its west and east hilltops were strongpoints Anne-Marie 1 and 2, occupied by 10th and 11th Companies and the command post of Major Thimonier's 3rd Thai Battalion. About half a mile due south of this feature on a lower, scrubby hillock was Anne-Marie 4 ('the Mercedes star'), which had a striking triangular layout. About 600yds east and slightly south of this, astride the Pavie Track at the north end of the airstrip, was Anne-Marie 3. These positions were held respectively by BT 3's 9th and 12th Companies. The Anne-Maries were separated from the main camp by flat rice-fields and scrub, and movement between them was possible only at night due to Viet Minh artillery fire.

From these isolated positions the Thais of BT 3 had watched the fall of Gabrielle, and their morale could hardly have been unaffected. Ever since their arrival they had been targeted by the Viet Minh for intense propaganda spread by infiltration of the local villagers, who had not been expelled from these peripheral hamlets like the central population of the valley. Moreover, the men of BT 3 were mostly White Thais, whose home region around Son La had also been occupied by the Viet Minh since the end of 1952. On 15 March the Viet Minh were able to get close enough to add direct appeals by loudspeaker to the leaflets smuggled in by murmuring villagers.[5] During that day Major Thimonier noticed signs of wavering; and on the night of 15/16 March there were many desertions from Captain Guilleminot's 12th Company at Anne-Marie 3, which had to be reinforced with légionnaires from I/2 REI.[6]

THE NIGHT 15/16 MARCH SAW another Viet Minh commando attempt on Haiphong–Cat Bi airbase, but this was foiled.[7] Heavy rain fell over the High Region in the early hours, and 16 March dawned overcast and drizzling. Despite this hindrance to air operations, there were those in Saigon who believed that an early onset of the true monsoon rains was actually desirable, in that they would hamper equally the Viet Minh resupply convoys on their primitive dirt roads. On 16 March General Navarre authorized an accelerated study of the possibility of provoking the rains artificially by seeding the clouds over RP41 with carbon dioxide crystals ('dry ice'); the scheme came to nothing.[8]

Meanwhile, back in the real world of Dien Bien Phu, the morning was initially quiet; and a Viet Minh officer under a flag of truce approached

Anne-Marie to announce that French wounded from Gabrielle would be left for collection at a point 600yds north of Anne-Marie the next day. The enemy could be seen entrenching to the west and north of Anne-Marie 1 and 2.

The most urgent business of the 16th was receiving air-drops of personnel, equipment and stores. The order of priorities was the new paratroop battalion, a replacement VHF beacon, medical supplies, two replacement howitzers, artillery ammunition, and infantry ammunition. The overcast obliged the pilots of the 42 troop-carrying 'Banjo' C-47s to fly in at wide intervals, but the drop of about 100 replacements for 1 BEP and 8 BPC and the whole 6 BPC began at around 11am and proceeded smoothly, although under intermittent shellfire; two pairs of Hellcats escorted the Dakotas, followed by Helldivers. By 7pm the 6th Colonial – which jumped 613 strong, of whom 322 were Vietnamese – were digging their first hasty foxholes on the bare west-facing headlands of Eliane 1 and 4 after a long trudge up from the southern DZ, and Captain Botella from the neighbouring 5 BPVN was pointing out the lie of the land to Bigeard.[9]

Colonel de Castries had also wanted the third battalion of GAP 1 – II/1 RCP – dropped immediately; but General Cogny retained it on stand-by for the time being. He hoped to use it as the nucleus for a whole new GAP with two other battalions returning from Laos.[10] Nevertheless, that afternoon Castries took the opportunity of Bigeard's arrival to issue a cheering order of the day along the lines of: 'We've taken some hard knocks and losses, but now we've received reinforcements and there are more where they came from; the artillery is intact, and when the weather lifts you'll really see what the Air Force can do; everything depends on us, and in a few more days we'll have won, and avenged our comrades.'[11] How many of the garrison found this entirely convincing is questionable, but the arrival of 'Bigeard's Boys' noticeably lifted the mood in the camp.

IN THE DAY'S CARGO DROPS priority was given to artillery ammunition. The expenditure of all ammunition had been shocking – about five days' planned supply in two nights – but that of the artillery particularly so, given that it was only shelling that seemed to have any real effect on the enemy human wave attacks.[12]

Before the battle began the total daily resupply requirements for GONO during a period of combat had been calculated at the equivalent of 15½lbs per man; in fact, they were now running at nearly twice that level – 26½lbs per man per day. The initial total figure of 80 tons per day accepted for Operation 'Castor' by Colonel Nicot had long been overtaken by events. True, thanks to US aid his Dakota fleet had now increased from a theoretical maximum of 69 to 88 aircraft, and the C-119s from five to 24. But he was still short of at least 12 Dakota and six C-119 crews; GONO had grown from the initial six to 12 battalions; and Nicot now had to satisfy simultaneous calls on his fleet from both the Delta and Operation 'Atlante' in Annam. The daily needs of Dien Bien Phu had been recalculated in February to 96 tons per day during intense combat. In fact, total supply drops between 16 and 30 March would achieve nearly 2,000 tons at an average of 120 tons per day; but since the actual daily requirement now averaged about 180 tons it would take until the end of March before artillery stocks were once more reasonably healthy.[13]

A point sometimes overlooked is that the cessation of cargo flights into the airfield from 13 March and the consequent reliance on parachute dropping of all loads instantly aggravated the tonnage problem by 12 per cent, since for every 220lb package loaded there was a 26lb penalty for the weight of the parachute pack itself. Regarding the whole question of planned air resupply, there is much evidence that although an interruption in the use of the airfield was foreseen, it was expected – as at Na San – to be reasonably brief before counter-attacks restored the air bridge. (One indicator that FTNV had expected any crisis to be of short duration was that Hanoi's initial stock of parachute flares for 'Luciole' flights was sufficient for only three nights' operations.)[14]

The routine for receiving ammunition resupply drops was for Sublieutenant Léonard at the main dump to apply to Lieutenant Patricot, commandant of the PIM camp, for however many labourers he needed (he tried to get the same men regularly if they proved cheerful and hardworking). The drop zones then had to be secured from interference – on 16 March, by a sortie from Isabelle. Air Force personnel from Major Guérin's PCIA then took a portable MF radio beacon out to the drop zone. The ammunition packages were shoved out of the side doors of C-47s with static-line cargo parachutes (for immediate automatic opening): either two boxes each holding two 105mm rounds, or two unboxed 155mm shells, or several cases of 155mm propellant charges. On the drop zone the PIMs ran out to unfasten the harness straps and manhandled the boxes into trucks for the drive to the ammunition dump, where other PIM gangs unloaded them for storage in the carefully sub-divided pens. At the dump Léonard checked all rounds closely for signs of deterioration or damage, and to ensure that the ammunition was stored together for issue in its 'manufacturing lots' as marked on the packaging: ideally a whole artillery shoot should be fired using shells from the same factory batch.[15]

Larger ton-weight packages were assembled for dropping out of the big tail doors of C-119 Packets under a G12 cargo parachute – 40 shells in 20 boxes – and these needed a good deal more time and effort to recover. The C-119s routinely delivered their six-ton cargoes either by dropping them from very low altitude – 330ft to 500ft – without parachutes if the load was not breakable (e.g. rolls of barbed wire and pickets); or if it was, then by parachute from between 1,650ft and 3,000ft. The loads were prepared at Haiphong–Cat Bi, where the Packets were based, by Lieutenant Pierre Guin's Compagnie de Ravitaillement par Air (CRA). This unit and its counterpart at Hanoi were among the unsung heroes; their work was exhausting, frenetic, and often frustrated by orders to unload and substitute alternative cargoes at the last moment, in the oven heat of parked aircraft. The classic load for a C-119 was six one-ton cubic packages, each rigged on a pallet which could be slid along the roller track inside the C-119's hull.

The technique for dropping was described by Lieutenant Marc Bertin as being a bit like getting a horse out of a horsebox by tipping it out the back, with the difference that in this case it was the horsebox which reared violently. With the big tail doors open, the chief despatcher pulled a quick-release strap, and the pilots simultaneously hauled back on the controls to point the nose up. As the huge packages rumbled down the track and out into thin air the removal of their weight made the aircraft leap upwards, while pilot and co-pilot struggled to get it trimmed level again. On more than one occasion a failure to keep the aircraft trimmed nose down once the doors were open resulted in loads tearing free and sliding out before arrival over the drop zone.[16]

By 16 March three howitzers already needed replacing, and others needed spare parts. When possible, repairs were carried out on the spot by Lieutenant Jourdonneau's teams from the Service du Matériel depot, helped by the crews; taking a two-ton gun to the workshop area involved much manhandling and rhythmic African work songs, due to the difficulty of getting towing trucks into the overcrowded and now shell-cratered gun lines.[17] On the 16th the artillery listed two of the 24 × 105s unserviceable, and one of the four 155s; from an original 28 × 120mm mortars, eight had already been destroyed in action.[18] The drops on the 16th brought two replacement 105s, and a third was dropped the following day. The guns were not disassembled in any way; they were strapped to a platform made of PSP, protected with large felt pads and a wooden frame built to collapse progressively, and dropped from C-119s under a G11 parachute or two G12s.[19] The lost 120mm mortars were not replaced; once four spare tubes previously acquired for 1 CEPML had been pressed into service, the total number serviceable would only decline.

The losses to shellfire among the camp's artillerymen were clear from the fact that GONO requested a new battery command team for Isabelle and the equivalent of eight complete replacement crews; they received just three – the only possible source was GM/35 RALP. Officers and men with specialist skills who were also parachute-qualified were in short supply, and individuals had to be dropped in as and when they could be found.[20]

AT ABOUT 4PM ON 16 MARCH a C-47 painted with prominent Red Cross markings ('P'tits Loups Zulu Zulu' of GT 2/62) made an approach, but shells falling on the runway forced the pilot to climb away; Lieutenant Héquet was willing to try again but the controller waved him off. Several other aircraft also failed to touch down; there were new AA guns on Béatrice and Gabrielle. Before Gabrielle fell the 37mm positions had been at least two miles from the airstrip; now some of them and many heavy machine guns could be placed on the axis of the runway much closer to its northern end, giving easy approaching and departing shots.[21]

Since the bombardment of 13 March it had become all too clear that casualties were going to be heavier and their evacuation more dangerous and uncertain than had ever been imagined. The camp's medical personnel needed urgent reinforcement, and the aid post at Isabelle could no longer count on being able to send serious cases up to the main hospital immediately. On the night of 14/15 March a 105mm shell had fallen on part of the hospital complex and killed nine patients, and a second destroyed the X-ray room; a few days later a 120mm mortar bomb would hit the triage room and killed another 14 men.[22] On 16 March the 3rd Parachute Surgical Team (3 ACP) under Lieutenant Dr Rézillot were accidentally dropped into a belt of barbed wire in the main camp, and had to face a dangerous truck journey to Isabelle – their intended destination – during a lull in the shelling. The following day Lieutenant Dr Vidal's 6 ACP were successfully dropped in to join Grauwin's and Gindrey's teams.[23] The Gendarmes of the camp's provost unit also volunteered their services; all were qualified in first aid and one had been an orderly in the Navy. For the rest of the siege they worked selflessly at the hospitals – scrounging rations and cooking for the casualties, escorting the evacuation vehicles to the airfield while it was open, and afterwards working in the hospital as stretcher-bearers and dressers; one, Pochelu, even served as a theatre orderly.[24]

Personal appeals were broadcast by Professor Huard – doyen of the Hanoi medical faculty and former teacher of many of the Viet Minh's doctors – that the enemy allow the air evacuation of wounded by machines clearly marked with the Red Cross, under guarantee that they would carry no military supplies or non-medical personnel.[25] However, during 17–19 March only three of eight attempted daytime 'casevac' sorties managed to land and pick up wounded, and these came under shell and mortar fire. The enemy's simultaneous handing back of French wounded, and denial of the opportunity to evacuate them, simply increased the burden on medical facilities and morale. Viet Minh accusations that Red Cross aircraft carried non-medical personnel in and out were true in a handful of cases, but not until after it became clear that the enemy artillery had no intention of respecting medical flights anyway.[26]

THE MORNING OF 17 MARCH revealed that enemy trenches were curling ever closer to Anne-Marie 1 and 2; and the spectacle of the agreed medical convoy driving past down the Pavie Track with 86 casualties from Gabrielle, whom the enemy had handed over as promised, did nothing to improve the confidence of BT 3. Early that afternoon some light shelling – about 20 rounds – finally broke the nerve of 10th and 11th Companies. A laconic radio message from the FOO, Sub-lieutenant Francois Pencréac'h, announced that 'The Thais are off...'; the men climbed from their trenches and leapt over the wire, and soon Anne-Marie 1 and 2 were occupied only by the French cadres and a handful of faithful Thai NCOs and riflemen. Frenchmen who had long served with them were shocked by this defection: the Thais were described affectionately as 'brave buggers'. But their talent lay in ranging their forest hills, not holding trenches under shellfire; and who knows what the enemy propaganda had told them about their family villages under Viet Minh occupation. Captain Guilleminot reported that 12th Company in Anne-Marie 3 were distinctly brittle; Captain Desiré claimed that his 9th Company in Anne-Marie 4 remained solid, but it seemed sensible to replace them and send them to a less exposed position (they went first to the Huguettes, and finally, on 19 March, to Isabelle).

On the afternoon of the 17th the few remnants fell back from Anne-Marie 1 and 2; the People's Army pushed forward to occupy the hill at once, under cover of shellfire, and the escapees were unable even to dismount and carry away their heavy weapons, reaching the central camp only after dark. It appears that 4th Company, 6 BPC were ordered north with a view to retaking the abandoned positions, but were stalled by machine-gun and RCL fire as well as shelling before they got anywhere near the hill.[27]

Castries and Langlais decided that the position would have to be abandoned: any attempt to retake it over open ground in full view of the new enemy positions had little chance. From that evening onwards the northernmost bastions of Dien Bien Phu would be Anne-Marie 3, rechristened 'Huguette 6', and Anne-Marie 4, now 'Huguette 7', held respectively by companies from I/2 REI and 5 BPVN (*see Map 13*). The collapse of BT 3 naturally cast doubt on the reliability of the 2nd Thai Battalion and the companies of Thai auxiliaries, but the drain on his infantry obliged Castries to continue to trust any which appeared fairly steadfast – at least for missions which would not expose them to brutal bombardments. BT 2 were left holding second-line positions in Claudine, with a limited counter-attack mission.[28]

The de facto destruction of BT 3 meant that on this fifth day of the battle the garrison had effectively lost three of its 12 battalions (replaced by two), and must have serious doubts about the staying power of a fourth;

but the implications for the artillery battle were even graver. The loss of Béatrice, Gabrielle and the northern Anne-Maries robbed GONO of its best ground observation posts, particularly for counter-battery fire on the northern and north-eastern hills (*see Map 12*). The loss of the northern ramparts opened up the whole valley to the enemy artillery and flak – not only to closer observation but also for the redeployment of weapons to shorter range. Before this only the howitzers, mountain guns and heavy mortars could reach targets inside Dien Bien Phu; now the People's Army could bring forward regimental 75mm RCLs for direct fire and 81mm mortars to thicken the indirect fire. Significantly, should they wish to take the opportunity, their artillery officers need no longer be limited to their original, rigid fire plans; improved observation should allow them to react at short notice to movements in the valley. One of the most vulnerable of these was the continuing attempt to fly seriously wounded men out of Dien Bien Phu, which became one of Colonel de Castries' central concerns during the second half of March.

A few Beaver liaison pilots were still making occasional daredevil landings and take-offs, but since the 13th the only C-47s which had risked landing at 'Torri Rouge' had been tasked with delivering medical supplies and evacuating casualties, and these had routinely come under shellfire. Typically, the enemy would wait until the moment when the ambulances and Red Cross-flagged trucks were approaching the taxiing aircraft at the northern end of the runway, and the wounded were hobbling or being carried to the door. Amidst a sudden flurry of shellbursts the pilots would have to open their throttles and race for take-off – sometimes empty, leaving the frantic wounded clustered under fire on the open field, sometimes with a few of the quickest or luckiest aboard. The photographer Jean Péraud (a survivor of the concentration camps) recorded behaviour which shocked him; and shamefully, a few able-bodied opportunists also tried to embark in the confusion.

On 17 March – with the replacement VHF radio beacon now functioning – two Dakotas got down, but only one managed to evacuate any casualties. At 1.50pm Lieutenant Ruffray of GT 2/62 landed with a load of plasma for the hospital. The controls were taken over by the previously stranded Captain Cornu, and despite attracting immediate fire (one shell landed hideously among a group of waiting wounded) he managed to make a 750yd take-off with 32 casualties crammed inside for a brief shuttle ride to Muong Sai. At 7pm Captain Darde's 'P'tits Loups Zulu-Tango' landed, and waited under fire for a full five minutes, but the ambulances could not get through the barrage to reach him; when he took off there were at least 19 holes in the aircraft, and the only man in the back was a flight doctor, Captain Lavandier, now wounded himself.[29]

TWO NIGHTS HAD NOW PASSED without a major Viet Minh assault, and while any respite was precious to GONO there were many officers – on both sides – who wondered why. Unknown to the French, a decision had been taken which marked the end of the first phase of the battle and a deliberate change of tactics.

Giap's casualties had indeed been severe, and the more so because of the siege army's limited medical facilities. Jules Roy later interviewed a senior Viet Minh doctor, Professor Thon That Tung, who was summoned to the front on 27 March as chief medical adviser on Giap's staff. At one improvised field hospital east of Dien Bien Phu he found – 17 days after the battle opened – just six assistant doctors overwhelmed by some 700 seriously wounded men who had still had no treatment other than immediate dressing and plastering; and this was not the only hospital. Head wounds due to the lack of steel helmets were particularly numerous and serious. Swarms of biting yellow flies were laying eggs in wounds which teemed with maggots; the hospital was infested with ticks, and muggy thunderstorms alternating with a hot, dry wind from Laos were wretchedly distressing for the wounded. Professor Tung carried out a continuous series of operations for an entire week, teaching techniques to a handful of young surgeons as he worked.[30]

To fill the anticipated gaps in his assault units General Giap had assembled at the end of February a reserve pool of 6,000–8,000 men; and radio intercepts showed that this total was raised soon afterwards to a requirement for 25,000 men – equivalent to the siege army's whole opening strength in infantry. To create this reserve men were called up from all over Vietnam, as far away as Lien Khu 5 in southern Annam, some of them with only a few weeks' service. It was noted that prisoners taken at Dien Bien Phu during April were often very young, and People's Army publications mention the youth and inexperience of new recruits reaching the siege army. These soldiers needed not only practical training but also relentless indoctrination by the unit political officers. Apart from rebuilding and encouraging the mauled ranks of Divisions 308 and 312, Giap also had to resupply his artillery; a large part of the ammunition stockpiled before 13 March had been used up by the 17th (Lieutenant Verzat's hopeful counting of chalk ticks had been justified), and radio intercepts confirmed that major new supplies were awaited from the Chinese frontier.[31] The French noted a slackening of fire in the second half of the month; and Giap later admitted that at times artillery fire had to be severely restricted – requests for shoots from infantry officers had to be passed up to the highest authority for approval, which was often refused.[32]

On 17 March the senior officers of the siege army were called together by Giap's Front Military Committee to receive the latest orders. These can be summarized as a reversion from immediate assaults to the patient creation of an extensive system of approach trenches for a future second phase of attacks, while the army was replenished with men and supplies. When the moment was ripe they would pass over to the offensive once again, attacking 'one strongpoint at a time, and if circumstances were favourable, two or three, but only when there was a guarantee of certain victory'.

Giap's decision to suspend the assaults following the capture of Gabrielle astonished some of his subordinates, who – perhaps influenced by the ridiculous ease with which the northern Anne-Maries had fallen into their hands – urged that the army press ahead and exploit its successes. Giap criticized this attitude, and his memories of the spring 1951 defeats and the check at Na San are clearly discernible behind the Party vocabulary:

> Certain comrades show signs of not having properly assimilated the recommended directing principles. Some wish to throw in a rapid offensive, attacking several positions simultaneously, neglecting preparatory work to press on at once to the third phase. Others are not sufficiently concerned with the need to reinforce and preserve our forces so as to be able to fight without interruption. This can be seen in delays – in rebuilding effective strengths, in reorganizing after each combat, in replacing the expended ammunition – and also in the insufficient importance they attach to gathering up the booty of war... Certain comrades, unaware of the actual situation and the forces involved, show subjectivity and

underestimate our adversaries, from which comes a weakening of our combat organization that can easily lead to defeat.[33]

The same source shows that on 20 March Giap addressed the new tactical situation. Getting within assault distance of the central camp and the hill strongpoints on the east bank would require gaining control of a wide margin of no-man's-land, which on the northern front was flat and open. The sapping tactics employed at Béatrice and Gabrielle would have to be extended on a vast scale. A sap is simply a trench – a narrow ditch deep enough to give shelter from enemy fire, and sometimes roofed over for part of its length – which is dug towards the enemy's positions. It offers only a narrow target for the defenders' artillery, and it zig-zags at short intervals to protect the diggers from lengthways fire. The spoil is thrown up on the exposed side to make a parapet, and historically the advancing head of the sap might be protected with earth-filled baskets – replaced in modern times by sandbags. When the sap reaches close to the enemy's defences it is used by assault infantry for their approach, reducing to a minimum the lethal moments they have to spend exposed above ground during their last rush. Digging siege entrenchments is exhausting and dangerous work, traditionally hated by infantrymen; but if a disciplined army can turn enough hands to the task then trenches can advance across open ground surprisingly quickly. The Viet Minh were highly disciplined, and had plenty of hands available.

Giap's order of the day for 20 March included this passage: 'Certain comrades are worried about asking our soldiers, already tired, to work to consolidate our lines, fearing to harass them and reduce their fighting spirit...' The rhythm of work involved may have justified such fears, but the Viet Minh's discipline and motivation were equal to it. Their trenching, like their fighting, was accomplished by night. One publication quotes an officer of Division 312:

> The soldiers know perfectly well what to expect – tens of consecutive nights without sleep, and one or two dead in every unit every night. The consolidation of strongpoints and shelters needed great quantities of wood, only available from kilometres deep in the forest. The orders were given: 'No trenches, no battle – Dien Bien Phu is trench warfare.' They worked without ever complaining. The timetable was unchanging:

return to unit area at 7am or 8am, eat, attend a work review meeting, then sleep from 9am to noon; cut and carry timber from noon until 3pm; another meal; then head for the trenches with picks and shovels, and work until long after sunrise.

We need not believe literally in only three hours' sleep in 24 to recognize that an exhausting tempo was maintained.[34]

On the alluvial plain of Dien Bien Phu an army of peasant farmers could make fast progress, and a French prisoner was able to observe the organization of the leading teams:

In utter silence and complete darkness, a survey team marked out the line of a trench every [20ins] with bamboo pegs which showed up on the darkest night. Close to each peg a second team scoured out an emplacement for a prone man, throwing up the spoil on the most dangerous side. A third team proceeded to deepen these holes to a man's height, and then join them up. So many men were used that a considerable distance was accomplished in one night.[35]

The diggings involved not only approach trenches from areas of cover towards the French wire, but also lateral communication trenches, shelters with overhead protection for infantry and support weapons, ammunition dumps and aid posts.

The aerial photos dropped into the camp every day soon revealed spiderwebs of new trenches on both northern and eastern flanks. On 18 March trenches about 1,000yds south of the Elianes had reached as far west as the river, marking the first serious obstacle to communications with Isabelle; and on the 19th others were spotted in front of Dominique 1 and 2. What aerial photos could not reveal were the camouflaged RCL and machine-gun positions being tunnelled into the slopes of Phoney and Baldy facing Eliane 2. On 20 March on Dominique 2, Sergeant Chief Cadiou's 425 CSM, a platoon of *supplétifs* from Phat Diem who were attached to III/3 RTA, came under fire from 57mm RCLs when they tried to halt work on the approaching trenches.[36] Out beyond the airfield, by 24 March a sap was within 50yds of the wire at Huguette 7, while other trenches multiplied opposite the western face of the camp.

Colonel de Castries naturally wished to hamper this work: local attacks to fill in the diggings and sow mines were carried out by various units on 24, 25 and 27 March, but with frustrating results. The filled-in trenches were simply re-dug the next night, and subsequent raids were met by pre-registered machine-gun and mortar fire. French artillery and mortars did not seem to slow down the trenching appreciably; the gangs were hard to locate despite flares, and usually revealed themselves only by the noise of their digging.[37]

DURING THIS SECOND PHASE of the battle, which lasted from 18 to 30 March against the background of parallel efforts by both sides to reinforce and resupply, patrol clashes took place outside the strongpoint perimeters – and sometimes with infiltrators well inside the camp – on most nights. As the noose of trenches tightened during the last week of the month daytime encounters developed into fiercer actions involving several companies and the tank platoons. The physical link between the main camp and Isabelle had to be maintained at the cost of almost daily road-opening skirmishes, which became steadily more serious. A simultaneous struggle to keep the air bridge open continued under selective but accurate Viet Minh shelling; and increasingly dangerous AA positions began to spread down the western and eastern flanks.

On 18 March, Lieutenant Rondeaux's 1st Company, 5 BPVN relieved Captain Desiré's 9th Company, BT 3 in Huguette 7 (though the latter had indeed proved solid). On Eliane 4, Major Bigeard learned that an officer of 6 BPC had been ordered to report to Lieutenant Colonel Langlais. Countermanding the instruction, he hobbled into the command bunker (he had sprained his ankle when he landed) and demanded that any orders for 6th Colonial were to be given through him alone. The two paratroop officers did not know each other, and both bristled with fury for a moment before Langlais lightened the mood: pointing to a solid roof pillar, he suggested that they both bang their heads against it: 'You're from Lorraine? I'm a Breton. Let's see who has the hardest skull!' Bigeard laughed; and from that moment on the two men would work together in harmony.[38]

Under cover of the morning fog, cutting and welding teams of Major Sudrat's engineers managed to repair enough of the shellholes in the PSP of the runway – reduced to 600 usable yards – to open it up again to 1,000yds. At 11.55am Lieutenant Biswang of GT 2/62 landed Dakota 'P'tit

Loups Zulu Sierra', and managed to take off for Muong Sai with a full load of 23 wounded. During the day two helicopter missions were attempted, drawing fire and evacuating only one casualty. The night of 18/19 March marked the successful introduction of new tactics – credited by Bernard Fall to Major Guérin – that enabled no fewer than four more Dakotas to land and take off with 19 casualties each. Dakotas approached in pairs, and one would fly over the valley as a noise decoy while the second drifted in from the south with all lights extinguished, the pilot peering out for a few shrouded runway lamps which were visible only from the correct angle and altitude. He then slipped down with engines almost feathered, and as the C-47 touched down the ambulances followed it north along the runway until it stopped and swung round to face south for take-off. Just five minutes were allowed for loading the wounded; then the Dakota throttled up for its take-off run, the noise covered by the sound of co-ordinated fire from the French artillery.[39]

During the last week of March, General Navarre criticized what he saw as a certain lassitude in the performance of the Air Force. The Généchef did not concern himself with such details as mandatory periodic engine maintenance; and it was unfortunate that during his visit to Cat Bi on 27 March an Air Force and a Navy officer had a violent altercation about the relative number of flying hours being logged by crews of the two services. General Lauzin vigorously rejected what he considered as an insult to his air and ground crews. As for the transport pilots, Colonel Nicot pointed out that the fleet was now logging 7,200 flying hours per month, a huge increase from 3,700 before 13 March.[40] This meant that each crew was averaging 94 hours per month, the equivalent of a sortie to Dien Bien Phu every single day; and in fact many crews were flying to the valley and back twice in a day. Since the 17th, Nicot had ordered them to drop cargo from safer altitudes than the optimum 650ft: 4,900ft was reckoned – usually correctly – to be out of reach of heavy machine guns, and 6,500ft – wrongly – the maximum range of the 37mm cannon. Some pilots continued to fly lower than these theoretically safe heights, however, and even above them many aircraft were still hit. As already mentioned, the accurate 'slant' range of the Russian 37mm gun was in fact more than 9,000ft and its shells did not auto-destruct until they had travelled another mile, so it is not surprising to read of some Dakotas being hit at 10,000ft.

Dropping from higher altitude had, of course, an attendant penalty in the wider scattering of loads and the consequent difficulty of recovering them – the higher a parachute opens, the more time it has to drift off the drop zone. The obvious answer was a delayed parachute opening device, but in 1954 these 'Timecutters' were available only in the USA and even there in small numbers. The air resupply staff in Hanoi began an intense search for a local solution, without waiting for General Cogny to pass the requirement up official channels. When he did so, on 26 March, the problem was already close to at least a makeshift solution, but the reply he received from General Navarre reveals the temperature at which their relationship was now conducted: 'I am amazed that you, responsible for the conduct and support of the battle of Dien Bien Phu, have waited until 26 March to face the problem of high-altitude parachute resupply and to alert me to your difficulties in this regard...'[41]

ON 18 MARCH COLONEL DE Castries ordered that in future those killed in action were to be buried on the spot. Inevitable delays in burying the dead in the designated cemetery had caused a horrifying stench and infestation of flies, and the graveyard and nearby open-air morgue area had been hit by shellfire with repulsive consequences. In future those who died in and around the hospital would be interred in mass graves scooped out by a bulldozer. The casualty rate even at quiet times was perhaps ten killed and 40 wounded each day by random fire.[42] With 'casevac' flights taking out an average of only a couple of dozen per night, the hospital was now treating some 500 wounded, and the hygienic disposal of piles of amputated limbs was sometimes a problem. A daily casualty report to Hanoi for one of the Legion battalions gives an idea of the typical trade coming into Dr Grauwin's dug-outs during a time of only intermittent shelling and no major assaults: 'Légionnaire Albus, Jean, killed by shell to head. Poualin, Pierre, wounded abdomen. Vaucher, Georges, killed. Sweibert, Stanislas, wounded thorax. Echevarry, Joue, wounded thorax. Collin, Hubert, wounded legs and left side. Gravenbrouck, Joseph, wounded right testicle. Schultz, Heinz, wounded left calf, multiple gasoline burns. Putters, Jean, wounded neck. Zirkel, Karl, wounded left shoulder, left pectoral, right thigh. Bressan, André, wounded right calf.'[43]

On 19 March, General Cogny broadcast to the Viet Minh in clear, announcing that a Red Cross aircraft would be landing to pick up wounded; this was not acknowledged, and nor were several other broadcasts over the coming days. The C-47, flown by Lieutenant Biswang of GT 2/62, was fired upon but managed to embark 23 casualties and get off again; two others, circling above, did not land. Five helicopter missions from Muong Sai were successful, though one H-19 was hit and damaged; but since the 'hélicos' could carry only four or five casualties their impact on the problem was strictly limited.[44] Some of these missions were seen by Viet Minh observers to be evacuating the unwounded but stranded Bearcat pilots of GC 1/22; the CO of the Combined Army Helicopter Unit (GFHAT) would later claim that this visible violation of the Red Cross led directly to further casualties among his crews.[45]

The Aéronavale put four Hellcats over the valley that day in the usual attempts to find and silence artillery; the CO of 11F, Castelbajac, lost his hydraulics to an AA hit and had to belly-land back at Cat Bi. However, on the night of 19/20 March the Air Force achieved a triumph which encouraged everyone: Lieutenant Colonel Descaves led a flight of Dakotas from GT 2/62 of which five managed to land, pick up a total of 95 casualties, and take off safely.[46]

THE BEARCAT MECHANICS AND other remaining Air Force personnel who were not needed to assist Major Guérin's air controllers were now attached to 4th Company, 1 BEP and issued infantry weapons. This was a trivial example of a significant process: during this invaluable lull between major assaults, 'Gars Pierre' was rationalizing the defences and putting every man he could find where he would be of the best use. Lieutenant Colonel Langlais ordered two new strongpoints constructed to north and south on the west bank of the river, to build some depth into the northern and eastern defences; they would also give true defensive positions to the paratroop counter-attack battalions, whose previous locations had been little more than heavily dug-in bivouac areas. In the north, between the southern end of the airfield and the Nam Youm, the old Dominique 4 was to be partially replaced by the new 'Epervier' ('Sparrowhawk'), held by Captain Tourret's 8th Shock. The south-east area of the central camp, Claudine 6, was now to be separated off as the new strongpoint 'Junon' ('Juno') for Major Guiraud's légionnaires of 1 BEP, together with some White Thais and Captain Jean Charnot's newly armed Air Force men (*see Map 11*).[47]

On 19 March, Langlais went to inspect Lieutenant Redon's quad-50s; he needed more firepower to support the Elianes, and decided to divide Redon's four mounts into two sections of two. This experimental unit had been undermanned from the start – Redon had just two senior NCOs and three telephone operators, plus four crews each consisting of a Vietnamese corporal chief and four men; now he found himself training six Legion paras drafted from Guiraud's battalion. The quad-50s now ceased to be controlled by the artillery's central PC Feux. To cover the Elianes one pair of mounts, under Redon, was towed south and installed at Junon, where Major Vadot put more men of I/13 DBLE at his disposal for heavy lifting. Warrant Officer Lemeur's section were given the new Legion paratroopers, a jeep for fetching ammunition and an SCR300 radio, and installed in Epervier to support the Dominiques.[48]

All over the exposed strongpoints during the third and fourth weeks of March men dug new communications trenches, previously neglected. For lack of anything better, tons of earth were shovelled on to the roofs of shelters, command posts and blockhouses. Field telephone lines were mended and buried deeper, and by night minefields were extended; Major Sudrat's two companies from 31 BG worked until they dropped. Mines were laid particularly (and under fire) on the approaches between Baldy and Eliane 2.[49] Patrols, morning road-opening and trench raids often produced local victories, and at night snipers equipped with infra-red sights and projectors lay out in wait for careless enemy sappers or commandos.[50] All these efforts gradually steadied morale at unit level: at least the garrison were doing something practical to help themselves, and during the lulls in the much less frequent shellfire they could cook hot meals and sometimes snatch a quick bathe in the Nam Youm.

A slight change in mood was even detectable in Colonel de Castries' exchanges with General Cogny; on 19 March he was as pessimistic as he had been on the 15th, but in the last week of the month a restored determination – though little actual confidence – was apparent. Writing of his men, he noted then that after the first shocks morale among the best of them – of all races – had hardened. Castries claimed to notice a reduction in what he defined as the 'inevitable' difference in morale between the

Viet Minh, a national army fighting for independence on its own territory, and French professional troops honouring their contracts far from home.[51] Of Lieutenant Colonel Langlais, Castries would write on 22 March that he 'has been remarkable – he took the defence in hand, reshaped it, and helped me greatly in lifting morale. I have designated him as my successor [i.e. in case Castries became a casualty]... but he has the faults of his qualities...' By this he no doubt meant Langlais' adversarial style of discussion with fellow officers: there would be tales of glasses of whisky thrown in faces and demands that disagreements be settled with fists. General Cogny's carefully worded testimony to the commission of inquiry would make clear that 'Gars Pierre' was a splendid fighter who nevertheless found it difficult to submit his opinions to questioning by his superiors in rank, let alone by anyone else.[52]

ON 20 MARCH, COLONEL PIROTH'S replacement, Lieutenant Colonel Guy Vaillant, was slipped into the camp on an ambulance aircraft. A survivor of cruel Japanese captivity in 1945, he had accepted the appointment despite being the widowed father of nine children. Vaillant was a Colonial officer, 49 years old but very fit, with long, mobile, humorous features and an affable though rather scholarly manner; his quiet realism inspired confidence.[53] Two days later Colonel de Castries would report: 'The artillery is improving – it had great need to...'[54]

Vaillant had not yet taken control when it was decided that the 155mm battery, which had been moved forward to Eliane 10 (where it had received no enemy fire, but appeared vulnerable to night raids by Viet Minh commandos), should be brought back to Claudine. Captain Déal would have preferred the cover of the morning fog, but was ordered to move that afternoon. On regaining their old positions the 11th Battery found that their crew and ammunition shelters – the latter particularly important for the 155's separately packed propellant charges – had been demolished for roofing materials by neighbouring units. They were still digging in and re-laying telephone lines when they received a fire mission. Déal explained why he needed an hour's delay, but the infantry commander insisted. The enemy artillery replied instantly to the first salvoes, and a shell fell among uncovered charges, killing three men and wounding others including Sergeant Chief Pierrel.[55]

Despite being themselves short of ammunition, the People's Army artillery seemed to give priority to shelling the French howitzers whenever they opened fire. Because of the obvious importance of safeguarding the daily air-drops the French gunners were instructed to concentrate on locating and shelling enemy 37mm flak positions, but this was extremely difficult. Although General Cogny ordered that each day's aerial photos should reach Colonel de Castries before nightfall this was hardly practical, since the habitual morning fog always delayed EROM 80's missions; indeed, 20 March was one of the days when weather conditions prevented the mission entirely. The only other reconnaissance resource was the flight of six Morane Criquets based at Muong Sai – 23 GAOA, reinforced by escaped crews from Dien Bien Phu's destroyed 21 GAOA.

Muong Sai was a primitive post with a new Dakota airstrip roughly scraped out beside a Meo village on a little plateau 2,300ft above sea level surrounded by jungle-clad peaks, some 80 air miles across the mountains south-west from Dien Bien Phu. The round-trip flight to the valley took two hours for the underpowered Criquets, so providing any continuity of observation required three Moranes to be in the air at any one time. After the fall of Gabrielle their spotting missions became lethally dangerous due to their low speed and altitude and the growing menace of AA fire, and consequently few useful results were recorded. Merely crossing the mountains was hazardous enough due to the uncertain weather, radio reception and navigation, and the Morane's practical ceiling of 3,900ft. On 19 March, Lieutenants Le Coz and Asselineau were given up for lost after five hours' absence in a storm so violent that at Muong Sai enormous hailstones holed the wings of parked Moranes; they eventually turned up on foot, having successfully crash-landed in the forest nearly ten miles away.

THE ABILITY TO MAINTAIN a constant flow of parachuted supplies was now fundamental to GONO's survival, and the basic problems of time and volume may be expressed in simple arithmetic. To consider only the C-47s that made up the great bulk of Colonel Nicot's fleet: a night's drop of say 100 tons involved 40 Dakotas. With a payload of about 2½ tons, each C-47 could drop some 25 packages of 220lbs each. These awkward parcels, weighing as much as a refrigerator, had to be manhandled out of the side door by the despatchers, which took a great deal longer than it did for a stick of paratroopers to jump out. Even while the large cargo drop zone (DZ Octavie) was still in use, only a proportion of the packages could be dropped in the time it took a C-47 to overfly the DZ, and a lot fewer once drops began over the battalion locations themselves (*see below*). Consequently each aircraft had to make as many as 12, sometimes even 15 separate circuits – and all the time potentially under enemy AA fire.[56] Some criticisms of the Dakota crews apparently failed to take into account the strain involved in turning back for a straight and level pass on a predictable course through the maelstrom of tracer bullets and shell flashes for, say, the tenth time that night, perhaps after being hit on an earlier pass. A total of 111 Dakotas would land with flak damage between 13 March and 7 May, apart from the four that were shot down.

Once on the ground, the total of around 1,000 separate packages had to be found, unharnessed, broken down and loaded on trucks during the hours of darkness and morning fog when the DZ gangs were free from observed – though not from random – enemy fire. The difficulty of accomplishing this led GONO to request on 18 March that in future some cargoes be dropped over six smaller DZs close to the battalion locations where they could be recovered directly by the troops, reserving a main DZ on the airfield for those loads needed in the central camp – e.g by the artillery, counter-attack force and hospital.[57] This system decentralized the problem but did not solve it, since drops near the perimeter strongpoints were more likely to be lost or to land under the gunsights of the enemy.

A major difficulty was, of course, the supply of parachutes. Their use at this rate – about 1,000 per day – had never been foreseen, and since they could not be returned after use the stock diminished rapidly; aerial photos of the camp show an ever increasing scatter of tiny white dots all over the landscape. By 20 March FTNV's Deputy Chief-of-Staff/Logistics, Major Baubeau, had been informed that only eight days' supply remained. The American MAAG in Saigon, now headed by General O'Daniel, were approached for help, and 'Iron Mike' responded with energy and generosity to this, as to every other French request during the battle. In a matter of hours he had organized an airlift of some 60,000 parachutes from bases in Japan and the Philippines; this was close to the total number used at Dien Bien Phu after 13 March. Lieutenant Colonel Pellerin, the theatre air resupply commander, was able to meet all demand from then on, although his two CRA companies at the Delta airfields were kept to a frantic pace of work – the pairs of women packers achieved a rate of one parachute every seven minutes. A massive programme of local procurement was also needed to manufacture all the packing and harnessing materials needed for the tens of thousands of cargo packages.[58]

BEFORE DAWN ON 21 MARCH a blast from out on the runway near Huguette 1 announced that a People's Army demolition commando had evaded the French patrols in the early hours; infiltrators had also thrown propaganda appeals into the positions of North African units. Judging that their most likely route in had been along RP41 between Dominique 1 and 2, Langlais ordered the construction of a blocking position in this gap. The 2nd Company, 5 BPVN were given the unenviable task of digging rudimentary trenches protected by meagre wire and a few mines, but this 'Dominique 6' was little more than a guard post (*see Map 14*).

During that day various outposts reported fleeting contacts, but the most significant action was triggered by the usual morning operation to keep the road open between the main camp and Isabelle. On the 19th the road-openers had encountered no trouble despite the evidence of trenching; but on the 20th commissars had warned villagers in the area to leave, and on the 21st the Viet Minh inserted a strong blocking force at Ban Kho Lai, the halfway point (*see Map 9*). Breaking through took most of the afternoon and the support of two tank platoons under Warrant Officer Carette from Claudine and Lieutenant Préaud from Isabelle. The cost was five dead, two missing and five wounded, the latter including a Legion sub-lieutenant named Alain Gambiez. A major operation to clear the Isabelle road was planned for the next day. That evening a senior general was making an overflight in a Dakota: Fernand Gambiez, Navarre's chief-of-staff. When his tasks were completed he asked the pilot of 'P'tit Loups Zulu Sierra', Lieutenant Biswang of GT 2/62, to fly over Isabelle. The plane took two AA hits, but it was the nearest he could get to his son, lying in Dr Rézillot's dug-out hospital.[59] After dark a patrol from I/2 REI had an inconclusive clash on the airfield; another completely disappeared between Huguette 7 and Francoise. Major Bigeard took part of 6 BPC on a strong overnight reconnaissance north up RP41; they ran into trouble close to Dominique and it took mortars and artillery to shoot them free before the early morning fog lifted.

The same day saw the first trials at Hanoi of a prototype delayed-opening device for cargo parachutes. The French forces had previously ordered a clockwork retarder (the 'Hesitator') from Japan, but this was not yet ready and its design was anyway too complex for mass production. A requirement for a device capable of rapid local production was issued on 19 March, and the first tests took place on the 21st. This remarkable speed of response was achieved by Lieutenant Deu of the Hanoi parachute main-tenance and packing platoon, with Captain Masson, an FTNV munitions specialist. The retarder was a detonator which cut a restraining strap around the canopy after a set delay; initiation was simply by measured lengths of slowmatch set alight by a friction igniter at the moment the cargo was dropped to fall free, and two detonators in cardboard housings were fixed to each parachute. Series production was ordered on 28 March at a rate of 1,000 per day, which was soon doubled. Finding local workshops able to make what was essentially a firework was not difficult in a country which celebrated Chinese festivals; materials were more of a problem. Daily requirements of 2,150sq ft of cardboard alone meant ransacking every military and commercial source – in particular those of the Bastos Cigarettes factory. Between 28 March and 8 May the unceasing production lines turned out 71,000 retarders, using up 50 miles of slowmatch, 140,000 igniters, and unguessable quantities of adhesive tape, hooks, cords, and luminous paint for night drops.[60] The retarders were first used on 28 March, for loads dropped from about 3,900ft with 25-second fuses. About half the loads went astray, and these devices were never more than a stopgap; throughout their use the failure rate was between 15 and 20 per cent, with canopies either 'Roman candling' or failing to open altogether, and a large minority nearly always drifted into the hands of the People's Army.[61]

THE MAIN BUSINESS OF 22 MARCH was the attempt by a strong force from 1 BEP, supported by Sergeant Chief Ney's tank platoon, to win back control of the road to Isabelle. The terrain south of Dien Bien Phu was mostly rice paddies divided by low dykes, with large areas of scrub and trees and the newly deserted native villages all offering plentiful cover. About halfway down to Isabelle, some 1.8 miles south of the camp, the

Huong Duoi Ta stream crossed RP41 at the twin villages of Ban Kho Lai and Ban Nang Nhai; and here Regiment 57 from Division 304 had thrown two trenches across the road. At about 7.30am the Legion paras came up against strong opposition from two Viet Minh companies, and despite their tank support they were unable to break through or effectively outflank the blockade. They were reinforced from Isabelle by Thai auxiliaries, Algerians from II/1 RTA and Henri Préaud's three Chaffees; but the Viet Minh stood and fought for nearly five hours, and it was not until Warrant Officer Carette's tank platoon from Claudine was released to join 1 BEP that they finally cleared the trenches and the village in the early afternoon. Only nine prisoners were taken, but Regiment 57 left 175 dead on the field. The French casualties were significant – 15 dead and 72 wounded.[62]

While the fight was still raging at Ban Kho Lai on the morning of 22 March, reinforcements for the artillery at Isabelle parachuted in – Lieutenant Yziquel with 15 men from GM/35 RALP. At 10pm that night Lieutenant Arbelet of GT 1/64 landed his Dakota and had taken aboard a full load of wounded when, from the darkness of the airfield, a stream of light machine-gun fire from an enemy infiltration patrol struck his cockpit. He was wounded in both legs, and his flight engineer was also injured; but Dr Grauwin patched them up, and under cover of the dawn mist on the 23rd the aircraft took off, followed by another flown by Lieutenant Rousselot and carrying 25 wounded.[63]

On 23 March the commander of Helldiver squadron 3F, Lieutenant Commander Andrieux, limped back to Bach Mai after taking a hit while diving on AA positions; no doubt his pilots offered him a restorative bowl of rice. This colourful officer was nicknamed 'Nha Que' (the term for a Vietnamese peasant) from his habitual diet and his precaution of wearing black Vietnamese 'pyjamas' under his flying suit, in case he had to evade capture.

A more serious setback that day was the loss to shellfire of Warrant Officer Bartier's H-19 at Isabelle, which led to an order halting all helicopter 'casevac' flights. The following day Castries' report would criticize the helicopter crews for putting down wherever they liked without taking note of the preparations made on the ground, which seems to have been at least part of the problem on this occasion. On the 23rd, Lieutenant Colonel

Lalande and Dr Rézillot at Isabelle had made everything ready for the arrival of a sortie; at 10am the approach of three helicopters was announced, but they apparently failed to check in with Major Guérin's air controllers before landing in the wrong place, ignoring light and hand signals from the ground. Bartier's crew left their machine and entered the hospital, becoming separated – one had a letter for Dr Rézillot. As shells began to fall near by the pilot was ordered to take off and move to the designated LZ, but he wandered off looking for his co-pilot, and before they could lift off their H-19 was destroyed. The crew survived, but patients had already been loaded: Sub-lieutenant Alain Gambiez, the general's son, was among those who were burned to death.[64]

The Sikorsky helicopters and their crews were neither equipped nor trained for night navigation across the mountains; but Captain Fauroux and his co-pilot Captain Butor suggested a way of resuming the evacuation flights. The idea was that several H-19s would fly in to Dien Bien Phu in late afternoon, timing their landings on prepared LZs for nightfall. Loaded with casualties under cover of darkness, they would take off individually, linking up again south of Dien Bien Phu to be guided to Luang Prabang by a Dakota. A trial was flown at Muong Sai on the night of 27 March, using a landing ground of the right size lit only by four shrouded lamps; to simulate a load of casualties Fauroux and Butor embarked two sergeant pilots, Henriot and Fillipi, and a mechanic, Sergeant Dehaux. Circling in the darkness to gain height, the helicopter crashed into a jungle-covered peak and all five men were killed.[65]

BAN KHO LAI, THE FIRST undeniable victory since 13 March, lifted French morale, and Colonel de Castries took satisfaction in reporting it to Hanoi at a time when the steady encroachment of enemy trenches was causing him growing concern. He returned to his fear, which had been quite widespread among French officers before 13 March, that Giap might choose to invest the camp so closely that he could 'stifle' it – prevent any useful activity, without risking further general assaults. Castries was also deeply worried about the rapidly accumulating casualties in the cramped hospital dug-outs; although he praised the 'sensational' Dakota pilots, the garrison's morale was inevitably affected by the failure to evacuate all the seriously wounded. He ended his signal to Cogny of 23 March: 'My resources and possibilities are now pretty near what they were on the 18th, and I don't see them improving unless the enemy's determination is itself worn down somehow... Without some new factor which I cannot foresee, I believe the situation can only get worse.'[66]

During the second half of March continued efforts were made to support Dien Bien Phu with air strikes on the surrounding siege army. GATAC/Nord was still handicapped by limited resources and simultaneous responsibility for interdiction of the Viet Minh supply routes, missions over Dien Bien Phu itself, and the continuing operations in the Delta. In all, between 13 and 25 March the two B-26 bomber squadrons flew 313 sorties over the valley; the Bearcats from the Plain of Jars flew 74 sorties, and the Navy's Hellcats and Helldivers a total of 250 – a typically high work rate by the *Arromanches* air group. By (inexact) comparison, there were only 39 sorties by B-26s over the Delta during the month of March, but 454 by Bearcats; and the 'battle of the roads' was more or less abandoned during the second half of the month, to the benefit of General Giap's logistics.[67]

The inadequacy of conventional means led the Air Force to experiment with unorthodox missions. The most valuable way to support the garrison would be to hit the People's Army in the nearby concentration areas where they rested and received supplies, and to burn off the cover around their artillery batteries. It was suggested that the weakness in conventional bombers might be made up by using transport aircraft to drop drums of napalm on the surrounding slopes. Between 20 and 26 March, C-47s flew 23 such sorties. Colonel Nicot, who naturally resented this drain on his overstretched command, reported that Dakotas were entirely unsuitable: there was no means of securing the drums safely, no means of aiming them, and in the absence of enough armourers unqualified volunteers had to be used as despatchers to wrestle the delay-fused drums out of the doors, with a consequently high level of risk. Nevertheless, the high command were apparently impressed by the early experiments, and in all Dakotas would fly 35 napalm sorties.

On 23 March it was decided to add the C-119's greater capacity to this project. Captain Soulat, the senior French C-119 pilot, chose French crews for two three-plane flights, and these received some rudimentary instruction by Lieutenant Mainguy, a B-26 navigator/bombardier. Taking off from Cat Bi late that afternoon, Lieutenant Clairé's No. 186 briefly came unstuck before thundering back on to the concrete and sliding for hundreds of yards on its belly in a terrifying shower of sparks: through a misunderstanding between pilot and co-pilot the undercarriage had been retracted too soon. Miraculously, neither the 1,500 gallons in the tanks nor the four tons of napalm in the cargo bay caught fire. The other five Packets flew to Dien Bien Phu at 13,000ft, led by Soulat and Mainguy in No. 136. When the tail doors opened and let in the roaring darkness the despatchers had the delicate task of unhitching the drums and getting them out into the cold void without fouling the detonator safety wires. The target was calculated by crude dead reckoning; and though a spectacular bloom of flame was seen, there was no way of evaluating the results. The short-lived blaze was apparently watched from the ground by Langlais and the newly arrived Lieutenant Colonels Lemeunier and Voinot.[68]

Subsequent missions over the next several days (the C-119s flew 78 napalm sorties in all) would produce the same lack of verifiable results. This experiment diverted transport aircraft from more urgent tasks; and several missions were aborted at the last minute, requiring the hazardous unloading of the napalm drums on the crowded airbases. There was at least one incident of a detonator safety wire being snagged during a flight, starting the delay fuse and requiring the pilot – luckily alerted at once – to break formation and dump his load.[69]

In this last week of March, Colonel Nicot's crews did not need any additional ways to risk their lives. On 24 March the C-47 flown by Captain Koenig of GT 1/64 was shot down in flames over Dien Bien Phu. On the 26th his squadron mate Captain Boeglin was forced by heavy flak damage to land his Dakota on Isabelle's airstrip, where enemy artillery soon destroyed it. That morning Lieutenant Héquet of GT 2/62 brought 'P'tit Loups Zulu Zulu' home from Dien Bien Phu with six hits, one of which set fire to the clothing of his despatcher; the same afternoon Héquet, now flying 'Zulu Sierra' over the Delta, was hit again eight times. On 27 March, No. 267 'Négros Novembre Kilo' of GT 2/63, flown by Captain Dartigues, was hit above Eliane 3 while coming in for his second casualty evacuation mission of the day; flames were seen streaming from the starboard engine before it crashed. Lieutenant Héquet's 'Zulu Kilo' was hit at 10,000ft; Captain Desailly's 'Zulu Delta' was hit twice and suffered an oil leak, and Lieutenant Ruffray's 'Zulu Coca' was also damaged. The previous night Captain Bouguereau of 2/62 had succeeded in taking 19 casualties out; on the 28th this veteran of several night evacuations was mortally wounded during a routine mission over the post at Kha Ly in the Delta. From that date the transport pilots began to be issued with body armour, the weight of the American 'flak jacket' adding to the discomfort of parachute, pistol and survival kit.[70]

JUST AFTER 7AM ON THE MORNING of 24 March, Lieutenant Colonel Keller, Castries' chief-of-staff who had suffered a nervous breakdown, was quietly flown out in an ambulance aircraft. The previous day the final member of the group of replacement staff officers, Lieutenant Colonel Voinot, had arrived by helicopter. This morning was therefore a natural time for a command conference in Castries' headquarters on the future conduct of the defence.

That thought tends to soften the colours of Bernard Fall's description of an incident which has taken its place among the legends of Dien Bien Phu. Whether this notorious '*putsch* of the paratroop mafia' ever took place in the terms that Fall quotes can never be known, due to the death or discretion of the participants. Quoting unnamed staff officers who were supposedly present, Fall states that Lieutenant Colonel Langlais and the commanders of the parachute battalions entered Castries' office 'fully armed' and announced that 'henceforth the effective command of the fortress would be in [Langlais'] own hands, but that as far as the outside world was concerned Castries would retain the appearance of command and would serve as an intermediary between the paratroop commanders and Hanoi.'[71]

Fall follows this dramatic passage by admitting that no other account supports it; that no formal passing of authority occurred; that Castries raised no objection; and that the relationship between Langlais and Castries remained excellent on both sides. It would be intriguing to know Fall's unidentified sources for this scene; the naked failure of Castries' staff must have hung shamefully in the air of GONO headquarters, and Pierre Langlais' abrasive bluntness cannot have left many hiding places for bruised self-esteem. Social class was still a real factor in the French Army of the 1950s, and there were some who regarded rough and ready paratroop officers with disdain. It is easy to believe that Langlais might also have expressed himself robustly to the officers newly flown in by FTNV, perhaps assuming that they were infected by the Olympian culture of the Hanoi Citadel. Langlais and Voinot certainly clashed, but the former later apologized and they reportedly worked well together thereafter. Fall notes that both of them continued to make up a four for bridge with Castries and Lieutenant Colonel Lemeunier every evening when circumstances permitted.[72]

The essential fact would seem to be that – perhaps after frank exchanges of views between the less than fully informed newcomers and an impatiently opinionated Langlais – the latter was now formally recognized as Castries' chief of operations. This simply put on a regular footing a situation which already existed in practice. This was the function which Langlais had been fulfilling since succeeding Gaucher in command of the central sector of the camp on the evening of 13 March. His responsibility for counter-attacks had been clearly specified in Castries' orders as early as 19 December; in the confusion of 13–15 March fine distinctions of role had become meaningless, and Langlais (and the staff of GAP 2) had assumed wider duties under the pressure of events.[73] That Langlais had retained them was a natural consequence of Castries' deferring to his much greater experience of positional infantry fighting, at a time when the death or dereliction of other officers robbed the GONO commander of the support he needed, and when his message traffic reveals his own sagging morale. His satisfaction with Langlais' expanded role is obvious from his comments on 22 March, quoted above.

As for the Cromwellian guard of battalion commanders described by Fall's source, the mention of the fact that they were armed is disingenuous at best – every combat officer at Dien Bien Phu went armed. It is not hard to understand the fears that might have prompted the paratroopers to crowd into the underground headquarters. The first disastrous 36 hours had seen collapse and indecision; but a week ago Dien Bien Phu had found the fighting man it needed. 'Gars Pierre' made decisions, and gave clear orders in language they understood; he took a grip on the defence, and gave them back some hope and self-belief. Concern that he might be shuffled aside by these new colonels whom Hanoi were slipping into the camp would surely be understandable. There is a lot of difference between exasperated soldiers in the grip of suspicion, and potential mutineers; but this difference may not seem so clear in a dimly lit cavern suddenly full of camouflage uniforms, blued steel and testosterone.

The new system which emerged on 24 March and took effect from the 27th does not look particularly smooth on paper, but was lubricated in practice by the personalities involved. (From this point on the senior figures seem to have agreed to drop most formal considerations of rank, and their conversations relaxed into the familiar *'tutoiement'* – a meaningful gesture for Frenchmen of their generation.) In practical terms Groupes Mobiles 6 and 9 had ceased to exist as separate entities, but Lieutenant Colonel Lalande's command of Isabelle was unaffected. Under Colonel de Castries, Lieutenant Colonel Langlais was the operations commander of the defence, with Lieutenant Colonel Lemeunier as his deputy, and Major Bigeard responsible for launching counter-attacks under Langlais' direction. From the former HQ bunker of GM 9, Langlais exercised personal command of operations in the eastern sector (the Dominiques and Elianes) and authority over the tanks and quad-50s. The western sector (the Huguettes) was taken over by Lieutenant Colonel Voinot, working from Lieutenant Colonel Trancart's former office in the main HQ. Major de Seguin-Pazzis retained command of GAP 2. Colonel de Castries signed a copy of these orders and sent them to Hanoi, where they raised only administrative eyebrows.

Jules Roy cruelly compares Colonel de Castries to a 'broken spring', but the respect and courtesy shown him by Langlais – and warmly returned – hardly supports this.[74] That he recognized his own limitations and Langlais' talents, and refused to hide behind his rank, surely did him credit. He was a cavalry officer, and armoured cavalry fight dispersed; his whole experience of command had accustomed him to giving his subordinates objectives and leaving them to make tactical decisions. It has been raised against him that he did not often leave the headquarters bunker and show himself to the troops in the strongpoints and hospitals; but everyone deals with the stress of battle in the way that works for him, and nobody who served with Christian de Castries ever cast doubt on his physical courage.

Questioned about Castries' role by the subsequent commission of inquiry, Langlais – never a man for the subtle choice of words – replied that 'he transmitted our messages to Hanoi', and these words were quoted mercilessly against Castries ever afterwards. Even taking them at face value, it is not impossible to imagine that they might have been meant thankfully rather than dismissively. Langlais was a goal-obsessed paratrooper, impatient to get on with running his battle without reference to anybody, least of all FTNV; he needed the more senior officer and smoother advocate to keep Hanoi off his back, and hoped that Castries' easy relationship with General Cogny would help GONO get the men and supplies it needed. In fact, Castries' contribution was far greater than that: he and Langlais worked together very closely, and Castries continued to shoulder the whole responsibility for the camp's daily survival – including the vital logistic aspects – while Langlais concentrated solely on deploying the combat units.

The scope of this relatively junior officer's authority over the operations of what was in effect an entire division may have been extraordinary, but the tone of Langlais' own comment on his situation is characteristic. In his memoir he wrote: 'Although I was only a simple paratroop lieutenant-colonel at the beginning of the battle, I had directly under my orders 10,000 men; but nobody in Hanoi or elsewhere sought to replace me in that handsome command, even though it would have been easy enough to get to Dien Bien Phu with a parachute on one's back – or indeed, until 29 March, in an aircraft.'[75]

GENERALS COGNY AND NAVARRE were hardly likely to concern themselves with any internal arrangements that Colonel de Castries chose to make for the defence of GONO. Navarre expected a second enemy offensive at Dien Bien Phu at any time after 19 March, but he was preoccupied with problems at a strategic level. As we have seen, the whole 'Navarre Plan' rested in great part on the build-up and improvement of the Vietnamese National Army, but he was now deeply disappointed by its showing in the second phase of Operation 'Atlante' in Annam.

Although General Cogny sent a long signal in an apparent attempt to raise Castries' spirits on 24 March, its utter lack of realism can only have had the opposite effect. Cogny made blithe tactical recommendations which ignored the physical realities at Dien Bien Phu completely, and given his continuing efforts to distance himself from GONO's fate one must wonder at his motives in filing such a document.[76] During the same week two of his senior aides confided in US Consul Paul Sturm that Cogny had 'never approved the concept of Dien Bien Phu, but accepted it as a "sporting proposition" when Navarre decreed its execution'.[77] It is clear that he was almost wholly absorbed by the escalating campaign by regionals and elements of Division 320 inside the Delta, which was tying down increasing numbers of his available troops. Between mid February and mid May no fewer than 59 Franco-Vietnamese posts would fall to attack, and in April Cogny would have to devote four complete Groupes Mobiles to protecting the Hanoi–Haiphong corridor alone. Vietnamese morale was badly affected; of the 59 lost posts, 35 had been garrisoned by local militias, but 28 by Bao Chin Doan gendarmerie, and 12 by Franco-Vietnamese regulars including TDKQ light units. On 25 March, General Cogny once again demanded reinforcements from Navarre, who replied on the 29th: 'I can only repeat what I have said many times before: that we are engaged in a general battle in which my absolute duty is to divide my forces between my senior subordinates in accordance with the missions which I have given them, and of which I must be the sole judge.' Some passages of this signal were couched in terms so patronizing as to be openly insulting.[78]

THE DAILY CLASHES WITH enemy infantry in trenches closing in on the battalion locations and on the Isabelle road were steadily increasing in size and cost, and Castries had been right to fear that the success at Ban Kho Lai would bring no lasting benefit. As so often, the various sources are sometimes contradictory about the exact details but the broad picture is clear enough. After a 48-hour pause, Lieutenant Trapp's 2nd Company, 6 BPC ran into stubborn resistance at Ban Kho Lai on the 24th, and once more the paratroopers needed tank and artillery support to break through during an action that lasted until noon; the Chaffee 'Posen' from Sergeant Chief Ney's platoon was immobilized by a bazooka and had to be towed home.[79] Lieutenant Bergot dates to the 25th a similar engagement which cost 1 BEP no fewer than 83 casualties including Lieutenants Bertrand and Lecoq. Bernard Fall has 1 BEP, with part of 5 BPVN and Ney's tank platoon, in action against penetrations around Eliane 4 on 25 March. He also records that Dominique 6 had to be temporarily abandoned under heavy fire on 24 March, but was reoccupied by 3rd and 4th Companies, 5 BPVN on the 25th while 8 BPC were fighting to 'aerate' Dominique 1.[80]

On 26 March two companies of 1 BEP made little progress in a push north of Huguette 6 until two platoons of tanks finally came up to blast a strong RCL and machine-gun position out of their path.[81] On the other hand, Captain Déal's 155mm battery achieved a rare success in destroying three enemy 75mm guns in a battery location designated 'YJ' east of Isabelle. On the 27th the approaches to Huguette 7 had to be cleared in a major operation led by Major de Seguin-Pazzis, involving parts of 1 BEP, 5 BPVN and Major Chenel's BT 2 (the Thais were still holding up better than their comrades in the 3rd Battalion); this sortie took 3rd Company, 5 BPVN back to the ford below Ban Khe Phai on the track to Gabrielle.[82]

The risks run by the Dakota pilots were brought home to everybody by the deaths of Captain Dartigues' crew on 27 March, and that afternoon Colonel Nicot ordered a halt to all parachute drops below 6,500ft in order to stop what he described as 'this carnage', which was having a bad effect on the nerves of his crews.[83] That evening the new GONO command structure stretched its muscles for the first time when Colonel de Castries ordered Major Bigeard to plan a major sortie against anti-aircraft positions to the west of Dien Bien Phu for the morning of the 28th.[84]

THE OBJECTIVE WAS TO DESTROY AA guns which had been pushed forward under cover of scrubland around the villages of Ban Ong Pet and Ban Ban, to within just under a mile of the camp (see Map 9). Major Bigeard was given 6 BPC, 8 BPC, and Warrant Officer Carette's tank platoon; 1 BEP would be in reserve on five-minute stand-by, backed by I/2 REI in position between Huguettes 1 and 4 in case the paratroopers needed cover for their withdrawal. Lieutenant Colonel Vaillant would support the operation with half his artillery, and Bearcat strikes were requested from GATAC/Nord. 'Bruno' Bigeard – a mere major – spent a sleepless night planning the whole interlocking operation by four battalions and the supporting arms; 6 BPC would be led on the morrow by his second-in-command, Captain Thomas. (Although new to Bigeard's clannish battalion, Thomas was regarded by the younger officers with friendly interest: at the cocktail hour on the eve of 'Castor' he had run, for a bet, down Hanoi's gracious Rue Paul Bert stark naked.)[85]

In the darkness before dawn on the 28th the paras, guided by légionnaires from I/2 REI, slipped silently out to their jumping-off positions:

6 BPC came from Eliane 4, 8 BPC from the central camp, 1 BEP from Junon and Claudine. Bigeard ordered his heavy weapons crews to remain on Eliane, firing on any promising targets and moving frequently to disguise their weakness. Tourret's 8th Shock would attack on the right, opposite Ban Ban; they moved up the Pavie Track to Huguette 1 before turning west. On their left Captain Thomas's 6th Colonial would make the southern thrust towards Ban Ong Pet; they formed up around Francoise, the 'doorbell' now held by Thais of BT 3 (see Map 12). Radio silence was maintained until 5.30am, and was only broken then to report arrival in position by a couple of clicks on the transmit button in response to whispered call-signs.

The waiting silence was ripped apart by the artillery preparation at 6am, just as the eastern hilltops were tinged with orange. Colonel Vaillant had allocated 12 of his 105s, two of the 155s, and 12 of the 120mm mortars to fire on three designated areas.[86] They fired for five minutes at 'maximum cadence' – a total of about 400 shells and many more mortar bombs – before falling silent for three minutes. Then they repeated the exercise, three times more. Shells fell about 300yds ahead of where the paratroopers lay in soggy ditches, behind dykes, in patches of scrub; through their knees and elbows they felt the ground trembling as if a Metro train was running beneath them, while dirt and pebbles occasionally pattered down on their helmets and shoulders.

The barrage moved forward slightly, then ceased; and at 6.30am the paratroopers got to their feet and advanced with the rising sun behind them, while the artillery waited for further fire missions to be called in at need by the FOOs accompanying them. The observer teams and gunners would have their work cut out over the next several hours, particularly Lieutenant Girault with 6 BPC. The day dawned clear and sunny at Dien Bien Phu, but the sky over the Delta airfields was overcast and the Bearcats – tasked with sealing off the forward edge of battle by hitting any visible enemy concentrations from 6.30am – would not actually arrive until 9am.

For the first time since 13 March, Tourret's and Bigeard's paratroopers were now able to fight the sort of action in which they excelled. Moving fast and aggressively despite the broken ground and heavy cover, they crossed streambeds and dykes, dodged around thick hedges and bamboo clumps, through tall scrub and tree lines as they vaulted forwards by squads and platoons, 1,200 men on a front of about a mile and a quarter. On the southern edge of Ban Ong Pet, 6th Colonial came up against stiff resistance from enemy trenches held by men of Division 308 (probably from Regiment 36), and heavy AA machine guns firing in the ground role. Mortar and artillery support was called in, and after a time progress resumed. The leading companies of both battalions got into the ends of east–west trenches which led to a long north–south system linking the AA positions, and began clearing them in World War I style, grenading and shooting their way from traverse to traverse. Lieutenant Le Vigouroux's platoon of Le Page's 1st Company, 6 BPC reached and destroyed two AA emplacements; the lieutenant was killed by a bullet in the head almost immediately afterwards.

At about 10am, Lieutenant Préaud's three Chaffees from Isabelle – 'Ratisbonne', 'Neumach' and 'Auerstaedt' – came up in support of 6th Colonial at a bad moment when a mortar barrage had exposed them to a counter-attack; and at around noon Warrant Officer Carette's tanks – 'Mulhouse', 'Bazeilles' and 'Douaumont' – blasted a path into Ban Ban for 8th Shock. The mentions of tank support risk becoming routine, but the intervention of the Chaffees made a crucial difference in this and many other actions at Dien Bien Phu.

The natural reaction of infantrymen in combat is to be comforted by the presence of tanks. Apart from the supporting fire of a heavy cannon and three machine guns against dangerous enemy positions, their general air of massive, ponderous power is a boost to confidence. The unsilenced roar of the slow-revving engine, the peculiar rumbling squeak of the tracks, the whiplash crack when the heavy gun fires, the stink of diesel and cordite, the heat radiating from the exhausts – all combine to create an impression of invulnerability. However, experienced soldiers are all too conscious of the drawbacks of getting too close to tanks. They are conspicuously valuable targets that draw heavy enemy fire; moreover, their drivers have very poor visibility, particularly at short distances, and infantry are rightly nervous of being crushed by the tracks.

For the five-man crews inside the Chaffees the (relative) safety of a thick armoured shell was bought at a high price in discomfort. From the outside a tank of World War II vintage may appear large, but once inside and battened down for combat each crew member had no more space to move than a man shut in a telephone kiosk. When they entered their hatches the crew had to wriggle into their cramped stations between masses of sharp-edged metal equipment protruding awkwardly from the steel walls. When the tank was on the move the turret crew were effectively blind and so unable to brace themselves in preparation for its wild lurches, which constantly threatened their heads, shoulders and knees with bruising impacts. In a typical engagement each tank fired between 60 and 100 shells, but the stowage racks held only 48; extra rounds were piled on the turret floor, adding to the clutter and discomfort.

The overwhelming impression was of heat, noise and blindness. Even on a summer's day in Europe the fighting compartment of a tank became stunningly overheated by a combination of sun on steel and the high temperature of the rear-mounted engine radiating forward through the bulkhead; in the tropics the discomfort was multiplied. Inside this pitching, wallowing oven the deafening bellow of the engine made speech impossible between men sitting close enough to touch. A few hours of this – aggravated by constantly straining to make sense of messages through the crackle and whistle of the headphones, and by the ear-splitting report of the heavy cannon two or three feet from their heads – was enough to cause chronic headaches. Even if the commander chose to risk standing up in the open turret hatch he was the only one enjoying any useful field of view; if enemy fire obliged the crew to 'button up', then their vision was limited to fleeting, distorted glimpses through periscopic gunsights or thick glass vision blocks – and the limited ventilation meant that engine speed had to be kept down to 3,000 revolutions per minute. In prolonged action the fumes from gunfire hung in the turret, combining with the general stink, heat, disorientation and unpredictable motion to bring on nausea.

BITTER FIGHTING AROUND BAN Ong Pet and Ban Ban lasted well into the afternoon, orchestrated by Major Bigeard over the battalion and company radios; all the para companies were fed into action progressively, since the mouths of all trenches leading into the enemy rear had to be occupied to prevent infiltration and encirclement. Enemy mortar fire became increasingly heavy and several counter-attacks were attempted, but were repulsed with the help of artillery and air strikes; there was a reported incident of a false Viet Minh surrender followed by treacherous firing, but given the confusion of close-quarter battle such stories seldom stand up to examination. French casualties began to mount as progress bogged down in the afternoon, and at about 3pm 'Bruno' called his hounds home; under covering fire the disengagement was achieved successfully.

The sortie had shocked the People's Army, and cost them the equivalent of perhaps a battalion of casualties: some 350 killed, an unknown number of wounded, and at least ten prisoners. Five 20mm AA cannon, a dozen 12.7mm AA machine guns, two bazookas or RCLs, 14 light machine guns and scores of small arms were reported taken or destroyed.[87] The French casualties were far fewer, but less easy to replace. Thomas' 6th Colonial lost Lieutenants Le Vigouroux and Jacob and 15 rankers killed, Lieutenant de Wilde and 35 men wounded (Wilde, commander of the Vietnamese 4th Company, had his right hand shot off by a heavy machine gun); in the 8th Shock, three paratroopers were killed, four officers and 50 men wounded – in total, 110 casualties, the equivalent of a company of Langlais' best soldiers.[88] Major Bigeard was conscious that the units' resilience would take time to recover from the high officer and NCO casualties. Indeed, most of the deaths or serious wounds must have left at least one of the survivors silent and thoughtful, perhaps sitting a little apart that night, suddenly lost without a friend on whose companionship he had long relied.

However high the price paid, many of the tired paratroopers returning to their trenches were elated by the success of the sortie: at last they had had a chance to 'show them!' It was not only GAP 2 who felt an access of confidence and hope, and the spreading news of their victory lifted the mood throughout the valley. Castries congratulated Major Bigeard, and reported the action in glowing terms to Hanoi, where Cogny was suitably delighted – if surprised. It was said that only a few hours earlier he had been holding one of his all too frank conversations with a couple of journalists, and had told them that 'Dien Bien Phu's carrots are cooked'.[89]

DESPITE THE VIET MINH ARTILLERY and anti-aircraft fire, between 13 and 27 March the Air Force had succeeded in flying a total of 324 wounded men out of Dien Bien Phu; but there would be no more.[90] At about 3.45am on 28 March, C-47 No. 434 'Boeufs Delta Coca' of GT 1/64

'Béarn', piloted by the squadron's second-in-command Major Maurice Blanchet and including among the crew the flight nurse Geneviève de Galard, put down safely between the few shrouded runway lamps. This was Blanchet's first night landing at 'Torri Rouge', and as he turned his Dakota at the north end of the runway the tail wheel became entangled in barbed wire. The loading of the wounded went ahead, but while attempts were made to cut the wheel free a bullet hit the starboard engine and punctured the oil tank. The wounded had to be disembarked, and sunrise found the Dakota stranded on the runway. At about 1pm, with 25 stretcher cases waiting in the shelter of the drainage ditch, the mechanics had to warm up the repaired engine; shells began to fall, and the third was a direct hit. When the aircraft was reported destroyed, GT 1/64's commanding officer Major Martinet radioed that he would fly in to pick up the crew the following night. He was unable to accomplish this; 'Delta-Coca' would be the last transport to land while Dien Bien Phu was in French hands, and no more would take off.[91]

Regiment 57 would again fight to cut the link with Isabelle on 28 and 29 March; and after the latter date GONO accepted that the daily road-opening battles were too costly to continue when there was no early prospect of reinforcements arriving. In total, the fighting of the third and fourth weeks of March had cost Castries 522 men killed and wounded – virtually equivalent to a fourth lost battalion to add to III/13 DBLE, V/7 RTA and BT 3 – for which he had received no replacements. He had asked for II/1 RCP, but General Cogny was still keeping Bréchignac's battalion under his hand while fobbing Castries off with vague promises to 'activate an airborne brigade'.[92]

On the ground and in the air the gateways out of Dien Bien Phu were now sealed, and the only way into the valley was under a parachute. After 29 March, Isabelle would fight the rest of the battle of Dien Bien Phu in complete physical isolation.[93] The battle between the French artillery and Giap's infantry was still in the balance, but that between the Colonial gunners and their People's Army counterparts had been lost decisively.

ALTHOUGH THE SUCCESS OF Bigeard's sortie had certainly confirmed the wisdom of General Giap's constantly reiterated warnings against underestimating the French, Colonel de Castries' fear that the People's

Army would continue a policy of 'stifling' his perimeter without risking the costs of further frontal assaults – expressed in his report to General Cogny transmitted on 23 March – was now to prove groundless. On 27 March, Giap had called his commanders together to give them their orders for the second phase of the offensive. Its objectives were to wipe out the eastern sector of the defences, to occupy the hilltops of the Dominiques and Elianes, and to transform them into jumping-off positions from which he could launch a third and final attack against the central camp.[94] His attempt to accomplish this would become known as the Battle of the Five Hills.

13. The Fifth Hill

*'The enemy's artillery pounded the interior
of his own position... to wipe out the
attackers, while his garrison remained
underground, to burst out at the opportune
moment; at the same time a barrage of shells
on our front line cut off all reinforcement
and communication. We had not foreseen
such tactics.'*

North Vietnamese official *account of action on Eliane 2, 30/31 March 1954*

THE DEVELOPMENT OF GENERAL Giap's attacks on Dien Bien Phu
from 13 March onwards roughly parallels the classic phases of attack on
any fortified place throughout history. First, the fortress is surrounded
and cut off from reinforcement and supply, and sorties by its garrison are
driven in. Then any outworks whose fire commands the approaches to
the walls are eliminated (Béatrice, Gabrielle and the northern Anne-Maries),
or invested so closely that their potential to interfere is stifled (Isabelle,
to some extent). After a period of sapping forward under cover of bombardment, assaults are launched on the weakest or the most important
sector of the defences, where the artillery has tried to make 'a practicable
breach'. At Dien Bien Phu the most important was the arc of five hills
guarding the east bank of the Nam Youm: from north to south, Dominiques
1 and 2, and Elianes 1, 4 and 2.

The objectives that Giap set for his commanders on 27 March differed from those of 13–15 March in two important respects. The previous assaults had each been limited to a single strongpoint, attacked by overwhelming numbers, and under cover of a single night – the classic Viet Minh tactic. Attacking the closely spaced bastions of Colonel de Castries' eastern wall would involve simultaneous assaults on these positions, so the artillery preparation would necessarily be divided. Capturing any of the hills would achieve direct observation of the central camp, and the opportunity to install mortars and recoilless guns overlooking other French positions at short range. However, if any one of the hills was captured alone, then the attackers who occupied it might come under close fire from the other heights, and would be vulnerable to counter-attack. Giap hoped to take all the Five Hills in a single night.

For this second phase of attacks, five infantry regiments each of three battalions would be employed. The two regiments which had captured Béatrice – 141 and 209 of Division 312 – were assigned the Dominiques. The Elianes would be the objective of Regiments 98 and 174 of Division 316; it seems significant that for this offensive Regiment 102 from the trusty Division 308 had also been brought across from that division's sector at the north-west of the siege army to be held in reserve in the centre, facing the gap between Dominique 2 and Eliane 1. Meanwhile, Regiment 36 from Division 308 would provide a diversion by making a secondary attack on Huguette 7, the 'star strongpoint' far to the west beyond the end of the airstrip. The operation was planned for the night of 30/31 March.[1]

ON 29 MARCH AN OUTRIDER OF the monsoon arrived over the valley; heavy rain drenched the defenders, turning the ochre earth to soupy mud – and also prevented any photo-reconnaissance missions. Perhaps its veil helped to hide a heroic ambulance driver who managed to get through to Dr Grauwin's hospital with some urgent casualties all the way from Isabelle. Still hoping for the resumption of the airlift, the surgical teams had 175 seriously wounded men on their hands. As well as the downpour, intermittent shelling kept most of the garrison underground. As the firing eased off with the approach of night, Lieutenant Colonel Langlais and Major Vadot came out of the old GM 9 command bunker for a little air, and when they looked to the east they saw an extraordinary sight: pinpoints of light in long lines, moving slowly eastwards up into the hills. This lapse of security, so unlike the People's Army, remains unexplained; perhaps the torches were carried by porters leaving the scene after delivering last-minute supplies.[2]

The rain continued all night and the next day, hampering the cargo drops (though also the Viet Minh flak), and many loads were misdropped behind enemy lines or too close to them to be recoverable. On the 30th, Langlais discussed with Colonel de Castries the idea of his hitching a ride on the next ambulance plane out, to confront General Cogny in Hanoi with a realistic situation report and insistence on a firm plan for resupply and reinforcement, before jumping back into Dien Bien Phu the following day. The failure of any aircraft to leave the valley no doubt saved Cogny from a memorable confrontation.[3] Instead, Langlais spent his day inspecting the eastern strongpoints, where he felt sure the enemy would strike soon (*see Map 14*).

The north–south arc of hills covered about 1,200yds, enclosing flats on the east bank of the river; this strip of low ground was of irregular width, but only about 400yds from east to west at the most. At the northern tip of the arc lay Dominique 1, close to the river-bank and rising about 130ft above it. South-east of this, across a 300-yard gap through which RP41 entered the valley, was the highest feature – the sprawling bulk of Dominique 2, 180ft above the valley floor; and between them, on the southern edge of the road itself, was the lonely outpost of Dominique 6. Another minor position, Dominique 5, was planted on hillocks to guard the next gap, which separated Dominique 2 from Eliane 1.[4]

The hilltop Dominiques had been entrusted to three companies of Algerian Tirailleurs of Captain Garandeau's III/3 RTA – tired, ragged, homesick, poorly equipped, and short of seasoned officers and NCOs.[5] Bernard Fall quotes a strength of 15 officers, 90 NCOs and 583 men, but does not specify a date; Erwan Bergot gives a very different picture. He states that the battalion had many men absent sick; that there were only about ten officers including the doctor, and some 20 French NCOs, none above the rank of sergeant. His source seems to be Sergeant Pierre Antonin, who at just 20 years old held the appointment of battalion sergeant major – a job for a grey-haired warrant officer. The battalion had only one elderly Reibel machine gun per company, and was short of filling machines for their 'camembert' magazines.[6] Morale had been affected by the fate of their countrymen on Gabrielle; Viet Minh propaganda teams had been playing on their nerves with loudspeakers; and, in the opinion of Major Bigeard at least, the battalion officers lacked the experience to provide the special leadership which North African troops needed.[7]

When Lieutenant Colonel Langlais inspected the Dominiques on 30 March with Captain Garandeau (who had influenza), he was alarmed by what he found (*see Map 17*). Dominique 1 was held by Lieutenant Chataigner's 11th Company with just 90 men; although they were supported by Legion mortars from 2 CMMLE, Langlais ordered that they be relieved by paratroopers – 4th Company, 5 BPVN. On Dominique 2 were Captain Garandeau's HQ, 9th and 10th Companies (Sub-lieutenant Lensch and Lieutenant Marie respectively) of III/3 RTA; but an important flank position was held by a platoon of shaven-headed teenage Roman Catholic auxiliaries from Phat Diem bishopric, armed with British rifles – the presence of this 425 CSM at Dien Bien Phu is unexplained. Langlais ordered Garandeau to replace them with some of his regulars; he also withdrew the Thais of 5th Company, BT 2 who were planted on Dominique 5 – when the People's Army attacked they would be able to achieve nothing there.

The Elianes, occupied by a mixture of the fairly well-regarded I/4th Moroccan Rifles and Vietnamese paratroopers, were slightly more reassuring. Eliane 1, only about 60ft high and just over 300yds south of Dominique 2, was held by a company of I/4 RTM. Immediately southwest of them and slightly lower – the two summits were separated by about 150yds – was Eliane 4, and here Langlais had planted Captain Botella's HQ, 2nd and 3rd Companies of 5 BPVN. A nameless hill immediately north of the saddle between Elianes 1 and 4 was not fortified, but stores and vehicle shelters were dug into its south-west foot.

Roughly 300yds south of Eliane 4 was Eliane 2, about 130ft above the river and a key strongpoint. Eliane 2 was oriented north-west to southeast, and formed the western arm of a crescent of three features, the other two of which were patrolled but not occupied except by French scouts. Eliane 2's low eastern slope was linked to Mont Chauve (Baldy), and northeast of Baldy stood Mont Fictif (Phoney); both these were roughly the same height as Eliane 2. Major Jean Nicolas had his HQ and two rifle companies of I/4 RTM on Eliane 2, surrounding a very strong summit position marked by a single skeletal banyan tree. This complex of bunkers and fighting positions had been built using rubble from the old governor's house; its concrete cellar, where the command post was installed, even had a shell-proof iron door. However, when Langlais asked Lieutenant Nicod about the morale of his 2nd Company, he was told that it depended upon their leaders: the Tirailleurs would hold as long as their officers and NCOs held, but if the cadres became casualties then nobody could guarantee their resolve.[8] Langlais was worried about the two unoccupied hills, which hid much of the enemy's preparations on this front; like most of the other hill features, they were partly surrounded by wooded gullies pushing in from the east. It had been impossible to take them into the perimeter – there were neither the materials to fortify them nor the men to hold them – and the artillery had been made responsible for keeping them clear. For about ten days now Major Nicolas's regular patrols to the two hills had been having difficulty; several had failed to return, their stripped corpses being found the next day, and by 30 March Phoney was simply unreachable. The lower eastern slope of Eliane 2 – nicknamed 'Champs-Elysées', for the broad, straight path it offered to the summit – was obviously vulnerable to attack from the gullies surrounding Baldy. Langlais was unconvinced that the Moroccan 2nd Company were secure in their relatively weak entrenchments on this lower shelf, dominated by the two brooding hills; he ordered their replacement by the Legion paras of 1st Company, 1 BEP led by Lieutenant Lucciani. When they took over they found the Moroccan trenches too shallow, and tried to deepen them with their folding spades, but discovered that this was about the only stony ground at Dien Bien Phu.[9]

Tracks negotiable by jeeps and trucks had been driven all over the flats between the river and the Five Hills, and led up to several of the hilltops; shelters for vehicles had also been bulldozed into the bottom of their western slopes. A number of other positions had been dug and wired into the flats, but these were more like bivouac areas than defensive locations. West of Dominique 5, covering the entry of RP41, was Dominique 3, guarded by a 105mm battery and a company of Algerian Rifles. Dotted between the Nam Youm and the hilltop Elianes were Elianes 12, 10, 11 and 3: west of Elianes 1 and 4 was Eliane 10, where Captain Pichelin's 2nd Company of 8th Shock waited in reserve; and by the Bailey bridge over the river, Eliane 12, occupied by part of the 2nd Thai Battalion. Behind Eliane 2 was Eliane 11, just south of the wooden bridge, with a company of the 31st Engineers; and Eliane 3, occupied by the last company from I/4 RTM, together with two Thai auxiliary companies led by Lieutenant Martinez. Langlais also kept most of Major Bigeard's 6th Colonial in reserve on the east bank, between Elianes 12 and 4, but he apparently ordered one company forward to reinforce 5 BPVN on the latter. On the previous day mounting casualties had forced Bigeard to disband his 4th Company and divide its survivors between the others.[10]

Lieutenant Colonel Langlais had now built some depth into his defence by ordering parts of the west bank transformed into defended locations for his counter-attack units, albeit weakly fortified. Between the river and the southern end of the airstrip, backing up the Dominiques, part of the former Dominique 4 had now become Epervier, home to Captain Tourret's 8th Shock, some remains of BT 2 in the old Japanese drainage ditch, and two of the quadruple 0.50in MG mounts. Further south the Elianes were backed by Junon, held by 1 BEP with some Thai and Air Force help, and Lieutenant Redon's other two quad-50s.

THE PEOPLE'S ARMY ASSAULT units left their staging areas east of the hills at around noon on 30 March, and made their way forward under continuing heavy rain. The downpour eased off in late afternoon; although low cloud clung to the hills, visibility was fair by about 5pm, when their artillery opened General Giap's second assault phase with the usual stunning bombardment on the Dominiques, the Elianes, and the French gunpits.

On Dominique 1 the shelling by 105mm batteries from the north-east began at the worst possible moment, as the Algerian 11th Company were in the act of handing over their positions to Lieutenant Martinais' 4th Company, 5 BPVN. The Tirailleurs had dismounted their heavy weapons and had begun to move out of their trenches, while the Vietnamese paras were still strung out in file up the mud-slick path on the reverse slope. All over the hilltop geysers of smoke and mud erupted, tossing up gutted sandbags, splintered timber and spirals of barbed wire, and filling the air with whistling fragments. Through binoculars Lieutenant Colonel Langlais distinctly saw Lieutenant Reboul's Legion mortar crews suffering terrible punishment before they could get into action; Reboul himself was killed (one of a number of artillerymen parachuted in as replacements whose names were never properly recorded in the personnel archives).

The barrage on Dominiques 1 and 2 was shorter than usual – the sources differ between 30 and 90 minutes. On Dominique 1 some of the III/3 RTA returned to their positions with the Vietnamese, but other Algerians jostled the paratroopers in their haste to get off the hill; at one point Lieutenant Martinais ordered his men to fire upon fleeing Tirailleurs, but to little effect. On both hills the first People's Army assault companies seemed to spring up out of the ground in the midst of their own shell-bursts; they had worked their way right up to the wire unseen, and now began pulling it apart with their bare hands – night-time infiltrators had loosened the pickets so that they could simply be plucked out and thrown down. Others carried long mats filled with earth, which they unrolled over the entanglements as bridges. So quickly did they close with the defenders that the shoots pre-arranged with 'Zulu Kilo' fell well behind them; the forward observer officers on both hills were soon wounded, and fire correction orders ceased to arrive at the batteries.[11]

There too the barrage was deadly; over the next 24 hours the French artillerymen would lose nine killed outright and 65 wounded, but would fulfil every fire order. When an accidental explosion knocked out half the crew of 6th Battery's No.1 howitzer the gun layer, Robert Stahl, kept it in action by loading, aiming and firing it himself; eventually it had to be manhandled to an empty gunpit because unexploded 120mm mortar bombs sticking out of the mud were preventing him traversing his piece.[12] Lieutenant Colonel Vaillant's batteries began the night of 30/31 March with 21 serviceable 105mm and three 155mm howitzers, backed up by 17 of the Legion's 120mm mortars. Three 105s, one 155 and three 120mm would be knocked out by 1 April – though the tireless repair crews would get some of the guns back in action, patching the punctured oil cylinders of the recoil mechanism and replacing shredded wheels with others taken from trucks. Ammunition expenditure would also be heavy. The relative calm during the second half of March had allowed stocks to build up to 875 rounds per gun for the 105s (21,000 in all), 600rpg for the 155s, and 880rpg for the heavy mortars. The calls for fire support during the next two nights' battles would be constant, and by evening on 1 April some 500 tons would have been consumed, including about half the 105mm stockpile. This would leave only some 10,500 rounds in hand – enough for one more hard night's fighting.[13]

On Dominique 1 only about 30 of the Algerian company stayed to fight alongside the Vietnamese paratroopers, with perhaps 40 Legion mortarmen now led by Lieutenant Poirier – fewer than 200 in all. They held out for perhaps three hours before going down under the waves of Regiment 209, but at about 9.50pm the radio fell silent. Over on Dominique 2 the collapse came even quicker; by 7pm Major Bigeard, watching from Eliane 4, radioed Langlais that he could see Captain Garandeau's Algerians streaming down the slopes in the last of the sunlight and running for the river. Others threw their weapons down and sat in the bottom of their trenches, hands on heads, waiting for capture. As Regiment 141 swarmed over the hilltop only 9th Company's blockhouse held them up with its stubborn fire. The HQ Company's heavy weapons crews had fled; young Sergeant Antonin and an 18-year-old Eurasian, Sergeant Chalamont, took a machine gun each. The two boys kept firing until they were outflanked – the weakness of internal barricades between sectors had proved fatal. Captain Garandeau fell among his last handful of men, and some time after 8pm Dominique 2 was engulfed. The eager surrenderers suffered for it: French artillery from Isabelle blindly lashed the slope where they had been herded, and their captors prevented them at gunpoint from taking cover in the trenches again.[14]

With the fall of both hilltop Dominiques a broad path seemed to have opened up, beckoning the People's Army into the heart of Dien Bien Phu. Between them and the river there lay only a single belt of wire guarding some insignificant earth parapets on the riverside flats.

ABOUT 300YDS SOUTH-WEST of where the now abandoned outpost Dominique 6 had stood guard on RP41 between the hilltop Dominiques, location Dominique 3 lay tucked between the southward sweep of the road and a 'dead arm' of the river (see Map 17). For some weeks – and so far free from enemy shellfire – the four howitzers of Lieutenant Paul Brunbrouck's 4th Battery, II/4 RCA had been emplaced here to cover the gap where the road ran between Dominiques 1 and 2. An old north–south drainage ditch, about 6ft wide and deep, provided a sunken lane down the middle of the battery position; the command post, shelters and ammunition dumps were dug into both banks and the sandbagged gunpits led off its eastern edge. The ditch was sealed off to the north by a heavy wire entanglement sown with mines, and another arched out to the east to protect the battery's front; the stagnant arm of the Nam Youm was only about 25ft west of the rear edge of the position. Lieutenant Filaudeau's 12th Company, III/3 RTA were dug in around the gunpits for local defence; Filaudeau had the luxury of a second company officer, Lieutenant Alix, and also a 0.50in heavy machine gun emplaced to cover the northern wire entanglement and minefield.[15]

In the last evening light of 30 March the West African gunners were bewildered to see the broken companies of Algerians fleeing back down the slopes of Dominique 2 only about 300yds ahead of them. Lieutenant Brunbrouck reported the retreat; and again, just before 10pm, the fact that his link with the last artillery observers on Dominique 1 had fallen silent. Most of the fleeing Tirailleurs stumbled on to the south, heading for the bridges to the west bank, but others sought refuge inside the battery's wire. Among them was a French sergeant from 5 BPVN, Bellencontre, shepherding his few surviving paras with gestures and grunts – terrible facial wounds from a grenade had cost him the power of speech.[16] When Brunbrouck again radioed his battalion HQ for orders in the face of imminent attack they refused to believe that both hilltop Dominiques had fallen.

The Colonial gunners had infantry weapons, and Warrant Officer Le Poitevin organized part of them for close defence; Brunbrouck was worried that his attached Tirailleurs might catch the contagion of fear from their beaten comrades, and drove out of his position any refugee Algerians who were not determined to fight. When the pursuing Viet Minh approached his position from due east a machine-gun duel began; no longer worried about firing on unrecognized refugees to his front, Brunbrouck was finally able to order Sub-lieutenant Baysset to open fire with small arms, which greatly lifted the morale of his African gunners. Surprised, Regiment 102 halted and went to ground; but the night and numbers were on their side, and they would certainly surge forward again soon.

Paul Brunbrouck was a gangling young man of 27 with a narrow, adenoidal face, beaky nose, pale protruding eyes and sandy hair. Over the past year this veteran of Na San had shown coolness, initiative, professional skill, and a talent for working easily with all ranks and races. At last managing to convince his battalion HQ of the seriousness of the situation, he passed new target co-ordinates to Major Knecht at the II/4 RAC command post and through him to the central PC Feux, who prepared shoots in his support by the two other batteries on the west bank. Any men who could be spared from the gunpits joined Le Poitevin's close defence platoon in the firing line with the Algerians.

When the Viet Minh infantry finally rushed the battery position, dimly lit up by parachute flares, Brunbrouck gave an order that was seldom heard in the 20th century: *'Débouchez à zéro!'* – 'Point blank!' The howitzer barrels were lowered to aim directly at the enemy mass and the fuses were set to minimum delay; the shells exploded just yards ahead of the muzzles, tearing bloody avenues through the closely packed *bo doi*. The French machine guns swept the battery's perimeter, the defence platoon worked bolts and triggers like men possessed; and at last the Viet Minh wavered back, leaving their dead piled along the wire. At this point the first enemy shells landed behind, ahead, and finally on the battery position; a number of them did not explode, and a perilous torchlight examination showed faulty fuses. Some lay flat on the ground as if, fired from well beyond the Dominique hills, they had ricocheted on the summits before falling here.

At perhaps 2am renewed human wave attacks were made by a fresh unit – Battalion 54 of Regiment 102 – which had looped around the long southern flank of Dominique 2 and came at them from the south-east. The gun captains fired at will over open sights, alternating impact and minimum delay fuses to blast both the front ranks and the columns pressing up behind them, while Captain André Combes at II/4 RAC brought down supporting fires from the 5th and 6th Batteries across the river. Again the People's Army were halted; but this respite surely could not last unless Brunbrouck's 180-odd gunners and Tirailleurs – the sole defence of Dien Bien Phu's north-eastern approaches – received more infantry support. Major Knecht renewed his demands, and was refused: desperate battles were raging simultaneously on the Elianes and the Huguettes, and there were simply no reserves to send him. Lieutenant Colonel Langlais came on the radio to speak directly to the young battery commander, and told him that if things became impossible he should sabotage his guns and retreat; Brunbrouck refused to consider it.

The 4th Battery kept firing, supported by shoots from its sister batteries and – with great effect – by Warrant Officer Lemeur's two quad-50 mounts behind them on Epervier, whose terrible streams of tracer tore up an enemy attempt to flank Brunbrouck from the north. Viet Minh infantry reached the drainage ditch, only to come under fire from the Algerian 0.50in crew in the blockhouse guarding the northern barricade. There was a pause in the attacks, although the battery was still under fire; Brunbrouck moved around his gunpits, checking, encouraging, advising, joking. The howitzers were burning hot to the touch, the crews clumsy with exhaustion, and the mud underfoot was treacherous. Some inevitably got on to the shell cases, and the breeches became fouled with a clogging residue of burnt explosive and earth which had to be scrubbed out with large wire brushes.

The enemy artillery groped for them again, at first inaccurately; but then a mortar bomb landed in the rear of one gunpit, and men screamed as violent flames roared up. Since most of the rounds were being fired with reduced charges for close targets, large numbers of discarded charge bags soon accumulated; three of the four gun captains had taken advantage of every lull to dump them in the Nam Youm, but one had not. Unconfined, the charges did not explode, but they inflicted terrible burns. Shortly after-wards another round fell directly on Sergeant Bernard Laurent's No. 4 gun, damaging the recoil mechanism beyond immediate repair; the battery must fight for the rest of the night with only three pieces. The 0.50in MG in the vital northern blockhouse, which had been firing incessantly, over-heated and jammed; Sub-lieutenant Baysset ordered the Algerian crew to urinate on its glowing barrel, which seemed to work. A 60mm mortar crew in a nearby foxhole – Moroccans from the 31st Engineers – were wounded. Warrant Officer Le Poitevin grabbed two gunners, rushed them over, gave them a few moments' instruction by the glow of the Luciole flares, and left them to it; soon an encouraging 'tonk!... tonk!' could be heard rejoining the defensive fire.

Repeated infantry attacks pressed up to the wire over the corpses of those who had gone before; Brunbrouck was again told that he could spike and abandon his guns, and again he refused. When the telephone lines were cut by shellfire he used the radio, speaking to Captain Combes at battalion HQ in an instantly invented slang based on the characters of their unit so that enemy listeners could not understand his reports on his status. The battery staff replaced reeling gunners in the crews; Sub-lieutenant Baysset took his turn lugging shells from the dump to the gunpits. Le Poitevin's close defence platoon of mixed gunners and Algerians now included several wounded men who insisted that they could still shoulder a gun or toss grenades. Viet Minh massing once more in a ditch close to the battery were killed in scores when Lieutenant Filaudeau triggered command-detonated charges which Langlais had had buried there – some 200 dead were found at this spot the next morning. Steadily, the enemy attacks lost momentum, and before first light Battalion 54 finally fell back altogether. Its commanding officer was reportedly dismissed for this failure.[17]

On 31 March, Lieutenant Brunbrouck was sent trucks to tow his howitzers back west of the river – his own vehicles were wrecked. Under steady rain, and harassed by occasional mortar bombs, the exhausted gunners returned to the artillery lines in Claudine, to find the terrain drearily transformed. They had not seen it since before the bombardments of mid March, and the trucks dumped them amid abandoned and stripped gunpits dissolving into a shell-cratered desolation. There was no time for rest; they had to turn to at once with pick and shovel to install their guns in these slimy wallows, ready for action. It was evening on the 31st before they could slump down on ammo boxes in the mud and grab a meal of cold canned rations. During the previous night's battle Brunbrouck's gunners had suffered no dead, three wounded, and a handful of burn casualties; during the day of the 31st, two were killed by enemy shelling.

During the night of 30/31 March these African soldiers had fired nearly 1,800 shells: 450 to 500 rounds from each of the four, later three guns in action. What that figure means in human terms is worth a moment's thought. The sheer labour involved in several hours of serving a gun (the apt traditional term) was considerable. Several dozen shells were usually stacked near each howitzer before an action, already removed from their fibreboard packing tubes and with the fuses screwed in. When these ran out, a constant supply had to be ensured by men stumbling back and forth along the trenches leading to the battery's main dump. Each complete crew consisted of a French NCO gun captain and eight men (though Brunbrouck's crews were probably smaller, given Le Poitevin's simultaneous need for riflemen); and half of them were basically ammunition carriers.

The 105mm shell was 'semi-fixed': the hollow steel head containing the explosive charge came already inserted (by a press fit) into the thin metal case resembling a giant rifle cartridge. To prepare it for loading, a crewman first had to pull the shell out of the case; then pull out – depending upon the order given – a number of the seven fabric bags of propellant explosive which were packed into the case, breaking the tape which linked them at the appropriate point. The unwanted charge bags were discarded, and the shell pressed back into the case. Its fuse, screwed into the nose, then had to be adjusted with a spanner-like tool for detonation on impact or a set time delay, again according to the specific order given (the fuse could not arm itself until the shell was fired, when the spin of its flight released a rotary safety device). Only then was the round ready to slide into the opened breech of the howitzer. The point of this possibly tedious description is that each round weighed 55lbs – as much as a large television set.

Brunbrouck's crews had each manhandled at least 450 of these, in darkness lit intermittently by parachute flares and amidst deafening concussions, while scrambling around a mud-slick gunpit rapidly filling up with empty shell cases, and for much of the time under enemy fire. Some of them had been forced to take up small arms and join a prolonged infantry fire fight against waves of attackers, after seeing other troops fleeing for their lives all around them. Under Paul Brunbrouck's leadership they had held off repeated attacks by two battalions from General Giap's most experienced division; and had prevented the panic collapse of the hilltop Dominiques from ripping through the north-eastern defences right down to the river-bank, to outflank the remaining Eliane strongpoints. Brunbrouck was granted an immediate award of the Knight's Cross of the Légion d' Honneur.[18]

THE CONSEQUENCES OF SUCH an outflanking of the Elianes would unquestionably have been disastrous for GONO. By the time Regiment 102 ran into Brunbrouck's stubborn gunners, Regiments 174 and 98 were already threatening to engulf the three southern hills too, giving General Giap the one-night victory for which he hoped.

The Moroccan company on Eliane 1 were in a position to witness the collapse of the Dominiques, and their morale crumbled under the bombardment. By 7pm Captain Botella, on Eliane 4 just behind them, reported seeing refugees falling back past his strongpoint. This company of I/4 RTM seem to have been overrun by the Tho soldiers of Regiment 174 in about 45 minutes, and GONO would report the loss of Eliane 1 at 7.30pm.

Few details are reported of the fighting on Eliane 4 on the night of 30/31 March, beyond the essential fact that Captain Botella's HQ, 2nd and 3rd Companies of 5 BPVN succeeded in defending their ground under bombardment and heavy infantry attacks from Regiment 174. The cost included the heavy weapons platoon wiped out, Lieutenant Gaven (3rd Company CO) and Lieutenant Marquèze killed, and Lieutenant Delobel of HQ Company wounded.[19] That the Vietnamese paratroopers held out all night – after other units had visibly collapsed to their left and front, and while a furious battle on Eliane 2 to their right remained in doubt throughout the hours of darkness – suggests that the reputation hung around their necks after the Gabrielle counter-attack was undeserved.

The first three hills had fallen; the fourth was holding out; but it was on Eliane 2 – which the People's Army called 'the Fifth Hill' – that the night would be decided.

TO APPROACH THE DEFENCES of Eliane 2, Regiment 98 had first to move up from their staging positions in the wooded gullies behind and around the flanks of Phoney, and to secure Baldy (see Map 17). This feature, disputed with French patrols for some ten days, had prevented them from digging their usual approach trenches up to the enemy wire. Moving off at about 5.30pm under cover of the bombardment, they occupied Baldy in an hour, and the regimental commander decided to infiltrate his men up a dry streambed to get close to the defences on Champs-Elysées. He had been given very heavy support for this assault: from Phoney, where concealed pits and deep tunnels in the forward slopes had been constructed over the previous weeks, the French positions would be raked at short range by two complete companies of recoilless guns, another two of 120mm mortars, two platoons of 82mm tubes, and machine guns.

These did great execution among the defenders in their shallow trenches; but the initial infantry assault was a disaster for Regiment 98.

Beginning their move on to Champs-Elysées in the dusk shortly before 7pm, the two lead battalions emerged from the streambed bunched too close together. Instead of cutting two widely separated lanes through the wire the columns advanced only about 30yds apart; this tight concentration was hammered into ruin by French shellfire from Isabelle, and Regiment 98 lost radio contact with Division 316 command.[20]

For firing upon infantry concentrations the French gunners had in their arsenal the option of VT-fused ('Pozit') high-explosive shells, fitted with tiny radar sensors which detonated them a few yards above the ground. These 'airbursts' are particularly deadly to infantry, since trenches and foxholes give no protection from the metal shards blasting downwards from above. The shells detonate with an orange flash followed by a puff of black smoke, an ear-splitting crack, and steel fragments that rain down for what seems an eternity – first those blasted downwards or sideways, then those blown upwards until their flight is halted by gravity and they fall in a widespread pattern. The infantry forming up to attack Eliane 2 were also in woodland; and the worst punishment of all is inflicted by 'tree bursts' – shells which explode in the treetops above sheltering troops – since these add big, wickedly spiked splinters to the metal fragments.

Despite the nightmare into which this bombardment plunged the first Viet Minh attackers, the weight of their own support fire from Phoney also caused many casualties among the defenders from Lieutenant Lucciani's 1 BEP company in the lower trenches on Champs-Elysées. At some time after 9pm Major Nicolas ordered him to pull his men back up the hill to join I/4 RTM in the stronger positions grouped closer to the command post on the summit. At about 9.50pm the enemy support fire lifted, and Regiment 98 rose from the battered trenches at the foot of Champs-Elysées and flooded up the slope. The infantry fighting was intense, and in little more than 20 minutes the Moroccans and Legion paratroopers were pushed back nearly to the hilltop.

Some time later, Major Nicolas in his cellar CP was in radio contact with Lieutenant Colonel Langlais. Langlais had just heard him report that a renewed Viet Minh assault was under way when call-sign 'Nicky' fell silent in the middle of a word. Previously this sudden breaking of contact during an action had meant that a command post had been captured or wiped out. Given the lethal danger which the loss of Eliane 2 would pose to the camp as a whole, Langlais did not hesitate: he ordered artillery fire on the summit of the strongpoint.

In the command post that he had installed on top of Eliane 4, Major Bigeard of 6 BPC was – characteristically – listening in to all the radio frequencies he could; reception was better up here than in the valley. From the patterns of muzzle flashes and grenade explosions he could see that Nicolas had in fact contained the immediate threat to Eliane 2; and this was confirmed by Lieutenant Bergot of 1 CEPML, who picked up a transmission from Lieutenant Lucciani over the artillery net.[21] Bigeard broke into Langlais' frequency to countermand the fire order. He also promised to send one of his companies to help the defenders of Eliane 2, even though his immediate responsibility to reinforce Botella on Eliane 4 at short notice made this a risky investment. Lieutenant Le Boudec's Vietnamese 3rd Company of 6th Colonial would arrive on Eliane 2 at about 1am.

The Viet Minh account states that their assault troops on the Fifth Hill were driven back by an artillery barrage and a two-pronged counter-attack with sub-machine gun and grenade. It goes on to describe French shellfire being called down within the French perimeter, alternating with sudden counter-attacks by defenders who charged out of shelters where they had been sitting out their own artillery fire. Meanwhile, other French shellbursts built a lethal wall behind the forward edge of battle, cutting all communication with the rear and preventing the reinforcement of the lead battalions. Regiment 98 'had not foreseen these tactics...'[22] This account suggests that some artillery salvoes were indeed fired before Langlais' order was countermanded; and reminds us that positions on Eliane 2, uniquely, had stone rubble 'bursting layers' in their overhead cover.

This success on Eliane 2 was only achieved by steadily reinforcing the defenders; and the night of 30/31 March presents the first example of a characteristic of the battle notable from then onwards – the cobbling together of piecemeal counter-attacks or reinforcements from successive individual companies of several units, rather than by moving complete battalions. This expedient was forced upon Langlais by the need to plug simultaneous gaps in his front while holding back men in the expectation of other breaches appearing, and all from a strictly limited pool of reserves. Faced with emergencies that would conventionally demand 600 men, he could afford only a hundred or two – and then perhaps another hundred an hour later. If it is confusing to the reader, then it must have been doubly so to the junior leaders on the ground; that they nevertheless won many tactical victories is hugely to the credit of the captains, lieutenants and senior NCOs of the parachute and Legion companies.

This aspect of the defence broke a number of basic military rules, and should have guaranteed confusion, muddled chains of command and dangerous failures to communicate. In fact, the nature of this battlefield and of these soldiers seem to have protected them from consequences that on paper look inevitable. In great clashes between entire divisions the conduct of junior soldiers can rarely have decisive effects; but Dien Bien Phu was an accumulation of strictly local struggles for individual strongpoints by half-battalions, even companies. The outcomes were determined by junior ranks – from Langlais and Bigeard downwards – taking extraordinary responsibilities, in the type of actions that can be swayed by the behaviour of a few dozen men.

This scrambling defence was being imagined into reality by paratroopers – the ultimate light infantry. Paratroopers have nothing on their side but aggressive energy and the instant grasp of opportunities; and these paratroopers were being commanded by a man who punched colonels and shouted at generals. They were opposed by soldiers whose training had shepherded them through a series of unvarying scenarios ten times over, led by officers who were discouraged from taking decisions and afraid of making mistakes. Although it is a striking reversal of their stereotypes throughout most of the Indochina War, the image of French terriers flickering around a Viet Minh buffalo must not be exaggerated: a shell travels faster than the most agile paratrooper, and on most battlefields God is indeed on the side of the big battalions. Nevertheless, this contrast between French opportunism and Viet Minh rigidity goes some way towards explaining the survival of GONO for far longer than could reasonably be expected.

On Eliane 2 that night Le Boudec's company from 6 BPC was followed by half of Lieutenant Martin's 3rd Company, 1 BEP. They were also joined by two tanks from Sergeant Chief Ney's platoon; in all five successive counter-attacks were made, and at around 3am Regiment 98 was finally fought to a standstill. Colonel de Castries – far from being a passive onlooker – was instrumental in persuading Langlais to reinforce and counter-attack at once, without waiting for the morning.[23] The survivors of Regiment 98's assault battalions fell back from about 4.30am; and the one fresh People's Army battalion brought up to occupy Champs-Elysées was able to hang on to only the smallest eastern toehold in the face of a last dawn counter-attack. At first light Lieutenant Trapp's 2nd Company from 6 BPC joined Le Boudec on the hill. Together the Moroccan Rifles, Colonial and Legion paratroopers – thinned out by casualties, filthy, dumb with fatigue, and hardly able to believe they were still alive – gazed over their parapets down the broad slope of Champs-Elysées, carpeted with the terrible dead.

WHILE THE FIRST BLOODY struggle for the Five Hills was taking place, General Giap did not leave the rest of the camp in peace. Down at Isabelle the infantry were forced underground by serious shelling in an attempt to silence the 105s whose fire was being brought down on the eastern slopes of the Dominiques and Elianes.

Meanwhile, at the opposite edge of Dien Bien Phu, a barrage was followed by an infantry attack upon Huguette 7. This – the former Anne-Marie 4, out to the west of the end of the airstrip – was now held by 1st Company, 5 BPVN. In shape it was a triangle: each of the three platoon positions at north-west, south-west and south-east was also roughly triangular, linked by trenches to a central command position (*see Map 13*). Attacked during the night by Regiment 36 of Division 308, the north-western position was largely overrun; Sub-lieutenant Thélot and his Sergeant Cloitre were both killed by an RCL shell through the embrasure of the command post, and at around 11pm the enemy pushed forward into the platoon's trenches. From the machine-gun blockhouse Sergeant Tournaye and other survivors maintained a desperate defence.

The 1st Company was led by Captain Alain Bizard, a big, cheerful cavalryman who just a month before had been an aide to the Army Chief-of-Staff, General Ely. When he volunteered to leave the delights of Paris in springtime for this, his third tour in Indochina, his friend Captain Botella had asked for him as battalion second-in-command; but Bizard was not parachute-qualified. He took care of that formality during four hectic days at Hanoi, and with his new wings in his pocket he jumped

THE FIFTH HILL   **471**

over Dien Bien Phu on 28 March, being sent up to relieve Lieutenant Rondeaux in Huguette 7.[24] Now, just 48 hours later, Bizard was shouting into his radio handset over the din of battle, reporting his situation to Major Clémencon – as CO of I/2 REI the Legion officer had operational control of the Huguettes. Clémencon radioed Langlais to ask for a company of paratroop reinforcements for Huguette 7; his request was curtly refused – Langlais was wholly focused on the threat to Dominique 3 and the Elianes, and if they fell then the fate of the Huguettes was sealed anyway. Clémencon did not argue: the Legion understood the principle of *'Démerdes-toi...'*[25] Bizard's Vietnamese rallied, and by 5.30am on 31 March they had recaptured their trenches by themselves. Heavy enemy fire continued to rake the platoon position, however, and Sergeant Tournaye faced another day without respite.

ALTHOUGH THE NIGHT'S immediate crisis had passed, Colonel de Castries was in no doubt that without the heroic exertions of a handful of junior officers and their men his ramparts would have been breached fatally. At midnight he appealed for the immediate dropping of a fresh parachute battalion: 'The situation will be difficult to restore without reinforcements from outside. We are doing the impossible.'[26] General Cogny – who had been reassuring Castries that he would be reinforced by a complete airborne brigade *after* he had held off the next heavy attack – was not at his desk when the signal arrived. Nor was he available to greet the C-in-C when General Navarre landed in Hanoi at 1.15am. The commander of FTNV had apparently been attending to a social obligation, and had left word that he was not to be disturbed by anybody.

Navarre irrupted among the drowsy FTNV night staff and, with Colonel Bastiani, drafted secret orders that were to be transmitted by Cogny to Castries. He assured the GONO commander that his men were defending the honour of France and Vietnam under the world's admiring gaze; that the rate of enemy casualties and the approach of the rains offered every hope; and that their continued resistance and the losses they inflicted on the enemy were of the first importance to the overall conduct of operations, by delaying to the maximum the moment when the important forces that they were tying down could be used elsewhere. (The implication – that a time would come when such forces would indeed be free to go elsewhere

– was not encouraging.) While calling for the preparation of the central camp and of Isabelle for eventual resistance alone should the outlying strongpoints be lost, Navarre ordered that Castries be reminded that all guns, tanks and ammunition must be destroyed rather than letting them fall into enemy hands. Castries was to be promised that everything possible would be done to evacuate his wounded (no practical suggestions were made), and to drop replacements for the casualties in his parachute battalions.[27] However, he was to be told that extra reinforcement units would be limited to one parachute battalion and a battery of 75mm RCLs; the promised entire airborne brigade should not be expected unless Navarre could be convinced that their commitment would not merely prolong the resistance, but would bring actual victory. Navarre's level of belief in such an outcome was clear from his final sentence: 'The commander of strongpoint Isabelle should be informed of these instructions in the event that, at a particular moment, he alone remains capable of resisting.'

When General Cogny finally arrived at the Citadel at 7.45am on the 31st, his meeting with Navarre turned into a blazing quarrel. The next time the theatre and regional commanders met, on the afternoon of 2 April, their mutual distrust and dislike would be expressed in terms which left the relationship beyond all healing. In the meantime Cogny had received a letter that Navarre had written him on 29 March. In insulting terms, it denied him the reinforcements for the Delta which he was requesting, stating that the forces at FTNV's disposal were quite adequate to fulfil his present mission, and adding that if any of the dire consequences that Cogny predicted did come about then Cogny would be entirely responsible, through his improper use of his resources. We must recall that at this date 'Axelle', the second phase of Navarre's cherished Operation 'Atlante' in Annam, was visibly failing depite the commitment of some 40 battalions, and that only days previously the Généchef had had to admit to General Ely the ruin of his hopes for the Vietnamese National Army (see Chapter 8). Cogny's written reply to this letter disputed each point; and stated that due to Navarre's lack of confidence in him he no longer wished to serve under him, but left the timing of his departure to the commander-in-chief.[28]

On 31 March the one decision taken of immediate concern to Colonel de Castries was authorization for the dropping into Dien Bien Phu of one fresh parachute battalion: Major Bréchignac's II/1 RCP, who were waiting at Hanoi–Gia Lam airfield. They would continue to wait: bad weather had closed in over the Delta.[29]

DAWN ON 31 MARCH FOUND Dominiques 1 and 2 and Eliane 1 firmly in the hands of the People's Army; and their installation on Dominique 2, looming over the whole valley, presented a particular menace. Before snatching a little sleep, Langlais had agreed with Castries, Seguin-Pazzis and Bigeard that they had no choice but to launch counter-attacks on the Dominiques and Elianes during daylight on the 31st, without waiting for the promised arrival of II/1 RCP.[30] The rhythm was now well established: the Viet Minh attacked by night, the French the following morning. Although Castries could not know it, the People's Army in this sector were just as drained by the night's fighting as the defenders. Bringing up the available units of Regiment 102 'Ba Vi' under the morning downpour, to take the place of the terribly mauled Regiment 98 in the gullies around Phoney and Baldy, was a slow business; it took them ten hours to cover just over four miles. Although neither B-26s nor Dakotas were able to take off from the Delta before 11am, French fighter-bombers did manage to get over the valley to harass their movements.[31] These troops would be the intended target of an operation planned to disrupt Giap's immediate threat to Eliane 2, using the only fairly fresh troops in GONO. From Isabelle, Lieutenant Colonel Lalande was to launch III/3 REI with his three tanks on a thrust up towards the eastern flank of Eliane 2 and the enemy's jumping-off positions around Baldy.

ALTHOUGH NOT YET SUBJECTED to many determined infantry assaults, the garrison of the southernmost location otherwise faced the same conditions as those in the main camp, aggravated by its small size and low-lying terrain. Less than half a mile across, Isabelle occupied a marshy oxbow on the west bank of the Nam Youm, which curled around its north-east, east and south-east perimeter. It had no hills, trees or areas of concealing scrub, and the water table was too high to allow deep digging. Even so, its commander Lieutenant Colonel Lalande – an ex-gunner, and a veteran of every World War II Free French campaign from Narvik onwards – had supervised his units closely in the construction of a strong system of trenches and shelters, with the best possible overhead cover. At some points the external wire belts were 100yds deep, and the seperate strong-points had internal wire dividers. The exception was Isabelle 5, 'Strongpoint Wieme', which was a last-minute extension across the river on the east bank towards the nearby auxiliary airstrip (*see Map 19*). By the time Lieu-tenant Wieme's two Thai Light Auxiliary Companies were added to the garrison there were few materials left; their chest-deep trenches lacked timber for strengthening, and the rudimentary wire and mines had to be backed up with traditional sharpened bamboo barricades.

By the beginning of April, Isabelle had a total garrison of around 1,500 infantry, plus just over a hundred gunners and tank men of Captain Libier's batteries and Lieutenant Préaud's Chaffee platoon. The major units were the 426 légionnaires of Major Grand d'Esnon's III/3 REI; and the 545 Algerian Tirailleurs of Captain Pierre Jeancenelle's II/1 RTA, to which were now attached 116 of Captain Gendre's V/7 RTA survivors from Gabrielle. There were also Captain Desiré's 200-odd Thais from 9th Com-pany, BT 3; and about the same number from Lieutenant Wieme's 431 and 432 CSLT.[32]

The main tasks of Isabelle were to defend the auxiliary runway about 350yds north-east of the river bend, and to house artillery which could sweep the eastern approaches to the Elianes and Dominiques. It would never seriously attempt the first (only two Dakota landings were ever made on the airstrip, whose use was impractical under the conditions which soon prevailed); but in the second it would be solidly successful. On 13 March Isabelle had had eight 105mm howitzers of 7th and 8th Batteries, III/10 RAC. Presciently, the battalion's Major Alliou had been concerned about the security of road access to the main camp, and had stockpiled about 12,000 rounds at Isabelle. The batteries had a bare minimum of personnel – fewer than 120 – and their officers and senior NCOs, like those of the batteries at Claudine, were pared away by the need to provide observers for the infantry units.[33]

The People's Army units committed to ensuring Isabelle's isolation were Colonel Hoang Khai Tien's Regiment 57 from Division 304, and Battalion 888 of Regiment 176 from Division 316. Entrenchments were dug around the strongpoint, most closely threatening Wieme's position on the east bank; but four battalions to two-plus were far from overwhelming odds. Unable to hold a continuous ring of trenches, Tien's infantry would be able to mount fierce but only limited attacks, and concentrated on blocking any movement north by the garrison.

When the battle opened on 13/14 March the main target had been Isabelle's artillery; the 8th Battery, in particular, was heavily bombarded, and ten casualties were suffered, but since as many as 40 per cent of the shells were duds all the guns survived the night. On 14/15 March gunner casualties were three times as heavy; and a determined infantry attack on Isabelle 5 and the nearby 7th Battery, where the enemy got close enough to fire rifle grenades into the gunpits, lasted all night. It was fought off with the aid of support shoots from the main camp, at the same time as Isabelle's guns were firing in support of Gabrielle. (This seemingly illogical arrangement – of guns separated by several miles firing simultaneously upon the infantry attacking each other – was quite normal.) In the main camp the specialists in supporting Isabelle were Captain Cabannes' 5th Battery, II/4 RAC at Dominique 4; this was the only battery which kept to its original positions throughout the battle, thanks to the very solid construction work of Warrant Officer Jullian (who would receive a battlefield commission). From 15 March onwards Isabelle's ammunition resupply was by direct air drop; by the same means they received three replacements for damaged 105s on 16 and 17 March, and were later able to reorganize their 11 guns into three batteries.[34]

During the second half of March the difficulties of road communication with Claudine had increased, with the same effects on Isabelle that the strangling of the airfield had on the main camp; these are exemplified by the story of Sergeant Leroy, a gun captain from 7th Battery. On 16 March, wounded around the kidneys by shell fragments, he was driven up to the main hospital, where Dr Grauwin operated on him. He was still in the hospital when it was shelled on the 18th, receiving further fragment wounds to the head and torso. Because of the disruption to the hospital, after receiving first aid Leroy was driven down to Isabelle again, to be operated upon there for his new wounds. At the moment of arrival the ambulance was caught in a shellburst and the driver killed, but Leroy was rescued from the burning wreck. On the night 19/20 March he had a stomach operation, and was registered for air evacuation. Since no ambulance remained, he made the now perilous journey back to the main camp in a truck on 22 March, and spent three nights in the drainage ditch beside the airstrip waiting his turn. At dawn on 25 March he was loaded on to a Dakota and flown out.[35]

The outbreak of the second offensive hit Isabelle hard. On the night of 30/31 March it suffered heavy bombardment; 12 gunners were killed, 18 wounded, shelters and command posts were wrecked, and the artillery was reduced to five serviceable guns. Wieme's men had to fight off infantry attacks all night long with the help of Captain Cabannes' gunners; the two Thai companies used 600 mortar bombs, at maximum elevation and minimum charge to drop just yards in front of their trenches.[36] The next day about 30 of the auxiliaries were found to have deserted from Isabelle 5 While the Legion battalion was mounting its sortie towards Eliane 2 on the 31st, Lieutenant Colonel Lalande was giving some of its mortarmen and those of II/1 RTA to the artillery for hasty training as replacement 105 gunners; and the artillery NCOs were supervising a frantic attempt to repair damaged howitzers, which by nightfall that day had nine of them back in action – though with only six qualified crews.[37]

Now, on the morning of 31 March, Major Grand d'Esnon's III/3 REI and Lieutenant Préaud's Chaffees left Isabelle at dawn. By about 9am they had run into heavy resistance on the site of the 1 BEP's battle of 22 March, where a stream crossed the road near the abandoned hamlets of Ban Kho Lai and Ban Nang Nhai. This blocking force were not tired from night fighting on the Five Hills; they were two battalions of Regiment 57, which made an aggressive pincer attack on III/3 REI with strong support from recoilless guns and bazookas. The tank 'Neumach' took a direct hit, and had to be towed back to Isabelle by another. By about 11.50am the légionnaires were in real danger, and had to call in artillery support just to disengage. With help from the gunners and from the Bearcats now wheeling overhead it might have been possible for Lalande's operation to punch its way through; but to what end? It did not take the top graduate of his class at the War College to deduce that there was little future in pushing a battalion already tired out by marching and fighting up to the unfamiliar wooded gullies around Baldy and Eliane 2, to meet unknown opposition, while the enemy closed the road behind them again. Lalande's légionnaires fell back on Isabelle, taking their 65 casualties with them. This was the last attempt by infantry from the southern enclave to take part in the battle for the main camp.

While Lieutenant Colonel Lalande was facing his decision, far to the north two counter-attacks were unleashed by Langlais and Bigeard to recapture lost positions in the eastern hills (*see Map 17*).

PART OF CAPTAIN TOURRET'S 8 BPC were assigned Dominique 2, while Eliane 1 was to be assailed from nearby Eliane 4 by companies of Bigeard's 6 BPC and Botella's 5th *Bawouan*. They would have support from two tank platoons and from the artillery; the barrage started at around noon and lasted an hour and a half. When they moved off at 1.30pm Captain Pichelin's 2nd Company of 8th Shock had to cross some 400yds under fire, following the creeping artillery and mortar explosions up the long western slope of Dominique 2. Although the People's Army had had well over 12 hours to consolidate their hold, progress was rapid; by 2.30pm the artillery had ceased fire and the paras were closing with the enemy on the summit in a final vicious struggle with grenade, bayonet and spade. His friend Captain Jean Pouget described Pichelin as a thoroughbred who would gallop until his heart burst: that day a Viet Minh machine gunner burst it for him, just before his men reached the summit, and his deputy Sub-lieutenant Pastor was also killed after a few moments in command.[38] On Eliane 1, Lieutenant Trapp's 2nd and Le Boudec's 3rd Companies of 6th Colonial, and part of 5 BPVN, were also successful in recapturing the summit from an enemy battalion; they, too, nearly paid for it with the life of a company commander when a bullet scored across Le Boudec's chest.[39]

Both hilltops were a shell-ploughed chaos of wrecked trenches and scattered corpses, with no intact positions left after many hours of French and Viet Minh shelling; and the latter now resumed. The paratroopers had taken significant losses, and it was obvious that they could not hold the ground they had recaptured against the determined counter-attacks that were sure to follow as darkness fell. They had taken the hills, but a fresh unit was needed to hold them – and Lieutenant Colonel Langlais had no fresh units. At about 3pm, from the foxhole on Eliane 4 where he had been crouching among his radio sets for 48 hours, Major Bigeard signalled Langlais that all objectives had been captured: was there any news of the arrival of II/1 RCP? 'Gars Pierre' replied to 'Bruno' – negative. Delayed first by the high command's indecision, then by the morning's bad weather, and throughout the clear afternoon by fear of a low-level drop in the teeth of People's Army flak, the battalion could never arrive and get into action by that night. Sick at heart, Bigeard radioed his bloodied companies about half an hour later: they must give up the ground they had won at such cost. Cursing, some weeping with rage, the 8th Shock fell back down Dominique 2, carrying the torn body of Captain Pichelin. At about 6pm, the last paras of 5 BPVN gave up Eliane 1 under renewed pressure from Regiment 174. Except for Lieutenant Le Page of 1st Company, all of 6 BPC's company and platoon commanders had now become casualties; in the past week the battalion had lost 43 killed and 183 wounded.[40]

The consequences of GONO's inability to hold the recaptured Dominique 2 were to be severe. The cause was the failure to provide Castries with at least one more parachute battalion before the second Viet Minh offensive phase; by the time his appeal reached Hanoi at midnight on 30 March it was already at least 48 hours too late. It might be argued that it was the reputation of the enemy AA gunners that had won the day rather than Regiments 141 and 174, and they underlined their deterrent value by shooting down two aircraft on the 31st. One was a Dakota flown by Warrant Officer Guiraud of GT 2/64 'Anjou'; the other was the naval Helldiver of Lieutenant Commander Andrieux – 'Nha Que', whose practice for escape and evasion did him no good in the end. The squadron leader of 3F was killed with his gunner, Petty Officer Jannic, when he came below the thick cloud ceiling stretching from 6,000ft down to 1,800ft at about 7.45am that morning. The disruption of the cargo drops had also left GONO perilously short of hand grenades and 81mm mortar bombs; the latter were in fact lying out on the drop zones, but it was to be three more days before they could be recovered.[41]

In Saigon at 6pm on the 31st, US Ambassador Donald Heath sent a digest of the most recent events at Dien Bien Phu to the State Department. He mentioned that bad morning weather had hampered drops of the badly needed paratroop reinforcements and an additional battery of '105s or 75s'. Could these be the mysterious battery of RCLs mentioned by Navarre, above? Heath judged that the latter were crucial, as in the previous night's fighting the French had 'lost seven guns at central redoubt and six out of

12 guns at Isabelle'.[42] The ambassador believed that if reinforcements could not reach GONO by that night then the remaining Elianes might well fall, presenting Navarre with the choice of reinforcing a doomed garrison or leaving them to their fate. The telegram reeked of impending disaster.[43]

On 31 March French intelligence suggested that General Giap was present on the battlefield in person, and with him the Chinese General Li Cheng Hu. It could only be presumed that he intended to complete his victory with another all-out assault on the last two French-held hills. At 10pm Lieutenant Colonel Langlais told Major Bigeard that he was free to judge whether or not Elianes 4 and 2 could be held throughout that night; 'Bruno' replied that he would cling on to them while he had a single man left.

COURAGE DID NOT GO unrewarded on the night of 31 March/1 April: persuaded by the determined French reaction during the day that the time was not yet ripe for an all-out assault, General Giap limited his operations to simultaneous attacks on Eliane 2 and Huguette 7.

As night fell, People's Army infantry emerged from behind Baldy and moved up to the foot of Champs-Elysées; these were two battalions of Regiment 102, and one of Regiment 98 – presumably the unit left out of battle the previous night. The whole of Eliane 2 was less than five acres in extent, and its summit defences measured only about 100yds on a side. The badly cratered eastern slope was scattered with corpses and parts of corpses; blockhouses which had been lost, recaptured and lost again were now roofless charnel pits, and little shelter could be found in trenches that were half filled in, their parapets blown away. Through this dismal landscape the Viet Minh columns surged forward yet again, up towards the first parapets of the summit defences.[44]

They were faced by a scratch force of defenders, the main units being the survivors of Major Nicolas's two I/4 RTM companies, Lieutenant Lucciani's 1st Company, 1 BEP, and that battalion's 4th Company led by Sub-lieutenant Boisbouvier.[45] There was certainly one, and perhaps two Legion infantry companies present: Captain Russeil died that night at the head of a composite company of I/13 DBLE from Claudine, and Lieutenant Rancoule of I/2 REI reportedly led a mixed company of légionnaires and

Thai auxiliaries from the Huguettes.[46] During the fierce fighting of that night other small elements were sent up to Eliane 2, including Sergeant Preignon with a 57mm RCL team from 8 BPC's HQ Company.

At about midnight, Captain Hervouët sent Sergeant Chief Ney's tank platoon across the Bailey bridge and up on to Eliane 2, where the Chaffees came under heavy fire from bazookas and recoilless guns. Ney's 'Ettlingen' was hit six times, and Sergeant Willer's 'Smolensk' twice, but both continued to manoeuvre and fire. At around 4am the continuing enemy pressure on the summit persuaded Langlais to commit Warrant Officer Carette's platoon as well, apparently led by Hervouët in person. Although virtually blind, the Chaffee crews engaged the enemy at close range, taking lethal risks in duels with the bazooka teams of the swarming Viet Minh infantry. At one point Sergeant Zurell and Sergeant Chief Novak of 4th Company, 1 BEP were both riding on Carette's closed-down tank 'Bazeilles', fending off infantry with the 0.50in MG clamped to its turret. Both survived when 'Bazeilles' was hit by a series of bazooka or RCL projectiles; the third hit started a serious engine fire, and the crew bailed out, Carette with an ankle wound.[47] 'Mulhouse', also hit by a bazooka, kept going; but 'Bazeilles' had to be abandoned for ever, high on the slope of Eliane 2.[48] This action in the early hours of 1 April seems to have been the occasion when Yves Hervouët was wounded for a second time, obliging him to lead his squadron from then on with both arms in plaster casts.

When the enemy tide ebbed back down Champs-Elysées at first light, the mixed garrison were still holding the summit of Eliane 2. In the overcast dawn the para and infantry légionnaires worked to repair their positions, and – until harassing artillery fire stopped them – scouted forward down Champs-Elysées, which now resembled in miniature some of the worst spectacles of the Great War. The night had cost the two 1 BEP companies 16 dead, four missing, and 27 wounded; in the past week the battalion had lost 40 dead, eight missing and 189 wounded, including five officers – one-third of its strength.[49] In a hole behind a parapet of enemy corpses, Zurell and Novak found the dead body of the burly Sergeant Chief Romanzin, company sergeant major of 4/1 BEP, beside an empty grenade sack; Zurell would claim that he still had his habitual cigar butt clenched in his teeth.[50]

While Eliane 2 had been fighting for its life, far away to the north-west in Huguette 7 the 1st Company, 5 BPVN had withstood yet another attack by Regiment 36 (*see Map 13*). Hammered by Division 308's mortars, Sergeant Tournaye's paratroopers were ordered at nightfall to pull back silently from the north-west sector; when the enemy assault battalion advanced they found the trenches and blockhouse empty, and exploited forward into the central complex. Captain Bizard withdrew his 90-odd men into the south-west and south-east platoon positions, abandoning the rest of the strongpoint to the People's Army. At about 11pm, when they had taken the bait, he called in a pre-arranged artillery shoot by the big 155s – given that the whole strongpoint was only about 150yds wide, this took faith. It was vindicated: enemy casualties were heavy, and at daybreak his Vietnamese charged out and recaptured the whole location, restoring their perimeter by soon after 10am on 1 April. Lieutenant Colonel Langlais was forced to admit that he had misjudged the 5th *Bawouan*; and later that day they were finally relieved, by another scratch company of légionnaires and auxiliaries led by Lieutenant Spozio of I/2 REI.[51]

WHILE VIETNAMESE PARATROOPERS with seasoned Colonial NCOs were proving reliable, other non-European troops were adapting less well to the undreamt-of ordeals of positional fighting. For some the mere prospect of having to hold trenches under artillery and massed infantry attack proved too much: at about 2pm on 1 April, Sergeant Chief Comte reported from the western 'doorbell' outpost at Francoise that his White Thais of 414th Company were fading away into the scrubland. The warning gave enough time for two Legion companies – 1st and 2nd of I/2 REI – to collect the abandoned heavy weapons and bring the remaining cadres back to the Huguettes. Lieutenant Colonel Langlais reportedly ordered that all remaining Thai auxiliaries apart from NCOs be disarmed and employed only as porters.[52]

This second enemy offensive at the beginning of April marked the point at which 'internal desertion' became a noticeable problem, which was to worsen during the rest of the month. Members of broken units and other individual stragglers drifted down to the river-bank, which was high enough at some points to provide shelter in cave-like burrows; and for this reason these despised figures passed into the legend of Dien Bien Phu as 'the rats of the Nam Youm'. They came out at night to scavenge ungathered parachute supply packs for food and *vinogel*, the unappetising wine concentrate that the French forces issued where liquid deliveries were impractical. Some 'rats' certainly robbed French corpses; others actually operated a black market in valuable items which they had recovered, bartering radio batteries or hospital supplies. The GONO provost unit was quite insufficient to tackle the problem, and at one point the enraged Langlais considered turning combat troops loose to purge the river-banks; but to what purpose? Bloodshed in such a cause would have been disastrous for morale, particularly among the non-European troops who were still holding up. Neighbouring paratroop and Legion units simply sealed off any communication trenches that led towards their lairs, so that in case of attack the 'rats' would either have to defend themselves or flee above ground, and could not disrupt the defence by running through fighting positions. The contagion of their example must have been damaging to that part of the 2nd Thai Battalion which held trenches in location Eliane 12 close to the river.[53]

The 'rats' were almost exclusively Indochinese and North African, though claims that a few white soldiers joined them cannot be dismissed. The Moroccans of the 31st Engineers and the West Africans of the artillery were as solid as oak throughout the battle. The collapse of III/3 RTA on the Dominiques and the melting away of Thai companies provided the nucleus of internal deserters, joined later by some Moroccans of I/4 RTM and by Vietnamese from the ranks of regular units. The latter were a sensitive subject, given the long controversy over the *'jaunissement'* of the Expeditionary Corps. There were some instances of wavering in mixed-race units; these were mostly checked by the NCOs, but not always, even in crack battalions like 6 BPC and II/1 RCP. In the latter this would lead, during a bombardment on the night of 11/12 April, to the 'fragging' of a dug-out full of French NCOs, and a ringleader being shot (as reported by Colonel de Castries on 13 April). From a few hundred in the first half of April the 'rat' population grew steadily, as units suffered increasing losses among officers and NCOs in confused night battles. In a signal to General Cogny on 14 April, Castries would report that combat effectives in the main camp had dwindled to about 3,500 infantry, among a total garrison of over three times that strength. Langlais and Bigeard would later put the final numbers of internal deserters at between 3,000 and 4,000, although others judge this figure to be exaggerated; 2,000-plus might be a conservative guess.[54]

Desertion was not exclusively a French problem; the camp continued to receive a trickle of *bo doi* whose morale had been so crushed by the losses suffered that they no longer believed in final victory. On the evening of 1 April the GONO intelligence team reported to Hanoi that one deserter had mentioned rumours in his unit to the effect that if the garrison held out until 15 April the siege army would withdraw.[55]

AT 9AM ON 1 APRIL A CONFERENCE between Generals Cogny, Masson and Dechaux, Colonels Nicot and Sauvagnac (Gilles' replacement at TAPI) and other staff officers took place at the Hanoi Citadel. Colonel de Castries had asked about the possibility of using the southern drop zones Octavie and Simone again, instead of the smaller DZs inside the main camp. (Given the strong enemy presence between the camp and Isabelle, Simone seems a puzzling suggestion.) The imminent attempt to drop II/1 RCP lent urgency to this discussion. Colonels Nicot and Sauvagnac both argued that the plan would expose the aircraft and the paratroopers to enemy fire for far too long.

Colonel Sauvagnac, a pioneer paratrooper since 1937, was sensitive to any attempt to mount airborne operations in an ad hoc spirit; always conscious of their special risks, he stood out against the cavalier culture which had developed in the Expeditionary Corps. He argued that given the extraordinary danger created by the 'flak alley' at Dien Bien Phu, no attempt should be made to drop a whole battalion at once by daylight; the troopers should jump in smaller parties, from irregularly spaced flights of Dakotas, under cover of night. This was agreed; General Cogny ordered that henceforth a major air-drop should only take place 'outside the valley, either in the form of a battalion which could attempt to join Dien Bien Phu, or by an extension of the battle through acting on [the enemy's] rear areas'. In this last phrase we may perhaps detect Cogny's stubborn yearning for diversionary operations to the benefit of his Delta forces.[56]

Whatever Cogny's motives in approving it, Colonel Sauvagnac's proposal was perfectly intelligible from the viewpoint of TAPI; unfortunately, it was irreconcilable with GONO's immediate needs. It was to starve Castries and Langlais of paratroop reinforcement except in penny packets, which would only ever keep up (if that) with daily losses, and would never give GONO the extra heavy punch they needed if they were to have a real impact on General Giap's battalions on the captured positions.

FROM THE NIGHT OF 1/2 APRIL a rebalancing of General Giap's offensive is evident. While attacks continued on Eliane 2, the fighting for the Huguettes intensified; having failed to make a decisive breakthrough in the Five Hills, the People's Army made a more determined effort to clip off the northern strongpoints guarding the airfield. That night the first blow fell on the isolated 'star strongpoint', Huguette 7.

The previous bombardments – by the enemy and, on the previous night, by French 155s – had so wrecked the defences that Lieutenant Spozio's newly installed company of légionnaires and Thais had little chance when two full battalions from Regiment 36 advanced at about 10pm. The attackers were able to infiltrate from crater to crater; this time they took care to clear out every dug-out rather than leaving any knots of resistance behind them, and by about 4am they had completely penetrated the position, reducing Spozio's hold to a single blockhouse. It was Captain Bizard of 5 BPVN who led a rescue mission to his former strongpoint; Major Clémencon ordered him to take whatever he could scrape together from Huguette 1. He assembled about a hundred men – two platoons from 2nd Company, 5 BPVN, one from 4th Company, I/2 REI, and the three scarred tanks of Carette's platoon, now led by Sergeant Boussrez. Their route led about 500yds up the airstrip to Huguette 6 at its northern end, then west some 600yds to Huguette 7, all across flat ground with only light scrub cover (*see Map 13*).

Meanwhile, from about 11.30pm, the company led by Lieutenant Rastouil of I/13 DBLE who were holding Huguette 6 had stood off their own first infantry attack, by Regiment 88. This had been repulsed by the time Bizard's rescue party passed their southern perimeter; he succeeded in reaching Huguette 7, and the Viet Minh fell back under the fire of the tanks' cannon. When Bizard got into the strongpoint he found the seriously wounded Spozio holding his lonely blockhouse with just 13 other survivors and three corpses. There was simply no way to restore

Huguette 7 to a defensible condition. At about 8am on the 2nd, Langlais grimly gave the order to abandon Huguette 7 for ever.[57]

LIEUTENANT COLONEL LANGLAIS' main concerns that night were the defence of Eliane 2 and – simultaneously and crucially – the arrival of the 'Banjos' carrying Bréchignac's II/1 RCP. Enemy artillery fire on the French howitzer pits at both Claudine and Isabelle was particularly effective on 1/2 April, and the next morning GONO would report to Hanoi that in view of the losses responsibility for counter-battery work would have to be passed to the Air Force and Aéronavale. Even with the consequent reduction in fire support, however, in the darkness Lucciani's Legion paratroopers once again fought off Regiment 102's attacks up Champs-Elysées, with the help of odd companies and platoons shuffled around to plug weak spots. That night the transfer of even a single pioneer flame-thrower squad from I/2 REI to Eliane 2 was a welcome reinforcement.

The first Dakotas were heard at about 10.30pm, and the Viet Minh AA batteries opened a savage fire. The designated drop zone at the southern end of the airstrip was too small to allow more than a few men from each plane to jump in one pass, forcing the pilots to make second, third, even fourth runs.[58] The paratroopers leapt into the night inside a cage of tracer fire, rising with deceptive slowness like strings of pearls. Five men were hit in mid-air. The aircraft were buffeted by the passage of howitzer shells, and from the ground the parachute canopies were lit up momentarily by the flash of artillery fire. The 'Banjos' had priority, but above them other flights of C-47s were circling impatiently – GONO's need for ammunition of all kinds was desperate. Soon the dropping of II/1 RCP had to be suspended when Luciole flares became essential to the defence of Huguette 7, and the cargo planes took their turn.[59] Only two platoons from 4th Company, part of HQ Company, and one replacement gun crew from GM/35 RALP got on to the ground before the mission was aborted.[60] Heavily laden with weapon valises and leg bags of ammunition, they came down hard, often into trenches and craters, on to barbed wire, aircraft wrecks or other obstacles. Corporal Chief Claude Sibille recalled to Howard Simpson that he was wounded by a shell fragment while trying to cut himself free of a wire entanglement. By the flash of explosions he spotted a Red Cross pack lying near by and crawled towards it, only to reach it at the same time as a wounded Viet Minh soldier. They shared the contents.[61] Lieutenant Colonel Langlais was incensed at this paltry rate of reinforcement, and began a prolonged and heated dialogue with TAPI. Their essential positions were, on Colonel Sauvagnac's part, that parachute jumps must be made over properly established and marked drop zones according to established procedures; and on Langlais', that in the current emergency the men should jump anywhere over the camp, taking the risk of landing injuries for the sake of getting them on to the ground quickly and in numbers.[62]

During the daylight hours of the 2nd, a sortie from Isabelle supported by the tank platoon destroyed approach trenches and weapons nests that were being pushed forward towards the perimeter; it would have to be repeated over the following days. In the main camp, drinking water began to run short; two of the holding tanks for purified water had been pierced by shellfire. (The Nam Youm was becoming an open sewer in which corpses bobbed; the carefree bathing of March was long forgotten.) With parachuted spare parts, Lieutenant Jourdonneau's repair teams worked like zombies to get the battered howitzers back into action, drafting nearby infantrymen to provide unskilled muscle; the dwindling number of qualified artillery NCOs was a lot harder to make up.

Those 105s which were serviceable did manage to find some targets among the Viet Minh emplacements on Baldy and Phoney, despite the deep tunnels which had been dug to hide the back-blast of the recoilless guns. On Eliane 2, the légionnaires and Moroccans profited by this to probe forward down Champs-Elysées; the results were promising enough for Major Bigeard to authorize a counter-attack by the whole of 1 BEP, while air strikes with napalm kept the enemy's heads down on the Dominiques and Eliane 1. By dusk the Viet Minh had been pushed right back into the neighbouring gullies; the cost to 1 BEP was 13 dead, nine missing, and 23 wounded including Major Guiraud – Captain Francois Vieulles took over the battalion command temporarily. However, Viet Minh artillery immediately began pounding the recaptured Champs-Elysées, and some of it had to be given up again. Giap's infantry exploited forward at about 10.30pm to maintain contact.[63]

BY THE NIGHT OF 2/3 APRIL most of the paratroop battalions available to Lieutenant Colonel Langlais for counter-attacks were down to about half their original strength: 1 BEP had about 300 fit men, 8 BPC some 400, 5 BPVN around 350, and 6 BPC perhaps 300. This figure was not appreciably improved by the paratroop drop that night. The Dakotas arrived early, at about 6.30pm, but only about half a dozen plane loads jumped. The first to land were replacements for the weakened howitzer crews: Lieutenant Juteau and 31 gunners from GM/35 RALP. They were followed by 74 men of 4th Company, II/1 RCP, giving Lieutenant Subrégis one full company to take over Eliane 3; but two complete sticks were misdropped over enemy lines and lost.[64]

That night Regiment 102 made yet another assault on Eliane 2, but was again repulsed. At about 4am this exhausted unit was withdrawn and replaced by Regiment 98, itself only partially reorganized after its terrible mauling on 30/31 March; the regimental commander contented himself with keeping a single company on Champs-Elysées to fend off any sorties by Lieutenant Lucciani's paratroopers, while the remainder stayed in the rear. On the northern face of the defences, however, the People's Army were far from stalled. On 2/3 April, Division 312 took over from 308, and its Regiment 165 'Dong Trieu' – veterans of the capture of Gabrielle – were thrown against the now completely isolated Huguette 6 (*see Map 13*). This irregularly shaped strongpoint was under direct observation and RCL and mortar fire from Dominique 2, which had cut up its barbed wire badly. Even so, this second assault by a rested unit was repulsed by Lieutenant Rastouil's scratch company: just 86 légionnaires, including some III/13 survivors from Béatrice, some from Captain Philippe's NCO training platoon, and others combed out from I/2 REI companies in Claudine.[65]

The weather on 3 April was very bad, and the majority of cargo flights signalled 'QRF' – 'Aborting mission'. Wet, tired, and strung-out by two consecutive nights of fighting against huge odds, the légionnaires in Huguette 6 were suspicious when they heard a Viet Minh loudspeaker broadcasting in German. They were being invited to take advantage of a short truce to go over to Huguette 7 and pick up some wounded from Lieutenant Spozio's Legion company. In the end, Sergeant Chief Katzianer and Sergeant Sterzing volunteered to take a party of stretcher-bearers: the precedents of Béatrice and Gabrielle were reasonably encouraging, after all. The truce was honoured, and they were not fired upon as they trudged the 600yds to the cratered smear of ochre mud which had been Huguette 7. There they found four stretchers laid out for them; these contained not wounded, but corpses, disgustingly mutilated. The People's Army was showing the other side of its character. At some time later that day, 12 légionnaires – all survivors of Béatrice – laid down their weapons and slipped out of Huguette 6.[66] The loss of a whole section was enough to weaken this tiny garrison appreciably, and they were replaced by a reserve platoon. This brought Lieutenant Rastouil about 30 men; the help of another officer, the young Lieutenant Francois; and (perhaps of more immediate impact) the '*Grossdeutschland*' veteran Sergeant Chief Bleyer – another Béatrice survivor, but an undaunted one.

ON THE NIGHT OF 3/4 APRIL, from some time after 7.30pm, Huguette 6 was again attacked by Regiment 165. The circuit of French trenches began to shrink alarmingly, and at about 10pm Lieutenant Colonel Langlais released a single meagre company to help Rastouil: Lieutenant Desmons' Vietnamese 4th Company of Tourret's 8 BPC, who had a thousand-yard approach march from Epervier up the runway drainage ditch. At least Langlais sent two tanks to accompany them; and as they arrived they had a stroke of blind luck – a bomb from their heavy mortar support shoot scored a direct hit on a Viet Minh command post well north of the strong-point. As the enemy hesitated, the paratroopers hacked into their flank with the Chaffees providing a base of fire, and before midnight Huguette 6 was secure again.[67] Desmons was unable to exploit his victory: the Luciole flares had ceased, since another prolonged attempt was being made to drop the rest of II/1 RCP at the other end of the airstrip, and GONO could not risk lighting them up either in the air or as they tried to assemble on the ground.

This night of 3/4 April was the occasion of a battle of wills between Lieutenant Colonel Langlais and an Air Force controller circling above the camp – a battle that the Breton paratrooper won. At about 8pm the Dakotas were flying a holding pattern while the Air Force officer, seeing the flashes of battle around Huguette 6, refused to give the drop order. Langlais, incandescent with frustration, insisted that the rule-book be thrown away on his own responsibility; he had a fuel drum set alight beside the Nam Youm, where the blaze would be reflected in the water, and demanded that the paratroopers jump on this marker – well south of the designated DZ on the airfield, and perhaps three-quarters of a mile from the fighting around Huguette 6. Langlais unleashed all of his considerable persuasive fluency, and the airman finally gave way; after the first thundering shadow passed between him and the stars the colonel distinctly heard the opening 'cracks' of the canopies only 900ft above him. The Parachute Chasseurs came down all over the camp; but casualties were only two dead and ten wounded or injured, and by dawn 309 of the battalion had landed. This represented all of Lieutenant Charles' 3rd Company, the rest of Lieutenant Abadie's HQ Company, and half of Captain Clédic's 2nd Company. Major Bréchignac himself came down in the wire, and arrived at Langlais' command post minus his trousers. Another 85 replacements for various units also jumped that night, among them Lieutenant Adenot and Sub-lieutenant Mengelle to take over the tank turrets of the wounded Captain Hervouët and Warrant Officer Carette.[68]

There was no rain at daybreak on 4 April, and little enemy shellfire. In the early morning light the men of II/1 RCP made an encouraging sight as they slogged across the camp to Eliane 10 and Dominique 3 under a blue sky; their camouflage fatigues were clean, their faces shaved, their equipment complete, and their eyes were not yet sunken with fatigue.[69] They offered a striking contrast with Michel Desmons' grubby, slouching little scarecrows of 8th Shock, making a wary return from Huguette 6 to their home at Epervier, where they lived a troglodyte life by day under the observation of enemy gunners on the hilltop Dominiques barely 1,000yds away. Epervier is memorably described by the eyewitness Lieutenant Bergot as a sort of *bidonville* or shanty town: a chaotic stretch of holes and hillocks, vaguely tied together with improvised communication trenches roofed over with plates of PSP (these were now spreading all over the camp, and were nicknamed 'the Metro'). Epervier had a gypsy population of paratroopers, quad-50 gunners, Algerian and Gendarmerie stretcher-bearers, Thai drop zone recovery gangs, and the whores of the 2 REI's field brothel, who had volunteered to work as nurses' aides.[70]

At about 2pm on the afternoon of the 4th came reports that the People's Army were pulling right back from the eastern slope of Eliane 2. Against an enemy at least six times as strong Major Nicolas and Lieutenant Lucciani had won their four-night, four-day battle, and their prize was hope – this was the first time that the enemy had actually abandoned ground to the defenders, beyond the ebb and flow of an individual fire fight. Patrols down Champs-Elysées reported counting about 1,500 enemy and 300 French dead scattered in the churned mud, each swollen and rotting under its obscene moving crust of blue-green flies; in the still air the stench was indescribable. Major Bigeard decided to leave Champs-Elysées as a no-man's-land; the trenches had been destroyed, and the slope could not be held under the gunsights of Phoney and Baldy.[71]

The Viet Minh account would admit failure at Eliane 2 in grudging terms: 'Our success was incomplete for various reasons. We had not known in detail the dispositions of the fortifications at the heart of the position, above all the formidable buried blockhouse at the summit, and the direct communications between Eliane 2 and the entrenched camp. The preparations for assault were thus insufficient.'[72] The excuse about communications is hard to understand, given the vantage points they enjoyed on Dominique 2, Eliane 1 and Phoney, all of which had lines of sight to the river bridges.

THE RESPITE WAS BRIEF; ON the evening of the 4th there was heavy rain, and Hanoi signalled that no attempt could be made that night to drop the remaining 212 men of II/1 RCP's 1st and 2nd Companies. That the postponement of such a small number of reinforcements was a disappointment is a reminder of just how seriously every man was needed by a garrison which now counted only about 4,700 fit combatants in the main camp.[73] The addition of two-thirds of a battalion to Langlais' fire brigade, and the enemy's acceptance that the Fifth Hill was for now beyond their reach, did not lift the threat to Huguette 6.

From 8.15pm on the night of 4/5 April a heavy bombardment fell on Huguettes 6, 1 and 5 from Division 308's heavy weapons backed by 105mm artillery (see Map 13). By 10pm Major Clémencon was reporting enemy infantry building up around Huguette 6; as usual, glimpses of movement and masses of flat helmets in the trenches were revealed by the parachute flares, and scouting parties began probing the wire and minefields. Once again, the attackers were Colonel Thuy's Regiment 165, and this time all three battalions seem to have been committed, attacking from north, west and east simultaneously.[74] This fourth assault was far stronger than the previous attempts, and Langlais and Clémencon fed a succession of reinforcements up the airfield during the night.[75]

At about 10pm, Lieutenant Viard's composite company from I/13 DBLE were sent up to assist Rastouil, but were soon confined with him in the southern part of the strongpoint by heavy infantry pressure. By about 12.30am on the 5th there was hand-to-hand fighting inside the position, whose fall seemed imminent. Shortly after 1am a second rescue force was ordered north up the drainage ditch: Lieutenant Bailly's Vietnamese 3rd Company, 8 BPC, with two tanks – Sub-lieutenant Mengelle's 'Conti' and Sergeant Chief Ney's 'Ettlingen'. About 300yds south of the strongpoint they ran into heavy resistance, including both artillery fire and bazookas; Bailly was shot twice in the thigh, and a number of his men were burned by white phosphorus shells. Some paratroopers may have managed to reach the south-west corner of the position, where they brought enemy mortar crews under fire, but the rest of the company remained pinned down in the ditch. 'Conti' was damaged by a mine; 'Ettlingen' took a bazooka hit that wounded Ney, but the tank remained in action.[76]

At about 3.15am, Langlais radioed Eliane 2 and ordered Captain Clédic to take his half-strength 2nd Company of II/1 RCP right across the camp to join the fight for Huguette 6. Despite the distance – about 900yds just to the southern end of the runway, crossing the river and a maze of unfamiliar earthworks and wire, and then another 1,200yds up the drainage ditch – Clédic came up with Bailly by about 4am. The last 50yds were across the runway, where the PSP seemed to shine like a mirror in the light of the flares; Clédic – a bull-like Breton – led his men across in a single charge into the southern part of the enemy lodgement, and by about 4.15am they had broken into the strongpoint in close-quarter fighting. They found perhaps 20 men of Rastouil's original garrison (including Herbert Bleyer) still holding out in one bunker. Regiment 165 soon resumed their attacks, and the odds were still heavily in their favour.

At about 5am, Lieutenant Colonel Langlais called Major Bigeard down from his eyrie on Eliane 4, and told him to put together a third counter-attack to secure and clear Huguette 6.[77] This he did in less than an hour, using two companies (about 160 men) from his 6 BPC led by Lieutenant Le

Page's 1st Company, with a company from 1 BEP in reserve. Le Page (another taciturn Breton) had the most experienced veterans in the battalion; moving off at 6am, they linked up at sunrise with Bailly's force outside the strongpoint. At about this time the enemy had reportedly committed yet a fourth battalion; but the counter-attack hit them hard, and daylight brought effective French artillery support.[78] By 8.30am on 5 April the attackers were falling back from around Huguette 6, and for once French aircraft caught them in the open. They left about 500 dead inside the strongpoint, another 300 outside, and 21 prisoners were taken. These proved to be very young, and when questioned they confirmed that barely trained replacements were now filling the gaps in Giap's regiments.[79]

The loss to the People's Army in this single action of the equivalent of a complete battalion killed (and therefore at least that many more wounded), added to the two battalions' worth of dead counted on Eliane 2, underlines the terrible cost to General Giap's siege army of this second offensive phase. All his assault regiments had now been in costly action at least once, most of them twice. During the first half of April radio intercepts would pick up orders that the rear bases put on the road for Dien Bien Phu replacements from among the 25,000 men most recently called up, which suggests serious pressure on Giap's manpower. So do other transmissions, calling to the front Regiment 9, the last unit of Division 304, which had been guarding the Viet Bac; and summoning two battalions, signals and heavy weapons companies of Independent Regiment 148, and a detached battalion of Regiment 176, back from operations in Laos.[80]

In the absence of verifiable Viet Minh records the estimates of People's Army casualties given in the various French sources invite caution; few cite their evidence, and there must be a natural tendency to exaggerate, particularly in accounts by participants. While a ratio of say two-to-one for wounded to killed is conventional, it may have been rather lower under the conditions of Dien Bien Phu, where fewer wounded may have been recovered from the field. Nevertheless, there seems no reason to discount French Second Bureau estimates, which were prepared by pragmatic experts whose sources included efficient radio intelligence. Bernard Fall quotes such an estimate to the effect that by 5 April the siege army had suffered about 10,000 killed and wounded – perhaps 45 per cent of Giap's infantry strength on 13 March.[81]

THIS FIRST BATTLE FOR THE FIVE HILLS and the northern Huguettes may be considered to have ended on the morning of 5 April, since the next few days saw a lull in activity by the People's Army. It was a time for both sides to take stock. For the thin battalions of GONO to have weathered the second offensive at all was a remarkable achievement; and on 7 April the War Ministry marked it by announcing a collective citation in Army orders for the entire garrison – the equivalent of a Croix de Guerre with Palm for every man. All individual citations and decorations in the gift of Generals Cogny and Navarre were signalled to the garrison.[82]

On 7 April General Giap discussed the situation with his senior officers. In effect, he asked if they were ready to pass to the all-out offensive stage, and then answered the question himself. Thanks to their past successes they had made good progress towards creating the necessary conditions. Nevertheless, some units had not accomplished their assigned tasks; therefore these conditions did not yet exist, and the army must continue its efforts for some time to come. They would resume the tactics of advancing their lines of encirclement and approach, tightening a stranglehold around the enemy positions. Errors were analysed and criticized, and new tactical instructions distributed; as mentioned above, it seems that unit commanders had been dismissed after the first attacks on Eliane 2 and Dominique 3 on 30/31 March.[83]

Again, Giap's handling of positional fighting had failed to reveal any flashes of originality. Once he committed troops to the assault his tactics had been as repetitive and costly as those of the reviled 'donkey' generals of World War I: bombardment followed by massed infantry frontal attacks, duplicated night after night. With the exception of the fourth assault on Huguette 6, these attacks had not even been mounted with the overwhelming concentration of numbers that might have guaranteed success. In terms of tactical skill, the French commanders at every level were clearly superior to their opponents, and their infantry were winning repeated local victories although greatly outnumbered.

The proof of one of the failures of the People's Army was the simple survival of the French artillery, even though units had sometimes been reduced temporarily to as low as 50 per cent serviceability.[84] Given their advantage in direct observation, it is surprising that General Vu Hien's 105mm howitzers had not by now completely silenced their French counterparts. Experienced artillerymen would have concentrated on each pit in succession until the gun was destroyed; when the captured Colonel Vaillant, shown the enemy guns, remarked defiantly that if the French and Viet Minh artillery positions had been reversed he could have wiped out the guns in the camp in 48 hours, he was speaking no more than the truth. In fact the incoming salvoes on any one objective were typically of 20 to 30 shells over three to four minutes, fired by a battery of three or four guns. Fire on the artillery lines was described by Captain Combes of II/4 RAC as raking quite large areas at a time; a few unlucky hits in the pits themselves caused the losses, but they were never enough to silence the supporting fire that caused such havoc among Viet Minh infantry attacking the strongpoints.

The inability to concentrate his fire on a succession of targets was the direct consequence of General Giap's decision to dig his guns into casemates, and of the inexperience of his artillery officers. Their inter-rogators would later congratulate captured French officers on the speed with which the Colonial batteries had been able to switch targets. During the April battles many of the burdens that were carried for the French by 'Zulu Kilo' had to be shouldered for the Viet Minh by their infantry, who paid an appalling price in consequence. There can be no doubt that the success of French counter-attacks by small numbers of paratroopers was often due to the inability of Giap's artillery to react quickly and accurately to new situations, despite their great advantages in direct observation.

In comparison with Giap's 105s, much more damage was done to the French artillery by 120mm mortars and, after the fall of the hilltop Dominiques on 30/31 March, by 75mm recoilless guns; their flat trajec-tory and accuracy made them far more dangerous than the dug-in howitzers. Whenever the French gunners opened fire during the day, a flurry of return fire would arrive in their lines, usually after only about three outgoing rounds – they became experts at rapid fire and diving for their shelters. In their turn, the French observers hunted for the RCLs' flash and back-blast before the crews had time to shift position; their task was aggravated by the enemy's trick of setting off decoy charges in false emplacements. Even the big 155s took part in these duels, sometimes at ranges as short as 700yds. Apart from the mounting casualties among the French gun crews and battery staff, the ammunition parties routinely suffered dead and wounded during their perilous journeys to and from the ammo dump. Many of the deaths among the PIMs – whose casualties would eventually reach about 1,200 – occurred during such missions, yet veterans recall their inexplicable willingness to continue this dangerous work day after day, without coercion.[85]

THE AREA NOW DEFENDED BY GONO had shrunk from an original extent of 1,186 acres to 642 acres.[86] The main camp was now vaguely triangular, with an isolated apex at Huguette 6 hundreds of yards up the open airstrip. The long, flat western face stretching down to Huguettes 5 and 4 and the ill-defined margins of Claudine had no natural defensive features. The lower part of the eastern face was anchored on the firm hill bastions of Elianes 4 and 2. North of these, however, where the area east of the runway stretched away into open space, the enemy-held Dominiques 1 and 2 overlooked the improvised mess of Epervier, where Lieutenant Colonel Langlais took the precaution of reuniting all four of Lieutenant Redon's quad-50 mounts on 5 April.[87]

Within this irregular perimeter the stockpiles of ammunition of all kinds were again dangerously low. On 6 April – when three C-119s misdropped their loads behind enemy lines – the 105mm howitzers had 2.6 fire units, or 455 rounds per gun; the 155s, only 120 rounds each; and the Legion's 120mm mortars, fewer than 110 rounds per tube. In all, this was barely enough for one more night's fighting by the howitzers, and only a couple of hours by the Legion heavy mortars; and the infantry were also very short of mortar ammunition and mines. In Claudine only four tanks were currently 'runners', and at Isabelle only two.[88] While another 177 men of II/1 RCP would arrive on 5/6 April, the overall rate of reinforcement by piecemeal night parachute drops was never more than barely adequate to keep pace with casualties. The cost of success to the four para companies which had been in action at Huguette 6 on 4/5 April had been about 220 all ranks; set against Castries' estimate of no more than 3,500 fighting infantry in Dien Bien Phu a week later, such losses were significant.[89]

The closing of the airstrip on 28 March had completely transformed the medical situation in the camp. The facilities had been planned purely to handle the first link in the classic chain of medical evacuation and treatment – evaluating and stabilizing casualties before sending them back down the chain for further treatment if necessary. Giap's artillery had cut the chain behind its first link, collapsing all its functions forwards on to the shoulders of the camp's small medical staff. Now they would have to perform every stage in the process themselves, here in their dug-outs: they would have to be their own advanced surgical hospital, casualty clearing station, base and hospital, providing all surgery, post-operative treatment and long-term care for an unknown number of cases, of whatever severity, for an unknown period of weeks or months. A week previously there had been 175 seriously wounded men in the hospital; by 7 April there were 590, and many others in the battalion aid posts.

Apart from actual wounds, the brutal tempo of fighting endured by the overstretched counter-attack units made combat exhaustion a factor. By the time the first battle for the Five Hills ended the paratroopers of GAP 2 had been under fire, or in immediate expectation of it for 25 days and nights. Most of the fighting took place after dark, so they had to snatch what sleep they could in the trenches during daylight, and this desire was usually frustrated. Companies were moved from one part of the camp to another at unexpected intervals; ammunition continually had to be carried out to the strongpoints; shelled trenches had to be dug out and repaired; there were always other men jostling their way through the narrow ditches, and intermittent gunfire was frequent.

In addition to the sleep deprivation that every combat veteran remembers, soldiers become exhausted by nervous tension. At Dien Bien Phu they seldom knew exactly when they would next have to clamber above ground and go deliberately into harm's way, or how long they had to rest in the meantime, so they could not regain real strength during pauses which might end abruptly at any moment. Such uncertainty also prevents men from pacing their feelings – from going methodically through whatever routine of mental deception has proved effective in controlling or displacing their fear. They simply never know what is going to happen next, how soon, or for how long. This process of cumulative mental fatigue advances in parallel with another: the repeated and irreplaceable withdrawals which battle forces each man to make from his strictly finite store of courage.

IT WAS ON THE NIGHT OF 5/6 April that an experiment was tried: the parachuting of volunteers who had not completed – or in many cases, even started – jump training. Lieutenant Colonel Langlais argued that any reasonably fit and agile volunteer making his first jump ran little increased risk. Colonel Sauvagnac opposed the suggestion, believing that it was suicidal to let men parachute into the middle of a battle at night without full ground and jump training. Parachute school statistics actually show fewer injuries on first than subsequent jumps; the essential factor in avoiding landing injuries is a very low wind speed. General Navarre informed Colonel de Castries, apparently on 5 April, that he had decided it was worth trying, with first-, second- and third-jump men. He asked for careful casualty returns, so that he could judge whether the experiment was useful on balance – there was no value in dropping men simply to clog up Dien Bien Phu's hospital. After the first trial that night, GONO reported no difference at all in injury rates between novice and trained parachutists.

When the idea was approved, volunteers stepped forwards in their hundreds from units all over Indochina. Of the 68 Algerian Tirailleurs at the lost V/7 RTA's rear base, 52 volunteered.[90] There was one collective battalion application from Major Cabaribère's II/3 REI, then fighting in the Delta; this was rejected by General Cogny because he suspected that many of the légionnaires had 'been volunteered' by their CO, and there was no point in risking refusals to jump when such men reached the door of a Dakota over Dien Bien Phu.[91] The eventual total of individual volunteers varies in the sources between 1,800 and just under 2,600, of whom about one in four are said to have been non-Europeans.[92] Of these, about 700 unqualified volunteers would actually be dropped during April and early May, the great majority making their first jump over Dien Bien Phu. In the event, door refusals by the volunteers would be remarkably infrequent.[93]

After a few hours' rudimentary ground instruction, these men often had to wait on the airfield for several days until the wind conditions allowed them to embark. Sometimes they were actually on their way to Dien Bien Phu when a change in the weather aborted the mission, and they had to return and endure another nerve-racking wait before they finally faced their door into the darkness above the flaming valley.[94] The officers and men who jumped in late April and early May can have had no delusions about their fate – Dien Bien Phu was now openly called *la cuvette*, 'the toilet bowl'; and some had no personal or unit connections with the garrison. Others were convalescents from the winter fights in the hills, or time-expired men awaiting the ship home, who simply decided that they wanted to be with their friends at the end. It would be grotesque to speak about 'the bravest men at Dien Bien Phu' – courage is not a competition; but the example of these individual volunteers remains astonishing. Pierre Langlais would later wage a two-year campaign against French Army bureaucracy to secure the award of their parachute 'wings' to any survivors who had made that first jump, though not the number officially needed to qualify. Sadly, the bureaucrats won their mean little victory.[95]

14. Verdun without the Sacred Way

'It's a bit like Verdun, but Verdun without the depth of defence – and, above all, without the Sacred Way...'
Colonel de Castries *to General Cogny, 22 March 1954*

GENERAL GIAP DESCRIBED THE fighting from the second week of April to the end of that month as *grignotage* – 'nibbling away'.[1] His failed attempt on Huguette 6 had reminded him of the risks of sending his assault infantry too far over open ground; their saps must be pushed forward right up to the barbed wire of French strongpoints that had been isolated from the support of their neighbours. Like his first pause, this next phase would see an ever tightening web of approach trenches dug towards and around French perimeter positions – this time, the Huguettes that now guarded the exposed north-western face of the camp; but the consequent fighting would differ in nature from the relatively cautious mutual probing of the second half of March.

It was as if the Western Front of 1915–18 had been recreated in the valley of the Nam Youm: trenches dug to within a few dozen yards of each other – sometimes even cutting into one another – were shelled, raided, defended, lost and retaken. Men clung to craters and ditches in a ravaged landscape saturated by rainstorms, unable to raise their heads in daylight for fear of mortars and snipers. On 13 April GONO actually requested trench periscopes, but Hanoi were unable to locate such antique equipment. The underground nature of the fighting would give the battle-field an extraordinary appearance of emptiness; although thousands of men were present, they could only be seen for brief periods. When they did clash face to face, the outcome would sometimes be decided not only with guns and grenades but with bayonets, daggers, and entrenching tools wielded like hatchets.

A special feature of Dien Bien Phu was the absence of a continuous battlefront; it was a series of individual, company-sized Verduns. Out to the north, west and south there still stretched large areas that were not occupied by either side, but merely stalked by the patrols of both. This illusion of freedom of movement, and their grip on some of the eastern hilltops, would keep the garrison's hopes alive throughout the month. Meanwhile, the attitude of the French high command to the continuing reinforcement of the camp would be marked by swings of mood, as the generals were forced to react to a series of changes in the wider picture. In France, the Easter recess closed parliament from 10 April to 2 May. For the garrison, the problem was at least straightforward: there was never a day when Castries and Langlais did not need more men and ammunition, and they kept up a constant stream of demands to Hanoi for their delivery to the valley by any possible means.[2]

DURING THE FIRST WEEK OF the month the transport aircrews were hampered by bad visibility over the High Region, sometimes down to little more than a mile. Combat aircraft still operated over the valley almost daily, however; on 2 to 4 April, B-26s of GB 1/25, Bearcats of GC 1/22 and the faithful Hellcats of 11F had all flown missions for GONO, bombing and strafing north and west of the perimeter bastions.[3] On the 6th the very last aircraft landed at 'Torri Rouge': a Morane spotter from Muong Sai, flown by Sergeant Ribière of 21 GAOA, was hit by machine-gun fire over Dien Bien Phu, and the observer Lieutenant Choue de la Mestrie of 23 GAOA was badly wounded. The pilot managed to make an emergency landing on the southern half of the runway, but the plane was immediately destroyed by enemy artillery; Ribière got out of the blazing wreck alive, but his officer did not.

That day orders were issued for a number of units to move position. Given the threat posed by the trenches snaking towards the flat south-western face of the camp and its weak defences, Major Jean Nicolas and the surviving couple of companies of his I/4 RTM were ordered across from the Elianes to carve a system of trenches and blockhouses out of the lower

Huguettes and upper Claudines. This was codenamed 'Liliane' ('Lili'): Claudine 1 became Lili 1, Lili 2 was entirely new, and Huguette 4 became Lili 3 (*see Map 18*). This system would take until 14 April to complete.[4] Major Knecht of II/4 RAC ordered the shifting of his 6th Battery from its position at Dominique 4, which he considered too exposed, back to the old artillery lines in Claudine.[5]

On 7 April, Lieutenant Colonel Langlais' order to disarm and disband several Thai auxiliary companies and, at Huguette 2, Captain Guilleminot's 12th Company, BT 3, was carried out; the bond between Thais and their French officers was personal, and since Guilleminot had been wounded his company was crumbling away. Although no effort was made to stop the Thais deserting, about 30 attached themselves voluntarily to the artillery as ammunition carriers.[6] (It should also be noted that at Isabelle, Captain Desiré's 9th Company, BT 3 fought on staunchly, as did most of Lieutenant Wieme's 200-odd survivors of the retreat from Lai Chau.)

Outside the valley, there was no immediate prospect of Generals Navarre and Cogny getting a whole new parachute brigade to quarrel over. On 8 April the C-in-C was advised in a telegram from Secretary Jacquet that the promised 7th Colonial battalion from France would not be arriving by air until about 25 April, and that the 3rd Foreign from Algeria, shipped aboard the *Pasteur*, would not be docking until perhaps 22 May. Under these circumstances General Cogny agreed to drop one more of the few in-country battalions into Dien Bien Phu; he apparently tried to fob them off with the Vietnamese 1 BPVN, but on the morning of 9 April Colonel de Castries sent a curt message directly to Navarre demanding the promised Legion paras of the 2nd Foreign – a first-class battalion, 677 strong (whose recent record is described in Chapter 5).[7] Once they were assured of getting them without further delay, Lieutenant Colonel Langlais and Major Bigeard could press ahead with an operation that was close to their hearts. On the evening of 8 April, Langlais approved Bigeard's plan for a second attempt to retake Eliane 1.

Heavy rain fell during the night of 8/9 April, but careful preparations for the attack continued throughout the next day. As men moved through the communication trenches to their jumping-off positions they looked up, as always, at the sound of aero engines, but today some probably wished that they had kept their eyes down. Hit by AA fire, Ensign Laugier of squadron 3F baled out, but opened his parachute too soon – it caught on the tailplane, and dragged him to his death when the Helldiver crashed near Claudine 5. Captain Capeyron's légionnaires from 3rd Company, I/13 DBLE went out and recovered the body. It would be one of the last to be buried in a coffin. Later that evening Captain Charnod's Air Force squad ventured out on to the open runway and extricated the charred remains of Lieutenant de La Mestrie from the burnt-out Morane.[8]

Despite rain on the night of 9/10 April, the 'Banjos' succeeded in dropping about half of Major Hubert Liesenfelt's 2 BEP: the HQ and part of Captain Picatto's HQ Company, two platoons of Lieutenant de Biré's 5th, three of Lieutenant Pétré's Vietnamese 8th, and the whole of Captain Delafond's 7th Company. Now that the paras were being dropped all over the camp it took hours to assemble and organize them; lights could be shown only fleetingly, and it was better for them to wait until morning rather than risk wandering into enemy lines. On 10 April they moved out to take up reserve positions at Epervier, where Corporal Antoine Hoinant of 8th Company recalled being shocked to find only knee-deep trenches and no proper shelters or blockhouses. The 7th Company were assigned to immediate counter-attack alert at Dominique 3; while reconnoitring the route there Captain Delafond was killed by shellfire, and Lieutenant Le Cour Grandmaison took over (by nightfall 2 BEP had already suffered 29 killed and wounded by random shelling).[9] All day, as they tried to improve their positions, they watched and listened to the battle to retake Eliane 1 a few hundred yards to the east.

THE VIET MINH OBSERVERS, snipers and rifle-grenadiers of the battalion occupying Eliane 1 had made life intolerable for the companies of 6 BPC and 5 BPVN on Eliane 4, which they overlooked from only 150yds away (*see Map 17*). Major Bigeard had been feeding disinformation to the enemy over the insecure radio net for some days, while he planned Eliane 1's recapture by his old battalion. Like any textbook assault of 1918, it would depend upon the objective being 'caged' by the fire of supporting units to isolate it from all help. The attack would be co-ordinated by Bigeard from a hole on the forward slope of Eliane 4, where he crouched with binoculars, maps, and eight radio sets. It would be a classic demonstration of the tactical skills for which he was already respected, and which he would later refine and extend in Algeria. Bigeard's own metaphor cannot be bettered: linked by radio to his companies, to Langlais and the reserves, to the mortars, artillery, tanks and forward air controller, he would conduct the whole action like an orchestral work.[10]

On the night of 9/10 April he had paid the enemy the compliment of imitation, having approach trenches dug out from Eliane 4 towards the base of Eliane 1. On the rear face of Eliane 4, he placed Lieutenant Allaire of 6 BPC's heavy platoon with 81mm mortars gathered from all the parachute units – 20 tubes in all; these would fire the opening salvoes of the barrage at 6am, in order not to betray the scale of the operation at once. They would be followed by drum fire from 12 howitzers at Claudine, eight at Isabelle, and the 120mm mortars – 1,800 shells were allocated for this 20-minute barrage.[11] Smoke shells to blind the enemy on Baldy and Phoney would signal the end of this phase; by that time four tanks would be on the road below Eliane 4 ready to engage Eliane 1's blockhouses, and the RCLs on Dominique 2, with their flat-trajectory cannon. The quad-50s at Epervier had also been given fire tasks, and from Eliane 2 six machine guns and 12 LMGs would lend their help.

Major Thomas's 6th Colonial Parachute Battalion had by now been reduced to an HQ company and three small rifle companies each of about 80 men. Lieutenant Hervé Trapp's 2nd Company would lead off, followed by Lieutenant René Le Page's 1st, with Lieutenant Perret's 3rd in reserve. All normal rules about the interval to be observed behind a 'friendly' barrage were thrown away. At 6.10am on 10 April Trapp's leading assault platoons, led by Lieutenants Samalens and Corbineau, rose from their approach trenches and dashed forward, following the shellbursts closely up the slope. Separate squads advanced in fluid rushes from shellhole to trench to shellhole, clearing them with small arms and grenades, bypassing stubborn positions where they dared, always exploiting forwards. It was desperate work – their breath sawing, hearts pounding, legs aching as they forced themselves up the slope, one hand clamping down a bouncing helmet, head constantly swivelling to catch a blurred movement out of the corner of an eye, raking bursts of half-aimed 'fire by instinct', clawing for a new clip or a grenade. Right on time, fighter-bombers appeared and began bombing and strafing the eastern slopes of the Dominiques and Elianes to seal the front line off from reinforcement.

Eventually, high on the slope, Trapp's company were checked by machine-gun blockhouses, and sealed off themselves by an enemy barrage of 120mm mortar bombs falling behind them. Alerted, 'Bruno' released Le Page's company, together with flame-thrower teams from HQ Company. Casualties mounted as the veterans of 1st Company worked their way up the slope by bounds, alternate squads using 'fire and movement' to cover each other. Bigeard had sent an extra light machine-gun section to cover the flame-throwers; the LMG teams were wiped out, but the flame-throwers made it to the upper slope and around the southern shoulder of the feature.

The US back-pack flame-thrower had a hand pipe with a lighting device at the muzzle, fed by two cylinders holding jellied petrol and a third cylinder of nitrogen propellant; it weighed about 70lbs – a serious encumbrance to a man trying to move fast uphill over broken ground. The operator facing heavy small-arms fire ran the risk of a horrible death himself if a hot bullet passed through the vapour in partly emptied fuel tanks. The cylinders emptied fast, since their five-gallon capacity gave only eight or ten seconds' firing time; but if the operator could get within 40yds of an enemy position his weapon was appallingly efficient, delivering a jet of liquid fire straight through bunker embrasures into the faces of the machine-gun crews. The gush of flame was like a huge orange feather, with little black-edged, curling streaks breaking away from the main blast, and it made an eerie, whistling roar which many men found terrifying. Beneath a dark veil of stinking petrol smoke the end of the flame fell away on the target in a shower of liquid drops, seeking out by gravity the crannies which were safe from bullets and shrapnel. It crackled as it fell on grass and brush, leaving small burning patches on the ground over which the attackers had to run.[12]

The fighting came to hand-to-hand range in the upper trenches, and by around noon 6 BPC were in control of the summit. The 2nd Company occupied the north of the position, 1st the south, and 3rd came up between them, together with Sub-lieutenant Prigent's 0.30in machine guns. No more than 180 men had captured the hill from a full battalion; the French would report a body count on the position of 300 enemy dead, and many wounded were seen being carried back. The commander of Regiment 174 was dismissed for this failure – he may have been reduced to the ranks, or even shot. Next day GONO would report 6th Colonial's casualties as 60 all ranks – perhaps 30 per cent of those who attacked the hill.[13]

Experience had taught that this level of casualties must be expected, and that it was essential to relieve the assault unit before it was hit by heavy counter-attacks. The People's Army gave the survivors of 6 BPC no respite to watch the Helldivers of 3F at work over Phoney; they sent in a first attack from about 1pm. The paratroopers clung on to Eliane 1 only with difficulty during the early afternoon; but at around 4pm Bigeard sent up two companies of II/1 RCP (Captain Charles' 3rd and Lieutenant Minaud's 4th), who managed to take over the torn-up position before an artillery barrage fell upon them at about 6.30pm. Between nightfall on the 10th and 4am on 11 April they held off four separate counter-attacks by Regiment 174 reinforced by two battalions from Regiment 98: at least three full battalions, perhaps 2,000 men even allowing for earlier casualties, outnumbering the Parachute Chasseurs by at least six, perhaps ten, to one. By 8pm close-quarter fighting was taking place, and both company commanders were wounded.

Lieutenant Colonel Langlais was as determined as Major Bigeard that the hill should not fall yet again, and for the first time he simply appealed to the other units to contribute what men they could. The first battalion to respond was 1 BEP, which sent Lieutenant Brandon's 2nd and Lieutenant Martin's 3rd Companies – companies in name only, since they numbered no more than 50 men each. Their advance up the slope of Eliane 1 that night provided one of the legends of Dien Bien Phu, which is confirmed by several eyewitnesses: onlookers were astonished to hear the légionnaires go into the attack singing the slow, Germanic cadence of their battalion marching song.[14] The next volunteers up the hill were 2nd and 3rd Companies, 5 BPVN. They sang too; but Vietnamese music does not lend itself to stern marches, so the *Bawouan* went into battle against their countrymen singing 'La Marseillaise'. By midnight the summit was secured; and at dawn Bigeard sent up Lieutenant Le Cour Grandmaison with his 7th Company, 2 BEP to join their fellow Legion paratroopers. The enemy body count on the position had now risen to perhaps 400; but the night had cost the II/1 RCP companies ten dead, 21 missing and 66 wounded, and the 1 BEP and 5 BPVN contingents also had about 100 casualties. Eliane 1 would continue to be held for the next 20 days.[15]

DURING THE NIGHTS OF 10/11 and 11/12 April the remainder of the 2nd Foreign Parachute Battalion jumped in. (Among the Dakota pilots who returned from these missions with flak damage we find the familiar names of some of the heroes of late March, including Lieutenants Héquet and Biswang; and on the 14th Captain Soulat's C-119 crew had to extinguish a cargo fire started by incendiary 0.50in rounds.)[16]

On the second night, Eliane 1 was first shelled, then assaulted, while infiltrators tried to cut the hill off from Eliane 4. Battalions 215 and 439 of Regiment 98 soon penetrated the wire and close-quarter fighting spread all over the position. The understrength 3rd and 4th Companies, II/1 RCP were reinforced by the alert company of 2 BEP, and by 1st and 2nd Companies, 6 BPC. By the time the Viet Minh fell back at around 4am the II/1 RCP companies had lost another 19 killed and 66 wounded including two officers (next day the 3rd and 4th would be amalgamated into a single company under Lieutenant René Leguère); and the 2 BEP company reported 47 casualties.[17] On 12 April, 1st and 2nd Companies, II/1 RCP (Lieutenant Périou and Captain Clédic) took over on Elianes 1 and 4. At least radio security now improved – they both spoke Breton. Other officers and radio operators tried to frustrate Viet Minh eavesdroppers by speaking English, German, Spanish or Arabic.

With Major Liesenfelt's battalion in place, companies of 2 BEP took turns to occupy the Elianes, relieving 1 BEP; 5th Company now spent three days and nights on the lunar desolation of Eliane 1. During company take-overs there was no question of simply filing through the communication trenches; the approach was a tactical movement, by four or five men at a time separated by wide intervals. In pitch darkness the NCOs had to take the men by the hand to lead them to the holes in the ground in which they would crouch throughout the daylight hours. Enemy surveillance was unremitting, and the RCLs were particularly deadly; their high velocity meant that the shells gave no warning whistle of approach before exploding on the position. When companies were relieved for a few days down at the 'Low Elianes' they were little safer; the shelling and mortaring was intermittent but just as deadly, and the men had to spread out in twos and threes. The stench of the enemy dead on the river flats, unburied since 31 March, was shocking.[18]

FROM 11 APRIL, LIEUTENANT Colonel Langlais reorganized the conduct of the defence into five *quartiers* or districts, each the responsibility of a single officer reporting to him. The Five Hills were the fief of Major Bréchignac of II/1 RCP. Behind him, Major Chenel of BT 2 took over the co-ordination of the 'Low' Dominiques and Elianes where immediate reserves for the hilltops were held. Captain Tourret of 8 BPC was the proprietor of Epervier in the north-east; and with his 1 BEP now shifted across to the Huguettes, Major Guiraud took command of the northern face of the camp. The west and south – Lili and Claudine – were supervised by Major Michel Vadot of the Legion, Jules Gaucher's former chief-of-staff. Major Bigeard was confirmed as Langlais' deputy with direct responsibility for counter-attacks, and henceforward shared his command post.

Each morning a 9am meeting was attended by all the 'district' commanders, Langlais, Bigeard, Lieutenant Colonel Vaillant of the artillery, Major Guérin of the Air Force, and Major de Brinon of I/13 DBLE, who had taken over responsibility for air-drop reception. Colonel de Castries did not attend in person, but was represented by a member of his staff, and Major Bigeard also made a point of reporting to Castries afterwards. Bernard Fall claims that the camp commander's 'progressive alienation, if not estrangement' from the battle dated from this time, in a gradual and unemphatic process; this interpretation has already been discussed in Chapter 12.

Generally, morale among the garrison seems to have been high during the week of 11–18 April, partly because of intelligence reports suggesting that it was low in the enemy camp. Radio traffic had been intercepted from People's Army unit commanders complaining of their troops' unwillingness to obey orders; and on the 15th an interrogated prisoner claimed that some *bo doi* had had to be forced into battle at gunpoint.[19] The loudspeaker propaganda war was not one-sided; an officer of Regiment 57 would later recall broadcasts from the camp in such terms as 'Oh enemy brothers, we feel sorry for you. Your infantrymen are nearly all dead. Only you are left, and your turn will come. Why don't you return to Hanoi with us, by aeroplane?... You have had enough. Give yourselves up. Your lives will be easier.'[20]

MAJOR JACQUES GUÉRIN WAS a sick man, and he also suffered from being the nearest target for the Army officers' frustration over Air Force failures, real or perceived. On 12 April, Lieutenant Colonel Langlais had an unanswerable complaint: from above the morning fog a B-26 had dropped a stick of six 500lb bombs across the middle of the camp. When he first heard the explosions Langlais' immediate reaction was that the Chinese Air Force had come into the war, as so many French officers from Navarre downwards had long feared. The bombs fell among the artillery gunpits, across the HQ area, astride the hospital and in Epervier, where one of them killed three and wounded two men of 2 BEP's HQ Company and destroyed two of their six 81mm mortars.[21]

A reminder of the dangers faced by the aircrews was not long in coming. A little before noon on the 12th, two of the big Navy Privateers were circling at about 13,000ft over the camp. One came below the high cloud ceiling and bombed from 9,000ft, while Lieutenant Manfanovsky in '28F-4' waited above. As he came down in his turn through 10,000ft, 'Caesar 4' was hit in the wing by 37mm fire; it veered off, dropping the rest of its load, and went into a spin. Manfanovsky seemed to correct this, but the Privateer then spun in the opposite direction, and crashed north-west of Anne-Marie. Three parachutes were seen, at least one of them 'candling'; but no member of the crew was ever heard from again.[22]

During the following night the price paid by the soldiers for the transport crews' mistaken cargo drops was emphasized when People's Army 105s shelled the camp using new US short-delay fuses, which were very effective at penetrating bunkers. The following day the Air Force salted the wound: two fighter-bombers dropped their ordnance on the camp, causing deaths and injuries and blowing up a precious depot of howitzer shells, while C-119s tipped their cargo of 105mm ammunition out over enemy-held Dominique 1. In a private transmission to General Cogny on 13 April, Colonel de Castries reported: 'In 24 hours we have sustained three [French] bombing attacks within our defensive perimeter. On the other hand the cargo of five C-119s, or a minimum of 800 artillery rounds, has been delivered to the enemy. No comment.' At one point artillery ammunition losses were so frequent that Langlais suggested that Hanoi should booby-trap shells and drop them deliberately over enemy lines, in the hope of destroying some guns when they were used (the idea was not pursued, for a fairly obvious reason).[23]

The weather over the High Region was unusually good from 9 to 16

April, and in fact record cargo tonnages would be achieved (217 tons on the 13th, 229 the next day – although inadequate packing caused some losses). Part of the problem over misdropped loads was that the American CAT pilots flying many of the C-119s spoke no French, and most ground controllers at 'Torri Rouge' little English. Radio facilities were limited, and when the PCIA was trying to control 30 or more aircraft at once in the daylight sky over the valley this led to delays in communication. In the face of enemy flak these were not only frustrating but dangerous; understandably, some pilots simply went ahead and dropped their loads by eye and experience without waiting for detailed instructions.[24]

The day would end in another tragedy. On 13 April, Major Knecht of II/4 RAC ordered that a gun of his 4th Battery try to hit a 75mm RCL spotted on Dominique 2. Although Paul Brunbrouck was not keen to draw fire in daylight he obeyed. Using Charge 6 to get the flattest possible trajectory, the gun captain missed with his first shot; after the RCL returned fire he tried again, and scored a surprising direct hit. Whether or not this incident drew some Viet Minh observer's particular attention cannot be known; but late that afternoon, out of the blue, a heavy enemy bombardment fell on 4th Battery's position, killing a shelter-full of men wounded the previous day. In a pause at about 7.15pm Sergeant Bernard Laurent made his way through the trenches to report to the battery command post. He found it wrecked; Sub-lieutenant Baysset told him that the battery commander was wounded, and that Father Trinquand was with him.

A shell with a short-delay fuse had penetrated the roof and exploded inside; Lieutenant Brunbrouck had taken large fragments in his back, and also parts of the acid battery from a smashed radio. He spoke calmly to his NCOs gathering around, but it was difficult to get the young officer out; a chicane wall protecting the entrance prevented them getting a stretcher inside, and he had to be manhandled out into the trench, which caused him great pain. Distressed African gunners helped carry him to the main hospital, where he died that night. Baysset asked Lieutenant Colonel Vaillant for a fire mission, to take the gunners' minds off their loss; and 4th Battery was taken over by Captain Manzoni, who had parachuted in a couple of days previously.[25]

IN THE HUGUETTES BOTH THE physical defences and the Legion garrisons were being ground away steadily by shellfire. By 14 April, I/2 REI had dwindled to 380 men, I/13 DBLE to 354; with 80 survivors of III/13, the main camp's Legion infantry now numbered just 814 – the paper strength of a single battalion. During the second week of April the units were reorganized (see Maps 13 and 18). Huguette 6 at the end of the airstrip was held from the 8th of the month by a Marching Company, I/2 REI – the former 1st and 3rd, amalgamated under Lieutenant Francois; and by Captain Bizard's 1st Company, 5 BPVN. Huguette 1, halfway down the runway, was occupied by Lieutenant Spozio's 2nd Company, I/2 REI. South of this, Huguettes 2 and 3 were held by 10th (Marching) Company, III/13 DBLE – the Béatrice survivors mixed with the regiment's old NCO training platoon, under Captain Philippe; and by 4th Company, I/2 REI led by Captain Bourges. The reserves for this sector were provided by I/13 DBLE and 1 BEP in the southern Huguettes and Claudines; and Moroccans of I/4 RTM held the Lilianes. As in the parachute battalions, most companies were now down to about 80 men.

The networks of Viet Minh trenches were gripping ever tighter. Each day's aerial photos revealed new tentacles spreading towards and around the strongpoints (in the end their total length would be estimated at about 60 miles). The artillery observers tried to bring fire down on the sap heads, carefully noting their latest advances by day for bombardment by night; but their task was frustrated by the lack of vantage points on the valley floor, and by the low allocation of shells for these shoots – priority had to be given to conserving ammunition for infantry support during Viet Minh night assaults. In the Five Hills an actual mine gallery was being driven under Eliane 2 by Regiment 98, whose soldiers included former coal miners from the Dong Trieu area; Hanoi dropped GONO improvised geophones – medical stethoscopes linked to dish-shaped split canteens – to enable them to track the progress of the tunnel. Even on the valley floor many of the approach trenches were partially roofed in, and some burrowed under and beyond the French wire.

On 11 April, Lieutenant Spozio made a daylight sortie to clear and destroy trenches from the west which were threatening to reach the runway and cut Huguette 1 off from both north and south. About three enemy companies sprang up out of the earth from concealed shelters, with supporting fire from sandbag machine-gun nests. Reinforcements, two tanks and artillery fire were needed just to get 2nd Company back into its position; one tank was bazooka'd; Spozio was carried in wounded, but Lieutenant Legros of 10th Company, III/13 had to be abandoned, in violation of a sacred law of the Legion. For the first time the enemy were not driven out of their trenches in daylight, and remained in control of the field. By 14 April Huguette 1's whole western wire would be confronted from a range of about 15yds by manned enemy trenches, and night infiltrators had cut a three-yd-wide gap almost through it.[26]

On the night of 13/14 April GONO reported that the runway 200yds north of Huguette 1 was actually being cut by a trench from the west; this seems to have been the work of a battalion of Regiment 88. They had approached the airstrip during the evening up trenches dug during previous nights, and for the sake of speed they came above ground as soon as darkness fell. The lead platoon split into three teams: the point squad had a light machine gun, the other men being fully armed with sub-machine guns, rifles and grenades, and the flanks were guarded by snipers. Digging forward yard by yard, occasionally dropping into their shallow diggings to avoid artillery and mortar fire, they reached the edge of the airstrip at about 11pm. As the holes were deepened and linked, one company was used solely to bring up planks and props, and overhead cover of timber and sandbags was raised at short intervals. Presumably they used explosives to cut the PSP, under cover of the sound of artillery. By 4am they had cut about 40yds across the runway. At first light a French counter-attack overran the lead company, killing the commander and driving the rest back. Another unit was sent up in support, but the completion of the trench had to be left until the next night.[27]

A VIEW OF THE PEOPLE'S ARMY entrenchments from the inside comes from a Legion prisoner taken that night. At about midnight on 13/14 April, Corporal Ortwin Preiss of 4th Company, I/2 REI returned to Huguette 2 to report an uneventful three-hour tour of duty in a listening post to the south-west. When Preiss assured him that he was not tired, Captain Guy Bourges gave him another mission: to take two men and scout the return route for two paratroop platoons then lying out in ambush between Huguette 5 and Huguette 1, and also to make contact with a 5 BPVN ambush on the airstrip. It was a still, mild night, with wisps of mist clinging to the barbed wire but bright stars overhead, when Preiss and his men moved out almost due north (*see Map 13*).

They had nearly reached the wreck of the Curtiss C-46 Commando halfway up the western edge of the airstrip when they heard Vietnamese voices, then a challenge in French. Thinking they had reached the 5th *Bawouan* patrol, they gave the password and advanced to be recognized – only to find themselves under the guns of a People's Army patrol hiding under the wings of the Curtiss. They were disarmed, and after a few minutes the patrol withdrew to the east with its prisoners: across the airstrip, down into the Japanese drain, then off north-eastwards. They passed for some 1,000yds alongside Viet Minh soldiers in about battalion strength who were busy digging a new trench on this axis.

Reaching the 12ft west bank of the Nam Youm, Preiss and his comrades were urged through an entrance camouflaged with woven bamboo, which led into a dark shelter under a log-propped earth roof about 6ft thick. Opening off this was a command post consisting of two candlelit chambers each about 15ft square. Preiss' men were left in the first, which was full of sleeping *bo doi*, while the corporal was taken into the second. The CP appeared to him to have been in use for some time. Several men without badges of rank were sitting on sandbags around a large table; one of them, using a US radio. The table bore a large sandbox model of that sector of the defences, and this was updated from the latest reports on the progress of the sapping as messengers came and went during the 30 minutes that Preiss was interrogated. His questioner spoke good French, did not bluster or threaten, and confined himself to the basics: name, rank, unit, where posted, purpose of mission, and so forth. After being given water, Preiss and his men were then marched off to the east under escort; the Viet Minh moved in single file, apparently unworried by the sound of aircraft circling overhead.

The Nam Youm was crossed on a footway sunk 15in below the surface of the water, and the party then entered a substantial trench. They moved at a good pace, though frequently halting to give way to units and individuals going up to the line. They passed many caches opening off the communications trench at right angles – short bays about a yard wide and several long, floored with bamboo and covered with matting; they were dug opposite trees and bushes, perhaps to mark their position. Their contents seemed to Preiss to be entirely recovered from French cargo drops, mixed up and bundled in anyhow, but well covered from the rain.

On the morning of the 14th the légionnaires and their escort rested in a deep trench sheltered by tall trees; individual sleeping burrows were dug into the trench walls, 5ft deep and under an impressive 9ft of earth cover. After the march resumed they passed a dressing station, also driven off the side of the trench and sheltering wounded on rustic stretchers; Preiss noted that some were receiving blood transfusions. At nightfall they reached RP41 and marched on up the road for some hours, passing busy foot traffic in both directions. Next morning a colonel questioned them for two hours; then the other two prisoners were marched off towards their eventual POW camp – Preiss never heard of them again. He himself was told that he would be held as a German interpreter to work at an interrogation centre.[28]

THE FRENCH 'COUNTER-ATTACK' which ran into Regiment 88's diggings on the runway on 13/14 April was in fact a heavily escorted ammunition and water party trying to reach Huguette 6 at the far end of the airstrip. The strongpoint's two-company garrison of légionnaires and Vietnamese paras was completely isolated and increasingly surrounded by the multiplying trenches of Regiment 165. Life in the northern Huguettes was monotonous but dangerous; by day there was intermittent shelling, mortaring and sniping, while the men tried to strengthen their positions and snatch some sleep. On 14 April a shell caught the officers of Huguette 6 during a meeting: Captain Bizard and Lieutenant Francois escaped, but Lieutenant Rastouil was killed and Sub-lieutenant Méric wounded. The day's one meal consisted of a mess-tin of rice – if there was water to cook it – with perhaps one tin of sardines between four men, or a tin of peas between ten. Food throughout the perimeter strongpoints became scarcer from 14 April, when shelling destroyed a large depot; from then on combat rations became the norm, and tobacco was very scarce. From about 5pm each afternoon the shelling became heavier and more focused, and it was time for the defenders to stand-to, tensed for a night assault.[29]

There was no large stockpile of munitions, nor of water, in these battered entrenchments, and over the third week of April the nightly expeditions to keep them supplied encountered increasingly heavy resistance. A large column of PIM porters would be assembled in the main camp, carrying ammunition boxes, rations, and awkward 5-gallon jerry-cans of water – Huguette 6 needed at least 20 jerry-cans a day. Escorted by one or two complete infantry companies and sometimes by tanks, the column would snake out through the chicanes in the camp's barbed-wire defences and on up the airfield drain from Epervier until they were opposite Huguette 1; then across the airstrip, and north again through communication trenches to Huguette 6 – after these were interrupted by new enemy diggings the final stage involved the escort in fighting the column through.

During the day of 14 April an operation to get through to Huguette 1 by paras of 6th Colonial and 8th Shock came under heavy mortar fire, and also encountered an unwelcome novelty: the enemy had started laying their own mines. That night 1 and 2 BEP each provided escort companies for a column of 50 porters; they were pinned down between Huguette 2 and Huguette 1 – a gap of about 300yds – for four hours under fire from trenches on the airfield. They eventually got through to Huguette 6 at about 2.40am on the 15th, but not without losing men and stores.

To get them back to the main camp in daylight required a major diversionary operation. Lieutenant Bailly's 3rd Company, 8 BPC from Epervier attacked the Viet Minh 'runway trench' across the airstrip, while Captain Philippe's 10th Company, III/13 DBLE pushed west from Huguette 2 against a strong enemy trench and blockhouse complex that had been created north of Lili 3. While the Legion paras made their way back from Huguette 6 both these companies had stiff fighting, and although Philippe was reinforced by Spozio's 2/I/2 REI from Huguette 1 neither of them managed to capture their objectives. The tank 'Ettlingen' took a bazooka rocket in the turret, killing two crewmen, but was soon repaired and back in action manned by parachuted replacements.[30]

The People's Army stranglehold on the northern Huguettes was becoming ever more confident. By contrast, there were still large gaps in the Viet Minh 'lines' through which patrols were circulating freely; that day a strong party from I/13th DBLE pushed west as far as Ban Ban, nearly a mile from the Huguettes. While the individual strongpoints were closely encircled, these and the enemy who clung to them were still islands on a sparsely inhabited plain.

ON 15 APRIL THE GOOD WEATHER continued, allowing cargo drops totalling an unprecedented 250 tons; but a significant amount was mis-dropped out of reach – the Air Force admitted 15 per cent, but some Army officers claimed it was nearly half. Nevertheless, food stocks were topped up to two days' supply, 105mm ammunition to five days', and bombs for the 120mm mortars to six days' theoretical needs. The three Legion mortar companies, whose work was so vital given the problems of the artillery, had suffered very heavy losses by this date. After the battle of the Five Hills the paratroop 1 CEPML had been pulled back from the 'Low' Dominiques and Elianes to the western edge of Claudine; here it was amalgamated with the surviving platoon of 2 CMMLE, under overall command of Lieutenant Erwan Bergot. Lieutenant Poirier's surviving platoon of 1 CMMLE was further north-east in Epervier; altogether, they had 15 serviceable mortars.[31]

The sailors who flew the Aéronavale fighter-bombers and dive-bombers were the most popular airmen at Dien Bien Phu: justly or not, they enjoyed a greater reputation for courage and skill than their Air Force counter-parts. On the 15th, however, one Hellcat 'penguin' was to mar this record. At about 5pm he was scheduled to free-drop GONO headquarters a pouch containing the latest aerial photos and maps of the whole valley, showing both updated French and the latest detected enemy positions. He had already slid his cockpit canopy back when he came under anti-aircraft fire, and during his evasive manoeuvres he somehow managed to drop the pouch behind enemy lines.[32]

That day the US Consul Paul Sturm, who was returning to the USA from Hanoi at the end of his tour of duty, reported to Washington on a farewell meeting with General Cogny. 'Delta Man' had been characteris-tically indiscreet: he had admitted that France did not have the aircrews to man the planes that she was constantly asking America to provide. Cogny was equally uninhibited about his disagreements with the commander-in-chief; he complained that Navarre should never have accepted battle in the remote jungle of the Thai country, since 'at Dien Bien Phu the seven-year battle for the Red River delta might very well be lost'.[33]

On the night of 15/16 April a strong escort was assembled from elements of 1 and 2 BEP and 6 BPC to take a column of about 60 porters up to Huguette 6. It was a massacre: 42 of the PIMs were killed or wounded, and only seven, with five jerrycans, reached the strongpoint – at most a pint of water for each defender, in the humid heat of spring.[34]

FRIDAY 16 APRIL 1954 WAS Good Friday, the most sombre day in the Christian calendar. There were many among the largely Catholic garrison of Dien Bien Phu who took comfort from the familiar observances, and the camp's chaplains conducted the rites proper to Our Lord's crucifixion.

At Huguette 2, Lieutenants Viard and Chounet, commanding two companies of I/2 REI, decided to start digging a trench north in an attempt to link up with Huguette 1, which was now completely surrounded by enemy works. GONO asked Hanoi to parachute mechanics and electricians to keep the precious generators and water purifiers working (the generators provided not only light and power, but ran the vital rechargers for radio batteries). Despite morning fog reaching up to 9,850ft, during the day about 215 tons of supplies were dropped, with at least 10 per cent going adrift.[35]

It was on 16 April that a concerted effort was made to neutralize the enemy flak batteries at least during priority drops, such as paratroopers. All observers were alerted before the day's resupply mission to watch for AA fire in their assigned sectors and report co-ordinates to the PC Feux. A fire plan was worked out, and from 17 April batteries were alerted by Major Guérin's air-control post before the Dakotas arrived. It was hoped that if all the howitzers and mortars switched to these targets during the parachute drops they should be able if not to destroy them, then at least to silence them for two or three hours. Major Le Gurun reported after his release from captivity that Viet Minh officers had told him that by day the batteries west of the camp were often neutralized for several hours by 'Zulu Kilo's' fire, and that light AA guns at the foot of the Dominiques suffered losses from shelling, mortaring and the quad-50 mounts. However, this was only achieved if all other fire tasks were ignored, and at a great cost in ammunition; there were simply too many AA guns.[36]

Good Friday did bring joy to some in the camp: the announcement of a number of battlefield promotions, signalled to Colonel de Castries the previous night. Castries became a brigadier general; Lieutenant Colonels Langlais and Lalande were named full colonels; Majors Bigeard and Seguin-Pazzis were promoted to lieutenant colonel, and – not before time – the parachute battalion commanders Captains Tourret and Botella became majors. A number of other officers were also promoted by one grade. The decisions had been taken at a high level, and were not without political undertones; for weeks now the French media had been splashing stories of the heroic defence of the camp, and public feeling was more engaged than at any time since October 1950.[37]

On the night of 16/17 April the usual supply run to Huguette 6 triggered a major action; fighting lasted until sunrise, and it took no fewer than three companies from 1 BEP and two from I/13 DBLE to link up with the strong-point at 6.15am. Simply keeping Huguette 6 supplied with daily necessities during the four nights of 13–17 April had now cost about 100 soldiers killed, missing and wounded, and probably the same number of PIMs. Such a haemorrhage was not sustainable for much longer; even though the abandonment of Huguette 6 would reduce the theoretical area of the drop zone for parachuted supplies and allow the enemy to push observers and AA guns even closer to the central camp, in practice the northern half of the airfield was already controlled by the People's Army. At 6.20pm on 17 April General de Castries and Colonel Langlais agreed that Captain Bizard's tattered little garrison should be extracted and brought home the next night. A small new strongpoint, 'Opéra', would be constructed on the drainage ditch north of Epervier to give some support to Huguette 1.[38]

DETAILS OF THE FIGHTING SOUTH of Huguette 6 on the night of 17/18 April are contradictory in various accounts, though all are agreed on its outcome. One source describes a first failed attempt to reach Bizard by two companies of 1 BEP, followed by a stronger second attempt co-ordinated by Lieutenant Colonel Bigeard at about sunrise on the 18th; others elide the two into a single operation lasting all night. However, it is clear that two companies (including the 1st) of 1 BEP and two (including the 4th) of 8 BPC, with two tanks, struggled for at least four and possibly eight hours that night to get past the Viet Minh dug in around Huguette 1 and across Regiment 88's 'runway trench'. At perhaps 2am they broke into this system, which had now been strengthened and enlarged to face both north and south; but they could make no further progress under heavy fire from mortars, RCLs and machine guns. 'Bruno' ordered his paratroopers to fall back at dawn. By 7.30am on 18 April, Castries and Langlais had reluctantly accepted that to persist in trying to send a rescue force up to Huguette 6 would cost unacceptable casualties with no guarantee of success.

Major Clémencon of I/2 REI radioed Captain Bizard and told him that he was on his own; speaking in English for security, he gave the strong-point commander the choice of either surrendering, or leaving his wounded and attempting to fight his way back with his remaining fit men. It was Easter Sunday morning, and Alain Bizard was 29 years old that day. He replied that he would try to break out at 8am, trusting to the cover of the morning fog. Francois' légionnaires and Bizard's Vietnamese paratroopers made their wounded as comfortable as possible, and smashed the heavy weapons and radios; the severely wounded Sergeant Horst Ganzer, the mortar liaison from 1 CEPML, volunteered to stay behind and give covering fire with the last machine gun. A number of the men slung sandbags to hang over their chests and backs as makeshift splinter vests, and all filled their pockets with grenades. They lined up in their southern trench; at exactly 8am Captain Bizard gave the order, and they leapt up and forward into the grey mist.

The Viet Minh in the nearest trenches were facing south, expecting a renewed attempt at rescue, and since they intended to assault Huguette 6 there were no mines or wire on the northern side. Bizard's men covered the first 200yds without being seen, jumped or scrambled across the trenches showering grenades in all directions, and dashed on down the runway. A group on the west of the line ran straight into a surprised enemy squad, but after a second's mutual hesitation they shot their way through. Behind them, Sergeant Ganzer died at his gun while buying his comrades as much time as he could, and French mortar bombs fell to guard their backs. They had another 200yds of open runway to cover, under a hail of fire; between the explosions Lieutenant Bergot heard Spanish voices yelling encouragement as they ran.

By 10.40am Captain Bizard was counting his survivors at Huguette 2. There is no record of how many men attempted the break-out; Pierre Rocolle states that about 60 reached safety. However, Bizard did note the figures for the whole period of his command at Huguette 6 between 8 and 18 April. Of about 300 men of both companies, 106 were dead (including Lieutenants Francois and Donadieu), 49 were wounded (including Lieu-tenants Cousin and Weinberger), and 79 were missing – which roughly confirms Rocolle's estimate. Dr Grauwin examined the survivors; Lieutenant Bergot quotes him as saying: 'They aren't wounded, but they have nothing left – they're dead men.'

The garrison had conceded another 60 acres to the People's Army, and that day enemy shellfire destroyed one of Captain Déal's three surviving 155mm howitzers. The weather was excellent, and the Air Force dropped Easter treats – liquor, cigarettes and chocolate.[39]

IT WAS FROM ABOUT THE EASTER weekend onwards that rumours began to circulate through GONO about a French relief force to be mounted from northern Laos. General de Castries seems to have been aware of the possibility earlier, but it was on 17 April that the C-in-C had a private letter dropped to the camp commander.[40] Castries had to be kept aware of the progress of planning for this Operation 'Condor'; its implications included the use of parachute units which he might otherwise have believed to be available for Dien Bien Phu. In the same letter General Navarre outlined ongoing discussions about a possible US Air Force intervention for the benefit of the camp, Operation 'Vautour'.

These parallel events far from the valley are covered in more detail in the next chapter, but they are mentioned here as contributing to the garrison's morale. In the second half of April there was widespread speculation in the Western media about possible US involvement in Indochina, and mail and newspapers continued to reach Dien Bien Phu by daily airdrops. On the 15th the French Secretary of State for the Air Force, M. Christiaens, had publicly announced that France was asking the USA for the loan of B-29 Superfortress heavy bombers for use in Indochina, with the pretence that French crews would fly them. Throughout spring 1954 there was free reporting of all examples of American assistance in the air: on 21 April it was revealed that US Globemaster transports would fly French paratroop reinforcements out from Paris–Orly airport; and the following day, that Vought AU-1 Corsair fighter-bombers had arrived at Tourane (Da Nang) aboard the US carrier *Saipan*.[41]

THE LOSS OF HUGUETTE 6 exposed Huguette 1, in its turn, to the full concentration of Division 308. On 18 April its current garrison -- Captain Bourges' 4th Company, I/2 REI – was due to be relieved, and at nightfall

Captain Chevalier's 4th Company, I/13 DBLE left Claudine 2. Most of the communication trenches on the airfield were now roofed over with PSP from the useless runway, turning them into dark and confusing rat-runs, but the undercover link from Huguette 2 to Huguette 1 started by Viard and Chounet on the 16th was not yet complete. At about midnight Chevalier's men were pinned down where the trench ended, by fire from the enemy cross trenches ahead of them that cut Huguette 1 off from the south, and from a new complex that the attackers had created to the west. Two hundred yards short of his objective, Chevalier had to wait for dawn to call in artillery and aircraft to shoot him through to Huguette 1. He broke through with their help at about 6.45am on the 19th, and Bourges' légionnaires pulled out – both companies took casualties in the process. By the time he was installed Chevalier had taken 14 hours to cover 1,500yds, and had lost two dead, six missing and six wounded. He found Huguette 1's defences smashed up by shellfire, most of the wire and mines destroyed, and very little water; the Viet Minh trenches were only half a dozen paces from his perimeter, and some saps had been dug right into his gapped wire.[42]

During 19 April the rest of I/13 DBLE relieved I/2 REI in Huguettes 2 and 3, though Major Clémencon and his staff stayed. Over to the east, 7th Company, 2 BEP relieved Clédic's 2nd Company, II/1 RCP on Eliane 1. Captain Bizard, with a dull-eyed remnant of 1st Company, 5 BPVN, took over Opéra from Lieutenant Pham Van Phu's 2nd Company; the 3rd, led now by the barely healed Captain Guilleminot, stayed in reserve. A strong fighting patrol of légionnaires and Moroccans struck out south from Claudine, and got nearly halfway to Isabelle before running into stubborn resistance. The reason for this attempt, and subsequent patrolling in late April, may have been connected with the plan for Operation 'Condor' to link up from the south.

ON THE 19TH A COLD FRONT reached the Delta, shrouding the airfields with *crachin* which would persist until 25 April. Take-offs were difficult and delayed, with the consequence that when the Dakotas and C-119s did reach Dien Bien Phu they faced a dangerously overcrowded sky which presented the People's Army with multiple targets. Yet on the eve of the monsoon the spring sky was still clear in the High Region; the rain usually stopped at dawn, the mornings were damp but fresh, and in the afternoons the sun blazed down, ripening the dead. It was hard for GONO to understand why the Air Force delivered only 100 tons that day. On the night of 19/20 April the C-47s managed to drop two sticks of volunteer parachutists behind enemy lines. There were grumbles that pilots had used ground artillery fire as an excuse to sheer off, on a night when the flak was unusually light. At 10am on the 20th General de Castries complained to Hanoi that during the past two days he should have received 60 loads from the C-119s, but had only had 23, of which three fell to the Viet Minh; food was now down to one day's supply once again.[43]

Soldiers and airmen never really empathize with one another's problems, however carefully they are explained. The period 6–26 April saw Colonel Nicot's S/GMMTA making their maximum effort, dropping a total of some 3,500 tons, and on most days they managed to put about 50 sorties over the valley. It seems unlikely that they could have achieved much more even if the shortage of aircrews had been less acute, since the base facilities in the Delta were already overstrained.[44] The fact that up to a third of those cargoes fell out of reach or into enemy hands (on some nights, such as 22/23 April, up to two-thirds) could not be blamed simply on a lack of competence or nerve among the pilots and despatchers. It took hardly anything to send the parachuted packages into enemy lines – the slightest error in angle of approach or in calculating wind speed and drift, or the irregular functioning of the extremely primitive delayed-opening device.

TUESDAY 20 APRIL SAW THE usual round of small incidents which characterized daily life at Dien Bien Phu. In the early morning darkness, Captain Bizard's paras at Opéra held off a probing attack with the help of the nearby quad-50s. At mid morning GONO appealed for air support to knock out recoilless guns on Dominique 1, which were doing great damage in the HQ and artillery areas. In the early afternoon a deserter from Regiment 209 ran over to Eliane 1; he claimed that his unit was half filled with raw recruits, that supplies were short and life in the forest was wretched now that the rains had started, that French artillery was still much feared – and that there was a Chinese soldier with every 37mm flak crew. That afternoon shelling set part of the ammunition dump on fire, but it was extinguished by an Air Force team. In late afternoon, seven

Thais deserted from Junon. With nightfall the tempo of enemy shelling picked up, and the daily stream of casualties arriving at the hospital quickened.

By the third week of April conditions in the hospital dug-outs were gruesome. Between 1 and 15 April a total of 751 wounded had been admitted, 310 operations had been carried out, and 76 patients had died. This rate of casualties – averaging 50 admissions and 20 operations daily – had threatened to overwhelm Dr Grauwin's 29 ACM and his colleagues of 44 ACM (Dr Jacques Gindrey) and 6 ACP (Dr Jean Vidal). There had been just five doctors and 13 trained nursing orderlies out of a total of fewer than 40 medical personnel, before an air-drop on 12 April brought them ten more pairs of skilled hands in the shape of Lieutenant Dr Hantz's 5 ACP. Another five orderlies parachuted in on 27 April; but during the third week of April daily casualties in the camp would rise to an average of 120 men.

In order to keep the movement of wounded men under fire to a minimum, three main medical facilities functioned for most of the battle. At the original hospital next to the GONO HQ area, the 29 and 44 ACM and (initially) 5 ACP surgical teams were responsible for casualties from the west bank of the Nam Youm. A second underground hospital for the eastern strongpoints was established by 6 ACP on the far bank of the river. Miles to the south, Dr Rézillot's 3 ACP did what they could for the wounded of Isabelle.[45]

There were also 18 battalion medical officers at their unit aid posts, who made every effort to treat lightly wounded men on the spot rather than subjecting them to the risks of transport under fire to the centre of the camp. About half of the total number of wounded reported during the battle would be dealt with at battalion aid posts, but any serious cases simply had to be carried to the hospitals. The unit MOs had no facilities for serious surgery, and each one was backed up only by a group of aides drawn from the ranks who had been trained in very basic first aid. Even if they reached the hospitals safely there were sometimes too many wounded to be brought underground; men lay outside on stretchers in the mud, and before a corner could be found for them some were wounded again, and some killed, by enemy shellfire.[46]

By the second half of April the intermittent night-time rain which had started on 29 March had become a feature of life in the valley, although it had not yet reached the unbroken intensity of the true monsoon. The floors of the hospitals, like every other trench, tunnel and dug-out in the camp, were soupy with mud, into which hurrying boots inevitably trod bloodstained dressings and human waste. The rain had not only aggravated the general squalor; it drove rats underground. The humid atmosphere in the dug-outs was compounded by a foetid stink of unwashed bodies, blood, vomit, urine and faeces; and on 17 April the first case of gangrene was recorded.

The electricity provided by the camp's 15 power generators kept essential equipment running – refrigerators, the X-ray unit, the lamps in the operating theatre – but elsewhere the lighting was dim and sinister, from occasional 40-watt bulbs. The 'wards' were caverns opening off a long central tunnel. On 14 April, at Grauwin's insistence that he must have more space, Lieutenant Colonel Langlais indulged his long-nurtured dislike of Captain Hébert's Commando Group 8 (whose main task was interrogating prisoners) by evicting the Meos and their families from their dug-outs on the other side of RP41. A roofed-over trench was dug across the roadway to link the hospital to the new dug-outs, which were modified to take 200 patients – though in dark, stifling catacombs which soon became infested with maggots from the nearby mass graves. To clean up the hospital properly would have required disinfectant in industrial quantities, and there was simply no space on the supply aircraft; Dr Grauwin tried to reassure his patients that the maggots were no threat, since they ate only dead tissue and thus kept the wounds clean.

Airlift priority had to be given to huge quantities of stored blood, and vital items such as a replacement X-ray machine. From 15 and 18 April the hospital received the equipment necessary to run a blood bank, taking, typing and storing donations taken directly from the garrison; the stored blood dropped in containers refrigerated with dry ice kept only for three days, and increasing delays in recovering parachuted supplies meant that it was sometimes useless by the time it was brought in. Despite the ever-growing pressure on the air-drop effort, before the first week of May the only medical supply stocks which ever caused serious concern were whole blood and plasma.[47]

WORKING WITH THE SURGEONS, the stranded flight nurse Geneviève de Galard earned the gratitude and soon the devotion of the wounded. Christening her 'the Angel of Dien Bien Phu' was, of course, a vulgarity committed by faraway journalists; but hurt and frightened men obviously take special comfort from the care of a woman. The round, girlish face of the 28-year-old Geneviève – as she was soon known to all – was deceptive. She was one of a number of young women from upper-class backgrounds who were to be found among the female volunteers in Indochina, and while they wore their combat fatigues with undeniable chic they were anything but dilettantes. Some had lived through experiences during World War II which made the comradeship of a combat zone more attractive than the social trivialities of a France where active careers were still not open to many women. The Convoyeuses de l'Air came originally from the aviation branch of the French Red Cross, but in Indochina they formed a distinct section of the Air Force's transport command. These 30-odd young women shared the dangers of long flights over jungle hills in all weathers, landing on dirt airstrips close to the fighting – and for years before the arrival of enough C-47s they did it in antique Junkers Ju52 trimotors. Several of this small group were killed, others wounded, and decorated for bravery.[48]

In the dank heat and stink of the overcrowded burrows Geneviève's serene competence earned her worshippers. She slept for the first three weeks in any available corner, on a stretcher which she folded out of the way when she awoke; she was deeply touched when Langlais, discovering this, had a tiny dug-out in the extension tunnels prepared for her and lined with parachute nylon. Some of the wounded could apparently be comforted only by her, and would call out to her continually as she inched her way between the bunks and stretchers – for water, for a bedpan, for help in moving, for a promise that they were not going to die. One Legion sergeant was a triple amputee; peeling off and replacing the dressings on the stubbornly unhealed stumps of his arms and leg took an hour and a half each time, and in his agony he often lost consciousness for hours afterwards. Geneviève was the only person who could do it without making him cry out; and on his better days she would help him to the entrance for a breath of air.

After washing her hands with antiseptic she might then turn – at least twice every day – to change the dressings of six abdominal cases who had undergone colostomies. This meant handling wads of gauze soiled with excrement; she did it with an unfailing smile, and a joke to ease the men's shame. Once the less seriously wounded had been stabilized they were returned to their unit aid posts, for lack of space in the main hospital; but Geneviève would brave the shellfire to visit them regularly, monitoring their condition and bringing small gifts of cigarettes, an orange, a tin of condensed milk.

Geneviève was a highly qualified professional, and her duties went far beyond simple nursing care; Grauwin and the other overworked surgeons relied upon her as an indispensable colleague. At any time of the day or night she might be confronted with yet another shocked stretcher case in mud-caked fatigues tagged with a label reading, say, 'Compound fractures of both legs – grenade; anti-tet-tox, morphine, half a mill units of penicillin.' She would not touch the initial dressings on his mangled lower legs, for fear of causing fatal secondary shock. The duty surgeon might order an injection of Phenergan and transfusion of two pints of blood. While she monitored the sinking blood pressure suitable veins had to be found quickly; this was difficult in the obvious spots like the inside of the elbows, since a traumatized body automatically directs its fluids towards the central organs, closing down the blood vessels just below the skin and in the limbs and leaving the body surface cold and pale.

Geneviève would soon have two bottles of plasma flowing, but not too fast: overloading the system with fluid can induce heart failure. The team would insert other needles into the patient's thighs, to carry Coramine, Syncortyl, K-thrombyl, anti-gangrene serum, and more penicillin. His blood pressure might fluctuate, falling through 60mm diastolic pressure towards the point at which the heart could no longer pump blood to vital organs; the doctor would order two drops of warmed blood a second and a half-dose of Phenergan. Two more blood bottles would be readied, and attached. Now the field dressings could be removed, with the sister watching for arterial bleeding indicating lesions of the larger vessels. After surgery the team would apply new dressings, then splints; blood pressure would be stabilized with a glucose saline drip; a small dose of heart stimulant might be injected – camphor solution or strychnine; and final injections of penicillin and streptomycin would guard against infection.

Doped patients would be carried from the operating theatre to be found a place on a bunk, or on a stretcher in one of the new tunnels which were constantly being excavated by the Moroccan sappers. Habitually stripped to the waist and running with sweat under his blood-spattered nylon apron, the bald, burly Dr Grauwin would wipe his spectacles and light up yet another of his perpetual series of cigarettes (partly against the stench); and Geneviève would turn at the sound of stumbling and cursing, as stretcher-bearers struggled down the slimy clay steps with the next agonized victim.[49]

ON THE NIGHT OF 20/21 APRIL, the paratroopers of II/1 RCP from the Elianes made an aggressive raid on Dominique 6, killing 19 of the enemy, wrecking machine-gun bunkers, and bringing back three prisoners and some automatic weapons (the following night men of 6 BPC did much the same on Dominique 5). The flak was heavy, and about 20 per cent of the dropped supplies fell beyond reach. A volunteer parachutist suffered a terrifying death when his canopy caught on the tail of a Dakota; the pilot tried to shake him off, but the parachute tore to shreds and he plunged to his death.[50]

At Huguette 1, Division 308 had now encircled the Legion strongpoint with trenches and heavy weapons emplacements. The French communications trench up from Huguette 2 had been completed, but new transverse enemy trenches cut it about 100yds short of Huguette 1. Nightly supply parties were taking several hours to fight their way through to Captain Chevalier's men, and on the night of 21/22 April the attempt failed.

The following night two companies of 6th Colonial tried to get through to Huguette 1, again without success, and at 2.10am Chevalier reported persistent infantry attacks from the nearby trenches. These were not massed charges at the wire: from several directions at once, groups of *bo doi* were bursting out of covered trenches and tunnels right inside his position, raking the defenders with automatic fire and hurling grenades. Chevalier sealed the tunnels with explosives, but more kept opening up; each close-quarter gunfight in the dark cost him more men, and he appealed for reinforcements. After about 2.30am on 23 April, Major Coutant's radio in Huguette 3 was no longer able to raise him. At first light one or two of Chevalier's légionnaires managed to crawl back to Huguette 2; they reported seeing their captain and his last few men fighting back to back on the roof of his command post. The People's Army would record with satisfaction the efficiency of the new tactics of encroachment, and the unit involved was decorated in the field.[51]

The shockingly rapid loss of Huguette 1 meant that almost the whole of the airfield was now dominated not only by General Giap's artillery but also by the machine guns, mortars and RCLs of his infantry (*see Map 13*). The size of the potential drop zone had shrunk yet again, at a time when the coherent system of central collection and distribution of supplies was already starting to break down – increasingly, units on the perimeter would be limited to whatever happened to fall near them. This situation was greatly aggravated on the night of 21/22 April by the loss to shellfire of the last three of GONO's 73 trucks; there were still a few jeeps running, but for the recovery gangs to gather up and transport 100 tons of supplies divided between 1,000 packages, with only a handful of ³/₄-ton jeeps to supplement human muscles, was simply impossible.

Early on the morning of 23 April General de Castries met with his latest chief-of-staff, Lieutenant Colonel de Seguin-Pazzis (Ducruix was seriously ill), Colonel Langlais and Lieutenant Colonel Bigeard to discuss a response to the fall of Huguette 1. Castries was of the opinion that it was vital to recapture the strongpoint and with it some measure of access to the centre of the airfield. The two paratroopers were doubtful if this could be achieved without unacceptable casualties, among men who would be needed to hold the Elianes against Giap's next offensive; and even if Huguette 1 could be retaken, how could it be held in the longer term? Nevertheless, Castries instructed them to plan a counter-attack for that afternoon; and by 8am the commander of the freshest and strongest parachute battalion – Major Liesenfelt of 2 BEP – was receiving his orders.

He was not overjoyed; at Dien Bien Phu the terms 'fresh' and 'strong' were relative, and after 13 days in the valley his 677 officers and légion-naires had already been whittled away to something between 350 and 380 all ranks. They had been serving in dispersed companies since they landed, and this would be the first time since 9 April that Major Liesenfelt had commanded 2nd Foreign as a unified battalion.[52]

THE HUGUETTE 1 COUNTER-ATTACK of 23 April was destined to be as bitterly debated as that on Gabrielle on 15 March, and its detailed timing demands attention, since some sources are contradictory over important points.[53]

Once the mission had been given him, it was Major Liesenfelt's right and duty to plan it in detail, in consultation with Lieutenant Colonel Bigeard. The plan was simple in essence: experience showed that it was pointless trying to charge up the open airstrip towards the Viet Minh 'runway trenches', so Liesenfelt planned to hit Huguette 1 from two different directions (*see Map 13*). The 7th and 8th Companies would move from Epervier up the drainage ditch past Opéra to a point opposite Huguette 1, and would assault from east to west across the airstrip. Meanwhile, on the west side of the runway, 5th Company would push north from Huguette 2 and clear the enemy transverse trenches around the wrecked Curtiss C-46 south of Huguette 1. From there, with the machine guns of HQ Company, they would provide a base of fire, engaging the Viet Minh positions to the west; and would move in to consolidate once Huguette 1 had been retaken. The 6th Company would be held in reserve at Huguette 3, with the rest of HQ Company and Major Liesenfelt's command post.

The attack would be preceded by a ten-minute air strike on Huguette 1, followed by a ten-minute artillery barrage. Major Guérin asked GATAC/ Nord for 12 fighter-bomber and four B-26 sorties, with another four B-26s to remain on stand-by; Rocolle states that Bigeard and Guérin requested that the strike begin at 1.45pm. The whole timetable for the attack depended upon that of the air strike, and Pierre Sergent (the historian of 2 BEP, who joined the unit shortly afterwards) suggests that Liesenfelt was ordered to begin his preparations before this time was established. After the air strike was set for 1.45pm, the artillery allocated 1,200 rounds for Huguette 1 from 1.55pm to 2.05pm. The 2nd Foreign would move out to begin their attack at 2pm, and this would be supported after the end of the artillery barrage by mortars at Huguettes 2 and 5 and Epervier. Three tanks would accompany 5th Company's western prong of the operation.

The first mistake was booking the air strike for 1.45pm, which did not give 2 BEP time to get into position. The battalion's companies were on the Elianes; organizing their relief by parts of II/1 RCP, 6 BPC and I/2 REI meant movements by at least ten and perhaps 14 separate companies, and radio traffic between 40 different sets. Apart from the delay involved, this signals traffic was insecure; and by noon, when most of the companies were in movement, there was a major increase in enemy shelling and mortaring right across the main camp, including short-delay and air-burst rounds. 5th Company's relief was late reaching Eliane 2, and 6th Company's did not arrive until 1pm. Because of the shelling the troops had to use the covered communication trenches of the 'Metro' for much of their journey, which was slow and confusing.

Pierre Sergent suggests that Major Liesenfelt was not told of the Air Force's timetable until 1pm, an hour and a half after his first companies began to move, and by which time it was clear that 2pm was very optimistic for H-hour. Rocolle states that at 1pm Liesenfelt's command post at Huguette 3 confirmed the 2pm deadline to his companies; Sergent, that at some point after 1pm Liesenfelt complained to Bigeard's CP that the scheduled timing was now impossible. By 1.30pm, 5th Company had only just begun arriving at Huguette 2; 7th and 8th had not reached the drainage ditch; and at the current rate, 6th would not arrive until 4pm. Major Liesenfelt did not speak to Bigeard in person; the latter, who had not slept for at least 36 hours, had taken to his bunk once the arrangements for the counter-attack had been agreed. Bigeard's deputy Captain Caillaud (a former officer of 2 BEP) told Major Liesenfelt that the air strike was on its way and could not be delayed; but that the artillery barrage would be postponed.[54]

At some disputed time after 1.30pm, Bigeard was awakened and drove a jeep across to Liesenfelt's CP at Huguette 3. Bernard Fall gives no timing, but states that General de Castries roused Bigeard by radio, telling him that from overheard radio traffic he had formed the impression that the counter-attack 'lacked punch' and ordering him to look into it. Bigeard's report would claim that he did not arrive until around 3pm, when the attack was well under way, and thereupon took control of the situation. The core of the later controversy is that Liesenfelt reported Bigeard's arrival as before 1.45pm. (If this is correct, then Castries' alleged wording is inexplicable – the attack had not yet started.) Bigeard was famous for his close personal control of every operation; on this occasion he allowed fatigue to loosen his grip – for a length of time which was later disputed – and he would deeply regret it. There is no way to reconcile the timing in his original report with that of Major Liesenfelt; for the sake of coherence, the following account relies upon the sequence of events researched by Rocolle and Sergent.[55]

At about 1.50pm, while Liesenfelt was still urging his companies to hasten to their jumping-off positions, the air strike arrived. The four B-26s bombed Huguette 1, followed by six Hellcats dive-bombing and strafing; the target was unmistakable and clearly defined, and on this occasion the aircraft were very effective. A People's Army source later confirmed that the company holding Huguette 1 was virtually wiped out and that the handful of survivors were in no state to resist an infantry attack. As the aircraft climbed away, however, the supposedly postponed artillery barrage began according to the original schedule. From Liesenfelt's command post, Bigeard radioed the fire-control HQ and remonstrated, but it was some moments before the ceasefire order reached the batteries and by then about half the allocated shells had been fired away. A huge cloud of dust and smoke was rising above Huguette 1; but although 7th and 8th Companies were now moving up the airfield drain and 5th Company were at Huguette 2, none of the infantry were yet ready to attack.[56]

The second flight of six Hellcats were now at work elsewhere in the valley, and at about 2.15pm Lieutenant Klotz, 'Savart Green Leader', led his wingman Petty Officer Goizet in a diving attack from 8,000ft with two 500lb bombs. Heavy machine-gun fire rose to meet them, and at about 6,000ft Goizet radioed that he could see flames from his leader's aircraft. Klotz acknowledged but continued his dive, dropping his bombs before climbing away and baling out. He came down with a dislocated shoulder in wet paddy-fields about 400yds south of Eliane 2; and as légionnaires of 10th Company, III/13 DBLE ran out to bring him in, from a Morane artillery spotter Lieutenant Henri Thiébaud saw Viet Minh racing to beat them to the prize. Thiébaud directed Goizet, whose strafing held the enemy back long enough for the rescue party to reach Bernard Klotz. It was led by Sergeant Chief Bleyer, the indestructible veteran of Béatrice and Huguette 6; this exploit cost him his third wound of the battle.[57]

Meanwhile, at Huguette 3, Major Liesenfelt and Lieutenant Colonel Bigeard agreed that H-hour for the attack on Huguette 1 would have to be postponed until 2.30pm, but that they could wait no later than that for the missing reserve company. At about 2.25pm, still with no sign of 6th Company, they called in the last five minutes' artillery barrage; and when they saw the final smoke shells, the paratroopers of 2nd Foreign leapt forward. During that half-hour delay the benefit of the air strike and of much of the barrage had been wasted: Division 308 had put fresh men into Huguette 1, and in all the surrounding positions on the airfield – and on the hilltops to its north and east – weapons crews were waiting for the obviously imminent assault.

Lieutenant Le Cour Grandmaison's 7th Company were first out of the drain, starting to skirmish across the 200yds of level ground which separated them from their objective; they were followed by 8th Company, now led by Lieutenant Garin – Lieutenant Pétré had already been wounded during the approach march. There were only a few shell craters on the runway to offer any cover, and the paratroopers at once came under heavy machine-gun fire from trenches ahead of them and on both sides. Particular damage was done on their left flank by a gun that had been hidden in the nose of the wrecked Curtiss C-46; its elevation perhaps 10ft above the ground gave it absolute dominance of the featureless airstrip. Amid bursting mortar bombs and a storm of automatic fire, the paratroopers simply had to throw themselves flat on the burning hot plates of PSP and shoot back as best they could, protected only by smoke and blowing dust. The Viet Minh machine guns were firing low, and many men were cut down by leg wounds; others were shot while kneeling or even lying flat. Inevitably, casualties mounted swiftly.

To the south, Lieutenant de Biré's 5th Company were trying to make progress up the west side of the runway from Huguette 2. North of that strongpoint their advance was slowed by a maze of trenches, tunnels and shell craters; they occupied these one by one, Great War style, under artillery and mortar fire and lashed by machine guns in bunkers out to their west. By perhaps 3pm, 5th Company were among the trenches just south of the Curtiss; Sergeant Kemencei's machine guns had been brought up, but it was hard to identify clear targets. Shortly afterwards Lieutenant de Biré was wounded in both legs; he radioed Liesenfelt's command post to report progress and request a replacement company commander. Captain Léonce Picatto of HQ Company made his way north, but before he reached them he was hit in the head and killed. Roughly bandaged, René de Biré continued to exercise command.[58]

Although Liesenfelt was in contact with 5th Company, he was out of touch with 7th and 8th and was apparently unaware that they were dangerously stalled. Both versions of the timetable have Lieutenant Colonel Bigeard at Huguette 3 by now. In Fall's account, he had just arrived after being roused by General de Castries, who had overheard urgent messages from the companies on the airstrip; but by Rocolle's and Sergent's interpretation, he had been there for more than an hour. Both versions agree that he asked Liesenfelt for a report on progess by the eastern prong of the attack; that Liesenfelt replied to the effect that it must be going well ('*Ca doit coller...*'), since no signals had been received; and that Bigeard then discovered that the battalion commander's SCR300 radio was incorrectly tuned.

The degree of incompetence or complacency that can fairly be ascribed to Major Liesenfelt depends upon the subjective wording chosen to describe this scene. On the first point, the 2 BEP commander's defence – that the company radios' performance had been disrupted by their use on a runway covered with 500 tons of steel plates – is entirely credible, and was confirmed as such at the time by Major Coutant, a former signals officer. Bigeard does not seem to have accepted it, even though his own 6 BPC had had exactly the same problem while trying to break through to Huguette 1 the previous night.[59] Sergent states that it took Bigeard up to 20 minutes to retune Liesenfelt's set successfully and make contact with Le Cour Grandmaison – which again argues that the mistuning was not a case of simple carelessness, and reminds us that 1940s vintage field radios were much less reliable than those of today. As to the charge that Liesenfelt should not have accepted the silence of his 7th and 8th Companies so passively, one can only say that he paid a price which many witnesses felt was unjustly harsh. The faulty radio link had only a minor effect on the outcome of events that afternoon; the delay between the air strike and the infantry attack was the decisive factor.

Lieutenant Colonel Bigeard learned at some time before 3.30pm that out on the runway 7th and 8th Companies of 2 BEP were hopelessly pinned down by enemy fire. The 7th Company commander reported that his and Garin's men had got to within perhaps 50yds of Huguette 1 (apparently the machine-gun nest in the Curtiss had been silenced); but that they were now nailed to the ground, scattered in any slight dips that they could find, and had taken between 115 and 123 casualties. Bigeard asked if they could get moving again if they received another artillery shoot, but Le Cour

Grandmaison and Garin replied that their paras were being slaughtered and that retreat was the only option. Liesenfelt apparently accepted this at once, Bigeard after some further exchanges; it was 4.30pm before he gave the order to withdraw. Some, including Captain Caillaud, believed that if 6th Company – now arrived at Huguette 3 – were committed, with proper support from the tanks, it might be possible to revive the attack; but neither Liesenfelt nor Bigeard was willing to sacrifice more lives on that chance. To cover the withdrawal Bigeard called in the four stand-by B-26s and obtained an additional artillery shoot.

The companies actually started pulling back at about 5pm, in the order 7th, 8th and 5th. Withdrawing from contact under fire is always a dangerous manoeuvre, and on the open airfield it was murderous, even though the French artillery 'caged' the Viet Minh in Huguette 1 to prevent them from pursuing. The 7th and 8th Companies fell back in small groups under heavy fire, and took further casualties. Lieutenant Garin of the 8th fell with both his legs mangled; when his légionnaires turned back to rescue him he waved them away – and when they persisted, he put his carbine to his head and blew his own brains out. At that moment Lieutenant Ysquierdo became 8th Company's third commander since noon; he managed to get about 40 of his men back to the drainage ditch, and finally to Epervier. Lieutenant de Biré of 5th Company got all the way back to the hospital on his own, using two pickaxes as crutches. The final butcher's bill was 154 officers and men: one captain, three lieutenants, three senior NCOs and 61 corporals and privates dead, and 72 wounded – at least 40 per cent casualties.[60]

This action was the last major counter-attack mounted by GONO, which now had no significant reserve of infantry left. To return to the original analogy of the 'oyster' defence, Dien Bien Phu's continued resistance to assaults would now demand the progressive sacrifice of its irreplaceable defenders – every day, the oyster would consume more of its own shell.

On 24 April the survivors of 1 BEP and 2 BEP were amalgamated into a single Foreign Parachute Marching Battalion – BMEP – under the command of Major Maurice Guiraud of 1 BEP. With companies led by Lieutenants de Stabenrath, Brandon, Le Cour Grandmaison and Pétré, this unit took over Huguettes 2, 3 and 5 and Lili 3.[61] (On the night of 28 April they would raise their spirits by sending a fighting patrol against new enemy trenches around Lili 3 and killing about 20 Viet Minh.)

Hubert Liesenfelt's reputation never recovered from this episode. Some of his officers felt that he had been harshly treated, since the failure of the operation was due to a number of cumulative mischances, and mistakes by several hands. Marcel Bigeard was not normally so intolerant of defeat in battle, and commentators have drawn their own conclusions.

WHILE IT HAS BEEN ESTIMATED that about 75 per cent of the wounds treated at Dien Bien Phu were caused by shell, mortar and grenade explosions, a higher than usual proportion of those suffered by 2 BEP on 23 April were gunshot wounds. These deserve a moment's thought, despite their assumed familiarity to any television viewer.[62]

The bullets fired from most rifles and machine guns at Dien Bien Phu were of 7.5mm–7.92mm calibre, equivalent to the British 0.303in and US 0.30in which were standard in both World Wars. The bullet is a cylinder tapering to a smooth point at the tip, about the size of a very short pencil stub, say an inch and a half long; but at about 1oz it weighs noticeably in the palm of the hand, because its core is of lead, skinned with a smooth copper or nickel alloy – the 'full metal jacket'. When fired, it leaves the muzzle of the rifle at a speed of at least 1,700mph. Because its base is heavier than its tip, the bullet would naturally turn around in mid-air, but the spiral rifling grooves in the barrel impart a spin which keeps it flying point first in a straight line until it hits something. When it does, the stabilizing effect of the spin disappears; and when it hits human flesh it can behave in a number of ways, transferring more or less of its energy and doing more or less damage depending upon speed, angle, the type of tissue it encounters, and other variables.

The 'million dollar' wound (as suffered by Hollywood heroes) is caused by a high velocity military bullet, undistorted and still encased in its metal skin, which passes straight through relatively elastic muscle tissue and out the other side, making a pencil-thin tunnel and leaving a star-shaped exit wound only about three-quarters of an inch across. However, the size of the tunnel caused by the bullet's passage varies due to yawing. For roughly the first 6in of its journey the fully jacketed bullet continues point first, and this may well be enough to take it out the far side; but because the heavier base of the bullet still wants to be at the front, after that distance it begins to turn around or cartwheel. When this tumbling reaches 90° the bullet is travelling sideways, thus enlarging the tunnel to more than an inch across. By the time it has travelled through tissue for about 15in it is moving base first, and the tunnel resumes its original width. Irrespective of the distance travelled inside the body, however, a bullet which hits major bones may break up; the metal jacket and soft lead core separate into irregular pieces, each of which travels on in unpredictable directions – as do the pieces of broken bone. In such cases the exit wound may be up to 5in across. Limb wounds which shatter the long bones can cause massive damage, particularly to the legs, where splintered bones threaten major blood vessels. Even a 'clean' penetration of the heart, liver or major blood vessels is usually fatal, and brain damage normally has devastating results even when the victim survives: apart from yawing and bone strikes, the amount of damage a bullet causes depends upon another effect known as cavitation.

Imagine a tennis ball, drilled through the centre and sliding freely along a pencil-thin rod. The rod is the tunnel made by the bullet – the 'permanent cavity'; the ball is the 'temporary cavity' caused all around that path by a brief but powerful shock wave following immediately behind the bullet. The tissue stretches away from the bullet's track, making a travelling cavity up to 7in across, which then collapses inwards again (the vacuum effect may also suck dirt through the entry wound into the bullet track). Some organs, such as the liver, can rarely survive this process; others, such as the lung, are less affected.

In muscle the crushed tissue of the permanent cavity and the stretched tissue of the temporary cavity are both, in effect, pulped, with their blood supply through minor vessels disrupted; if left untreated the flesh will rot (necrotize), producing an ideal breeding ground for bacteria. The surgical treatment therefore involves debridement – the cutting away of the dead tissue and of a margin of healthy tissue around it; this is more or less radical depending upon individual circumstances, and the correct timing and degree of debridement are matters of professional discussion among trauma surgeons. In the best case, new healthy tissue will grow inwards all around the debrided wound. In the worst case, sepsis will occur – gangrene – and the patient's prospects become seriously worrying.

BY 24 APRIL THE LOSS OF MUCH of the airfield had reduced the total area controlled by GONO to less than half what it had been on 13 March – it was now only about 520 acres, ever more tightly ringed not only with anti-aircraft guns, but also some artillery. There were 105s on the former Anne-Maries and behind Baldy and Phoney, and by the 30th there would be 75mm RCLs both east and west of Isabelle (though interestingly, General Giap's 120mm mortar ammunition seemed to be in cripplingly short supply in the second half of the month). Opéra was now abandoned, but Captain Bizard's company began trying to construct a small new position – 'the nameless strongpoint' – actually in the drainage ditch above Epervier. Since this was now waist-deep in water, with banks the consistency of chocolate pudding, the position resembled something from Passchendaele in autumn 1917. The Vietnamese paras would hold it for two weeks; their wounded had to be propped up to keep their heads above water, and their dead sank.[63]

That day a signal to Hanoi gave the total of fit infantry as 3,250, plus 402 'lying' and 676 'sitting' in the main hospital; Bernard Fall gives another 878 in the battalion aid posts. Isabelle had 1,400 fit, plus 117 wounded.[64] On the 24th the dispositions and rough strengths of the individual units were as follows, in clock-face order from Epervier at the north-east, down the east side, across the south and up the west:

Epervier was held by Pierre Tourret's 8th Shock with about 400 men, plus Alain Bizard's company of 5 BPVN at the 'nameless strongpoint', and a couple of Thai platoons from BT 2 – perhaps 530 in all, plus Redon's quad-50 mounts. Eliane 1 and 4 (the 'High Elianes'), with Eliane 3 behind and below, were occupied by some 550 paratroopers – about 400 of Jean Bréchignac's II/1 RCP, plus Pham Van Phu's 2nd Company, 5 BPVN. Some 300 légionnaires of Major Coutant's I/ and III/13th DBLE were on Eliane 2. At Dominique 3 and Eliane 10 on the flats behind the hills were about 650 paras, Algerians and Thais: the remnant of Major Thomas' 6th Colonial, Filaudeau's 12/III/3 RTA, and perhaps 350 from Chenel's BT 2. Junon was occupied by 180 men – mostly White Thais under Captain Duluat, but including Captain Charnod's little Air Force platoon. Both Junon and Eliane 10 now began to receive increasing numbers of lightly wounded who were still able to handle a gun.

In the centre and south of the camp Claudine was occupied by Major

Clémencon's I/2 REI, perhaps 400 in number (who were noted for pushing out strong patrols to the west and south during the final week of April). In the new location Lili, Major Nicolas still had about 250 Moroccans of his I/4 RTM; and another company of them under Captain Nicod shared the Huguettes with Major Guiraud's composite Foreign Parachute battalion – say 640 men in all.

Ignoring the discrepancies that are inevitable given the constant ebb and flow of casualties and piecemeal replacements, these figures give the whole camp an absolute maximum strength for 'bayonets' of about 4,900 men, guarding some 2,100 wounded; and an incalculable total of about another 4,000 who were either non-infantry combatants, service troops or internal deserters.

Between 17 and 30 April GONO's total casualties – killed, missing or seriously wounded – would be about 1,430; and during this period the camp would receive 683 parachuted replacements.[65]

BY THE END OF APRIL THE MEN defending this shell-pocked swamp were exhausted, many of them dangerously dull-witted from lack of sleep; the frequent issue by the medical officers of Maxiton – an 'upper' with effects comparable to Dexedrine – had only temporary benefits.[66] Troops under constant pressure for days and nights on end crave any opportunity to rest, eat warm meals, and wipe the worst of the filth off their bodies, even though hot water is a distant dream. Even when not directly under fire the dwindling companies had to spend much of their time digging, or carrying heavy ammunition boxes up to the strongpoints. Nearly all movement was limited to the squalid maze of trenches, which by now often resembled sewers: they were knee-deep in liquid mud, and men who are constantly under fire defecate where they are rather than risk finding their way to a latrine trench. For at least 48 hours at a time the paratroopers and légionnaires had to take their turns under shellfire, mortars and sniping in the crumbling perimeter strongpoints; and when pulled back a little to notional safety on the banks of the Nam Youm, they had to expect that at short notice they might be roused and sent stumbling off to meet some emergency hundreds of yards away. Most had now been in action for at least 45 days – the point after which, according to World War II studies, fatigue begins to drag a man down from dangerous carelessness into nervous exhaustion. It is remarkable to read in the testimony of the repatriated wounded that, despite everything, the shreds of the parachute and Legion battalions maintained their discipline to the end.

It is extraordinarily hard to grasp the fact, attested by many survivors, that well into the first week of May many of these soldiers believed they could still break the enemy and win this battle. Lieutenant Bergot recalled that those who had been in the valley from the first were sometimes surprised to learn from newly arrived volunteers of the pessimism which reigned in Hanoi. There, a pervasive culture of defeatism caused instinctive hesitation to throw any more men and resources to an inescapable fate. In the valley the paratroopers looked no further than the next fight, and saw any failure to give them what they needed as inexplicable, almost criminal. The enemy must be just as tired as they were, and his losses were much higher; after mid April there were frequent instances of *bo doi* surrendering when bested in combat, and claiming to have been marched up from Thanh Hoa after only a few weeks in uniform. As long as the Elianes were held there was always hope – hope of another couple of parachute battalions, hope of some politicians' deal at Geneva, hope of the relief column from Laos, even hope of the rumoured intervention of the US Air Force.[67]

BY CONTRAST, VIET MINH morale was flagging. Before one even considers the impact of their heavy casualties, their daily conditions of life had become harder with the beginning of the rains. The People's Army could rotate their infantry units between the trenches and rest areas in the surrounding forest – if not daily, as they later boasted to their captives, then certainly on a fairly regular basis; but this brought only the most relative comfort. Colonel Pham Duc Doi recalled that he and his comrades slept on the ground with only a bamboo mat or banana leaves on a plastic sheet as a bed. Very few of them had mosquito nets, and malaria was the norm; Colonel Pham suffered attacks usually lasting a week – sometimes two attacks in a month, sometimes at longer intervals. They had very little quinine to treat it, and several men would pass around a cup of water in which one tablet was dissolved. During mild attacks the men worked as usual, but were weak and had no appetite. Colonel Pham describes the diet as rice, sometimes with salt, sometimes with a little buffalo or monkey meat.[68]

Any *bo doi* of Division 316 who did not sometimes doubt that they would ever take the defiant Elianes must have been superhuman; and the northern Huguettes, though finally captured, had demanded no smaller sacrifice from individual units. Many soldiers of the assault battalions had survived the experience of seeing their units slaughtered around them by shocking French firepower – some of them, during several separate actions on different strongpoints. They, too, were disheartened by having to leave their dead and dying behind them. General Giap's infantry had by now suffered about 50 per cent casualties in six weeks. Although the blood tax had not fallen on all units equally, many soldiers were now surrounded in the ranks not by trusted comrades but by bewildered and half-trained boys. French intelligence believed that in terms of numbers the losses had been replaced, and more. However, prisoner interrogations revealed that some replacements had been drafted only in early March; they had walked to Dien Bien Phu in groups of about 100, and when they reached their units each recruit had been put with two veterans to teach him the ropes.[69]

In a telegram of 16 April to Secretary Jacquet, General Navarre was already claiming that the Viet Minh troops at Dien Bien Phu were 'showing great lassitude, and some of them give the impression of being at the end of their moral and physical strength'. This comment was based largely upon interrogation of prisoners taken at Huguette 6 and Eliane 1 on 5 and 10 April; but in fact the crisis of morale struck the People's Army in the second half of that month, after the hard fighting for Huguettes 6 and 1. General Giap did not seek to hide the fact in his memoir of the battle:

> The principal trait of that phase of the battle had been the violent character of the combat... the battle having lasted a very long time, more troops – who had had to fight without interruption – became fatigued, worn, and subject to great nervous tension... Our forces had not been able to avoid decimation... It was precisely at these moments when rightist tendencies appeared among our cadres and soldiers – in the fear of suffering many casualties, [in giving way to] fatigue, in subjectivity, in overestimation of the enemy... The Political Bureau, which closely monitored the condition of our combatants, judged that

the recent important victories had created the fundamental conditions permitting [them] to overrun the entrenched camp... [But] these rightist tendencies remained serious, and partly limited the scope of our victories...[70]

As we have seen, 'subjectivity' and 'rightist tendencies' could mean whatever the Party chose them to mean; but here the jargon clearly indicates that officers and men in the ranks of mauled battalions were drawing fearful conclusions from their own direct experience. The divisional commissars held a self-criticism session to study the causes and remedies for this wavering of morale, and on 27 April they agreed to launch a campaign 'to mobilize morale and rectify rightist tendencies', stressing the land reform programme. Some propaganda sessions were watched through binoculars by French officers, who in the late afternoons saw large gatherings of troops being harangued by commissars on Gabrielle and Béatrice. In the meantime, Giap's orders of the day encouraged marksmen, machine gunners, mortarmen and artillerymen to kill the enemy one by one – 'for each bullet fired, an enemy killed' – and promised decorations for the most successful.[71]

The slump in Viet Minh morale in the second half of April is a credible reason for Giap's delay in unleashing his third offensive phase. His logistic preparations were complete by 26 April at the latest.[72] In theory he could thus have opened his third offensive then, to coincide with the opening of the Geneva Conference. But he chose to wait: the conference was the ultimate reason why he could not afford to launch his assault prematurely – to fail under the eyes of the world would have incalculable consequences.

At the highest level of command, there was no reason for the Viet Minh to feel wholly confident of victory even after the appalling sacrifices of the past six weeks. After nearly 50 days the French garrison – representing less than 4 per cent of the total CEFEO and ANV forces – were still holding out, and tying down about 60 per cent of the People's Army regular force (and thus about 20 per cent of their total forces). Western media speculation about American air intervention in Indochina was no secret, and many senior officers in the hills around Dien Bien Phu must have watched the sky even more nervously than usual.

FROM THAT SKY THE DAKOTAS were dropping their cargoes by day with 40-second delay fuses from at least 8,500ft, with predictable consequences; the resupply programme was being strangled by the combination of bad weather, enemy flak and shrinking drop zones. On 23 April, 117 tons were dropped, but at least 15 per cent went astray; Captain Soulat's Packet was hit yet again – a despatcher was wounded, and would lose his leg. That night 72 parachutists jumped into the valley. It was a normal working day for the Air Force; but the picture would soon darken further.

On 24 April, of six B-26s of GB 1/19 that flew low-level flak suppression missions, three were hit; Major Villetorte flew home without use of his flaps, and Navy Lieutenant Loizillon, whose No. 447 lost its hydraulics, had to land at Cat Bi with a full bombload and his jammed nose-wheel flaming. On the same day a C-119 flown by the CAT crew of Wallace Buford and chief pilot Paul Holden was hit by a 37mm shell in the right side of the cockpit, nearly costing Holden his arm and blowing out part of the roof; a second shell passed through a tail boom but did not explode. Buford completed the mission, but the incident brought a simmering problem to the boil.[73]

Routinely, the daytime C-119s had been coming in high over the outer flak ring and then diving for a single dropping pass as low as 300ft. During the three minutes or so they spent in the danger area it was not uncommon for 50 per cent of the aircraft in the flight to be hit. The Americans' contracts specifically excluded combat missions; yet they were continually flying into the sort of fire normally associated with bomber sorties, and they were often dissatisfied with the support they received from French combat aircraft. Understandably, they became increasingly reluctant to fly; equally understandably, the French C-119 pilots – who faced the same dangers for reasons of patriotic duty rather than the high wages paid to the foreign civilians – tried to cajole or shame them into continuing, with the ambiguous support of the company's management.[74]

After returning to Haiphong–Cat Bi from the 24 April mission the CAT crews refused to fly again, thus cutting the C-119s' important contribution to the overall resupply effort by two-thirds (during April the Americans had flown about 428 sorties, representing roughly 2,500 tons). While intense efforts were made to change their minds, Saigon took until the 26th to authorize the transfer of ten French Dakota crews back to the

Packet Detachment; consequently air-drops averaged only 60 tons over the next three days – about a third of what was needed, even if it had all been recovered.

On 25 April the true monsoon finally arrived; it brought huge slabs of stratus cloud to both the Delta and the High Region every morning, which sometimes lifted in the afternoon but might persist all day. On the 25th there was low cloud over the Thai Highlands from 3pm to 11pm, and since no flak suppression missions could be flown, neither were low-level C-119 sorties by Captain Soulat's crews. There were hours of torrential rain daily, and when aircraft did manage to fly missions they often faced dangerous thunderstorms when returning to the Delta late in the afternoon. From this point onwards the resupply programme would progressively fail.

Monday 26 April was the worst day of the battle for the combat squadrons. At 10.30am the Hellcat of 20-year-old Petty Officer 'Baby' Robert was brought down by guns on Anne-Marie during a strafing run; he baled out safely, but was captured. Soon afterwards the B-26 flown by Lieutenant Caubel of GB 1/25 was shot down; only the flight engineer, Sergeant Texier, managed to bale out, and he too was taken prisoner. That afternoon another GB 1/25 patrol lost Lieutenant Iteney's aircraft; only Captain Rigal of this crew would return from captivity. Both these bombers were shot down by 37mm fire at altitudes as high as 9,000ft; and the next day General Lauzin ordered that priority be given to flak suppression. On 28 April – a rare clear day – no cargo drops took place at all. In the C-47 squadrons night-time cargo missions had to replace 'Banjos', and on the night of 26/27 April only 36 men were dropped into the camp.[75]

The great difficulties faced by the transport pilots are discussed earlier in this chapter, but some of the misdrops were less excusable, and did appear to be due to a pilot's anxiety to avoid 'going round again'. Of Isabelle, Colonel Lalande reported: 'It is inadmissible, even criminal, to knowingly parachute 105mm ammunition to the enemy for the sole reason of keeping to a timetable. It was not rare for such incidents to take place, when those responsible disobeyed direct orders to stop their dropping. Many crews proved their discipline and courage, but the proportion of failures was too high.' Colonel Nicot, who was fiercely protective of his transport crews when he thought the Army's complaints unjustified, did later confirm to

Pierre Rocolle that there had been a slump in 'moral determination' in one of his squadrons; he removed the commander and 'soaped the heads' of the other officers.

By 28 April the state of the aircrews of GT 2/62 'Franche-Comté' was reported to be 'very bad. The commander, his deputy, plus eight pilots are *hors service'* – in other words, 35 per cent of the squadron were grounded.[76] During the whole month of April the crews of GT 2/62 had flown 439 sorties, totalling 1,226 operational flying hours by day and 516 by night. If we assume (generously) that 25 aircraft were available, these figures give the appearance of a monthly average of 18 missions per Dakota – that is, three missions over two days over an acceptable monthly total of 69 flying hours per aircraft. But aircraft numbers were not the deciding factor: crews were. At one point during April there were apparently only 55 crews available for Nicot's whole fleet of (theoretically) 101 Dakotas, so the averages per crew must have been nearly twice that many hours and missions – some pilots certainly flew up to 120 hours during the month, without co-pilots. It was commonplace for a crew to fly two missions in a day, and by the last week of the battle one night-time and two daylight missions over 24 hours – that is, ten hours in the air – were not unknown. If most of those sorties involved repeated circuits through the flak over Dien Bien Phu, then combat exhaustion was inevitable. We should recall that GT 2/62 were the 'Little Wolves'; still flying with this squadron were courageous officers like Lieutenant Biswang, who had made two daylight landings and take-offs under fire to rescue full loads of wounded, and Héquet, who had taken fourteen flak hits in two separate missions on 26 March.

Colonel Nicot would later claim that by the end of the battle all his crews were suffering from extreme fatigue, that 30 per cent of them had been grounded, and that the rest of them would have been if they had allowed themselves to be examined by medical officers. He was characteristically frank in his final report:

> If I refused to send them in low by daylight, to certain death, it was [for the following reasons]: the sacrifice would have been useless, since they would have crashed before being able to drop their cargoes. My means and personnel were limited, and the losses could not be replaced from

France and North Africa, where there were only 40 crews in reserve.
[And finally,] the war would not end for us with the fall of Dien Bien Phu,
and I had no right to completely break the air transport command there.[77]

MEANWHILE, THEIR CORRESPONDENCE during the last ten days of
April confirms that the relationship between Generals Navarre and Cogny
had sunk to a level of icy mistrust. While Navarre was confronted by
strategic and political problems at national and international level, Cogny's
willingness to commit his opinions to paper narrowed to a self-defensive
concentration on his mission to defend the Delta.[78] He still favoured a
thrust into the enemy base areas, which he apparently believed would
benefit the Delta, and pretended would also benefit GONO. Navarre
continued to deny him these resources, pointing out that they would not
benefit Dien Bien Phu at all, nor even the Delta. While the passionate
Cogny seems to have resigned himself to GONO's fate, Navarre, the sac-
rificer of pawns, still saw advantages in keeping Dien Bien Phu alive. It
was tying down the majority of the Chu Luc, weakening its potential for
future operations elsewhere; and it gave France a card at Geneva. If the
conference succeeded, there might be a reprieve for GONO; if it failed,
then the USA might be persuaded to offer direct support.

On 24 April, Navarre confronted Cogny with his responsibilities in a
series of blunt questions. How long could Dien Bien Phu hold out, either
with or without reinforcement? If Cogny favoured reinforcement, then
did he recommend the continued dropping of individuals, or a complete
battalion? And finally, was he in favour of the planned Operation 'Condor',
to break through to GONO from Laos? On the 26th, Cogny replied: he
believed Dien Bien Phu could survive another two or three weeks if reinforced and if the Viet Minh did not launch a general assault, but only eight
days if not reinforced. He favoured continuing the dropping of individual
replacements for the next week, followed by another full parachute
battalion; and he thought 'Condor' was worthwhile if it was initiated
straight away.[79] An added problem for both Cogny and Navarre was that the
French public were now transfixed by the drama of Dien Bien Phu, and
would never understand any argument that its importance was secondary
to the general situation in the Delta or beyond. The media-friendly Cogny,

in particular, was paying the price for allowing the camp to become a symbol while remaining personally uncommitted to it, thus attracting a wave of public pressure which distorted purely military calculations.

IN THE VALLEY, THE MONSOON downpours that had begun on 25 April increased the garrison's misery; by the 29th they would report an average of 3ft of water in the trenches.[80] Radio traffic suggested movement by enemy units, and every night brought trenching and probing all around the perimeter from the Elianes to the Claudines. Small-scale clashes, sniping and mortaring were punctuated by occasional artillery shoots which wore away the precious ammunition. Responding to a raid on the High Elianes on the 25th cost Colonel Vaillant 750 rounds of 105mm and 50 of 155mm; and a howitzer duel during heavy rain on the following night saw one of the last two 155s knocked out.[81] Aggressive Legion patrolling continued until the end of the month, however; on the night 24/25 April, I/2 REI got men as far as Ban Co My nearly two miles to the south-west, and the following night they pushed up the Pavie Track all the way to the ford below Ban Khe Phai. That night of 26/27 April the noise of many truck engines was heard; under cover of the rainstorm the enemy were moving munitions and artillery closer.[82] Down at Isabelle, new 75mm RCL batteries would soon be adding to the trials of Colonel Lalande's garrison, whose swampy position did not allow the digging of a 'Metro' of deep communication trenches; and on 26 April that impressive officer seems to have made his only serious misjudgement during his lonely defence.

ALTHOUGH THE PEOPLE'S Army adopted tactics of strangulation rather than all-out assault on Isabelle, there had been occasional sharp combats during April. These occurred both during Viet Minh attacks on the perimeter – nearly always on the weak, waterlogged trenches of Isabelle 5 ('Strongpoint Wieme') on the east bank – and during sorties by the infantry and the tank platoon to clear and destroy advancing trenches and heavy weapons (see Map 19). The location was shelled heavily on most days, keeping the garrison underground much of the time – apart from the unfortunate artillerymen, whose value in supporting the Five Hills was well understood by General Giap – and during April the incoming shells were no longer the duds of mid March. Since neither side's radio traffic was secure, the GONO Second Bureau were able to forewarn Isabelle of several commando raids aimed at knocking out the howitzers; conversely, after these had been repulsed, a storm of 120mm mortaring would follow shortly after any fire order radioed to Isabelle's gunners by the PC Feux.

The location became so torn up that some defenders gave up trying to repair field telephone cables and communicated by shouting or runners; Sub-lieutenant Ducourneau counted one crater in every square metre of his 9th Battery position. Isabelle's tiny size made the air-drop recovery problem particularly acute; it took eight days to replace the 105mm ammunition expended in the battles of 30 March to 1 April. Although the theoretical time it took a Dakota to overfly Isabelle itself was just two seconds, volunteer replacements for the Legion battalion, the artillery and the tank platoon were parachuted in near by. On the other hand Isabelle had a low priority for Luciole flare missions, and usually had to rely on less effective artillery star shells to light up attacks.[83]

The west bank location, roughly half a mile across by a quarter of a mile deep, was divided into four strongpoints, with Colonel Lalande's command post, Dr Rézillot's hospital and the artillery on very slightly rising ground in the centre. Isabelle 1 in the north-west was held by Captain Jeancenelle's Algerian Tirailleurs of II/1 RTA. In the south-west Isabelle 2 accommodated troops whose morale was not completely trusted: nearly 120 Gabrielle survivors of V/7 RTA under Captain Gendre, and the Thais of 9th Company, BT 3 withdrawn from the Anne-Maries. Isabelle 3 and 4 in the south-eastern and north-eastern quadrants were occupied by the légionnaires of III/3 REI.[84]

By 15 April the constant pressure had ground away at least half of Lieutenant Wieme's Thai auxiliaries in Isabelle 5; they had suffered 10 per cent killed and 40 per cent missing, and Wieme asked Colonel Lalande to relieve them from their wretched outpost. Captain Desiré's faithful 9th Company, BT 3 replaced them; this was dangerous, since it involved crossing the small, exposed bridge that the engineers had built from Isabelle 4, and the changeover attracted shellfire. The popular Desiré was among the wounded, and Lieutenant Siauve took over his shaken company in Isabelle 5 (to be killed himself on the 21st). Attacks on the east bank position continued, and sorties by légionnaires with tank support brought only short-term relief.

On 19 April a good deal of Isabelle 5 was lost, but most of the ground was retaken by Thais, légionnaires and tanks within 12 hours; a successful sortie beyond the perimeter before dawn on the 20th hit Battalion 265 of Regiment 57 particularly hard. On the 19th the garrison as a whole ate its last hot meal, and on 20 April rations ran out temporarily. Strength that afternoon was reported as 490 men of II/1 RTA plus about 100 of V/7 RTA, 400 of III/3 REI, and 370 Thai regulars and auxiliaries; eight guns and two tanks were operational; and the accumulated killed and missing were totalled as 136 up to that date.[85]

On 26 April, under the full weight of the monsoon, Colonel Lalande told Captain Jeancenelle to pick his four best II/1 RTA platoons for a sortie against a trench north-east of Isabelle 5. It turned out that there were two mutually supporting trenches, and the Algerians fell back in disorder after losing six killed and 22 wounded. Lalande now made an uncharacteristic error of judgement: perhaps worried about a contagion of defeatism from the Gabrielle survivors, he ordered the platoon commanders of the unsuccessful sortie to designate two men each for court martial on charges of cowardice in the face of the enemy – a crime with only one possible punishment. Lalande referred to Castries for permission to convene the court, but the general insisted on leaving the decision up to him.

Worried NCOs came to their officers – particularly to 8th Company's commander Lieutenant Cheik Belabiche – and warned that the Tirailleurs would not accept this World War I barbarity, and were prepared for armed mutiny. Allegedly, Captain Jeancenelle was surprisingly unresponsive; so Belabiche went direct to Colonel Lalande. The location commander had by then recovered his senses, and a form of trial took place only after the assurance that the verdict would be acquittal. To judge by the eventual casualty figures, the Algerians and Thais at Isabelle in fact fought just as hard as the légionnaires.[86]

On 27 April, with little artillery support from Claudine, III/3 REI and the Thais would try in vain to clear the rest of the enemy penetration of Isabelle 5. On the night 29/30 the Viet Minh shelling was particularly heavy, including new American short-delay 105s which smashed up many dug-outs; the tank 'Ratisbonne' was damaged by two 105mm shellbursts, but remained operational. Although the flak was light, seven circling C-47s dropped only 65 men in all. Artillery ammunition was worryingly short; ever since the 20th, Isabelle had been asking for 1,700 rounds of 105mm to be dropped daily, but had been getting an average of only 348 rounds. On 30 April, General de Castries demanded uninterrupted drops of 8,000 shells on Isabelle, adding an unnecessarily cutting remark about the aircrews' willingness to share the infantry's risks.[87]

IT WAS EARLY ON 27 APRIL that the Air Force dropped the first batch of body armour vests – to the People's Army; that afternoon they tried again, and got 200 into the main camp and 100 to Isabelle. Priority for issue went to the artillery crews, but some were also shared among paratroopers and légionnaires in exposed positions on the High Elianes – Captain Clédic's company of II/1 RCP got one between each two men. GONO had only requested this well-proven US equipment on 14 April; the US authorities processed the request in just five days, but it then took the French another eight days to drop them into Dien Bien Phu. Had these 'flak jackets' been requested as soon as the counter-battery threat was revealed in mid March, a large number of the casualties in the gunpits could have been avoided.[88]

The latest batch of aerial photos showed trenches branching between the lower Huguettes, and even towards Eliane 3 on the river flats; the sap heads were being covered with overhead beams and sandbags to protect the diggers as they progressed. On Eliane 2 the sounds of mining were clearly audible. That night there was a full moon, but thick stratus clouds above the valley; only Captain Erhart of GT 2/64 managed to drop his stick of 24 légionnaires over Isabelle, and 20 other Dakotas returned to Hanoi with their tense volunteers still aboard. On the High Elianes paras from II/1 RCP and 5 BPVN raided Viet Minh trenches, destroying bunkers, killing 12 of the enemy and bringing back three prisoners. The People's Army were suffering from the monsoon as badly as the French; that day the four-battalion Engineer Regiment 154 were summoned all the way from Nghe An province to work on maintaining Route Provinciale 41.[89]

On 28 April the camp's defences continued to melt under the monsoon rain. Thick clouds closed the sky over Dien Bien Phu; no supplies were dropped and no combat air patrols were flown. Even so, morale was reportedly good among the troops, due to widespread rumours about Operation 'Condor'. It was not helped, however, by air-dropped copies of *Le Figaro* of the 23rd, which carried an article speculating about the Air Force's inability to sustain GONO and American unwillingness to do so – this story was also carried by Radio Hirondelle, which could be heard in the camp. That night the Dakotas dropped 30 tons of supplies and flew six 'Banjo' missions, but no parachutists jumped. At 10pm Legion paras of BMEP crawled out from Liliane 3 through deep mud to raid enemy trenches, killing at least 20 and getting back with only four men wounded. After a brief bombardment of approach trenches a fighting patrol on the High Elianes found about 40 enemy dead.[90]

On the 29th, after a night of unbroken rain, the order was broadcast that the garrison would henceforward be on half rations. The troops in the central redoubt never ran short – indeed, there were some inevitable cases of pillage and drunkenness; but the units in the perimeter strong-points found it increasingly difficult to send regular ration parties to collect what they needed, and tended to scoop up whatever fell near by. (In the first week of May the paras of II/1 RCP would get only bread and tomato sauce.)[91] Gathering up the packages by night could be perilous: enemy machine gunners registered the position of any interesting-looking bundle, and fired on these lines if they heard movement after dark. Such combat rations as were available were stuffed in every corner of the French dug-outs; before going on patrol men would gobble a few mouthfuls of canned meat – 'monkey' – and hard biscuits, a bit of nougat or a few sweets. If evening found them under cover and able to heat up a mug of water, then coffee (with a slug of rum, for the lucky or provident) washed down a supper of canned sardines and stewed fruit.[92] It kept them alive, but it did not warm up the body core enough to fight off their accumulating exhaustion. The infantry seldom got any sort of hot meal now, and their rain-soaked clothing never had a chance to dry.

The morning of 29 April revealed on Dominique five newly installed recoilless guns, apparently hidden in tunnels dug right through from the reverse slope. They were supported by a widespread artillery barrage which blew up a batch of shells in the ammunition depot. Major Tourret called 'Zulu Kilo' for shelling on trenches advancing on Epervier, and then raided with men of his 8 BPC and 5 BPVN from the 'nameless' mud-hole near by. A lone légionnaire took it upon himself to crawl out from Eliane 2 and blow up an enemy blockhouse. That evening the tank 'Douaumont' was duelling with the RCLs on Dominique when it received a direct hit on the glacis plate from a 105mm shell, killing or wounding the whole crew (one, Private Lecry, had only parachuted in on the 24th); the M24 was towed to Huguette 3 and used as a fixed pillbox.[93]

On the evening of 29 April, Colonel Langlais called Geneviève de Galard to his headquarters; there she found General de Castries, Lieutenant Colonels Lemeunier and Bigeard and Major Vadot, gathered to congratulate her on the award of the Knight's Cross of the Légion d'Honneur – since the higher award demanded it, Castries also pinned a Croix de Guerre to her camouflage blouse.[94]

LIKE A BLESSED GIFT FOR THE Foreign Legion's feast-day of Camerone, 30 April dawned dry, though hot and humid; and that day the American CAT pilots agreed to resume missions over Dien Bien Phu. They would drop only delay-fused parachutes from 'medium' altitude, which meant around 10,000ft, and with a guarantee of better flak suppression escorts. (The French C-119 crews would still fly low-level missions by night.) That day almost 100 transport sorties dropped 212 tons; the Air Force would admit to 65 tons going astray, GONO claimed it was nearly half the total, and the truth probably lay in the middle – like the tantalizing packages scattered between French and enemy lines.

Few were more attractive than two identifiable crates of *vinogel* lying in no-man's-land on the edge of Champs-Elysées, under the sights of Viet Minh machine-gun nests and the fascinated gaze of I/13 DBLE on Eliane 2. They kept their eyes on them all day, through intermittent shelling, reports of activity outside Junon, and a bickering fight which broke out at Dominique 3. Camerone without a drink was unthinkable; and although General de Castries had generously sent the battalion his last four bottles of wine, even in their weakened ranks one bottle between each company would be hardly enough to drink *'la poussière'* – the 'dust-layer'. At about 10pm Major Coutant laconically reported a successful trench raid which had blown up two bunkers and damaged another, returning without loss. Apart from the vital pink jelly, the fighting patrol – selected from among clamouring volunteers – brought back a 16-year-old prisoner who did not know the number of his unit, and had been conscripted only on 8 March.[95]

The celebration of Camerone was a drier affair for I/2 REI down in Claudine, but the Legion did what they could to honour their ancestors and their comrades. The most senior Legion officer in his rank was Lieutenant Colonel Lemeunier, who somehow contrived to be in immaculate uniform when he greeted his guests in his command post: General de Castries, Colonel Langlais, Lieutenant Colonel Bigeard, and Mlle de Galard. The Foreign Legion does not lightly invite outsiders – even distinguished combat officers – on to the rolls of its brotherhood by awarding them honorary rank; but on Camerone 1954, Geneviève de Galard was named an honorary *légionnaire de 1ère classe*, alongside Lieutenant Colonel Bigeard of the 6th Colonial Parachute Battalion.[96]

Maurice Lemeunier's most public duty that day was to read over the radio net to all Foreign Legion personnel at Dien Bien Phu *'le récit'*, the brief traditional account of the first Camerone. It had not been Austerlitz, but a company action – Rorke's Drift with a grimmer ending; it was fought not to save a throne, but a pay convoy. In Mexico on 30 April 1863, three officers and 62 men led by a captain with a wooden hand sold their lives dearly to 2,000 attackers, holding a ruined farmyard all one blazing day without water or hope. When it was almost over, each of the last five men fired his last cartridge; then they charged out at their tormentors with fixed bayonets. Astonished, a Mexican officer spared the lives of the three survivors. Militarily, Camerone was without significance; but in its name the Legion celebrates obedience to the given mission, unto death.

'L'armée Francaise assiéga Puebla...'; as Lemeunier began to read out the familiar words the légionnaires in the mud of Dien Bien Phu were bonded with légionnaires all over Indochina and the wider world – in the column struggling up from Laos, on the Delta airfields where the volunteers waited, on the deck of the *Pasteur* somewhere in the Indian Ocean, in Morocco and the Algerian Sahara, and on the square at Sidi bel Abbès where Captain Danjou's wooden hand was being paraded before the great globe of the Monument to the Dead.

After the solemnities, Camerone is a day for feasting and drinking. For most légionnaires at Dien Bien Phu there was pathetically little to feast upon – a shared tin of sardines, a couple of cigarettes if they were lucky, and a puddle of *vinogel* at the bottom of a canteen cup to drink the toast to

'Our friends beneath the sands'. But they could still sing, and the cheerful nonsense words and fine thudding rhythm of the Legion's march rose above the sandbags:

'*Tiens,* voilà du bou*din,* voilà du bou*din,*
Pour les *Al*sa*ciens,* les *Suisses* et *les – Lor – rains...*'[97]

THE NEXT DAY MARKED another feast, and from their trenches the légionnaires would see red flags brandished and hear the *Internationale* broadcast over tinny loudspeakers to celebrate May Day – General Giap could hardly have picked a more auspicious date for his final offensive. Several thousand of the garrison of Dien Bien Phu were still ready to fight like wolves; but to their commanders it had been clear for weeks that any hope of salvation lay with politicians, airmen and soldiers far outside the valley. These external factors may conveniently be summarized together in the next chapter.

15. Deus Ex Machina

'The B-26 squadrons did not attack the enemy: they transported bombs.'
General de Champeaux de la Boulaye, *1987*

ONE OF THE BASIC ARGUMENTS on which the air–ground base concept had been founded was that the French Air Force would be able to sway any battle in the defenders' favour. It was believed that the artillery and combat aircraft would together form a hammer to smash the People's Army on the anvil of the ground defences. In the event, only two genuinely successful direct air support missions seem to have been provided: that at Huguette 6 early on 5 April, and that wasted before the Huguette 1 counter-attack on 23 April. The failure of the concept in practice demands examination.

Firstly, dispersal of effort continued to weaken the impact of General Dechaux's squadrons on the ground battle. GATAC/Nord's limited number of aircraft were still subject to the simultaneous and conflicting demands of the Delta, the attempt to cut General Giap's supply routes, and the tactical problems of GONO. The relative priorities given to these types of mission varied according to successive orders emanating from Generals Navarre and Lauzin, whose relationship was prickly before the battle started, and did not improve.[1]

To consider first the numbers and work rate of the fighter-bombers: during the month of April the Air Force Bearcats flew a total of 641 sorties during 1,041 flying hours. Of these, only 198 sorties were for the benefit of Dien Bien Phu, while 184 were attacks on the lines of supply, and no fewer than 259 were over the Delta.[2] The theoretical total strength of GC 1/22 and 2/22 in Tonkin and northern Laos was 40 Bearcats – per squadron, 16 plus four spares, so the operational maximum was 32.[3] The present author has been unable to confirm the number of pilots actually available; but assuming that Far East Air Forces' overall figure of 23 per cent personnel shortfall in flying units applied to the Bearcat squadrons, we arrive at a rough guess of 25 pilots each flying about 26 missions totalling 41 hours during April – equivalent to one mission on six days out of every seven. (Once again, the limitations of averaged figures are acknowledged.) However, as we have seen, only 198 missions in all – 30 per cent of this total – were to Dien Bien Phu.[4]

By comparison, the naval Hellcats of 11F each averaged 58 flying hours in April. The apparent significantly higher work rate than the Bearcats is deceptive – the Navy fighters, with longer endurance, flew from the Delta coast, while a proportion of the Bearcat flights were from Xieng Khouang, 110 miles nearer than Haiphong–Cat Bi; an extra 35 minutes in each direction for the Aéronavale would account for the difference in flying hours. However, while the Hellcat and Helldiver pilots flew an average 24 missions each during April, they recorded a total of 569 sorties to Dien Bien Phu that month. Compared with the Bearcats' 198 sorties, they would thus have been nearly three times as visible to the troops on the ground as the Air Force fighters, which may account for their better reputation.[5]

As for the work they did over the valley: in simple terms, there are two kinds of air support for ground troops in battle. 'Direct' support involves aircraft attacking the enemy troops confronting a friendly unit, either at an agreed time as part of a co-ordinated operation, or at short notice to provide emergency support against a sudden enemy assault. 'Indirect' support strikes at the enemy anywhere on the battlefield where he is vulnerable, according to a general doctrine based on information and experience, in order to cause him the greatest damage. At Dien Bien Phu the first type of support was virtually never delivered.

The most obvious reason was that the great majority of People's Army attacks took place at night, and any retreat by failed attackers was usually covered by the morning fog. Pilots did fly daylight missions in support of specific French ground operations such as the recapture of Eliane 1 on 10 April; but most of these struck general areas of identified or supposed Viet Minh activity. GONO called them in on probable concentration areas in the late afternoon before anticipated enemy attacks, as an extension of the camp artillery's 'counter-preparation fires'; but the limitations of fighter-bomber attack on forested terrain have already been mentioned.[6] The aircraft were also employed to seal off sectors of the battlefield from immediate reinforcement, and to blind or neutralize enemy artillery by attacks on Dominique 2, Baldy and Phoney.

However, Dien Bien Phu does not offer examples of the kind of strictly controlled supporting attacks on pinpoint targets close to advancing or threatened friendly troops that characterized America's Vietnam War of the 1960s. Such attacks demand very tight communications between the commanders of the ground units and the leaders of the air strikes, and this facility was entirely absent at Dien Bien Phu, where the central PCIA controlled all air activity. The fighter-bombers could not be called in at short notice on exact targets, clearly marked and distinguishable from friendly troops close by; and Viet Minh infantry commanders were well aware of the measure of protection thus offered by 'hanging on to the Frenchman's belt' – by closing up to the defenders as quickly as possible.

The sheer difficulty for single-seat fighter pilots in delivering accurate attacks on pinpoint targets with bombs, napalm or unguided rockets has already been discussed in Chapter 11 in relation to the Bearcat strikes of 14 March. 'Indirect' support – typically, more or less freelance strafing by Bearcats and Hellcats – did sometimes achieve success, but its impact was limited. There were few fighters over the valley at any one time, and in the face of plentiful light flak their attacks were necessarily fast and brief. While low-level air attack is terrifying to troops in the open, the People's Army seldom allowed themselves to be caught out of their trenches in daylight, and on those rare occasions strafing by half a dozen fighters did not actually kill many of them.

Even those pilots who did reach the valley had too many different jobs to do: their missions were divided between attempts to silence the Viet Minh's artillery, the suppression of anti-aircraft fire in support of air-drops (particularly by the low-flying C-119s) and tactical support for the infantry. Moreover, their original briefings were sometimes countermanded while they were in flight: until 17 April Colonel de Castries had the prerogative of overruling Hanoi's selection of targets when the aircraft arrived over Dien Bien Phu.[7] This might seem sensible; but he (or Langlais) often diverted missions to infantry support at the last moment, and without much understanding of the problems this involved for the unbriefed pilots. Soldiers seldom grasp the near impossibility of identifying a particular group of tiny, drab-coloured figures on an unremarkable piece of ground, through a scratched plexiglass cockpit canopy set directly above a pair of broad wings, from several hundred feet up, while travelling at between 200 and 300 miles per hour.

When the airmen took over from 'Zulu Kilo' the task of countering General Giap's artillery they had to try to locate heavily camouflaged casemates in thick woodland, and even if they scored a lucky hit their 500lb bombs were unlikely to penetrate the many feet of overhead protection. The difficulty of hitting the even smaller AA guns has already been touched upon; and these were mobile targets, which could be shifted and recamouflaged without much labour if their position was identified. The lessons of World War II suggest that only large numbers of bombers dropping 'carpets' of 1,000lb bombs would have been really effective against the Viet Minh artillery, and General Lauzin's Far East Air Forces were quite unable to provide support on this scale.

The five (later, four) Privateer heavy bomber crews at Haiphong–Cat Bi flew missions by both day and night; their total of 176 sorties in April seems to give each crew an extraordinary average of at least 35 missions – a figure that would have been impressive for fighter pilots at the height of World War II, and was never achieved by heavy bomber crews.[8] Normally the Privateers flew in rotating patrols of two; the ground staff worked at the same frantic pace as the aircrews, turning a bomber round between missions in about 45 minutes, and it was not unknown for a crew to fly three missions in 24 hours. But despite the naval aircrews' remarkable stamina, pairs of bombers dropping 6,000lb loads from about 10,000ft could have no decisive effect on the battle; and the Norden bombsight could be blinded by fog and cloud just as easily as the human eyeball.

For the great majority of their bomber support, GONO relied upon the Air Force B-26 squadrons; and an analysis of their operations also suggests reasons for the wider failure of combat air support at Dien Bien Phu.

IN 1987 SUCH AN ANALYSIS of the operations of one of the two B-26 squadrons – GB 1/25 'Tunisie' – was published by General de Champeaux de la Boulaye, a veteran of a 1951–2 combat tour in B-26s who returned to Tonkin just before the end of the battle. His extensive documentary research and interviews with veterans led him to conclusions which make bleak but illuminating reading.[9]

The two bomber squadrons, GB 1/19 and 1/25, were equipped with American B-26 twin-engined medium bombers (formerly designated A-26 – the Douglas Invader). The first 25 had arrived in Indochina in January 1951, and the US provided a second batch of 22 during January/February 1954. On 13 March the two squadrons had a total of 34 aircraft on strength; the majority were the B-26B model with a solid nose mounting eight 0.50in heavy machine guns, and a minority the B-26C with a glazed nose for a bombardier. (A master bombardier flying in a B-26C led each flight, and all released their loads on his signal.) In April, GB 1/25 alone had 23 aircraft; yet in practice this inventory was meaningless – the number actually available for the squadron's missions averaged only 11 bombers on any one day, and individual missions were very seldom flown by as many as seven together.

The Air Force was chronically short of mechanics, but by March 1954 this need had been met to some extent by 200 seconded American ground crew.[10] The actual serviceability rate achieved during April should have allowed GB 1/25 to record about 1,450 flight hours. A two-way mission between Cat Bi and Dien Bien Phu, including say 30 minutes over the target, took just under three hours; so from the viewpoint of serviceable aircraft this squadron should have been able to achieve a monthly total of 483 sorties. In fact the squadron's total combat flight time in April was just over 773 hours, in 297 sorties – a shortfall of 47 per cent in flying hours and 39 per cent in sorties.

This was due in large part to a lack of aircrews. In mid February the unit's recorded personnel strength should have provided 21 trained three-man crews; but the actual number was 16 crews, and during April the average number who made themselves available for missions was 11 crews.[11] General de Champeaux judged that the squadron should have been able to achieve 450 sorties during the month if all personnel had pulled their weight, and up to 100 more if they had thrown away the rule-book – as they were authorized to do on 15 March. In the latter case – with each of 16 crews averaging only just over one mission each day – this would have put about six patrols each of three bombers over the battle-field every day, from this one squadron. In fact, nothing like this rate was ever achieved by the two B-26 squadrons together, which during April flew a total of 423 sorties over Dien Bien Phu and 80 over other targets. The average crew thus flew two sorties every three days, the burden on those who did fly being increased by those who did not.[12]

THE BOMBLOADS CARRIED obviously had major consequences for the effectiveness of missions. The B-26 had a maximum capacity of 8,000lbs when eight 1,000lb general purpose (blast plus fragmentation) bombs were loaded; but this 3½-ton capacity fell off when larger numbers of smaller bombs were fitted to the bomb bay shackles – to 5,000lbs (ten × 500lb), 3,000lbs (12 × 250lb), and so forth. During the whole battle, not one B-26 ever carried more than 4,000lbs – half its capacity. From his examination of armourers' logs General de Champeaux concluded that the variations in numbers and sizes of bombs loaded were arbitrary choices, independent of any calculations of weather or target. He suggested that the overall limits were due to an excessive concern with safety, which had become habitual since 1951 when the runway at Cat Bi was only 1,420yds long. Yet it had since been lengthened to a much safer 2,620yds; flying with full loads would not even have required General Lauzin's authorization of 15 March for his crews to disregard all safety norms under current war conditions.

General de Champeaux claimed that an even greater degree of *'je-m'en-foutisme'* governed the fitting of the various types of bomb fuse. The effect of bombs dropped from high altitude is greatly diminished when they fall on soft ground at hundreds of feet per second, burying themselves deeply before they explode; for this reason air forces use 'instantaneous' impact fuses (one-thousandth second delay after hitting the ground). A range of different American delay fuses were delivered to the B-26 squadrons along with the bombs; but due to lack of training and supervision, GB 1/25's armourers seem to have selected fuses 'with indifference', most often fitting 0.025-second delays – four times the optimum delay – which allowed many bombs to bury themselves uselessly in the mud before exploding.

There was worse. America had also supplied quantities of advanced 'Variable Time' fuses – in effect, miniaturized radar sensors which could detonate the bomb several feet above the ground; such airbursts were devastating to infantry and to open gun positions. To avoid accidents in flight the VT was fitted with a retarder which armed the fuse only after the bomb had fallen clear of the aircraft – an interval which could be set between one second and 58 seconds.[13] For safety reasons the fuses were delivered to the units with the retarder set at the maximum interval; it was the armourers' job to turn it back to the desired delay when loading for a mission. Unfortunately, the squadron personnel never bothered to read the instruction manual; and throughout the battle the potentially devastating airburst fuse was dropped still set for nearly a minute's arming delay – when it took bombs just 15 seconds to fall 10,000ft.

TO TURN FROM THE TECHNICAL to the operational: the People's Army at Dien Bien Phu simply did not match the 1944 European scenario that seems to have shaped the expectations of too many staff officers. The targets at Dien Bien Phu were either skilfully hidden – the artillery, and the infantry massing in the forest rim; or ephemeral – infantry occupying narrow trenches following night battles. Merely to scatter a few dozen bombs hopefully over an area of perhaps 160 square miles, unevenly inhabited by some 50,000 enemies, was futile; yet probably 15 per cent of the B-26 daylight sorties bombed entirely blind from above the clouds, out of AA range. At night, when they were needed most, they were almost wholly absent. Night missions were flown only at moments of crisis, such as the first two nights of the battle for the Five Hills, when 19 sorties were put over the valley. Their inaccurate bombing is hardly surprising, since targets had to be designated by dead reckoning estimated from the 'Torri Rouge' radio beacon – not a method to employ when friend and foe are in close contact.[14] Effective air support, especially by such a small bomber force, demanded accurate target location, quick reaction, concentration of effort, close liaison with the ground troops, and a mastery of all the complex techniques of ground-attack flying. All of these seem to have been lacking at Dien Bien Phu.

From 28 March the choice of objectives and the allocation of aircraft was made at General Cogny's headquarters in Hanoi by a co-ordinating committee (CCF) which included artillery, Air Force and intelligence officers. It met at 6pm each evening to identify the priorities – throughout the Tonkin war zone – for the following day. About an hour later the committee reconvened to agree a provisional programme balancing the demands and resources of all parties. At about 4.30am the next morning, with the previous afternoon's reconnaissance photos and the night's radio reports to hand, the committee met to fix a definitive plan for the day. Orders went out to the air bases at about 6am for the morning's missions; only then was the arming of the aircraft started – a process taking about two hours. At approximately midday the committee met again to fix the afternoon's missions, with the benefit of further study of the previous day's photos, but not of any detailed report on the morning mission's results. This routine limited the bombers to a maximum of two missions a day.

The orders sent to GATAC/Nord's squadrons – more than 12 hours after the reconnaissance photos had been taken – specified the objectives and the timing of missions. The objectives selected during the first half of April included (rounded off) 46 per cent support missions, i.e. attacks on enemy troops; 44 per cent flak suppression; and 9 per cent attacks on artillery positions. But during the second half of the month the figures were 13 per cent support, 68 per cent AA suppression, and 21 per cent artillery.[15] Thus, during the height of the battles for the Huguettes and while Giap's troops were closing in for the final offensive, attempts to suppress enemy flak and artillery had far greater priority than supporting the infantry – yet with very little verifiable result. There is no firm evidence that any single enemy artillery piece was destroyed during these attacks; and since anti-aircraft guns were moved out of the forested hills and closer to the entrenched camp from 20 April, the deterrent effect of air attack on AA Regiment 367 cannot have been great.

Apart from the choice of bombloads and fuses, the altitude was also left to the squadron commanders. General de Champeaux collated the daily weather data for morning, midday and evening throughout the siege. Making all due allowance for the weather, Champeaux could find no reason for the high altitudes selected except for unwillingness to face the flak.

While General de Champeaux stated that target marking by artillery smoke shells never seems to have been attempted, several other sources certainly confirm use of this standard technique. However, it was of limited value without direct radio contact between bomber formation leaders and individual strongpoint commanders, rather than through Major Guérin's air control team (PCIA) at GONO headquarters – who might be a mile from the target and rarely had any view of it. Given that the low-altitude spotter planes from Laos could not loiter in the sky over the valley by daylight, this may have been the most significant weakness in the whole system. Without reliable target marking coupled with a direct radio contact on the spot to talk the pilots through such missions in 'real time', close support strikes were highly problematic. Aircrews did not dare to drop their loads too close to the last known limits of friendly positions – information which, due to the CCF's routines, might now be 24 hours out of date. We should bear this in mind when considering Colonel Lalande's complaint: 'We asked for interventions on targets, which were hit after unpredictable delays. It was not rare to see bombing near our position in zones where our constant patrols had never reported any enemy. Trying to correct bombing by the use of smoke shells was unfruitful because of the lack of direct radio contact with the aircrews.'[16]

The Air Force also suffered from a failure to report the results achieved, which might have enabled them to correct failure or exploit success. At squadron briefings lead bombardiers never received any general intelligence on the enemy's latest dispositions in relation to friendly lines, the position of his heavy weapons, the greatest concentration of his infantry, his concealment and camouflage, or information on People's Army tactical practice.

FINALLY, GENERAL DE CHAMPEAUX did not shrink from stating in the most robust terms that professional standards in the bomber squadrons were not high. Bombing as a speciality had been neglected for years; since the role of the French Air Force within NATO was entirely defensive, it had been discontinued for economic reasons. Most airmen in the B-26 units were ex-transport crews, and GB 1/25 was a former Dakota squadron converted to the bomber role – not the ideal background for ground-attack pilots. The process of conversion had also been less than rigorous: the crews got a few weeks' flight training, but no instruction at all in the complex technical and operational skills of the bombing trade.

General de Champeaux paid tribute to the USAF instructors who accompanied the initial batch of B-26s in 1951, hammering as much information as they could into the first four crews from GB 1/19 during an improvised six-week course at Saigon–Tan Son Nhut. (By comparison, he noted that at that date British RAF bomber crews had to pass a number of specialist operational courses lasting a full year.) Further theoretical study and actual combat experience brought the original crews up to an acceptable level of skill which was gradually diffused throughout the unit. But when veterans finished their 18-month tours their skills went home with them; incredibly, there was no systematic programme for them to instruct their replacements, and by 1954 the B-26 crews had 'turned over' twice. The absence, before the very last days of the battle, of a specialist bomber commander ranking above the squadron level no doubt had a negative effect on this, as on other aspects of the B-26 operations.

General de Champeaux reported a 'detestable' atmosphere when he and a few other experienced crews were briefly called back to Indochina in the last days of the battle; he stated frankly that unit commanders and their crews were slack, unmotivated, and unprepared for the risks of battle. Too many of them simply went through the motions; it was considered impossibly boring actually to read the technical manuals provided; and Champeaux remarked tartly upon *'une épidémie de maladies psychosomatiques'* which had coincided with the revelation of the enemy's formidable AA artillery. The older officers – many of them reservists recalled for a limited period – were poorly trained and had no career incentives to improve themselves. The younger officers did not understand what they were doing in this sinister tropical backwater, instead of making a future for themselves flying jets back in Germany.

At Dien Bien Phu the B-26s achieved so little success that by the late stages of the battle the soldiers of GONO formed the impression that bombing raids had become a largely symbolic gesture of solidarity on the part of the Air Force. General de Champeaux's final conclusion was that given the available numbers of men and machines, the B-26s could have been at least ten times more effective at Dien Bien Phu than they actually were. It is a subjective judgement; but the judge's qualifications invite respect.

IF THE EXPECTATIONS PLACED upon French air power had proved vain, there remained, in some minds, one last great hope. The relationship between the French and United States governments was complex –

and aggravated as much by questions over France's attitude to NATO as by her Asian policies. Yet during late March and April 1954 there seemed to be a possibility that the Eisenhower administration might escalate American support from the financial and logistic to the point of actual commitment of US air forces for the rescue of Dien Bien Phu.

Early in 1954 a hint of diplomatic blackmail can be detected in some of the contacts between the two governments: if the USA did not step up its support France might be obliged, reluctantly, to explore a separate nego-tiated peace with the Communists, despite the inconvenience to America's Asian policy as a whole. French representatives advanced the view that – even with US material aid – a military solution was beyond France's unaided capability, for reasons of manpower and domestic politics. On 5 January, Ambassador Heath had quoted speculation by Commissioner General Dejean that provided funds became available (from an unspeci-fied source), and provided Chancellor Adenauer could be persuaded to agree (by unspecified friends), then perhaps six new almost completely German regiments of the Foreign Legion could be raised for the Expeditionary Corps. On 21 January, Heath had reported a meeting with Secretary Marc Jacquet. Jacquet had claimed that if General Navarre did not produce some victories within a few months then the French parliamen-tary opposition would force negotiations with Ho Chi Minh. If the C-in-C could achieve a bloody defeat of the Viet Minh at Dien Bien Phu then the problem would be postponed; but no decisive victory in Indochina was possible without US participation, perhaps in the form of a 'foreign legion' of pilots and other specialists.[17]

The announcement on 18 February of the forthcoming Geneva Conference on 26 April concentrated the minds of the Laniel government. France needed to go to Geneva not visibly desperate for a ceasefire, and with the confidence that if the conference failed to produce one she had a fallback position – the hope of American intervention. On 11 March, two days before the bombardment of Dien Bien Phu, the National Defence Committee met to hear Defence Minister Pleven's report on his tour of Indochina. It was agreed that Washington must be informed of the French conclusions before the Geneva Conference. Briefly, these were that a military solution was not achievable in the short term, and that a diplo-matic solution should be sought; that in parallel to this search, any

improvement in the military balance depended upon the rapid development of the Vietnamese National Army, which could be brought about
only through increased US aid; and that France remained worried about
the possibility of direct Red Chinese intervention, and sought assurances
of US assistance should this occur.

Between 20 and 26 March (while Castries and Langlais were rebuilding GONO to face the forthcoming Viet Minh second offensive), this
message was carried to Washington by the Chief of the Defence Staff,
General Ely, who was granted access to President Eisenhower, Secretary of
State John Foster Dulles, and Admiral Arthur B. Radford, Chairman of
the Joint Chiefs-of-Staff, among others. The broad US response to the
French position was to urge the indivisibility of the South-East Asian
problem; to argue that no fruitful negotiations could be pursued with
China or the Viet Minh until France's military position had been improved,
and to promise accelerated aid, while at the same time continuing to
criticize aspects of French policy in Indochina.[18] However, in his last
meeting with General Ely on 25 March, the Chairman of the Joint Chiefs
surprised him by going a good deal further.

It was now nearly a fortnight since Giap's unveiling of powerful
Chinese-supplied artillery and flak, and Admiral Radford believed that
US intervention could be presented as a reasonable counter-escalation.
He raised the hypothesis of B-29 heavy bombers from the Philippines
attacking Viet Minh supply routes, escorted by jet carrier fighters.[19] This
was the scenario which would soon be christened Operation 'Vautour' (to
the Americans, 'Vulture'). The hope that it might enjoy support beyond
the Pentagon was raised two days later when Secretary Dulles made a
speech to the Overseas Press Club in New York; he called for unified action
to halt the aggressive expansion of Communism in South-East Asia, by
the USA, Britain, Australia and New Zealand, France and the Associated
States, Thailand and the Philippines.[20] While falling far short of a commitment to US military action, this speech must still have given the Viet
Minh leadership some pause.

On 29 March a meeting of the restricted war cabinet took place in
Paris; no minutes were kept, but it is reported that General Ely gave his
opinion that a formal request to Washington might bring US intervention, perhaps including the bombing of the actual siege army at Dien Bien

Phu. It was agreed to send a trusted Air Force staff officer, Colonel Raymond Brohon, to seek General Navarre's opinion.[21] Brohon arrived in Saigon on 1 April, while the battle of the Five Hills was raging at Dien Bien Phu. Over the next two days he discussed 'Vautour' with Generals Navarre, Bodet and Cogny and Commissioner General Dejean. To his surprise, the Généchef's response was unenthusiastic – not because he did not believe the operation to be feasible, but because he feared retaliation by the MiGs of the Chinese Air Force against his vulnerable Delta airfields.

In a secret telegram of 3 April, however, General Navarre was more positive. He believed that the battle was now delicately balanced and could be tipped either way by relatively minor factors. He intended to resupply GONO by parachute to meet an eventual Viet Minh final offensive, but lacked the capacity to send in major troop reinforcements: 'I estimate that under these circumstances ['Vautour'] could have a decisive effect, above all if it were carried out before the Viet Minh assault.'[22]

Navarre's hope was for a hammer blow not on Giap's siege army, but on their lines of supply. Operation 'Vautour' could seriously hamper the expected third Viet Minh offensive only if it were carried out while Giap's necessary supplies – perhaps 25,000–30,000 tons – were still on the road through chokepoints such as Co Noi, or stockpiled at rear depots around Tuan Giao. The C-in-C was all too aware that French Air Force operations against the supply lines had been negligible since 13 March.[23] The prospect of several successive raids by 60 B-29s of the US Far East Air Force from the Philippines, each carrying up to nine tons of bombs, on roads which must soon become precarious with the arrival of the monsoon proper, was surely enticing; and Navarre's fear of Chinese retaliation could be stilled if US carrier fighters from the Gulf of Tonkin were also available to cover his airfields. The Superfortresses, massed in that strength, offered true strategic 'carpet bombing'; they could darken the sky, and release a thunder over the Thai Highlands that would make General Lauzin's little tactical air force seem like a toy. But however attractive this scenario, if 'Vautour' was going to come to Dien Bien Phu's rescue then it had to happen soon.[24]

On the same day that Navarre sent his more enthusiastic telegram to Paris, in Washington Secretary Dulles and Admiral Radford were presenting the outline of 'Vulture' to a group of eight Congressional leaders. They sought a joint resolution of Congress allowing the president freedom to commit air and naval forces to Indochina at his judgement. Reactions to the idea of unilateral US action were negative – particularly from Senator Lyndon B. Johnson of Texas, the Senate Minority Leader – and the request for the enabling resolution was denied. Congressional support for 'Vulture' would be forthcoming only if a coalition including the British Common-wealth and several Asian nations would also commit themselves to military participation in the Indochina War – a vanishingly unlikely prospect. While Vice President Richard M. Nixon, Chairman of the Senate Armed Service Committee, was in favour of Radford's plans, President Eisenhower was unenthusiastic about another Asian commitment so soon after the end of the Korean War; and Army Chief-of-Staff General Matthew B. Ridgway – an Asian specialist – was deeply opposed.

A summary of Chinese assistance to the Viet Minh – including the presence of a military mission with Giap's army at Dien Bien Phu – would soon arrive via Ambassador Dillon in Paris. This would be used as ammu-nition by both sides in the debate; but General Ridgway argued that dead Chinese generals would be another reason for fearing that air strikes would lead to mutual escalation. He predicted that increasingly large numbers of US ground troops would inevitably get sucked in, and argued vigorously against the United States getting caught up in another Asian land war.[25]

On the night of 4/5 April (while Sergeant Chief Bleyer and his 20-odd comrades were holding out in the last blockhouse on Huguette 6, overrun by four enemy battalions), Prime Minister Laniel made a formal request for American air intervention, both through Ambassador Dillon in Paris and directly to Admiral Radford in Washington.[26] Dillon's secret cable to Secretary Dulles described an emergency meeting with Laniel and Foreign Minister Bidault; he had been told that 'armed intervention by US aircraft at Dien Bien Phu was now necessary to save the situation'. This was the occasion when the ambassador was handed the analysis (referred to above) from General Navarre, summarizing all Chinese aid to the Viet Minh over the previous year. Dillon reported that Georges Bidault had specifically accepted the risk of consequent Chinese retaliatory attacks on the French air bases; and that he had stressed that France was making this very serious request because the outcome of the Geneva Conference would turn on the outcome of the siege of Dien Bien Phu.[27]

While awaiting the US response French staff officers exchanged flurries of telegrams concerning the practicalities of such joint action, some of which must now seem faintly absurd.[28] General Navarre and his naval commander Admiral Auboyneau had conversations with Admiral Hopwood, chief-of-staff of the US Pacific Fleet; and on 10 April the carriers USS *Boxer* and *Essex*, cruising near by, were deployed to the Gulf of Tonkin. During this first half of April the C-in-C was also called away from Saigon to deal with a crisis of confidence suffered by the Cambodian government in the face of Communist successes. For several days General Navarre was preoccupied by shadowy contacts via Vietnamese intermediaries between officers of the Expeditionary Corps and the Viet Minh, specifically excluding the civil government from explorations of possible future armistice terms. Paris retrospectively authorized these contacts on 18 April (the day that Alain Bizard had to leave his wounded with Sergeant Ganzer and run his survivors down the airstrip from Huguette 6). This shadow dance came to nothing, as the Vietnamese intermediaries and the Viet Minh decided to pursue direct contacts at Geneva.[29]

Despite French pressure, no definite response to the request for USAF intervention was received from Washington, where an intense round of consultations was taking place between the White House, the State Department, Congress and the Pentagon. When General Earle E. Partridge, commanding the US Far East Air Force, arrived in Saigon on 14 April it emerged that his orders were solely to prepare a study, and lacked both precision and urgency. On the 20th a mission headed by Partridge's bomber commander General Joseph D. Caldera threw themselves energetically into making such a study; and on 23 April (the day of 2nd Foreign Parachute Battalion's crucifixion on the steel plates outside Huguette 1), Navarre signalled General Ely that the operation could be launched at 72 hours' notice. Both USAF generals had misgivings over apparent French ignorance of the scale of destruction involved in unleashing a wing of Superfortresses, and over the apparent indifference at the prospect of the inevitable French 'collateral' casualties. General Caldera flew over Dien Bien Phu three times (twice, apparently, in his personal B-17 Flying Fortress, a nostalgic souvenir of World War II); and despite the inadequate guidance and navigation facilities available, he believed 'Vulture' to be feasible as a daytime operation.[30]

In Paris on 24 April, two days before the Geneva Conference convened, Foreign Ministers Bidault of France and Anthony Eden of Great Britain had a meeting with Secretary Dulles to review the possibility of Allied intervention in Indochina. Dulles had to report that Congress would not allow a US military commitment unless Britain, her Commonwealth and the nations of South-East Asia also undertook to send troops to assist the French on the ground. From Great Britain's point of view this was impossible; and on 27 April, Prime Minister Churchill (whose wartime leadership had, after all, survived the much costlier fall of Singapore) told the House of Commons that Britain would not undertake to intervene militarily in Indochina before the results of the Geneva Conference became clear.

At a meeting on 29 April in Washington, Secretary Dulles and Admiral Radford were heavily outnumbered by senior political and military figures who opposed the adventure, and at a subsequent press conference President Eisenhower ruled out unilateral US military action.[31] On the previous day, General Ely had already had to inform General Navarre that there was, after all, no chance of Operation 'Vautour' taking place in time to be of any help to the garrison of Dien Bien Phu.

The agony of the soldiers in the valley was cruelly felt in Hanoi, Saigon and Paris; in Washington and London it was regrettable, naturally, but just one more piece on the global board. Although the US government had a long list of demands concerning France's Asian policy, they had been prepared to consider helping the French militarily if they had a reasonable chance of winning. However, in view of reports received during April the Pentagon and State Department no longer believed that their intervention could achieve anything more than postponing the inevitable fall of Dien Bien Phu. The Eisenhower administration was fully alive to the Communist threat to South-East Asia, but the immediate reality was the Geneva Conference, which must take its course. America's position, at that conference and in the wider world, could only be harmed by associating herself openly with a French military defeat that seemed inevitable, with or without USAF intervention.[32]

THERE HAS BEEN HEATED speculation that the dropping of atomic bombs was discussed during the Franco-American negotiations over Operation 'Vautour/Vulture'. Jules Roy states flatly that it was always intended to be a nuclear attack; that the carriers *Boxer* and *Essex* had such weapons aboard; and that General Navarre's denial that the use of atomic bombs was contemplated was 'a childish lie'.[33] Navarre's then aide, Captain Jean Pouget, vigorously denies that the possibility was ever raised with the C-in-C even in veiled terms. Although Roy did not cite his source, Bernard Fall believed it to be General Cogny who told Roy that General Ely's emissary Colonel Brohon had mentioned during his visit of 1–2 April that the use of 'several atomic bombs' in the Dien Bien Phu area was contemplated. Foreign Minister Bidault would later claim that the possibility of the US making two bombs available had been mentioned to him by Secretary Dulles during a meeting in Paris on 14 April.[34]

If these claims are true, then we may at least say that both parties to the talks seem to have displayed a failure of imagination. To consider only the most immediate practical effects, USAF participants in the discussion of 'Vautour' as a conventional bombing operation were struck by French stoicism over possible friendly casualties; but had atomic bombs been dropped close enough to Dien Bien Phu to neutralize the People's Army, it is hard to see how the French garrison was expected to survive.

Given the late Howard R. Simpson's ties over many years with US government agencies concerned with foreign policy in Asia, his summary written in 1994 is perhaps sufficient here:

> A persistent official haze still hangs over the proposed use of tactical nuclear weapons to save Dien Bien Phu. The relevant documents remain classified, but enough has seeped out through personal comments and written memoirs to suggest that such a proposal was seriously considered. Fortunately for the garrison of Dien Bien Phu, the project was abandoned. The comparatively crude nuclear weapons of 1954 risked wiping out the defenders as well as the attackers, and the second use of US nuclear weapons in Asia would have had disastrous and long-lasting political consequences.[35]

IF THE FATE OF GENERAL DE Castries' garrison would not be decided beside the Potomac, there were still some who hoped that it might be negotiated on the banks of Lake Geneva. General Navarre's briefing document for Georges Bidault's delegation to Geneva was dated 20 April. In summary, Navarre believed that without 'Vautour' Dien Bien Phu could not survive; he had no realistic hopes for a breakthrough to the camp by ground forces from Laos; and he saw the continued parachuting of men and munitions solely in terms of prolonging the defence in case the Geneva Conference could achieve a general ceasefire before the darkness finally closed over the garrison.

If diplomacy failed and GONO were wiped out, Navarre foresaw a continuation of the war until winter 1954/5 as conceivable, given the losses that Giap's main force had suffered at Dien Bien Phu. However, a military solution would be entirely conditional on either a massively increased French national effort to match Giap's new weapons and capability (an effort which Navarre clearly regarded as incredible); or on the 'internationalization' of the war, with the USA taking over the military burden on top of her current financial and material contribution.[36]

France's choice of tactics at Geneva presented a problem in itself: whether to try to secure a rapid ceasefire, followed by prolonged negotiations over a detailed settlement, during which no further military pressure could be applied; or whether to continue military operations and negotiations in parallel, in the hope of improving the military balance and thus the terms of an eventual ceasefire. The latter choice carried the obvious danger of a collapse of morale among the Expeditionary Corps and particularly the ANV – would soldiers continue to risk their lives when a ceasefire was obviously imminent? Foreign Minister Bidault and the majority of the French government favoured playing for time, while his deputy Paul Reynaud advocated a diplomatic dash for a ceasefire. General Navarre did not definitively recommend either course to Paris; on 21 April he stressed the importance of keeping up the pressure, but on the 30th his emphasis was that only a quick ceasefire could save Dien Bien Phu, and that in its absence he would authorize an attempt to break out towards Laos.[37]

In fact, France's negotiating tactics were irrelevant: control of the pace of discussion did not lie in her hands. The first week of the conference was taken up by diplomatic fencing over procedural questions – essentially, the admission to the talks of the Viet Minh and Associated States delegations. The former did not join the conference until 4 May; it was only on the 8th that all nine delegations sat down together; and the senior Viet Minh delegate Pham Van Dong then proceeded to spend another two days arguing for the admission of representatives of the Pathet Lao and the Cambodian Communists. Significant negotiations did not begin until 10 May – by which date not only French tactics, but the Laniel government itself had been rendered irrelevant by the turn of events in the High Region.[38]

IN THE ABSENCE OF ANY HOPE of American intervention in the air to transform the balance of advantage, or of an immediate general ceasefire to freeze the battle lines where they stood, the only remaining card to play was a link-up with GONO by French forces from northern Laos.

In December 1953 an operation codenamed 'Condor' had been planned to exploit an anticipated defeat of the People's Army at Dien Bien Phu. Its planners foresaw the movement north-eastwards of infantry from the Nam Ou valley, up the Nam Noua to rendezvous with paratroop units dropped near Sop Nao; the whole force would then advance through the frontier hills via the Col des Calcaires pass to arrive in the Nam Youm valley south of Dien Bien Phu (*see Map 8*).[39]

In the first three months of 1954 various other contingencies involving paratroop insertions south or east of Dien Bien Phu had been studied.[40] So too had possible plans for a break-out from Dien Bien Phu to the south ('Xénophon' and 'Ariane', mentioned in Chapter 8) associated with such an operation. On about 6 April, General Navarre sent the commander of Land Forces Laos, Colonel de Crèvecoeur, a small staff to assist him in planning a version of 'Condor', whose final architect would be Colonel Then, Crèvecoeur's staff officer for operations. 'Condor' always centred on a march north-east by troops from the Nam Ou valley towards Dien Bien Phu, but the picture of its exact intended strength and objective – and above all, its timetable – wavered during April, depending upon the shifting pattern of the units and resources that could be committed to it.[41]

The essential military geography of Upper Laos was shaped by river valleys; there were no viable roads in the thickly wooded hills. From Dien Bien Phu the Nam Youm flowed south for about six miles before one branch turned west through the Massif des Calcaires, and meandered about 28 miles to Ban Loi on the frontier, where it joined the Nam Noua. This flowed south for some 20 miles, past Sop Nao, before it entered the bulging north-east loop of the much larger Nam Ou near the village of Pak Noua. The western leg of the loop – the Nam Pak – led from the strategic Muong Khoua, roughly 12 miles upstream from the confluence; on the eastern leg, Muong Ngoi lay perhaps 30 miles downstream from Pak Noua. The total distance between Dien Bien Phu and Muong Khoua was between 50 and 70 miles, depending upon whether troops followed the river bends or cut across country; but all these distances are approximate 'crow's flight' figures – a marching column had to cover a great deal more ground.

This was the stretch of country through which Major Vaudrey's troops had advanced north to Sop Nao in Operation 'Ardèche' of November–December 1953, to meet Langlais' 'Régate' sortie from Dien Bien Phu in Christmas week. Since then it had been ravaged by Giap's Division 308 during its southward thrust in February, which had destroyed the garrison of Muong Khoua and, when it fell back to Dien Bien Phu, had left behind it regional units to play a merciless game of hide-and-seek with pro-French Meo and Lao partisan bands. These bands still existed, however, and Lieutenant Colonel Mollat's 800-odd Laotians and Meos with a tiny French cadre were available on the east bank of the Nam Ou. Scattered on both the west and east banks of the Nam Noua north of the Nam Ou bend were additional groups led by teams from Lieutenant Colonel Trinquier's Mobile Intervention Group (the ex-GCMA): these included 'Aréquier' west of Sop Nao, and east of the river 'Pamplemousse' and 'Banana'. These partisans were to form the advance scouts for Operation 'Condor', and were to secure drop zones for the planned airborne element.

Colonel de Crèvecoeur's dispersed forces for 'Condor' numbered just over 3,000 men; of these, nearly 1,700 were Laotians, and only one battalion was European – II/2 REI. This Legion unit and 4th Laotian Chasseurs (4 BCL) would advance up the eastern leg of the Nam Ou bend, commanded by Lieutenant Colonel Godard; meanwhile 5 BCL and 1st Laotian Parachute Battalion (1 BPL), led by Major Coquelet, would march up the Nam Pak towards Muong Khoua. The original plan called for these columns to advance up both valleys to a link-up around Pak Noua; the unified force, under Godard's command, would then move up the Nam Noua, to rendezvous in turn with paratroopers dropped west of Sop Nao; together they would march the final leg through the Massif des Calcaires, to emerge into the valley six miles south of Isabelle.[42]

Lieutenant Colonel Godard got his units moving on 14 April, in exhausting heat; their march was slowed by his inability to gather enough porters, mules and pack-saddles in this already pillaged countryside. He did not even have enough jerrycans to carry water, let alone the inflatable rafts he needed for stream crossings; on 18 April General Navarre ordered mules and 500 PIMs to be airlifted to him, thus laying the first extra burden on Colonel Nicot's overstretched Dakota fleet just as bad weather closed in over the Delta.[43] The first phase of 'Condor' – before the rendezvous with the paratroopers – was clearly going to take at least 15 days, so the air-drop phase would have to be scheduled for the last days of April, and Godard could not hope to reach Dien Bien Phu before about 7 May. While Godard's troops struggled painfully through the Laotian forest, skirmishing with the Viet Minh in their path, staff conferences in Hanoi confronted the difficulties of executing this airborne phase.[44]

The dilemma was cruelly simple: in order to mount an air-drop to give the rescue column the weight it needed to punch through, and to keep it supplied by air during its advance, it would be necessary to deny Dien Bien Phu itself the paratroop reinforcements and the cargo drops that it depended upon just to survive from day to day. Since the fresh paratroopers of 7th Colonial from France were not due to land at Saigon until 24 April, there were in practice only three parachute battalions in Tonkin potentially available for either task: 1st Colonial (1 BPC), and the Vietnamese 1 and 3 BPVN. Colonel Langlais was demanding 1 BPC to reinforce the camp, and rejected the two ANV battalions. To drop them for a link-up with Godard would require the diversion of every available Dakota for at least 24 hours, leaving only the C-119s to maintain Dien Bien Phu's lifeline. This was at a time when GONO had desperate need of constant ammunition resupply flights to build up stocks before General Giap's third offensive, which was expected daily from 10 April onwards.[45]

The pro-French partisans were active in the forest ahead of Godard's columns; and by 22 April radio intelligence and questioning of prisoners suggested that – in anticipation of an air-drop around Sop Nao – strong enemy forces were concentrating between the Nam Ou valley and the plain of Dien Bien Phu, astride the Col des Calcaires pass. In tortured terrain that lent itself perfectly to the tactics of ambush and delay, four or five battalions confronted Godard's single battalion of légionnaires and three rather hesitant Laotian units. Two battalions from Independent

Regiment 148 had been identified, one from Regiment 82 (formed from Pathet Lao guerrillas), and further north a battalion from Giap's Regiment 176; north of the pass Godard would also face Regiment 57. On the same day, General Navarre – acting on Colonel Nicot's report that he was unable to fulfil the demands of both GONO and 'Condor' – ordered the postponement of the latter's airborne phase until further orders, to be revived only on five days' notice.[46]

On 23 April, Godard's II/2 REI established a bridgehead north of the Nam Ou around Pak Noua; and on the 25th, the western column reached Muong Khoua. Colonel Then's plan for 'Condor' was now modified to take account both of the anticipated opposition and the postponement of the paratroop operation. He would abandon the Sop Nao area as the site of the airborne insertion, and shift it to Muong Nha, on an eastern tributary of the Nam Youm and north-east of the Massif des Calcaires. He now planned to disperse and mislead the enemy: between 25 April and 1 May the column would show itself south of the mountains, drawing Viet Minh attention and giving the impression that it was heading for the Col des Calcaires on the obvious route to Dien Bien Phu. Then, leaving only a screen of partisan units noisily active astride the direct route, Godard's battalions would swing away south-eastwards along the southern edge of the hills to reach Muong Nha and join up with the parachute element. Together they would march for Dien Bien Phu, reckoning to arrive on perhaps 25 May.

This timetable made 'Condor's' prospects of reaching GONO while the camp was still holding out extremely marginal; and the next few days would see them eliminated altogether. On 27 April, General Navarre approved Colonel Then's modified plan; but he ordered that Godard's force be reinforced by two battalions that were to be airlifted from central Laos up to Muong Nam Bac, a good 30 miles south of Muong Khoua. Given the strain on the Dakota fleet, and the length of the reinforcements' subsequent march, this would seriously delay 'Condor's' already almost impossible schedule. On 28 April, Colonel Nicot reported to General Lauzin that he would have great difficulty in providing the aircraft simultaneously to drop parachute reinforcements into Dien Bien Phu and at Muong Nha, maintain the resupply of GONO, and supply Godard's column on its march to the valley. The monsoon rains had now started in earnest;

and (as mentioned in the previous chapter) since the 24th the American crews for his C-119s had refused to fly, forcing him to transfer ten Dakota crews back to the Packet Detachment.[47]

On 29 April, General Navarre sent a confidential signal informing Colonel de Crèvecoeur that the airlift difficulties would prevent the execution of the airborne phase of 'Condor' for another seven or eight days. Oddly, the C-in-C gave the colonel no firm orders, leaving it up to him to judge his next move; but the truth could no longer be avoided. Without the paratroopers Godard's troops could never hope to fight their way through to Dien Bien Phu in time. On 30 April, while the Legion celebrated Camerone on the battlefield, General Navarre informed General Ely in Paris that if the Geneva Conference produced no early ceasefire, he was inclined to approve an attempted break-out by the garrison towards Godard's force in Laos.[48]

16. 'Tell Gars Pierre we liked him a lot'

'Langlais sang the Marseillaise *for 56 days.
Well, he had to...'*
Colonel Bigeard, 1966

AT A MEETING OF THE FRONT Military Committee on 22 April, General Giap outlined his intentions for the third offensive phase. The absolute necessity of presenting Pham Van Dong at Geneva with a clear-cut victory, and the combination of combat fatigue and inexperience in the ranks of his infantry, dictated a relatively cautious approach.

This was not to be the final assault; the objectives for 1–5 May were the capture of the High Elianes, and of the newly reorganized Huguettes on the western face. This would be followed from 6 to 10 May by a period of consolidation on the captured positions, while approach trenches were dug, artillery and AA guns were brought in closer, and the remaining defended area was denied all resupply. Only then would the final assault on the central positions be launched. On that same day General Navarre had informed General Ely in Paris, on the basis of radio intercepts, that Giap envisaged the siege continuing throughout the duration of the Geneva Conference, perhaps until the end of June.[1]

DURING THE NIGHT OF 30 April/1 May a battalion from Division 308 took some boggy trenches at Huguette 5, but at 2.30am the Legion para-troopers counter-attacked in driving rain, with artillery support from Isabelle. By first light the attackers showed signs of wavering; Captain Bourges led his company of I/2 REI up through the 'Metro' and emerged to clear the enemy's approach trenches outside Huguette 5, which was secure again by 8am on 1 May. Major Guiraud reported his casualties to Lieutenant Colonel Trancart, who was now in charge of personnel matters: the night had cost his battalion 12 dead, eight missing, and 68 wounded – these days, the whole strength of a company.[2]

The rain stopped in the early morning of May Day. The Viet Minh artillery kept up a sporadic fire, and small clashes took place where the opposing trenches were close together, but generally it was a quiet day for Dien Bien Phu. However, celebratory red flags and recorded martial music were not the only noticeable activity. From Huguette 5, French look-outs with binoculars saw enemy reinforcements moving about (including some artillery, unusually exposed by daylight, on the old Anne-Maries), and radio traffic suggested a good deal of preparation. On the sodden valley floor the People's Army found it just as cumbersome to move units around through half-flooded trenches as did the French; it took a battalion 12, sometimes 24 hours to shift from the east face of the siege ring to the west.[3]

GATAC/Nord gave priority to flak suppression that day; B-26s dropped napalm and 'Hail Leaflet' flechette bombs, and the soldiers saw the first appearance of a new type of aircraft – the big Vought Corsair fighter-bomber, with its long cylindrical cowling, W-cranked wings and ungainly afterthought of a tail. The USS *Saipan* had delivered 25 loaned AU-1 Corsairs to Tourane (Da Nang) a week previously, for Aéronavale Flotille 14F; Lieutenant Commander Ménettrier's personnel were flown out from Karouba in Tunisia. Battered veterans of the Korean War, 24 of the Corsairs were immediately declared not airworthy, as was the last one after a brief test flight. The ground crews slaved to get them in shape for combat flying, and they were shuttled up to Hanoi–Bach Mai in batches; by 1 May the squadron were able to put 11 sorties over Dien Bien Phu.[4] This was not a reinforcement, however, but a replacement: the pilots of 11F had flown themselves and their patched-up old Hellcats to a standstill, and they were now taken off operations.[5]

There had been little flak during the night, and the attentions of the fighters and bombers muffled it during 1 May; over the 24 hours starting at midnight Hanoi would load 197 tons of supplies for GONO, but about half of this was misdropped. The camp had three days' stocks of food, perhaps two nights' worth of 105mm shells, but only enough 120mm for a couple of hours' firing.[6] This was quite insufficient for Colonel Vaillant to face the forthcoming third offensive with confidence; and the gunners were also noticing that a growing proportion of the air-dropped ammunition was damaged when it reached the batteries – dented shellcases and bent mortar-bomb fins had to be hammered back into shape with improvised tools.[7]

At 5pm on May Day, Colonel Langlais' long-distance quarrel with Colonel Sauvagnac over the dropping of paratroops reached a climax in a message whose language betrayed both extreme strain and a sense of isolation: '... We shall win this battle without you and in spite of you... This will be the last [message] I shall address to you.'[8] The slow trickle of individual replacements – however heroic – had uneven levels of combat experience, and were inevitably thrust into the ranks among unfamiliar comrades and leaders, with little chance to settle in or master the special local knowledge that they needed if they were to live through their first night. What Langlais had been demanding was the dropping of a complete battalion, to give him once more a credible counter-attack force in time for the obviously imminent third wave of assaults on the eastern hills.

SHORTLY AFTER LANGLAIS' exasperated rant was transmitted to Hanoi in the late afternoon of 1 May, a thunderous artillery and mortar barrage began to fall on the perimeter strongpoints, the central area and the gunpits. It would last a full three hours, longer than any previous bombardment, and some recalled it as more violent – 'an earthquake'. Thanks to French air-drops, Giap's gunners now had a choice of fuses: impact, bunker-busting short-delay, or murderous airburst. At Dominique 4 the unusually solid command dug-out of II/4 RAC's 5th Battery rocked and trembled, and one ear-splitting blast left the battery staff deafened for hours afterwards.[9] All over the valley and the eastern hills men simply curled up under whatever notional cover they could find, buried their helmeted heads in their arms, and tried to ignore the shrugging of the earth all around them; they prayed for the barrage to end, but they knew what that end would bring. There was a new moon, and the night of 1/2 May would be dark.

General Giap's plan was for a first thrust to take the remaining strongpoints on the High Elianes, and part of the northern river flats in order to drive a salient between the hills and Epervier. Regiment 174 from Division 316 would assault Elianes 1 and 4, while Division 312's Regiment 141 thrust south-westwards to take Dominique 3 in the valley. Eliane 2 remained the key to the south-east defences; but Regiment 98 – to be hurled once again at this bastion on whose glacis they had already left so many of their dead – had not yet completed the approach saps which they were digging from the south. Neither was the mine tunnel ready; it needed to extend at least 50yds, to bring it under the summit blockhouse, before it could be packed with a ton or two of TNT.

On the western face, Division 308's Regiment 88 was tasked with capturing Huguette 5, and Regiment 36 with Lili 3 – the ex-Huguette 4. Taking these objectives would put the People's Army within 500yds of the French artillery lines. Finally, down at Isabelle, Regiment 57 would make yet another attempt to eject the defenders from the evil swamp of 'Strongpoint Wieme'.

In each case the Viet Minh assault infantry would enjoy a superiority of anything between five and eight to one. Since the French companies had been worn away to about 80 men each, the strongpoints were held by no more than double companies. If the Viet Minh regiments each committed two battalions to the assault (as was normal), then fewer than 200 defenders would face at least 1,000 attackers, with another 500 or more in reserve.[10] The outcome would turn, as so often before, on the question of whether this disadvantage could be balanced by 'Zulu Kilo'. Colonel Vaillant still had 19 howitzers and 15 heavy mortars in action, though their crews had suffered heavily from the direct fire of the RCLs on the Dominiques, and the mortars were short of ammunition. A number of Captain Hervouët's tanks were still serviceable enough to provide fire support, but reportedly only one in the main camp was still in condition to fight on the move.[11]

ELIANE 1 – LOST BY THE Moroccans to Regiment 174 on 30/31 March, recaptured but abandoned by paratroopers the next day, and retaken by 6th Colonial on 10 April – had been under relentless fire for the three weeks since. Its trenches were vaguely traceable ditches among the overlapping shell craters, its summit a muddy desolation strewn with debris and ghastly human remains – sometimes buried, exhumed, dismembered and scattered by repeated shelling. The enemy were dug in only 10yds from the now purely theoretical perimeter wire, and the least movement drew fire. It had been impossible to rebuild the defences under such close observation, and any attempt to 'aerate' the front line had led to vicious hand-to-hand fighting. Major Bréchignac's II/1 RCP – reduced to three miniature companies, which rotated on and off the hill every 48 hours – were worn down by losses and exhaustion, and some of the odds and ends filling the gaps in the ranks did not know the men they fought beside. On the night before 1 May an attempt had been made to strengthen the parapets with sandbags – actually, local sacks made from *cai phen*, coarsely woven reeds; but these were slippery in the rain and refused to pack together properly, and during the day 57mm RCLs and mortars had smashed the parapets once more.[12]

On the evening of 1 May the summit was held by Lieutenant Leguère's 80-strong 3rd Company, II/1 RCP. Just behind them on Eliane 4 were Lieutenant Pham Van Phu's 2nd Company, 5 BPVN, and the command post for the High Elianes shared by Bréchignac and Major Botella, who acted as his second-in-command for this sector. From the forward trenches of Eliane 1 the paras could see an orderly series of small marker flags which Regiment 174 had planted to mark battalion assault lanes. It will be recalled that this regiment's commander had been dismissed and disgraced after they lost the hill on 10 April and failed to recapture it by four separate counter-attacks against II/1 RCP the next day; tonight the Tho soldiers from the hills around Lang Son had a score to settle with the Chasseurs Parachutistes.

When the long bombardment lifted and the first assault companies of two battalions rose from their trenches at about 8.20pm, the defenders saw hundreds of dark shapes with eerie pale muzzles under the rims of their flat helmets – each man was wearing a gauze mask over his nose and mouth.[13] Regiment 174 hurled themselves forward at the thinly held French trenches, firing and shouting their war-cries, and after about a quarter of an hour 3rd Company were already being forced back from the summit. Colonel Vaillant's 105s gave some fire support, but the shellbursts were too few and too dispersed to make a real difference. Lieutenant Leguère took a head wound that exposed his brain; for a while about 50 of his men clung on to the reverse slope around the sheltered trench that led back to

Eliane 4, but by 9pm these had been reduced to a weak section under Sergeant Chief Lair. Major Bréchignac sent Lieutenant Périou's 1st Company across, but mortar fire from the north raked the slopes; Périou was soon killed and his company were ground away. By about 1am Regiment 174 were simply mopping up; the survivors were closely pursued and showered with grenades as they tried to fall back, and Bréchignac managed to recover fewer than 20 of his 180 men, all wounded. He called down artillery on Eliane 1, which was officially reported lost at 2.07am on 2 May (*see Map 20*).

At about 2.30am Regiment 174 surged forward again over the 150yd saddle which now separated them from Eliane 4. By the intermittent light of flares and the flashes of explosions, confused and savage fighting – sometimes at hand-to-hand range – lasted for about an hour and a half, while artillery of both sides continued to shell the High Elianes. Under the eyes of their CO, André Botella's *bawouans* held their ground, and at about 4am the assault slackened. By dawn two hours later Pham Van Phu and his paratroopers had pushed Regiment 174 right back off Eliane 4.

Despite Eliane 2's secondary role that night, the légionnaires of I/13 DBLE were not left in peace to provide supporting fire for the paratroopers to their north. An attack towards the southern blockhouse was repulsed at about 3am; and there was an attempt by a 'death volunteer', loaded with explosives but rather bizarrely shrouded with pale parachute nylon, to infiltrate and blow up the central bunker. (He was not the first; the Legion snipers had dropped several others in no-man's-land, and légionnaires would crawl out to recover their explosive charges.)[14]

WHILE REGIMENT 174 WERE storming Eliane 1, on the flats to the north-west Regiment 141 smashed into Dominique 3. Since their losses during the capture of Béatrice on the first night of the battle, the 'Hong Gai' Regiment had had a fairly easy victory over the Algerians of III/3 RTA on Dominique 1 two weeks later; there were probably a good number of veterans still in the ranks that night who remembered Na San in December 1952. There, men of this regiment had driven the 2nd Thai Battalion off their strongpoint in 20 minutes; tonight they would meet once again. With its back to the 'dead arm' of the river, Dominique 3 was now defended by a ragged little garrison mostly from Major Chenel's BT 2: French NCOs and a few score Thai stalwarts, together with Captain Filaudeau's Algerians of 12/III/3 RTA – the same company who had fought here beside Paul Brunbrouck's gunners on the night of 30/31 March.

Since nobody had much faith in these soldiers, shortly after the Viet Minh attack on them opened at about 7.30pm Major Thomas of 6 BPC sent Lieutenant Perret's 3rd Company north from Eliane 10 to stiffen them. In fact, the Thais and Algerians fought as they had never done before, and repulsed the first attacks with heavy loss. The People's Army responded with a renewed artillery and mortar bombardment from about 8.30pm, followed by a second wave of assaults. The position was captured yard by yard over the next six hours; Dominique 3 received no artillery support, and by midnight the western part had been overrun. Some time in the early hours Lieutenant Perret radioed his CO with a calm situation report: he told Thomas that the blockhouse had been knocked out with Chinese grenades, that there was fighting in the transverse trench leading to the command post, and that he was about to lead a counter-attack. Overhearing the signal, Lieutenant Hervé Trapp of 2nd Company, 6 BPC sent him Sergeant Chief Flamen with another small platoon – 16 of his 57 men – but this was no more than a gesture of comradeship. The defenders of Dominique 3 fought until their ammunition ran out; the end came some time well before dawn.[15]

After taking BT 2's position at Na San under the full moon of December 1952, Regiment 141 had been hammered mercilessly by Colonel Gilles' artillery, and then driven off by a whole battalion of counter-attacking Legion paratroopers. History did not repeat itself under the new moon of May 1954, when the 'green berets' had other preoccupations.

WHILE THESE ACTIONS RAGED on the east bank, the western face of the camp was under attack by Division 308 (*see Map 18*). Here the strongpoints were shelled by 105mm howitzers installed on the old Anne-Maries, and the mortaring that night also left no doubt that General Giap had solved his 120mm ammunition shortage.

In the middle of the evening an infantry attack struck Lili 2 and 1, but by about midnight the two Moroccan companies of I/4 RTM had driven the enemy back from their wire. Lili 3 was held by a company of the Foreign Parachute Marching Battalion led by Lieutenant Lucciani, the hero of the 'Fifth Hill' – now wounded for a third time, and with an empty eye socket heavily bandaged. His Legion paras stood off two separate waves of attack by Regiment 36 at 8.30pm and 1.50am. There was confused hand-to-hand fighting on the position at around 2.30am, but by daybreak the enemy had been driven out, with the aid of supporting fire from one of the tanks, légionnaires from Huguette 3, and Moroccans from Lili 2.

On this front, however, the night's major attack fell upon Huguette 5, sticking out like a thumb at the north-west corner of the French perimeter. Tightly surrounded by approach trenches, this position was occupied only by two 'platoons' of Lieutenant Alain de Stabenrath's BMEP company. These veterans of the old 1 BEP comprised Sub-lieutenant Boisbouvier, Sergeant Chief Novak, Sergeant Zurell, and exactly 26 corporals and privates; Stabenrath had already been wounded on 17 April, and Boisbouvier three times in the past 15 days. This position too was pounded by guns on the Anne-Maries, and at perhaps 2am infantry attacks were launched by Regiment 88 'Tam Dao' – the mauled victors at Gabrielle on 15 March, who had gone on to garrotte Huguette 6 with their 'runway trenches' a month later. At about 3.30am Novak radioed that he was virtually alone; the 'Tam Dao' Regiment had taken an hour and a half to overrun 30 men. At some point 50 légionnaires of I/2 REI from Huguette 2 tried to counter-attack, but they were caught in the wire by enemy artillery and driven back.

At dawn on the 2nd they were astonished to see Zurell and two other mud-caked survivors crawling up to their perimeter, dragging the helpless Lieutenant de Stabenrath: Corporal Granta had snaked across the position while it was actually being consolidated by the victorious Viet Minh, found his officer badly wounded in a shellhole, and had got him clear without being spotted.

Shortly before midnight General de Castries' situation report to FTNV stressed the lack of reserves, the terrible fatigue of all his units, and his absolute need for a complete and solid battalion to be parachuted on the following night if GONO was to survive. By dawn the night would have cost him 331 men killed and missing and 168 wounded – the equivalent of a battalion.

It was on 2 May that FTNV received confirmation that USAF Globemasters of the 62nd Troop Carrier Wing were beginning to airlift 450 more paratroop replacements from France. They were expected to arrive in Saigon only on 7 May; and most of them were coming directly from their qualification at the Pau and Vannes parachute schools.[16]

DURING THE NIGHT OF 1/2 MAY the Viet Minh bombardment of Isabelle lasted for about 3½ hours. The légionnaires tried to unbalance the coming infantry attack by making a sortie against trenches 200yds north-west of the perimeter. However, at around midnight Regiment 57 launched their own assault on the north-east corner of Isabelle 5 – still called 'Strongpoint Wieme', although now held by a mixture of Algerians, 11th Company of III/3 REI and two of Lieutenant Préaud's Chaffees (*see Map 19*). By 2am there were Viet Minh inside the position, and the tanks led a counter-attack. Some of the lost ground was retaken by around 8.20am, when 100 enemy dead were counted in the wire.

By noon on 2 May only six of Isabelle's 11 howitzers were serviceable. Further counter-attacks were sent forward on the east bank during the day; one in the early afternoon failed to make much ground, but at about 4.10pm another push finally recaptured the enemy's night-time gains. However, the cumulative effect of flooding and bombardment had reduced Isabelle 5 to a chaotic swamp full of trash and corpses; it was indefensible, and Colonel Lalande decided to pull west of the Nam Youm everybody except listening posts and an 'alert' patrol. Even they would be evacuated under heavy shelling during the night of 2/3 May.[17]

THE RAIN RETURNED ON 2 MAY, and cumulo-nimbus storm clouds over the High Region forced pilots to fly at 17,000ft; one source states that the Navy Corsairs, at least, were not provided with oxygen equipment, so this caused difficulties. Despite the rain-clouds GATAC/Nord managed to get 41 sorties to Dien Bien Phu: 13 bombers and six fighters flew support missions, four of each hunted for the enemy artillery, while ten fighters, four B-26s, and two Privateers provided flak suppression.[18]

In Hanoi, the relationship between Generals Navarre and Cogny sank to a new low on 2 May, when the C-in-C threatened his subordinate with an investigation by the military security branch into his alleged defeatist press leaks.[19] Nevertheless, Navarre decided that Castries and Langlais should have their new battalion. Of the three possible units this was the strongest and best – 1st Colonial, who had fought at Dien Bien Phu in November and December. Colonel Langlais had rejected the alternatives, 1 and 3 BPVN; it was planned to hold at least one in reserve until the arrival in Tonkin of 7th Colonial and 3rd Foreign allowed the formation of a complete new brigade.

Now commanded by Captain Guy de Bazin de Bezon, 1 BPC had had little rest since being pulled out of the valley a couple of days before Christmas. On 26 December they had been flown to Seno, and had carried out operations in central Laos for the following six weeks. In mid February they had jumped at Muong Sai to bolster that remote post during Division 308's threatening march south, returning two weeks later to take over airfield guard duties at Gia Lam and Cat Bi and local security operations. The 1st Colonial were alerted at their barracks at Gia Lam at 9am on 2 May, but they could not be flown to the valley in a single lift. GONO was simultaneously desperate for ammunition and other supplies, and it would in fact take the limited number of transport crews three separate missions to get about two-thirds of the battalion to Dien Bien Phu.

In the valley, hope lifted when the night of 2/3 May brought no major activity by the People's Army. Heavy rain hampered the air-drops, however; among 122 parachutists only the first 107 men of Lieutenant Marcel Edme's 2nd Company, 1 BPC managed to drop that night. Eight C-119s aborted their missions; only 53 tons of cargo were dropped, of which perhaps 45 tons were recovered. The perimeter units sent out aggressive fighting patrols, and men from I/13 DBLE blew up an enemy bunker on Eliane 2. That night they could no longer hear digging from the mine shaft, which was worrying – were the miners ready to fill it with explosive?[20]

MONDAY 3 MAY, A DAY OF overcast skies and intermittent rain, brought the same pattern of activity: irregular bouts of enemy shelling, punctuated by small-scale skirmishes around the perimeter. Colonel Vaillant's howitzers carried out a parsimonious shoot against Eliane 1; General Giap's worked over the Claudines with a more generous hand, adding to the misery of men digging in mud and water up to their waists at Claudines 4 and 5. All over the camp the patient, skilful engineers of 31 BG repeatedly exposed themselves to fire as they rebuilt, repaired, patched, improvised; they had set such a standard that they were taken for granted, but it was a miracle that they kept electric power and clean water flowing. At Isabelle, Colonel Lalande's légionnaires pushed out strong patrols to both west and east. The first cleared enemy trenches in hand-to-hand fighting and brought in about 20 weapons; the second topped this, returning in triumph dragging a 75mm RCL.[21]

This was reportedly the day when an appeal was shouted through Dr Grauwin's hospital that any of the wounded who were fit enough should return to the front lines.[22] Many responded, choosing to face whatever was coming beside their mates in the trenches rather than helplessly, among strangers, in this stinking labyrinth. Scores of soldiers hobbled off through the yellow mud with helmets clapped over bandaged skulls, plastered or splinted limbs jerking awkwardly, and empty sleeves flapping. Grauwin tried to dissuade many of them; they thanked him – he was their saviour – but they kept going, fading away into the veil of rain.

In the Hanoi Citadel that day, FTNV staff officers were obeying General Navarre's orders to work on a plan in which such soldiers as these could play only one part: the role for which Sergeant Horst Ganzer had volunteered at Huguette 6 two weeks previously.

A CONTINGENCY PLAN FOR Operation 'Albatros' – a break-out attempt by at least the strongest part of the garrison, when it seemed unavoidable – had been under consideration for some days. General de Castries had been kept informed of the developments surrounding Operations 'Vautour' and 'Condor', and when the latter lost its airborne component and stalled north of Muong Khoua on 30 April the C-in-C had confirmed to Paris that 'Albatros' now had to be taken seriously. For obvious reasons of morale and discipline General de Castries kept secret his discussions on this subject with Hanoi; it seems unclear exactly when he took his senior officers into his confidence, but it cannot have been later than 5 May. General Navarre received authorization from General Ely on 2 May, and General Cogny's staff began planning at once; but several senior figures were deeply opposed, including Cogny himself.

In broad outline, 'Albatros' foresaw a break-out by perhaps 2,000 to 3,000 of the fittest surviving men in three groups: the paratroopers led by Colonel Langlais, the légionnaires from the main camp by Lieutenant Colonel Lemeunier, and the garrison of Isabelle by Colonel Lalande. Their departure would be covered by the Air Force, the artillery, and a sacrificial rearguard – a few men from each company, the Thais and North Africans, and all the lightly wounded – under the command of General de Castries. All the wounded would naturally have to be left behind, in the care of the medical staff; and once the break-out force was clear, the rearguard would destroy all equipment and munitions.

The attempt would commence late in the day to allow the columns, carrying only small arms and four days' rations, to reach the cover of the forest by nightfall. The original plan seems to have envisaged the three groups following different routes but all basically south-eastwards, to link up with the partisan elements of Lieutenant Colonel Godard's force – 'Pamplemousse', 'Banana' and Group Mollat – in the area of Muong Nha. These scouting groups would start north only at the last possible moment so as not to alert the Viet Minh in northern Laos; after the rendezvous they would guide and screen the break-out forces south to the Nam Ou valley, along routes previously planted with caches of rations, medical supplies and radio batteries. It was hoped that the People's Army units in the south of the valley would be unable to mount a rapid pursuit in strength because of the need to prepare their own logistics (though this would still leave many Viet Minh in the refugees' path, and they would have to make a wide eastwards hook to Muong Nha – *see Map 8*). At first Colonel de Crèvecoeur believed that the partisans could reach the rendezvous area by 15 May, but he quickly revised this to 20 May.[23]

On 3 May, with General Giap's third offensive only 48 hours old, it seemed extremely doubtful that the camp could hold out long enough for that to be a realistic date; and anyway, there were strong objections in Hanoi to the principle of 'Albatros'. GONO had held out heroically for more than six weeks, earning admiration throughout the Free World, and a failed attempt to escape by only part of the garrison would 'tarnish their glory'. This was not pretension: one must make allowance for Gallic phrase-making, which cannot function without the sound of trumpets. The nightmare shared by General Cogny and his chief-of-staff Colonel Bastiani was a repetition of the ugliest aspects of 'the disaster of RC4' in 1950 and of the much more recent retreat from Lai Chau. They anticipated with real horror the spectacle of exhausted men – these particular men, who had endured so much already – left wandering in the jungle lost, starving and sick, only to be hunted down in handfuls and killed or caged like rats. Not all would disappear, of course; but Lieutenant Colonel Levain, chief of General Cogny's Second Bureau, shrank at the prospect of what Viet Minh propaganda and the left-wing press would make of the pitiable state of the survivors – and of captured paratroop and Legion officers who would be said to have 'abandoned their helpless wounded'.

Cogny believed that resistance until the very end of the garrison's resources would be preferable, although Castries should give individual unit commanders the freedom to try to break free at the end if they thought their men were up to it. One is prompted to wonder whether this kind of *sauve qui peut* would have presented any less demoralizing a spectacle. In the event, it was Colonel de Crèvecoeur's timetable and the consequent impossibility of launching 'Albatros' before about 15 May that convinced General Navarre to order – on 4 May – that preparations for it should continue, but that in the meanwhile FTNV should play for time by continuing to drop reinforcements into the valley.[24]

ON THE NIGHT OF 3/4 MAY only seven C-119s and sixteen Dakotas completed their resupply missions, dropping just 57 tons of which about 40 per cent was reckoned to have gone astray. (Between 1 and 7 May as a whole it is believed that 800 tons were dropped, of which a majority either fell directly into the hands of the People's Army or was not recoverable from no-man's-land.) Pilots reported that the enemy had now installed searchlights – certainly one on Anne-Marie, which dazzled them as they made the usual south-to-north dropping run, and apparently two more near the main camp and Isabelle.[25]

Colonel Langlais received his next small increment of 1 BPC: part of Captain Francois Penduff's HQ Company, and the whole 125-man 3rd Company led by Captain Jean Pouget. This cavalry officer and ex-*maquisard* in the Savoy hills had volunteered for the paratroopers and Indochina. He had later served for several months as General Navarre's aide-de-camp; but in January 1954 he had requested a transfer to a combat unit, and had taken part in 1 BPC's jump over Muong Sai on 13 February. Pouget's exalted former appointment and his choice to resign from it naturally attracted some comment among his colleagues. He later published a vivid description of his jump that night:

The plane turned very high above the 'toilet bowl'. All lights were extinguished except for the greenish glow of the instrument panel... A flaming T at the bottom of a dark shaft marked the limit of the DZ and the angle of approach. Six men could jump at a time so long as there was no hesitation. I knew that the crossbar of the T was in the perimeter wire... The aircraft dived steeply to the jump altitude of about 900ft, aligned on the axis of the T. The despatcher gripped my shoulder: 'Get ready to jump – steer only for the long stroke of the T. Pay no attention to the green light – the pilots are incapable of judging the right moment...'

At the same instant, from all around the edges of the 'toilet bowl' the flak opened up, firing at the sound only, on the preregistered and unavoidable line of flight... The tracers rose towards us like wobbling strings of pearls... On the invisible ground below me, shells were bursting in big, ephemeral corollas of fawn-coloured light...[26]

After landing Captain Pouget found his way to Colonel Langlais' command post, where Lieutenant Colonel Bigeard told him to wait until the morning light allowed him to assemble his company; he should then take them to Eliane 3, in reserve for Eliane 2. Pouget went next to the main GONO command bunker, where he found the floor so deep in mud that Lieutenant Colonel de Seguin-Pazzis was walking around in bare feet, and General de Castries had to lean on his shooting stick and pull his feet out at every step. While they were talking – inevitably, they asked him questions he could not answer about the latest news from Geneva – a radio call came in from Lili 3, held by Captain Lucciani's Legion para company reinforced by some Moroccans.

At about 2.30am on 4 May, hard on the heels of a bombardment which also blanketed the supporting batteries in Isabelle, a major infantry assault fell upon Lili 3 (see Map 20). Pierre Rocolle believes that the attackers were Regiment 36 probably supported by a battalion from Regiment 88, so the infantry columns could have totalled either three or four full battalions against one weak company. Regiment 36 were the unit bloodied by Bigeard's famous sortie against the western flak batteries on 28 March; one of its battalions had been tricked by Captain Bizard of 5 BPVN into an artillery barrage inside Huguette 7 in the early hours of 1 April, but had finally taken it the next night; and it was probably this regiment that had overrun Captain Chevalier's Huguette 1 on 22/23 April, and held it against the 2 BEP counter-attack on the 23rd.

They had been occupying flooded trenches on the valley floor ever since the monsoon began; now they emerged from them, making fast progress despite the boggy ground, and the lead companies were soon grenading and raking Captain Lucciani's perimeter positions. Because the paras of 1 BPC were dropping over the central camp the Luciole flares had to be stopped, and in the darkness the enemy overran the northern part of Lili 3. During an immediate counter-attack to retake it Lucciani was wounded in the head yet again; but People's Army radio traffic intercepted at about 3am betrayed heavy casualties, confusion, and the replacement of more than one unit commander in the thick of the fighting. The message that Captain Pouget overheard in GONO headquarters about half an hour later was from a lieutenant commanding a platoon of I/4 RTM. He appealed for reinforcement, saying that only about ten men were still holding out around the CP; then the transmission broke off with what seemed to be the young officer's death-cry, and Lili 3 fell at about 3.45am.[27]

Major Guiraud's other companies of the BMEP could not mount an immediate counter-attack, since the last sticks of 3rd Company, 1 BPC were still dropping. At about 6am on 4 May he scraped together perhaps a hundred Legion paratroopers and Moroccans with one tank in support. Remarkably, they got from Huguette 3 to the very edge of Lili 3, but on this flat expanse of mud a heavy enemy crossfire supported by artillery and mortars prevented their getting into the strongpoint. The attempt was abandoned at 9am, and Lili 3 was shelled by the French artillery. The night had cost General de Castries another 164 dead and missing and 58 wounded from among his best remaining infantry; and the enemy now had men digging in 750yds from his headquarters bunker. Captain Le Damany reported 1,260 wounded in his hospitals.[28]

DURING DAYLIGHT ON 4 MAY the pattern of harassing shellfire, small-scale infantry clashes, and French artillery shoots on enemy concentrations was repeated. Through continual heavy rain and sporadic shelling, Captain Pouget led his newly arrived company of 1 BPC from

Epervier to Eliane 3; it took six hours for them to cover approximately half a mile. When they arrived they tried to organize themselves fighting positions amid what Lieutenant Bergot described as a *'cour de miracles'*, a sort of Bedlam Fair occupied by a crowd of mud-plastered gypsies, many of them swathed in filthy bandages. A large part of the position was taken up by the flooding burrows of Dr Vidal's 6 ACP, crammed with about 300 wounded. Many more lightly injured or convalescent men were outside in the rain-lashed trenches; Bergot describes one-legged soldiers manning machine guns in the blockhouses, being fed ammunition by their one-armed and one-eyed comrades. Soldiers of all units, ranks and races – paratroopers, légionnaires of 13 DBLE, Thais, Algerians – spontaneously formed themselves into combat squads, which sometimes included armed PIMs who had presented themselves as volunteers for the Legion.[29]

At 9am on the 4th, General de Castries sent a signal to FTNV that reflected his frustration. All witnesses agree that – after he recovered from the shocks of 13–15 March – the commander had always been master of himself: reasonable, calm and courteous, he had brokered co-operation between subordinates of very different characters, and maintained excellent relationships with rougher diamonds such as Langlais and Bigeard. During this late stage of the battle several instances suggest that he had found a new wellspring of firm leadership, but his urbane manners were proving unequal to the strain of Hanoi's evasions and irrelevancies:

Our provisions of all kinds are at their lowest; for 15 days they have been reduced little by little. We don't have enough ammunition to stop enemy attacks or for the harassing fire that must continue without pause; it appears that no effort is being made to remedy this situation. I am told of the risks to the aircrews, but every man here runs infinitely greater risks – there cannot be a double standard. Night supply drops must begin at 8pm instead of 11pm. The morning hours are lost because of the fog, and due to the planning of night drops with long intervals between aircraft the results are ridiculous. I have absolute need of provisions in massive quantities.

The very small size of the centre of resistance, and the fact that the elements holding the perimeter cannot leave their shelters without coming under fire from snipers and recoilless guns, means that more and more of the cases dropped are no longer retrievable. The lack of vehicles and porters obliges me to employ exhausted units for recovery tasks; the result is detestable – it also causes casualties. I cannot count on recovering even half of what is dropped, although the quantities sent to me represent only a very small proportion of what I have requested. This situation cannot go on.

I insist once again on having the broad authority in the matter of [medal] citations that I have requested. I have nothing to sustain the morale of my men, who are being asked for superhuman efforts; I no longer dare to go to see them with empty hands.[30]

The camp commander's inability to decorate men with any symbol more powerful than a slip of paper noting their recommendation was painfully evident that day, when he and Colonel Langlais spent many hours visiting the main hospital. This now presented a scene worthy of Goya: men lay crowded together so that their limbs overlapped, in dim caverns ankle-deep in mud and haunted by bold jungle rats. The air was heavy with the stink of putrefaction; there were many gangrene cases, and the constant shelling made it dangerous to take amputated limbs and buckets of debrided flesh above ground for disposal in lime pits. Castries spoke to every single one of the many hundreds of wounded, and a further signal to FTNV that night showed how deeply he was moved by their wretched conditions.[31]

Artillery expenditure over this 24 hours was 2,600 of the precious 105mm shells, 40 rounds by the sole remaining 155mm, and 1,180 mortar bombs by the Legion's 120mm crews. The rain kept the fighter-bombers on the ground in the Delta. That afternoon General Cogny sent Castries a long signal with the details of the plan worked out by FTNV for the 'Albatros' break-out. A last personal message was received: Captain Desiré of BT 2, lying wounded in the aid post at Isabelle, was informed that his wife had given birth to a healthy baby girl – they had already decided to name her after his original strongpoint, Anne-Marie. During the day Desiré was joined in the hospital by the Reverend Tissot, who had baptized his new rank of honorary légionnaire with shell fragment wounds. Outside the bunker in the monsoon downpour, a strong sortie to the west by men of III/3 REI ran into a waiting ambush; they fell back into Isabelle at nightfall after taking 32 casualties, including two officers.[32]

It rained throughout the night of 4/5 May; only about 40 tons of resupply was recovered, and at about 2.40am five Dakotas managed to drop just 73 more men of 1st Colonial, from Captain Tréhiou's 4th and the HQ Company. One of them was the CO; Captain de Bazin's frank complaint on his arrival at the command post that he could not understand why they had been dropped into this toilet, since his tired men could do nothing to save the camp, triggered an equally frank outburst from Colonel Langlais. According to Bigeard's memoir, Langlais told Bazin to keep his opinions to himself – he was there simply to fight and if necessary die alongside them. The new men were assigned to join Captain Clédic of II/1 RCP on the High Elianes, but Captain de Bazin had his thigh smashed by a shellburst almost immediately, and Captain Pouget of 3rd Company took over as acting CO of 1st Colonial.[33]

That night a handful of soldiers from a I/4 RTM platoon sharing Claudine 5 with Captain Schmitz's company of I/2 REI deserted and gave themselves up to the enemy. They cut a lane in the perimeter wire in order to do so; and the People's Army troops opposite the strongpoint at once opened a sustained fire on this gap. Trying to close it cost Sergeant Chief Kosanovic plus seven other légionnaires killed and Sergeant Lunquik and 12 others wounded, and despite these heavy casualties the wire stayed unrepaired. Furious légionnaires disarmed the rest of the Moroccans and kicked them out to go and join the 'rats of the Nam Youm'. The incident thus cost Claudine 5 two platoons: at Dien Bien Phu in the first week of May, a scale of loss that could have disastrous consequences for any strongpoint.[34]

DURING 5 MAY, A DAY OF VIOLENT rainstorms, the available men of 1 BPC redeployed on to the High Elianes – the freshest men in the garrison were an obvious choice for its most vital bastions. Part of HQ Company and Captain Tréhiou's 4th went up to Eliane 4, while Captain Pouget took 2nd and 3rd Companies to Eliane 2. Pouget's paratroopers replaced the few score remaining légionnaires of Major Coutant's I/13 DBLE; 3rd Company took over the summit and Lieutenant Edme's 2nd the defences on the lower southern and eastern slopes. The Great War appearance of the position came as a shock to 1 BPC: they found trenches and blockhouses ruined, the roofs, parapets and firing loopholes patched with anything to hand – bits of field bunks, old lockers, ammo boxes and canteens, even the barrels of smashed weapons – anything that could be filled with earth and might slow a bullet. The departing légionnaires told them about the enemy mining, and Sergeant Chief Chabrier of 2nd Company was relieved when he heard the digging start up under his feet that morning: the tunnel was obviously not yet ready for the filling of its charge chamber. Chabrier would recall that during the day Sergeant Clinel took a patrol to try to blow up the mine's entrance, but they were caught in the open and wiped out.[35]

On 5 May hopeful rumours spread through the camp that Lieutenant Colonel Godard's 'rescue column' from Laos had reached Sop Nao, only 30 miles to the south-west; the immediate spark seems to have been a report broadcast by Radio Hirondelle. It was referred to as the 'Crèvecoeur column' – Colonel de Crèvecoeur's long service in Indochina, dating back to before VJ-Day, had made him something of a legend – and hints of its progress had been current for several days; with extraordinary disregard for security, *Le Monde* had published reports of Operation 'Condor' as early as 24 April. The rumour was cruelly unfounded. Some of Godard's partisans were indeed in the forest south of the Massif des Calcaires; but after the C-in-C's signal on 30 April about the cancellation of the airborne phase had left Godard dangling, Crèvecoeur had ordered his regular units to fall back and dig in on the north bank of the Nam Ou bend. This was done over the next three days, and continuing partisan activity in the forest to the north was simply intended to screen this withdrawal against pursuit. 'Condor' itself was now history; in an attempt to deceive Viet Minh radio monitors Godard's mission was now rechristened Operation 'Ariège'.

General de Castries and his senior officers knew this perfectly well on 5 May, but they could not risk breaking their men's morale by crushing the rumour. Indeed, the spirit of the best troops remained so determined that some staff officers, resigned to the inevitable, were worried that units still full of fight would refuse to accept any ceasefire order, and would battle on until they got themselves massacred. Among the junior ranks there was a widely expressed belief that the war itself hung on Dien Bien Phu, and that 'they' simply could not allow it to be lost by leaving GONO to its fate.[36]

On or by 5 May the senior officers who had roles to play in 'Albatros' were informed of the plan, although bad radio reception that day kept Colonel Lalande at Isabelle short of details of the overall picture. Preparations were made for the issue of maps and survival rations to the break-out force. At 4.15pm a message from General de Castries to General Cogny insisted that the number of men involved and the cramped tracks to the south dictated that the three groups would have to sortie in different directions in order to move fast and divide the Viet Minh reaction; GONO would take the final decisions, and for security reasons would not be informing Hanoi. Remarkably, the fact that the rendezvous force could not be at Muong Nha for another two weeks does not seem to have been regarded as decisive. Castries requested final authority to launch 'Albatros' when he felt the time was right, and at 9pm he received that permission from General Cogny, whose message finished with the words: 'Needless to underline inestimable value from all perspectives offered by the prolonged resistance on the spot which now remains your glorious mission. Very cordially, Cogny.' To the very end, Cogny's frank priority was tying down as many enemy troops as possible, for as long as possible, as far as possible from his Delta.[37]

In strongpoint Junon, Sergeant Paygnard, an NCO with Captain Duluat's White Thai auxiliary companies, finally succeeded in persuading their wives to leave the camp for their own safety. They drifted out that night, unmolested by the Viet Minh.[38]

ON 5 MAY LITTLE RESUPPLY reached the camp; the C-119s did appear, but only over Isabelle. During the past week 'Zulu Kilo's' ammunition dumps had been emptying inexorably. The difficulties of finding and recovering the ammunition boxes, and of bringing them in through the mud and sometimes deep water in the trenches, had further exhausted men who were already moving like zombies, and these trips under fire cost the lives of PIMs and Frenchmen alike. But the gunners still delivered what support they could to the infantry, who expressed their gratitude for its accuracy if not for its volume.[39]

On that day the French artillery still had 18 serviceable 105mm howitzers each with several hundred rounds of ammunition; the one remaining 155mm and the 15 heavy mortars had very little left. The survival of such a significant number of French guns until 48 hours before the final collapse may seem extraordinary, but it was an inescapable consequence of the limitations of the Viet Minh artillery deployment, as already discussed. In theory General Giap had had the means to achieve a complete artillery dominance, but he rarely chose to attempt this between 15 March and 6 May. Artillery-versus-artillery fighting was a complete novelty to him, and his deployment of this precious but unfamiliar asset in hillside caves had been wholly defensive. People's Army mortar and recoilless gun units had advanced with the infantry front lines, but there had been very little movement of field guns. A few had taken up better positions to dominate the airstrip after the fall of Béatrice and Gabrielle, and later some had been deployed to Anne-Marie, but the great majority had remained in their casemates. Guns reported further south are unidentified (*see Map 10*), and seem more likely to have been the relatively more portable 75mm pack howitzers than 105s.

Despite the enemy's relative failure to concentrate his counter-battery fire, however, the 'billhooks' slashing across their gunpits had still taken a dreadful harvest of the French artillerymen whenever they left their shelters to save beleaguered companies of paras and légionnaires. By the end of the battle the 155mm battery had suffered 60 per cent casualties, and II/4 RAC, 41 per cent, while the Legion 120mm mortar companies had lost more than 50 per cent of their personnel.[40]

EARLY ON THE NIGHT OF 5/6 May a heavy bombardment ploughed up Eliane 2; Captain Pouget's paratroopers tensed for an infantry assault that never came, and when the shelling finally ceased they could hear the renewed sounds of digging from the mine tunnel. A half-hearted enemy probe at Eliane 3 was repelled by paras of 6 BPC; more serious attacks on the Huguettes were fought off by the Legion paras, who cleared out enemy penetrations successfully in two counter-attacks.[41]

From about 4am on the 6th the 'Banjos' began dropping more men of 1 BPC. Between 90 and 100 paras of 4th and HQ Companies jumped; but heavy flak slowed the drop, and at first light around 5.20am the mission was curtailed. Those 90-odd troopers of 1st Colonial were the last men to jump into Dien Bien Phu, and Captain Faussurier's 1st Company were carried back to Hanoi. The battalion had got a total of 383 men into the 'toilet bowl', including 155 Vietnamese soldiers. The rump which remained in the Delta were now the only uncommitted French parachute unit in Tonkin.[42]

THE MORNING OF THURSDAY 6 May broke dry, and after the fog dispersed a warm sun shone from a clear blue sky. As the day progressed GATAC/Nord laid on a maximum effort to support the cargo drops, keeping the flak crews preoccupied by repeated dives on their positions. At last the arrival of an experienced bomber commander, Lieutenant Colonel Dussol, resulted in massed use of the B-26s: 47 sorties, supported by four by Privateers, 16 by Helldiver dive-bombers, 18 Corsair sorties, and 26 by the Bearcats.[43] Colonel Nicot's 25 C-119s and 29 Dakotas managed to drop a handsome 196 tons; but since many of the packages fell in full sight of the enemy infantry, GONO would have to await the cover of darkness before trying to recover them.[44]

Despite the relatively light flak, it was on the 6th that the American C-119 crews suffered their worst loss. The CAT pilots had volunteered to fly a low-altitude ammunition drop over Isabelle; one of them, Art Wilson, took a 37mm hit in his left tail boom, lost elevator control, but completed his run and nursed his Packet safely back to Cat Bi. Next into the circuit was James B. McGovern, a pilot with a particularly colourful past flying for the Chinese Nationalists. This huge, bearded man – nicknamed 'Earthquake McGoon' after a character in the popular American comic strip *Li'l Abner* – was flying his 45th mission over Dien Bien Phu that day, with Wallace Buford in the co-pilot's seat and two French crewmen behind them. He had just turned in for his drop run when his C-119 was hit in the port engine; he immediately feathered it, but then a second shell struck the tail. McGovern could not control the aircraft, so he restarted the feathered engine for the sake of the little extra power it could still give, and the C-119 wavered off to the south-east, yawing badly.

His colleague Steve Kusak followed 'Earthquake', and they managed to reach Muong Het about 75 miles away before it became clear that McGovern and Buford could no longer keep the Packet in the air. Reportedly, McGovern was reluctant to bale out and 'do all that walking again' – once in China he had come down far from friendly lines. Both crews searched for suitable ground for an emergency landing, but McGovern was losing altitude rapidly; he managed to lift the C-119 over a last ridge, and was flying along a narrow river valley when his port wingtip touched the slope. His last words to Kusak were, 'Looks like this is it, son.' The aircraft flipped over twice and exploded, with its full load of ammunition still aboard.[45]

ON THE 6TH THE LATEST AERIAL photos showed new trenches radiating out from Dominique 3 towards the Low Elianes, and from Baldy and Phoney towards Eliane 2. Colonel Langlais held a briefing for his 'district' commanders and those unit COs who were able to leave their positions, and tried to present the most encouraging picture he could. Bernard Fall implies that Langlais repeated the claim that Godard's force was indeed only 30 miles away. He pointed out that the day's bountiful air-drops had delivered 70 tons of infantry and 50 tons of artillery ammunition – much of the latter the desperately needed 120mm – although admittedly most of it could not be recovered until that night. He reminded them that GATAC/Nord and Colonel Nicot's transport squadrons had put more aircraft into the sky above the valley that day than most of them had ever seen before. He spoke of the imminent arrival of the remaining paras of 1st Colonial, and reminded them that at any day the Geneva Conference might produce a ceasefire.

He was still speaking when Captain Noël came in and handed Langlais a signal: the Saigon Second Bureau's radio monitors confirmed that the People's Army would mount a general assault on Dien Bien Phu that night. If they followed their invariable practice of a bombardment starting between 5pm and 6pm and lasting at least two hours, followed immediately by infantry assaults, then there would be no time for GONO to recover the parachuted shells and mortar bombs. The meeting broke up; Captain Yves Hervouët walked over to the hospital, where he asked Dr Grauwin to cut the plaster casts off his two broken arms so that he could get back into a tank turret.[46]

That afternoon Langlais and Bigeard toured the strongpoints on the east bank, sitting in the command posts and passing a brandy bottle around while they took stock (*see Map 20*). Up on Eliane 4, under fire from RCLs and heavy AA machine guns on Eliane 1, Majors Bréchignac and Botella had their tired companies from II/1 RCP and 5 BPVN and, facing south-east, Captain Penduff's HQ and Captain Tréhiou's 4th Companies of the fresher 1st Colonial. The 1 BPC's 3rd and 2nd Companies were on Eliane 2 with Captain Pouget and Lieutenant Edme.[47]

Behind them, the only barriers on the enemy's path to the river and the central camp were the weak 'strongpoints' of the Low Elianes: from north to south, Elianes 12, 10, 11 and 3, all held only by the debris of various virtually destroyed units. The most exposed was Eliane 10, behind Eliane 4 and just west of the main road, where Major Thomas had Lieutenants Le Page and Trapp with 1st and 2nd 'Companies' of his 6th Colonial. In fact these were platoons – Trapp had 32 men, of whom one-third had already been wounded. They were backed up by so many injured men from other units that Eliane 10 was nicknamed the 'strongpoint of the wounded'. The 6 BPC command post itself was manned by wounded but still capable officers and NCOs – men such as Lieutenant Le Boudec, wounded on Eliane 1 on 31 March, and Sergeant Chief Flamen of Trapp's company, who had survived the forlorn hope to Dominique 3 on the night of 1 May. Propped up beside the radios and the scrawled-on mosaics of aerial photos, they had been living on little more than black coffee, Maxiton and stubborn hope – the last partly based on the presence of Lieutenant Allaire, who now had the remaining 81mm mortars of all the parachute battalions grouped here.[48]

Lightly wounded men had also been sent to Elianes 12 and 11. With his back to the river, Major Chenel occupied these mud wallows with remnants of his BT 2 and the Algerian III/3 RTA, and the Moroccan sappers of 31st Engineer Battalion under Captain Fazentieux.[49] Level with Eliane 10 and further south, behind Eliane 2, was the *'cour de miracles'* – Eliane 3, held by Major Coutant's surviving légionnaires of I/13 DBLE, Captain Nicod's weak company of I/4 RTM brought across from Lili, plus another mixed crowd of wounded.

On the west bank, the remnants of Major Tourret's 8th Shock occupied Epervier/Dominique 4 with 5th Battery, II/4 RAC, and two quad-50s; the nearby 'nameless' position in the flooded drainage ditch was still held by Captain Bizard's little company from 5 BPVN. In Junon down to the south were Captain Duluat's two companies of White Thais (who had held up remarkably, despite the low expectations of everybody except Duluat); the small platoon of Air Force personnel under Captain Charnod; and just over 600 wounded men. (That day Major Coutant was also in Junon with survivors of I/13 DBLE, but they would soon be sent across to Eliane 3.) Junon also seems to have had two of the four quad-50 mounts once again.[50]

The west and south faces of the camp were now defended by a mixed assortment of Moroccans, Legion infantry and paratroopers. Major Guiraud's BMEP in Huguettes 2 and 3 now numbered perhaps 160 men, and Lili 1 and 2 were held by two nominal companies of Major Nicolas's I/4 RTM; in Claudine the remnant of I/2 REI were led by Major Clémencon and Captain Coldeboeuf, but some of their squads had been sent north to reinforce Nicolas' Tirailleurs.[51]

The artillery in the central camp now had very uneven stocks of ammunition: one of the howitzers of 6th Battery reported only 12 shells left. They had not had 'Pozit' airburst fuses for some days, and had to use time-delay fuses instead – drawing enemy return fire using exactly the same ordnance, thanks to the misdropped supplies. The guns themselves were battered and scarred, the shields holed, the wheels like fretwork, and the recoil cylinders patched and repatched. Major Knecht chose the 5th Battery of his battalion to be the 'stay behind' unit, delivering shoots to cover the 'Albatros' break-out. The battery commander Captain Cabannes accepted the decision calmly; in spring 1945 he had marched with the Alessandri column on its epic retreat into China.

The only commander at Dien Bien Phu whose ration strength was actually increasing was, of course, Captain Le Damany, the chief medical officer: on 6 May his hospitals reported 1,310 wounded under care.

FROM ABOUT 4PM ON 6 MAY the Viet Minh artillery brought down a constant harassing fire on the French positions to cover the assembly of their assault infantry. It seems to have been this part of the afternoon that saw the unleashing of a wholly new weapon in Heavy Division 351's armoury: the 'Stalin organs'. These six-tube banks of Chinese rocket projectors announced their presence with a monstrous screeching – first one, then others joining in to overlap in a terrifying chorus as the rockets were fired in rippling salvoes. The particularly unnerving quality of this banshee shriek can be attested by Allied veterans of World War II who faced the German *Nebelwerfer* ('Moaning Minnie' or 'Screaming Meemie') on which the later Chinese design was based. The shattering explosions that followed were louder and often more destructive than those of shells of larger calibre – the explosive made up a much greater proportion of the rocket's weight than that of a howitzer round. Normally such weapons did not have the penetration to destroy fortifications; but the melting dug-outs of Dien Bien Phu could hardly be classed as 'hard targets', and many collapsed under the rocket barrage, particularly at Claudine 5.[52]

Sources differ over which specific damage should be attributed to the rockets and which to shelling, but the barrage on the evening and night of 6 May would cause serious destruction of irreplaceable stores; part of the ammunition dump was hit, as was the medical supplies depot. Later that night Captain Le Damany signalled Hanoi: 'Situation of the wounded extremely precarious due to flooding and collapse of several dug-outs... Urgent need of all medical supplies; my stocks are destroyed.'[53]

The camp's ordeal by rocket had lasted perhaps an hour when heavy clouds closed in over the mountains once again; the first downpour of the night flooded the trenches, and their defenders shivered in the sudden chill. The rocket projectors were a relatively inaccurate area weapon, and some time between 5pm and 5.30pm the Viet Minh's conventional artillery added its more focused malevolence. The 'Stalin organs' ceased fire altogether at about 6pm – presumably because their inaccuracy made them dangerous to use when friendly troops were near by. Since the first assaults were scheduled for 7pm some movement was necessary in daylight; Regiment 98 had to reach their front-line trenches facing Eliane 2 by 5pm, and Regiment 174 moved off towards Eliane 1 at around 6pm.[54]

For the night of 6/7 May, General Giap did not significantly alter his dispositions of 1 May. Division 316 would assault the key High Elianes – Regiment 174's objective was Eliane 4, and Regiment 98 would make yet another attempt on Eliane 2. At the same time Division 312 would strike the Low Elianes guarding the two bridges across the Nam Youm: Regiment 165 would attack Eliane 10, and Regiment 141 would thrust past it to hit Eliane 12. On the western face, Division 308's Regiment 102 would attack Claudine 5; the division's other two regiments, 36 and 88, would simply maintain contact, presumably being held back for a final assault.

General Vu Hien's artillery would support these assaults in a slightly different manner than they had on 1 May, at last making real use of their dominance. A heavy concentration of 120mm and other mortars would be devoted to silencing the French howitzers at Isabelle, to prevent their interference on the approaches to the High Elianes. Other mortars – perhaps as many as 50 – were massed behind Baldy to saturate the defences of Eliane 2, coupled with the direct fire of recoilless guns installed on the hill itself.[55]

ELIANE 2 WAS THE FIRST strongpoint to be attacked that night; darkness had not yet fallen when, at about 6.45pm, a battalion of Regiment 98 clambered out of their trenches and advanced (*see Map 21*). They did not take the butcher's road up Champs-Elysées, but hooked around the southern end of the slope with the intention of capturing the western face of the hill and cutting it off from any reinforcement.[56] Naturally the artillery observers had prepared fire plans, and at first they were able to bring down a murderous barrage on the People's Army infantry; the gunners hardly needed specific orders for shoot 'Saxo 411' by now – they knew the co-ordinates by heart.[57] So heavy were enemy casualties that the two platoons of 1 BPC defending this slope, under Lieutenant Julien and Sub-lieutenant Paul, were able to hold off the enemy without real diffi-culty for several hours. The Viet Minh account speaks of a machine-gun blockhouse supported by another MG position pinning the assault companies down; their own RCLs had no success in silencing these, and their assault sappers took heavy casualties.

However, the artillery support for Eliane 2 dwindled steadily during the evening as a sustained bombardment continued to fall on the battery positions at Isabelle. By about 10pm three 105s and their crews had been knocked out by direct hits and only three howitzers were still firing, of which two more had been silenced by 11pm.[58] On the southern and south-eastern faces of the hill another battalion of Regiment 98 infiltrated forwards under cover of the supporting fire from Baldy, waiting to launch a more general attack when the mine was blown.

The various sources give contradictory times for this event, over a span from 8pm to 11pm; but Pierre Rocolle's research and interviews suggest that the explosion took place at about 9.30pm.[59] Veterans recalled a muffled rumbling and a shuddering under their feet, followed after a distinct pause by a great fountain of earth and stones hurled into the air. Again, the exact site of the explosion is located differently by different sources. Bernard

Fall publishes a sketch map from a Viet Minh source that puts it on the south-west shoulder of the hill, which would seem to place the tunnel entrance at a point controlled by French fire rather than in the siege trenches. More convincingly, Colonel Rocolle places it some way below the summit on the north-east slope.[60] Other facts are not disputed: that the tunnel had not been dug long enough to reach under the key French block-house dug into the summit; that although Lieutenant Edme's 2nd Company took serious casualties in the explosion, this failed to disrupt the defence as a whole; and that the People's Army failed to exploit it.

The enemy on the eastern face of the hill seem to have hesitated for as long as an hour and a half; one can perhaps imagine lengthy exchanges about the failure of the mine to destroy the blockhouse, and the implications for the infantry plan. Meanwhile, other units of Regiment 98 renewed the pressure on the southern face, at least some now struggling up Champs-Elysées as so many of their dead comrades had done before them. At an unidentified time Sergeants Bruni and Ballait, from 1 BPC's 2nd Company, climbed into the abandoned hulk of the tank 'Bazeilles' and got one of its machine guns back into action to support the defenders on this flank.[61] At perhaps 11pm additional Viet Minh units hit both the northern and eastern slopes, and Captain Pouget's men had to fight on three fronts at once. On the east slope Pouget led a platoon to the lip of the mine crater, which their fire dominated, but on the south face he soon had to pull his men back from Champs-Elysées to the summit.

It seems to have been at about this stage that his appeal for reinforcement prompted Colonel Langlais to contact Major Guiraud at the Huguettes, which were not under direct attack. From Huguette 2, Guiraud ordered Lieutenant Le Cour Grandmaison to take his 20-odd Legion paras to Eliane 2 – a journey of only three-quarters of a mile, but which Captain Pouget knew would take at least an hour. Pouget's mood was not one of despair but of frustration: he was convinced that with just one more company he could clear Eliane 2. By midnight Regiment 98 had made such good progress that he was hard pressed from all three directions. Nevertheless, the machine guns in the blockhouses amid the brick ruins of the 'governor's house' were proving as deadly as ever before, and Pouget launched several successful counter-charges with sub-machine guns and grenades to drive the enemy back.

In the early hours of 7 May, as so often happened when the Viet Minh's assaults were held up by stubborn resistance, the units of Regiment 98 paused to regroup and to reorganize their artillery support. The assault was then renewed, with the help of 'caging' artillery fire that cut Eliane 2 off from any hope of reinforcement. By about 2.30am much of the summit seems to have been penetrated, although confused fighting continued for at least another two hours, particularly in the northern part of the position. Captain Pouget had been trying to follow from overheard radio traffic the progress of Le Cour Grandmaison, but by 3am it was clear that he was making very little ground.

At about 4am, with perhaps 35 of his men still fighting and their ammunition almost finished, Pouget was unable to reach Colonel Langlais but got through to Major Vadot at GONO main headquarters. Vadot told him calmly that there was not another man nor shell to send him; whatever could be scraped up was already on its way to Eliane 4, which was in equally great danger of being overrun. After acknowledging this message, Pouget announced his intention to sign off and wreck the radio. A Vietnamese voice immediately broke into the net and told him not to destroy the set just yet – they would play him some music. Through the static Pouget heard a recording of the 'Song of the Partisans', a wartime anthem of the French Resistance. The irony was not lost on him.

Jean Pouget put three bullets through the radio, then left the cellar to join his men. Their small-arms ammunition and grenades ran out soon afterwards, and Regiment 98 swarmed over the hilltop mopping up. At between 4.40am and 5am Captain Pouget and his last handful of men were surrounded and captured. Sergeant Chief Chabrier of 2nd Company, 1 BPC would claim that the last French gun firing on Eliane 2 was the machine gun in the hulk of 'Bazeilles'.

Regiment 98 did not try to penetrate any further west into the camp; the surviving *bo doi* consolidated on the captured position and gave supporting fire to their comrades of Regiment 174, who by daybreak still had not taken Eliane 4 some 300yds to the north-west.[62] Their thoughts as they gazed down into the valley at last, with the rising sun at their backs, can only be imagined: after five weeks, six separate assaults on the High Elianes, and probably at least a thousand dead and seriously wounded, their regiment had at last taken the bloody 'Fifth Hill'.

THE INFANTRY ASSAULT ON Eliane 4 had commenced much later than on Eliane 2, at about 9.30pm. The first wave of attackers from the north-east were driven back by Captain Guilleminot's 30-odd Vietnamese of 3rd Company, 5 BPVN, with effective mortar support from Lieutenant Allaire down at Eliane 10. Soon afterwards Regiment 174 threw themselves at the slopes again; Major Botella brought Lieutenant Pham Van Phu's 2nd Company round from the southern flank at about 10.30pm, but the Viet Minh managed to push them back to the summit. Major Bréchignac radioed Colonel Langlais for any help he could send; 'Gars Pierre' called upon Major Guiraud's BMEP, and Lieutenant Michel Brandon with a 60-man company was ordered to start across the camp for Eliane 4.[63] Bréchignac knew that it would be hours before he could hope to see them, and in the meantime he launched a series of counter-charges by 5 BPVN and II/1 RCP. These managed to contain the enemy until about midnight – they were still on the summit, but had not overrun it. When Captain Clédic of II/1 RCP called for artillery fire on a People's Army concentration visible on Eliane 1, 'Zulu Kilo' gave him three rounds – the 105s were now down to about 300 shells each, the 120mm mortars to a couple of dozen bombs per tube.[64]

Jacques Le Cour Grandmaison's small platoon spent at least two hours getting across the camp via the sheltered trenches of the 'Metro', braving enemy fire as they crossed the bridge, and then forging on across the mud-flats for Eliane 2. They took casualties not only from artillery and mortar fire, but from Viet Minh small arms and even grenades – the east bank was infested by parties of the enemy. Soon after they reached highway RP41, at some unconfirmed time but clearly after all hope had been given up for Pouget on Eliane 2, Lieutenant Colonel Bigeard radioed a change of objective: Le Cour Grandmaison was to take his surviving handful of légion-naires to Eliane 4 instead. When he arrived, Major Bréchignac ordered them to spearhead another of his counter-attacks to try to clear the crest. Incredibly, this succeeded; by first light the Viet Minh held only a 20yd toehold on the eastern summit, and the situation on Eliane 4 seemed to be under control. Le Cour Grandmaison's 'company' now consisted of himself, his radio operator, and two unwounded paratroopers. At about 7am, although they were running short of ammunition, the summit was still held by its mixed remnant from the Vietnamese, French and Legion parachute battalions.[65]

GIVEN THAT IN SIZE THE GROUPS of reinforcements sent from the west bank actually resembled fighting patrols more than formed units, the difficulty they encountered in reaching the High Elianes may seem surprising; but their paths led directly through a furious fight which was raging around Eliane 10 (*see Map 21*). This strongpoint was attacked from about 10pm onwards by Regiment 165, who penetrated the position perhaps an hour later. The survivors of Major Thomas's 6 BPC and the mixed crowd of wounded men were soon holding off repeated attacks on a reduced enclave around three blockhouses; when Lieutenant Allaire's mortar ammunition ran out his men fought on as infantry. If Eliane 10 fell, the way to the bridges would be open and the men on the High Elianes and Eliane 3 would be cut off from all retreat.[66]

It was while this struggle was taking place that the Dakotas arrived overhead to make yet another attempt to drop 1st Company of 1st Colonial. The Luciole aircraft was lighting up the battlefield with a constant stream of flares, which would have to be interrupted before the paratroopers could jump. Colonel Langlais passed the decision all the way down to Lieutenant Le Page of 6 BPC, whose platoon was at that moment the most hard-pressed in Eliane 10: drop reinforcements in the dark, or turn them away for the sake of light to fight by? Le Page replied that if his men were left in the dark they would be overrun in moments. The C-47s were turned away, and flew back to the Delta carrying perhaps the luckiest paratroopers in Indochina, while the fighting for Elianes 2, 4 and 10 raged on.[67]

Always conscious of the threat to the Bailey bridge, Langlais took reinforcements for Eliane 10 from Epervier, ordering two 40-man companies of 8 BPC led by Lieutenants Jacquemet and Bailly to try to get through to Major Thomas. Jacquemet's platoon was destroyed near the river crossing; Bailly's managed to reach Eliane 10 by about 3am, and found Thomas with perhaps 20 men of 6th Colonial still holding out in the radio bunker. At 3.30am another handful of help arrived – Lieutenant Weinberger with two platoons of Legion walking wounded from Eliane 12.[68] A Viet Minh account by an officer of Regiment 165 described the fighting for Eliane 10 as particularly severe; three assaults were mounted, each of them repulsed, and each followed by a French counter-attack. At 5am, awaiting reinforcements which never came, one of the Viet Minh battalion commanders reported his men's morale wavering in what he astonishingly called 'an unequal fight'.

Equally astonishing was Colonel Langlais' unbroken spirit. When Eliane 10 was still holding out at daybreak on 7 May, he considered using it as the base for a counter-attack to recapture Eliane 2; if that position could be retaken and held only until nightfall, it might give 'Albatros' a slim chance of success. At about 8am he scraped together every man in the central camp who could hold a rifle and walk, and ordered them to start for Eliane 10.[69]

WHILE THE PARATROOPERS died in the defence of the Elianes, on the opposite side of the camp the last of Giap's planned attacks for the night of 6/7 May was rolling over the légionnaires. After a heavy bombardment, Claudine 5 was assaulted by Regiment 102 shortly after 10pm (*see Map 21*). The remnant of 2nd Company, I/2 REI were pushed back, and Major Clémencon threw every man he could find into a counter-attack; these included a platoon of Captain Philippe's III/13th survivors from Claudine 4, and the battalion's platoon of bearded pioneers. These few dozen légionnaires managed to re-establish some kind of front in the shell craters by about 10.30pm; but from around 2am they were overrun by weight of numbers, and resistance in Claudine 5 had ceased by daybreak on 7 May.[70]

PERHAPS MERCIFULLY FOR THE individuals involved, on the morning of 7 May the People's Army gave Colonel Langlais no opportunity to attempt his beggars' crusade against Eliane 2. Shortly after 8am, preparatory bombardment heralded the renewal of the assaults on both Eliane 4 and Eliane 10, now held by a few dozen tottering ghosts.

The north-east face of Eliane 4 gave way soon after 9am. The ammunition was virtually finished, and there was not a man anywhere on the hill who could be spared to plug the gap. Majors Bréchignac and Botella and Dr Rouault, the 5 BPVN medical officer, would not attempt to escape. The only able-bodied men who tried to leave the position and reach Eliane 10 were Captain Clédic of II/1 RCP with two lieutenants and a handful of paratroopers, but most of them were captured almost as soon as they got off the hill. At about 9.30am Bréchignac radioed Bigeard: 'Brèche to Bruno. It's the end. Don't shell us – there are too many wounded.' Then

Botella took the handset from Bréchignac: 'Dédé to Bruno. It's all over – they're at the command post. Goodbye – tell Gars Pierre we liked him a lot.'[71]

DOWN ON THE FLATS, ELIANE 10 was overrun shortly afterwards. A handful of individuals – including Lieutenant Le Page – evaded capture and managed to make their way back across the Bailey bridge, which was guarded by two of Hervouët's semi-disabled Chaffees and the fire of quad-50s at Epervier. While the Viet Minh consolidated at Eliane 10 they allowed many of the wounded simply to walk back across the Nam Youm, carrying the worst injured (who now included Lieutenants Le Boudec of 6 BPC and Bailly of 8 BPC). Dr Rivier, 6th Colonial's MO, led this column of half-naked, bandaged, mud-covered apparitions to Dr Grauwin and passed on the message he had been given by his captors: 'Tell your doctor we're coming soon.' Le Boudec would be the last man on Paul Grauwin's operating table before the camp fell.[72]

The morning fog was burning off, and 7 May promised to be another fine day. By about 10am nothing remained between the People's Army and the river but the improvised positions at Elianes 12, 11 and 3, where a few score demoralized Thais and Moroccans, and convalescent wounded, were gathered around a skeletal armature of légionnaires from 13 DBLE's lost battalions.

AT ABOUT 10AM GENERALS de Castries and Cogny had a long radio conversation. Castries reported the loss of Elianes 2, 4 and 10, and listed as well as he could the latest status of his various units. Since the fall of Claudine 5 the Viet Minh had been within perhaps 400yds of his command post; the best that he could hope for was to hold the west bank of the river until dark, and then to attempt the planned break-out the next night, 7/8 May. He stressed the importance of holding on to the water purification plant; and once again he asked for, and received, Cogny's unambiguous authority to launch 'Albatros' at his own judgement. This – and their last conversation at about 5pm that afternoon – were both taped; the recordings were later edited, but transcripts made at various stages allow a recon-struction of most of what was said. General de Castries' voice was that of a man who had lived through too many 'white nights'; he stumbled

over words and repeated himself, but kept his emotions under gentle-
manly control apart from one tiny catch over the phrase '... before the
end'.[73]

General de Castries asked for a maximum effort by the Air Force to
help buy him a few hours, and was promised it, thanks to the fine weather.
Lieutenant Colonel Dussol led 25 sorties by the B-26s, supported by 30
Bearcat and 16 Corsair sorties; Langlais later claimed to have been told
that these caused serious casualties. GONO's supply staff were still asking
Hanoi for ammunition drops at 2.40pm; but all these missions were, of
course, far too late to have any significant effect.[74]

At around noon, Colonel Langlais gathered in his command post the
COs of the units whose men were to take part in the attempted break-out
that night. While they sat around drinking the warm soup that Langlais
had brought from the nearby hospital kitchen, Lieutenant Colonel Bigeard
outlined the plan. For GONO's purposes he had given it a codename which
perhaps reflected his view of its chances: Operation 'Percée de Sang' –
'Bloodletting'. It would not involve the 2,000–3,000 men that Hanoi had
originally assumed. From the main camp, the remnants of the Legion and
airborne battalions would form eight 'marching companies' of about
70 or 80 men each, in two columns. According to Bernard Fall, it was
envisaged that these would break out in different directions, and straws
would be drawn to decide which would go westwards (with a slim chance)
and which to the predictable south (with virtually none). This attempt by
some 650 men would have to be covered not only by the shreds of the
North African and Thai units, but also by 200–300 good infantry who
would have to be left behind.

All the battalion commanders rejected the plan, on the grounds that
their remaining men were so exhausted that it would be suicidal. The
latest aerial photos dropped by a Corsair showed three new belts of enemy
trenches astride the Nam Youm south of Junon; it was unthinkable for
men in their state to mount the kind of bloody assaults that would
be necessary to fight their way through. The survivors would then face
the horrors of a jungle evasion march lasting many days, in the uncertain
hope of an eventual rendezvous. Soon after 1pm General de Castries was
informed that no break-out from the main camp was feasible.[75]

MEANWHILE, AFTER A COUPLE of hours' pause to digest their latest conquests, the People's Army on the east bank were cleaning up Elianes 12 and 11 (*see Map 21*). In Eliane 12, Captain Fazentieux of the 31st Engineers saw some of his previously reliable Moroccans waving white cloths on their rifle barrels from the front-line trench. Eliane 12 was overrun with little resistance shortly after noon by Regiment 141 'Hong Gai' of Division 312; and at about 2pm the same unit was ordered to move against Eliane 11. The Viet Minh account states that this position was attacked after a short bombardment at about 3pm, and that its fall was hastened when some of its defenders left their trenches to join the 'rats of the Nam Youm' who were streaming back towards the central camp. An immediate attempt by a Viet Minh unit to wade the river was driven back by the wounded men at Junon. The Bailey bridge was still covered by quad-50s at Epervier, their raised firing platforms now surrounded by dunes of spent cartridges and links.

East of the river this left only Eliane 3; for the time being it was ignored, presumably because it was irrelevant – it was too far south for its small-arms fire to command the Bailey bridge about 500yds away to any significant degree. The few unwounded soldiers in its garrison were further weakened from about 3pm when Captain Nicod's company of I/4 RTM joined the flight of the 'rats'; the 13 DBLE survivors would not be able to hold out for long after this desertion.[76]

AT AROUND NOON ON 7 MAY the People's Army were obviously no longer working to General Giap's original plan, envisaging a pause of several days before a final fourth offensive on 10/11 May; but they certainly expected some sort of lull for consolidation before storming the west bank. General de Castries still contemplated leading the resistance of much of the garrison at least until the morning of the 8th. However, by about 3pm that afternoon the commanders on both sides had realized that Dien Bien Phu could not hold out even until nightfall.

As always, the Viet Minh account appears to have been tidied up retrospectively, and the French version is confused between various sources – such untidiness being entirely consistent with truthfulness. Bernard Fall couples in Langlais' report to Castries at 1pm or 1.30pm the fact that no break-out was possible, and the opinion that further resistance was therefore pointless.[77] But Pierre Rocolle records a radio message to Colonel Lalande at about 2pm in which the GONO chief-of-staff Lieutenant Colonel de Seguin-Pazzis discussed Isabelle's part in 'Percée de Sang'. They had had a preliminary conversation that morning; now Lalande was told that resistance in the main camp would continue through the night until perhaps 7am on 8 May, in order to cover the sortie. In a second message at about 4pm, Seguin-Pazzis – speaking in English for security – told Lalande that there would, after all, be no break-out from the main camp, and that resistance would cease in an hour or two.[78]

The Viet Minh account has General Giap alerted in the early afternoon to the unexpected possibility of a French collapse by reports of the flight from the east bank of the large numbers of 'rats' (whom his observers had no way of knowing were not combatants), and the desertion and surrender of other troops from the Low Elianes. Giap later claimed to have radioed the commander of Division 308, Vuong Thua Vu, telling him that there were signs of confusion in the enemy ranks and that he should stick closely to the French so as not to give them any chance to break away.[79] Pierre Rocolle states that Giap was in fact absent from his headquarters when the information was assessed; and that it was his deputy chief-of-staff General Thanh, with responsibility for the eastern face, who at about 3pm issued orders in his name to maintain the momentum: 'The Commander of the Front to divisional commanders – Commence immediately general offensive on Muong Thanh – Pointless to wait until nightfall.' Units of Division 312 subsequently crossed the river on to the west bank, and Division 308 advanced from the west to meet them. Witnesses noted that the force from the east bank included units who seemed to be dressed entirely in new French combat fatigues.[80]

The second conversation between Colonels de Seguin-Pazzis and Lalande confirms that before 4pm the decision to cease fire had been taken; and the conversation at 5pm between Generals de Castries and Bodet (*see below*), that a time of 5.30pm had been agreed. Colonel Langlais' headquarters was to broadcast the announcement to the People's Army; meanwhile Seguin-Pazzis would contact all French units in time for them to make their preparations. He began making these calls at 4.30pm, in each case waiting for a clear acknowledgement that his orders had been understood.[81]

Alone on the east bank, Eliane 3 was an island in an ocean of enemy movement, and apparently still unmolested. At some time during the afternoon an officer who had escaped the fall of Eliane 10 and found his way to this last outpost radioed Langlais' headquarters. It was Lieutenant Allaire, the weapons platoon commander from 6th Colonial who had lost his mortars and ammunition on DZ Natacha on the long-ago first morning of 'Castor'. Now he asked his old CO, Lieutenant Colonel Bigeard, what they should do: 'do a Camerone', or take to their heels? Bigeard told him not to try anything – the ceasefire would be fixed soon. A man's sense of proportion often becomes skewed under the strain of prolonged combat, and Allaire then made an extraordinary request: he wanted the ceasefire order in writing – for all the world as if he might one day be called to account for surrendering his handful of scarecrows, amid the collapse of ten thousand men. Bigeard humoured his boy, and told him he could have his written authorization if he sent a runner.

Somehow a man got through to the command post, and back to Eliane 3 with a piece of paper on which was scrawled: 'For Allaire – Ceasefire at 17.30 – Don't fire any more – No white flag – See you soon – Bruno'. Above the signature are a few words that suggest that even Bigeard's iron self-control was crumbling at last: 'Poor 6th – Poor paras'. Some time later Allaire radioed laconically, 'They're coming at us without firing.' The loss of Eliane 3 was confirmed at about 4pm, by which time enemy units were infiltrating between all the positions on the western front of the camp.[82]

EXACTLY WHAT HAPPENED IN various parts of Dien Bien Phu between 2pm and 5.30pm is obscure; accounts are fragmentary, and few people outside the headquarters had any reason to note exact times. Different radio operators were in contact with different departments in Hanoi, which has confused the record for those seeking some kind of orderly and co-ordinated process; there was none. There are contradictory versions of how long firing continued from Epervier and Junon; equally, it is unclear to what extent the People's Army shelled the west bank that afternoon, if at all. For the reader, just as for so many of the soldiers of GONO, this indistinct fading away of the fighting leaves a baffling sense of anti-climax. Apparently, over about three and a half hours on its 56th day, the battle of Dien Bien Phu just... stopped.

The last French mortar and artillery ammunition was fired away; presumably what Major Le Gurun described as this 'final fireworks display' brought some reply?[83] General de Castries gave orders for the 31st Engineers to destroy whatever could not be fired, and all other useful equipment apart from that needed to keep electricity and clean water flowing; they were also told – optimistically, as it turned out – to stand by for orders to begin repairing the surface of the runway.

All requests for air combat support and drops of ammunition were cancelled just after 4pm; GONO now wanted only food and medical supplies, and an air-drop for the morrow was requested, so that after the surrender a day's worth of rations could be distributed. Some aircraft were already in the air on their way to the valley, however; at about 5.05pm, Privateer 'César 7' announced to 'Torri Rouge' control that he was about 30 seconds from arrival with his bombload. The ground operator told him to abort, then called up his wingman 'César 5': 'At 5.30 we're blowing everything up – goodbye to our families... Adieu, César.'[84]

As the ceasefire warning reached the various parts of the camp, men destroyed all the weapons and equipment they could. Gun barrels were burst by sticking them into the mud and firing a last round. The engines of the last tanks were drained of oil and raced until they seized. Artillerymen smashed their sights, threw their breech-blocks into the river, and let off incendiary grenades inside the barrels. Against a background of stuttering explosions large and small, plumes of smoke rose from every part of Dien Bien Phu as anything burnable – including all paperwork – was set alight.

At the hospital, Dr Grauwin ordered his staff to get back into some sort of proper uniform clothing with Red Cross armbands, and then continued operating. The shrinking of Dien Bien Phu had brought many hundreds more wounded from the aid posts of lost positions to crowd into the central area, like animals driven up a hill by rising floodwater. In every trench, dug-out and blockhouse they lay or sat in the mud, and an interminable file of them still stretched all the way back to the front lines. The new arrivals stumbled over the helpless and the already dead. Men who were unwounded but completely bewildered joined the queue for the hospital automatically, and as soon as they sat down they fell asleep.[85]

This theme of men finally giving way to their craving for sleep – simply dropping their weapons and webbing, lying down, and surrendering to exhaustion – recurs in several accounts. Others, however, still had more urgent concerns. In Claudine, Thai soldiers were already getting rid of their uniforms by 3pm, and Captain Hébert's Meos were slipping out of the camp and away – they knew what the Viet Minh intended for them. Others made less dramatic preparations, destroying or trying to hide their few personal possessions. Colonel Langlais burned his red beret rather than let some *bo doi* take it as a souvenir; Bigeard wrapped a silk escape map round his ankle. The Viet Minh knew his name well and would exult in capturing him, but 'Bruno' rejected Castries' suggestion that he make a break for it.[86]

For those soldiers who still had the strength and will to keep fighting in their own defence – perhaps a thousand? – one of the most shocking impressions was the number of others who now emerged from the shelters where they had been sitting out the battle.[87] Gazing at this passive crowd, how could the paratroopers and légionnaires not remember the hilltops, and the comrades, lost for lack of a hundred fresh men at the right moment. After eight long weeks spent focusing solely on the task of denying the People's Army this valley – weeks which had drained them of almost every physical and psychological resource; weeks during which they had seen almost every one of their friends killed or maimed – the collapse of their whole mental world within a few quiet hours was simply incomprehensible. Many of the paratroopers, in particular, felt not just stupefaction but also a sense of injustice. For 56 days they had given everything, endured everything; they had achieved the impossible, not once but again and again. They *deserved* to win; and if they were now being robbed of victory, then the real thieves were not the People's Army, the 'rats of the Nam Youm' or anyone else in the filth of this last valley, but men who slept between clean sheets far away.

SHORTLY BEFORE 5PM, General de Castries spoke over the secure Z13 radio link to Hanoi, telling the C-in-C's deputy, General Bodet, that he intended to make preliminary radio contact with the People's Army before sending emissaries to them at 5.30pm. His whole concern was to ease the plight of his wounded, and he hoped that the Viet Minh would allow Red

Cross planes to land the next day. Asked about the possibility of Operation 'Albatros', he simply replied, 'Isabelle is going to try it.'[88]

A conversation that has attracted much more attention took place a few moments later. From Hanoi, General Cogny came on the air, perhaps prompted to do so by the mention of emissaries – emissaries who must, by definition, carry a white flag.

'Old boy, it has to finish now, of course; but not in the form of a capitulation. That is forbidden to us. There mustn't be any raising of the white flag; the firing must be allowed to die away – but don't surrender. That would debase everything magnificent that you've done up to now.'

Both Jules Roy and Bernard Fall state that the surviving recording and transcripts have been cut and edited at this point. Roy, quoting Sergeant Kubiak of III/13 DBLE, believes that a white flag had indeed been raised over GONO headquarters by this time, but was later removed. The recording gives Castries' next words as: 'All right, general, only I wished to protect the wounded' – and the use of the past tense *voulais* does seem to support Roy's assertion. General Cogny went on to explain:

'Yes, only, I have a paper here [an instruction left with him by Navarre before he left Hanoi]; I haven't the right to authorize you to make this capitulation. Do whatever's best. But this mustn't finish with a white flag. What you've achieved is too good for that. Do you understand, old boy?'

'All right, general.'

'Well – au revoir, old boy.'[89]

GIVEN THE PRACTICAL SITUATION that Castries and his soldiers actually faced, it is hard to grasp exactly what subtleties of behaviour Navarre and Cogny were urging upon him. They clearly attached great importance to the symbolism of military honour; it is equally clear that in General de Castries' mind, honour now depended solely upon saving the lives of his surviving troops, and sparing his wounded any more avoidable agony. Whatever the high command's sensitivities, witnesses attest that many white flags were indeed raised; soldiers know all too well that the moment when they are trying to get their surrender accepted can be the most dangerous of all – any ambiguity is lethal.

Various survivors described the moments when they came face to face with the troops of Divisions 312 and 308 as they spread out all over the camp, and a pattern emerges. Many remarked upon the youth of the enemy infantrymen, and upon their wary behaviour. Some were as nervous as the men they were taking prisoner; Lieutenant Allaire recalled that his captor asked hesitantly, 'It's all over?' – 'Yes, it's all over.' 'No more shooting?' – 'No more shooting.'[90] No doubt there were cases of unnecessary killing, but there is plenty of anecdotal evidence of self-conscious correctness, even spontaneous humanity. The first Viet Minh soldier to burst into one shelter full of badly wounded Legion paras asked if they had any water, and when Corporal André pointed to their jerrycan the *bo doi* made to take it. André protested that he should only do so if he promised to bring it back refilled; and two hours later, he did.[91]

At 5.32pm Sergeant Millien, General de Castries' personal radio operator, transmitted to Hanoi: 'In five minutes everything will be blown up here. The Viets are only a few metres away. Good luck to everybody.' A few moments later the first Viet Minh assault squad entered the GONO headquarters bunker, and General de Castries and his staff were herded out at gunpoint. The camp commander leaned heavily on his stick, and appeared to have aged in the past three months. By 5.40pm a large red, gold-embroidered Viet Minh flag had been raised over the command post, in which General Vuong Thua Vu of Division 308 would soon install himself. The People's Army attached great importance to the capture of General de Castries in person, and in a memoir General Giap stresses his orders that the French commander be identified with certainty. He even sent a jeep with a photograph of Castries to Generals Do and Thanh, insisting that they confirm his capture with their own eyes; he apparently feared that Castries might be impersonated by another officer. It was, after all, the first time that the Viet Minh had ever captured a French general.[92]

Shortly afterwards the strongpoints of Claudine were occupied; the last to be taken was the I/4 RTM command post of Major Nicolas, at about 6.20pm. By then the very last message from the main camp had already been sent to FTNV, at about 5.50pm; perhaps fittingly, it was from the unglamorous, tirelessly practical 31st Engineers, station 9-DMO: 'We're blowing everything up. Adieu.'[93]

THERE REMAINED, OF COURSE, Isabelle. Throughout the night and early morning of 6–7 May its bombardment by enemy artillery, mortars and RCLs had continued, while Colonel Lalande's command post listened over the radio to GONO dying by inches. He had discussed the break-out plan in guarded terms with Lieutenant Colonel de Seguin-Pazzis during the morning and again at about 2pm. That afternoon, as he watched the fires and explosions all over the north end of the valley, he had ordered the destruction of Isabelle's own stores and equipment. By the time of their conversation at about 4pm, when he was told that no sortie would be launched from the main camp and that he was free to make up his own mind whether or not to attempt 'Percée de Sang' alone, Lalande no longer had a choice, since his men no longer had the means to defend themselves. He had already decided who would go and who would stay; rations had been distributed and kit lightened. GONO headquarters advised him that the south-east direction was likely to be less well guarded by the enemy than the south-west, and that some GMI partisans were already in place in the overlooking hills. His last serviceable howitzer was ordered to cease fire missions for the benefit of Claudine from 5pm.[94]

A little less than an hour after General de Castries informed General Bodet at about 5pm that Isabelle would try a break-out, General Cogny spoke to Colonel Lalande directly to discuss the details; oddly, he did not mention that the main camp had already fallen, but this was confirmed to Lalande at about 6.30pm. Shortly afterwards a Viet Minh radio on the same frequency repeated this, and demanded the surrender of Isabelle; the artillery bombardment intensified. During the early evening the strong-point commander remained in two minds about the best route to attempt; at one stage he considered breaking not directly south, but north towards the main camp before turning westward, in the hope that Regiment 57 might have been drawn away north. (In fact, it seems that the regiment was being reinforced by three battalions, probably from Division 308.) Colonel Lalande radioed FTNV via a Dakota relay aircraft asking for the latest information on enemy dispositions around Isabelle, but he received no reply.

At about 8pm the leading companies began to leave Isabelle (*see Map 19*). The plan was for the escapers to follow both banks of the Nam Youm southwards until they reached a known track. The légionnaires of 11th Company, III/3 REI, accompanied by Henri Préaud's tank crews, headed down the west bank; 12th Company crossed the Nam Youm and moved off down the east bank; and some of Lieutenant Wieme's Thai auxiliaries joined each party. After a few miles the west-bank company ran into heavy resistance, and a confused fire fight broke out. Nothing could be heard from the east bank, so Colonel Lalande ordered the bulk of the force to follow that route.

This was a slow process: the night was extremely dark, the trenches deep with mud, and there was a lot of barbed wire through which the légionnaires had to grope their way before they could reach the flat paddy-fields east of the Nam Youm. While they waited their turns to slip out of the strongpoint shells were still falling on Isabelle, where a B-26 overhead reported seeing major explosions of ammunition dumps at about 9.40pm. Ahead of them, to the south, the men in the column could hear heavy firing.[95]

At about 11pm, when the tail of column still had not left Isabelle, Viet Minh troops began to infiltrate it. The difficulty of identifying friend from foe caused a lot of confused shooting and contradictory orders to fire or cease fire. The east-bank column was completely dislocated; some were killed, others captured, and still others turned back to Isabelle in the hope of organizing a renewed defence behind its barbed wire. At about midnight Colonel Lalande did consider trying to rebuild a defence; but his positions were ruined, his heavy weapons destroyed, the enemy were already infiltrating his perimeter, all communication with his units had been lost, men had become separated from their officers and NCOs, and he had more than 250 wounded to protect. In the midst of this chaos, People's Army envoys arrived demanding to see Colonel Lalande; they were allowed through at about 1am, and after a brief discussion Lalande ordered his men to lay down their arms. His last message, sent at 1.50am, was picked up by the relay aircraft and heard in Hanoi: 'Sortie failed. Cannot communicate with you any more.'[96]

It has been claimed that the order to cease firing never reached Warrant Officer Louis Foucherau and a handful of Moroccan gunners manning the last serviceable howitzer of III/10 RAC. They still had 125 rounds stacked in their gunpit, and when they saw enemy infantry approaching at first light they opened fire. After a pause the Viet Minh made an assault; if the story is true, then Gunner Mohammed ben Salah may have been the last man killed in the battle of Dien Bien Phu.[97]

THE ATTEMPTED SORTIE FROM Isabelle also caused confusion in Hanoi. At Haiphong–Cat Bi that night, four French-crewed C-119s of Captain Soulat's Packet Detachment were on alert, loaded with rations and medical supplies in accordance with GONO's request of that afternoon. At 10pm Captain Soulat took a telephone call ordering him to have the aircraft unloaded and reloaded with ammunition for Isabelle. The detachment commander argued against this order in emphatic terms, since he believed such a mission to be unachievable and a futile risk of his crews' lives. So determined was his resistance that the telephone was passed first to Colonel Nicot of S/GMMTA, and finally to General Dechaux in person. When Captain Soulat pointed out that the order was both pointless and potentially suicidal, the commanding general of GATAC/Nord reportedly appealed to him to accept it as a sacrifical mission; and Soulat responded that since this would be his last mission, he therefore had a special request – that a general officer should accompany him. One may imagine a silence over the telephone line.

Nevertheless Henri Soulat did take off that night, alone. He flew his No. 143 all the way to the valley, and then circled slowly over Isabelle. There was no radio contact, and Hanoi ordered him to turn back.[98]

The battle was over at last; now the dying would really start.

17. L'Addition

'The method is excessively simple, like the
repeated dripping of water. After the subject
has been brought to the point of despair, he
is shown a glimmer of hope to give him his
second wind. Then he is taken once again to
the very edge; and each time he sinks a little
lower. This game blunts the willpower of even
the firmest character.'

Dr J.-L.Rondy, *1 BEP, survivor of Viet Minh Prison Camp No. 1*

ON THE LATE AFTERNOON AND evening of 7 May the infantrymen
of Divisions 308 and 312 took possession of the battlefield. They hurried
all their prisoners who could walk or hobble – and many stretcher cases
– on to RP41, and began marching them out of the north-east corner of
the valley. At this stage the mass of prisoners were simply herded, and
only the most superficial searches were carried out; many soldiers still
had pocket knives, compasses and other valuable items – some even had
hidden pistols and grenades.[1] The senior officers from the command posts
were segregated and driven off in trucks and jeeps. Many officers had their
hands tied behind their backs – some for refusing to answer questions,
others apparently on general principle – as did anyone else who made any
show of defiance or disobedience.

The first march lasted well into the evening, and after about ten miles
the prisoners were halted near a water source in a large clearing, where

they slept in the open air under a light rain. At this transit camp, over the next few days, they were sorted into separate groups of 50s, 100s and 400s by race and rank, before being put on the road to march at least 300 miles – and in some cases, half as far again – to their eventual prison camps in the South Delta Base and the Viet Bac. Officers and senior NCOs were separated from their men; all Vietnamese officers and soldiers were marched away, and even the different main nationalities within the Legion's ranks were divided. It was during this early stage that the first systematic interrogations of officers took place; the interrogators appeared to be line officers, who showed great interest in all details of the conduct of the defence.[2]

During this sorting process a few of the obviously most serious casualties were allowed to return to the valley, where Dr Grauwin and the other medical staff would find themselves at the centre of a painful game of cat and mouse over the next three weeks. On the evening of 7 May his hospital was inspected by the senior surgeon of Division 308. The two doctors quickly established a mutual respect; the Viet Minh wounded were clearly in an even worse plight than the French, and Grauwin shared some of his small stock of drugs and instruments. It was agreed that the French wounded should be brought into the open air, where shelters were rigged for them using parachute canopies. For the time being the French medics could continue to treat their patients; but the plane-loads of rations and medical supplies which the Air Force dropped every day did not reach the French hospital.

In keeping with their guerrilla tradition the People's Army were meticulous in recovering from the battlefield anything which could be of use, and over the next few days search teams were tasked with gathering particular items. Plenty of small arms were taken from the 'rats of the Nam Youm', but very few heavier weapons remained intact; only two 105mm howitzers and one quad-50 mount had escaped sabotage, along with three wheeled vehicles and the engineers' bulldozers. But no matter how mundane the booty, everything was grist to the Viet Minh mill: not just weapons, munitions and medical supplies, but the tens of thousands of discarded parachutes that lay all over the valley, clothing, tools, telephone cables, even odd straps and buckles.[3]

NOT ONLY WERE THE FRENCH wounded denied the air-dropped medical supplies – it was understandable that the People's Army preferred to give these to their own sparsely supplied and much fuller field hospitals; but after two days Viet Minh political commissars took charge. While the casualties continued to suffer and die under the minimal care that the French doctors could bring them, their captors used them as a bargaining counter.

Securing Viet Minh agreement to the air evacuation of the wounded was the CEFEO's main priority and was also pursued at Geneva; there the victors made humane noises, but in the valley they held all the delaying cards. A request for negotiations by General Navarre finally secured the arrival by helicopter on 13 May of a French delegation headed by the widely respected Professor Huard, dean of the Hanoi university medical school.[4] Tortuous bargaining over the fate of at least 1,500 seriously wounded lying outside the hospital continued over many days, with each team referring contentious issues back to their superiors. The Viet Minh were determined to extract the maximum advantage for their agreement, and their main demand was a halt in French Air Force activity both within six miles of the valley, and over major stretches of RP41 – on which their own troops marching back towards the Delta would be mixed with columns of French prisoners and trucks full of Viet Minh wounded.

Eventually the French were forced to agree; but Viet Minh delaying tactics meanwhile became more threatening. While a very few of the most serious cases were allowed to be flown out by helicopter and Beaver, and the main airstrip was very slowly de-mined and repaired to take Dakotas, the commissars demanded that no Vietnamese CEFEO wounded be included in the deal. They also interfered with the treatment and evacuation of the wounded on political rather than medical grounds, insisting that non-European rankers must have first priority, and European officers last. It was 17 May before an agreement was finally reached in principle: 858 seriously wounded could be evacuated, selected on medical grounds irrespective of nationality. For this concession the French had to agree to drop demands for neutral observers to monitor the valley or the POW columns. However, before and during the evacuations further pressures were brought on the French medical staff to write various documents for the Viet Minh propaganda effort. Like those presented to POWs during their captivity, these typically admitted the guilt of the colonialist oppressors and begged for the forgiveness of 'Uncle Ho'. Geneviève de Galard was one of those who resisted this blackmail, but eventually Dr Grauwin authorized the signing of anything that would hasten the release of the hostage wounded.[5]

Tragically, on 22 May three B-26s bombed and strafed RP41 just south of Co Noi, killing and injuring numbers of both Viet Minh and French POWs. This set back the evacuation by another week, and led to reprisals against Grauwin's medical personnel. Geneviève was flown out on 24 May, and Grauwin with the last of the French wounded only on 1 June.[6]

The criteria for direct evacuation enforced by the Viet Minh were harsh and often medically uninformed; as a result, many wounded whose weakness should have saved them from the long march to the camps were held back, while men with more obvious injuries were flown out even though they had in fact healed well and regained much of their strength. A preliminary French Medical Service report on the condition of these evacuees stated that it was 'remarkable that in less than eight days the great majority were stabilized, in respect of both medical conditions (amoebic dysentery, malaria) and septicaemia'.[7] At least 3,000 wounded were put on the road to the camps, completely dependent on the unskilled care of stronger men; these included not only minor injuries but serious stretcher cases – recent amputees, men with head, chest and stomach wounds, and compound fractures which had not been immobilized. The majority of these casualties had never reached the hospitals in the first place and had received nothing but basic care at unit aid posts. Some were marched or carried only as far as Tuan Giao, where they spent the rest of their captivity; very many others were marched the whole way to the Viet Bac.

The number of men who fought for the French at Dien Bien Phu, and the casualties that they suffered, have been variously calculated and debated, but precision is impossible. Under the circumstances – the drifting in of survivors of the Lai Chau garrison, the piecemeal airborne reinforcement of GONO during the battle, and the lack of casualty records for 6 and 7 May – it would be unsafe to rely upon any of the statistics that have been published, some of which are difficult to reconcile. The following figures are those arrived at by Pierre Rocolle:

Effectives 13 March: 10,813

Parachuted in later: 4,277

Total: 15,090

Casualties up to 5 May:

Known killed 1,142 (7.6 per cent)

Missing in action 1,606 (10.6 per cent)

Wounded treated 4,436 (29 per cent)

  Of which died 429

Total casualties: 7,184 (47.6 per cent)

These figures raise several questions. What proportions of those listed as 'missing' were killed or captured cannot be estimated; the same is true of the probably two thousand 'internal deserters' not listed here; and included in the 'wounded' total are an unknown number who returned to the line after dressing and were subsequently killed on 6–7 May. Rocolle suggests that approximately another 400 killed and 400 wounded is a reasonable estimate for the desperate final battles of 6–7 May; and on that basis he suggests that roughly 5,500 men fell into Viet Minh hands unwounded and perhaps 4,500 wounded – 10,000 in all.[8] Subtracting the 858 seriously wounded who were evacuated from the battlefield, and a margin for those who died there after 7 May, leaves a tentative figure of something over 9,000 prisoners who were marched away, of whom at least a third were wounded or sick to some degree.

Their captivity lasted only four months; but during that time perhaps half of them would die or disappear. Like the great majority of the 12,000-odd Viet Minh and French soldiers who already lay in the yellow mud of the Nam Youm valley, they would have no known graves.[9]

OF THE 2,440 PIMS WHO WERE held in the camp on 13 March, about half are believed to have become casualties. Although their treatment by the French seems to have been as decent as circumstances allowed, their docility – even loyalty – under fire was extraordinary. Although guarded by only one officer and eight Moroccan rankers, and necessarily unsupervised during much of their work all over the camp and on the drop zones, only 30 are known to have made a break for it; and there are no known instances of PIMs secreting weapons – which would not have been difficult after the first days of April. The Viet Minh announced that they would try as war criminals any French intelligence officers, those who had worked with the GCMA/GMI partisans, and PIM guards; yet on the fall of the camp the compound commander Lieutenant Patricot, known by sight to almost every prisoner, was never denounced.[10]

MEANWHILE, THE NEWS OF the fall of Dien Bien Phu rippled outwards across the world. In northern Laos on the early afternoon of 7 May, Commando 'Pamplemousse' reported villagers as saying that a large People's Army force was soon expected to move south from the Nam Youm valley. On the northern fringes of the Nam Ou bend Lieutenant Colonel Godard began to take precautions against attack, such as mining the trails from the north. At some time on the morning of the 8th – the delay is unexplained – General Cogny transmitted to Colonel de Crèvecoeur the agreed phrases signifying that GONO had fallen, and that Godard's 'Ariège' force should retreat at once to Muong Sai: 'The fruits are ripe... Austerlitz'.[11] Godard's men now faced a forced march of about 80 miles, without air cover or support of any kind. Several of his outposts quickly reported determined Viet Minh probes; Godard led his battalions out at once, not along his earlier approach route but cutting a new trail – a wise decision which took them clear of a major ambush. Even so, 4 and 5 BCL both suffered significant casualties before they reached Muong Sai. The mood of Godard's French and Legion officers and men was reported to be bitter: they had made huge exertions, but had been prevented from coming to the aid of GONO. As for the Laotian troops, they deserted in droves.

The Viet Minh regionals, regulars and political teams throughout the High Region were naturally put on the alert for fugitives. The number of members of GONO who slipped away from Dien Bien Phu in the confusion of 7 May and attempted to make their way towards safety can never be known, since only those who succeeded left any record. In all it is thought that 78 survived to reach French troops; but of these only 19 were European, and the rest were almost entirely Thais, who had the obvious advantages of inconspicuous appearance, local language and knowledge of the terrain. Few European soldiers had any training in jungle survival skills, and without plentiful food, clean water, weapons, maps, compasses (and spare boots) their chances of walking 100 miles through the jungle – even if they evaded their hunters – were slim. Comparison of the stories of the successful escapers suggests that those who kept to the crests and met highland Meos had the best chance of being given food and guidance; those who took the less obviously exhausting choice of sticking to the valleys and watercourses usually encountered Thai villagers who turned them in to the Viet Minh – or simply killed them.

The only officer to get away was Sub-lieutenant Makowiak of the 3rd Thai Battalion, who had long experience of these hills and spoke good Thai. After fighting at Eliane 3 he slipped away to the west into Laos, and on 31 May he met a party of pro-French partisans. Most refugees headed south, hoping to reach Muong Sai (*see Map 8*).

A party of tank crewmen from Isabelle, later joined by a few légionnaires, managed to fight off two Viet Minh patrols on 10 and 13 May; they took casualties, but five reached friendly Meos and rafted down the Nam Pak river to Muong Sai by the end of May – a remarkable achievement for non-infantrymen with no jungle experience.[12]

Sergeants Willer and Ney of the tank squadron at Claudine escaped from a POW column on 14 May; on the 21st they reached a village on the Nam Noua river, where they met a larger party of sappers and Légionnaire Kienitz of 1 BEP. Sergeant Chiefs Ryback and Cablé and Sergeants Jouatel and Le Roy of 31 BG had been held at Dien Bien Phu for a week to lift mines; they thus had a chance to gather useful kit before fleeing on the night of 13/14 May. Together this party headed west, avoiding Thai villagers and being aided by Meos; they made a wide hook through the jungle, and after some 125 miles and many ordeals they were in bad shape when, within two days of Muong Sai, they were spotted by a French helicopter on 3 June. (Sergeant Willer still had his camera with him, with photos taken during the trek.)[13]

Gunner Georges Nallet, who escaped from a POW column on 15 May, also headed west, and on the 24th linked up with four other escapers including the remarkable Sergeant Chief Sentenac of 6 BPC, who were being fed by friendly Meos. This confident paratrooper advised that the party rest for two weeks to get up their strength for a jungle march and let the hue and cry die down a little. Setting off for Muong Sai only on 8 June, they were picked up by a helicopter on 2 July in surprisingly good condition.[14]

Others who took the westward route along the crests into Laos were Sergeant Delobel and Corporal Charrier of GM/35 RALP, who had dropped on 3 April as replacements for II/4 RAC. They started with a third man, but he became so ill that they were obliged to abandon him. Eventually Delobel too became sick, and stayed at a friendly village as Charrier pressed on. He reached a French post, was picked up by helicopter, and later guided his CO Captain Le Gall in a Dakota to identify Delobel's village, where the helicopter soon rescued him.

Two Vietnamese corporals marched neither west nor south, but east for the Red River, straight through 185 miles of enemy territory, and on 10 July they reached a friendly post on the edge of the Delta.[15]

THE NEWS OF THE FALL OF DIEN Bien Phu found the commander-in-chief at Hue, where General Navarre was reckoning up what troops he could take from Land Forces Central Vietnam (FTCV) for transfer to Tonkin (Operation 'Atlante' was suspended for this purpose).[16] The next day, 8 May, he was back in Hanoi to take the salute at the usual VE-Day parade, but it was a sad affair watched by thin crowds. The resident wives and families of members of GONO were frantic for news which nobody could give them.

That morning General Navarre broadcast an unconvincing attempt to spin sad pride into determination. The garrison had been fighting at odds of five to one, and had tied down 30 enemy battalions for five months; their courage and endurance had saved from invasion both Upper Laos and the Delta. Defeat was blamed on Communist China's provision of the 'means for modern warfare new to the theatre of operations'. The garrison of Dien Bien Phu had fulfilled the mission assigned to them, adding a most glorious page to the long history of French arms; they had given the French and Vietnamese forces a new pride and a new reason for fighting – 'The struggle continues.'[17]

Because of the seven-hour time difference the news reached Paris at about noon on 7 May. The National Assembly had been in Easter recess for the whole period from 10 April to 2 May, but immediately after the deputies' return from this lengthy holiday a vote of confidence on 4 May had seen the government's majority plunge. The chamber was packed when, at 4.45pm on the 7th, Prime Minister Laniel rose to announce the fall of Dien Bien Phu. The Archbishop of Paris ordered a solemn mass; television cancelled its evening schedule, and radio entertainment programmes were replaced with solemn classical music such as the Berlioz *Requiem*. Some theatres, cinemas and restaurants closed; the news was the only topic of conversation, and people felt obscurely that they should cancel social engagements as a mark of respect.[18]

At 6.15pm, in Geneva, Foreign Minister Bidault had the excruciating task of rising to address the conference with an acknowledgement of the defeat, under the eyes not only of the world's press but of Pham Van Dong, Chou En Lai of China and Vyacheslav Molotov of the Soviet Union. The USA was represented by Undersecretary Walter Bedell Smith, since John Foster Dulles had flown home. As he neared the close of a speech choked by emotion, Bidault proposed 'that the Conference should, first of all, declare that it adopt the principle of a general cessation of hostilities in Indochina based upon the necessary guarantees of security...' Four days later, on 11 May, the Laniel government survived another challenge by only two votes.[19]

Apparently ignorant that a mood of shocked despair was sweeping France, coupled with anger at the political and military authorities and fear for the fate of the prisoners, General Navarre was still studying his chess board. While the Geneva Conference continued it was his duty to maintain as favourable a military balance as he could. The situation was not irretrievable if everybody kept their heads, and the C-in-C's immediate correspondence with Paris envisaged FTNV being able to stand off Viet Minh attacks on the Delta during June and July by combing out about ten battalions from other fronts. This would mean adopting a static posture throughout the rest of Indochina, and France sending out serious reinforcements to confront the People's Army in the autumn 1954 campaign season. Navarre conceded that the CEFEO might eventually have to give up the southern and north-eastern parts of the Delta in order to concentrate the available forces more densely in the essential areas surrounding the Hanoi/Haiphong corridor. On 15 May Paris instructed him to take no steps towards such an evacuation – orders that were repeated by the new Chief of the Defence Staff, General Ely, when he flew in to Saigon on 18 May.[20]

General Navarre's confidence might appear surprising, but in coldly mathematical terms he had some arguments on his side. In terms of matériel the loss of Dien Bien Phu was not nearly as costly as had been the collapse in October/November 1950. True, the fall of GONO had cost 16$\frac{1}{2}$ parachute and infantry battalions, of which 11 were of high quality, and the equivalent of perhaps another four battalions of support and service troops; and these 15,000 men represented about 3.3 per cent of the numerical strength of the CEFEO and the Associated States' armies. The 'disaster of RC4' had cost some 2.6 per cent of the CEFEO's then manpower of *c.* 182,000; but in October 1950 the People's Army losses had been modest and quickly replaceable at a time of expansion, while at Dien Bien Phu General Giap had burned away perhaps 25,000 of his best regulars, who would now be very hard to replace.[21] The survivors of his Dien Bien Phu divisions were tired out and far from the Delta, and the rainy season still had months to run.

Surprisingly, there were even some successes to show on the ground: on 8 May, too late for Dien Bien Phu, Lieutenant Colonel Trinquier's partisan bands had at last been able to strike real blows against the Viet Minh rear areas whose garrisons had been reduced to caretaker levels by the needs of the siege army. The Meos and Thais of the 'Cardamome' force had actually recaptured the important Chinese border post of Lao Cai; the Thai capital of Lai Chau had also been retaken, and even far to the northeast Cao Bang was under siege by Meo and Man guerrillas.[22]

The balance of forces was thus not impossible to re-establish, if France would repeat the surge of will and resources given to General de Lattre to retrieve the situation in winter 1950/1. Apart from the two parachute battalions already in theatre or arriving within days, plans were in place to send out a new North African Groupe Mobile and three tank squadrons. There had even been discussion of forming three new light divisions for autumn 1954 if the obstacles to sending conscripts to the Far East could be overcome. At the end of May, Navarre did not believe that the Viet Minh could mount an assault on the Delta until perhaps 20 June; they were arriving back in their base areas, but would need weeks to rest and to rebuild their logistics. He did not believe he faced any other immediate threat except in the Central Highlands, where new enemy units had been committed. He conceded, however, that the 'black point' was the morale of the Vietnamese population and the ANV, which was at a 'worryingly low level due to uncertainty over the Geneva Conference and the shock caused by the fall of Dien Bien Phu'.[23]

In fact, of course, for General Navarre to concern himself with these calculations was an exercise in futility: he was not de Lattre, and this was not 1950. Whatever the numerical strength of the CEFEO and ANV on paper, it was absurd to imagine that General Nguyen Van Hinh's nervous conscripts would stand up to an army that had wiped out 11 of the best battalions in Indochina and in the process had virtually destroyed the French airborne reserve; and Dien Bien Phu had also called into question the combat value of the remaining North African units. It was similarly unthinkable that any French government could command the votes to send young conscripts to the Far East. That Dien Bien Phu had been a tactical but not a strategic defeat was lost upon French voters; they were not staff-college graduates, and nor were their politicians.

The capture of a French general and 10,000 of his men was horribly reminiscent of June 1940, and the Frenchman in the street saw this defeat as evidence that the People's Army had achieved a decisive military advantage – indeed, that it was intrinsically superior to the CEFEO. For French voters of most shades of opinion, as for the prisoners in the Viet Minh camps, the torment of hope repeatedly disappointed had indeed worn away the resolve of 'even the firmest characters'. The idea of allowing the generals to set up the chess board for yet another game was simply unbearable, and their politicians understood their mood. The only promise that they dared to offer the electorate was to end it now – the whole wearying, shaming, eight-year outpouring of treasure and lives – and to end it on any terms that they could get.

The nakedness of this collapse of national morale guaranteed that those terms would not be glittering, and that France's moral obligation to the peoples of North Vietnam would be discarded with humiliating speed. During June the formal proceedings of the Geneva Conference dragged on without any immediate signs of progress; but behind the scenes conversations had been taking place between the military members of the French delegation and their Viet Minh counterparts since 19 May.[24]

ON 4 JUNE 1954, LIEUTENANT General Henri Navarre was relieved of his command of the Indochina theatre. Both he and Commissioner-

General Maurice Dejean were replaced with effect from 8 June by General Paul Ely, who had been in the country for two weeks. Although he had proconsular powers there was nothing of de Lattre about General Ely, an obedient instrument of the will of Paris (and for once that will was discernible). Ely's military deputy was none other than *'le Chinois'* – Navarre's predecessor General Raoul Salan, whose next meeting with Navarre must have been one of the more embarrassing of the latter's career.

Despite Paris' hesitation two weeks previously over the idea of evacuating part of the Delta, almost General Salan's first move was to order General Cogny to make preparations to do just that. This appears to have been an entirely political decision: there were no signs of offensive moves by General Giap's regulars; and the Delta's internal security situation, chaotic as ever, did not display any critical new signs of *pourrissement* in the southern zone.[25]

On 15 June the zone commander, Colonel Vanuxem, received top-secret orders to prepare for Operation 'Auvergne': the abandonment of the southern part of the Delta below a line roughly from Hung Yen to Ninh Giang and on to the coast south of the Thai Binh river (*see Map 5*). This area – well over one-third of the Delta – included the towns of Phu Ly, Nam Dinh, Thai Binh, Ninh Binh, and the loyal Roman Catholic regions around Phat Diem and Bui Chu. Vanuxem already had about 7,000 French and North African troops and 32,000 Vietnamese, including the Moroccan GM 8, an armoured and an amphibious group, and plentiful artillery. To help cover his withdrawal he would be given GM 4 (whose backbone was II/13 DBLE, now the only surviving battalion of this famous Legion regiment), more tanks, artillery and engineers, and a large air, road and river transport fleet.[26] Facing him across the indistinct southern reach of the De Lattre Line were People's Army Division 320, a regiment from 325, two independent regiments, and regionals to the equivalent of 14 battalions – a force potentially capable of turning a withdrawal into a bloody rout, which might rip all the way up to the vital road and rail links between Hanoi and Haiphong.

Colonel Vanuxem was ordered to prepare for launching 'Auvergne' on 1 July. To prevent a complete collapse of ANV morale and chaos among the population these preparations had to be made with great speed but complete secrecy. Extraordinary precautions were taken, using the pretext that the region was to be transferred to ANV control and that French units were simply concentrating at fewer points further north. There was much strengthening of roads and bridges; river and air transport began evacuating families and non-essential personnel, and by 30 June Colonel Vanuxem's troops had already successfully transferred 32,000 people and 11,000 tons of stores and equipment. The Viet Minh showed no signs of suspicion until 27 June, when Vanuxem named the 28th as D-Day for 'Auvergne'.

During the next six days the zone commander carried out a masterly fighting withdrawal planned on the principle of several different 'collapsing bags', extricating his men not only up RC1 and RP10 towards Hanoi and Haiphong but by boat down the rivers to the coast. He manoeuvred his units at high speed, alternating retreats with fierce counter-attacks by armour, artillery and aircraft to keep the pursuing People's Army off his back. On 30 June, Phat Diem was evacuated by river; now every movement order started a new race against the Viet Minh, with Vanuxem juggling timetables and battalions at short notice. On the evening of 1 July the consolidated units from Nam Dinh, Thai Binh and Bui Chu boarded landing craft that would take them down the Red River. On the 3rd, six converging battalions of People's Army regulars threatened Phu Ly on RC1; Vanuxem fought a brisk counter-attack battle on three fronts simultaneously, with complete success. The last road columns fought their way through a succession of villages deserted by all but the Viet Minh, and it was all over by the night of 3/4 July. Colonel Vanuxem had evacuated 68,000 military and (carefully selected) civilians, for a loss of 38 dead, 129 wounded and 26 missing, and had saved 97 per cent of the matériel.[27]

This withdrawal through guerrilla territory, pursued by enemy regular forces, was an extremely difficult and dangerous enterprise, haunted by the constant risk of units becoming cut off and dragging would-be rescuers to disaster. Colonel Vanuxem had proved that the CEFEO were still perfectly capable of successfully conducting classic operations in terrain where they had elbow room to manoeuvre and make use of their firepower. But although 'Auvergne' was a tactical masterpiece it was still a retreat – not even by a defeated army, but by a defeated government, deserting most of the civilian population as it pulled back to the ports from which it would soon sail away.

That government was not the administration of Joseph Laniel, which had finally been despatched by the National Assembly on 12 June; but its successor was defeated nonetheless, since its first pronouncement had been to declare its own helplessness. On 17–18 June the cabinet of Pierre Mendès-France took office, and the new prime minister immediately made a public pledge that he would resign if he had not achieved a ceasefire in Indochina within one month, by 20 July. This pronouncement hardly assisted French diplomats at Geneva in wringing concessions from Pham Van Dong's delegation.[28]

In conducting these negotiations the French were in any case handicapped by an imbalance between each side's knowledge of the true strengths and weaknesses of the other's positions. The factions and divisions of opinion within the conspiratorial world of French politics were transparent. But the French intelligence agencies, though historically successful in discovering the strength, movements and short-term intentions of the People's Army, could not provide insights about the Viet Minh national leadership – the policy differences at the highest level, the compromises that individual leaders might tolerate, or the intimacies and stresses of the relationships with China and the USSR. It was a poker game which the French played with their cards face up and their few chips showing, while their opponent kept his under the table.[29]

WHILE COLONEL VANUXEM had been demonstrating the CEFEO's strengths in the Delta, a very different lesson was being repeated down in the Central Highlands of Annam (*see Map 1*). In this sinister wilderness the significant units were limited to Groupe Mobile 100 at An Khe, and the Vietnamese GM 42 at Pleiku and GM 41 at Ban Me Thuot. Since they had responded to Operation 'Atlante' by taking the offensive in these hills in February the excellent local Viet Minh units had enjoyed the initiative, carrying out a traditional hit-and-run campaign at separated points along the meagre road network to lure the French into repeated ambushes. They had a total strength of about ten battalions plus ten regional companies, built around Regiments 108 and 803, but no artillery or heavy mortars.

An Khe on the eastern slope of the Highlands had been cut off from Pleiku, about 55 miles to the west, for several weeks; but the 'air bridge' functioned well, and the town was not closely invested by the enemy.

Nevertheless, in the aftermath of Dien Bien Phu it was decided to evacuate the garrison to Pleiku, despite the objections voiced by the local commander General de Beaufort.[30] Operation 'Eglantine' would involve two forces, Group East and Group West; the former was the An Khe garrison, which would move west along RC19, while the latter moved east along the same road from Pleiku to meet it at the Man Yang Pass, the joint force then returning to Pleiku.

The withdrawing Group East consisted of Colonel Barrou's GM 100, the Vietnamese light infantry unit TDKQ 520, and irregular scouts. Although much harried over the past five months this motorized brigade had a fine reputation; its infantry were the two-battalion Régiment de Corée – the former French UN battalion from the Korean War, expanded by local recruitment – and BM/43 RIC, a good unit enlisted mainly from ethnic Khmers from western Cochinchina. Coming to meet them in Lieutenant Colonel Sockeel's Group West were GM 42, built on three *montagnard* battalions recruited among Rhadés from around Ban Me Thuot; each brigade had the usual 105mm artillery battalion and a few Stuart tanks from the 5th Cuirassiers.[31] Group West also had a small airborne brigade: GAP 1, commanded by Lieutenant Colonel Romain-Defossés, with 7 BPC (Major Balbin) and 3 BPVN (Major Mollo).

The airlift of equipment and non-combatants and other obvious preparations warned the Viet Minh of the imminent departure from An Khe, and their Regiments 108 and 803 gathered along RC19; in particular, a strong ambush was set up over nearly two miles around Kilometre 15. French intelligence reports of movement caused the evacuation to be brought forward by one day to 24 June, and GM 100 began leaving the town at 3am that morning. The large column travelled in four separate convoys, the first two only ten minutes apart but the third and fourth each half an hour behind the one in front – the rearguard was delayed by harassing attacks from the moment it started out.

At 2pm the first elements reached Kilometre 15, where the road wound through an expanse of tall elephant grass; and here BM/43 RIC, some of the artillery, TDKQ 520 and Colonel Barrou's mobile HQ were ambushed in great strength. Many vehicles were set ablaze by mortars and bazookas, blocking the advance of the Régiment de Corée. The fighting became general, and at 3.15pm the order was passed to leave the road. Only darkness brought a lull in the Viet Minh attacks, and in small groups the survivors were able to make their way south, then west to Kilometre 22 during that night and 25 June. The wounded (including Colonel Barrou) had to be abandoned on the road with volunteer medics; casualties were reckoned at about 35 per cent of the men, most of the vehicles and all the artillery and heavy equipment.

Group West had already placed an advance battalion at Kilometre 22; Lieutenant Colonels Sockeel and Romain-Defossés decided to create a defended reception zone here for GM 100, leaving a small force behind them to hold the Man Yang Pass about five miles to the north-west. The last of the survivors of GM 100 who had evaded or shot their way through the enemy pursuit reached the paratroopers by nightfall on 25 June; the joint force then returned to the pass, fighting their way through repeated ambushes. With Man Yang Pass occupied and air resupply drops received, the joint column resumed the march west towards Pleiku early on the 27th. The wooded terrain made it almost impossible to leave RC19, but infantry were sent ahead to picket the most threatening heights, and the column had the cover of four Morane spotters with plentiful combat aircraft on call.

On the morning of the 27th a Morane reported solid ambushes and roadblocks ahead of them at two points. The column lost about another 80 men while fighting their way through with air support, and reached Dak Ryunh that night. The paratroopers pushed on another six miles after dark to seize in advance an important crossroads, which they held by dawn. At about midday on the 28th the bulk of the column were about halfway between the night's stop and GAP 1's position when they were very heavily attacked along more than a mile of road. For an hour and a half infantry, tanks, artillery and aircraft were all engaged in repeated actions. Progress was maintained by engineer vehicles pushing blazing trucks off the road, and at about 1.30pm the Viet Minh suddenly fell back. Pushing on to join up with GAP 1, the column reached a camp east of Pleiku that night. The three infantry battalions of GM 100 had been reduced to between 350 and 500 men each; vehicle losses were 85 per cent, and all the artillery had been abandoned.[32]

The ordeal of the battered Régiment de Corée was not over. Despite the shocking destruction of GM 100 as a mobile force, a couple of weeks later zone HQ at Nha Trang ordered Operation 'Myosotis' ('Forget-me-not') against Viet Minh units which had infiltrated along RC14 between Pleiku and Ban Me Thuot. Lieutenant Colonel Sockeel was unconvinced that anything could be achieved by yet another road column through rugged terrain, but on 12 July he led his GM 42 south from Pleiku as ordered. He had the remnant of I/Corée (about two and a half companies) as well as his *montagnards*, but no supporting paratroopers and very little air cover. At dawn on 17 July they left Ea Long and pushed south down RC14 into the Chu Dreh hills. The *montagnard* infantry got through the dangerous Chu Dreh Pass without trouble, while I/Corée and the artillery formed the rearguard; but at 10.50am, after leaving the southern end of the pass, 8th Montagnard Battalion (8 BM) and the brigade HQ group were attacked by a Viet Minh battalion.

Half an hour's fighting, supported by artillery fire from the rearguard and by a few fighter-bombers, drove the enemy off; but this bought time for the People's Army to bring up two more battalions. The aircraft had to leave the convoy in order to refuel, so there were no Moranes overhead at 12.15pm when the bulk of the column were emerging from the southern end of the pass. They were struck by a massive ambush including heavy bazooka, mortar and RCL fire; dozens of vehicles were destroyed, and two companies of 8 BM and 4th Company of I/Corée were butchered in the pass itself. North of the chokepoint I/Corée's HQ and 1st Companies tried to fight their way back northwards by leap-frogging bounds. All their radios were knocked out; at the south end of the pass most of GM 42 were holding out thanks to the belated arrival of air support, but were ignorant of I/Corée's plight. Eventually tanks of the 5th Cuirassiers turned back to help them, and took heavy losses.

When I/Corée finally got back to Ea Long the battalion numbered 54 able-bodied men and 53 hospital cases. The destruction of this fine unit over the past three weeks might stand for that of the whole Expeditionary Corps in microcosm, whenever it ventured outside the Delta.[33]

UNSURPRISINGLY, THE VIET MINH delegation at Geneva dragged the French right up to the final moment of their self-imposed deadline, but the armistice which ended the French Indochina War was effectively agreed on 20 July. Various formal instruments were signed over the following week, and a general ceasefire came into effect in most parts of Indochina on 27 July 1954.

The terms agreed at Geneva were shocking to many, both French and North Vietnamese; the Bao Dai government reacted with fury, but was largely ignored. In stark terms, a military armistice would be followed by a temporary partition of the country at the 17th parallel just north of Quang Tri, flanked by a 'demilitarized zone'. The French would withdraw from the North, leaving Hanoi on 9 October, and the Viet Minh from the South. For 300 days – until 18 May 1955 – free movement of the populations between North and South would be allowed. Partition would last only until July 1956, when countrywide elections would be held to decide the political future of Vietnam; until then, the CEFEO would continue to protect South Vietnam. The fulfilment of these Geneva accords would be supervised by an International Control Commmission provided by neutral states.

A vital clause for the French had always been that governing the exchange of prisoners of war. In Tonkin the release of some 11,000 French POWs began at Viet Tri on 18 August and continued until October. The Viet Minh extracted as much propaganda value from the occasion as they could. Some prisoners had been given new blue overalls and cheap pith helmets to replace their rags. They were clapped along the path to the hand-over point between ranks of People's Army troops, under banners proclaiming international friendship, while white-aproned Viet Minh nurses (the first the POWs had ever seen) smiled demurely. Some of these gaunt, hollow-eyed spectres were even told to shake hands with the commissars for the cameras, but the paratroopers looked straight ahead and ignored the out-thrust hands. Lieutenant Colonel Bigeard stalked to freedom with the proud red beret characteristically tipped far over his left ear like a tile. When the haggard General de Castries was handed over to sailors of the riverine unit *Dinassaut 12* on 31 August he asked Commander Bourdais, 'Is it true that they want to shoot me?'[34]

From the first, the French reception parties were shocked by the physical condition of many of the returning prisoners, and not just of that pitiful handful who had survived four years in captivity since being captured on RC4. Many men who had been in Viet Minh hands only since Dien Bien Phu in May bore a terrible resemblance to the photographs from

Buchenwald or Changi Jail in 1945. Of the 61 returned prisoners who died within three months of their release, 49 had been captured at Dien Bien Phu. The authorities chose not to make any public protest for fear of the Viet Minh holding back prisoners not yet released; and when the hand-overs trickled to a close with thousands of French names remaining unaccounted for, the French government was still unwilling to place any difficulties in the way of the smooth working of the agreement. It was from the released prisoners themselves that the CEFEO discovered what had happened to the 9,000 French soldiers who had been herded out of the valley of the Nam Youm on the evening of 7 May.[35]

THE PRISONERS WERE PUT ON the road for the camps over a number of days. Their captors were keen to get them as far as possible from the chance of French rescue, and some were sent off immediately; others – mostly specialists such as engineers – were held back for a week or more to maintain the camp's machinery or to lift mines. On 14 May a number of POWs were returned to the valley in order to take part in reconstructed scenes of the 'fall of Dien Bien Phu' staged for the cameras. These were mostly North Africans, some of them given camouflage fatigues to imper-sonate paratroopers; when Bigeard was told to play-act his surrender, coming out of the CP with his hands up, he is said to have replied curtly, 'I'd rather die.' The resulting film footage and stills have been widely cir-culated ever since, but to the informed eye their lack of authenticity is usually obvious; the cameramen were particularly careless about the back-grounds to supposed 'battle scenes', and it takes some practice even to act a corpse convincingly. At one point fairly early in the journey to the camps thousands of the POWs were also made to march for many hours in broad columns past a dais erected for Communist cameramen and journalists; the pictures survive, but various memoirs give widely differing dates and places for the event.[36]

The destinations of the march for various batches of POWs were either a belt of camps along the lower Song river in Thanh Hoa province, about 300 miles to the south-east by road; or the larger concentration in Bac Kan province of the Viet Bac north of Tuyen Quang, up to 450 miles away. Once begun, the march was undertaken in stages of about 12 miles a day, and the journey took the prisoners anything between one and two months.

They were stripped of all their possessions, and some did not even have shoes. Before they started marching all the combat troops were exhausted by an eight-week battle on short rations and little sleep, and during the journey their health deteriorated sharply. Many suffered from malaria and other tropical illnesses, and since they nearly always received unboiled water amoebic dysentery became commonplace; this caused dangerous dehydration, muscular weakness and startling weight loss. Ulcerated sores, blisters and skin diseases made walking a torture for many.

The food was an unrelieved diet of husked rice, which working parties of prisoners had to collect in bulk sacks, often from long distances, at the end of each day's march. This lacked many essential nutrients, and was insufficient to keep up the strength of men unused to such a diet.[37] It was supplemented only on very rare occasions even by salt. One account mentions an issue of ten peanuts every tenth day; Dr Rondy of 1 BEP recalled receiving half a banana on one occasion, and on another day two sardine-sized fish heads discarded after the guards' meal, during a march of six weeks.[38]

Roughly one in three of the POWs were wounded or diseased to some extent, and their injuries ranged from healing minor flesh wounds, through amputations, to serious head, thoracic and abdominal wounds (none of these cases would survive). Carrying a stretcher required two relays of four men each; unless a casualty was accompanied by his own close comrades men were not always willing to weaken themselves in this way, and numbers of wounded were simply left to stagger along as best they could. The captured doctors were kept with the other officers and not allowed to give even minimal care to the French wounded. The limit of the care provided by the Viet Minh was occasional washing, and very occasionally a little thin tea; the reason given for witholding nutritious food and drugs from the wounded was French air raids. Memoirs of the march include many hideous instances of suffering – a man dying of gangrene because the wire bonds round his wrists were never loosened, a double amputee trying to keep up with the column on his hands and stumps, a soldier cutting off his own gangrenous arm with a pocket knife. Not everyone behaved well; there are stories of inspiring fortitude and unselfishness, but others of great callousness. From the first days the Viet Minh commissars accompanying the column made every effort to play off the prisoners against one another and to destroy any group loyalties, encouraging a culture of every man for himself.

Wounded, sick or merely exhausted soldiers who lost the will to live dropped out of the column and were simply left to die. Their friends were not allowed to bury those who perished on the march; the guards prodded them back into line at gunpoint to shuffle on, leaving what had been a comrade for the rats and ants. One who died beside the track was the 20-year-old Navy Hellcat pilot, Petty Officer 'Baby' Robert; it was noted that men in their 30s and 40s often held up better than the youngsters. Another who died, on 21 July, was Captain Yves Hervouët of the tank squadron.[39]

Actual beatings were not usual, except in the case of would-be escapers who were recaptured (as most were). The columns were not guarded in great strength and it was not impossible to pick a moment to slip away into the undergrowth. However, for a weakened man without stored food, a weapon or even a water canteen the jungle was a deadly place; most of these fugitives soon ran foul of enemy patrols or allowed starvation to lure them into approaching hostile villagers. The photographers Jean Péraud and Pierre Schoendoerffer were being driven after dark in a truck full of officers, their hands tied behind their backs, when they managed to cut their bonds with an overlooked pocket knife. At a bend in the road near the Black River crossing at Ta Khoa they jumped, but a wall of bamboo stopped them getting out of sight before the next truck's headlights swung round the corner. Schoendoerffer was recaptured and beaten unconscious; Jean Péraud got away, but was never seen again.[40]

Several paratroopers made stubbornly repeated attempts; one who reckoned he had a good reason to try was Sergeant Kemencei of 2 BEP. In 1950, after being captured on RC4 with the 1st Foreign, he had been among the few seriously wounded men to be handed back, but only after signing a parole that he would not take up arms again. In May 1954 he was worried about being recognized or investigated, so he gave a false name and took every opportunity to escape. The first time he was caught he was simply pushed back into the column with his hands tied; the second time he was badly beaten with rifle butts, but was actually relieved that this made his face unrecognizable. Other recidivist escapers, such as Komencei's comrade Sergeant Szegedi, were punished by having their boots confiscated – he never received footwear again during the whole of his captivity. Sergeant Chief Flamen of 6 BPC also escaped twice, and on the second occasion headed east and got all the way to the southern edge of the Delta before being recaptured. Robert Mallet, an NCO of 2 BEP, made three attempts; on the last occasion he was rescued by a People's Army patrol from villagers who were about to hack him to death, and reckoned that he got off lightly with a beating and a spell tied up in a bamboo cage.[41]

THOSE WHO SURVIVED TO reach the camps soon found themselves in an environment just as lethal as, but subtly different from, the Japanese camps of World War II. The death rate from disease was comparable with that suffered in the camps of the infamous Burma Railway, but the sadistic cruelty of their guards was absent. Unlike the Japanese, the Viet Minh did not hold POWs in racial hatred or in contempt for allowing themselves to be captured, and only a minority seemed to take pleasure from inflicting fear and pain. Instead there was an unnerving contrast between their earnest determination to engage with their prisoners at an ideological level, and their utter disregard for the value of individual lives.

The first camps had been set up in late 1950 after the RC4 victory brought the People's Army prisoners in large numbers for the first time. Physically they resembled villages of flimsy native huts, without barbed wire or guard towers; their remoteness, their hill and jungle setting, and the hostility of the surrounding population were walls enough. Most Dien Bien Phu prisoners were not given even the most basic equipment – only the officers' Camp No. 1 was provided with pots to boil water. Before they learned for themselves how to improvise with bamboo and banana leaves men had to drink water directly from streams, and as a result the death rate from water-borne intestinal diseases was extremely high. Weak from their long march and the rice diet, and made to carry out daily physical labour, the prisoners succumbed in large numbers during the few months of their captivity – malaria and amoebic dysentery were the routine killers, but typhus, bronchitis and pneumonia, beri-beri, oedemas, and leptospirosis (from rats' urine in unwashed rice) also took their share, singly or in combination.

Prisoners were all regarded as having the same status, healthy or sick, and if they did not work then they received no rations. These were the usual two *cai bat* of rice, with a little salt every second day. An inmate of the officers' camp recalled one good meal, immediately after he arrived – warm rice with a little pork fat; thereafter, on occasional Communist holidays they also received perhaps 18lbs of buffalo or monkey meat between 400 men (less than an ounce each); or 11lbs of lentils or one live chicken between 50 men. Rations were routinely withheld for disciplinary reasons.

A man who fell sick and could not take his place in the timber party got no food; without food he quickly became weaker still. For a while a friend might work a double shift to draw rations for him, but he soon lost his appetite for the endless rice anyway. A cold highland night would chill him on his pad of branches on the floor, or he might have to stagger to the latrine trench in the rain; he would catch a fever and, reduced to half his body weight, he would go out like a light. At morning roll-call his body had to be carried out by the living so that all could be counted together; then his comrades' first fatigue of the day would be to bury him. Under the monsoon rain the little mound, marked only by a sliver of bamboo with his name in indelible pencil, would soon dissolve into invisibility.[42] Among the paratroop officers named in this text who died in captivity was the heroic Sub-lieutenant Boisbouvier of the 1st Foreign.

Each camp had an 'infirmary' – a hut where the obviously dying were dumped to end their journey, staffed by a French orderly of uncertain training who might have a lancet and a tiny and irregular supply of quinine tablets. (All the French doctors were sent to Camp No. 1 with the other officers.) The Viet Minh set up a few rudimentary field hospitals near clusters of POW camps in January 1954, and there was reportedly a Hospital Camp No. 128 staffed by captured Frenchmen; but few prisoners were ever transferred from their own camps in time to reach these alive, and surgical care was virtually unknown. Of the roughly 11,000 POWs from all periods released in autumn 1954, it was found that only 81 had received any surgical intervention during their captivity, and 38 of these without anaesthetic. It must be remembered that a proportion of the POWs arrived in the camps with major battle trauma that had been completely neglected for months, with the most pitiable, even grotesque consequences.[43]

The inevitable outcome of this regime of privation and neglect may be summarized by a few examples from both before and after Dien Bien Phu. In March–September 1952, Camp No. 5E had lost 201 dead from 272 inmates; in June–December 1953, Camp No. 123 had lost 350 of about 700 prisoners. In the four months following his arrival from Dien Bien Phu, Robert Mallet of 2 BEP reckoned that half of his intake to Camp No. 73 died; and over the same period in Disciplinary Camp No. 42, Erwan Bergot counted 244 deaths among the 327 men who had survived the march.[44]

FROM THE FIRST DAYS OF THE march deliberate efforts were made to break down the psychological solidarity of the POWs, by separating them from their leaders and degrading them in their own eyes. This softening-up was the first stage in their 're-education', by stripping them of their inner certainties and sources of self-respect. It was accompanied by an open and constantly repeated threat: they were all war criminals who deserved to be shot, and their lives hung on the thread of Uncle Ho's great mercy, which might be broken at any moment by the slightest sign of defiance. (In a number of cases it was: while death sentences handed down by tribunals were not normally carried out but kept hanging over prisoners' heads, repeated escape attempts or other acts of resistance could bring transfer to the punishment camp at Lang Trang, from which none returned.) The prisoners were well aware that their ordeal was completely open ended: they had no recourse to the protections of the Geneva Convention, and no guarantee that they would ever be released – only a fragile hope, which their captors manipulated ruthlessly.

The process of 'brainwashing' was an ideological assault on a man's identity for the purpose of enlisting him in the Marxist–Leninist cause – to serve it not here in Indochina, but after he was released. He was told that his hope of that release depended entirely upon his progress and sincerity in putting off the 'old man' he had been – a blind mercenary of colonialism and a tool of international capitalism – and embracing his new identity as enlightened proletarian man. Uncle Ho was going to give him this chance to transform himself because, in his infinite clemency, he understood that even a wretched war criminal was merely the cynically manipulated creature of the imperialists. It was generally believed by its practitioners that this process of renewal took six months for common soldiers, 18 months for NCOs, but several years for officers. One of these last who wrote an account of the first four months of this procedure was Dr Rondy of 1st Foreign Parachute Battalion.[45]

The first or softening-up stage continued with the POWs' arrival at the camp. At the officers' camp on 21 June, Dr Rondy's intake were given a better meal than usual, and then addressed by the senior commissar: 'You are here for an indeterminate period, to be re-educated by work. You will live the life of those you have oppressed; you will suffer like them, and come to understand them. We will guide you on your search for the truth, and we hope you find it. We will let you go when you have put off the old man and abandoned your capitalist and colonialist prejudices.'

Each day began with a gong at dawn, morning roll-call, and the burial of the most recent dead. Then the labour parties were sent out for several miles to gather timber. After they returned the officers ate their meal, and were allowed to rest. Occasionally reading matter was distributed, limited to Communist publications (the airmail edition of *L'Humanité* was prized as a source of cigarette and toilet paper), and carefully slanted news bulletins were issued. In the afternoon the teams of commissars resumed their work; apart from endlessly repeated mass propaganda lectures the officer prisoners were instructed on an individual basis, by men of some education who were sometimes even familiar with their individual military records.

Dr Rondy called the second stage 'the catechism'. The subject was repeatedly led through an analysis of the errors and crimes of his class, which proceeded from obvious truths, through half-truths, to more or less subtle non-sequiturs, and finally to rigid Communist dogma. He could not merely listen dumbly, preserving his mental defences: he had to respond to questions, and his answers were noted, to be twisted into arguments against his resistance to admissions during future interviews. In his answers the subject had to copy the interrogator's use of the language of Marxist–Leninist dialectic; once accustomed to repeating these turgid phrases parrot-fashion, he was then treated as if he really meant them, and any contradictions led to a maddeningly patient repetition of the lesson. The aim was to make the prisoner admit the guilt of his nation and class, his own guilt, and thus by logical extension that of his comrades in the camp.

The third stage was compromise, which was again a matter of small increments. Whenever a man gave way over a minor point out of exasperation or fear, it was easier for his interrogator to force a further concession by apparently logical argument. The fear was soundly based – not of beating, but of deprivation of food, or of medicine for the sick. The commissars played on their captives' hunger and weakness by repeatedly granting or withholding small rewards. These might be directly linked to the prisoners' co-operation, but were sometimes random in order to instil uncertainty: after a few days of better food or easier work details, all the prisoners would suddenly be put on punishment regime – supposedly in reprisal for some crime committed by a prisoner in another camp.

It was during this third phase that the emphasis on group learning and group discipline – 'camp solidarity' – became the major theme. If a man had really understood and repented his crimes he must take part in public self-criticism, so that everyone could help him correct his past mistakes and watch for any backsliding in future. Refusal or even passivity was an offence against camp solidarity, for which all must suffer; and to bring punishment to an end proof of sincerity was needed – say, the denunciation of other prisoners. At a certain stage prisoners were asked to sign some anodyne letter, appealing for peace or thanking Uncle Ho for his 'haute clémence'; and when they had compromised once, they could be pressured into signing ever more political confessions and petitions. Hanging over the language of political theory was the very practical and immediate threat of deprivations that meant life or death to the sick.

After their release few prisoners wished to remember the humiliations and small betrayals of their months in the camps, let alone the ghosts of their dead; but the relative brevity of their ordeal seems to have saved the French officers of GONO from long-term psychological effects specifically linked to the brainwashing process. A number of those unfortunates who had been in enemy hands for four years before release in 1954 did suffer badly, their mental trauma presenting in ways which have become familiar since the end of the American war in Vietnam.

In the camps for enlisted ranks the process seems to have been more collective and less subtle. Mass propaganda lectures were the norm, in language supposedly adapted to the men's educational level. The hope of repatriation was held out, with selection to be made on the criteria of work performance as well as political receptiveness. In Disciplinary Camp No. 42 an East German lectured German-speaking légionnaires for two hours at the beginning of each morning. He got their attention by offering

– in return for their learning their lessons well – the chance of direct repatriation to their countries of origin, now behind the Iron Curtain. A fairly large number were indeed sent home from the camps in this way – perhaps as many as a thousand – though to what kind of reception is unclear.[46]

Robert Mallet, in Camp No. 73, found the political lectures very naive. Some of the commissars were completely ignorant of life in the West and knew no European language but French, which allowed POWs to play various dangerous but satisfying games. Some introduced solemn-sounding nonsense into their self-criticism sessions, for the amusement of their fellow prisoners; and when urged to sing revolutionary songs the légionnaires substituted ribald army lyrics in various languages. (Interestingly, Mallet reported that some of the interminable political assemblies were also attended by local villagers.)

So convinced were some commissars of their success in indoctrinating their captives that after the ceasefire announcement in late July some officer prisoners were warned not to mix with released enlisted ranks, whose new political enlightenment might prompt spontaneous attacks on their former oppressors. A handful of POWs are rumoured to have made full defections (as also occurred in Korea and the American Vietnam War), but in their great majority paratroopers, légionnaires and other French regulars from Dien Bien Phu seem to have been entirely insincere in any shows of conversion. Reportedly, a significant number of the better educated among the North African prisoners were more receptive. As Muslims they were not susceptible to Communist dogma; but the simple appeal to nationalism – 'Why do you fight for the French in our country, instead of fighting against them at home and getting your own country back?' – was unanswerable. A number of Dien Bien Phu veterans, including some officers and senior NCOs, would soon be valuable recruits to the Algerian National Liberation Army.[47]

SINCE THE NUMBER OF MEN captured during the battle and at the fall of Dien Bien Phu was never recorded, and there is no way of allocating between the dead and the prisoners the 1,600 listed as missing, the number of those who died in captivity can only be guesswork. There is only one relatively firm figure: a French representative on the International Control Commission estimated in March 1955 that the number of prisoners from the Dien Bien Phu garrison handed back by the Viet Minh was 3,900, or some 43 per cent of the prisoners taken from the valley.[48]

The number of direct repatriations of captured légionnaires to Communist countries of origin is unknown although, as mentioned above, a figure as high as 1,000 has been claimed. Even if we accept and subtract that figure, it is clear that at least 4,100 men died or disappeared in captivity. The darkest interpretation would therefore suggest that of the men who served in French uniform in the valley of the Nam Youm in spring 1954, no more than four out of every ten ever went home, wounded or unwounded. On the face of it, a death ratio of 60 per cent is a statistic to rival the very worst battles of the 20th century.[49] Behind these figures hide others, however, which may point to a rather less or an even more ominous conclusion, and it is most improbable that we shall ever know which. These are the breakdowns by race.

An estimate of the ethnic composition of the garrison gives the following numbers for the initial strength and the parachuted reinforcements combined; they total 15,105 – convincingly close to the 15,090 cited above. As always, the bare figures raise some questions, but the overall picture is still useful:[50]

French mainland	2,810 (18.6 per cent of GONO)
Foreign Legion	3,931 (26 per cent)
North African	2,637 (17.5 per cent)
West African	247 (1.6 per cent)
Vietnamese (regular)	4,052 (26.8 per cent)
Vietnamese (auxiliary)	1,428 (9.5 per cent)

As far as the present author is aware, no ethnic breakdown of the roughly 3,900 Dien Bien Phu prisoners who returned from captivity has been published. But such analyses have been made of the totals of CEFEO prisoners taken during the whole war who were handed back after the 1954 ceasefire; the following figures and rounded-off percentages include as 'Vietnamese' only regular soldiers on the strength of CEFEO or Associated States units:[51]

Total POWs, 1946–54:   36,979

Of which:

Non-Vietnamese	21,220
Vietnamese	15,759
Total repatriated	10,754 (29 per cent of all POWs)
Total unaccounted for	26,225 (71 per cent of all POWs)

Of POWs unaccounted for:

Non-Vietnamese	11,901 (56 per cent of non-VN POWs)
Vietnamese	14,324 (91 per cent of VN POWs)

It is hard to think of any reason why the proportion of Vietnamese prisoners released after capture at Dien Bien Phu should have been any higher than this general figure of 9 per cent for the war as a whole. The fate of perhaps 2,250 of these 'puppet' troops from Dien Bien Phu therefore remains open to uneasy speculation. How many of them were eventually released after 're-education', and how many died in the hands of the Viet Minh? They were, after all, regarded as traitors; and even General Giap would admit that the years immediately following partition were marked by atrocities.

DURING THE GENEVA CONFERENCE, France's willingness to abdicate control over the future of Vietnam was already apparent; but it was not shared by the US State Department, whose policy was support for an independent, non-Communist regime. The problem was to identify credible leaders for such a government amid the factional chaos that naturally reigned following Mendès-France's declaration of intent. Since the beginning of April, Bao Dai's usefulness even as a figurehead had been reduced by his absence; he was relaxing at one of his properties in the South of France, and showed no inclination to share his country's trauma from any closer range. On 14 May Secretary John Foster Dulles sent his Geneva delegation instructions that if their urging failed to persuade Bao Dai to return, he must be made aware that US policy towards his regime would be re-examined. Six days later a CIA National Intelligence Estimate from Saigon reported that in Bao Dai's absence extreme factionalism was tearing the regime apart; the Vietnamese government was virtually paralysed, and might easily disintegrate altogether during June.[52]

Under US pressure Bao Dai now appointed a new prime minister: Ngo Dinh Diem, a portly 52-year-old with a detached and scholarly air. This devoutly Roman Catholic politician had previously held a ministerial portfolio, but was strongly identified with anti-Bao Dai circles and had spent two years in prudent exile in the USA in 1950–2. During this period he had made important contacts, and to some eyes he was a plausible helmsman for an anti-Communist Vietnam. On 26 June he arrived in Saigon, where a team led by the CIA's legendary Colonel Edward Lansdale were waiting to assist him. Lansdale had arrived on 1 June, ostensibly as assistant air attaché, but with a reputation for buccaneering operations in the Philippines as an aide to President Magsaysay during a Communist uprising. He would head a group with the cover title of Saigon Military Mission (SMM), which was regarded with some suspicion by both the US Embassy and MAAG, but which had the blessing of both Secretary Dulles and his brother Allen at the head of the CIA.[53]

While the Geneva negotiations dragged on, Lansdale's mission was to help establish a viable Vietnamese national government; his methods would be propaganda, psychological warfare, and the organization of para-military groups for 'unconventional' clandestine operations, in co-operation with elements of the Vietnamese National Army but not with the French. The USA was not a signatory of the Geneva accords at the end of July, but gave its reluctant approval, and let it be known that any renewal of Communist aggression would be regarded 'with grave concern' as a 'serious threat to world peace'. After the partition of the country was announced the emphasis of the SMM's operations shifted to encouraging and assisting the emigration from the North to the South of as large a number of refugees as possible, coupled with implanting 'stay-behind' paramilitary groups in Tonkin, where some sabotage was carried out before the French with-drawal in October 1954. While this mission was pursued in Hanoi a second team also remained at work in the South.[54]

During the months of August and September 1954 unprecedented but wholly predictable chaos gripped both North and South. The French had foreseen perhaps 30,000 refugees from Tonkin before partition, but these were soon registering in their hundreds of thousands. Fear of the future under a Communist regime was encouraged by the SMM's propaganda, some of it distinctly 'black' (though the future would in fact confirm its accuracy). Whole populations from the Roman Catholic provinces decamped for the South led by their priests and bishops. The French transport facilities were completely overwhelmed, but Colonel Lansdale – jubilant at the propaganda value of this spectacle of anti-Communists voting with their feet – helped organize US Navy shipping to carry the throngs of pitiable refugees south from Haiphong. He also secured a contract on 18 August for CAT to airlift a proportion of them; Operation 'Cognac' would see 12 Curtiss C-46s with CAT crews fly some 20,000 refugees south between 22 August and 4 October. The precise numbers who fled were unrecordable; there were at least 680,000, and the figure of 1 million has been claimed. There were simultaneous movements from South to North as Viet Minh troops were assembled at Can Tho and My Tho and tranferred in French landing craft to Cap St Jacques, whence they were shipped north in Polish and Soviet vessels.[55]

In the South, meanwhile, the always murky labyrinth of power alliances was thrown into complete disarray, as different factions, commercial interests, religious sects and armed gangs struggled to secure their future in a new and unpredictable world. While the USA supported the Diem government, the French sought to undermine it through the activities of the SDECE Action Service, and the prime minister also faced hostility from the Chinese and French business communities. A strong pro-Bao Dai faction within the ANV, led by chief-of-staff General Nguyen Van Hinh, were openly insubordinate. The CIA had to work hard to shore up Diem's confidence and grip on power, though he eventually summoned up the resolve to dismiss Nguyen Van Hinh (who returned to France and his interrupted career in the Air Force). An uneasy joint Training Relations Instruction Mission of French and US officers was formed to oversee French withdrawal from the ANV and a simultaneous American takeover.

During that summer the American information officer Howard Simpson was unofficially attached by the embassy to Diem's fledgeling press relations office. When he first visited the prime minister at the Norodom Palace, Simpson was struck by the emptiness of its echoing corridors and the unfamiliar absence of French officials. On later occasions he noticed a progressive accumulation of US visitors – officials from the embassy, shadowy figures from Colonel Lansdale's SMM, fellow members of the US Information Service, and officers of the MAAG. Constant presences were Diem's younger brother Ngo Dinh Nhu and his elegant and formidable wife – the future 'Dragon Lady'.[56]

By late 1954 a growing number of US representatives of various diplomatic, military, intelligence, commercial, academic and media organizations were flocking to Saigon to become deeply enmeshed in the support of the Diem regime. Often well-meaning and intelligent, many of them were nevertheless entirely unprepared for this steamy swamp of conspiracy and corruption. The vast upheavals of population caused by partition, with its attendant dislocation of so many lives, offered opportunities for huge sums of money to be made, and it was inevitable that in the process some of the worst elements in the South became enriched and entrenched.

It was widely believed – in both North and South – that the agreed July 1956 elections would be won by those demanding a unified Communist Vietnam. In view of this conviction the southern leadership (with some US encouragement) held a pre-emptive referendum in the South in October 1955; the result was the declaration of an independent Republic of Vietnam with Ngo Dinh Diem as president. Once confirmed in power Diem proved to be a stubborn bigot; the transfer of northern refugees had at least doubled the Roman Catholic population in the South, who now received special favours from the regime. This caused a steady aggravation of tensions between Catholics and Buddhists, and the consequent problems of the Diem government would demand ever increasing American involvement. Diem declared that since his government had not been party to the Geneva accords he was not bound by them, and proceeded to violate many of the terms. The influx of Tonkinese refugees had included perhaps as many as 6,000 hard-core Viet Minh cadres and fighters; the ostensibly departing People's Army had left in the South many caches of arms and a solidly entrenched infrastructure; and Diem's rule provided a fertile seed-bed for what would become known to the world as the Viet Cong.[57]

ON THE COLD, DAMP, WINDY morning of 9 October 1954 the last French troops withdrew over the Paul Doumer bridge towards Haiphong as the *bo doi* of People's Army Division 308 'Viet Bac' entered Hanoi. Dodging International Control Commission patrols, Howard Simpson took photographs from a jeep that he was sharing with three SMM agents led by the colourful Colonel Lucien Conein ('Black Luigi').

Neatly turned out in new uniforms and packs, the veterans of Gabrielle and the Huguettes filed along the deserted streets almost silently in their rubber-soled shoes. Gawping at the tall buildings of a city the like of which few had ever seen before, they were tightly disciplined by their officers and commissars, and Simpson was struck at first by the utter lack of drama attending the end of one world and the birth of another. Slowly, as the shuffling columns moved deeper into the city, red flags began to blossom from the windows of the buildings that they had passed, and he heard singing and clapping. Viet Minh block committees were shepherding their people out on to the pavements, and small crowds began to form. Some units of soldiers halted, and sang with them; but for the liberation of a capital city by a victorious army at the end of an eight-year war, it all seemed weirdly unspontaneous and puritan. Was this what the *bo doi* had dreamt it would be like, as they lay in the mud of the Nam Youm valley?[58]

When the last armoured cars fell back along the great steel bridge and faded into the distance down the road to the sea, the anti-Communist cells that Colonel Conein had organized in Hanoi were not the only Vietnamese who were being abandoned to a short and grisly future.[59] France's withdrawal from Tonkin only two months after the announce-ment of the ceasefire had condemned the GMI partisans in the highlands, and their French leaders, to a lingering death. They had simply been told to make their way to safety in the South, which was quite impossible for most of them; or, failing that, to surrender – as if they had not already been condemned to death by the Viet Minh. Air supply drops were halted, and they were abandoned in the jungle with their dwindling ammunition and fading radios, to be hunted down and exterminated by Viet Minh tracker units over the months to come. One of the most horrible legends of Indochina is the report that an aircraft flying near the border picked up a last desperate message from one of these French NCOs a full two years after Dien Bien Phu, cursing them for not dropping ammunition so that the fugitive survivors could at least die like men.[60]

THE LAST TROOPS OF THE CEFEO left South Vietnam in April 1956. A few weeks previously, on 12 March, the last unit of the Foreign Legion had embarked – the 2nd Battalion of the 5th Foreign Infantry, the 'Régiment de Tonkin'. They left behind them the graves of just over 10,000

légionnaires. The whole war had cost the multi-racial Far East Expeditionary Corps some 92,000 men killed, missing in action, and prisoners
unaccounted for. The comparable total for the French-led Associated States
armies was nearly 27,000.[61] No figure for the Viet Minh is recorded, but
a total of at least a quarter of a million dead has been suggested.

When they sailed away down the Saigon river, II/5 REI were bound for
the Algerian naval base of Mers-el-Kébir. The first co-ordinated attacks
by the Front for National Liberation had taken place in the Aurès and
Kabylie highlands on the night of 31 October 1954, three weeks after the
French withdrawal from Hanoi. Paratroopers of III/1 RCP had been among
the first troops deployed, and by the time II/5 REI climbed the gangplanks
légionnaires of 3 REI had been in action in the mountains for more than a
year. The 5th Foreign, based around Tlemcen in the Oranais to guard the
Moroccan frontier, would be commanded by Colonel Favreau – the one-
eyed officer who had held the hilltop strongpoint PA26 at Na San in
December 1952. Some of the most remote Legion posts in the deep desert
were held by the Saharan motorized companies, the CSPLs; and photos
taken at the 'Beau Geste' forts of Ouargla and Laghouat over the coming
years would show a number of Vietnamese faces in the ranks.

WITH THE DEPARTURE OF THE French from Tonkin and northern
Annam, Ho Chi Minh's government could at last proceed with transforming North Vietnam into a fully Communist state. After ten years of
relative caution due to the need to avoid alienating those who supported
the cause of independence but not the Marxist–Leninist programme of the
Revolution, the Party could now apply its principles to the mass population of the Delta. The land collectivization reforms that the commissars
had promised to the weary porters along the supply roads and the battle-
shocked soldiers on the slopes of Béatrice and Gabrielle would now be
delivered. In summer 1955 packs of young Revolutionary cadres spread
out from Hanoi and set about destroying the age-old social order of village
society. The population was divided into categories, from the self-evident
class enemies of category A (the rich landlords and mandarin families),
and the 'rich peasants' or small independent farmers of Class B, through the
poorer categories C and D on down to the landless labourers of Class E.

The men who applied these principles in practice were rigid, ignorant and brutal. Tribunals with unlimited powers were given quotas of 'class enemies' to find within each village; definitions of guilt were altered repeatedly to ensure that the quotas were met, and informers profited from the confiscated goods of those they denounced. Tens of thousands of innocent men and women were accused, beaten, tortured, driven from their homes or killed. The agricultural base of the country descended into anarchy, and famine was not far behind. Estimates of the total number who were executed or who starved vary between 30,000 and 100,000. The disastrous failure of the programme caused panic among the officials responsible, who responded by launching ever more cruel and senseless witch hunts, both in the Delta and in the tribal highlands: since the Party line was infallible, its failure must be due to sabotage.

As the Party leadership slowly grasped what was happening in the countryside, recriminations began to be traded in Hanoi. Cliques manoeuvred to avoid blame, and scapegoats were designated and punished; but the moral credit of Ho Chi Minh's new state had largely been wasted in its first two years of existence. At the 10th Plenum of the Party, 27–29 October 1956, General Giap – now deputy prime minister and minister of defence – performed the necessary official act of contrition:

> Cadres, in carrying out their anti-feudal mission, created contradictions between the tasks of land reform and the Revolution, in some areas treating them as if they were separate activities. We failed to recognize the need to achieve unity with Class C; we should have formed an alliance with Class B instead of treating them as if they were Class A. We indiscriminately attacked all families owning land. Many honest people were executed. We saw enemies everywhere and resorted to widespread violence and the use of terror.
>
> In some places, in our efforts to implement land reform, we failed to respect religious freedoms and the right to worship. We also failed to respect the customs of the Montagnard tribes, and attacked their leaders and their hierarchical system too strongly. We placed too much emphasis on class origins rather than political attitudes. We resorted to disciplinary punishment, to expulsion, to execution. Worse still, torture came to be regarded as a normal feature of the Party's methods... There were grave errors...

In November 1956 armed rebellions broke out in Nghe An province in the old South Delta Base; and at Vinh – close to Ho Chi Minh's birthplace – some 3,000 rebels fought for three days before being crushed by two divisions of the People's Army. Hundreds were killed, about 2,000 executed, and twice that many imprisoned.[62]

ONE OF THE MOST PERNICIOUS consequences of Dien Bien Phu was its effect on the relationship between the French state and the professional core of the French Army. During most of the Indochina War a series of governments were believed to have let the army down; they had sent it to perform a task for which they were unable or unwilling to provide the means, and which they lacked the courage either to prosecute seriously or to abandon decisively. The climax of this failure was perceived as being Dien Bien Phu, where soldiers had been asked to sacrifice themselves to buy time for a government that was already planning to negotiate away everything they thought they were dying for. Even among those soldiers who accepted that withdrawal from Indochina was now inevitable, the politicians' apparent lack of interest in the fate both of the thousands of missing French prisoners, and of the loyal North Vietnamese whom they were largely abandoning, was seen as deeply dishonourable.

When the relationship between a polity and its armed forces is long matured such episodes may be, if not forgiven, then at least endured until the pain fades; but in the years following 1945 the reborn French Republic had accumulated little moral credit with its army. The many disappointments suffered during the terms of 19 successive administrations, culminating in the hurried scuttle from South-East Asia, left the political loyalty of many officers partial, qualified and wary. The damage that this caused might have been limited had the army as a whole felt unified by a single self-sustaining legend; but it did not.

All armies embrace traditional rivalries, which can be entirely positive when they surface as *esprit de corps* – a competitive regimental spirit; and these are deeply engrained by the ancestor worship that is the religion of all good armies. But the ancestor cults arising from the events of 1940–45 were to some extent divisive, and Indochina bred a whole new set of resentments. The CEFEO veterans resented those who had pursued their careers safely at home; and the paratroopers and Legion officers resented those whom they believed had left the 'real' fighting to them. Some French soldiers came home too cynical for the health of their future units; and some, so determined to learn ways of countering this new type of revolutionary enemy that their next test would lead them down dark paths. Since they faced that test almost immediately, there was no time for them to absorb and reconcile their experiences.

The officers and senior NCOs who returned from Indochina were the long-term career soldiers, not the nation-in-arms as was the case in the post-1945 British Army; they were not the conscripted sons, brothers and husbands of the nation as a whole. These scarred survivors, upon whom the French state immediately placed a new responsibility for crushing the rebellion in Algeria, were the leaders and the setters of tone within the spearhead units. Their whole experience in Indochina had created a sense of separation from the political class and, to some extent, from the civilian population and the mass of the conscript army drawn from it.

Despite the alienating effect of guerrilla warfare, many members of the CEFEO had acquired genuinely protective feelings towards the non-Communist Vietnamese and the tribal peoples whom they had come to know in the North. In 1954 they were forced to abandon these peoples to an uncertain fate, and their suspicions would soon be proved all too accurate. Thrust immediately into the turmoil of Algeria, they were encouraged to make absolute promises to the white population and the non-hostile Algerians (of whom there were many) that France would never abandon them. Under terrorist attack the white settler community – much larger and more entrenched than that in Indochina – became terrified, furious and intractable. The irreconcilables on both sides silenced the liberals by murder and exemplary terror. Trapped between the demands of the absolutists – Algerian, French and *colons* – French governments proved as helpless to chart a mutually acceptable course as they had been in Indochina. In 1958 the legitimacy of the Republic was rejected at the barricades; there were calls for the army to take power, but it was the long-retired General de Gaulle who left Colombey to stride on to the stage once more. Many in the army and among the settlers believed that their vision was safe in his hands, but in pursuing his much more far-sighted agenda he would prove an even chillier realist than General Navarre.

Militarily, the French Army won the Algerian War decisively, at some cost not only in blood but also to their good name; but having won it, it became clear to those whom the novelist Jean Larteguy called 'the centurions' that they had been turned into liars. Once more the army were to be pulled out, abandoning not only the graves of their dead, but also one and a half million European civilians – with whom many soldiers identified closely – to often destitute exile. More horribly, they were to leave scores of thousands of loyal Algerian *harkis* to the monstrously cruel revenge of the ALN. A small minority of them found this new dishonour intolerable; the result was the so-called *putsch* of April 1961, with its tragic consequences for France and her army.

At the head of the bloodless coup in Algiers was the 1st Foreign Parachute Regiment, rebuilt from that 1 BEP which had been wiped out on RC4 in 1950 and again at Dien Bien Phu in 1954. This final time it would be the French government that destroyed the 1st Foreign; in a modern Western state they had no realistic option, but the true responsibility for that third annihilation did not lie with the paratroopers. Notwithstanding the murderous gangsterism that followed the failure of the mutiny, and the distinctly mixed character of the group who launched it, it is undeniable that officers such as Major Denoix de Saint-Marc of 1 REP were men of transparent decency.[63]

Faced by the drama of April 1961, it is tempting to draw broad conclusions about the unwisdom of politicians abusing their army so repeatedly and so carelessly that its deepest sense of identity is outraged. True as that may be, the longer historical perspective argues – always – against generalising from the particular. The French Army of 1961 was the product of a unique life-story that began in 1789, and was shaped in fundamental ways by 1870–71, 1916–17, 1940 and 1943–5; and a particular group within that army were the product of their experiences in Indochina. Among those bitter memories, they had come to see Dien Bien Phu and its aftermath as the defining moment. They responded with that terrible cry of pain which pretends to free a man from his sworn duty, and promises such chaos to come: *'Nous sommes trahis!'* – 'We are betrayed!'

Notes and Sources

1 *La Formule*

The epigraph is quoted from Jacques Favreau &
Nicolas Dufour, *Nasan, La victoire oubliée
1952–53 – Base aéroterrestre au Tonkin,*
Economica, Paris (1999) p.183.

1 Simpson, *Tiger ...,* p.47+

2 Apart from its usual 9 × light machine guns/
automatic rifles and pairs of 0.30in Brownings
and 60mm light mortars, 11th Company had
been allocated 6 × extra rifle-calibre MGs (apparently Reibel M1931As); and 2 × heavy 0.50in M2
Brownings. (Favreau & Dufour, p.128)

3 Apparently a battalion from Regt 88 'Tam Dao'.

4 The experimental Foreign Legion Composite
Company (CMLE), with 4 × 120mm and
12 × 81mm tubes, had been rushed together in
late October 1952, from about 150 officers and
men of 3 & 5 REI and 13 DBLE. Commanded by
Lt Bart of 3/I/5 REI – which provided most of the
légionnaires – the company fought very effectively
at Na San, but for administrative reasons it was
disbanded following the battle. On this occasion
Lt Bart had only 6 × 81mm and 4 × 120mm under
his immediate control. (Favreau & Dufour,
page 114+)

5 Letestu, once a young casemate chief in 146th
Fortress Infantry, would rise to command 3rd
Foreign Infantry, and later to general's rank and
appointment as Commandant of the Foreign
Legion. (Favreau & Dufour, p.127+)

6 The guns were flown in one by one on a single
Bristol 170 freighter requisitioned from a civilian
airline; see also Ch.9 below. The last para bn to
arrive was 5 BPC. (Favreau & Dufour, p.194)

7 The attackers were reportedly Bn 165, Regt
141 from Div 312.

8 The 57mm RCL ('recoilless rifle') was a
bazooka-like infantry support weapon which
could be fired over the shoulder or from a tripod
mount. See fuller discussion in Ch.4 & 5 below.

9 Reportedly, Bonnet's company was attacked
by two bns of Regt 209 and Bn 428 of Regt 141,
all from Div 312. Enemy weapons recovered
included 2 × mortars, 3 × heavy and 39 × light
machine guns, 45 × sub-machine guns, and
scores of rifles.

10 Regt 174 of Div 316, plus Bn 2, Regt 88 from
Div 308.

11 The accounts of all these actions draw most
heavily on Favreau & Dufour, Ch.9, but also on
Rocolle, p.147+, and Gaujac, *Histoire...,* p.361+.

12 Favreau & Dufour, p.173+

2 The Three *Ky*

1 General physical and historical descriptions in
this chapter largely follow Florence & Storey's
'Lonely Planet' guide *Vietnam,* and Brig Peter
Macdonald's biography *Giap.*

2 To put this into rough perspective for British
readers: rainfall in the Hoang Lien Son
mountains over a six-month monsoon season
can reach 98in, while average annual rainfall in
mainland Great Britain is about 41in.

3 Florence & Storey, p.13+

4 Normally a Vietnamese is given three names
at birth. The first is one of the relatively few
clan/family names, e.g. Ngo, Pham, Nguyen. The
second may be purely ornamental; may follow a
family tradition; or may indicate the sex. The
third is the individual given name by which the
person is addressed, normally coupled with a
range of titles depending upon sex, age and social
status. This text refers to 'Giap' and to 'Ho'
simply because these are the most familiar forms
to Western readers. (Florence & Storey, p.595)

5 Macdonald, p.42+

6 By the 1930s, 2.5 per cent of the population of the south owned more than 45 per cent of the land; and of the 6,530 landowners in the whole country who held more than 125 acres, 6,300 were in Cochinchina. (Macdonald, p.49)

7 *ibid*, p.46+

8 *Encyclopaedia Britannica*, 1961

9 Lewis, Ch.VI, IX

10 *The Peoples of Mainland Southeast Asia*, Cartographic Division, National Geographic Society (1971); and Lewis, p.278+

11 Only 10 per cent of Vietnamese children received any schooling at all, and only 4 per cent of those any beyond primary grade. Between 1918 and 1939 just 827 Vietnamese graduated from the lycées with the baccalaureate. By 1945, 1,134 had gained university degrees, of whom 408 were lawyers, 337 engineers, 229 doctors, and 160 teachers. One of the lawyers, in 1937, was Vo Nguyen Giap; but he was unable to obtain a certificate to practise, and had to take employment as a history teacher at a Hanoi private school. (Macdonald, p.21+)

12 Labrousse, p.19+

13 Macdonald (p.51+) gives some 780 executions, 90 per cent of them summary; 546 sentences of life imprisonment, and some 3,000 internments.

14 This whole summary of the wartime and immediate post-war years draws heavily upon Héduy (ed.), *passim*; O'Ballance, Ch.II & III; & Macdonald, Ch.2 & 5.

15 Bergot, *Les 170 Jours ...*, p.55

16 See Ch.5, note 34.

17 The 53rd, 60th, 62nd & 93rd Armies, and the 23rd, 39th & 93rd Independent Divisions. (Macdonald, p.63)

18 Ca Mau, Bac Lieu, Soc Trang, Can Tho, Kien Giang, Rach Gia, Ha Tien, and parts of Chau Doc and Long Xuyen provinces. (O'Ballance, p.58)

19 He was not alone in this opinion; his aide Jean Lacouture would later say, 'I never met any well-informed man down there who had any doubt of the necessity to negotiate the conditions of an inescapable Vietnamese emancipation with the Viet Minh – who were the only serious spokesmen.' (Labrousse, p.29). Maj Philippe de Hautcloque, an aristocratic cavalryman, had taken the *nom de guerre* 'Leclerc' to protect his family in France when he declared for de Gaulle in 1940. In 1942, while stationed in the remote wasteland of Chad, French Equatorial Africa, the charismatic Leclerc led a column of 2,500 mostly African troops

across 1,500 miles of the Sahara Desert to join the British campaign against Rommel.

20 Dr Jean Roland, III/21e RIC, quoted Héduy, (ed.) *La Guerre...*, p.41

21 Macdonald, p.69

22 *ibid*, p.74+. The VM claimed figure of 6,000 dead is now thought to be hugely exaggerated.

3 The Dirty War

1 In Sept 1939–Aug 1945 French civilian deaths were about 470,000. For comparison, UK military casualties 1939–45 from a population of 47.5 million were 305,800 killed and missing, 277,100 wounded and 172,600 POWs, and 60,600 civilians were killed. From a US population of just over 129 million, military dead and missing Dec 1941–5 were 405,400, wounded 670,800, POWs 139,700, and civilian casualties were insignificant. (Ellis, *The World War II Data Book*, Aurum, 1993; p.253+)

2 From Sept 1944 onwards French military or civilian courts examined 160,287 cases of alleged collaboration. About 45 per cent resulted in dropped charges or acquitals; 25 per cent in forfeiture of civil rights ('national degradation'); and 7,037 in death sentences, of which only about 1,500 were carried out. (Ousby, pp.250+, 304, 310)

3 Rocolle, p.101. The cost of the war was calculated in 'milliards', one milliard being one thousand million old francs (one billion, in US usage). The total multiplied from 3 milliards in 1945 to 27 milliards in 1946, and on up to 308 milliards in 1951 and 535 milliards in 1952. For 1953/4 figures, see Ch.5, note 21.

4 Bodin, *RHd'A*, 1979/3

5 The brief summaries of annual events throughout this chapter are taken mostly from O'Ballance, and Héduy (ed.), *La Guerre...*, with additional material from Rocolle, Fall (*Street...*), and a number of the other sources listed in the Bibliography.

6 Gazin, *RHd'A*, 1955/4

7 The bridging weights of some main US vehicles used by the CEFEO were: Dodge WC54 ambulance, 5.8 tons; GMC 'deuce-and-a-half' truck, 9 tons; M8 Greyhound armoured car, 7.5 tons; M3 series half-track, 10 tons; M5A1 Stuart tank, 16.5 tons; M24 Chaffee tank, 18 tons.

8 From 1948, in the main river deltas and on the coast of Annam, the CEFEO made innovative use of the small US M29C Weasel as a combat reconnaissance vehicle and of larger LVT-4 and -(A)4 'amtracs' as infantry transports and fire support

vehicles. Christened 'Crabs' and 'Alligators' respectively, these were mainly operated by Foreign Legion cavalry squadrons. (Dunstan, *Vietnam Tracks*, Ch.1)

9 Gazin, *RHd'A*, 1955/4

10 Porch, p.544

11 Lewis, pp.184, 208

12 Simpson, *Tiger...*, p.79+

13 Couget, *RHd'A*, 1978/3

14 2/I/3 REI had three officers, 101 NCOs and men, 1 × 81mm and 2 × 60mm mortars, and 2 × M1916 37mm light infantry cannon (their attackers also had 37mm as well as 75mm, the latter probably Japanese mountain guns). Capt Cardinal and Lt Charlotton were killed, among 23 dead and 48 wounded; S/Lt Bevalot – just 15 days off the boat – commanded most of the defence, and had 39 men on their feet when Lt Col Simon arrived on 28 July 48.

15 Apparently from Regts 36, 88, 165, 174, 175, 209, and regional units. Some sources believe that more than 20 bns were committed.

16 'Groupement Bayard': 1 BEP, 1 and 11 Tabors Marocains, 1 Bn de Marche/8 RTM plus irregulars.

17 III/3 REI, 3 Tabor Marocain plus irregulars.

18 It was calculated that Gen Giap captured 13 field guns, 125 mortars, 950 machine guns, 1,200 sub-machine guns, and 8,000 rifles – enough to arm a whole division; in addition some 1,300 tons of supplies and munitions and 450 vehicles were also abandoned. (O'Ballance, p.118)

19 The command was offered first to Gen Juin, then to Gen Koenig; both declined, the latter over the government's refusal to send French conscripts to Indochina (Dutrône, *Militaria* No. 193). As France's youngest general, de Lattre had commanded 14th Inf Div in 1940; when Germany occupied Vichy France in 1942 he resisted, and was imprisoned. Escaping to North Africa in Oct 43, he was put in command of what became French 1st Army, which he led in the South of France invasion of Aug 44, in the Colmar Pocket in Jan/Feb 45 and in the drive across southern Germany, reaching the Swiss border early in May. (Windrow & Mason, *A Concise Dictionary of Military Biography*, Osprey, 1975)

20 Tran Hung Dao was a 13th-century Vietnamese admiral who resisted a Mongol invasion. For a summary of the classic phases of Communist revolutionary warfare as defined by Mao Tse Tung, see pp.145–7.

21 *Tet* is the Chinese lunar New Year in mid February.

22 Napalm was first used in Indochina near Tien Yen on 22 Dec 50; the VM were not yet familiar with its effects.

23 Fall, *Hell...*, p.167

24 De Lattre's part in the formation of the Vietnamese National Army (ANV) is mentioned in Ch.5, below.

25 O'Ballance, p.138+; Favreau & Dufour, p.38+

26 Fall, *Street...*, p.176+; Gazin, *RHd'A*, 1966/1

27 For the concrete, a total of more than 14 million cubic feet of crushed stone was needed in the Delta alone – i.e. some 2,950 metric tons to be supplied and transported *every day* for a year. (Gazin, *RHd'A*, 1966/1)

28 The alleged quotation inspired a long, satirical piece of blank verse which circulated throughout the CEFEO. This anonymous masterpiece lists all the types of troops and characters to be found in the Expeditionary Corps, and ends with the catchphrase, *'Dans le béton, les plus cons'* – 'And in the concrete, the real c***s'. (Dutrône, *Militaria* No.193)

29 Gaujac, *Histoire...*, p.269+

30 Rocolle, p.45+

31 Gaujac, *Histoire...*, p.344+

32 Fall, *Street...*, p.273. Gaujac (*Histoire...*, p.248) gives 91 dead and missing from 6 BPC. Fall (p.71) says 'three-fifths of the battalion' were casualties. The contradictory numbers may be due to confusion between members of 6 BPC and other Franco-Vietnamese troops retreating with them. Gaujac has 417 officers and men of the unit decorated at Hanoi; as 6 BPC jumped with 667 men, casualties cannot have been higher than 250, or 38 per cent.

33 Eric Morgan, 2 REI (*Images of War*, 51/4, p.1418; interviewed by Vicky Thomas)

34 Morgan (*Images of War*, 51/4, p.1416)

35 See also Ch.17.

36 O'Ballance, p.179+; Rocolle, p.166. The units ambushed at Chan Muong were 4/7 RTA, II/2 REI and BMI infantry, and RICM tanks.

37 1 and 2 BEP, 3 and 5 BPC; III/3 and III/5 REI; II/1 RTA, II/6 RTM; TD 55; BM/BT 1, BT 2 and 3; 5 GAVN (2 btys), IV/41 RCA (1 bty), CMLE. (Favreau & Dufour, p.193)

38 People's Army units present appear to have been: *Div 308*, Regts 88 and 102; *Div 312*, Regts 141 and 209; *Div 316*, Regts 98 and 174. (Favreau & Dufour, *passim*)

39 Favreau & Dufour, Ch.9 and *passim*; Rocolle, p.147+; Gaujac, *Histoire...*, p.365+

40 Rocolle, p.150; Fall, *Hell...*, p.25+

41 Rocolle, p.152+

42 The third regiment was surrounding the small post of Muong Khoua, which had repulsed attacks and delayed the division's advance. The garrison held out from 13 Apr until overrun on 18 May. (Rocolle, p.150; O'Ballance, p.190)

43 Gaujac, *Histoire...*, p.368+. Para units on the Plain of Jars were 3 and 6 BPC, II/1 RCP, 2 BEP, and 3 BPVN.

4 The People's Army

1 Macdonald, p.82, on the explicit acceptance of murder and torture, and the policy of patient infiltration and subversion.

Throughout this text the Communist political leadership are referred to as either the Viet Minh or the Party, irrespective of their exact current title. The armed forces are referred to arbitrarily as either the Viet Minh or the People's Army; political and military control were integrated throughout the war, and in practice exact distinction between the two terms is unnecessary. (Labrousse, p.35)

2 Instruction was in *Quoc Ngu*, the phonetic form of Vietnamese transcribed in Latin script, which had been devised by the remarkable 17th-century missionary Alexandre de Rhodes. (Florence & Storey, p.592)

3 Labrousse, p.40+

4 *ibid*, p.62+

5 *ibid*, p.49

6 *ibid*, p.344

7 *ibid*, p.53, quoting Giap, *Récits de la resistance vietnamienne*, Maspéro, Paris (1966) p.72.

8 Rocolle, p.84+

9 There was one shining exception to the fragmentation of Catholic resistance in the south: the island province of Ben Tre, where a remarkable Eurasian, Col Jean Leroy, was given a free hand to push through social and economic reforms that genuinely addressed the peasants' grievances. His reward was a highly motivated local militia which kept Ben Tre free from the Viet Minh throughout the war. (Labrousse, p.185+)

10 *ibid*, p.57+

11 The Cong An 'political investigation service' had representatives at every level of the VM territorial administration; its manpower in a typical

province was between 600 and 1,000, and it was authorized to make 'preventive arrests'. (Labrousse, p.124)

12 *ibid*, p.62+

13 Rocolle, p.72+

14 *ibid*, p.86+

15 Labrousse, p.74+

16 Macdonald, p.70

17 A detailed listing of regional regt and bn deployments in Tonkin, and the VM regular order of battle, can be found on websites *http://members.lycos.co.uk/Indochine/vm/vm OB1.html* and... *Indochine/vm/chuluc.html*. The former is taken from an FTNV 2nd Bureau report of 1 Apr 54, now filed in SHAT 10H614.

18 Rocolle, pp.80, 87

19 Labrousse, reprinted from Gen Navarre, *Agonie de l'Indochine*, Plon, Paris (1958) pp.45–6.

20 Rocolle, p.81+

21 *ibid*, p.128+. Even the strongest concrete forts in the De Lattre Line were not always safe from attack once the VM got heavier weapons; e.g. at Gia Loc, 6 Dec 53, four blockhouses out of six were overrun, and at Linh Dong on 13 Jan 54 two out of four were captured.

22 Rocolle, p.82+

23 Duval, Alain, 'Actions du Corps Expédition-naire', p.330+, in Héduy (ed.), *La Guerre...*

24 Lewis, Ch.XX

25 Boissau, *RHd'A*, 1989/4

26 O'Ballance, Ch.XII

27 Macdonald, p.92+

28 CIA report quoted by Conboy & Bowra, p.5. The approximate strength totals given here are a synthesis from a number of sources, incl. Gen Yves Gras, *Histoire de la Guerre d'Indochine*, Plon, Paris (1979), and André Tuelière, *Historia* Hors Série No.24, Tallandier, Paris (1972).

29 Simpson, *DBP...*, p.18

30 Labrousse, p.113+. The main camps were at Wenshan, Longzhou, Jingxi, Yulin, Dongxing, Guangyan, and Haikou on Hainan Island.

31 O'Ballance, p.112; Labrousse, p.85

32 Rocolle, p.88. Chinese mortars were made in 82mm calibre so that captured Western 81mm ammunition could be used, but not vice versa.

The sources are puzzling about the numbers of MGs/LMGs in an infantry battalion. Labrousse (p.116) quotes Capt Jacques Despuech, translator of Ngo Van Chieu's *Journal d'un combattant vietminh* (Seuil, Paris, 1955), that a VM bn in 1953 had 500 × rifles, 200 × SMGs, but no belt-fed machine guns *(mitrailleuses)* and only 20 × light machine guns *(fusils-mitrailleurs)*. Since the normal scale is roughly one LMG per 10–15 riflemen, 20 would seem very low for a battalion – only one per 35 men.

33 Rocolle, p.89, quoting Giap, *Guerre du peuple, armée du peuple,* Maspéro, Paris (1966) p.136.

34 Labrousse, p.83+; Rocolle, p.90+, quoting 2nd Bureau report of early winter 1953; website *http://members.lycos.co.uk/Indochine/vm/chuluc.html.* Note that official formation dates may precede the date of availability for combat by some months.

35 Rocolle quotes the title 'Viet Bac' from VM sources. Western sources often give it as 'Capital'; 'Iron Div' has also been suggested, though 'Steel and Iron Divs' was also applied collectively to Divs 304–325 inclusive.

36 Macdonald, p.93. The high number of 'officers' quoted may be mistranslated from 'cadres', covering all line and political leadership grades.

37 Rocolle, p.99

38 The phrase 'captured in Korea' raises the question, 'From whom?' During the initial retreat of summer 1950 there were only a handful of US Army 105s in Korea. In the winter 1950/51 retreat some guns were certainly left behind, but the US Army is not known for abandoning ordnance without disabling it thoroughly. The ROK Army had just 45 × 105mm guns in 1950, and though all seem to have been lost, at least some must presumably have been disabled first. The ROK did not receive replacement artillery until mid 1952, after which date there were no further Communist breakthroughs.

39 Labrousse (p.126) identifies the general staff recce unit as Bn 426; Rocolle (p.171), as Bn 468.

40 Rocolle, p.92. Divs 330 and 338 were formed in 1954–5 from southern VM shipped north at the time of partition.

41 *ibid,* p.67+; Labrousse, p.113+

42 Rocolle, pp.68+, 97

43 An extra 1.75oz was issued to men carrying radios, and 3.5oz extra to stretcher-bearers.

44 It was calculated that on level ground each porter could carry 55lbs of rice or 40lbs of other loads, for 15 miles in a day or 12 miles by night, both load and distance being halved in mountain country. The difference between load types was because rice sacks mould to the body and are easier to carry than, say, an ammunition box. The porters were rewarded with 2.2lbs of rice per

carrying day, since this had to last until they reached home. (Rocolle, p.98; Macdonald, p.93; O'Ballance, p.113; Chapelle, *RHdA,* 1959/1)

45 Labrousse, p.111

46 *ibid,* p.113+

47 *ibid,* p.115, quoting Gen Henri Jacquin, *Guerres secrètes en Indochine,* Olivier Orban, Paris (1979) p.203

48 Macdonald, p.94

49 This was a copy of the sturdy Russian PPSh41, identifiable in thousands of WWII photos by its wooden butt, slotted barrel jacket and big drum magazine – the Chinese version used a curved 'banana' box magazine instead. Rate of fire was 700–900rpm. The other main SMGs supplied to the VM were the Soviet PPS43 with a folding skeleton butt and its Type 51 Chinese equivalent.

50 The 120mm mortar used by the People's Army is assumed to be the Russian M1943; this weighed up to 1,320lbs when rigged for travelling. At 34lbs its bomb was slightly lighter than the French equivalent, and at $3^1/2$ miles its maximum range very slightly less.

51 The Chinese Type 51 copied from the US M20 3.5in 'super bazooka' had a calibre of 87mm; it may be significant that in a letter to Mshl Juin on 14 Dec 53, Gen Navarre mentioned the enemy's '90mm bazookas'. (Rocolle, p.169)

52 SKZs are invariably described in French sources as being of 75mm calibre, but may have included several slightly varying Russian and/or Chinese models. The technical distinction is that bazookas are loaded with an electrically ignited self-propelled rocket, while recoilless guns ('RCLs') have an opening breech and are loaded with a shell in a perforated case. See also Ch.5 note 23

53 The use of badges actually declined with the growth of the Chu Luc. A complete sequence of collar and sleeve rank insignia – yellow stars, bars and chevrons on red backing – was noted by French intelligence in time to appear in soldiers' handbooks in 1949, but seems to have disappeared after 1950. (Dutrône & Grojan, *Militaria* Nos.177 and 180)

54 Rocolle, p.90

55 *ibid,* p.91. See also Ch.8, pp.286–7

56 Labrousse, p.94. French intelligence claimed that up to 90 per cent of VM traffic was normally intercepted. As a general rule VM radio security was poor; transmissions were routinely made for months on end on the same wavelengths, with the same call-signs, and at the same times of day. (Puy-Montbrun, Déodat, in Héduy (ed.), *La Guerre...*, p.264; Babet, *RHd'A*, 1967/1)

57 Rocolle, p.149+

58 Fall, *Hell...*, p.152

59 Rocolle, p.96+

60 *ibid*, p.99

61 Labrousse, p.96+

62 Brancion, p.282; Simpson, *DBP...*, p.52. French artillery officers who reported on their interrogations included Col Vaillant, Maj Le Gurun, and Capt Noël, the former battery commander from 7/III/10 RAC who served as GONO's chief of intelligence from 21 January.

5 The Expeditionary Corps

The epigraph is quoted from Prof Bodin's paper 'Inadapté ou inadaptation? Le CEFEO 1945–54', in *Revue Historique des Armées*, 1979/3.

1 The following section draws heavily upon Clayton, *France ...*, Ch.1 & 2 *passim*.

2 *ibid*, Ch.10

3 Huge resentment was caused by Royal Navy shelling of the French fleet at Mers-el-Kébir in July 40, which killed some 1,300 Frenchmen. It was inflamed by the abortive attempt on Dakar in West Africa in Sept 40; and even more so in June–July 41 by the successful British Commonwealth and Gaullist invasion of Syria and Lebanon, which inflicted some 3,350 dead and wounded on the Vichy garrison. The Gaullist force – mainly Foreign Legion and black African units – could still field only one brigade. Offered the choice between joining it or repatriation, only about 10 per cent of the 35,000-odd prisoners taken in the Levant enlisted with the Free French.

4 Clayton, *France...* , p.137+

5 *ibid*, p.142

6 Le Goyet, *RHd'A*, 1974/4

7 Gaujac, *Militaria* No.149

8 The regular schedules for rotation of CEFEO personnel did *not* include provision for making up combat and other losses, only for replacing men who had reached the end of their tour. Thus, in e.g. 1952 the totals of killed, missing, and repatriated wounded and sick were 587 officers, 1,756 NCOs, and 2,132 enlisted men. To make up such losses successive C-in-Cs had to beg Paris for additional drafts, and such appeals were routinely resisted with stubborn ingenuity. (Rocolle, p.102)

9 Rocolle, p.102. In addition, on 1 Jan 53 French Air Force strength in the Far East totalled 7,100, and French Navy strength 10,900.

10 Rocolle, p.103+. An infantry battalion should have had at least 18 officers & 60 to 80 French NCOs; in fact most were lucky if they had 12 & 40 respectively, and the average ratio of unit officers to men was 1 to 30, compared with 1 to 20 in Europe and North Africa.

11 Blondieau, *Insignes...*, Tome I, Planche 5 notes

12 Clayton, *The Wars*, p.56; Dutrône, *Militaria* No. 193

13 Lewis, p.290: for pay rates see also note 38.

14 Despite determined efforts at the highest levels to hush it up, the scandal broke in the National Assembly in Dec 53. Devaluation of the piastre to 10 francs the previous May hit the Indochinese population and local troops badly, distorting the price of staple foods. (Bail, *L'Enfer...*, p.112)

15 O'Ballance, pp.109, 114; Rocolle, p.63. US recognition of the Associated States in 1949 qualified Vietnam for direct American aid under the Mutual Defense Assistance Act of that year; and the new prime minister, Nguyen Phan Long, applied for $146 million. The French, deeply opposed to direct US interference in their colonies, insisted that everything had to pass through their hands (though not unreasonably, given the local levels of corruption). Nguyen Phan Long was replaced with the more tractable Tran Van Huu; in May 50 a US mission arrived in Saigon, and in June the first aid followed. The Americans insisted on improvements in the French norms of maintenance if they were to supply aircraft and vehicles.

16 The French *treillis mod. 1947* was not general issue throughout the CEFEO until 1952.

17 French 7.5mm, 7.62mm, 7.65mm and 8mm, Chinese 7.92mm, US 0.30in long and short, US 0.45in, British 0.303in and 9mm.

18 8mm Berthier M1907/15 rifles.

19 Kemencei, *Homme de Guerre* No.3, letter p.46

20 7.62mm Reibel M1931A machine guns on US M2 mounts.

21 During 1950–51 US aid represented about 15 per cent of the total cost of the war to France (O'Ballance, p.122); but by autumn 1953 America had agreed to fund approximately three-quarters of the following year's costs, forecast at 626 milliards (626 billion 'old francs'), of which Metropolitan France would be responsible for

only 136 milliards (Rocolle, p.101). By July 54 the total cumulative cost of US aid was about $954 million, and of French expenditure, some $11 billion; but together, these figures for an eight-year war represent only about half the US expenditure on the three-year Korean War. (Fall, *Street...*, p.314)

22 Browning 0.30in guns were the M1919A4 with M2 tripod, or M1919A6 with bipod and shoulder stock.

23 Flat trajectory – i.e. the projectile leaves the muzzle at such high velocity that its track to the target is virtually straight, rather than a shallow drooping curve; this gives superior accuracy for firing at pinpoint targets, rather than relying on the destructive blast and fragmentation radius of hits in their general area.

Like a bazooka rocket-launcher, the recoilless gun operates by venting the hot gas from its discharge backwards at the same instant as the projectile leaves the barrel forwards. The disadvantages are a dangerous back-blast; the inability to fire at a high angle of elevation unless a channel for the back-blast is first dug in the ground behind the breech; and – worst of all – a very visible 'signature' of flame and dust when the weapon is fired, making concealment impossible. The M18 57mm RCL used by the French could be fired over the shoulder or from an M1917A1 machine-gun mount, the M20 75mm only from the latter.

24 Le Troadec, *RHd'A*, 1956/3

25 Bodin, *RHd'A*, 1979/3

26 Morgan, *Images of War*, p.1418

27 Lewis, p.20+

28 *ibid*, p.284

29 Perhaps 2 million Vienamese were confessing Roman Catholics, mainly in the north.

30 Venereal diseases accounted for between 20 and 30 per cent of all medical cases, despite the CEFEO's best efforts (Forissier, *RHd'A*, 1989/4). Untroubled by Anglo-Saxon neuroses, the French Army had long accepted that prostitution should be tolerated, but supervised by the Army medical department. For this reason the famous BMCs – 'mobile field brothels', staffed by Algerian and Indochinese women – circulated between units in the field. More permanent establishments were provided in the cities, operated by local entrepreneurs under the watchful eye of the medical service and the military police.

31 Fall, *Hell...*, p.250+

32 Regional soldiers proved the more tractable, and were usually held as PIMs at unit level. Even regulars could be 'turned' in internment camps,

however; one camp in Tonkin held some 2,000 People's Army prisoners in 1952–4, and was able to release 1,100 of them, of whom 900 enlisted in the ANV. No doubt individual opportunism played a far greater part than ideological conversion; but these figures do at least show that Communist indoctrination did not always penetrate deeply. (Rocolle, p.99+)

33 Vietnamese – *Kinh* – is a tonal language, intensely difficult for Europeans to master, since any one of six different inflections of each syllable completely alters its meaning. Questions are asked in the negative; an affirmative answer is given as a double negative, and a negative answer as an affirmative. (Florence & Storey, p.592+)

34 The universalist Cao Dai sect, founded in the 1920s by a seer named Ngo Minh Chieu, was centred on Tay Ninh north-west of Saigon. Numbering between 1 and 2 million adherents, it was a baffling mixture of Confucianism, Buddhism, Taoism and the outward trappings of Catholicism. The church was led by a 'pope', and numbered not only John the Baptist and Joan of Arc but also Victor Hugo and the Jade Emperor among its saints. The slightly less numerous Hoa Hao sect of Chau Doc province was founded by an occultist Buddhist monk in 1939. Both movements were to some extent encouraged by the Japanese during their occupation. (Lewis, p.33+; Florence & Storey, p.61)

35 Labrousse, p.183

36 A Viet Minh agent told Norman Lewis (p.300) that grenade attacks were usually to make an example of owners who had failed to pay protection money.

37 Many knowledgeable pre-war intelligence personnel had been dismissed as part of an anti-Vichy purge, and it took time to rebuild reliable networks. After 1950 the Service de Documentation Extérieure et de Contre-Espionage (SDECE) was officially given a co-ordinating authority over the alphabet soup of other agencies operating in Indochina: military security; the Second Bureau, military intelligence; the Fifth Bureau, and the Service de Renseignement Opérationnel (SRO), both reporting directly to the commander-in-chief; the Sûreté or police security service; and the Bureau Technique de Liaison et de Co-ordination (BTLC), both working under the civil government. Needless to add, the turf wars continued unabated.

38 As early as 1946 the Bataillon de Marche/16 RIC had only one company of Frenchmen; by 1952 the 11, 21 and 22 RIC each had one French and two Vietnamese battalions.

Apart from the shortage of French volunteers, local recruitment was relatively cheaper: in

Tonkin in 1950 a French private received 586 piastres per month (just under 9 pounds sterling, at the official rate of 60 piastres to the pound), a Vietnamese regular 410 piastres, and an auxiliary only 270 piastres. (Clayton, *France...*, p.326; Dutrône, *Militaria* No. 194)

39 Labrousse, p.179+, quoting the memoirs of Gens Raoul Salan and Lionel Chassin.

40 Dutrône, *Militaria* No. 194; Rocolle, p.107. The figure of 800 officers seems to be seriously deceptive – see note (47) below; most of these appear to have been interpreters given equivalent military rank rather than trained soldiers qualified for line command.

41 For example, the 2e Bataillon de Marche d'Extrême-Orient (2 BMEO) was redesignated *Tieu Doan* 66; the Bataillon des Forces Côtières du Tonkin (BFCT) became TD 72; and the 2e Bataillon Muong, TD 73. (Blondieau, *Insignes...*, Planches 10 & 12 notes)

42 The contradictory assessments of the military prowess of Cambodians are striking. In 1950 Gen des Essars, the French commander in Cambodia, told Norman Lewis that he despaired of making fighting men out of pacifist Buddhists each one of whom spent a year as a mendicant novice monk (*Dragon...*, p.204+). However, several sources including the US observer Howard Simpson speak highly of Cambodian volunteers in Vietnamese units, recruited among the (perhaps acculturated?) Khmer minority living in western Cochinchina. Notoriously, by the 1970s the Khmer Rouge had become the most savage of all the Indochinese Communist guerrilla movements.

43 For instance, TD 62, 63, 64 & 65 were formed from 1er & 2e Bataillons de Marche/11 RIC, I/22 RIC & II/22 RIC respectively; TD 68, 75 & 76 from IV/13 DBLE, IV/5 REI & V/3 REI respectively. (Blondieau, *Insignes...*, *passim*)

44 Rocolle, p.95. The Viet Minh exerted itself to plant a two- or three-man *Dich Van* cell within each ANV unit, to gather intelligence, foment discontent, and lead mutinies if the opportunity offered. The work of such infiltrators could be particularly dangerous in units dispersed as post garrisons.

45 Rocolle, p.102. Within Indochinese units as a whole, the total of attached French personnel in Jan 54 was 882 officers & 3,450 NCOs – perhaps 9 per cent of the whole French manpower in the CEFEO; of those, in Mar 54 the ANV alone accounted for 780 officers and 2,847 NCOs.

46 Simpson, *DBP...*, p.60

47 Rocolle, p.106+. On 1 Jan 54, Associated States units had only some 300 Indochinese line officers,

6,500 senior NCOs & *c.*1,000 interpreters given equivalent military ranks. In Mar 54 fewer than 300 candidates came forward for a planned 500-student class at the ANV's Dalat officer school.

48 Simpson, *Tiger...*, p.31+

49 One slogan picked for this project has the unmistakable ring of civilian advisers in some far-away air-conditioned office: the TDKQs were to implant themselves in the community 'with a guitar under the left arm, a sub-machine gun under the right'...

50 Simpson, *Tiger...*, pp.78–81; Nguyen Van Hinh, in Héduy (ed.), *La Guerre...*, p.239

51 Rocolle, p.108+

52 Lewis, Ch.VI, IX. The Mois' solemn welcome to a stranger, *'Nam lu'*, has been translated as 'Let's get drunk'.

53 Blondieau, *Insignes...*, Planche 10 notes

54 *The Peoples of Mainland Southeast Asia*, Cartographic Division, National Geographic Society (1971)

55 Sergent, *Paras-Légion*, Ch.XVIII. This passage also draws upon Gaujac, *Histoire...*, p.354+ & *passim*.

56 Appel & Beebe, 'Preventive Psychiatry: An Epidemiological Approach'

57 There were no troop-carrying helicopters available. The first two light Hiller 360s had been acquired in 1950; by spring 54 only 32 helicopters had been delivered to Indochina, of which at the time of DBP only 23 seem to have been serviceable (mostly Sikorski S-55s, termed H-19 by the French). These were officially dedicated entirely to casualty evacuation, although individual rescue missions were occasionally flown, e.g. during Operation 'Pollux' in Dec 53. (Forissier, *RHd'A* 1989/4, & Rocolle, p.112)

58 Gaujac, *Histoire...*, p.337

59 Bail, *L'Enfer...*, p.21. Fall (*Hell...*, p.5) gives the strength of II/1 RCP for the actual DBP jump as 569 – a proportion of each unit always remained at the depot. The figures for 1 BEP are from Fall, *Hell...*, p.16.

60 Former Sgt Johann Wallisch, 2 BEP, in conversation with the author.

61 Porch, Ch. 25 *passim*

62 The Milice Francaise, raised in 1943 and led by Joseph Darnand, was the most active Vichy security force. The Légion des Volontaires Francais contre le Bolshevisme fought on the Russian Front, 1941–4, with an initial strength of about 3,000; some LVF survivors passed into the

French SS Volunteer Assault Brigade 'Charlemagne' in Sept 1944.

63 The few published memoirs are well known (Colin John, *Nothing to Lose*; Henry Ainley, *In Order to Die*; Adrian Liddell Hart, *Strange Company*, etc.); but Eric Morgan, a Welshman who served in Indochina with 2 REI in 1951–3, never met another British or American légionnaire (conversation with the author).

64 For instance, at Na San in winter 52/53, III/3 REI's 12th Co was Vietnamese.

65 A reference to the Legion's 'holy day' – 30 April 1863 – when an understrength company fought to the last against huge odds at Camerone in Mexico during the Emperor Maximilian's French-sponsored claim to that country.

Indochina would be the Legion's costliest war; the official totals of killed 1946–54 were 309 officers, 1,082 NCOs and 9,021 corporals and privates.

66 Porch, p.545+. A Pole named Stefan Kubiak, who had deserted in 1947, allegedly fought as 'Major Ho Chi Tuan' with Div 312 at strongpoint 'Béatrice' on 13/14 Mar 54. (Fall, *Hell...*, p.270)

67 Clayton, *France...*, Ch. 9 *passim*

68 An anti-French demonstration in this Algerian town on VE-Day 1945 became uncontrollable when panicky shots were fired. More than a hundred European civilians were butchered; and over the following weeks French troops and vengeful colonist lynch-mobs killed some 3,000 Muslims more or less at random. This episode was astonishingly little discussed in France, but provided important encouragement for the nascent Algerian independence movement.

69 It is worth making the point that in the Armée d'Afrique enlisted men had to learn French if they hoped for any advancement; in the Indian Army, all British regimental officers were obliged to learn the relevant Indian languages.

70 Apart from the Tirailleurs and Spahis units, in the CEFEO many North African troops served in mixed-race artillery, engineer, logistic and other service units, though their low literacy rates limited some of these opportunities.

71 Apart from various Bataillons de Marche de Tirailleurs Sénégalais, d'Afrique Occidentale Francaise & d'Afrique Centrale Francaise, African troops made up a high proportion of 6 RIC, and served in artillery, support and service units. (Clayton, *France...* p.326)

72 West African units that proved themselves in battle included 30e Bn de Marche/Tirailleurs Sénégalais at Vinh Yen in 51; and I/24e Regt de Marche TS at Yen Vi in 53. (Bodin, *RHd'A* 1989/4)

6 The Air-Conditioned General

The epigraph is quoted from *Le Nouveau Candide*, Paris, 17–24 October 1963.

1 Rocolle, p.118+; Fall, *Hell...*, p.27+

2 Rocolle, p.20+.

3 Rocolle, p.120+; Fall, *Hell...*, p.28+; Fall, *Street...*, p.62

4 These aims were later confirmed by the Laniel cabinet in a communication to Navarre dated 21 Nov 53: 'the objective of our action in Indochina is to lead the enemy to recognize that he cannot hope for a military solution...'

5 Rocolle, p.25+

6 *ibid*, p.51+, p.109+

7 *ibid*, p.124. This offensive would materialize as Operation 'Atlante', which opened on 20 Jan 54 – see Ch. 8 below.

8 *ibid*, p.110. On 1 Jan 54 the static defence of the Red River delta by 917 posts accounted for 1,076 CEFEO officers, 7,515 NCOs & 73,879 men.

9 *ibid*, p.115+. Navarre would eventually receive eight-plus battalions; but his additional demand for replacements to rebuild his weakened units was denied – he would be sent only a fraction of the cadres he needed, and even these only *as an advance* against the next rotation of time-expired men, not an addition. The Air Force provided only 700 of the 4,000 men he requested, and no resources for improving the network of airfields. The Navy did provide additional coastal and transport vessels, and agreed to the permanent – rather than intermittent – stationing of an aircraft carrier in the Gulf of Tonkin.

10 *ibid*, p.59+. Navarre's doubts about defending Laos would soon be known to the VM: the minutes of this meeting were leaked to the journalist Roger Stéphane, who quoted them in *France-Observateur* on 30 July.

11 *ibid*, p.62

12 *ibid*, p.54+; le Troadec, *RHd'A*, 1956/3

13 Rocolle, pp.127, 130

14 Fall, *Hell...*, p.33. This contentious question would later lead Cogny and Navarre into legal confrontation over the finer points of their respective intentions for DBP in mid Nov 53; there is no evidence that either general made these distinctions in writing at the time.

15 Rocolle, p.178; Bail, *Les Combats...*, p.77+

16 Rocolle, p.163

17 Fall (*Hell...*, p.31+) suggests that Cogny's opinion was expressed at a regional commanders' conference in Saigon on 16 June which reviewed the plans that Navarre would shortly take to Paris. Certainly Cogny never denied this position, and confirmed it once more in articles published in *L'Express* in Nov–Dec 1963.

18 Déodat Puy–Montbrun et al, in Héduy (ed.), *La Guerre...*, p.264+; & Trinquier, *RHd'A* 1979/2.

19 Simpson, *DBP...*, p.19+. Apart from White, Black and Red Thai, Meo and Nung, groups of Man (Yao) and Lolo were also active in this programme. Rocolle (p.156) suggests that the claim of *c.* 15,000 in total is exaggerated.

20 Rocolle, p.156. Morale faltered if these bands were forced to withdraw from their own immediate region, but without their territorial motivation the programme could never have existed at all.

21 Trinquier, *RHd'A*, 1981/4

22 Favreau & Dufour, p.194: BT 1, BT 2, BT 3, III/1 RTA, part II/4 RAC & CMLE.

23 Rocolle, p.161+; Trinquier, *RHd'A*, 1979/2; Favreau & Dufour, p.170+. All GCMA operations remained strictly classified, leading Jules Roy to ascribe VM failure to interfere with the evacuation to a banal error on the part of an enemy radio operator – Rocolle was similarly misled.

The price of the withdrawal in equipment and stores was 34 vehicles, 150 tons of munitions, 142 tons of rations, and 35 cubic metres of fuel destroyed, and 150 pack ponies set free. Naturally, the prefabricated PSP surface of the airstrip was also abandoned; the plates would be lifted by the VM and efficiently employed during their work to drive new trails through to Dien Bien Phu. They would also recover and put to good use large numbers of mines which French Air Force bombing failed to destroy (Fall, *Hell...*, p.34); and – according to an SDECE agent – some 105mm shells and the latest US fuses, whose demolition charge failed to work. (Brancion, p.284)

24 Rocolle, p.170

25 *ibid*, p.171

26 Héduy (ed.), *La Guerre...*, p.347

27 Rocolle, p.174. The maps for all operations within the Delta were prominently marked with 10km circles indicating the range from the nearest battery of 105mm howitzers.

28 Fall, *Hell...*, p.33

29 Rocolle, p.175

30 Fall, *Hell...*, p.9

31 Rocolle, p.177

32 It seems more rewarding to examine what did happen, and how, rather than who might or might not have predicted its happening; but on this single point there is a (mildly) intriguing discrepancy in the sources. Rocolle (p.178) reports Bastiani's memorandum – a copy of which Bastiani showed him – in the terms quoted, though with an additional comment downplaying the importance of the DBP rice crop. Fall (*Hell...*, pp.35–6) gives a more dramatic version which continues: 'I am persuaded that DBP shall become, whether we like it or not, an abyss for battalions, with no possibility of large-scale radiating out from it as soon as it will be blocked by a single VM regiment...' (sic). If Bastiani really issued a serious warning of disaster to (as opposed to wasteful use of) the troops inserted at DBP, it is puzzling that Rocolle does not mention this, given his personal interview with Bastiani and sight of the original document. Bastiani must, of course, be credited with predicting that DBP would suck in reinforcements, if not actually that it would be annihilated.

33 Rocolle, p.179+

34 *ibid*, p.181

35 Fall, *Hell...*, p.4

36 *ibid*, p.37

37 Rocolle, p.184

38 Roy, p.31+

39 Distances are from US Defense Mapping Agency 1:1,000,000 scale Operational Navigation Chart, sheet ONC J-11.

The note on civilian requisitions is from Brancion, p.274+, which lists companies and types. In winter 50/51 Gen de Lattre reorganized the Aviation Directorate of the High Commission to allow periodic military requisition of aircraft and crews from civil aviation firms operating in Indochina, and this still applied in 53/4.

40 Rocolle, p.185+. Contributions to this meeting were recorded in a succinct summary made by Col Bastiani; and in notes taken by Capt Yves Rocolle, Col Pierre Rocolle's brother, who was an officer on Gen Navarre's staff.

7 Castor

The epigraph is quoted from Jules Roy, *The Battle of Dien Bien Phu*, Faber & Faber (1965) p.51.

1 This is the name used in all Viet Minh documents of the day; and Nam Youm is the Thai name for what the Vietnamese call the Nam Rom river.

2 Fall, *Hell...*, p.22+; Roy, p.36+

3 Holmes, page 204+

4 Bergot, *Les 170 Jours...*, p.35

5 Weeks, pp.25+ & 40+. The static line of the T7 pulled the canopy out of the pack first so that it started to deploy immediately; the shock was considerable, but it gave great safety in case of a low jump. Only 10 per cent casualties were suffered among men mistakenly dropped from only 175ft at Noemfoor, New Guinea on 3 July 1944. The author is shamelessly indulging himself by adding that in contrast, the contemporary British X-type Statichute was a 'canopy last' design; the static line pulled the canopy out still restrained by a sleeve, allowing the full length of the shroud lines to pay out before it was finally released to deploy. In Col Weeks' words, '... the man feels no jerk at all, and the stories of parachutists landing with bruises on their shoulders and legs... have never applied... with a Statichute or its derivatives.' With due respect to rank and immeasurably greater experience, some 30 years ago the present author would have begged to differ.

6 The foregoing follows Bail, *L'Enfer...*, p.20+; Bergot, *Les 170 Jours...*, p.25+; Brancion, p.30+; Fall, *Hell...*, p.1+; and Rocolle, p.199

7 Racca, *RHd'A*, 1968/1

8 Rocolle, p.30

9 *ibid*, p.218

10 Maj Segrétain's second in command, Capt Jeanpierre had served with the Legion since 1936 except for a period with the Resistance in 43–4 which ended in Mauthausen concentration camp. In Algeria in Mar 57 Lt Col Jeanpierre would take command of 1 REP, the enlarged unit born from the ashes of 1 BEP's second annihilation at DBP; he led it with great energy and success until his death in action in May 58.

11 Bergot, *Les 170 Jours...*, p.35

12 The military parachutes of the 1940s–60s bore no resemblance to today's sports rigs, which more or less guarantee a 'stand-up landing' every time. A loaded paratrooper of that era hit the ground as if he were jumping from an upstairs window, and the training in rolling to spread the impact was definitely necessary. The most common injuries were broken ankles, crushed heels, and compression fractures of the lumbar vertebrae.

13 Gaujac, *Histoire...*, p.267; and Trinquier, *RHd'A*, 1981/4. The title 'Shock' was in homage to a famous Free French airborne unit raised in North Africa in 1943.

14 The US M20 75mm RCL, had a theoretical maximum range of 6,800yds or 3.8 miles, but a much shorter practical battle range for accurate fire on pinpoint targets.

15 Brancion, p.271. 1 CEPML was formed in Sept 53 largely from 1 BEP with some attached artillery personnel. The Brandt M1949 120mm mortar had a removable two-wheel carriage and could be towed by a Bernardet 'scooter', of which there would be only two at DBP. The mortar weighed 1,010lbs, nearly half a ton, but could be broken down into four loads, each of which could be manhandled – with some difficulty – by three men. Each mortar bomb weighed 38lbs, in comparison to 55lbs for a 105mm howitzer shell. The strongest propellant charge – Charge 7 – was not used at DBP, so the maximum range of the mortars was about 4 miles, against 6 miles for the 105mm howitzer. Over the usual battle ranges at DBP the 120mm mortar bombs of both sides were comparably destructive to 105mm shells; they also arrived without any warning whistle.

16 Bail, *Les Combats...*, p.47; Fall, *Hell...*, p.16

17 Gaujac, *Histoire...*, p.405 & *passim*

18 Fall, *Hell...*, p.17

19 Roy, p.51

20 Fall, *Hell...*, p.53

21 Trinquier, *RHd'A*, 1981/4.

22 The VM did not consider the counter-guerrilla threat to be over, however; during the battle of DBP at least four battalions were deployed to guard the rear areas of the siege army from interference, and other regional units were deployed further to the west for the same reason. (Rocolle, p.157)

23 *ibid*, p.227+

24 Fall, *Hell...*, p.21

25 Bail, *Les Combats...*, p.51; Rocolle, pp.202, 309. The 22,800 PSPs and 15,000 pickets needed to fix them weighed a total of 510 tons – more than 200 loads for C-47s or 85 for C-119s.

26 Fall, *Hell...*, p.41

8 Torricelli and the Front Supply Commission

The epigraph is quoted from Patrick Facon, 'L'Armée de l'Air et Dien Bien Phu', in *Revue Historique des Armées*, 1985/1.

1 Rocolle, p.190+

2 *ibid*, p.194, quoting *Contribution à l'histoire de DBP*, Hanoi (1965) p.7.

3 *ibid*, pp.197, 209 – but not, in fact, Div. 304. 308's move on 28 Nov from its staging area north of the Delta uncovered the approaches to the Viet

Bac. Giap therefore moved Div 304 – less Regt 66, detached at Thanh Hoa – up from the South Delta Base to take 308's place between 27 Nov and mid Dec 53.

4 *ibid*, p.206

5 *ibid*, pp.43+, 60. Turpin, whose duties gave him access to decoded telegrams from Navarre, used a *Libération* journalist named Baranés as a conduit to the French CP. Some senior officers had long been uneasy about the security of the NDC permanent secretariat. A more direct link with the USSR was Georges Paques, a civil servant under the Mayer, Laniel and later Mendès-France cabinets, whose trial in 1963 revealed that he had been handing over intelligence to his Soviet handlers twice a month since before VE-Day. Whatever practical effect these leaks and betrayals may or may not have had on Giap's conduct of the campaign is unconfirmed.

6 *ibid*, p.33. The piece, by the Swedish journalist Svante Löfgren in *Expressen*, was reprinted in *Le Monde* on 1 Dec, and Ho Chi Minh would repeat more or less the same message in a broadcast on 19 Dec.

7 *ibid*, p.208, quoting *Contribution...*, p.41.

8 Fall, *Hell...*, p.127; Rocolle, p.209

9 Rocolle, pp.209, 250

10 Simpson, *DBP...*, p.33

11 Rocolle, p.248; Fall, *Hell...*, p.126

12 Fall, *Hell...*, p.128; Rocolle, pp.70, 213, 240

13 Rocolle , p.219+; Fall, *Hell...*, pp.41+, 222

14 Rocolle , p224+; Fall (*Hell...*, p.39+) criticizes Cogny as if he had ordered the building of a continuous 31-mile perimeter around the valley – which, obviously, he had not.

15 Fall, *Hell...*, p.44. Navarre formalized these instructions in his Directive No.949 of 5 Dec 53. (Rocolle, p.265)

16 Rocolle, p.226

17 Fall, *Hell...*, p.129. Rocolle (p.212), states that between 5 and 20 Dec, of 434 tons of supplies reaching Tuan Giao only 74 tons were transported by portage or bicycle, the rest on vehicles.

18 Rocolle, p.240

19 Fall, *Hell...*, pp.128+, 133.

20 Rocolle, p.213

21 Fall, *Hell...*, p.129, quoting Giap, *Dien Bien Phu*, Hanoi (1964 edn.)

22 Rocolle, p.210+; Fall, *Hell...*, p.129

23 Variously identified by the codenames 'Hail Leaflet' and 'Lazy Dog'.

24 Rocolle, p.211; Simpson, *DBP...*, p.34+

25 Rocolle, p.112; Bail, *Les Combats...*, p.93

26 Bail, *L'Enfer...*, p.48; *Les Combats...*, p.75; Rocolle, p.111

27 Rocolle, pp.112+, 317; Champeaux de la Boulaye, *RHd'A* 1987/4. See also Ch.15 below.

28 Formerly the Royal Navy's HMS *Colossus* (13,300 tons standard), a veteran of the Pacific Fleet in 1945. Loaned to the French Navy in Aug 46 and sold outright in 51, the *Arromanches* was on her fourth Far East tour.

29 Simpson, *DBP...*, p.86; Bail, *Les Combats...*, p.241

30 Rocolle, p.310+. The 'technical difficulties' included the proximity of too many powerful radio transmitters in Hanoi. The work of the CCF is described in more detail in Ch.15.

31 Rocolle, p.314

32 *ibid*, p.320. In addition, those Bearcats based at DBP and Xieng Khouang flew 526 sorties in direct support of the garrison.

33 *ibid*, p.318+; Champeaux de la Boulaye, *RHd'A* 1987/4

34 Fall, *Hell...*, p.129+

35 See Gen de Champeaux's analysis of B-26 bombload practice in Ch.15 below.

36 Rocolle, p.315

37 The other battalions were 2 BEP & 3 BPVN. (Gaujac, *Histoire...*, p.412)

38 Rocolle, p.244+; Simpson, *DBP...*, p.45+: Bail, *Les Combats...*, p.70

39 Rocolle, pp.222, 246, 321+

40 *ibid*, p.242

41 *ibid*, p.243

42 Simpson, *DBP...*, p.47; Fall, *Hell...*, p.49

43 Rocolle, p.241; Fall, *Hell...*, p.104; Simpson, *DBP...*, p.49

44 Rocolle, p.265

45 Fall, *Hell...*, p.85; this is a very slight editing of Fall's translation. He cites no source for this quotation, nor for another from the report by Lt Col Denef to which Bastiani's note was attached.

46 Fall, *Hell...*, p.45+

47 Rocolle, p.125. GMs 41 & 42 were raised in the Central Highlands, and GMs 11 & 21 in Annam and Cochinchina. The French brigades were GMs 10 & 100; the core of GM 10 was a regiment of Algerian Tirailleurs shipped in from Germany. GM 100 was built around the former

French UN battalion which had fought with the US 2nd Div in Korea, now expanded by local recruitment into the two-battalion Régiment de Corée. See also Ch.17, p.634+.

48 *ibid*, p.125. The then-forming ANV GM 32, and GMs 2, 3 & 7.

49 Including independent Regts 96, 108 & 803, regional Regts 84 & 120, and regional Bn 89. (Héduy (ed.), *La Guerre...*, p.173)

50 Bail, *Les Combats...*, p.80

51 Rocolle, p.270. The phrase was 'Nous avons pratiquement réglé et achevé dans les conditions générales de temps prévues la première phase de l'opération *Atlante...*'

52 Rocolle, pp.124+, 246+, 270, 412; Fall, *Hell...*, p.45+; Simpson, *DBP...*, p.45+

53 Rocolle, p.412

54 *ibid*, pp.213, 315

55 *ibid*, p.318. Rocolle's definition of terms seems unclear, but his figures show that of one series of 751 sorties, 88 per cent were flown either in formations of three, by pairs or by single aircraft.

56 *ibid*, p.317+. The officer requested was a Col Michaud, but the commander of the unified bomber group which operated during the last 48 hours of the battle was Lt Col Dussol.

57 Rocolle, pp.314 & 318, quoting the report compiled by Air Force Maj Feuvrier for Third Bureau (Ops) of Gen Navarre's staff. See also analysis of B-26 operations by Gen de Champeaux de la Boulaye in Ch.15.

58 Fall, *Hell...*, p.132+; Simpson, *DBP...*, p.28

59 Bail, *Les Combats...*, p.74+; Caillot, 'La 11-F'

60 Bail, *Les Combats...*, p.80

61 Rocolle, p.214

62 *ibid*, p.250

63 *ibid*, p.323+. China provided 1,700 tons of rice via the Black River and Lai Chau; more came up the Song river from Thanh Hoa, and *c.* 3,000 tons were gathered by local requisition in the High Region.

64 *ibid*, p.250+, including quotation from *Contribution...*, Hanoi (1965) p.43.

65 *ibid*, p.92. There have also been persistent claims that Chinese AA personnel served at DBP with the 37mm batteries of Regt 367; some were seen by the captured Capt L'Hostis. (Brancion, p.258)

66 Simpson, *DBP...*, p.53, quoting his interview with Gen Giap on 18 Mar 91.

67 Rocolle, pp.215, 255+, 263

68 During a night mission over Muong Sai one Privateer crew nearly fell victim to an attempt to mislead them into bombing their own troops; the VM had 'hacked into' the ground/air HF wavelength used by the Navy bombers. Much the same would happen in early March during a Privateer mission over DBP. Given the Viet Minh's overall lack of sophistication in the use of radios, the French found these incidents startling. (Bail, *Les Combats...*, p.88+)

69 Rocolle, p.257+

70 *ibid*, p.260

71 A reference to the notoriously bloody revolt on that island against the Angevin kings in 1282. Rocolle, p.37+; the report was undated.

72 Rocolle, p262+. Gabions were the earth-filled baskets used in historic times for the same purposes as modern sandbags.

73 Brancion, *op cit* p.282+; and Brancion, *RHd'A* 1992/4, illustration p.115

74 *ibid*, p.283

75 Rocolle, p.251+; Simpson, *DBP...*, p.52

76 Rocolle, p.252. The artillery historian Gen de Brancion does not mention this incident.

77 Rocolle, 261+

78 Brancion, p.281:
Regt 45 = two battalions, each of four companies, each with 3 × 105mm: Bn 950 (Cos 60, 64, 66 and 68), and Bn 954 (Cos 80, 83, 86 and 89).
Regt 675 = Bn 175 (Cos 754, 755 and 756, each 3 × 75mm); Bn 275 (Co 751 with 4 × 120mm; Co 753 with 3 × 75mm; Co 756 with 4 × 120mm); & Bn 83 (Cos 111, 112 and 119, each 4 × 120mm; Cos 113 and 115, each 3 × 75mm).

79 Rocolle, p.241+

80 The 37mm Russian M1939 AA gun was broadly similar to the classic Swedish/British 40mm Bofors. Since the practical rate of fire was up to 80rpm, 44,000 rounds could theoretically be expended in an accumulated total of some 15 minutes' firing by 36 guns. In practice, of course, consumption would be much slower – guns do not fire continuously; but it is still hard to imagine the People's Army contemplating the start of an anti-aircraft battle with 44,000 rounds divided between any more than 36 guns.
  The heavy MGs are always described generically as '12.7mm' (0.50in), suggesting the Russian DShK M1938, but may have included slightly larger types such as the 14.5mm ZPU-1. There are no obvious Soviet bloc candidates for the reported 20mm cannon, but they may have been

Oerlikon guns captured from the Nationalist Chinese or purchased on the open market.

81 Rocolle, p.340. Even if the entire 200-ton additional convoy had been 120mm mortar bombs, stocks would only have totalled *c.* 320rpg – little more than one hour's continuous firing. Further shipments must have arrived during March.

82 *ibid,* p.263+, quoting from *Contribution...,* Hanoi (1965) p.45.

83 *ibid,* pp.270+, 339. To dignify Luang Prabang, Muong Sai and Pleiku with the description 'air–ground base' would seem optimistic; but this document was an exhortation rather than an analysis. On 8 Mar the C-in-C issued a memorandum discussing replacing chains of small Delta posts by fewer, larger entrenched camps with airstrips.

84 *ibid,* p.332+

85 *ibid,* p.272

86 *ibid,* p.340

87 *ibid,* p.343; and see Appendix 4 at the end of this book. At this stage he had three complete regts each from Divs 308 & 312 (2 × 3 × 3 = 18 bns); one regt from Div 304 (= 3); two regts from Div 316 (2 × 3 = 6); plus one bn from Regt 176, Div 316 (whose other two bns were operating against the partisans alongside Indpt Regt 148).

9 GONO

1 Fall, *Hell...,* p.56+; Gaujac, *Histoire...,* p.291

2 Fall, *Hell...,* p.55+; Rocolle, p.235+. The slightly venereal overtones of the acronym were not lost on the French.

3 Brancion, p.80. Gen de Brancion, then a captain, was wounded in this incident.

4 Williams, *The Reach of Rome,* pp.38–9

5 Fall, *Hell...,* p.96

6 Simpson, *DBP...,* p.38

7 Rocolle, p.104+

8 Bergot, *Les 170 Jours...,* p.114+

9 Perhaps drawing on an FTNV telegram of late Nov 53 (Rocolle, p.330), which describes it as a 'proven' unit in contrast to the other Thais, Fall (*Hell...,* p.113) states that BT 3 distinguished itself during Op 'Mouette'. However, Paillard (*RHd'A,* 1984/4) quotes the subsequent inquiry report to the contrary. He identifies the attackers as Bn 884/Regt 48 & Bn 722/Regt 64 from Div 320.

10 Rocolle, p.331

11 Bail, *L'Enfer...,* p.35; Léonard, *RHd'A,* 1956/3. The recently retitled repair unit – drawn from men of 5 REI under cadres from the Service du Matériel's 1st Repair Bn at Saigon – was still known to the troops by its former (and easier to pronounce) acronym 'CRALE' – 'Foreign Legion Automobile Repair Company'. The tank airlift was not the first of its type: Op 'Rondelle I' had seen M5A1 Stuarts flown into the Plain of Jars aboard C-119s in spring 1953.

The DBP garrison had 44 jeeps, 47 Dodge 4 × 4 and 6 × 6 trucks and 26 GMC 2½-ton trucks. These were sufficient for internal liaison and supply distribution, but not for engineer tasks. (Rocolle, p.276)

12 Fall, p.95+. There were four 4-ton water purifiers, 15 generators and five battery chargers. Two more generators were later parachuted in to replace those destroyed by shellfire, but one smashed on the DZ and the other proved too heavy to be recovered under fire.

13 Some accounts state that the two Legion infantry mortar companies had mixed equipment of 81mm and 120mm tubes: Gen de Brancion (*op cit,* p.61) is clear that both were equipped solely with the 120mm Brandt M1949; and confirms (p.113) that only Lt Clerget's platoon of 2 CMMLE were based on Gabrielle by 13–15 Mar 54, the other remaining in the artillery area of Claudine.

14 TD 301, withdrawn from Lai Chau, was also based at Isabelle for two or three weeks from 23 Dec 53, when it was shifted there from Anne-Marie (Bergot, *Les 170 Jours...,* p.300). Poor morale signalled by desertions led to its removal from DBP to Muong Sai in mid Jan 54. The other main unit from Lai Chau, 2e Tabor Marocain (Maj Borie), were flown out of DBP to Hanoi on 4 Jan. (Blondieau, *Insignes...,* notes to Plate 16)

15 Each of the 12 battalion localities should have had 500 tons of wire; since only 3,000 tons were provided for the whole camp, each battalion had well under half its requirement.

16 Favreau & Dufour, pp.128–3, 146–7

17 Simpson, *DBP...,* p.36, for comments by an officer of V/7 RTA.

18 Rocolle, p.275+

19 *ibid,* p.277

20 Fall, *Hell...,* p.88+

21 Rocolle, p.275+

22 According to Roy (p.312), Capt Bordier left DBP a couple of days before the battle started, 'in search of dental treatment'.

23 Fall, *Hell...,* p.63. Op 'Léda'; the principal units flown out, by 183 × Dakota sorties, were a

Senegalese HQ detachment, TD 301, 2e Tabor Marocain, BT 2, and a paratroop company. Simpson (*Tiger...*, p.102) states that a large store of munitions in a schoolhouse was in fact forgotten, and that an engineer team had to be helicoptered to Lai Chau at the last moment to destroy it. Deo Van Long and his household reached asylum in France – apart from some female ballet dancers, who by mischance found themselves trapped at DBP throughout the siege.

24 References rarely make clear distinctions between CSLT 'auxiliaries' and GMI 'partisans'; an unrecorded number of the latter were present in the forest during the withdrawal and were able to guide some stragglers to safety.

25 Fall, *Hell...*, p.66+; Bail, *L'Enfer...*, p.62. Guillermit's seven companies were overrun on 8–10 Dec; his Sgt Arsicaud continued to lead survivors south, at one stage gathering about 600 under his command, but was last heard of on the 19th. Ulpat's six companies were wiped out on 18 Dec near Pou Koi, though he and a dozen other survivors were rescued later. Blanc's three-plus companies were encircled and annihilated at Muong Pon on 12–13 Dec. The last French survivor to reach safety is believed to have been Cpl Chief Roger Vigier, a GMI radio operator, who arrived at the Laotian post of Muong Outay, 87 miles from Lai Chau as the crow flies, on 1 Jan 54.

26 431, 432 and 434 CSLT

27 Fall, *Hell...*, p.64+; Bail, *L'Enfer...*, p.62; Rocolle, p.228

28 Bergot, *Les 170 Jours...*, p.50

29 Simpson, *Tiger...*, p.101

30 Bail, *Les Combats...*, p.49. Howard Simpson (*Tiger...*, p.97+) describes accompanying a similar 6 BPC patrol some four miles northwards, though the date is not recorded. The former GI was impressed by the unit's pace, by the austerity and energy of its commander, and by its fieldcraft. However, some French commentators (e.g. Bail, *Les Combats...*, p.57) note that the paratroopers of the 1950s were sometimes guilty of the same carelessness as their US successors in Vietnam, in that they discarded cigarette packets, ration cans, etc., in the field, thus making themselves easy to follow.

31 Bergot, *Les 170 Jours...*, p.40

32 Bail, *Les Combats...*, p.55+

33 Fall, *Hell...*, p.58+

34 Bergot, *Les 170 Jours...*, p.41+

35 Simpson, *DBP...*, p.25+

36 Artillery support was provided by the Laotian battery and the newly arrived 9/III/10 RAC, under overall command of Capt Castaignet – see Ch.10. (Brancion, p.49)

37 Fall (*Hell...*, p.69+) states that Tourret's men linked up with Langlais at about 2pm on the 12th, and that it was they who led the way into Muong Pon; Bergot (*Les 170 Jours...*, p.49) puts the link-up only on the night of the 13th. There appears to be confusion over the two separated elements of 8th Shock.

38 Both Fall (*Hell...*) and Bail (*L'Enfer...*) say that the French dead were left on the field; Bergot (*Les 170 Jours...*, p.48) states that all corpses had been removed, adding to the sinister desolation of the scene. His sources for this chapter seem to include his fellow Legion paratroop officers Lt Martin and Capt Cabiro, who were present.

39 Brancion, p.50+

40 Simpson, *DBP...*, p.27

41 5e Tabor Marocain, II/2 REI & 5e Bataillon de Chasseurs Laotiens.

42 Rocolle, p.230+; Simpson, *DBP...*, p.29+; Brancion, p.64

43 Roy, p.121

44 Navarre had visited DBP on 29 Nov & 17 Dec; he would do so again on 3 & 26 Jan 54, 18 Feb & 4 Mar. (Rocolle, pp.236, 273)

45 Henri IV of Navarre, r.1589–1610

46 Bergot, *Les 170 Jours...*, p.53+

47 Racca, *RHd'A*, 1968/1

48 Simpson, *DBP...*, p.42+

49 Racca, *RHd'A*, 1968/1. The soldiers who staffed such depots, under the authority of the Intendants Militaires, were designated Commis et Ouvriers Militaires d'Administration, COMA. (Bunel, *RHd'A*, 1957/4)

50 Bail, *Les Combats...*, p.72

51 Simpson, *DBP...*, p.43+

52 Bail, *Les Combats...*, p.73

53 Bergot, *Les 170 Jours...*, p.61. On 13 Mar there were a total of 7 Vietnamese and 11 Algerian prostitutes at DBP; four of the latter would be killed by shellfire, and all apparently volunteered as nurse's aides. (Macdonald, p.135)

54 Simpson, *DBP...*, p.46.

55 Green would describe Castries' 'neat, dark, histrionic features'; and his angry insistence on the camp's offensive role, in contrast to the defensive character of Na San (*The Spectator*, 10 Apr 54.

A list of principal visitors drawn from Rocolle (pp.236 & 273) and Fall (Hell..., p.106+) is as follows:
22 Nov 53: Gen Cogny; 24 Nov: Gen Spears; 26 Nov: Gen Cogny; 29 Nov: Gens Navarre & Cogny, US Gen Thomas Trapnell (MAAG); 9 Dec: Gen Cogny; 11 Dec: Gen Dechaux (GATAC/Nord); 12 Dec: Gen Cogny, Gen Bodet (Deputy C-in-C), Col de Crèvecoeur (FTL), Graham Greene; 17 Dec: Gens Navarre & Cogny; 19 Dec: US Gen Trapnell; 24 Dec: Gen Navarre; 29 Dec: Gen Cogny, Gen Bodet, Gen Lauzin (FAEO), Gen Pennacchioni (Insp Arty CEFEO); 1 Jan 54: Gen Cogny; 3 Jan: Gens Navarre & Cogny, Commissioner Gen Maurice Dejean; 14 Jan: US Gen Trapnell; 15 Jan: Gen Cogny; 22 Jan: Gen Cogny; 26 Jan: Gens Navarre & Cogny, Gen Blanc (Army C-of-S), Commissioner Gen Dejean, Marc Jacquet (Sec for Assoc States); 1 Feb: Gen Cogny; 2 Feb: US Gen John O'Daniel (incoming chief MAAG); 7 Feb: Gen Cogny, Alain de Chevigné (Sec for Ground Forces); 14 Feb: Gen Ely (Chief of Defence Staff), Sec de Chevigné; 18 Feb: Gens Navarre, Cogny & Jeansotte (Army Surgeon Gen), Col Dr Terramorsi (chief MO, FTNV); 19 Feb: Gen Cogny, Gen Fay (Air Force C-of-S), René Pleven (Defence Minister); 28 Feb: Gen Cogny; 4 Mar: Gens Navarre & Cogny; 6 Mar: Malcolm McDonald (Brit High Commissioner SE Asia); 12 Mar: Gen Cogny.

56 Bail, Les Combats..., p.71; Bergot, Les 170 Jours..., pp.52, 76

57 Simpson, DBP..., p.42 et passim. Cameraman André Lebon and photographer Daniel Camus jumped in with the first wave of paratroopers; photographers Jean Martinoff and Jean Péraud and cameraman Pierre Schoendoerffer flew or jumped in later. Martinoff was killed by shelling, and Lebon lost a foot and was evacuated, on 12 Mar; Camus and Schoendoerffer both survived the battle and the Viet Minh prison camps, but Péraud disappeared. Schoendoerffer later became a respected film director, recalling his time in Indochina in 317e Section, Le Crabe Tambour, and finally in Dien Bien Phu (1992).

58 Rocolle, p.66

59 Simpson, DBP..., p.61; Fall, Hell..., p.108+. An amphibious warfare specialist in the Sicily, Anzio and South of France landings, 'Iron Mike' had served alongside the French as commander of the US 3rd Inf Div at the Colmar Pocket in Jan–Feb 45. He commanded the US Army's Infantry School in 1945–8, and I Corps in Korea. (Boatner, Biographical Dictionary of World War II, Presidio Press, 1999.)
Several US officers spent time at DBP. Cols John M.Wohner & Richard F. Hill, US Army, were temporarily attached as observers to 13

DBLE. When it became clear that 37mm AA guns might be on their way to DBP the French requested an advisory mission by US officers familiar with them from Korea. Between 22 & 30 Jan, Maj Vaughn, Capts Lloyd & Mickey, USAF, studied the ground. The view of a joint Franco-US group chaired by an AA officer, Lt Col Sousselier, and including Capt Robert F. Lloyd, was that 37mm guns could not be hidden effectively from the air; their report (29 Jan) concluded that 'the study .. permits one to envisage with optimism the continuity of resupply by air...' (Rocolle, p.291)

60 French dead and missing between 20 Nov 53 and 5 May 54 = 498; Vietnamese = 661 (Fall, Hell..., p.483). The colour photos by Lt Dr Rondy mentioned at the beginning of this passage appeared in Hommes de Guerre magazine No. 18, May/June 1989.

61 Rocolle, p.268+

62 ibid, pp.334+, 339. Gen Blanc was exaggerating by a month the expected onset of the monsoon in May.

63 Roy, p.142

64 Rocolle, p.337+

65 ibid, p.338, quoting Gen Paul Ely, Mémoires – L'Indochine dans la Tourmente, Plon, Paris (1964)

66 Bail, Les Combats..., p.76

67 Simpson, DBP..., p.56+; Fall, Hell..., p.79+

68 Fall, Hell..., p.80; Bail, Les Combats..., p.81

69 Brancion (p.116) puts Hill 674 further north. Rocolle and Roy omit an operation between 10 & 12 Feb altogether; Fall (Hell..., p.82+) gives 10 & 11 Feb; Bail (Les Combats..., p.81+) gives 11th & 12th. Bergot (Les 170 Jours..., p.64+) omits exact dates but says the operation ended on the 15th, as does Simpson (DBP..., p.57). It is possible that they, Fall and Rocolle (p.269) elide separate engagements between 11 & 16 Feb into a single operation; or equally, that Bail (p.83) is mistaken in treating fighting on the 15th–16th as distinct.

70 Rocolle, p.269. On p.271 he mentions a further sortie on 21 Feb, but there is no other reference to it.

71 An ACP's equipment was divided into 32 packs with a total weight of 2,600lbs, and two Dakotas could drop the whole unit. During their month at DBP, 1 ACP triaged and evacuated 207 wounded and 75 accidental injuries.

72 It is often assumed that Dr Grauwin was the senior medical officer at DBP; in fact he was officially responsible only for his surgical team. He was not a regular officer, but a reservist who had been granted major's rank as a member of the Corps de Liaison Administratif d'Extrême-Orient, which recruited medical personnel on temporary contract. The senior medical officer in the camp was initially Col Terramorsi, then Capt Rives of GM 9 until 20 Feb, and thereafter Capt Le Damany of GM 9. (Rocolle, p.303)

73 Forissier, *RHd'A*, 1989/4; & Rocolle, p.304

74 Fall, *Hell...*, p.121

75 Roy, p.138

76 Galard-Terraube, in Héduy (ed.), *La Guerre ...*, p.162+. The flight nurses were provided by a special branch of the French Red Cross attached to the Air Force – Infirmières, Pilotes & Secouristes de l'Air (IPSA).

10 Zulu Kilo

The epigraph is quoted from Brancion, *Dien Bien Phu: Artilleurs dans la Fournaise*, Presses de la Cité, Paris (1993) p.87.

1 Bail, *L'Enfer...*, p.60; *Les Combats...*, p.54

2 Brancion, p.77

3 *ibid*, pp.46, 59+, 134

4 *ibid*, p.65+. Note that these were short-barrelled 155mm howitzers, resembling enlarged 105s – not the famous long-barrelled 155mm 'Long Tom' guns. Each 5½-ton piece had to be broken down into loads for two C-47s and one Bristol 170, and the crews, tools and initial ammunition supply filled another 17 Dakotas. Calculated as a proportion of the daily airlift capacity in Indochina, moving this single battery represented perhaps 20 per cent of the available sorties.

5 On 13 Jan, 7/III/10 RAC also moved to Isabelle; on 2 Feb, 9/III/10 RAC returned to Claudine. (Brancion, pp.81+, 94, 223, *et passim*)

6 Among the variables which constantly had to be updated in order to keep a fire plan effective were – obviously – wind speed and direction; but also humidity, barometric pressure, and even the 'Coriolis effect' of the earth's rotation. Some of these were determined daily by releasing a meteorological balloon from DBP; others were radioed from Hanoi.

7 Bergot, *Les 170 Jours...*, p.36

8 Brancion, page 277+. After the ceasefire an officer of GM/35 RALP came across thick sheaves of good pre-1939 maps of the DBP area in a store at Dalat.

9 *ibid*, p.48

10 Rocolle, p.287+

11 Fall, *Hell...*, p.101+, quoting Pierre Schoendoerffer. On 16 Dec 53, Piroth told Col de Winter that to support a division he should have had three rather than two battalions of 105s, and a whole battalion of 155s; yet on 26 Jan 54, during the visit by Gen Blanc and Sec Jacquet, he refused an offer of reinforcement.

12 Favreau & Dufour, p.77+ *et passim*

13 Experiments were made with colour and infra-red film, including special Eastman camouflage detection stock, under supervision by Capt Hill, USAF, who was based at Hanoi from 23 Jan to 2 Mar; the results were disappointing. (Fall, *Hell...*, p.103; Bail, *Les Combats...*, p.94)

14 Brancion, pp.39+, 269+. Neither the first Second Bureau report in Oct 53 that the VM had acquired a regiment of 105mm howitzers, nor a report on 3 Jan 54 by Gen Pennacchioni on the inadequate means of target location at DBP, prompted any serious attempt to improve the SRA there or elsewhere in Indochina. Hanoi apparently gambled everything on the effectiveness of aerial photo interpretation.

15 Brancion, p.67+

16 Bail, *Les Combats...*, p.74+

17 Brancion, p.84

18 *ibid*, pp.87, 282+. Gen de Brancion believes that the first shots were fired on 1 Feb 54. Simpson (*DBP...*, p.54), whose source is Col Bui Tin, dates them to late afternoon 26 Jan, and states that at any one time only a single 75mm gun fired ranging shots to perfect the VM fire plan. Rocolle (p.263) and Bail (*Les Combats...*, p.76) date the first shots to 31 Jan 54.

19 Brancion, pp.87+, 95, 273

20 Fall, *Hell...*, p.103; Brancion, p.155

21 Brancion, pp.79, 92 & 218

22 Roy, p.138+

23 Fall, *Hell...*, p.104

24 Brancion, p.99

25 Bail, *Les Combats...*, p.73; Fall, *Hell...*, p.304

26 Rocolle, p.144

27 Bail, *Les Combats...*, p.73

28 *ibid*, p.62; Bergot, *Les 170 Jours...*, p.44

29 US National Intelligence Estimate 91, 4 June 53, listed S/GMMTA's fleet as 28 × C-47 & 3 × Ju52 in Tonkin, 5 × C-47 & 8 × Ju52 in Annam, and 16 × C-47 & 4 × Ju52 in Cochinchina.

30 Brancion, p.275+; and Air America Association

– History, University of Texas Archives, accessed via *http://www.air-america.org/About/History.htm*

31 *ibid,* p.134+. Capt de Brancion was one of those in whom Col Piroth confided, at Thai Binh on the night of 3 Dec 53, shortly before the VM commando attack on their divisional CP.

32 Fall, *Hell...,* p.105

33 Brancion, p.101+; Fall, *Hell...,* p.99+. Each 'quad-50' was mounted in an M45C Maxson skeleton turret of the type normally seen on the M16 half-track, but here fixed to an M20 two-wheel trailer, the combination designated M55. Its electrical traverse and elevation were powered by two six-volt batteries charged by an integral generator and 'Little Joe' petrol engine. The trailer was jacked up off its wheels for firing; accurate horizontal range was about 1,650 yards – the M18 reflex AA sights were not ideal for ground combat, but made little practical difference for indirect fire missions. Feed was from 210-round belts in large metal 'tombstone' cases.

34 Fall, *Hell...,* p.85+

35 Bergot, *Les 170 Jours...,* p.72

36 The sources are contradictory over the dates of a number of patrol actions and sorties. Brancion dates this action to 12 Mar, and the V/7 RTA's skirmish at Ban Khe Phai to the 11th; Bail (*L'Enfer...,* p.85) dates the latter to 13 rather than 12 Mar – which seems unlikely.

37 Roy, p.155; Simpson, *DBP...,* p.62+; Brancion, p.103

38 Bergot, *Les 170 Jours...,* p.77+. By comparison, the normal strength of parachute companies was three officers, 16–18 senior NCOs, 28–30 corporals, and at least 105 privates.

39 Rocolle (p.349) states that French radio had intercepted orders for a VM raid on the night 10/11 Mar on Isabelle, to try to reach the artillery; and that on 11/12 Mar, Div 316 Trinh Sat were ordered to reconnoitre artillery and tank positions in Claudine with a view to attacking them on 12/13th. This did not take place, but may have been attempted on 13/14th.

40 Rocolle, p.327+

41 *ibid,* p.341+; Roy, p.151. Navarre apparently suggested inserting a new strongpoint between Claudine and Isabelle.

42 Col de Castries disliked the staff's term 'entrenched camp', and came up with the more positive alternative 'prepared battlefield'. (Rocolle, p.233)

43 *ibid,* p.329

44 *ibid,* p.329; Fall, *Hell...,* p.110

11 Béatrice and Gabrielle

The epigraph is quoted from Rocolle, *Pourquoi Dien Bien Phu?,* Flammarion, Paris (1968) p.354.

1 Roy, pp.161, 169

2 Bergot, *Les 170 Jours...,* p.80+. Coincidentally, this had been the very aircraft used by the French to take the Sultan of Morocco into exile the previous year.

3 Fall, *Hell...,* p.134

4 Bail, *L'Enfer...,* p.89+

5 Rocolle (p.309) says the problem was water, quoting Gen Dechaux's report of 20 May 54; Fall (*Hell...,* p.134+) attributes it to blowing dust getting into the fuel.

6 Bail, *L'Enfer...,* p.92

7 *ibid,* p.89

8 *ibid,* p.91+

9 Fall, *Hell...,* p.136+; Bergot, *Les 170 Jours...,* p.80+

10 Bail, *L'Enfer...,* p.91; Fall, *Hell...,* p.155; Brancion, p.14+

11 Bergot, *Les 170 Jours...,* p.85+

12 Anonymous British soldier, Worcestershire Regt, Normandy, 1944, quoted Berlin, *I Am Lazarus.*

13 Bowen (ed.), *Emergency War Surgery NATO Handbook*

14 In 1934 a book entitled *Covenants with Death,* edited by T. A. Innes & Ivor Castle, was published in Britain by the *Daily Express;* they were determined that the public should understand something of the reality of the Western Front in 1914–18, which had been carefully hidden during the war years. Several pages of photographs of battlefield remains and of the pitiful survivors of the most extreme wounds were held closed by a paper band, as a warning to sensitive readers. Once seen, these pictures unfortunately can never be forgotten; and most of them show the effects of shellfire.

15 Fall, *Hell...,* p.139

16 *ibid,* p.94

17 Rocolle, p.327+

18 Fall, *Hell...,* p.139

19 Brancion, pp.13+, 112. Later examination of duds showed two types: one had broken fuses, the other had none. The latter – the latest US munitions, presumably captured in Korea or perhaps at Na San – were intended to receive radar proximity VT fuses ('Pozit', in French terminology), but had been fired with the socket empty.

20 Brancion, p.110+; Bergot, *Les 170 Jours...*, p.90+

21 Brancion, p.268. At the outset of the battle the artillery and 120mm mortars were administratively separated into three task groups (see Map 11): *Group A* for direct infantry support (Maj Alliou): 9/III/10 RAC at Claudine, 7/ and 8/ at Isabelle; 1 CEPML at Claudine and Dominique 2; 2 CMMLE at Claudine and Gabrielle. *Group B* for direct infantry support (Maj Knecht): 4/, 5/ and 6/II/4 RAC at Dominique 3 and 4; 1 CMMLE and quad-50s at Dominique 4. *For counter-battery* (Capt Déal): 11/IV/4 RAC at Claudine and Eliane 10. From 23 Mar 54 at latest this formal division of tasks disappeared, and all assets were used to benefit the overall defence.

22 Brancion, p.18

23 The strongpoint numbers and company dispositions are contradictory in Rocolle, Fall, and Bail, *L'Enfer...* Here we follow the Legion officer Erwan Bergot, *Les 170 Jours...*, pp.85+ & 305; his sources include Lt Turpin, CO 11th Co.

NB, Capt Nicolas, 10/III/13 DBLE, should not be confused with Capt, later Maj Jean Nicolas, CO I/4 RTM.

24 Rocolle, p.352+; Bergot, *Les 170 Jours...*, p.57

25 Rocolle, p.348+

26 *ibid*, p.350

27 Quoted by Bergot, *Les 170 Jours...*, p.91+; his timings are generally later than other accounts. Additional material is from Rocolle, p.350+ (including published Viet Minh timings, which often seem too early); Fall, *Hell...*, p.139+; Brancion, pp.13+; and Simpson, *DBP...*, p.67+, who briefly quotes Capt Nicolas.

28 Fall, *Hell...*, p.140, and Bergot, *Les 170 Jours...*, p.112, state that two 105s were actually destroyed on 13/14 March, but Brancion does not confirm the second loss.

29 Fall, *Hell...*, p.139+

30 Rocolle, p.357

31 Rocolle states that Regt 209, suffering particularly from French shellfire, did not actually occupy B3 until 10.30pm.

32 Rocolle quotes Kubiak, *Képi Blanc* (1962 passim), to the effect that 9th Co's radio sent its last message at *c.* 12.15am; but also a message from GONO to FTNV at that time, stating that the survivors had already reached Dominique. He adds that Castries received nothing from B1 after 10pm. Fall follows Kubiak's timings; Bergot states that 9th Co's radio fell silent at *c.* 11pm.

33 Simpson, *DBP...*, p.69+, quoting Gen Tran Do. Again, the reference to MGs is puzzling: did the company have only 2 × LMGs? See Ch.4, note 32.

34 Brancion, p.106+; Simpson, *DBP ...*, p.73

35 Bergot, *Les 170 Jours...*, p.105

36 Rocolle, p.359+

37 Rocolle, p.358. Bergot (*Les 170 Jours...*, p.109) gives the number of recovered wounded as 14; Fall (*Hell...*, p.142+) quotes eight, but is clearly misinformed over the number of dead.

38 Rocolle, p.144. The expected number of days of rainfall at DBP were only six in April and 11 in May, rising to 14 in June and 17 in July. After 14/15 Mar 54 intermittent heavy rainfall seems to have returned only on 29 Mar, and continuous monsoon downpours did not begin until 25 April.

39 Bergot, *Les 170 Jours...*, p.110+

40 Fall, *(Hell...*, p.143) identifies the aircraft as a DHC Beaver; Bail (*L'Enfer...*, p.88), as a Siebel NC701.

41 Brancion, p.114+

42 This account is from Bail, *L'Enfer...*, p.96, which has convincing details. Fall (*Hell...*, p.134+) states that 12 × F8Fs were on the airfield on 13 Mar; and that Sgts de Somow and Barteau flew five missions each before flying to Vientiane *that* day. Fall, Bergot (*Les 170 Jours...*, p.113) and Bail (*Les Combats...*, p.104) all say that Lt Parisot, Sgts Bruand and Fouché managed to take off only on the afternoon of the 14th. Rocolle (p.309), drawing on the report of Gen Dechaux (20 May 54), has nine fighters present and three getting off under cover of morning mist on the 14th. It therefore seems that Somow and Barteau flew missions on both days (the fact that only their two aircraft were serviceable on the 13th accounting for their large number of sorties that day); that all-night work to clear the fuel systems allowed Parisot, Bruand and Fouché to escape on the 14th; that Somow and Barteau flew their final mission on the afternoon of the 14th before flying to Vientiane; and that the remaining four F8Fs were destroyed by shellfire.

43 Both VHF 'gonio' and MF 'radiophare' transmitted identifying Morse signals; these could be picked up by All Direction Frequency receivers in the aircraft, which were tuned until the strongest signal indicated the course to the beacon. Both were 'line of sight' signals whose strength and range were affected by terrain and altitude. The VHF, which probably also had a 'countdown' ranging facility, was the more stable signal, and at a normal altitude of *c.* 9,500ft had a range of *c.* 40–50 miles; the less reliable MF signal could be picked up only *c.* 20 or even 10 miles from the beacon. Both signals faded into a 'cone of silence' immediately above the transmitter.

44 Capt André Botella, CO 5 BPVN (promoted major on 16 Apr) should not be confused with Lt Antoine Botella of 2nd Co, V/7 RTA.

45 This officer's name is spelled Kha by Rocolle, but Kah by Fall, Bergot and Bail.

46 Not counting 68 NCOs and men at the battalion rear base at Phu Ly.

47 Bergot, *Les 170 Jours...*, p.115+

48 Fall, *Hell...*, p.145

49 Bail, *L'Enfer...*, p.46

50 Not to be confused with Capt André Botella, CO 5 BPVN.

51 Brancion, p.116

52 *ibid*, p.113

53 The account which follows draws upon Rocolle, p.363+; Fall, *Hell...*, p.145+; Brancion, p.116+; Bergot, *Les 170 Jours...*, p.115+, which seems to depend partly upon Lt Sanselme; and Bail, *L'Enfer...*, p.91+.

54 Rocolle (p.365) states that this process proved very slow, taking perhaps five hours – i.e. until *c.* 11pm – before the assault trenches reached the wire. All other accounts put the first infantry assault much earlier, and Rocolle must be referring to the later attack by Regt 165 from the south-east.

55 Brancion, p.117

56 The time of the destruction of 4th Co's CP and the death of Lt Moreau is variously reported. Fall (*Hell...*, p.146) has him dead in his wrecked blockhouse by 10pm; but Bergot (*Les 170 Jours...*, p.125) – whose source seems to be Lt Sanselme – reports that Moreau was killed by an RCL round through the vision slit of his CP during the renewed assaults some time after 3am.

57 Lt J. -M. Moreau, 6/II/4 RAC should not be confused with his namesake who commanded 4/V/7 RTA.

58 Brancion, pp.111 & 123. See also note on VM ammunition stocks in Appendix 4.

59 Bail, *L'Enfer...*, p.95; see also note 56.

60 Fall, *Hell...*, p.151+

61 'Pour tenter de *conserver* Gabrielle ou au minimum de *recueillir* le reliquat de la garnison...'(author's italics); Rocolle, p.373, quoting p.4 of Gen de Castries' supplementary report to the commission of inquiry.

62 The most detailed analysis of the counter-

attack is that of Rocolle, who interviewed several of the principals to clarify his documentary research (*op cit*, pp.295+, 371+). Additional comments are drawn from Bergot, *Les 170 Jours...*, p.130+, which quotes Capt Botella; Bail, *L'Enfer...*, p.95+; Fall, *Hell...*, p.151+; Brancion, p.127+, and Simpson, *DBP...*, p.78+.

63 Presumably Regts 209 & 174 respectively?

64 Brancion, p.128

65 Both Fall and Bergot state that the Vietnamese battalion was selected first, and that two companies of 1 BEP were added later. However, Rocolle (p.375), who questioned both Lt Col Langlais and Maj Guiraud, is clear that the reverse was true.

66 Bail (*L'Enfer...*, p.95) identifies the gunner as Tirailleur El Naze; Bergot (*Les 170 Jours...*, p.144, quoting Lt Sanselme), as Cpl Chief Slimane.

67 Fall, *Hell...*, p.151

68 Bergot, *Les 170 Jours...*, p.145. Figures for those who remained on the hill vary widely in different accounts. Rocolle (p.377), normally careful, gives *c.* 80 killed, *c.* 350 captured and *c.* 150 escaped, leaving some 300 unaccounted for – one might suspect a misprint in the figure for dead. However, Fall (*Hell...*, p.154) also quotes about 80 killed among '*c.* 500 missing'. Bail (*L'Enfer...*, p.95) puts the dead at 483, the missing (mostly captured) at 175, and the survivors fit for further service at *c.* 120, including Capts Carré and Gendre and Lt Antoine Botella – giving a total which comes closer to the ration strength. Roy (p.176) numbers the escapees at 170, presumably before medical triage. None of these authors cites their sources, and the division between dead, missing and captured can only be approximate; it is natural that the DBP veteran Lt Bergot gives them the benefit of the doubt.

Major Kah died of his wounds in captivity on 27 Mar 54; Sgt Chief Abderrahman survived, later fighting the French with the Algerian ALN and attaining the rank of major.

69 Simpson, *DBP...*, p.79

70 Roy, p.186. Rocolle (p.404) cites an official report of the debriefing of French wounded from DBP. Fall (*Hell...*, p.154) suggests that Langlais was party to the decision to disarm and effectively disband part of 5 BPVN. None of these has Bergot's quoted interview with Capt Botella.

71 Bergot, *Les 170 Jours...*, p.155

72 Rocolle, p.377

73 It seems that only Lt Col Lalande at Isabelle had indeed planned and practised counter-attacks with his infantry officers and tank commanders in any detail (Rocolle, p.297). This is only one of several instances which prompt one to wonder how events might have differed if the central camp had been able to employ this officer's services.

74 Rocolle, p.296

75 *ibid*, p.295+. They had already been sent.

76 The insertion of a few officers by ambulance aircraft was ordered only after it became clear that the Viet Minh would not respect the Red Cross. (Fall, *Hell...*, p.171)

77 Roy, p.179; it was with his intelligence chief, Col Fleurant.

78 Rocolle, p.378+

79 Rocolle, p.380: '(a) The fall of DBP is a bad reverse but not a disaster; it is not even a defeat which will have grave military consequences. We have lost less than 5 per cent of our regular forces and less than 3 per cent of our total forces in Indochina. (b) The defeat is very relative: the enemy has had losses at least equal to ours, and most of theirs are dead, while most of ours are prisoners. For the first time the best VM units have been broken; it will take them a long time to rebuild their experienced divisions. (c) Our reverse is not without balancing success – since November we have immobilized 36 VM battalions by this *abcès de fixation*, facing 12 of ours. If it had not been for Dien Bien Phu the VM could easily have invaded Laos and taken Luang Prabang...'

Following the actual fall of DBP in May the French parliament, press and public found these arguments unconvincing.

80 Brancion, p.132+; Fall, *Hell...*, p.156+; Bergot, *Les 170 Jours...*, p.147

12 Gars Pierre and Torri Rouge

The epigraph is quoted from Pierre Rocolle, *Pourquoi Dien Bien Phu?*, p.296.

1 Fall, *Hell...*, p.155); Brancion, p.130+

2 Bail, *L'Enfer...*, p.113; Bergot, *Les 170 Jours...*, p.146. Fall (*Hell...*, p.155) confuses Sahraoui's unit with the Navy flight. Bail (*Les Combats...*, p.107) states that Capt Aubel's B-26 No. 487 from GB 2/19 was also shot down on 15 Mar, but does not give a position – see Appendix 3.

A Navy aircraft returning from a sortie that day had a flight deck accident in bad weather; this prompted Capt Patou to transfer the embarked squadrons from *Arromanches* to Cat Bi (11F) and Bach Mai (3F) airfields thereafter, which gave them shorter flights and more loiter time over Dien Bien Phu.

3 Fall (*Hell...*, p.155) quotes the air recce estimate.

Maj de Mecquenem estimated that Gabrielle cost the VM 1,500 dead and thousands more wounded. A later VM prisoner would say that one of the battalions which attacked at Gabrielle suffered 240 dead – about 30 per cent fatalities (Rocolle, p.394). Bail (*L'Enfer ...*, p.95) suggests 2,000 dead on 14/15 Mar; Bergot (*Les 170 Jours...*, p.144) offers a breakdown by regiment which totals 2,400 dead for the same night. Neither gives any source, and Bergot includes units (Regts 36 & 141) which Rocolle does not confirm were committed that night.

4 Bergot, *Les 170 Jours...*, p.148

5 Rocolle, p.383. Such appeals would be broadcast increasingly during the battle, in French, Vietnamese, Arabic or German depending upon the unit targeted.

6 *ibid*, p.382+

7 Bail, *Les Combats...*, p.110

8 Rocolle, p.411

9 Fall, *Hell...*, p.158. Bail (*Les Combats...*, p.110) states that 6 BPC jumped near Isabelle; and that the replacement VHF 'gonio' was dropped by Capt Soulat from C-119 No.562. (Bail, *L'Enfer...*, p.120)

10 1 BPC & 3 BPVN; with 2 BEP, then in the Central Highlands, these were TAPI's last battle-ready reserves.

11 Fall, *Hell...*, p.160

12 Brancion, p.280. Rocolle (pp.202 & 285+) gives the opening stock of ammunition on 13 Mar as 21,000 × 105mm; 2,800 × 155mm; and 26,400 × 120mm. Some 17,500 × 105mm had been used up by 16 Mar, together with 2,200 × 155mm and 9,600 × 120mm; these figures represented 83 per cent of the 105mm stockpile, 79 per cent of the 155mm, and 64 per cent of the 120mm. Artillery ammunition was calculated in 'fire units' of a certain number of rounds per gun: 175rpg for the 105mm, 100rpg for the 155mm, and 110rpg for the 120mm mortar. These were set at a theoretically sufficient level for 12 hours' combat; but during intense fighting at DBP, a 105mm howitzer could consume two or even three fire units in a night. By 16 Mar there was less than one fire unit left for the 105s and about one and a half units for the 155s; only the 120mm mortars, much reduced in number, still had more than four units per tube.

13 Brancion, p.279+, quoting report of 6 July 54 by Maj Baubeau, FTNV Deputy Chief-of-Staff/ Logistics; & Ruffat, *RHd'A*, 1984/4. Since 105mm shells weighed 55lbs each without their packing or parachute, and the payload of a C-47 was about 2½ tons, 17,500 rounds (see note 12) represented about 175 Dakota sorties.

14 Rocolle, p.298

15 Brancion, pp.108+, 114+

16 *ibid*, p.276, quoting Bertin, Marc, *Packet sur Dien Bien Phu*, La Maison du Livre-Aviation (1991); Bail, *Les Combats...*, p.61

17 Brancion, p.139

18 Rocolle, p.284, quoting Maj Le Gurun. Three new 105s were dropped on 16 & 17 Mar, to Isabelle, where 7/ & 8/III/10 RAC thereafter had a maximum of 11 × 105s.

19 Brancion, p.275+. All these materials were provided by a US base in Japan, as were instructors for the rigging. The G11 cargo canopy measured 7,530sq ft, the G12 3,980sq ft.

20 Fall, *Hell...*, p.158; Brancion, pp.138 & 141; Bergot, *Les 170 Jours...*, p.171

21 Bail, *L'Enfer...*, p.120

22 Rocolle, p.305

23 Forissier, *RHd'A*, 1989/4

24 Salaun, Capt, in Héduy (ed.), *La Guerre...*, p.165

25 Rocolle, p.387. Prof Huard had successfully negotiated a limited number of serious casualty repatriations following the disaster of RC4 in Oct 50; but not, it seems, on this occasion.

26 Rocolle (p.389) states that two of eight day missions were successful; Bail (*Les Combats....*,) lists three, one by Lt Ruffray & Capt Cornu and two by Lt Biswang.

27 Rocolle, p.384. A VM source states that 232 Thais came over with their weapons. Rocolle dates the 6 BPC attempt to the afternoon of the 17th; Bergot (*Les 170 Jours...*, p.153), to the 16th.

28 Fall, *Hell...*, p.164+; Rocolle, p.385

29 Bail, *L'Enfer...*, p.120; in his *Les Combats...* (p.115) he gives Darde's rank as major and dates this landing to 18 Mar.

30 Roy, p.226+

31 Rocolle, p.393+

32 *ibid*, p.326

33 *ibid*, p.392, quoting *Contribution à l'histoire de DBP*, p.51; Simpson, *DBP...*, p.90

34 Rocolle, p.395 and Simpson, *DBP...*, p.103, both apparently quoting Gen Tran Do.

35 Rocolle, p.396

36 Bail, *L'Enfer...*, p.120

37 Rocolle, p.396+

38 Roy, p.190. Bergot (*Les 170 Jours...*, p.151+) and Fall (*Hell...*, p.160) both date the ordering of

one company of 6 BPC towards A-M 1 & 2 to 16 Mar soon after their arrival, and Bergot offers this as the reason for Langlais' and Bigeard's confrontation; but this seems to be an elision of two separate incidents. Rocolle (p.384) is clear that A-M 1 & 2 were not deserted until the 17th, when Wilde's 4/6 BPC was briefly ordered there – see note (27) above.

39 Forissier, *RHd'A*, 1989/4; Bail, *L'Enfer...*, p.120

40 Facon, *RHd'A*, 1985/1; Rocolle, p.322

41 Bail, *L'Enfer...*, p.120; Simpson, *DBP...*, p.97

42 Rocolle, p.407

43 Simpson, *DBP...*, p.87

44 *ibid*, p.88, quoting telegram from US Consul Paul Sturm, Hanoi, to US State Department.

45 Fall, *Hell...*, p.170+

46 *ibid*, p.170. Bail (*Les Combats...*, p.115+) gives the other pilots as Capts Vannier & Schmilewsky, S/Lts Joachim & Hubert. Three other C-47s were unable to land, and Capt Maubert's 'ZG' was hit by flak.

47 Fall, *Hell...*, p.192

48 Brancion, p.142+, is muddled; but his map on p.194 is clear and is supported by other sources which place the quad-50s as described.

49 Rocolle, p.400

50 Bergot, *Les 170 Jours...*, p.159+. The US Sniperscope M1 fitted to the T3 modification of the 0.30in M1 carbine was approved in Mar 1944; improved M2 and M3 models appeared from June 45 and Aug 51. It is not clear which were supplied to the French, but all these kits consisted of an IR telescopic sight and a big projector lamp clamped to the carbine, linked by a cable to a separate satchel holding a power pack including a transformer and a six-volt rechargeable battery. The equipment was heavy and awkward, and a second man often carried the power pack. The effective range was only about 400ft. Most snipers at DBP carried the MAS49 semi-automatic rifle with conventional telescopic sights.

51 Rocolle, p.407

52 *ibid*, p.296

53 Brancion, p.143

54 Rocolle, p.350

55 Brancion, p.151+. Rocolle (p.386) dates this move to the night of 16/17 Mar, but Gen de Brancion's account seems more circumstantial.

56 Ruffat, *RHd'A*, 1984/4

57 Fall, *Hell...*, p.167; Ruffat, *RHd'A*, 1984/4

58 Brancion, p.279+; Rocolle, p.297+; Léonard, *RHd'A*, 1956/3. Even anti-American French commentators admit that during the battle for DBP the conditions formerly attached to US aid were abandoned; as far as physically possible, the USA provided everything the French asked for, generously and at short notice. Parachutes used 13 Mar–7 May totalled 56,750, including 820 large cargo canopies. During mid Apr usage would rise to 2,300 parachutes per day, largely as a result of the breakdown of the C-119s' one-ton loads into 220lb packages from about 1 Apr, to ease the work of the DZ gangs – although it greatly increased that of the CRAs at the air bases. The total used 20 Nov 53–7 May 54 was about 68,350 (many initially returned and reused, for a total of about 83,000 deployments).

59 Bail, *L'Enfer...*, p.121. Fall, (*Hell...*, p.172) dates this action at Ban Kho Lai to 20 Mar.

60 Léonard, *RHd'A*, 1956/3

61 Rocolle, p.300. From 5 Apr the altitude was increased to 8,500ft and the delay to 40 seconds; and in the last two days of the battle, to 9,800ft and 50 seconds.

62 Figures from Rocolle (p.407), quoting message traffic. Fall (*Hell...*, p.175) seems simply to misread his source in quoting 151 French dead, and is followed by Simpson (*DBP...*, p.92). Castries' satisfied report of the action would be inconceivable if 1 BEP had lost two companies wiped out; and a dead-to-wounded ratio of two-to-one would defy all logic in this type of combat.

63 Bail, *L'Enfer...*, p.121; in *Les Combats...* (p.118+) he dates Lt Arbelet's landing to the night 21/22 Mar, but Capt Rousselot's to 22/23 Mar.

64 Rocolle, p.390. Fall (*Hell...*, p.175+) gives a slightly different sequence of events, and Bail is uncharacteristically silent, but the main facts are not in dispute. In total, between 14 & 23 Mar, 101 casualties had been successfully evacuated to Muong Sai by H-19s of the Groupement de Formations d'Hélicoptères de l'Armée de Terre. (Forissier, *RHd'A*, 1989/4)

65 Brancion, p.149+.

66 Rocolle, p.399

67 *ibid*, p.397+

68 Bail, *L'Enfer...*, p.121+, *Les Combats...*, p.119+; Fall, *Hell...*, p.176. The other pilots on the first mission were Bertin (No. 147), Courrèges (No. 187), Rols (No. 537) & Secretant (No. 536).

69 Rocolle, p.398; Bail, *Les Combats...*, p.123

70 Bail, *L'Enfer...*, p.130, *Les Combats...*, p.121; Bergot, *Les 170 Jours...*, p.169. Fall (*Hell...*, p.183) differs slightly, but Bail's Air Force sources seem more detailed.

71 Fall, *Hell...*, p.176+. Jules Roy does not suggest that any specific incident took place, which may be significant given the *ad hominem* nature of his book. Howard Simpson (*DBP...*, p.94+) accepts the broad sense of Fall's version but without the confrontational details; it is perhaps worth noting that Simpson remained in touch with Gen Bigeard over many years, and that Bigeard had considerable respect for Castries. Erwan Bergot, personally acquainted in 1954 with many Legion paratroop officers and later with Bigeard, omits any such episode from both his cited books; and Rocolle is also silent.

72 Fall, *Hell...*, p.178

73 *ibid*, p.96

74 Roy, p.195

75 Fall, *Hell...*, p.177, quotes a very slightly different translation from Langlais, *Dien Bien Phu*, France-Empire, Paris (1963), p.249.

76 Fall, *Hell...*, p.179+

77 Simpson, *DBP...*, p.94

78 Rocolle, pp.130, 409

79 Fall, *Hell...*, p.181

80 *ibid*, p.182

81 Bergot, *Les 170 Jours...*, p.166+; Fall, *Hell...*, p.182

82 Fall, *Hell...*, pp.183, 189

83 *ibid*, p.185

84 Bergot dates this operation to 28 Mar in both his books cited, one of which is specifically endorsed by Gen Bigeard. Rocolle (p.402) mentions 26 Mar, but this seems to be a simple misprint since on p.401 he follows most other sources in dating it to the 28th. Bail (*Les Combats...*, p.122) gives 26 Mar, but elsewhere (*L'Enfer...*, p.130), the 28th.

85 Bergot, *Les 170 Jours...*, p.174

86 *ibid*, p.171. The serviceable strength of the artillery on 21/22 Mar was reported by Maj Le Gurun to have been 25 × 105mm (thanks to the third new gun parachuted at Isabelle on 17 Mar), 4 × 155mm and 17 × 120mm; there are no reports of any further losses before 28 Mar. (Rocolle, p.284)

87 Sources differ in details, but these are the mean figures. The '20mm cannon' are unidentified but are listed by all sources. The '12.7mm' (0.50in) machine guns may have included some heavier calibre Russian weapons.

88 The summary of this action draws upon Rocolle, p.402+; Fall, *Hell...*, p.186+; Bergot, *Les 170 Jours...*, p.173+, & *Bn Bigeard*, p.123+. Ban Ban was sometimes referred to as Ban Pe.

89 Bergot *(Bn Bigeard*, p.127) identifies them as Michel Descamps and Joël Le Tac of *Paris Match.*

90 Rocolle (p.304) says 316; the total of 324 for fixed wing and helicopter evacuations is from the later research of Forissier *(RHd'A,* 1989/4). Of these, 223 were evacuated by 15 successful C-47 missions, 12 or 13 of them night sorties – see note (26) above. For helicopter evacuations see note (64) above.

91 Bail, *L'Enfer...,* p.130; Fall, *Hell...,* p.190. Mlle de Galard's (unsought) subsequent celebrity tended to overshadow the other members of her crew: navigator Sgt Cuinet (died in captivity), radio operator WO Larriot, and flight engineer WO Chauvin.

92 Fall, *Hell...,* p.189

93 Rocolle, p.407

94 *ibid,* p.399

13 The Fifth Hill

The epigraph is quoted by Rocolle (p.425+), from *Contribution à l'histoire de Dien Bien Phu,* Hanoi (1965), pp.75–6.

1 Rocolle, p.415+

2 Fall, *Hell...,* p.193

3 *ibid,* p.194

4 Various different heights have been quoted for the Five Hills; those given here are adjusted from Bergot *(Bn Bigeard,* p.119) and Lassus *(MI,* No.18). The valley floor around Muong Thanh was between 1,475ft and 1,550ft above sea level, higher at the airfield and Claudine; approximate hill heights *above the river-bank* are used in this text. Similarly, published sketch maps vary greatly in lateral distances; those quoted in this text have been checked where possible against aerial photos, but can only be approximate.

5 12th Co (Filaudeau) were guarding 4/II/4 RAC in Dominique 3 – see below.

6 Fall, *Hell...,* p.116; Bergot, *Les 170 Jours...,* p.183

7 Rocolle, p.418.

8 Brancion, p.209, quoting Gen Pierre Daillier, *Le 4e RTM – Les Bataillons de marche en Indochine 1947–54,* Service Historique de l'Armée de Terre (1990), p.310.

9 Rocolle, p.419+; Bail, *L'Enfer...,* p.130

10 Map, Fall, *Hell...,* p.166; Bail, *Les Combats...,* pp.103, 127; Bergot, *Bn Bigeard,* p.294 – which does not record that the 6 BPC company ever actually moved on to E4 before that night's

fighting. The shapes and limits of these 'low' Dominiques and Elianes are only approximately indicated on the sketch maps and aerial photos in various sources.

11 Rocolle, p.421; Fall, *Hell...,* p.196; Brancion, p.267; Simpson, *DBP...,* p.105

12 Rocolle, p.421; Brancion, p.197+. Another 11 casualties were suffered among the artillery FOO teams with infantry units.

13 Fall, *Hell...,* p.200; Rocolle, p.286; Brancion, p.200; Simpson, *DBP...,* p.116. On 30 Mar there were 5 × fire units of 105mm, 6 × 155mm and 8 × 120mm in hand. Fall (p.200) quotes 13,000 × 105mm fired 30 Mar–1 Apr, 855 × 155mm and 1,200 × 120mm. Simpson gives 9,500 × 105mm fired on 30/31 Mar alone, and Fall (p.123) 4,500 on 31 Mar/1 April.

14 Fall, *Hell...,* p.196; Bergot, *Les 170 Jours...,* p.185+. Fall *(Hell...,* p.118) misplaces 11th Co on D2 rather than D1.

15 Brancion, p.158; Bergot, *Les 170 Jours...,* p.183

16 Bergot, *Les 170 Jours...,* pp.191+. Lost in the dark after leaving the battery, Sgt Bellencontre finally met up with Lt Trapp's 2nd Co, 6 BPC, where his wounds were treated. Bellencontre recalled to Bergot the first words of the company medic, Cpl Chief Lecoq, when he shone his torch on the sergeant's ruined face: 'Well, *mon vieux,* you're amusingly arranged, aren't you?'

17 Rocolle, p.422, quoting report of Maj Le Gurun of conversations during his interrogation.

18 Brancion, pp.159+, 177; Ch.8 *passim*

19 Fall, *Hell...,* p.472; Gaujac, *Histoire...,* p.405

20 Rocolle, p.424

21 Bergot, *Les 170...,* p.195. The failure of Maj Nicolas' signal may have been due simply to its wandering off the wavelength – a weakness of the 1940s generation of field radios.

22 Rocolle, p.425.

23 Bergot *(Bn Bigeard,* p.133) says 'about 50' men of Lt Martin's company; but in *Les 170 Jours...* (p.199) he seems to misidentify Martin's command as 2nd Co. Bail *(Les Combats...,* p.130) and Fall *(Hell...,* p.199) identify the 1 BEP reinforcement as from 2nd Co, under Lt Fournier; neither is clear on their time of arrival.

24 Roy, p.197+; Bergot, *Les 170 Jours...,* p.202

25 Sometimes rendered more delicately in print as *'Vous êtes légionnaire? Alors, débrouillez-vous...',* this old slogan means roughly, 'You're a légionnaire, aren't you? Sort it out for yourself.' (Fall, *Hell...,* p.200; Rocolle, p.427)

26 Rocolle, p.427+

27 The French government was still trying, through the International Committee of the Red Cross, to get VM agreement for free passage of ambulance aircraft, but without response. Castries made direct offers, by released prisoners and radio transmissions in clear, to hand over 60 VM wounded. A more limited *exchange* of wounded was all that the VM would agree to, and this eventually took place on 7 & 9 Apr; it was not to be repeated. (Rocolle, p.452; Fall, *Hell...*, p.229; Simpson, *DBP...*, p.113+)

28 Roy, p.215; Simpson, *DBP...*, p.114

29 Rocolle, p.427+

30 Fall, *Hell...*, p.200

31 Simpson, *DBP...*, p.109; Rocolle, p.426

32 Fall (*Hell...*, p.279) quotes 1,809 total, without date; on p.284, for 2 Apr, he lists 1,663 of which 1,547 infantry (incl 410 Thai) and 116 artillery, and 50 'miscellaneous'.

33 Rocolle, p.514+; Fall, *Hell...*, p.279+; Brancion, Ch. 11 *passim*. 8/III/10 RAC (Capt Riès) was installed on 24 Dec 53; 9/ (Lt Santonja) on 5 Jan 54; and 7/ (Capt Dumoussaud) on 13 Jan. On 2 Feb, 9/ returned to Claudine.

34 Brancion, pp.212, 228

35 *ibid*, p.229+

36 Fall (*Hell...*, p.284) identifies the VM unit as Intelligence Co 63. To use a divisional Trinh Sat unit as assault infantry seems strange employment for these valuable specialists.

37 Brancion, p.232

38 Rocolle, p.430; Bergot, *Les 170 Jours...*, p.204

39 Bergot, *Bn Bigeard*, p.137

40 Rocolle, p.430; Fall, *Hell...*, pp.204, 208; Bergot, *Bn Bigeard*, p.139

41 Fall, *Hell...*, pp.204, 473

42 The reference to the dropping of 75mm RCLs to GONO during the battle is intriguing. Fall (*Hell...*, p.224) states that at 2pm on 5 Apr a C-119 misdropped a load including two RCLs south of DBP; and that the next day légionnaires pushed 3km south-west to Ban Co My and recovered them. On p.473 he lists 4,000 × 75mm among a French estimate of artillery ammunition misdropped to the VM; this calibre would not have been dropped unless the garrison had 75mm RCLs. On p.335 he mentions briefly a I/2 REI 'patrol' on 26 Apr north towards Gabrielle being accompanied by 'recoilless rifle teams from 35 RALP', which suggests 75mm rather than 57mm guns – although the former would be extraordi-

nary for a 'patrol'. The present author is unaware of any other references.

43 Simpson, *DBP...*, p.109

44 Rocolle, p.431; Bergot, *Les 170 Jours...*, p.206

45 Bergot, *Les 170 Jours...*, p.208

46 Lt Rancoule's company is mentioned by Rocolle (p.431) and Fall (*Hell...*, p.205). They do not mention Russeil, but Bergot's source (*Les 170 Jours...*, p.206+) is apparently Russeil's radio operator, Lég Guenzi, who carried his officer's body off the hill after he was killed by mortar fire.

47 Fall, *Hell...*, p.207; Bergot, *Les 170 Jours...*, p.208+. The 75mm high-velocity tank cannon was provided with a 'canister' anti-personnel round, but it was not particularly effective.

48 Rocolle, p.432. It rests there to this day – see photograph 26 in this book.

49 Fall, *Hell...*, p.207+

50 Bergot, *Les 170 Jours...*, p.210

51 Rocolle, p.432+; Fall, *Hell...*, p.207; Bergot, *Les 170 Jours...*, p.203

52 Fall, *Hell...*, p.208. This order was obeyed only selectively; the Thai *supplétifs* of Legion battalions continued to fight in *ad hoc* mixed companies. The Legion would certainly have regarded such a decision as a family matter, and Langlais was, after all, a Colonial.

53 Rocolle (p.385) states that the morale of BT 2 was now very low, and that from 31 Mar they played little part in the battle, staying in their trenches.

54 Rocolle, p.405+; Fall, *Hell...*, pp.209, 248

55 Fall, *Hell...*, p.213

56 *ibid*, p.210

57 Rocolle, p.433; Fall, *Hell...*, p.214

58 The DZ measured 1,000m × 400m; at 105mph a C-47 travelled 1,000m in 15 seconds, in which time a maximum of six men could jump even with the most urgent haste – only three, at normal tempo.

59 Ruffat (*RHd'A*, 1984/4) states that from 30 Mar to 5 Apr deliveries averaged 90 tons per day, about 20 per cent going adrift due to high delayed drops; and that three cargo planes were shot down in eight days. He gives no details, and other sources confirm only one, that of WO Guiraud of GT 2/64. Sources sometimes fail to distinguish between aircraft losses over DBP and simultaneous losses elsewhere in Tonkin; see Appendix 3.

60 Fall, *Hell...*, p.210+; Gaujac, *Histoire...*, p.417; Rocolle, p.453

61 Simpson, *DBP...*, p.115+

62 Fall, *Hell...*, p.211

63 *ibid*, p.214

64 Gaujac, *Histoire...*, p.417; Fall, *Hell...*, p.215

65 Bergot, *Les 170 Jours...*, p.214+

66 Rocolle, p.434; Fall, *Hell...*, p.216; Bergot, *Les 170 Jours...*, p.215

67 Rocolle, p.434; Bergot, *Les 170 Jours...*, p.218

68 Fall, *Hell...*, pp.217+; Rocolle, p.454; Gaujac, *Histoire...*, p.419. It is a strange statistical fact that paratroopers do not suffer as many landing injuries at night as by day. The colder air is more supportive, slightly slowing the rate of descent; and a man who cannot see the ground is less likely to tense his muscles.

69 Fall, *Hell...*, p.218. Fall is unclear in his sequence of events between the nights of 3/4 Apr and 4/5 Apr, for which Rocolle and Bergot seem better sources.

70 Bergot, *Les 170 Jours...*, p.217

71 Fall, *Hell...*, p.219

72 Rocolle, p.433, quoting *Contribution...*, pp.80 & 168–70

73 On 4 Apr, GONO reported a strength of 6,295 able-bodied combatants. Of these 1,613 were at Isabelle. (Bail, *L'Enfer...*, p.138; Fall, *Hell...*, p.226)

74 Rocolle, p.434; Fall, *Hell...*, p.220

75 Sources differ over the sequence, as discussed by Fall (*Hell...*, p.473); this account follows Fall (p.220+) and Bergot (*Bn Bigeard*, p.140+; *Les 170 Jours...*, p.220+), with some confirmation from Gaujac (*Histoire...*, p.266).

76 'Conti' was recovered, and later used as a static pillbox south of the airfield. (Dunstan, *Vietnam Tracks*, p.29)

77 Rocolle, p.435

78 Fall (*Hell...*, p.221) identifies this as Bn 14, which does not appear in known VM orders of battle.

79 Rocolle, p.436

80 Rocolle, p.346; Fall, *Hell...*, pp.223, 243+. Regt 9 would not in fact be committed at DBP, and may have been deployed to protect the rear of the siege army; the staff and other units of Div 304 would be engaged, arriving from 27 Apr. The detached unit of Regt 176 was Bn 970; the Regt 148 units were Bns 910 & 920, 523 Sigs & 121 Hvy Wpns Cos.

81 Fall, *Hell...*, p.225

82 Rocolle, p.464; the award would be gazetted

in the *Journal Officiel* on 25 Apr. In Indochina the basic award was the *Croix de Guerre TOE* – for 'exterior theatres of operations' – differenced from the WWII award by its pale blue and scarlet ribbon; a citation in Army orders was marked by a bronze palm branch on the ribbon. It is notoriously difficult to compare the decorations of different countries, but in British terms the CdeG was very roughly equivalent to a Mention in Despatches; it was also routinely awarded for serious wounds. A US comparison, equally inexact, might perhaps be a combination of the Bronze Star and Purple Heart.

83 Rocolle, p.436+, quoting *Contribution...*, p.55; and Fall, *Hell...*, p.225. The dismissals were revealed to Maj Le Gurun during his interrogation.

84 We lack a serviceability calendar for 31 Mar–9 Apr; but Fall (*Hell...*, p.223) quotes a report that on 5 Apr, III/10 RAC had six of 12 guns u/s.

85 Rocolle, pp.282, 287; Brancion, pp.187, 282+

86 Ruffat, *RHd'A*, 1984/4

87 Brancion, p.183

88 Rocolle, p.286; Fall, *Hell...*, p.226. The tanks were 'Mulhouse', 'Douaumont', 'Posen', 'Ettlingen' – plus 'Smolensk', immobilized by gearbox failure on an unconfirmed date; and 'Auerstaedt' & 'Ratisbonne' at Isabelle. (Dunstan, *Vietnam Tracks*, p.29)

89 The companies of Viard, Bailly, Clédic and Le Page. Gaujac (*Histoire...*, p.418) quotes 23 dead, no fewer than 86 missing, and 112 wounded, including four officers.

90 Bergot, *Les 170 Jours...*, p.116

91 On 21 Apr, Gen Cogny signalled Gen Navarre that Maj Cabaribère – 'upon whom rested the will of the II/3 to be parachuted' – and two other officers were among 23 members of the unit killed that day in an action against VM Regt 42 on RC5. Cabaribère was an indomitable officer who had recently escaped from VM captivity after his previous command, II/2 REI, had been badly mauled in northern Laos at the beginning of Feb 54. (Simpson, *DBP...*, p.132)

92 Fall (*Hell...*, p.218) gives 2,594 of whom 2,048 whites, 451 North and West Africans and 95 Vietnamese. Gen Navarre (*Agonie de l'Indochine*, Plon, Paris, 1956, p.237) gives 1,800, of whom 800 French, 450 Legion, 400 North African and 150 Vietnamese.

93 Rocolle (p.455) states 709 non-qualified volunteers jumped; Fall (*Hell...*, p.218), 680. At jump schools, where everything conspired to bolster the novice's confidence, a door refusal rate of about 3 per cent was expected; Col Sauvagnac

calculated that over DBP the rate was less than 10 per cent. (Rocolle, p.457)

94 Rocolle, p.455+

95 Bergot, *Les 170 Jours...*, p.265

14 Verdun without the Sacred Way

The epigraph is quoted from Rocolle, *Pourquoi Dien Bien Phu?*, p.344. The *Voie Sacrée* was the single road for supplies and reinforcements leading from Bar-le-Duc to Verdun, upon which the French defenders relied in 1916.

1 Rocolle, p.466

2 *ibid*, pp.40+, 453

3 Bail *(Les Combats...*, p.138+) records the loss of Lt Beglin's B-26 on 2 Apr, but gives no position; since two of the crew, rescued by French troops, returned to Cat Bi on 4 Apr they cannot have come down anywhere near DBP. Sgt Bourdelon's Bearcat disappeared on 3 Apr, after GC 1/22 put 13 sorties over the approach roads and eight over DBP; this exemplifies the difficulty of defining how many aircraft were actually lost 'at DBP' – see Appendix 3.

4 Fall, *Hell...*, pp.226+, 232

5 Brancion, p.202+

6 Fall, *Hell...*, p.228; Rocolle, p.385

7 Simpson, *DBP...*, p.123; Fall, *Hell...*, p.230; Sergent, p.186

8 Roy, p.226; Fall, *Hell...*, p.232

9 Roy, p.228; Sergent, p.192

10 Fall, *Hell...*, p.232. In Algeria, 1955–8, Col Bigeard would command with great success 3rd Colo Para Regt. He was among the pioneers in the use of helicopters to insert and manoeuvre rifle companies on the battlefield.

11 Fall *(Hell...*, p.231) times the barrage 5.50–6.10am; Bergot *(Bn Bigeard*, p.144), 6–6.20am; Rocolle (p.468), only 6–6.10am, which seems too short for the ammunition expenditure even at 'max cadence'. The assault in fact began before the barrage ended.

12 The M1A1 and M2 models were essentially identical. In most wars since their introduction by the German Army's Guard Pioneers in February 1915, soldiers carrying flame-throwers have found it difficult to surrender alive; some who succeeded had bitter reason to regret it.

13 This account of the action follows Rocolle, p.468+; Fall, *Hell...*, p.231+; and Bergot, *Bn Bigeard*, p.145+. Several French officers learned

of the dismissal while in captivity. During his lengthy interrogation, Lt Col Bigeard was pressed on the details of the attack; his captors did not believe that it had been achieved by only two French companies. Fall *(Hell...*, p.233) gives 13 killed, ten missing, and 26 wounded including three officers = 49. Bergot (p.148) gives no overall figure, but 15 dead and 22 wounded in Trapp's company alone, where all platoon commanders and most section leaders became casualties. Six Vietnamese paratroopers deserted that night; it is unclear whether these are included in GONO's total of '60 *hors de combat*'.

14 Rocolle, p.469. Gen Lucciani confirmed that it was the 1 BEP song *'Contre les Viets'* (Simpson *DBP...*, p.125).

15 Rocolle, p.470; Fall, *Hell...*, p.235+; Bail, *L'Enfer...*, p.139.

16 Bail, *Les Combats...*, p.146+

17 Fall, *Hell...*, p.240; elsewhere (p.330) he dates the II/1 RCP amalgamation to 24 Apr.

18 Sergent, pp.193, 199+; Brancion, p.187

19 Fall, *Hell...*, p.236+

20 Roy, p.236

21 Rocolle, p.70; Sergent, p.195

22 *http://www.netmarine.net/forces/aero/flo/ 28f/histoire/ant28.htm.*

23 Fall, *Hell...*, p.241; Simpson, *DBP...*, p.116+

24 Brancion, p.280; Fall, *Hell...*, p.241, 247+. A replacement electricity generator smashed on the DZ; and jerrycans of fuel were dropped full to the brim, so that they burst on impact.

25 Brancion, p.206+

26 Fall, *Hell...*, pp.237+, 243

27 Rocolle, p.471, quoting *Contribution à l'histoire de Dien Bien Phu*, Hanoi (1965)

28 Champeaux, *RHd'A*, 1989/4. While acting as interpreter Cpl Preiss was held in a small, well camouflaged camp about 12 miles NW of DBP. Apart from a reduced rice ration he received no harsher treatment than the guards; he was beaten only once, when he tried to intervene in the beating of a would-be escaper. German-speaking Legion prisoners were held for 24hrs, and questioned for several hours, without threats or manhandling. As far as he could tell the interrogators' primary interests were the layout of the DBP strongpoints, updated on a series of sand tray models and reported up the chain of command by frequent despatches; the effect of VM weapons; and garrison morale. (In the CEFEO only aircrew were given any precautionary training in how to behave under interrogation.)

29 Bergot, *Les 170 Jours...*, p.227+; Fall, *Hell...*, p.247+

30 Fall, *Hell...*, p.253; Dunstan, *Vietnam Tracks*, p.29

31 Brancion, p.213; Rocolle, p.284

32 Fall, *Hell...*, p.255

33 Simpson, *DBP...*, p.135

34 Fall, *Hell...*, p.256

35 Bail, *Les Combats...*, p.148

36 Brancion, p.212; Rocolle, p.292

37 Rocolle, p.464+

38 *ibid*, p.472. Fall (*Hell...*, p.257) does not mention heavy fighting on 16/17 Apr, but Rocolle quotes from two separate progress reports from GONO to Hanoi. 'Opéra' has been published in some sketch maps as a substantial position opposite the northern part of H2, but late aerial photographs show only modest and separated trenches.

39 Rocolle, p.473+; Fall, *Hell...*, p.259+; Bergot, *Les 170 Jours...*, p.243+; Roy, p.238; Simpson, *DBP...*, p.136

40 Rocolle, p.501

41 Rocolle, pp.67, 461; Bail, *Les Combats...*, p.151. Maj Balbin's 7 BPC embarked on USAF Douglas C-124 Globemasters at Orly in civilian clothes, due to the sensitivities of some of the countries where they would be landing to refuel. They arrived at Saigon on 24 April.

42 Fall, *Hell...*, p.262+

43 Rocolle, p.144; Bergot, *Les 170 Jours...*, p.153

44 Ruffat, *RHd'A*, 1984/4

45 Forissier, *op cit*, seems to transpose the positions of 3 & 6 ACP, which are attested in several other sources including Fall and Roy. Rocolle (map 14) initially places 5 ACP in southern Claudine, but later with 6 ACP on the east bank. His map suggests that 6 ACP was in location E10; Bergot (*Les 170 Jours ...*, p.278) states that it was in E3. For Isabelle, Rocolle (p.305) gives total wounded as 564, of whom 215 needed operations before the end of the battle.

46 Forissier, *RHd'A* 1989/4. Probably *c.* 2,200 casualties were treated only by unit MOs.

47 Galard-Terraube, in Héduy (ed.), *La Guerre...*, p.162+; Fall, *Hell...*, p.244+; Simpson, *DBP...*, p.138. Plasma is blood with the red corpuscles separated out; it can be used to transfuse most patients of all blood types for a limited period before it becomes essential to give them whole typed blood.

48 Geneviève de Galard had insisted upon flying the 27 Mar mission because she did not consider that her previous day's flight – which had been forced to take off under fire without embarking wounded – should 'count'. During her four years in Indochina she completed 149 medical evacuation missions.

Some 2,000 French women volunteers served with the CEFEO, and a number were decorated. For example, the prestigious Médaille Militaire was awarded to the nurse Geneviève Grall, who twice within a month parachuted to work under fire with small, surrounded units. The most celebrated was the extraordinary Capt Valérie André of the Air Force, who in 1976 would become France's first woman general. A surgeon, physician, pilot (both fixed wing and helicopter) and parachutist, Capt André piloted one of the first two helicopters in the country, and by her return to France in 1953 had saved 165 lives in the course of 120 missions, often in circumstances of extreme danger. The Algerian War would take her total missions to 496.

49 Laffin, p.171+, translated from Grauwin. The triple amputee, Sgt Haas, survived DBP, to greet Geneviève at Paris reunions.

50 Fall, *Hell...*, p.268

51 Rocolle, p.474+; Fall, *Hell...*, p.267+

52 *ibid*, p.475; Fall, *Hell...*, p.272; Sergent, p.105. Lt Col Ducruix would die in captivity.

53 This account relies partly upon Rocolle (p.476+), whose own sources include the after-action reports by Lt Col Bigeard and Maj Liesenfelt; but also upon the detailed commentary by 2 BEP's historian Capt Pierre Sergent (p.206+).

54 Rocolle, p.477; Sergent, p.207

55 Rocolle (p.477) quotes Maj Liesenfelt, and Sergent (p.208) agrees. Fall, who reconstructs Gen de Castries' words (*Hell...*, p.276), gives no time, but states that the call to Bigeard was provoked by hearing radio traffic from 2 BEP companies in action; if true, this would support Bigeard's 3pm timing. Bergot's timings (*Les 170 Jours...*, p.248+) are later than all the others by at least an hour, and seem untenable. Like Fall and Bergot, Rocolle is apparently anxious not to accuse the respected Lt Col Bigeard of massaging the record to lessen his responsibility for events; he hints diplomatically that both Liesenfelt's and Bigeard's timings may err, thus shortening the gap between them. Simpson (*DBP...*, p.143) quotes from Bigeard's much later memoir, *Pour une parcelle de gloire*, Plon, Paris (1975): 'Despite my weariness, I should simply have taken personal command of the operation. The wonderful officers of the 2 BEP were as good as mine, as those of Bréchignac or of Tourret, but that day the

orchestra conductor... was missing. I therefore consider myself responsible for this defeat.'

56 Rocolle, p.478; Fall, *Hell...*, p.277; Sergent, p.208

57 Fall, *Hell...*, p.278; Brancion, p.188+; Bail, *L'Enfer...*, p.139. Herbert Bleyer would survive DBP and the POW camps.

58 Rocolle, p.478

59 *ibid*, p.478; Sergent, p.211

60 Sergent, p.212+; Simpson, *DBP ...*, p.143. Fall (*Hell...*, p.276+) has Bigeard ordering the retreat at 3.25pm, but this is not supported elsewhere. The artillery 'supplement' brought the total expenditure in this action to 1,600 × 105mm, 80 × 155mm, & 1,580 × 120mm.

61 1st Co BMEP (Stabenrath) was formed from 1st & 4th, 1 BEP; 2nd (Brandon), from 2nd & 3rd, 1 BEP; 3rd (Le Cour Grandmaison), from 5th & 7th, 2 BEP; 4th (Pétré, despite his wound), from 6th & 8th, 2 BEP; plus Weapons Ptn (Lt Nomura). (Sergent, p.215)

62 The following passage draws upon Bowen, *op cit*, pp.13–34; & Gilbert, Adrian, *Sniper One-on-One*, Sidgwick & Jackson, London (1994), pp.122–31. (As so often, the present author is indebted to Will Fowler for these references.) It is emphasized that the description which follows has no relevance to soft-nosed ammunition, or to the current generation of .22FMC/5.6mm or Soviet 5.45mm military rounds.

63 Ruffat, *RHd'A*, 1984/4; Fall, *Hell...*, p.329+

64 Fall, *Hell...*, p.328; Rocolle, p.479

65 24 Apr strengths & deployments from Bergot, *Les 170 Jours...*, p.260+; Rocolle, p.480. These figures do not exactly match the differing totals given by Fall (*Hell...*, pp.328 & 482) – the latter apparently distorted by a misprint. Casualties and replacements from Fall, p.351.

66 Holmes, p.247

67 Holmes, p.214; Rocolle, p.481; Bergot, *Bn Bigeard*, p.154

68 Macdonald, p.149

69 Fall, *Hell...*, p.329. A quoted estimate of 35,000 VM infantry at this date is not believed by Rocolle (p.518).

70 Rocolle, p.482+; Fall, *Hell...*, p.278 – both quoting Giap, *Dien Bien Phu*, Editions en Langues Etrangères, Hanoi (1964), p.131+. (Fall's translation slightly edited by present author.)

71 Simpson, *DBP...*, p.143

72 Rocolle (p.484) mentions a convoy arriving at Son La on the 24th with 4,000 × 105mm, 3,000 × 75mm, 1,600 × 120mm, 1,000 'rockets' of 82mm (possibly bazooka rounds?), another 1,000 rounds of unspecified calibre, plus 12 × 75mm recoilless guns. Supplies of fuel were assured on 25 April by the arrival at Tuan Giao of a 200-vehicle convoy carrying 2,400 barrels.

73 Bail, *Les Combats...*, p.156+; Fall, *Hell...*, p.327

74 CAT pilots were paid $35 per hour flying pay, for a minimum of 60 hours per month. This was high by French standards; but the US pilots stressed that they did not enjoy disability benefits, nor their families any death compensation entitlement.(*http://www.air-america.org/About/History.htm*)

75 Bail, *Les Combats...*, p.160+; Fall, *Hell...*, p.337+

76 Rocolle, pp.484+, 513

77 Bail, *Les Combats...*, p.165; *L'Enfer...*, p.76; Rocolle, p.512+. Rocolle (p.319) makes a calculation that the Dakota crews in fact averaged well under a normal rate of 80–100 flying hrs/month; but this seems to the present author to be based on unsafe definitions and averages.

78 Rocolle, p.489

79 Fall, *Hell...*, p.332+

80 *ibid*, p.344

81 Rocolle (p.284+) quotes Maj Le Gurun's report that on 27 Apr serviceability was 19 × 105mm, 1 × 155mm, 15 × 120mm; and ammunition stocks on 30 Apr, 875rpg × 105mm, 300rpg × 155mm, & 330rpg × 120mm – i.e., in heavy combat, about two nights' supply only for the 105s, (marginally) one night's for the 155, and a couple of hours' for the heavy mortars.

Small-arms ammunition was normally in good supply; depots were set up in each strongpoint and topped up by parties sent back to camp in quieter periods. However, hand and rifle grenades and mortar bombs often ran short; a strongpoint under attack could use up 2,000 grenades and many hundreds of 60mm mortar bombs in a night. (Rocolle, p.513)

82 Fall, *Hell...*, p.340

83 Brancion, Ch.11 *passim*

84 Fall, *Hell...*, p.283; his map on p.282 seems incorrect, and this description follows an aerial photo in Bail, *Les Combats...*, p.184.

85 Fall, *Hell...*, Ch.VIII *passim*

86 *ibid*, p.286+; Rocolle, p.516. The latter gives final casualties of 56 dead & 313 wounded for II/1 RTA plus V/7 RTA; 258 dead & wounded for III/3 REI; 56 dead & 79 wounded for BT 3; and 70 dead & wounded for Lt Wieme's CSLTs.

87 Fall, *Hell...*, p.290

88 *ibid*, p.249. The French Bn de Corée that had served in Korea – where armour vests were one of the great successes of the war – had been in Indochina since Dec 53, so GONO's failure to request them sooner is puzzling. They stopped 75 per cent of all projectile fragments, and all SMG bullets, though not high-velocity rifle rounds. In Korea USMC statistics showed that the vests prevented 60–70 per cent of all abdominal and chest wounds. (Dunstan, *Flak Jackets*, p.18+)

89 Bail, *Les Combats...*, p.161; Fall, *Hell...*, pp.129, 340+

90 Bail, *Les Combats...*, p.163; Fall, *Hell...*, p.343+

91 Rocolle, p.513+

92 Racca, *RHd'A*, 1968/1; Fall, *Hell...*, pp.247, 256

93 Fall (*Hell...*, p.327) has the whole crew casualties, and states that 'Auerstaedt' was thereafter the only operational Chaffee. Dunstan (*Vietnam Tracks*, p.29) – whose source is Lt Préaud – gives three dead in 'Douaumont'; and states that 'Mulhouse', 'Posen' and 'Ettlingen' were operational in the main camp until 7 May, plus all three tanks at Isabelle.

94 Fall, *Hell...*, p.346

95 Bail, *Les Combats...*, p.165; Fall, *Hell...*, p.347+

96 Fall, *Hell...*, p.348; Rocolle, p.517. Gen de Castries and Col Langlais were both named honorary corporals; at Isabelle, Col Lalande made Father Guidon and Chaplain Tissot – the only Protestant priest at DBP – honorary légionnaires 1st class.

97 'Hey, here's some sausage, here's some sausage/ For the Alsatians, the Swiss and the Lorrainers...' – the verse continues with a disobliging comment about the Belgians. The words probably date from the Franco-Prussian War, 1870–71; the tune is older, and was first formally arranged by Bandmaster Wilhelm in the early 1860s.

15 Deus Ex Machina

The epigraph is quoted from Gen de Champeaux de la Boulaye, 'Les B-26 à Dien Bien Phu', *RHd'A* 1987/4.

1 Facon, *RHd'A*, 1985/1

2 Rocolle, p.442; Facon, *RHd'A*, 1985/1. Over 1–7 May, the Bearcats would fly 71 sorties for DBP, 40 against the supply lines and 38 over the Delta (Rocolle, p.509). DBP's main competitor for F8F sorties seems to have been Col Paul Vanuxem, zone commander in the southern Delta. This hulking, red-bearded hero of Vinh Yen combined a master's degree in philosophy

with a forceful personality; it took a brave Air Force controller to deny him Bearcats when he demanded them for one of his units in trouble.

3 Assuming (unrealistically) 100% serviceability, this gives an average of 32.5 flying hrs per aircraft during Apr. Rocolle (p.319) divides the total by 40 rather than the correct 32, giving an average of 26 hrs.

4 Facon (*RHd'A*, 1985/1) quotes the 23% shortfall from a report of 1 Jan 54.

5 Rocolle, pp.319, 510. The latter reference appears to confuse the Helldivers with Corsairs in 14F, which in fact flew missions to DBP only in May.

6 Rocolle, p.508; Champeaux, *RHd'A*, 1987/4

7 Rocolle, p.509

8 Total flying hrs were 673, giving an average crew total of 134 hrs and average mission endurance of 3.8 hrs.

9 Champeaux, *RHd'A* 1987/4. It should be borne in mind that Gen de Champeaux's own former squadron was GB 1/19.

10 On 29 Jan 54 the US President's Special Committee on Indochina approved sending 200 uniformed USAF mechanics qualified on the B-26 and C-47 to augment MAAG, to serve on bases where they would be 'secure from capture and the risks of combat'.

11 Complete three-men aircrews on GB 1/19 & 1/25 combined totalled 33 on 13 Mar. (Facon, *RHd'A*, 1985/1)

12 Rocolle (p.442) gives Apr B-26 sorties as 423 to DBP, 58 in the Delta & 22 over VM supply lines. Gen de Champeaux quotes (from an annexe to Gen Lauzin's after-battle report) total B-26 sorties 13 Mar–7 May as 1,047 during 3,617 flying hours. Gen de Champeaux assumes an average 22 available *aircraft*; but the overall figure of 33 *aircrews* gives averages for the whole battle *per crew* of roughly 32 sorties in 110 hrs spread over 56 days, i.e. two three-hour sorties in every three days. As mentioned in Ch.8, this compares with 1944 French AF day bomber norms of up to 25 missions (each lasting about five hours) in 30 days, in the face of Luftwaffe fighters and NW European levels of flak.

13 In a striking phrase Gen de Champeaux confirms that up to 10 per cent of VT fuses of this vintage tended to detonate '*un peu n'importe quand*'. A catastrophic accident during the 'battle of the roads' in winter 1953–4 had destroyed two B-26s in flight, killing (with five other airmen) Maj Helliot, the most experienced bombardier in Indochina.

14 Rocolle, p.508

15 During the first week of May the ratio was 31 per cent support, 48 per cent anti-AA, and 18 per cent anti-artillery.

16 Rocolle, p.509

17 Simpson, *DBP...*, p.49+. Dejean does not seem to have wondered where the vast numbers of new officers and NCOs could be found for 18 new Legion battalions.

18 Rocolle, p.413

19 Fall, *Hell...*, p.298

20 Simpson, *DBP...*, p.110+

21 Rocolle, p.415; Roy, p.202

22 Rocolle, p.439.

23 Rocolle, p.441–2. Of 503 total B-26 sorties in Apr, only 22 were against the supply roads.

24 Fall (*Hell...*,p.300) quotes from official US sources that in fact 98 × B-29s with 14-ton bomb-loads were potentially available, from both Clark Air Force Base and a second wing on Okinawa, with cover from *c.* 450 jet fighters. Navarre and AF Gen Lauzin remained nervous of possible Chinese reaction – a sensitivity not eased on 7 Apr, when a flight by jet fighters over Tonkin was only belatedly identified as a US training mission of which the French had not been warned.

25 Simpson, *DBP...*, p.118; Fall, *Hell...*, p.300+

26 Rocolle, p.438+

27 Simpson, *DBP...*, p117+

28 Rocolle, p.444+. There was considerable dis-cussion about the markings the bombers should carry; and Gen Navarre suggested on various dates that USAF aircrews should fly without documents or insignia, or be officially enlisted in the Foreign Legion.

29 Rocolle, p.459+

30 Rocolle, p.443+; Fall, *Hell...*, p.305; Simpson, *DBP...*, p.118+

31 Fall, *Hell...*, p.310+; Simpson, *DBP...*, p.147

32 Rocolle, p.445. He quotes in support, from Pres Eisenhower's memoirs, a memorandum to this effect sent by Sec Dulles to Gen Ely as early as 23 Mar. Dulles' dishonest attempt in June 54 publicly to blame Britain for US failure to intervene was unconvincing even to the American press. (Fall, *Hell...*, p.312+)

33 Roy, pp.198, 211, 215, 222

34 Fall, *Hell...*, pp.30, 299, 475

35 Simpson, *DBP...*, p.119

36 Rocolle, p.487+

37 *ibid*, pp.493, 500

38 *ibid*, p.494

39 Fall, *Hell...*, p.315

40 Rocolle, p.410

41 *ibid*, p.458

42 Fall, *Hell...*, p.318+; Bail, *Les Combats...*, p.161

43 Rocolle, p.497; Fall, *Hell...*, p.319

44 A meeting by Gens Cogny & Dechaux & Col Sauvagnac on 16 Apr first considered possible alternatives to 'Condor'. Cogny was still arguing for another raid on Phu Doan; and a drop on RP41 to cut VM supply lines at the Meo Pass was also considered but rejected. (Rocolle, p.463)

45 *ibid*, p.464

46 Rocolle, p.498+; Fall, *Hell...*, p.321

47 Rocolle, p.501; Bail, *Les Combats...*, p.163

48 Rocolle, p.500+; Fall, *Hell...*, p.321. Gen Navarre did not, of course, express a blunt intention; his words were '... [je] m'orienterai peut-être vers sortie garnison *si réalisable'* – author's italics.

16 'Tell Gars Pierre we liked him a lot...'

The epigraph is quoted from an interview with Col Bigeard by Col Pierre Rocolle, reported in the latter's *Pourquoi Dien Bien Phu?* (p.296).

1 Rocolle, p.485+

2 Fall, *Hell...*, p.349; Bergot, *Les 170 Jours...*, p.265

3 Rocolle, p.517

4 Bail, *Les Combats...*, p.156+. The squadron's own F4U-7 model Corsairs, less suitable for low-altitude work than the AU-1, were left at Karouba.

5 Fall, *Hell...*, p.357; Bail, *Les Combats...*, p.167. 11F transhipped to the newly arrived *Bois-Belleau* (ex-USS *Belleau Wood*) on 3 May, but boiler trouble took the carrier and its Hellcats to Hong Kong from 9 to 23 May.

6 Fall (*Hell...*, p.350) gives 14,000 × 105mm, 275 × 155, & 5,000 × 120mm; but Rocolle (p.287) gives '100 rounds each' for the 120mm mortars = 1,500. For comparison, during 36 hours 13–15 Mar, the 105s had fired 14,300 shells, the heavy mortars 13,000.

7 Brancion, p.244

8 Fall, *Hell...*, p.351

9 Rocolle, p.521; Fall, *Hell...*, p.352+; Brancion, 236+; Simpson, *DBP...*, p.150

10 Rocolle (p.518) calculates that Gen Giap now had 28 rebuilt battalions each with approx 500 riflemen – significantly fewer than their probable original strength of *c.* 800 – and thus *c.* 14,000 first line combatants, while Gen de Castries had 2,000–3,000 still in condition to fight.

11 Rocolle (pp.519, 525) and several other sources give 'Auerstaedt' as the last fully serviceable tank at Claudine. However, Dunstan (*Vietnam Tracks*, p.29) – whose source is Lt Préaud – names 'Auerstaedt', 'Neumach' & 'Ratisbonne' as the Isabelle ptn, and states that in the main camp 'Mulhouse', 'Posen' & 'Ettlingen' were to some extent serviceable until the end. He distinguishes them from the M24s used as static pillboxes, i.e. 'Conti' south of the airstrip & 'Douaumont' at Huguette 3. Since at least partial repairs were made on a daily basis, any particular tank's claimed status as 'the last in action' can only be temporarily accurate before 7 May. The tanks averaged 1,500 × 75mm rounds fired during the battle, and recoil mechanism failure became frequent; on 7 May three guns were unserviceable. (FTNV report, quoted Yves Buffetaut, 'Les Blindés Francais en Indochine', *Steel Masters* No. 58, Aug 2003.)

12 Bergot, *Les 170 Jours...*, p.267+; Rocolle, p.520, quoting WO Cordier.

13 Bergot, *Les 170 Jours...*, p.268. These may have been worn against smoke and dust, but had the added advantage of distinguishing friend from foe at night.

14 Rocolle, p.521; Bergot, *Les 170 Jours...*, p.269; Fall, *Hell...*, p.352+; Simpson, *DBP...*, p.150

15 Rocolle, p.522; Bergot, *Les 170 Jours...*, p.270, & *Bn Bigeard*, p.158.

16 Fall, *Hell...*, p.354+; Bergot, *Les 170 Jours...*, p.272. Fall times the loss of H5 to midnight; Bergot believes the attackers were Regt 102; Rocolle (map 27) identifies Regt 88. Lt de Stabenrath survived VM captivity, but died shortly after repatriation.

17 Fall, *Hell...*, p.290+

18 *ibid*, p.357+; Bail, *Les Combats...*, p.167

19 Fall, *Hell...*, p.358

20 Gaujac, *Histoire...*, p.454; Rocolle, pp.505, 523; Fall, *Hell...*, p.359

21 Fall, *Hell...*, p.290+

22 Roy, p.258

23 Rocolle, p.500+; Fall, *Hell....*, p.324

24 Rocolle, p.504; Simpson, *DBP...*, p.154+

25 Ruffat, *RHd'A*, 1984/4; Bail, *Les Combats...*, p.171

26 Rocolle, p.456+; author's translation from

Pouget, Jean, *Nous étions à Dien Bien Phu*, Presses de la Cité, Paris (1964), p.326+. In the original Pouget wrongly refers to the 'T' marker as a cross.

27 Rocolle, p.524. Fall (*Hell...*, p.363) gives the attackers – unconvincingly – as Regt 36 entire, plus three bns from Regts 88 & 102, plus one bn from Div 312. A force of seven bns would have been pointlessly unwieldy for such a small objective.

28 Rocolle, p.525; Fall, *Hell....*, p.364

29 Fall, *Hell...*, p.364; Bergot, *Bn Bigeard*, p.162 & *Les 170 Jours...*, p.278. Bergot places 6 ACP in E3 – see Ch.14 above, note (45).

30 Simpson, *DBP...*, p.152; original slightly edited by present author.

31 Fall, *Hell...*, p.365+; Simpson, *DBP...*, p.154

32 Roy, p.261; Fall, *Hell...*, pp.290+, 367

33 Simpson, *DBP...*, p.155, trans. Bigeard, Marcel, *Pour un parcelle de gloire*, Plon, Paris (1975); Rocolle, p.523; Fall, *Hell...*, p.368

34 Fall, *Hell...*, p.370

35 Rocolle, p.527; Fall, *Hell...*, p.368+; Bail, *Les Combats...*, p.172

36 Rocolle, p.525; Roy, p.263; Fall, *Hell...*, pp.322, 371

37 Rocolle, pp.505, 526; Fall, *Hell...*, pp.323, 371

38 Bergot, *Les 170 Jours...*, p.278

39 Brancion, p.243+

40 Rocolle, p.283. 11/IV/4 RAC had 33 killed, 21 wounded from 89 all ranks; II/4 RAC had 49 killed, 179 wounded from 556 all ranks (totals of original establishment plus parachuted replacements).

41 Rocolle, p.527; Fall, *Hell...*, p.372

42 Rocolle, p.523; Bail, *Les Combats...*, p.172; Fall, *Hell...*, p.372. 'French' here means as opposed to Indochinese.

43 Fall, *Hell...*, p.373. Bail (*Les Combats...*, p.172) gives fewer fighter-bomber and Helldiver sorties, but is imprecise.

44 Rocolle, p.526. Ruffat (*RHd'A*, 1984/4) gives the area of DBP still in French hands on 6 May as 333 acres.

45 Fall, *Hell...*, p.373; website *http://www.air-america.org/ About/History.htm*; Roy, p.265. Bail (*Les Combats...*, p.172) states that three French aircrew died with McGovern and Buford, but that a young paratroop sub-lieutenant who was also aboard survived to be captured – he gives no names, explanation or source.

46 Fall, *Hell...*, p.374+; Roy, p.265; Bail, *Les Combats...*, p.173

47 Fall, *Hell...*, p.376: Roy, p.265. Fall states that the High Elianes were defended by *c*. 750 paratroopers; this suggests that II/1 RCP & 5 BPVN together had *c*. 370 men still in the line.

48 Rocolle, p.527; Bergot, *Bn Bigeard*, p.162+

49 Fall, *Hell...*, p.382

50 Fall (*Hell...*, p.375) puts an unspecified number of the quad-50s at Epervier, and Bergot (*Les 170 Jours...*, p.278) at Junon, on 6 May. Originally all four were at Epervier; on *c*. 20 Mar, two were sent to Junon; on 5 Apr, all four were reunited at Epervier (Brancion, p.183). However, supporting Bergot is the fact that in 1996 Kieran Lynch photographed the debris of one quad-50 mount at Junon; it is plausible that two should have been moved back south to cover Elianes 4, 2 & 3.

51 Bergot, *Les 170 Jours...*, p.278; Fall, *Hell...*, p.375+

52 Rocolle, pp.519, 529; Brancion, p.245+; Fall, *Hell...*, p.377. Some survivors claimed that the rockets had been fired first on 5 May, but most sources give 6 May. Use of the slang names 'Stalin organ' and 'Katyusha' has misled several writers into identifying these as the truck-mounted 12-tube 120mm projector banks used by the Soviet Red Army in WWII. The weapon displayed in the Dien Bien Phu section of the Hanoi War Museum is a Chinese-made 86mm M1950 launcher, with two flat rows of three tubes mounted on a gun-style carriage (the author is indebted to Kieran Lynch for a photo). They were apparently dispersed in sections of two, one being carried on a truck which towed the other. They were later seen by French prisoners a couple of miles north of Gabrielle, and other survivors (Rocolle, p.529) claimed to have located a battery near Béatrice. The rockets had a considerable blast effect, but their enormous back-blast and noticeable smoke trails made concealment almost impossible.

53 Rocolle, p.306. Col Léonard (*RHd'A*, 1956/3) describes the ammo dump as in three sections totalling 62 'cells' divided by internal walls, their roofing covered with earth. After bombardment began on 13 Mar there were frequent small fires in the dump, and these became continuous from the end of March, but most were quickly stifled by the fall of the earth roofing ballast. There were losses of ammunition but, thanks to the compartmentalized design, no major explosions.

54 Bergot, *Bn Bigeard*, p.163; Fall, *Hell...*, p.377; Rocolle, p.529

55 Rocolle, p.529

56 The following account of this action generally follows Rocolle, p.530+. Fall (*Hell...*, p.378+) misidentifies the assault unit as Regt 102, which fought on the west bank that night.

57 Bergot, *Les 170 Jours...*, p.274. Rocolle identifies the senior FOO as Lt Robin, and Brancion (p.247) names Lt Juteau as FOO for the 105s and WO Poulain for the 120mm mortars.

58 Rocolle (p.529) gives midnight; Fall (*Hell...*, p.379) cites Col Lalande's signal of 11pm.

59 Rocolle, p.531. Capt Pouget wrote 8.30pm, but apparently agreed with Rocolle after further discussion. The Viet Minh account in *Contributions...* elides the times of the explosion and the delayed next assault, to 11pm; and Fall (*Hell...*, p.383) follows this. The relative timings of events following the mine explosion are thoroughly confused in all the sources.

60 Fall, *Hell...*, p.385; Rocolle, map 29. Bergot (*Les 170 Jours...*, p.281) also locates the crater on the north-east face.

61 Bergot, *Les 170 Jours...*, p.281; Fall, *Hell...*, p.383. Fall mentions the 0.50in MG; this was externally mounted on the cupola, while the hull and co-axial turret MGs were 0.30in calibre.

62 Rocolle, p.532; Fall, *Hell...*, p.386+

63 Fall, *Hell...*, p.382. It is unclear what happened to them – there is no mention of their arrival at Eliane 4. Brandon survived the prison camps.

64 Rocolle, p.532+; Fall, *Hell...*, p.380+

65 Rocolle, p.533; Fall, *Hell...*, p.387+; Sergent, p.218+. Rocolle mentions the counter-attack; Sergent simply has the platoon arriving four men strong.

66 Fall, *Hell...*, p.382

67 Rocolle, p.533. Cargo drops were also attempted on the night 6/7 May. 16 × C-119 sorties were flown: of the first five a/c three were hit, so the next six were ordered to abort; five more arrived, two dropping accurately but the others being turned back by flak. (Bail, *Les Combats...*, p.176)

68 Fall, *Hell...*, p.387

69 Rocolle, p.533+

70 Rocolle, p.535; Fall, *Hell...*, p.379

71 Rocolle, p.534; Fall, *Hell...*, p.391+

72 Fall, *Hell...*, p.394; Bergot, *Les 170 Jours...*, p.283

73 Rocolle, p.535; Fall, *Hell...*, p.395+

74 Rocolle, p.536; Bail, *Les Combats...*, p.178

75 Rocolle, p.536+; Fall, *Hell...*, p.398+

76 Rocolle, p.537+, quoting *Contributions...*, p.179; Fall, *Hell...*, p.397+

77 Fall, *Hell...*, p.400

78 Rocolle, p.544+

79 Fall, *Hell...*, p.391, quoting Giap, 'Quelques

souvenirs de Dien Bien Phu', in *Contributions...*, p.136

80 Rocolle, pp.486 & 538, quoting *Contributions...*, p.179; Fall, *Hell...*, p.400

81 Fall (*Hell...*, p.405) quotes the order as forbidding any further French firing from 5pm, not 5.30pm.

82 Bergot, *Les 170 Jours...*, pp.276 & 285 – the original note is reproduced on p.290; Fall, *Hell...*, p.400

83 Rocolle, p.540. On the morning of 7 May there were 6 × 105mm serviceable in the main camp, plus 2 × 105mm at Isabelle; 1 × 155mm, & 6 × 120mm. The 105s had some hundreds of shells left, the sole 155 about 30, and the 120s only about 25 bombs each. However, the 105s at Isabelle still had 1,700 rounds (Rocolle, p.284+).

84 Bail, *Les Combats...*, p.178. Rocolle (pp.511 & 547) & Fall (*Hell...*, p.415) state that on the night 7/8 May Privateer '28F-6' was shot down over RP41; Bail (*Les Combats...*, pp.145, 193; *L'Enfer...*, pp.48 & 144) places it at Son La and names the pilot as Lt Montguillon. Fall implies that the whole crew died; Bail names two survivors, Petty Officers Keromnès and Carpentier, whom Fall incorrectly gives as survivors of Lt Manfanovsky's '28F-4' shot down on 12 Apr – see p. 508 above.

85 Rocolle, p.538, quoting Grauwin, Paul, *J'étais médecin à Dien Bien Phu*, Éditions France Empire, Paris (1956) p.337

86 Fall, *Hell...*, p.401

87 Rocolle, p.549

88 Rocolle, p.539

89 Rocolle, p.539+; Roy, p.282; Fall, *Hell...*, p.406+; Kubiak, *Képi Blanc*, serial article Aug–Dec 62. Several days later, when the People's Army reconstructed many scenes of the 'fall' of the camp for the Soviet cameraman R. L. Karmen, they did not show a white flag over the command post.

90 Bergot, *Les 170 Jours...*, p.286

91 Sergent, p.221

92 Rocolle, p.541+, quoting Giap, 'Quelques souvenirs de Dien Bien Phu', in *Contributions...*, p.138+. Capt Ta Quang Luat and squad leaders Van and Chu Ta The were officially credited with the capture of Gen de Castries.

93 Rocolle, p.541+; Fall, *Hell...*, p.407+

94 Fall, *Hell...*, pp.292 & 412; Rocolle, p.544+

95 Rocolle, p.546; Fall, *Hell...*, p.412+

96 Rocolle, p.547

97 Brancion, p.249

98 Bail, *Les Combats...*, p.184+

17 *L'Addition*

The epigraph is quoted from 'Les méthodes Viet-Minh de lavage de cerveau' in *RHd'A*, 1989/4.

1 Bergot, *Bn Bigeard*, p.170; Sergent, p.224+; Bail, *L'Enfer...*, p.177

2 Fall, *Hell...*, p.320+; Bail, *Les Combats...*, p.175

3 Rocolle, p.540

4 Fall, *Hell...*, p.425. As president of the Red Cross throughout Indochina Dr Huard had a long record of impartiality; he had a Vietnamese wife, and spoke the language well.

5 Fall, *Hell...*, pp.425+, 430

6 *ibid*, p.431; Bail, *Les Combats...*, p.190. Mlle de Galard flew back to France from Hanoi a few days later.

7 Rocolle, p.307

8 Rocolle, p.548+. The total number of wounded recorded between 13 March and 5 May was 4,436, of whom 429 died. Of this total, 2,280 were treated solely by battalion aid posts, including 287 who subsequently died. 2,156 were treated by the surgical teams at the hospitals, who carried out 1,154 operations; 142 of these men died. These figures are from Forissier (*RHd'A*, 1989/4) quoting the official history *Le Service de Santé en Indochine 1945–54*, published by the Director of Medical Services/Far East, Saigon (1955). Rocolle (p.307) quotes for the surgical teams 2,265 patients, 934 operations, and 319 died, from a source apparently pre-dating the official history's calculations.

Fall (*Hell...*, p.483) gives the following breakdown by origin of casualties between 13 March and 5 May; 'Vietnamese' is limited here to regulars in French units and 5 BPVN:

	killed	wounded	missing	
French mainland	269	+ 974	+180	= 1,423
Foreign Legion	318	+1,266	+738	= 2,322
North African	191	+983	+433	= 1,607
West African	15	+53	+1	= 69
Vietnamese	307	+1,011	+213	= 1,531
Totals:	*1,100*	*+4,287*	*+1,565*	*= 6,952*

Fall and Rocolle both list an additional 1,161 known deserters; as quoted elsewhere, Col Langlais believed that the actual total was far greater. The 'rats' from combat units were primarily members of BT 2 and BT 3, Thai auxiliary companies, III/3 RTA and, later, I/4 RTM. In justice, it must be stressed that many members of these units fought to the end; and that the 'rats' also included a small number of légionnaires and perhaps other Europeans.

9 Fall, *Hell...*, p.448; Simpson, *DBP...*, p.169; and see note (21) below. The ceasefire terms of July 54 allowed both sides to send graves registration teams into each other's territory. In May 55 a Franco-VN team had begun work at DBP to recover bodies for an ossuary; but South Vietnamese President Diem broke this term of the Geneva accords (among many others), and in retaliation the work at DBP was stopped. Today many of the dead lie under the new town and airfield, and although monuments have been raised there is only one small cemetery in the vicinity of Eliane 2.

10 Fall, *Hell...*, p.250+

11 Rocolle (p.506) says 10am; Fall (*Hell...*, p.322), 1pm – perhaps the time when the message was relayed to Lt Col Godard.

12 Fall, *Hell...*, p.442+

13 Bail, *L'Enfer...*, p.145; Fall, *Hell...*, p.446

14 Fall, *Hell...*, p.446. Three years later Sgt Chief Sentenac would find a tragic fame through the photos of war correspondent Marc Flament. Serving once more under Col Bigeard with 3 RPC, his death from wounds on a sand dune at Timimoun in the Sahara on 21 Nov 57 would provide one of the iconic images of the Algerian War.

15 Brancion, p.253; Fall, *Hell...*, p.447

16 Rocolle, p.556+

17 Fall, *Hell...*, p.421+

18 Mme Thérèse Naskidaschvili, in conversation with the author.

19 Rocolle, p.40+; Fall, *Hell...*, pp.415, 423+; Macdonald, p.157

20 Rocolle, p.558+

21 *ibid*, p.553+. Gen Navarre's intelligence sources suggested total VM casualties of 20,000 dead and *evacuated* wounded, so an estimate of *c.* 10,000 dead and up to 15,000 wounded was plausible. Gen de Castries was told in captivity that VM casualties had in fact totalled 30,000; and other Frenchmen who had contact with the VM during Control Commission meetings were told the same.

22 Simpson, *DBP...*, p.170

23 Rocolle, pp.555, 559; Simpson, *DBP...*, p.175

24 Apparently between Col de Brébisson and Col Ha Van Lau; the outline for a partition agreement was emerging by 24 June. (Rocolle, p.562+, quoting Francois Mitterrand, *Présence Française et Abandon*, Plon, Paris, 1957, p.40; & J. Lacouture & P. Devillers, *La fin d'une guerre*, Le Seuil, Paris, 1960, pp.118 & 211–15).

25 Rocolle 560+

26 GM 4's other infantry units were III/6 RTM,

& BMI – the locally recruited Bataillon de Marche Indochinois, which had earned three citations in Tonkin.

27 Fonde, *RHd'A*, 1980/2

28 Rocolle, p.41

29 *ibid*, p.47

30 *ibid*, p.564

31 GM 42's infantry were 1er, 5e & 8e Bataillons Montagnards, the artillery 4 GAVN, the armour 1 tank ptn from 3/5 RC plus 1 ERVN, an ANV recce unit. GM 100's artillery were II/10 RAC, its armour 2 ptns from 3/5 RC.

32 Sockeel, *RHd'A*, 1977/3; Fall, *Street...*, p.207+. After-action strengths: I/Corée = 452; II/Corée = 497; BM/43 RIC = 345.

33 Sockeel, *RHd'A*, 1977/3; Fall, *Street...*, p.235+

34 Bail, *L'Enfer...*, p.150+. Apart from Maj Kah and Lt Col Ducruix, all senior staff and battalion commanders named in this text survived captivity.

35 Sergent, p.177+; Macdonald, p.160; Bail, *L'Enfer...*, p.159

36 Fall, *Hell...*, p.433; Bail, *Les Combats...*, p.192. Dates quoted for the 'march past' range from 14 May to 14 July.

37 The usual daily ration quoted during captivity is 28oz (Racca, *RHd'A*, 1968/1), but Fall (*Hell...*, p.432) quotes 14oz during the march; and Dr Rondy (see below) says that deliberately small rations were given to encourage quarrels, theft and a breakdown of solidarity. On 28oz daily the problem was not lack of bulk starch, but of essential vitamins.

38 Rondy, *RHd'A*, 1989/4

39 Fall, *Hell...*, p.437+; Bail, *Les Combats...*, p.157; Sergent, p.224+

40 Fall, *Hell...*, p.436

41 Sergent, p.224+; Bergot, *Bn Bigeard*, p.172; Simpson, *DBP...*, p.172

42 Rondy, *RHd'A*, 1989/4; p.218+.

43 Fall, *Street...*, p.299

44 Fall, *Street...*, p.295+; Bail, *L'Enfer...*, p.158+; Simpson, *DBP...*, p.173

45 The following passage draws heavily on Rondy, *RHd'A*, 1989/4, but also upon Fall, *Hell...*, p.439+; Sergent, p.232+; and Rocolle, p.551.

46 Fall (*Hell...*, p.440) quotes a report in the *New York Times* of 19 Dec 54, in which a New York-based E. European exile organization lists the names of 1,000 E. European légionnaires reportedly forced to return to Communist countries in this way; the USSR admitted providing aircraft for this purpose. Sgt Wingens, 2 BEP, escaped back from E. Germany to France, and rejoined what was now 2 REP in Algeria after collecting several years' back pay and the Escaper's Medal. (Sergent, p.232)

47 It has sometimes been implied that N. African POWs, relatively amenable to 'brainwashing', received preferential treatment. However, of 5,007 N. African NCOs and men believed captured during the war, only 2,865 were repatriated; and of well over 200 from V/7 RTA captured at Gabrielle on 15 Mar 54, only 65 returned. (Ferrari & Vernet, p.153; Bergot, *Les 170 Jours...*, p.145)

48 Bail, *L'Enfer...*, pp.144 & 158, adds all the missing to the captured and quotes the returned prisoners from DBP as 3,290 (but does not give his source); he suggests that nearly 72 per cent of DBP POWs died or disappeared in captivity.

49 Rocolle, p.547+. From say 15,100 total, 324 wounded evacuated pre-28 Mar, + 858 evacuated post-7 May, +?1,000 repatriated to Communist bloc, + 3,900 released = 6,082, or just over 40 per cent survived. Even if we (unrealistically) omit all Thai auxiliaries from the garrison total, the percentage returned is still only 44 per cent. While the danger of comparing like with unlike is freely acknowledged, the proportion of British dead and died of wounds in the annihilation of 1st Airborne Div at Arnhem in Sept 1944 was roughly 15 per cent.

50 Fall, *Hell...*, p.481+

51 Rocolle, p.550

52 Simpson, *DBP...*, p.176+

53 Simpson, *DBP...*, p.177; *Tiger...*, p.111+

54 Air America Association – History, University of Texas Archives, accessed via *http://www.airamerica.org/About/History.htm.*

55 Simpson, *Tiger...*, p.121+; Bail, *Les Combats...*, p.232, *L'Enfer...*, p.152; *http://www.airamerica.org/About/History.htm*

56 Simpson, *Tiger...*, p.118

57 Macdonald, p.167+

58 Simpson, *Tiger...*, p.123+

59 The SMM were generally unsuccessful in establishing an effective underground network; when the US and European agents left on 9 Oct 54 the well-informed Viet Minh security branch began an immediate and efficient campaign of arrests and executions.

60 Simpson, *Tiger...*, p.135; Rocolle, p.564. Pierre Schoendoerffer's feature film *317e Section* memorably reconstructs the ordeal of a small GCMA team trying to reach French lines.

61

	Killed	Missing	Unreleased POWS	Wounded
French, Legion, N. & W. African	22,860	9,951	18,507	45,256
Vietnamese in CEFEO units	14,093	12,830	13,200	26,924
Totals	*36,953*	*22,781*	*31,707*	*72,180*

Sources: Héduy (ed.), *La Guerre...*, p.21; Clayton, *The Wars...* p.74

62 Macdonald, p.171+

63 Among hundreds of officers whose careers were destroyed during the arrests and purges that followed this episode were Cols Jean Nicot and Yves Godard and Majs Maurice Guiraud, Jean Bréchignac and André Botella. Gens Lalande and Langlais and Col Bigeard negotiated these treacherous waters safely; later Bigeard also became a general, and a junior defence minister.

Select Bibliography

BOOKS, SPECIFIC

Bail, René, *Indochine 1953–54 – Les Combats de l'Impossible*, Lavauzelle (1985)

Bail, René, *L'Enfer de Dien Bien Phu*, Éditions Heimdal (1997)

Bergot, Erwan, *Bataillon Bigeard*, Presses de la Cité (1977)

Bergot, Erwan, *Les 170 Jours de Dien Bien Phu*, Presses de la Cité (1979)

Blondieau, Christian, *Les Insignes de l'Armée Française: La Guerre d'Indochine – Tome I*, Copernic (1983)

Brancion, Henri de, *Dien Bien Phu: Artilleurs dans la Fournaise*, Presses de la Cité (1993)

Clayton, Anthony, *France, Soldiers and Africa*, Brassey's (1988)

Clayton, Anthony, *The Wars of French Decolonization*, Longman (1994)

Dunstan, Simon, *Vietnam Tracks: Armor in Battle 1945–75*, Osprey Publishing (1982)

Fall, Bernard, *Street Without Joy*, Pall Mall Press (1964)

Fall, Bernard, *Hell in a Very Small Place*, Vintage Books/Random House (1968)

Favreau, Jacques, & Dufour, Nicolas, *Nasan, la victoire oubliée 1952–53 – Base aéroterrestre au Tonkin*, Economica (1999)

Ferrari, Pierre, & Vernet, Jacques M., *Une Guerre Sans Fin: Indochine 1945–54*, Lavauzelle (1984)

Galard, Geneviève de, with Beatrice Bazil, *Une femme à Dien Bien Phu*, Editions les Arènes (2003)

Gaujac, Paul (ed.), *Histoire des Parachutistes Francais*, Éditions d'Albatros/Société de Production Littéraire (1975)

Grauwin, Paul, *J'étais médecin à Dien Bien Phu*, Éditions France-Empire (1956)

Héduy, Philippe (ed.), *La Guerre d'Indochine 1945–54*, Société de Production Littéraire (1981)

Labrousse, Pierre, *La Méthode Vietminh – Indochine 1945–54*, Charles-Lavauzelle (1996)

Lewis, Norman, *A Dragon Apparent*, Jonathan Cape (1951), Eland Books (1982)

Macdonald, Peter, *Giap – The Victor in Vietnam*, Fourth Estate (1993)

O'Ballance, Edgar, *The Indo-China War 1945–54*, Faber & Faber (1964)

Ousby, Ian, *Occupation – The Ordeal of France 1940–44*, John Murray (1997)

Pissardy, J.-P. *Paras d' Indochine 1944–54*, Société de Production Littéraire (1982)

Porch, Douglas, *The French Foreign Legion – A Complete History*, Macmillan (1991)

Rocolle, Pierre, *Pourquoi Dien Bien Phu?*, L'Histoire Flammarion (1968)

Roy, Jules (trans. Robert Baldick), *The Battle of Dien Bien Phu*, Faber and Faber (1965)

Sergent, Pierre, *Paras-Légion – le 2ème BEP en Indochine*, Presses de la Cité (1982)

Simpson, Howard R., *Tiger in the Barbed Wire*, Brassey's Inc (1992)

Simpson, Howard R., *Dien Bien Phu – The Epic Battle America Forgot*, Brassey's Inc (1994)

BOOKS, GENERAL

Berlin, Stephen, *I Am Lazarus*, Galley Press (1961)

Bowen, Brigadier General Thomas E., MD (ed.), *WSURG – Emergency War Surgery NATO Handbook* (2nd US edn.)

Conboy, Kenneth, & Bowra, Kenneth, *The NVA and Viet Cong*, Elite series 38, Osprey Publishing (1991)

Dunstan, Simon, *Flak Jackets – 20th Century Military Body Armour*, Men-at-Arms series 157, Osprey Publishing (1984)

Ellis, John, *The World War II Data Book*, Aurum Press (1993)

Florence, Mason, & Storey, Robert, *Vietnam*, Lonely Planet Publications Pty Ltd, 6th edn. (2001)

Henry, Mark R., *The US Army in World War II (1): The Pacific*, Men-at-Arms series 342, Osprey Publishing (2000)

Hogg, Ian V., *British and American Artillery of World War Two*, Greenhill Books (2002)

Holmes, Richard, *Firing Line*, Penguin Books (1987)

Laffin, John, *Combat Surgeons*, Sutton Publishing (1999)

Smith, Joseph E., *Small Arms of the World*, Stackpole Books (1973)

Weeks, John, *Airborne Equipment – A History of its Development*, David & Charles (1976)

Williams, Derek, *The Reach of Rome*, Constable (1996)

JOURNALS

Revue Historiques des Armées, quarterly; articles listed alphabetically by author, issues as *RHd'A,* year/number:

Babet, Général, 'Les Transmissions en Indochine de 1945 à 1954', *RHd'A,* 1967/1

Bodin, Professor Michel, 'Inadapté ou inadaptation? Le corps expéditionnaire en Extrême-Orient 1945–54', *RHd'A,* 1979/3

Bodin, Professor Michel, 'Les Troupes Africaines en Indochine', *RHd'A,* 1989/4

Boissau, Général Raymond, 'Le Bataillon 303', *RHd'A,* 1989/4

Brancion, Général Henri de, *'Dien Bien Phu – le choc de deux artilleries',* *RHd'A,* 1992/4

Bunel, Intendant Militaire de 3e classe, 'L'Intendance Militaire en Operations en Indochine', *RHd'A,* 1957/4

Champeaux de la Boulaye, Général de, 'Les B-26 à Dien Bien Phu', *RHd'A,* 1987/4

Champeaux de la Boulaye, Général de, 'Un centre d'interrogatoire Viet-Minh à Dien Bien Phu', *RHd'A,* 1989/4

Couget, Georges, 'Le Train dans la bataille de la RC4, zone frontière du Tonkin 1947–50', *RHd'A,* 1978/3

Facon, Patrick, 'L'Armée de l'Air et Dien Bien Phu', *RHd'A,* 1985/1

Fonde, Général J.-J., 'Opération Auvergne – Rétraction de la zone sud du delta tonkinois 18 juin–4 juillet 1954', *RHd'A,* 1980/2

Forissier, Régis, 'Le Service de Santé en Indochine', *RHd'A,* 1989/4

Gazin, Général, 'Le Génie en Extrême-Orient', *RHd'A,* 1955/4

Gazin, Général, 'Le Génie au Combat...', *RHd'A,* 1966/1

le Goyet, Colonel, 'Libération de la France – L'unification des forces armées', *RHd'A,* 1974/4

Léonard, Colonel, 'Quelques aspects typiques du rôle du Matériel en Indochine', *RHd'A,* 1956/3

Paillard, Jacques, 'L'Affaire du GM4, Indochine, 1953', *RHd'A,* 1984/4

Racca, Intendant Militaire de 3e Classe, 'L'Intendance en Indochine – l'Approvisionnement en Vivres des Combattants de Dien Bien Phu', *RHd'A,* 1968/1

Rondy, Jean-Louis, 'Les méthodes Viet-Minh de lavage de cerveau', *RHd'A,* 1989/4

Ruffat, Hubert, 'Le ravitaillement par air de Dien Bien Phu', *RHd'A,* 1984/4

Sockeel, Général Jacques, 'Après Dien Bien Phu: les derniers combats au Vietnam sur les plateaux Montagnards', *RHd'A*, 1977/3

Trinquier, Roger, 'Les maquis d'Indochine: (I) L'évacuation de la base aéroterrestre de Na San en août 1953', *RHd'A*, 1979/2; '(II) Comment nous sommes allés à Dien Bien Phu', *RHd'A*, 1981/4

le Troadec, Général, 'Le Service du Matériel d'Indochine 1949–51', *RHd'A*, 1956/3

OTHER JOURNALS

Appel, J. W., & Beebe, G. W., 'Preventive Psychiatry: An Epidemiological Approach', *Journal of the American Medical Association*, 131 (1946), p.1470

Buffetaut, Yves, 'Les Blindés Francais en Indochine', *Steel Masters* No. 58 (August 2003)

Caillot, Frédéric, 'La 11-F', *Marines Internationales*, April 1980

Dutrône, Christophe, '1951, l'année de Lattre', *Militaria* Nos. 193 and 194 (August and September 2001)

Garros, Louis, 'La Légion – Grandeur et Servitude', Hors Serie No. 3, *Historama* (November 1967)

Gaujac, Paul, 'Une victoire amère... juin 1945–janvier 1946', *Militaria* No. 149 (December 1997)

Kemencei, Janos, 'Mourir (pour rien) à Dong-Khé', *Hommes de Guerre* No. 3 (December 1987)

Lassus, Denis, 'Dien Bien Phu', *Military Illustrated Past and Present*, No.18 (April–May 1989)

Morgan, Eric, 'Back to the Jungle' (interview, Vicky Thomas), *Images of War*, Vol. 4, No. 51

Appendix 1

French Staff and Commanding Officers

A: SENIOR COMMAND STAFF, FRENCH INDOCHINA:

FRENCH FAR EAST EXPEDITIONARY CORPS (CEFEO), HQ Saigon:
COMMANDER-IN-CHIEF FAR EAST General Henri NAVARRE
Deputy: General Bodet
Inter-Service and Army Chief-of-Staff General Gambiez
Deputy Chief-of-Staff/Operations Colonel Berteil
Commander, Airborne Troops (TAPI) (–Feb 1954) General Gilles
                                     (Mar 1954–) Colonel Sauvagnac
Inspector/Artillery General Pennacchioni
COMMANDER, FAR EAST AIR FORCES (FAEO) General Henri LAUZIN
COMMANDER, FAR EAST MARITIME FORCES (FMEO) Admiral AUBOYNEAU

LAND FORCES NORTH VIETNAM (FTNV), HQ Hanoi:
Commander General René COGNY
Deputy General Masson
Chief-of-Staff Colonel Bastiani
Deputy Chief-of-Staff/Operations Lieutenant Colonel Denef

TACTICAL AIR GROUP NORTH (GATAC/Nord)
Commander General Jean DECHAUX
Commander, Air Transport Command (S/GMMTA) Colonel Nicot

LAND FORCES LAOS (FTL)
Commander Colonel Boucher DE CRÈVECOEUR

B: PROMINENT STAFF OFFICERS AND UNIT COMMANDING OFFICERS AT DIEN BIEN PHU (ranks pre-16 April 1954)
CO, Operational Group North-West (GONO) Colonel DE CASTRIES
CO, Mobile Group 6 (GM 6) Lieutenant Colonel LALANDE
COs, Mobile Group 9 (GM 9) Lieutenant Colonel GAUCHER
                                     Lieutenant Colonel LEMEUNIER

COs, 2nd Airborne Brigade (GAP 2) Lieutenant Colonel LANGLAIS
Lieutenant Colonel DE SEGUIN-PAZZIS
Commanders, artillery Colonel PIROTH
Lieutenant Colonel VAILLANT

GAP 2:
CO, 1st Foreign Parachute Battalion (1 BEP), &
Foreign Para Marching Bn (BMEP) Major GUIRAUD
CO, 8th Para Shock Bn (8 BPC) Captain TOURRET
CO, 5th Vietnamese Para Bn (5 BPVN) Captain BOTELLA

GAP 1:
COs, 6th Colonial Para Bn (6 BPC) Major BIGEARD
Captain THOMAS
CO, 2nd Bn/1st Para Light Inf Regt (II/1 RCP) Major BRÉCHIGNAC
CO, 2nd Foreign Para Bn (2 BEP) Major LIESENFELT

CO, 1st Bn/2nd Foreign Inf Regt (I/2 REI) Captain CLÉMENCON
CO, 1st Bn/13th Foreign Legion Half-Brigade (I/13 DBLE) Major COUTANT
CO, 3rd Bn/13th Foreign Legion Half-Brigade (III/13 DBLE) Major PÉGOT

CO, 2nd Bn/1st Algerian Rifle Regt (II/1 RTA) Captain JEANCENELLE
CO, 3rd Bn/3rd Algerian Rifle Regt (III/3 RTA) Captain GARANDEAU
CO, 5th Bn/7th Algerian Rifle Regt (V/7 RTA) Major DE MECQUENEM
CO, 1st Bn/4th Moroccan Rifle Regt (I/4 RTM) Major NICOLAS

CO, 2nd Thai Bn (BT 2) Major CHENEL
CO, 3rd Thai Bn (BT 3) Major THIMONIER

CO, 2nd Bn/4th Colonial Artillery Regt (II/4 RAC) Major KNECHT
CO, 3rd Bn/10th Colonial Artillery Regt (III/10 RAC) Major ALLIOU

Appendix 2

French Order of Battle

Operational Group North-West (GONO)
Dien Bien Phu, March–May 1954
with abbreviations used in this text:

PARACHUTE INFANTRY

II/1 RCP...*2e Bataillon/1er Régiment de Chasseurs Parachutistes*
    2nd Battalion/1st Parachute Light Infantry Regiment
1 BPC...*1er Bataillon de Parachutistes Coloniaux*
    1st Colonial Parachute Battalion
6 BPC...6th Colonial Parachute Battalion
8 BPC...*8e Bataillon de Parachutistes de Choc*
    8th Parachute Shock Battalion
1 BEP...*1er Bataillon Étranger de Parachutistes*
    1st Foreign (Legion) Parachute Battalion
2 BEP...2nd Foreign (Legion) Parachute Battalion
5 BPVN...*5e Bataillon de Parachutistes Vietnamiens*
    5th Vietnamese Parachute Battalion

INFANTRY

I/2 REI...*1er Bataillon/2e Régiment Étranger d'Infanterie*
    1st Battalion/2nd Foreign (Legion) Infantry Regiment
III/3 REI...3rd Battalion/3rd Foreign (Legion) Infantry Regiment
I/13 DBLE...*1er Bataillon/13e Demi-Brigade de la Légion Étrangère*
    1st Battalion/13th Foreign Legion Half-Brigade
III/13 DBLE...3rd Battalion/13th Foreign Legion Half-Brigade

II/1 RTA...*2e Bataillon (de Marche)/1er Régiment de Tirailleurs Algériens*
    2nd (Marching) Battalion/1st Algerian Rifle Regiment
III/3 RTA...3rd (Marching) Battalion/3rd Algerian Rifle Regiment
V/7 RTA...5th (Marching) Battalion/7th Algerian Rifle Regiment
I/4 RTM...*1er Bataillon (de Marche)/4e Régiment de Tirailleurs Marocains*
    1st (Marching) Battalion/4th Moroccan Rifle Regiment

....2e Bataillon Thai – 2nd Thai Battalion
BT 3...3rd Thai Battalion
GMPT (1)...*(1er) Groupement Mobile des Partisans T'ai*
(1st) Thai Mobile Partisan Group (*c.* 11 companies)

ARMOURED CAVALRY
3 EM/1 RCC...*3e Escadron (de Marche), 1er Régiment de Chasseurs à Cheval*
3rd (Marching) Squadron, 1st Light Horse Regiment
(Composite squadron, incorporating 1 ptn from Moroccan Colonial Infantry
Regiment – 10 × M24 Chaffee tanks)
At Claudine – command tank 'Conti';
Ptn Carette (RICM) 'Mulhouse', 'Bazeilles', 'Douaumont';
Ptn Ney (1 RCC) 'Smolensk', 'Posen', 'Ettlingen'
At Isabelle – Ptn Préaud (1 RCC) 'Auerstaedt', 'Neumach', 'Ratisbonne'

ARTILLERY
II/4 RAC...*2e Groupe/4e Régiment d'Artillerie Coloniale*
2nd Battalion/4th Colonial Artillery Regiment
(3 batteries of 4 × = 12 × HM2 105mm howitzers)
11/IV/4 RAC...11th Battery/4th Battalion/4th Colonial Artillery Regiment
(4 × HM1 155mm howitzers)
III/10 RAC...3rd Battalion/10th Colonial Artillery Regiment
(3 batteries of 4 × = 12 × HM2 105mm howitzers)
GAACEO...*Groupe d'Artillerie Antiaerién Coloniale d'Extrême-Orient*
Colonial Far East Anti-Aircraft Artillery Battalion (platoon)
(4 × quad M2 0.50cal MGs, M55 trailer mounts)
(Plus many individual replacements from
GM/35 RALP...*Groupe de Marche/35e Régiment d'Artillerie Légère Parachutiste*
Marching Battalion, 35th Parachute Light Artillery Regiment)

HEAVY MORTARS
1 CEPML...*1ère Compagnie Étrangère Parachutiste de Mortiers Lourds*
1st Foreign (Legion) Parachute Heavy Mortar Company – ex 1 BEP
(12 × 120mm mortars)
1 CMMLE...*1ère Compagnie Mixte de Mortiers Lourds Étrangère*
1st Foreign (Legion) Composite Heavy Mortar Company – ex 3 REI
(8 × 120mm mortars)
2 CMMLE...2nd Foreign (Legion) Composite Heavy Mortar Company – ex 5 REI
(8 × 120mm mortars)

ENGINEERS
31 BG...*31ère Bataillon du Génie*
31st Engineer Battalion (2 companies)

SERVICE UNITS
3 ACP...*3e Antenne Chirurgicale Parachutable*
3rd Parachute Surgical Team

5 ACP...5th Parachute Surgical Team
6 ACP...6th Parachute Surgical Team
29 ACM...*29e Antenne Chirurgicale Mobile*
    29th Mobile Surgical Team
44 ACM...44th Mobile Surgical Team

342 CPT...*342ème Compagnie Parachutiste des Transmissions*
    342nd Parachute Signals Company
2/822 BT...*2ème Compagnie, 822ème Bataillon des Transmissions*
    2nd Company, 822nd Signals Battalion
2/823 BT...2nd Company, 823rd Signals Battalion
5 CMRLE...*5e Compagnie Moyenne de Réparations de la Légion Étrangère*
    5th Foreign Legion Medium Repair Company (platoon)
1 GEO...*1ère Groupe d'Exploitation Opérationnel, Service de l'Intendance*
    1st Exploitation Battalion, Quartermaster Corps
730 CR...*730ème Compagnie de Ravitaillement, Service des Essences*
    730th Fuel Resupply Company
3 CM...*3ème Compagnie des Munitions*
    3rd Ammunition Resupply Company (part)
712 CCR...*712ème Compagnie de Circulation Routière, Train*
    712th Traffic Company, Service Corps
3 CTQG...*3ème Compagnie de Transport de Quartier Général*
    3rd General Staff Transport Company
3 LM/GRGM...*3ème Légion de Marche, Garde Républicaine/Gendarmerie Mobile*
    3rd Marching Battalion, Republican Guard/Gendarmerie (provost)
    (part)
403 BPM... *403ème Boîte Postale Militaire*
    403rd Military Post Office

AIR FORCE
DB 195...*195ème Détachement de Base*
    195th Base Detachment
CT 21/374...*21/374ème Compagnie des Transmissions*
    21/374th Signals Company

INTELLIGENCE
GC 8...*Groupe de Commandos 8, GMI*
    8th Commando, Mixed Intervention Group
    (Plus detachments, *Securité Militaire,* and *6ème Section, SDECE*)

(Sources: Fall, *Hell...,* p.479+; Bergot, *Les 170...,* p.292+; Bail, *L'Enfer...,* passim)

Appendix 3

Air Units and Air Supply

A: AIR UNITS OPERATING IN SUPPORT OF DIEN BIEN PHU

AIR FORCE *(ARMÉE DE L'AIR)*
Bomber squadrons
GB 1/19...*Groupe de Bombardement 1/19 'Gascogne'*
    (Douglas B-26B and C Invader)
GB 1/25...*Groupe de Bombardement 1/25 'Tunisie'*
    (Douglas B-26B and C Invader)

Fighter squadrons
GC 1/22...*Groupe de Chasse 1/22 'Saintonge'*
    (Grumman F8F-1 Bearcat)
GC 2/22...*Groupe de Chasse 2/22 'Languedoc'*
    (Grumman F8F-1 Bearcat)

Transport squadrons
GT 2/62...*Groupe de Transport 2/62 'Franche-Comté'*
    (Douglas C-47 Dakota)
GT 2/63...*Groupe de Transport 2/63 'Sénégal'*
    (Douglas C-47 Dakota)
GT 1/64...*Groupe de Transport 1/64 'Béarn'*
    (Douglas C-47 Dakota)
GT 2/64...*Groupe de Transport 2/64 'Anjou'*
    (Douglas C-47 Dakota)
Détachement Packet
    (Fairchild C-119A Packet)

Various
21 and 23 GAOA...*21er & 23e Groupes Aériens d'Observation d'Artillerie*
    21st and 23rd Artillery Air Observation Squadrons
    (Morane 500 Criquet)

EROM 80...*80e Escadrille de Reconnaissance Outremer*
   80th Overseas Reconnaissance Flight
   (Grumman F8F-1 Bearcat)
ELA 52 and 53...*52e & 53e Escadrilles de Liaison Aériennes*
   52nd and 53rd Air Liaison Flights
   (various, incl. DHC Beaver, NC701 Siebel)
GFHAT...*Groupement de Formations d'Hélicoptères de l'Armée de Terre*
   Combined Army Helicopter Unit
   (Sikorsky S-55/'H-19')

NAVAL AIR ARM *(AÉRONAVALE)*
3F...*3e Flotille d'Assaut Embarquée*
   3rd Carrier Attack Squadron
   (Curtiss SB2C-5 Helldiver)
11F...*11e Flotille de Chasse Embarquée*
   11th Carrier Fighter Squadron
   (Grumman F6F-5 Hellcat)
14F...14th Carrier Fighter Squadron
   (Vought AU-1 Corsair)
28F...*28e Flotille de Bombardement*
   28th Bomber Squadron
   (Convair PB4-Y2 Privateer)

B: AIR SUPPLY OF DIEN BIEN PHU

Transport squadrons of *Sous-Groupement des Moyens Militaires de Transport Aérien* (S/GMMTA)

November 1953–May 1954
Groupe de Transport 2/62 'Franche-Comté'
   Call-sign *P'tits Loups* ('Little Wolves'); yellow nose cones.
GT 1/64 'Béarn'
   Call-sign *Boeufs* ('Bullocks'); red nose cones.
GT 2/64 'Anjou'
   Call-sign *Seigneurs* ('Lords'); blue nose cones.
Détachement Packet
   Call-sign 'Bird', later 'Pigeon'

Plus from February 1954
GT 2/63 'Sénégal'
   Call-sign *Négros*; green nose cones.

Transport aircraft (& crews) available to S/GMMTA for whole Indochina theatre

November 1953:
C-47 × 69 (crews × 68), C-119 × 5 (crews × 5)

December 1953:
C-47 × 91 (crews × 60), C-119 × 15 (crews × 5)

January 1954:
C-47 × 94 (crews × 60), C-119 × 15 (crews × 10)

February 1954:
C-47 × 90 (crews × 74), C-119 × 15 (crews × 4)

March 1954:
C-47 × 88 (crews × 76), C-119 × 24 (crews Fr × 6, US × 12)

April 1954:
C-47 × 101 (crews × 55), C-119 × 29 (crews Fr × 5, US × 12)

May 1954:
C-47 × 103 (crews × 49), C-119 × 29 (crews Fr × 10, US × 12)

Tonnage of cargo landed and parachuted at Dien Bien Phu

Operation 'Castor', 20–25 November 1953:
Requested = 600 tons (daily average = 100 tons)
Delivered = 682 tons (daily average = 113 tons)

26 November 1953–31 January 1954:
Requested = 11,600 tons (daily average 173 tons)
Delivered = 11,055 tons (daily average 165 tons)

1 February–12 March 1954:
Requested = 4,600 tons (daily average 115 tons)
Delivered = 3,608 tons (daily average 90 tons)

13 March–7 May 1954:
Requested = 10,200 tons (daily average 182 tons)
Delivered = 7,120 tons (daily average 127 tons)
(but: 30 March–5 April, *c.* 90 tons dropped daily;
after 30 April, *c.* 50–80 tons daily)

TOTALS 20 November 1953–7 May 1954:
Requested = 26,700 tons (daily average 158 tons)
Delivered = 22,465 tons (daily average 133 tons)

Total personnel parachuted 14 March 1953–6 May 1954:
3,597 jump-qualified, ?680 to 709 unqualified

(Sources: Ruffat, *RHd'A*, 1984/4; Facon, *RHd'A*, 1985/1; Bail, *L'Enfer...*,
pp.76 and 78, and *Les Combats...*, pp.29 and 141; De Brancion, p.279+)

C: AIRCRAFT SHOT DOWN DURING MISSIONS OVER DIEN BIEN PHU

Various sources have claimed that up to 50 aircraft were shot down 'during the battle', but fail to define these in terms of time or place, or to cite evidence; some seem to be straightforward VM propaganda. As mentioned in the text, it is difficult to define which combat aircraft to include, since these were sometimes given multiple targets – e.g. it was commonplace for missions to be routed to and from DBP along RP41 to hit VM lines of supply. Should aircraft lost during flights to or from the valley be counted as 'at DBP'? Thus, to the following list of losses from 13 March to 7 May should possibly be added: 2 × B-26 (15 Mar, Aubel – see note 2, Ch. 12; 2 Apr, Beglin, see note 3, Ch. 14); and 1 × Bearcat (3 Apr, Bourdelon – see note 3, Ch. 14).

4 × C-47 Dakota: 24 Mar (Koenig), 26 Mar (Boeglin – forced landing),
   27 Mar (Dartigues), 31 Mar (Guiraud)
1 × C-119 Packet: 6 May (McGovern)
2 × F8F Bearcat: 13 Mar (pilot unknown), 15 Mar (Sahraoui)
2 × B-26 Invader: 26 Apr (Caubel and Iteney)
3 × F6F Hellcat: 15 Mar (Lespinas), 23 Apr (Klotz), 26 Apr (Robert)
2 × SB2C Helldiver: 31 Mar (Andrieux), 9 Apr (Laugier)
2 × PB4Y Privateer: 12 Apr (Manfanovsky), 7/8 May (Montguillon)

It is unclear how many of the *c.* 10 × Morane 500 Criquet light observation aircraft of 21 and 23 GAOA that were lost can properly be described as 'shot down', apart from Ribière and de la Mestrie's aircraft on 6 April.

   The minimum total is thus 16 aircraft, the maximum excluding Moranes possibly 19.

Appendix 4

Vietnamese People's Army

A: VIETNAMESE PEOPLE'S ARMY
Dien Bien Phu, March–May 1954

Identifications are incomplete: e.g., there is no identification of a divisional artillery battalion for Div 308, and territorial titles for most units have not been published – there is some evidence to suggest that these were borne by sub-units down to company level.

Front commander General Vo Nguyen Giap
Chief-of-Staff General Hoang Van Thai

Division 304 'Nam Dinh', part (General Hoang Sam*)
(*until November 1953, Gen Hoang Minh Thao)
   Inf Regt 9 (Bns 353, 375, 400)
   Inf Regt 57 (Bns 265, 346, 418)
   Arty Bn 345

Division 308 'Viet Bac' (General Vuong Thua Vu)
   Inf Regt 36 'Chapa' (Bns 80, 84, 89)
   Inf Regt 88 'Tam Dao' (Bns 23, 29, 322)
   Inf Regt 102 'Ba Vi' (Bns 18, 54, 79)
   Arty Bn?

Division 312 'Ben Tre'* (General Hoang Cam**)
(*later 'Chien Tang', 'Victorious') (** until ?1953, Gen Le Trung Tan)
   Inf Regt 141 'Hong Gai' (Bns 11, 16, 428)
   Inf Regt 165 'Dong Trieu' (Bns 115, 542, 564)
   Inf Regt 209 (Bns 130, 154, 166)
   Arty Bn 154

Division 316 'Bien Hoa' (General Le Quang Ba*)
(*Fall, p.239, gives Gen Vu Manh Hung)
  Inf Regt 98 (Bns 215, 439, 933)
  Inf Regt 174 (Bns 249, 251, ?)
  Inf Regt 176 (Bns 888, 970, 999)
  Arty Bn 980
  Hy Wpns Co 812

Independent Infantry Regiment 148, part
  Bns 910, 920
  Hy Wpns Co 121

Heavy Division 351, reinforced *(General Vu Hien)*
  Eng Regt 151
  Hy Wpns Regt 237
  Arty Regt 45 (Bns 950, 954)
  Arty Regt 675 (Bns 83, 175, 275)
  AA Regt 367
  Field Rocket Unit

(Sources: Fall, *Hell...,* p.486+ *et passim;* Rocolle, *passim;* Favreau & Dufour, p.126; website *http://members.lycos.co.uk/indochine/vm*). See also Ch.8, note 78.

B: ARTILLERY STRENGTH

(1) In October 1953 the first report by the French Second Bureau of the Viet Minh's acquisition of 105mm howitzers mentioned a possible figure of three battalions each of 12 pieces. A further report of January 1954 on the strength and organization of Heavy Division 351 is the basis for Gen de Brancion's figures (*op cit,* p.281):
Regiment 45 Total 24 × 105mm.
Two battalions, each of four companies/batteries, each 3 × 105mm:
  Bn 950 (Cos 60, 64, 66 and 68), and *Bn 954* (Cos 80, 83, 86 and 89).
Regiment 675 Total 18 × 75mm (incl. 12 × Japanese Type 94 mountain guns, 6 × US M3A1 pack howitzers), 20 × 120mm mortars (Russian and French).
Three battalions:
  Bn 175 (Cos 754, 755 and 756, each 3 × 75mm);
  Bn 275 (Co 751, 4 × 120mm; Co 753, 3 × 75mm; Co 756, 4 × 120mm); and
  Bn 83 (Cos 111, 112 and 119, each 4 × 120mm; Cos 113 and 115, each 3 × 75mm).
Regiment 237 Presence at DBP unconfirmed (30 × mortars, 82mm and/or 120mm)
AA Regt 367 (Approx. 100 × 12.7mm machine guns, plus unknown number – 36 ×? – 37mm cannon).

From 3 March 1954 there were intelligence reports of a 37mm AA regiment being driven from the Chinese border towards DBP, but total strengths in 37mm guns remained unconfirmed. This report may have referred to the heavy batteries of Regt 367, or conceivably to a second unit; if the latter, this unit may have been dispersed along the lines of supply, where 37mm fire was reported by pilots. This question is discussed in the text on pp. 294–5.

(2) On their return from captivity, several French artillery officers – including Col Vaillant, Maj Le Gurun and Capt Noël – who had been interrogated by their Viet Minh opposite numbers reported being told that there had in fact been three battalions of 105mm howitzers present, i.e. 36 guns. However, official Viet Minh sources later gave the figure as 24 guns.

(3) After interviewing Gen Giap in 1990, Brig Peter Macdonald wrote in his invaluable biography that in 1953 Division 351 had received from China 48 × 105mm howitzers, most of them 'newly captured in Korea', and that 36 of these – nine batteries/companies each with four pieces – were indeed on the strength of *Regt 45* at Dien Bien Phu. He also stated that:

Regt 675 had 24 × 75mm guns, not 18 ×, plus its 20 × 120mm mortars;

Regt 237 had indeed been present, equipped with 120mm mortars; that there had also been 60 × 75mm recoilless guns (presumably with infantry unit heavy companies); but that *AA Regt 367* had only 36 × 37mm guns. (Macdonald, *Giap. ..*, p.133)

Artillery ammunition

Rocolle (p.340) quotes the C-in-C's Saigon Second Bureau as reporting on 10 March that ammunition stocks *'amené à pied-d'oeuvre'* ('in hand') included 15,000 × 105mm and 5,000 × 75mm.

Brancion (p.284) states that in estimating 105mm stocks held near DBP on 13 March at 8,800 rounds, the FTNV Second Bureau at Hanoi was 'close to the figure of 9,000 rounds given in Viet Minh sources'. However, he states elsewhere (p.24) that an FTNV Second Bureau report dated 2 April retrospectively estimated that on 13 March the 105mm stock had stood at 10,400 rounds; presumably the figure of 8,800 was the latest available to GONO on 13 March.

Much of this ammunition supplied by China must have been from pre-1950 Nationalist stocks, perhaps thus in poor condition; but they presumably had a proportion of newer shells captured, along with guns, in Korea; and also an unknown quantity captured at Na San when the French demolition charges failed. Presumably about two-thirds of the 75mm ammunition was for the Japanese Type 94, and thus at least nine years old; the number of 'duds' remarked at DBP is hardly surprising.

This stockpile and the resupplies of 17–29 March were practically used up in the first two attack phases of 13–15 March, and 30 March–5 April respectively. It took Giap (like the French) another three weeks to rebuild his stocks a third time for the final battles. From early April, when the French Air Force had to parachute supplies from medium altitude with delayed opening, the People's Army benefited from strayed drops of the latest 105mm ammunition. The large number of duds reported by the French in the early stages of the battle tailed off; during the second half of April the use of effective short-delay fuses increased, together with proximity airbursts (i.e. 'Pozit' or VT-fused shells). Fall (*Hell...*, pp.451 and 473) quotes French estimates that in all *c.* 3,500 × 105mm rounds were misdropped to the People's Army, and 8,500 rounds for other weapons of 75mm and upwards, i.e. 81mm and 120mm mortar bombs but also perhaps 75mm RCL – see Ch.13 note 42.

The French estimate of total Viet Minh artillery ammunition expenditure at Dien Bien Phu was *c.* 30,000 × 105mm and *c.*100,000+ other calibres. This represents between 1,300 and 1,700 tons of artillery and heavy mortar ammunition delivered to the battlefield by the Viet Minh logistic organization. For comparison, total French artillery and heavy mortar expenditure 20 November 1953 to 7 May 1954 was estimated at 95,000 × 105mm, 8,500 × 155mm and 38,000 × 120mm.

INDEX

W